A. J. HOLMAN COMPANY

DAILY BIBLE COMMENTARY

Romans —Revelation

A. J. HOLMAN COMPANY
DIVISION J. B. LIPPINCOTT COMPANY
PHILADELPHIA AND NEW YORK

© 1973 Scripture Union
First published 1974
Reprinted 1977

U.S. Library of Congress Cataloging in Publication Data

Daily Bible Commentary: Romans to Revelation.
   Reprint of the ed. published by Scripture Union,
London.
   1. Bible. N.T.—Commentaries. I. Cundall,
Arthur Ernest.
BS2341.2.D33   1977   227'.07   76–46442
ISBN–0–87981–071–8

Printed and bound in Malta by
Interprint (Malta) Ltd

Contents

Co-ordinating Editor: Arthur E. Cundall, B.A., B.D.

Maps: Jenny Grayston.

Photographs: Rev. A. E. Cundall, P. W. Marsh, Rev. A. Thompson.

List of Standard Abbreviations

AV (KJV)	Authorised Version (King James), 1611.
c. (circa)	about
cf., cp.	compare
e.g.	for example
f.	verse following
ff.	verses following
Gk.	Greek
Heb.	Hebrew
i.e.	that is
J.B.	Jerusalem Bible, 1966.
LXX	Septuagint (Greek Version of the O.T.)
NEB	New English Bible, 1961 and 1970.
NT	New Testament
OT	Old Testament
p.	page
pp.	pages
RSV	Revised Standard Version 1946 and 1952.
RV	Revised Version (American Standard Version) 1885.
s.v.	(*sub voce*) 'under that word'
v.	verse
vs.	verses
viz.	namely

Maps

Photographs

General Introduction

The overwhelming response to the Scripture Union Bible Study Books, when originally issued during the period 1967–71, has led to the demand for their preservation in a more compact and durable form.

It will be recalled that the original intention of this series was to encourage the daily study of the Bible at greater depth than was possible with the Bible Study Notes. This allowed fuller discussion of introductory, textual and background material, whilst still aiming at devotional warmth, sound exegesis and relevance to daily life. It is heartening to know that this aim has, in considerable measure, been achieved. Moreover, the Bible Study Books have been widely used as the basis for group discussion in homes, colleges and churches, and some volumes have even been used as prescribed texts in Bible colleges! It is hoped that the new format will find an equally encouraging reception.

It remains true, however, that the principal aim of this series is to stimulate personal daily Bible study. Each main section contains material for a three-month period. The one exception to this is the section Corinthians-Galatians which contains readings for a four-month period. Where it is suggested that two sections should be read together in order to fit a two or three-month period, they are marked with an asterisk. There is, of course, no obligation to adopt this suggestion. This particular volume, therefore, provides material for a period of approximately fourteen months. The complete series of four volumes will provide for daily readings over a five-year cycle, and will form a complete Bible Commentary. It is appreciated that few students will have the time available for a full consideration of all the questions set for further study. But since these are placed at approximately weekly intervals it would be stimulating and refreshing if time could be set aside once a week for the study of one or more questions.

The authors of the individual sections have been allowed the necessary liberty of approach within the general scope of the series. This provides for a certain variation which we trust will prove stimulating rather than disconcerting. All authors are united within the circle of evangelical, conservative scholarship and are widely respected within this field.

Opportunity has been taken to correct errors which escaped attention in the earlier edition and also to make limited revisions where necessary. The inclusion of introductory articles and maps, will, we trust, add to the value of this volume as an aid to the study of God's Word.

The World of the New Testament

Harold H. Rowdon

The world of the New Testament was not the geographical world, but the Roman world, an enormous area stretching from Spain all the way around the Mediterranean Sea to North Africa. Its supreme ruler was the Emperor. Technically he was no more than first citizen, but his power was supreme. He was commander-in-chief of the armed forces, his instructions acquired the force of law, and he possessed powers which gave him rights of legal veto and appellate jurisdiction.

The Roman empire comprised some 40 provinces which fell into two categories. Those which were situated in frontier or unsettled areas were under the authority of the Emperor. They were governed by senatorial legates with the title of pro-praetor, or by nobles who were known as prefects or procurators. All were directly responsible to the Emperor. More settled provinces were ruled by proconsuls appointed by and responsible to the Roman senate. This was an old established institution going back to Rome's republican days which still retained some power under the empire.

The Roman world was plentifully supplied with cities. Many of them had been founded in the days of the Greek empire. They served as centres of government and administration, contained lavish provision for recreation and social intercourse, light industry and trade, and provided a kind of focus for the surrounding countryside. In some ways they were rather like English market towns. They contained many voluntary associations, or guilds, which brought together people with common interests in matters of business or social life. The banquets held by such associations, like the general civic festivals, contained religious overtones and created problems of conscience for Christians. Citizenship of a notable city was a source of special pride. The holding of municipal office might carry with it Roman citizenship. This was also given in recognition of outstanding services to the empire, and might be purchased.

Some cities which were formed by settlements of Roman citizens, often discharged soldiers, were known as *coloniae*. Others, which had been free cities before they were incorporated into the Roman empire, were allowed to retain their independent status, and were termed *municipiae*.

Radiating from the city of Rome was a superb system of roads which was better than anything before or since till the eighteenth century. Built for military purposes, they were maintained at the public expense and provided a unique system of communications—even if the

8

motive power was only horse power! Travel by sea was also relatively easy, for the Mediterranean had been almost entirely cleared of pirates. Navigational aids were few, however, and it was necessary to hug the coast. Travel by sea was hazardous in bad weather and impossible in winter.

Judea had been incorporated into the Roman empire during the first century B.C. Herod, son of Antipater, an Idumean who had been appointed procurator by Julius Caesar, ingratiated himself with Rome and was given the title of King of Judea. He tried to secure Jewish support by marrying Mariamne, heiress of the Jewish priestly house, and by rebuilding the Temple on a magnificent scale. But he also built a temple to Augustus in Samaria and founded the city of Caesarea in honour of Caesar. He created a new nobility of royal officials, and there emerged among the Jews a party of Herodians.

On Herod's death in 4 B.C. the three of his sons who had survived the murderous intrigues of his reign succeeded to his domain. Philip ruled the area north-east of Galiliee. Herod Antipas became tetrarch of Galilee, with Perea, east of the river Jordan. He built Tiberias in honour of the Roman emperor of that name, but lived as a practising Jew and even showed some regard for John the Baptist. Antipas was married to the daughter of Aretas, king of Nabatea, but this did not deter him from forming a liaison with Herodias, who was daughter of one of his half-brothers and wife of another. On the death of the emperor Tiberius, Antipas petitioned Caligula, his successor, for the title of king. Instead, he was banished on the ground of treasonable charges that had been brought against him by his nephew, Herod Agrippa I, who was rewarded by being given the territory ruled by Antipas.

Judea and Samaria, the greater part of Herod the Great's kingdom, went to his son Archelaus. He proved a thoroughly incompetent and unpopular ruler who managed to clear himself from one set of charges by a personal visit to Rome, but was eventually deposed in A.D. 6.

Thereafter, Judea was placed under the control of a succession of Roman procurators responsible to the Emperor, except the years A.D. 41–44 when almost all the territory once ruled by Herod the Great was entrusted to Herod Agrippa I. He made a bid for Jewish support by persecuting the Christians, until his sudden death, recorded in Acts 12. The procurators, of whom Pontius Pilate was one (A.D. 26–36), resided in Caesarea, but in times of potential unrest, such as the Jewish feasts, made their headquarters in Jerusalem. They commanded a standing army of 3,000 men who were recruited from the non-Jewish sector of the population. One cohort was stationed in Jerusalem in the castle of Antonia which had been built by Herod and overlooked the Temple. The procurator was responsible for taxation as well as law and order, but in general the Jews were self-governing.

Judaism was not confined to Palestine. Far from it. From the time of the Old Testament captivities the Jews had become widely dispersed in the ancient world. In the first century A.D. there were probably more Jews outside Palestine than within it. In some cities they constituted a sizeable proportion of the population. The Jews of the dispersion practised their religion, though in a modified form. Synagogue worship, with its prayers to Jehovah, Scripture reading and exposition, and lofty moral teaching, attracted numerous Gentiles. Those who did not become Jewish proselytes—and they were many—often proved receptive to the Christian message.

The ancient world was exceedingly religious. As a topic of conversation, religion was an excellent starter! It pervaded every aspect of life, political, social and family as well as personal. It was like cement which did almost as much to bind together a heterogeneous empire as the military might of Rome.

State religion was frankly polytheistic, and often purely formal. It was concerned with retaining the favour of the gods by showing them due honour. Since first-century religion was essentially syncretistic, it was not difficult to equate the traditional gods of Rome—Jupiter, Mars, Minerva and the rest—with Zeus and the other gods of Greece. The worship of the state gods was essentially civic, and all loyal citizens were expected to be present at festivals in honour of the gods.

The first century saw the development of another form of state religion, even more sinister from the Christian point of view. The Emperor came to be regarded as a kind of incarnation of the spirit of the imperial dynasty, and the saviour and lord of Rome. Highly successful Emperors, like Augustus and Vespasian, came to be included in the number of those who should be worshipped as divine. From the end of the first century Emperors came to expect divine honours during their lifetime, if only as a token of loyalty to the Roman empire.

There were innumerable forms of private religion. Diana of the Ephesians enjoyed a wide vogue. Asclepius, god of healing, was almost a universal favourite. Lares and Penates, symbolic of hearth and home, called forth the religious devotion of many a family. Religious practices merged into the frankly magical. In the countryside, religion was almost animistic. Shrines were set up wherever there was some manifestation of life or power, such as a spring of water, a range of mountain peaks or a grove of ancient trees. To such shrines offerings of milk, cheese, grain or flowers were brought.

The first century saw the introduction into the Roman empire of new religions from the east, particularly the mystery religions with their sacred myths and their promise of 'rebirth for eternity'. Their initiation ceremonies included purifications, robings and sacramental meals. They bear superficial resemblances to Christianity, but their main importance is as witnesses to something approaching a spiritual vacuum.

As a rule, Rome allowed individuals freedom to practise private religion unhindered provided it was neither antagonistic to the official cult, politically subversive nor grossly immoral. It was taken for granted that the devotee would continue to observe the state religion.

Despite their rigid monotheism, the Jews had contrived to secure toleration. Theirs was a national religion, they were of great commercial importance to the empire, and they had influence in high places. Christianity at first shared in the toleration granted to Judaism, but with its increasingly obvious separation from that faith it was compelled to stand on its own feet. It came to be regarded by those who had no intimate knowledge of its adherents as undesirable on political, religious, social and even moral grounds!

If Latin was the universal language of government and law within the Roman empire, common Greek was the *lingua franca*, at any rate in the towns. It was used in commerce and general social intercourse. Many examples of correspondence in Greek have come to light and show that it was widely used.

Greek philosophical thought had passed its peak, but in the first century the figure of the travelling philosopher was a familiar one. He might be a charlatan, offering cheap entertainment with his subtle logic-chopping. On the other hand, he might give careful instruction in one of the schools of Greek thought. Epicureanism extolled the pursuit of happiness. Cynicism despised external trappings of any kind and easily led to contempt for authority and morality as well as religion. Stoicism propounded a kind of pantheistic materialism which identified the divine principle with reason, and urged men to live a life in accordance with the dictates of reason. The old philosophy of Platonism, later to enjoy a revival in the form of Neo-Platonism, taught that ultimate reality belonged not to the material but to the spiritual world. Some Christian thinkers were to regard it as having prepared men's minds for the Christian revelation.

The area shown on this map was especially important in the growth of the Church in New Testament times.

PALESTINE AND SYRIA—areas of early Christian activity, based on Jerusalem, reaching Phoenicia, Cyprus and Antioch. Note the extensive area referred to in Acts **2.**9–11 to which converts must have returned from Jerusalem.

ASIA MINOR AND THE AEGEAN—area of Paul's missionary journeys. He claims to have 'fully preached the gospel of Christ' from 'Jerusalem and as far round as Illyricum' (Rom. **15.**19). Acts and the epistles give many details of this activity as it concerned the provinces of Cyprus, Galatia, Asia, Thrace, Macedonia and Achaia.

BLACK SEA

Byzantium

BITHYNIA & PONTUS

SIA
amum
Thyatira
Sardis
• Philadelphia Antioch (Pisidia)
  Laodicea
IS
  Colossae
  / PISIDIA   Lystra   Derbe
    Attalia PAMPHYLIA Cilicia
  LYCIA   Perga
atara   Myra   Trachea Seleucia

GALATIA

Lesser Armenia

CAPPADOCIA

CILICIA   Commagene

Iconium

Tarsus

• Antioch

OSROENE

KINGDOM
OF
ARMENIA

PARTHIAN

EMPIRE

CYPRUS
Paphos • Salamis

SYRIA

Sidon
Tyre   Damascus
Ptolemais Caesarea Philippi
Caesarea
Joppa Samaria
Lydda Judea
Gaza Jerusalem

Seleucia

Babylon

Alexandria

EGYPT

Nabataean Kingdom

BITHYNIA, PONTUS, AND CAPPADOCIA—addressed in 1 Peter.

PATMOS—where John wrote the Revelation. Ephesus was the centre of activity of the apostle John, and the Epistles of John were written to churches in the neighbourhood.

ALEXANDRIA—the home of Apollos: the church there probably originated in New Testament times, but by what means is unknown.

ROME—church there when Paul arrived. Its existence shows how Christianity had expanded, in ways not mentioned in Acts, by the agency of other apostles (cf. 1 Cor. **9.**5, Rom. **15.**20) and by the private migrations of individuals.

The Teaching of the New Testament

Donald Guthrie

Because the New Testament is a collection of books, written at different times to different people and with different purposes, it does not present the reader with a systematic account of what Christians believe. It is nevertheless the only source of Christian doctrine. It provides the raw material out of which the unity of the New Testament can be brought to light, and it is the task of theology to investigate its various strains to discover how that unity can exist in the midst of diversity. There are two main ways in which such a task can be approached. The first may be called the analytical method which analyses the emphases of the various groups of books, and the second is the thematic method which classifies the main teaching into categories. In a brief treatment it is clearly impossible to do justice to the former method, but the latter offers the opportunity to present a concise survey of the contents.

Any arrangement of theological ideas must start with *God*. The most important initial question on this theme is whether the Old Testament shows a different revelation of God from the New Testament. Much is undoubtedly the same, for the New Testament stresses the love and mercy of God in a similar way to the Old Testament. Moreover, the character of God as righteousness is carried over into New Testament thought. The judgement of God is basic to a right understanding of the whole mission of Jesus. He Himself taught that God is holy (John **17.**11; Matt. **6.**33). The creatorship of God is another aspect carried into the New Testament from the Old Testament. Not only is this everywhere assumed (cf. Rev. **4.**11), but the New Testament specifically states that God in Christ upholds all things (Col. **1.**17; Heb. **1.**3). The most remarkable feature of the New Testament teaching on creation is the way in which Christ is linked with God in creative activity.

The most distinctive aspect of the New Testament view of God is His Fatherhood. Although this idea is not wholly absent from the Old Testament, it is viewed within the covenant relationship. God was seen as Father to His people Israel. He called them collectively 'my son' (Hos. **11.**1). But Jesus carried the idea much further into the realm of personal relationships. God the Father shows providential care for all men, but has a special regard for His children (cf. Matt. **6.**32f.). Throughout His life, Jesus shows the importance to Him of the Father's will and thus provides a pattern for His followers. Yet He drew a distinction between His own filial relationship to God

14

and that of His followers (John **20**.17). Whereas Jesus serves as a pattern, His own relationship was unique by reason of His person and of His perfect fulfilment of the Father's will (cf. Matt. **11**.27). It is important to note that the teaching on the personal aspects of Fatherhood was addressed by Jesus to His disciples. It is not surprising that the theme of the Fatherhood of God constantly recurs throughout the epistles. It comes in the opening salutation to every one of Paul's epistles. Indeed, there is no New Testament book (except 3 John) in which the title 'Father' is not used of God.

Another feature is the idea of God as King, which is particularly brought out in the teaching of Jesus about the Kingdom of God. Here again there is strong background influence from the Old Testament idea of the theocratic king, but the distinctive feature of the New Testament Kingdom teaching is that members of the Kingdom are those who have committed themselves by faith to Jesus Christ.

Of great importance for a right assessment of New Testament thought is the decision made about the nature of *Jesus Christ*. This can be done by a comparison between what He Himself claimed and what others claimed for Him. There has been much discussion over this most important centre of New Testament thought, but it will only be possible to summarize the statements of the New Testament itself.

Jesus' view of Himself is best seen in the titles which He used of Himself, and of these the most important is 'Son of Man'. On many occasions Jesus used this title, and without doubt meant Himself. Sometimes it is used when He could have said 'I' (as in Matt. **16**.13, cf. Mark **8**.27), sometimes when He was making important statements about His death (as Matt. **20**.18), and sometimes when He was thinking of events relating to His second coming (as Matt. **19**.28). The question arises over what He meant by the term and why He chose to use it. It is generally agreed that it draws special attention to the humanity of Jesus and is in some way linked to the Servant spoken of by Isaiah. It is doubtful whether the people who listened to Jesus understood fully His reason for using it. The most acceptable view is that He preferred it rather than 'Messiah', because of the materialistic ideas associated with the latter title.

Although Jesus never specifically called Himself Messiah, He undoubtedly regarded Himself as the fulfilment of all the noble Messianic hopes of the past. The Christians at once acknowledged this and the New Testament reflects the strong belief of the early community that many of the Old Testament predictions, including many that the Jews treated as Messianic, pointed to Jesus Christ. The fact that throughout the New Testament the title 'Christ' is used

15

by others when speaking of Jesus testifies to the strong conviction that He was the true Messiah. His mission was not, however, to deliver Israel from the domination of their enemies as the Jews currently believed, but to save men from their sins. The Messianic hope had become spiritual and universal.

On many occasions Jesus spoke of Himself as Son, while the title Son of God is frequently used of Him in the New Testament. As well as being perfect man, He claimed to be equal with God (John **10.**30; **14.**8–11). The apostle Paul speaks of Him as the image of the invisible God (Col.**1.**15), in whom the fullness of God dwells (Col. **1.**19; Eph. **1.**23), who thought equality with God a prize not to be snatched at for it already belonged to Him (Phil. **2.**6). The New Testament becomes intelligible only when Jesus is regarded as both human and divine.

There is a close link between what Jesus is and what He came to do and this is high-lighted by His name, for Jesus, as Matthew points out, means 'Saviour' (Matt. **1.**21). But the aspect of salvation with which Jesus was concerned was not national but spiritual. It had to do with sins, not with political status.

This exalted view of Jesus is at the basis of all New Testament theology. The Christian Church was not founded on a mere man, but on the risen Christ. Special attention will now be given to the mission of Jesus to bring out His significance.

What Jesus did for man may be gathered up into the New Testament doctrine of *salvation*. This, broadly speaking, comprises the doctrine of the Atonement and its application. What the New Testament teaches about the Atonement is too many-sided to be stated concisely but some general idea may be given. Jesus Himself made many significant statements which after His death were seen to be important for His own understanding of the meaning of the Cross. There is no doubt that He saw the Cross as the main purpose of His mission. For Him it was no accident. In His first specific mention of His coming sufferings He made it clear that He *must* suffer death (Matt. **16.**21), which shows that He regarded the passion as a divine necessity. This at once disposes of any theories of the Atonement which regard the death of Christ as accidental or unforeseen. Closely linked with this are statements which bring out the voluntary nature of the death of Jesus, of which the most notable is John **10.**18, where Jesus the Shepherd takes full responsibility for laying down His life for the sheep.

The announcement of John the Baptist that Jesus was the Lamb of God which takes away the sin of the world (John **1.**29) is of great importance because it shows that Jesus had come as a sacrifice, and because it is directly related to man's universal sin. This sacrificial idea is developed in the New Testament epistles. Another figure of

16

speech which was used by Jesus in describing His mission and which was further developed by the apostles was that of the ransoming of a slave (cf. Mark 10.45). The central idea is of the deliverance of the slave from a life of bondage to a life of freedom, a vivid illustration of the liberating power of the gospel. In order to bring out the effect of His passion, Jesus used the picture of a seed of corn which has to be buried in order to become productive. It was left to the apostles once again to bring out the full significance of the illustration. The existence of the Christian Church itself was a witness to the basic necessity of Christ's death. He Himself had become the only foundation (1 Cor. 3.11).

The motive behind the Passion, in the mind of Jesus, was love (cf. John 3.16; 15.13), an aspect of the mission of Jesus which has always fired Christian imagination. This is backed up by the considerable emphasis in the Gospels on the compassion of Jesus, seen most vividly in the healing miracles. In the epistles also the love behind the giving of Jesus is brought out (cf. Rom. 5.8; 8.34 f. 2 Cor. 5.14ff.). It is noticeable that the testimony of His enemies unwittingly contributed to an understanding of His death, as when Caiaphas declared that it was more fitting for one to die for the people than for the whole people to perish (John 11.50ff.). This substitutionary view of the Atonement is developed in various ways in the apostolic understanding of the event. Caiaphas was nearer the truth than he knew. The main focus of Jesus' thought about the application of His work is found in the Last Supper where the words of institution show that the passion is to be central in the continual memory of the Christian community. The bread was broken and the wine poured out, to bring out the sacrificial significance. The coming passion was 'for the remission of sins' (Matt 26.28). Moreover, it was viewed by Jesus Himself as the inauguration of the New Covenant.

In the epistles of Paul the main lines of interpretation can be summed up under the great themes of justification, redemption, reconciliation and sanctification. The Atonement is central in the doctrine of justification, as the key passage, Rom. 3.21ff., shows. In this passage Paul describes the death of Jesus as a propitiation which God had provided to enable sinful man to approach Him. The condition of acceptance is not man's own efforts (which Paul calls 'works of the law'), but God's gracious provision which is received by faith. This is closely linked to the doctrine of redemption. Here again the act of Jesus in redeeming man is tied to His work on the cross (cf. Eph. 1.7). It is worth noting that this Pauline theme also recurs in 1 Peter (cf. 1.18f.). The believer is no longer his own, but belongs to God who has redeemed him. Although he had been delivered from the power of sin, the apostle

17

still saw himself as a slave—but now to Jesus Christ (Rom. **1.**1). It is perhaps reconciliation which looms largest in Paul's thought. He saw himself as a minister of reconciliation to those who had become alienated from God (2 Cor. **5.**17ff.), a reconciliation which had somehow been effected by Jesus becoming a curse for us (cf. Paul's equally mysterious statement about Christ becoming a curse for us in Gal. **3.**13). The New Testament does not claim to explain fully the mission of Jesus. There is at the heart of it what Paul calls a 'mystery' (cf. Rom. **16.**25; Eph. **1.**9).

Paul's doctrine of sanctification may be summed up as his teaching about the application of Christ's work. Indeed his practical advice is integral to this doctrine. He conceived of the Christian life as the working out of that salvation which Jesus had obtained (Phil. **2.**12). The new life is essentially a life in the Spirit and for this reason Paul has much to say about the activity of the Spirit in the life of the believer (cf. especially Rom. **8**). The ethical teaching of the apostle is rich in down-to-earth, practical advice which is nevertheless based on his understanding of the saving work of Christ.

The other books of the New Testament are equally strong in practical advice. The epistle of James concentrates on this aspect and does not mention the atoning work of Christ. But the intensely practical advice assumes a basis of right relationship with God. Although works are brought into the discussion on justification, faith is not excluded and the works are the works of mercy which are regarded as the natural outcome of the faith (cf. Jas. **2.**18). In the epistle to the Hebrews, in which approach to God is the main theme, the necessity for the sacrificial work of Christ is seen throughout. His sacrifice is, moreover, distinguished from all others because it was offered 'through the eternal Spirit' (Heb. **9.**14). The outcome of Christ's work is clearly seen in Heb. **10.**19ff., where again the objective work of Christ has a practical effect in the life of the believer. The consummation of the mission of Jesus is portrayed in the book of Revelation, in which He is seen as the triumphant slain Lamb who puts all His enemies under His feet.

Mention has already been made of the work of the *Spirit* in the life of the believer. In the Gospels the activity of the Spirit is frequently brought out in the ministry of Jesus (e.g. Mark **1.**12; Luke **4.**1, 14) and figures as an important subject in the farewell discourses in John's Gospel. Jesus made it clear that the disciples were to be dependent on the Spirit for knowledge of the truth, for guidance, for convicting the world of sin and for leading men to faith (cf. John **14.**15 f., 25f.; **15.**26; **16.**7f.). The risen Christ breathed on the disciples and exhorted them to receive the Spirit (John **20.**22). It was on the day of

Pentecost that the Spirit descended in power on the waiting disciples (Acts **2**) and the record of the development of the Church in the book of Acts is a record of the special activity of the Holy Spirit. In the Pauline epistles the work of the Spirit is strongly emphasized, for apart from the Spirit no one can believe (Rom. **8.**9), nor can he produce fruit in his life (Gal. **5.**22). Moreover, the Spirit gives special gifts to believers (1 Cor. **12.**4–31), and believers are exhorted to seek the fullness of the Spirit (Eph. **5.**18). It was through the Spirit that Jesus offered Himself (Heb. **9.**14), and through the Spirit that John received his revelation of Jesus Christ (Rev. **4.**2). It would be true to say that the teaching of the New Testament would be unintelligible apart from the work of the Spirit.

The New Testament idea of the *Church* is twofold. Local groups of believers form Christian communities in specific places and the totality of these local groups comprises the universal Church. On two occasions Jesus spoke of His Church, once in the universal sense (Matt. **16.**18) and once in a local sense (Matt. **18.**17). The book of Acts gives insight into the formation and operation of many Christian communities, although it is the Pauline letters which provide most information about local problems. At an early stage some pattern for the ministry is apparent. A system of elders operated from the earliest journeys of Paul and existed still earlier in the Judean churches. Bishops were elders with specific functions (Tit. **1.**5ff.). An order of deacons was also established as 1 Tim. **3.**8 shows. There is some evidence also for deaconesses (Rom. **16.**1) and 'official widows' (1 Tim. **5.**9ff.).

The New Testament speaks of two ordinances of the early Church—baptism, which followed confession of faith, and the Lord's Supper. Little is known of the worship patterns of the early Christians, but it is certain that Scripture reading and hymns formed part of their services (cf. 1 Tim. **4.**13; Eph. **5.**19; Col. **3.**16). In practical matters a communal system was tried in Jerusalem (Acts **4.**32ff.), but there is no evidence for it elsewhere. Paul organized a collection scheme among the Gentiles for the relief of poverty-stricken Christians in Judea (Rom. **15.**25ff.; 1 Cor. **16.**1ff.; 2 Cor. **8.**1ff.). The Christian communities took seriously their social responsibilities towards their less fortunate brethren.

A belief in the *final consummation* of all things is integral to New Testament teaching. The second coming of Christ is basic to the various books, although more apparent in some. Jesus Himself predicted His return (cf. John. **14.**3). He gave special teaching regarding the end of the present age (cf. Matt. **24,25**); Mark **13**; Luke **21**), while many of the Kingdom parables are related to the end-time (e.g. the 'harvest' theme in Mark **13**.26ff.). Various events must precede the coming (cf. also 2 Thess. **2**), but the consummation will be marked by ultimate victory (cf. the whole theme of the book of Revelation). All enemies will be put under the feet of Christ (1 Cor. **15**.25; Phil. **2**.10). This picture of the final triumph of Christianity is a great encouragement to those who are persecuted for their faith. The New Testament presents the future hope as a relevant factor for present living, since it has a purifying effect (1 John **3**.3).

Romans

INTRODUCTION

The authorship of the Epistle to the Romans went undisputed until 1792. It can be certainly attributed to Paul. The place and date of writing can be determined with some certainty from internal evidence. Paul had not yet been to Rome (1.11,13,15), where a mixed church of unknown origin (Acts 28.15) was already functioning, but he intended to pay a visit, after a forthcoming journey to Jerusalem, whither he intended to carry contributions from Macedonia and Achaia (15.23–32). This intention was in his mind during his residence in Corinth (Acts 19.21). Ten years of vigorous evangelism were over, and he purposed a major new move after the visit to Jerusalem to which he looked forward with justifiable apprehension. He made this journey, and he made it from Corinth (Acts 24.17). When he wrote to Rome, Timothy, Sosipater, Gaius and Erastus were with him (16.21,23). Gaius was, at least for part of his Corinthian residence, his host (1 Cor. 1.14). Erastus was a Corinthian, perhaps a prominent figure in the city (16.23; 2 Tim. 4.20), and had served Paul in Macedonia (Acts 19.22). In Acts 20.4 we read that Timothy, Sosipater (Sopater) and Gaius were with Paul in Corinth. Phoebe, who appears to have carried the letter to Rome, and who may have also been hostess to Paul, lived in the marine suburb of Corinth, Cenchreae (16.1). Set these biographical data in order, and it appears that the letter was written in the winter of A.D. 56,57. This said, the great document may be left to tell its own story, of Christian truth, and its mighty exponent.

Photo: The Via Appia—Rome—lined with ancient monuments

Photo: Forum at Rome

Romans 1.1–4   Paul's Vocation and Credentials

Paul was no waster of words. Every ancient letter began with a note of the one who sent it, and a clear statement of the person or persons to whom it was addressed. The discovery this century of the thousands of papyrus letters, which the arid sands of Egypt have preserved, has revealed that the New Testament epistles conform to the pattern of the letters of their time. The deep matters of the faith required nothing more than the common forms of communication and the simplicities of daily intercourse in which to express themselves. They need no more today. Christ can find demonstration in our conversation, in the normal conduct of our lives and our activities. The common bush can be 'aflame with God'.

Paul passes promptly to his credentials. He is a slave of Jesus Christ, not his own, but 'bought with a price', and bound in wondrous servitude to the King of kings. It was an ancient and honourable title. Moses had carried it (Josh. 1.1 f.), and so had the prophets (Jer. 7.25). It implied a dedication to the doing of a master's will. The beautiful story of Abraham's servant on his mission to Haran is a perfect illustration (Gen. 24.1–66). And like Abraham's servant Paul was a special messenger, an 'apostle,' one sent to fulfil a particular task. The purpose and the vocation are emphasized in the closing words of the first verse. It was Paul's conviction that he was 'set apart' for the gospel of God, not merely by the formal commissioning of his fellow-Christians (Acts 13.2), but in the long-laid plan of God Himself (Gal. 1.15). In both contexts the same Greek verb is used.

Then, in swift economy of words, Paul proceeds to state the essential facts of the good news of God. He is apparently addressing in the Roman church a group of Jews and their converts. He can rely on an Old Testament background. Hence the emphasis in two verses on the Lord's earthly royalty, His power and divine Sonship, confirmed by the Holy Spirit, and sealed by the resurrection. The incarnation without the resurrection is meaningless. The two basic doctrines of the faith move together. Paul never wavered from this position. And without God revealed in Christ (John 1.18), a Christ risen from the dead, there is no Christianity.

A Meditation: 1 *Cor.* 15.12–19.

Romans 1.5–8   'All One in Christ Jesus'

Grace, the free unmerited favour of God, was the gift to all Christians. Apostleship was limited to those fitted for a special task. This clear distinction should be observed. In writing to the Corinthians Paul devotes a whole chapter to the division of labour, and variety of vocation in the Church (1 Cor. 12). Intrusion into another's sphere of service breeds frustration and ineffectiveness, and at the same time leaves the proper task undone.

Paul's task was to summon men to 'the obedience of faith'. The genitive ('of faith') is one of definition. Obedience consists in faith (Acts 6.7). To believe, and to commit the life to that belief, is to obey. God asks no more, no less, and in the act is involved both trust and the disciplined living which demonstrates the trust. 'The first law that ever God gave to man,' said Montaigne, 'was a law of obedience; it was a commandment pure and simple, wherein man had nothing to enquire after or dispute, for to obey is the proper office of a rational soul, acknowledging a heavenly benefactor.'

Now comes (7) the salvation, warm in its wording. 'Called to be saints' means saints in virtue of His calling. This fact is no warrant for the tactless claim to sainthood which a watching and listening world will interpret in other than Biblical terms. The coinage of speech can become debased, and the term 'saint' cannot be presumptuously used by any Christian, true though it is that God in His grace calls Christians thus.

'Grace and peace', the second the fruit in mind and heart of a proper understanding of the former, are the total of Paul's wish to the Christians of Rome. In the words are combined an echo of the common greeting of Greek to Greek, and the common (still common) greeting of Israeli to Israeli—'Shalom'—'Peace'. Paul moves into his wider sphere of witness in his very salutation.

And Jesus Christ—Jesus the Messiah—finds its fifth mention in eight verses. There is no Christianity, let the plain truth be again repeated, without the Christ of the New Testament, no deluded and defeated dreamer from Galilee, done viciously to death by collaborating priests and occupying authorities, but the Risen Son of God, from all time envisaged.

Meditation: John 1.14–18.

Romans 1.9–12   'And so to Rome'

Paul was writing his letter to Rome, probably in Corinth, where he spent three winter months at the end of A.D. 56 and the beginning of 57 (Acts 20.3). The Italian peninsula did not seem far away. Many years before a grand plan had taken shape in his mind, no less than a strategic attack on the Roman Empire. Cyprus had prompted the thought. He had first put it into motion when, to the annoyance of the junior member of the party, he had abandoned the sea-port, and made for Antioch of Pisidia, the bastion of Roman power in central Asia Minor (Acts 13.13 f.).

Nine years had passed since that adventure in evangelism, and Paul had seen the fulfilment of much of that which he had set out to do. Christian churches, 'cells' of witness, were planted in the great centres of power, religion, learning and trade, in the eastern half of the Empire. He wrote from Corinth, the nodal point of central Mediterranean communications. There were Christians in Athens, intellectual hub of the world. There was an active church in Philippi, old fortress of northern Greece. Ephesus, religious centre of Asia, and proconsular seat, had its witness. Paul hoped to see the message thus placed radiate down the roads and trade-routes, permeating the vast power-system for Christ.

It was a magnificently imaginative idea. There remained the central core of the Empire, Rome itself, and the western bastion, Spain, which was to provide Rome with Emperors, as it had already provided men of accomplishment and letters—Seneca, for example, philosopher and tutor of the Emperor, and Lucan, the decade's best known poet. Spain was Paul's next objective, with Rome *en route*. Paul was not to know the painful and circuitous route by which he was to come to Rome (Rom. 15.24–28). The pilgrimage to Jerusalem, on which he had set his heart, lay ahead, and against all opposition and advice he set out on that path—a fruitless errand, if the brief account be read aright, but one which God turned to good, for all that tumult in Jerusalem and prison in Caesarea lay in the way.

Observe in vs. 11 f. that Paul speaks humbly of gaining blessing and comfort in Rome, as well as bestowing it. Students in class, and congregations in a church, should remember that there is a two-way commerce in spiritual things, a giving as well as a getting. And could this (an awesome thought) be also true of God and us? Is this why He made us free?

Exercise: Trace the pattern of Paul's churches on a map.

Romans 1.13–17   A Gospel of which to be Proud

Paul owed, he said, a debt 'both to Greeks and barbarians'. It is curious to find the RSV persisting in this meaningless translation. Words change their meanings, expand and contract, as they pass from people to people, century to century. A 'barbarian' in the ancient Greek conception, and the language which gave it voice, was simply one who did not speak Greek. The word implied no cultural inferiority. The Greeks called the Persians and the Romans 'barbarian', while acknowledging the superiority of both, the former in material culture, the latter in political power. The 'natives' of Acts 28.2, the 'barbarous people' of the AV (KJV), are in the Greek text *barbaroi*. Both versions miss the point. Paul simply refers to the Phoenician-speaking Maltese. In the present text the word means those who did not share completely in the Mediterranean civilization. He found such people at Lystra (Acts 14.11). He probably met others in Illyricum (Rom. 15.19). 'Greeks' would include Romans, for Greek was their second tongue. Paul sensed an obligation to those of his own culture and those outside it. He felt, what Jowett in his little classic called 'a passion for souls'; or as F. W. H. Myer put it in his poem on Paul:

> *'Then with a rush the intolerable craving*
> *Shivers throughout me like a trumpet call:*
> *Oh, to save some, to perish in their saving,*
> *Die for their life, be offered for them all.'*

One had already died, and in vs. 16 f. Paul speaks of the gospel which is to be the theme of his epistle. He had preached it proudly in two continents. It brought 'salvation'. In the mind's depths, for all the materialism and self-delusion which obscures reality, man is still conscious of a need for a hand reaching down. Death in this century is a less present and pressing reality than it has been in other ages. Medicine has postponed it and softened its impact. It is nevertheless true that the whole approach to life would be vitiated, and society gravely injured if all thought of another life and of ultimate justice were stamped out from the consciousness of men.

Sin still presses on mind and body for all the words used to take away its sting. Frustration and despair are still real. A sense of helplessness before forces beyond control is still a reality. Hell can be a present experience for those enslaved to evil. Christ gives purpose, 'life more abundantly', a sense of being real, clean, useful—Christ *saves*.

Thought: . . . *'The Good, the True, the Pure, the Just—Take the charm "For Ever" from them, and they crumble into dust'* (Tennyson).

Romans 1.18–21   The Reality of Natural Theology

Paul insists that, apart from the Bible and God's self-revelation in Christ, God is manifest to those with minds open to receive Him, in the works of His creation. The wonder of the world, the evidence of law, order, and purpose interwoven with all nature are evidence enough of an Intelligence behind the visible world. The first verse of John's Gospel says as much . . . 'In the beginning was a Mind which expressed itself . . .'

Furthermore, if it is clear in the world around us that Mind came before matter, it is also clear that the planning mind seen in created things also demanded obedience to certain laws. The human body can be abused, the laws of its operation disregarded, and pain follows. The land which provides our sustenance, the air we breathe, the waters upon which all life depends, are given to mankind on fixed conditions. There are laws to be observed, the selfish flouting of which, as the world is learning to its cost, brings inevitable retribution. Dust bowls, dead lakes, polluted waterways, chemical-ridden produce, smog-laden air, all carry death and pain. The planet itself could be rendered uninhabitable by its rebellious inhabitants. God put man in a garden, 'to serve it', says Gen. 2.15, literally translated, and it is part of man's reverence for his Creator to treat reverently His creation.

Paul speaks truth. Not only is the goodness of God manifest in nature, as he told the peasants of Lystra (Acts 14.15–17), but as truly, the wrath of God. So, too, in human experience. As James Froude, the historian, remarked a century ago, there is one clear lesson on which history insists, 'that the world is somehow built on moral foundations, and that, in the long run, it is well with the good, and, in the long run, it will be ill with the wicked'. Herbert Butterfield, historian of our own century, agrees. The 'wrath of God', God's inevitable reaction against rebellion and sin, is a reality, as everyone who is willing to see can see, written into life and history. Apart, therefore, from the ultimate revelation of God, which Paul was urgent to preach, man, he maintains, had the elements of truth before him. Given the desire it was possible to find God.

Romans 1.22–25   The Folly of Idolatry

We have already mentioned Paul's excursion into natural theology at Lystra. He also touched on the theme before a much more intellectual audience at Athens (Acts 17.22–31), and a remark reported by Luke from that address has significance here. God, Paul maintained to the philosophers, set man in a context of order and purpose, 'that they should seek God, in the hope that they might feel after Him and find Him' (27).

In the quest, something went awry. In arrogance and selfishness man sought a deity to tame and to serve him, instead of a Being to whom he could give himself in worship and surrender. He made God in his own image, as the psalmist chided: 'You thought that I was one like yourself' (Psa. 50.21). The beauty of Greek art could

26

not conceal the fact that the lovely statues of Apollo, Zeus, and Athene were only Greeks as the Greeks saw themselves in their moments of self-exaltation, while the myths and legends which surrounded them told of caprice, sensuality, cruelty and pride.

Idols were the result of this perversion in man's quest for God, and they revealed the point Paul makes, man's self-willed misreading of the evidence which God had set before him. And idols were everywhere. It is difficult for a modern Christian to grasp the pervasive nature of the paganism with which his spiritual forbears had to deal. Many pages in Tertullian reveal vividly the practical difficulties which at every turn confronted the Christian in the ancient world. 'Why, even the streets and the market-places,' he writes, 'the baths and the taverns and our very dwelling-places, are not altogether free from idols. Satan and his angels have filled the whole world.' It was worse than this. The conscientious Christian had to absent himself from public festivals. They opened with pagan adoration and sacrifice to an idol. His membership of a trade guild, and in consequence his commercial standing and goodwill, involved the awkwardness of 'sitting at meat in the idol's temple'. His very shopping raised the problem of meat which had been sacrificed to idols. And still worse, man becomes like the object of his worship, especially if it is a projection of his own evil. This is the purport of the climax in v. 25.

Meditation: We shall be like Him.

Romans 1.26–32 The Contemporary Scene

Paul was writing during the principate of the young profligate Nero when Roman society was sunk in hideous vice. It has been left to the present day to produce again on the stage the nude and open sexuality which scandalized the more sober writers of Nero's day. Petronius, so ably portrayed in Henryk Sienkiewicz' historical novel *Quo Vadis*, was writing, at about the same time as Paul, a piece of fiction which has partly survived. It concerns the base doings of three Greek scamps in the sea-ports of Campania, and is dark confirmation of all Paul here writes. Anyone who seeks evidence in support of the apostle's grim description can read Petronius' *Satiricon*, Seneca's *Letters*, Juvenal's *Satires*, Tacitus' historical works, and Suetonius' *Lives of the Caesars*. Paul was writing to dwellers in Rome, some of them 'of Caesar's household' (Phil. 4.22), who had all this before their eyes.

The close of this chapter is a warning to all peoples and all ages. To read it in our own 'permissive society' is to encounter a challenge to be strong in faith, determined in our committal to God, urgent in our evangelism. Paul is describing a society which had abandoned God. He is diagnosing the malady from which Rome was to die, for no great nation has ever yet been destroyed by a foe from without which has not already destroyed itself by corruption within. Such sin carries its own penalty, its own damnation. The time is here when Christians must show, as they were called upon to do in Rome, by word, act, and manner of life, their difference.

The last verse expresses ultimate rebellion. Sin falls under four heads. First stands fleshly sin, so obvious, so disreputable and withal, at times, so pitiable. Secondly comes spiritual sin, pride, vanity, lust for power and the legion of the like, respectable, yet treacherous, too often well concealed, and altogether damnable. Thirdly follows diabolical sin in which evil becomes an object of love for its own sake, sin's judgement on itself, the final fruit of unrepentant wickedness. Finally, comes blasphemy, that conscious hostility to God which the Bible defines in its final consummation as the 'sin unto death', and which finds no repentance because it is never committed until all desire for repentance has been wilfully rejected.

Questions for further study and discussion on Romans ch. 1

1. 'True freedom consists in service.' Apply this to the life of the Christian.
2. 'The Incarnation without the Resurrection is meaningless.' How do the Gospels illustrate this truth?
3. Study 'grace', its definition and various meanings. Consult the dictionary and Bible commentaries.
4. How are obedience and faith linked?
5. From what is the Christian 'saved'?
6. What is 'natural theology'? What does creation teach of God?
7. How does Psa. 50.21 illustrate idolatry?
8. How does 'permissiveness' in ethics and morals run counter to Christianity?
9. Why must sin, tolerated and cherished, grow more heinous and destructive?

Romans 2.1–4 'All Have Sinned'

In the next chapter Paul makes one of the great evangelical statements of Scripture: 'All have sinned and fall short of the glory of God' (3.23). Christianity maintains that at some point of time man, self-conscious and free, set his will in opposition to the will of God, and that ever since humanity has followed suit. Nor can individual man shift the burden of that responsibility on to history, heredity,

28

environment. Professor Butterfield, the historian already quoted, says with striking simplicity: 'It happens to be a fact that I can recognize responsibility or freedom in myself—I can feel more internally sure about the fact that it was possible for me to have helped doing this or that than I can about the matters that belong to external scholarship.' No honest man will deny the personal application of that remark. We are all, in our more candid moments, conscious of the fact that we bend more easily to ill than good, that we seek with greater ease the good of self than the good of others, that our very virtues are based more on fear of punishment than on love of good, and that pride, self-assertion, arrogance, the very element and essential of all sin, mingles itself like a pervading poison with all our pretence and practice of good. In short, to apply a famous dictum, if there were no doctrine of a Fall and of Original Sin, 'it would be necessary to invent one'.

Paul finds it necessary, before proceeding to this assertion, to meet an objection. He has described in vivid terms the moral breakdown in contemporary society, but he is also conscious of a counter-argument, and pictures himself in debate with an objector. There were, firstly, good pagans. We have mentioned Seneca, destined like many Christians, to die at Nero's hands. He wrote at the same time as Paul was writing, and his attitude to moral evil was so uncompromising that Tertullian spoke of him as 'often one of us'. But Seneca, for all his goodness, illustrates Paul's point. His tutelage of the youthful Nero led him into horrifying compromises which betrayed all his aspirations, and revealed his dire need.

Secondly, came the Jew, confident in his election, certain of his righteousness, proud of the Law. Paul will soon proceed to show what the Law really signified, and the hollowness of all Jewish pride.

Romans 2.5–10 Paul and James

The last verse of yesterday's reading spoke of a tremendous responsibility. Man can presume upon the grace of God, and imagine that His love is mere indulgence. The first verse of today's reading expresses in awesome terms how heavy a load such trifling with eternal things is upon the soul of man. To treat the grace and kindness of God lightly is to encounter the inevitable severity of God's hostility to sin.

Paul proceeds to insist upon certain principles. First, God will 'render to every man according to his works' (6). This verse must be steadfastly borne in mind by those who study the great doctrine of this epistle—justification by faith. There is no contradiction between Paul and James. To Paul, it was no faith which did not issue in deeds, conduct, and character.

The next two verses open the theme of God's impartiality. There is no covenant of indulgence for those who had known God best, indeed responsibility is deepened. For Paul, a rabbi and a Pharisee, such a notion was revolutionary, and emphasizes the transformation which Christ had brought to his mind. In the strength of God's Spirit a whole way of thought, a life-long pattern of conviction, had been broken. When Peter was summoned to Cornelius' home in Caesarea, the same conviction gripped him, and filled him with wonder (Acts 10.34 f.). And for us who read their words the wonder is that Christ could command such obedience, and induce such change. It prompts us to ask how deep the transforming influence of the indwelling Christ has penetrated into our prejudices, our modes of thinking.

The 'factious' of v. 8 are the rebellious. This is the essence of sin, for man has chosen sin in open and self-willed rebellion against God. 'One of the greatest deficiencies of our time,' remarks Professor Butterfield, 'is the failure of the imagination or the intellect to bring home to itself the portentous character of human sin.' André Gide is expressing the mind of 'factious' or 'contentious' (AV[KJV]) man, when, in *The Prodigal Son*, he extols the will to independence as the birth of human freedom and of man's responsibility for his own life. In the notion that human independence can only be secured by severance from God lies the fount of all disaster, and along that path come the fiercest of temptations.

Romans 2.11–16 God's Impartiality

Verse 11 forms a text which is expanded in the remainder of the passage. It is a theme which we could wish had been more fully developed, but Paul was content to make his main point, and that was that the mere possession of the Law conveyed no special privilege. In fact it sharpened responsibility.

In v. 13 are echoes of a rabbinical debate of the sort beloved by the scribes. Some quoted: 'If you will diligently hearken . . .' (Exod. 15.26) as a proof that doing was less important than hearing. Paul generally was reflecting the nobler view of the school to which he belonged, the Pharisees. 'Not learning, but doing is the Leader', runs one Pharisaic commentary. The interest which emerges from thus closely marking Paul's words is his intimacy with the forms and language of current theological debate.

There is also apparent to anyone familiar with Greek thought, another clear indication of the same versatile scholar's complete

30

familiarity with Greek thought. This is a phenomenon which is notable in 1 Cor. 1—4, a passage of sustained irony which could not have been written by anyone unfamiliar with Plato and the Stoics.

Paul's knowledge of the Stoics, the noblest school of philosophy active in the world at the time, was clear in his address to the Athenian Court. It is as obvious here. The Stoics had much to say on a law naturally written in the heart, and were the first Greeks to use the term 'conscience' in Paul's sense. And it was four centuries since Aristotle had written in his *Ethics:* 'The truly educated man will behave as if he had a law within himself.' It was five centuries since Sophocles had made Antigone confront the tyrant, who demanded obedience in all he said, with the magnificent remark that 'there are unwritten and irrefragable ordinances of Heaven', which those conscious of them cannot break.

Paul was aware of such ideas and the passage is further evidence of his familiarity with the patterns of thinking in the world to which he brought the gospel. An example lies therein. Paul's famous word to the Corinthians, written six or seven years before (1 Cor. 1.18–31), implied no abandonment of all available means of communication with his contemporaries.

Romans 2.17–21 What of Example?

C. H. Dodd calls this passage 'fiercely satirical'. It is better described as ironical. Human pride, the most elusive and persistent of man's vices, can turn into a boast the very grace which should humble and the privilege which should inspire a lowly gratitude. It transforms the standing with God which the sinner has done nothing to merit or to win into a claim to excellence.

In v. 18 the grounds of the Jew's pathetic boasting was reviewed. They knew the will of God and 'approved what is excellent'. The R.S.V. translation is not good. Phillips' 'appreciate moral values', and the phrase 'aware of moral distinctions' of the NEB, are nearer to the Greek. Paul uses the words again in Phil. 1.10. Read vs. 9 f. in that chapter. The passage may be rendered: 'This is another prayer I pray, that your love may increase more and more in discernment and all manner of perception, so that you may judge what is right and wrong, and be sincere and safe from stumbling until the day of Christ. . . .'

That is, discernment and perception are needed if we are to judge right and wrong. The phrase, here and in the Philippian letter, means literally 'test out things which differ'. It is the verb of Rom. 12.2: '*prove* what is that good, acceptable and perfect will of God'

31

(AV[KJV]). It referred, in its common Greek use, to auditing and scrutinizing the accounts and conduct of office. Both AV and RSV assume that 'things which differ' are things which are better than ordinary, and this is the rendering in both passages. But 'things which differ' are surely more likely to be ethical opposites. Hence the Jew's boast. He had the Law, which prescribed for him the clean and the unclean.

It was a fact that, as no other nation, he had a notion of the holiness of God. It was true that he was, or could have been, 'a guide to the blind, a light to those who are in darkness, a corrector of the foolish, a teacher of children . . .' Such enlightenment should have made his nation that which it was from all time designed to be—a missionary people. Isaiah had glimpsed and preached that truth. It was part of the promise to Abraham (Isa. 45.22; 52.10; Gen. 18.18; 22.18; 26.4; 28.14). It was a privilege and a responsibility. To corrupt it into a theme for pride was heinous sin.

Romans 2.22–26   The Testimony of Israel

Among the greater characters of Israel there was always a realization that the honour of their God was in their hands. Note the significant phrase in the story of Abraham and Lot (Gen. 13.7-9)—'the Canaanites and the Perizzites dwelt in the land'. It was this which made strife in the camp of Abraham serious. Observe, too, Ezra's remark (Ezra 8.22). He had boasted of his God.

And now Paul in v. 24 quotes the Septuagint rendering of Isa. 52.5. In the prophetic passage it is the degradation and misery of Israel which forms the basis for the Gentiles' scorn. What sort of God, they said, so abandons His people? This is more than once the theme of O.T. prayer.

Paul gives the words another twist. Like people, like God. If Jews have a reputation for vice, then the Gentiles' response will inevitably be that their God is base. There was some reason in the assumption. Man becomes like the object of his worship, and if man creates an object of worship out of his own mind, that deity inevitably reflects its origin, and courts rejection.

Paul is writing, no doubt with some knowledge of Roman Jewry, and there is some contemporary evidence that all was not well with the reputation of the Jews. Probably a decade later than the writing of the letter to Rome, Joachin ben Zakkai spoke with scorn of Jewish morals. The date might imply that it was a reaction to the terrible experience of the Great Rebellion (A.D. 66–70), and the destruction of the Temple, Jerusalem and Palestine. Matt. 23, however, suggests that the roots of moral corruption went deeper in time, and found their ground in a religion turned legal, formal and unspiritual.

This was stern language. Of what use the Law if the Law was flouted by its advocates? Nor is this irrelevant to those emancipated from the Law in Christ. Christ is dishonoured if those without Him walk more righteously than those who profess His name. As John wrote many years later: 'The one who professes to abide in Him *is bound* to walk as He walked' (1 John 2.6). There is a debt of love, a binding obligation, and doctrine is tested by its fruit. So we prove the validity of religious experience. Unless that experience involves a reorientation of the will, a setting of the affections in the direction of the moral excellence revealed perfectly in the Person of the Lord, it is no true experience of God, but a sham, a futile stirring of the emotions, self-exaltation, and a pose.

Romans 2.27–29   Outward Sign or Inward Reality

'The men of Nineveh,' said Christ, 'will appear at the Judgement when the men of this generation are on trial, and ensure their condemnation, for they repented at the preaching of Jonah' (Luke 11.32, NEB). Paul is saying in the technical language of Judaism, that the Gentile, if he observes the moral law as conscience reveals it to him, wins the favour of God, but that the Jew, in spite of, indeed because of, the physical sign in his body, falls under condemnation if he fails to keep the Law which has been divinely given him.

It is a moot question how far the highly specialized language of the Judaistic debate should be kept in translation. Involved in the whole process is the other question—when translation becomes paraphrase. Other modern translations should be looked at here. RSV is conservative in its rendering. A. S. Way's little known translation concludes the passage well: '*He* is the Jew who is so in his secret soul; and his is the true circumcision—that of the heart, consisting in the Spirit's presence, not in observance of the written letter. Men may have no praise for such a man—God has'. This is paraphrase, but legitimate.

The argument appears remote from today and its ways of thinking. In the particular form in which we find it, it *is* remote. But consider two points. First, imagine its impact in the Roman Jewish community. A Jew, Paul points out, can be a transgressor of the Law, in spite of his possession of the Law, and the physical mark of the Covenant in his body. He has an outward sign which does not vary as may the condition of his heart. That sign can be a reminder, a challenge, an encouragement. Hence an undoubted blessing, and an advantage. Hence, too, a responsibility.

Secondly, remote from everyday thought though this argument may be with its symbolic language and strange imagery, the principle applies to the Church. No outward formality, no ritual of worship, no religious attitudes or practice of Church observance, no form or ceremony, no membership of organization or system, no right of birth, nothing devised of man, can replace the true experience of Christ in rebirth and salvation, genuine committal to Him, and continued practice of His presence.

Romans 3.1–4 The Jew's Advantage

This passage is a brief preview of chs. 9—11. Paul seems to pause at his last conclusion, wondering whether he has hit his fellow countrymen too hard. Some might imagine that he had concluded that the Jew had no special privilege whatsoever, and that the sign of the Covenant had no significance apart from a change in the heart.

In fact, that statement comes very near the truth. But Paul was a 'Hebrew of the Hebrews' (Phil. 3.4–6), and also remembered, perhaps, a word of Christ (John 4.22). On both counts he felt impelled to say a word of encouragement. The first question literally runs: 'What has the Jew over the rest?' It continues: 'What help is the sign in his body?'

He sums it up in v. 2. The Jews have the records of God's own self-revelation. Why then 'To begin with'? Paul has in mind the whole rabbinical argument of the three later chapters (9—11), and the list of advantages abruptly cut short in this verse could be completed from 9.4 f. To be the guardians of God's revelation of His Person and His Plan for man was an immense privilege.

Then Paul remembers the thread of his earlier argument. The Jews had much at God's hand, but they used it ill. They were given commandments, not privileges. Special choice involves a special duty. Some, to be sure, failed to see this. They did not believe (3). Paul is treading carefully. It was a remnant only who believed, and to this fact the O.T. is witness. And now it was 'the Remnant' again, who had grasped the truth that Christ fulfilled, concluded, and gave significance to the Law.

Did the vote of 'some', even of a majority, invalidate truth? God forbid. This is the gist of Paul's argument. The verdict of the multitude is no expression of basic truth—neither in time past nor now. God works through minorities. It is a truth worth remembering when alone, or when a tiny band faces overwhelming odds. It is worth remembering in society at large. It is worth considering in the context of history, when so many seek cheap accommodation with secular thought. To belong to 'the Few' is a privilege.

Romans 3.5–8 A Theological Quibble

It has been remarked before that anyone sensitive to the ways of Greek thought recognizes in Paul's writing, in a host of subtle ways, his Greek outlook, which complements his equally obvious Jewish insights. The imaginary debate with a Jewish objector which is the key to this passage is typical of some of the writings of popular Stoicism.

The objections brought up by the supposed antagonist appear in this passage at their most obscure, but the argument Paul deals with is one which was not uncommonly advanced against his own doctrine of salvation by grace, and he was peculiarly sensitive to it.

It was simply this: if a man sins, his sin is a foil to God's righteousness, the contrast setting God's holiness in higher relief, just as darkness would not be known without light, and pleasure is made more comprehensible by pain. Therefore, the pernicious conclusion follows, if a man's sin enhances the glory of God, why should he be condemned for it?

The rift in the logic is obvious. If God could take joy in another's sin, because thereby He was exalted, it would follow that God was imperfect Himself. The whole argument is absurd, and Paul is almost apologetic in advancing it (5): 'I speak in a human way', that is: 'This is common argument.'

But although the logic seems absurd, and the very drift of the argument almost blasphemous, is not the same sin apparent in more than one sphere of modern theological thought? By one means or another, by diminishing man's responsibility or by misrepresenting God, man, the sinner, seeks to avoid the admission, in all heinousness, of his sin. The modern theologian, compromising with 'permissiveness', murmuring excuses about 'situation ethics', speculating on God's 'involvement' in the world, and avoiding the Bible's downright condemnation of sin, has no cause to be impatient with his ancient counterpart.

Questions for further study and discussion on Romans chs. 2—3.8

1. How does man 'fall short of the glory of God'?
2. How is sin related to rebellion? What is 'the Fall'?
3. 'A privilege always carries a duty or a responsibility.' How can this be illustrated from the Jews?

4. What place should ethics have in Christian preaching? Illustrate from Paul, James and Peter.
5. 'The doctrine of the Remnant.' Where does the Bible, in both Testaments, speak of this? What is its significance today?
6. 'All sin is accompanied by a faulty conception of God.' Is this true?
7. Are moral standards variable in accordance with 'the situation'?

Romans 3.9–12   All Equal in Sin

As the imaginary discussion continues, Paul returns to the equal condemnation under which both Jew and Gentile stand. Both are 'under the power of sin' (9). The RSV rightly renders it thus. The Greek phrase simply says 'under sin'. It occurs again at the end of 7.14, and in Gal. 3.22. It occurs in Eph. 1.22: 'under His feet', and in 1 Pet. 5.6. In all such contexts it implies subjection, reduction to impotence, and bondage. In both Christ's teaching and Paul's, sin is a bondage and a servitude (John 8.34). Rank and station are a mockery among slaves. Hence the equality of Jew and Gentile, sharers of a common tyranny.

Paul then proceeds to a 'catena', or 'chain' of quotations. Two or three points of interest emerge. First, note Paul's identity with the manner and form of scribal and rabbinical debate. In the interplay of theological argument during the Passion Week between the Lord and those who thought to discredit Him, O.T. texts were used in this fashion. See, for example, Matt. 22.42–44 and John 10.34–36. The latter context is striking. The Lord's use of a text, while not entirely unrelated to the original setting of the word, was considerably adapted. Adopting the rabbis' line of argument, He struck them down with an O.T. phrase.

When quoting O.T. scriptures it was not the practice to give particular attention to all aspects of the context. This is the second point to note. Paul's quotation in vs. 10–12 is from Psa. 14.1–3, where nothing attaches the words peculiarly to Jews. This, however, was not an illegitimate use of O.T. quotation. It was an accepted use of sacred texts, and must not be judged by alien standards of argument. A Jew would regard a quotation as authoritative irrespective of context. It must also be noted that Paul was himself writing what was to be Scripture. His use is sanctioned by divine authority.

The O.T. made the mental background of the Jews to whom Paul primarily wrote. Christ's conversation with Nicodemus can be properly understood only if it is realized that the learned rabbi knew by heart Ezek. 36.26 —37.10. The letter to the Hebrews reveals the same intellectual background in those addressed.

For us, in the third place, there is a solemn warning not to treat the O.T. with less than the reverence it claims. We have here another illustration of how inextricably woven is the Old with the New.

Romans 3.13–18 The Old Testament Speaks

Verse 13 is an exact quotation of Psa. 5.9, as it appears in the Greek O.T., the Septuagint. The original appears to be directed by David against the rebels in his kingdom, if Pss. 3—6 are correctly ascribed to the time of the monarch's retreat before Absalom.

Verse 14 is a freely quoted version of Psa. 10.7, of unknown reference, while vs. 15–17 are selectively extracted from Isa. 59.7 f. It is interesting to observe the workings of the mind of a man taught to think and express himself within the framework of O.T. language and thought. It is important always to remember, in reading Paul's letters, the Epistle to the Hebrews, Peter's five addresses in the opening chapters of the Acts, and also much of what the Lord Himself said, that the communication presupposed such habits of thought and expression, and such a frame of reference.

The purpose of this catena of O.T. quotations is to establish, by appeal to the very oracles of which the Jews were the custodians (2), the sinfulness of Jewry, and the potency of such quotation in the argument is beyond doubt. Nor must it be supposed, easily though the words of the O.T. came to his lips, that Paul's quotation was haphazard. . . .

First, he establishes by quotation the charge of universal sin (10 f.). He proceeds to reinforce it (12), and to illustrate the rebellion of the heart by the baleful utterances of the lips, words fraught with death and corruption, tongues dedicated to deceit, and malice that kills in their words (13). Their speech betrayed the noble functions of speech, calling down harm, and giving expression to the bitterness of the godless personality which sought such self-revelation (14). It is word and deed which betrays the soul's condition. Words are the revelation of thought, and that which lays hold upon the mind turns inevitably into action (15). The world's violence begins in the mind. And the evil abroad in society at large is only the collective outcome, the total individual wickedness. Ruin and misery are inevitable results (16). Peace vanishes, in the life of men and society (17), and all because men fail to 'stand in awe, and sin not' (18 and Psa. 4.4, AV[KJV]). A devastating build-up of quotations, in fact.

Romans 3.19, 20 The Purpose of the Law

These two verses round off a section of the letter which began at 1.18. We shall take them in turn: *Verse 19.* Paul has been quoting

37

from the Psalms and Isaiah. His reference to 'the Law' obviously refers to these passages. It follows that he is using the term in a special sense. The Law is referred to some seventy times in the letter, and is used in four different senses (i.e. the Pentateuch, 3.21, where it is distinguished from the prophets; a principle, 3.27; 7.21,23,25; 8.2; the law of God, 2.17 ff., 23 ff.; and in the present passage, where it obviously refers to the O.T. in its entirety). The meaning of this verse is that, if those who have God's revelation are condemned by that very revelation, how can anyone else claim righteousness?

Verse 20. Hence arises a daunting thought. Of what use is the Law? The question opens up a whole important facet of Pauline and Christian thinking. The Jew believed that he was just in God's eyes if he kept the Law. That was the position of the rich young man who came to Christ with a vital question (Luke **18**.18–27). His shallow thinking imagined that he had actually kept the Law, until Christ's probing showed how imperfect he was. The disciples' question and Christ's obscure answer were a foreshadowing of what Paul is to make clear in this epistle—the true purpose of the Law, the dilemma of conviction of sin, and God's remedy—justification by faith.

Paul had pondered long over the meaning of it all. As a Pharisee he had dedicated his life to the keeping of the Law (Phil. 3.4–6), and yet had no peace nor satisfaction (the theme closes ch. 7). But the Law was not without purpose, impossible though it was meticulously to keep it. In a flash of revelation Paul saw the truth. The Law revealed man to himself, showed him the righteousness of God, and how far short he fell of its demands, set before him the nature and the seriousness of sin, and therefore, by immediate implication, his dire need of a Saviour. The first necessity if a man is to come as a penitent to God must be a deep realization of his natural helplessness. This, Paul saw, was the prime function of the Law.

Romans 3.21–25a   The Universal Condemnation

The way is now clear for the great affirmation. It has been demonstrated that Jew and Gentile stand alike condemned, and that the only advantage the Jew had was the clear proof of his need by the very impact of the Law and the revelation of divine demands implicit in it. Nor, says Paul, was this alien to the O.T., in both the Pentateuch and the Prophets, had they been properly read and understood (21). This is important. Paul implies that the legalistic Judaism from which he was emancipated by his conversion, was not a true development of the O.T., but a sterile perversion of it. There was another tradition, traceable to Abraham, who later is to provide a striking illustration of the theme (ch. 4), and also prominent in the message of the prophets, who in no way saw the Law as the final revelation of God (Isa. 1.1–18). Paul was abundantly right. The theme of the N.T. emerges again and again in the O.T. (Psa. 51.16 f.). Hence the heresy of Marcion in the second century, calling on the Church to abandon the O.T. Hence the need today to reaffirm the unity of the Bible. Paul was preaching no new version of God's revelation. He was calling Jewry back to their real heritage, from the blind road into which Pharisaism had led it.

God's righteousness is shown to be unattainable by the Law. To fall short of His glory is to betray the prime function of our being, to demonstrate the marring of the divine image in which we were created. Hence a clear definition of sin (23). See Psa. 4.4 and Isa. 43.7 for the germ of Paul's thought in his comprehensive statement.

Justification (24) is, as the Westminster Shorter Catechism puts it, 'an act of God's free grace, wherein He pardons all our sins, and accepts us as righteous in His sight'. This is through 'the redemption which is in Christ Jesus'. Redemption, in the meaning of the Greek word, is the act of buying a slave out of bondage to set him free. A ransom, in other words, is paid, just as Israel was redeemed from bondage in Egypt (Deut. 7.8) and in Babylon (Isa. 51.11). See also Gal. 3.23—4.7. Our justification rests on the fact that God, of His own free grace, has intervened to rescue His people from bondage to sin. It follows that the redeemed are those who accept emancipation. It follows, too, that they must *believe* to do so.

Romans 3.25b–27   The Sacrifice

Verse 25 has been divided to secure a logical end to yesterday's note, and a firm beginning for today's exposition. It will be necessary, however, to go back to one term in yesterday's note. The word rendered 'expiation', the 'propitiation' of the AV (KJV), derives from a verb which most commonly means to 'expiate' a sin, that is, by some act of ritual or sacrifice, by some payment or satisfaction given, to annul the guilt incurred by the commission of a sin. In the O.T. the formalities whereby the priesthood or the people were cleansed from defilement are described as 'making propitiation' or 'atonement'.

In the present passage Christ is set forth as the means by which moral guilt may be annulled, and that is obviously an act which God alone could determine and perform. This is why the RSV avoids the term 'propitiation'. The word suggests the placating of

an angry God, and although God's implacable opposition to evil
in all its forms may properly be described as 'wrath', that is not the
whole theological picture. Paul here means that God 'puts forward'
the means whereby the guilt of sin may be removed and He does this
through Christ.

It was 'by His blood' because Christ had to die to make such
atonement possible, the last, complete and all-satisfying sacrifice.
Again the O.T. is drawn into union with the N.T. And yet again,
how could such sacrifice be effective in its operation unless those
for whom it was made regarded it as such and received it? Faith is
that act of receptivity and committal whereby God's means of grace
is received in gratitude and appropriated into the life. Where grace
meets faith, there is redemption.

We have passed through three word pictures. God justifies: He
takes the part of a judge who sets the prisoner free, absolving him
from guilt. God redeems: He pays the slave's ransom and liberates
him. God cleanses: He takes the place of the priest who makes
expiation. To those trained in the imagery of the O.T., each metaphor
was vivid and complete.

Thus God can redeem without loss of righteousness (25,26),
without betrayal of principle, without ceasing to be Himself. He is
'faithful and *just* to forgive us our sins' (1 John 1.9, AV[KJV]).
God remains God, no whit of His holiness diminished. The judge
is not unjust; the emancipator pays the full price; the expiation is
complete.

Meditation: Isa. 45.22. '*I looked until I could have looked my
eyes away. There and then the cloud was gone, the darkness had
rolled away and I saw the sun*' (C. H. Spurgeon).

Romans 3.28–31   A Firm Conclusion

'Therefore we conclude. . . .' (28 AV[KJV]) is a better rendering
of the opening phrase than that of the RSV ('For we hold that').
The words ring with the confidence of the writer. Such firm conclusions were wrought out in anguish of soul in the years of retreat
and searching which followed the shattering event of the Damascus
Road. 'A man' (28) means any human being, and leads to the fuller
definition of the next verse .There cannot be two distinct religious
systems, one based on the Law and applicable to a Chosen People,
and the other based on faith, and available for the other division
of mankind, as the Jew conceived mankind. Paul is anticipating
and closing a desperate breach in his line of argument which his
continually present and imaginary Jewish objector might be likely
to make.

And why? There were those of his race who imagined a monopoly on God. Paul's view of God was based on the old covenant, and Abraham, in this closely woven epistle, is never far from his thinking. 'In you all the families of the earth shall be blessed' implied a religion far wider than one race, and presupposed a God who was God of all men. Jew and Gentile could, by the same argument, have only one way of salvation.

Paul knew very well, from his own agonizing experience, how difficult it was for his fellow Jews to cast off the deep preoccupations of a narrow belief which had penetrated from childhood all their thinking, their whole personality, their complete view of God and God's world. He drives his argument about salvation by faith with ruthless honesty and urgency to its only possible conclusion but he passes on the same comforting thoughts which had come to his aid when he found himself thrust to his vast reappraisement of all he had believed.

Quite clearly the Lord's word, contained in the oral tradition, was in his mind. He came, He said, not to annul the Law, but to fulfil it. Hence the closing verse of this chapter, and the conclusion of a main line of the whole argument of the letter. The Law only finds meaning if it be thus bound to the ultimate revelation of God's long-standing purpose. Two further lines of proof are to follow, one in ch. 4 and another in chs. 6 to 8. The just demands of the Law, by no means made void, are met in believers only.

Questions for further study and discussion on Romans 3.9–31

1. Where, and why, does the N.T. speak of sin as servitude?
2. In modern apologetics and preaching are texts from the Bible enough?
3. What does the story of 'the rich young ruler' teach about the Law and grace?
4. How is the O.T. essential to the N.T.?
5. How does faith differ from credulity? Does doubt negative faith?
6. What is 'propitiation'? See reference books.
7. How can God be 'just' in forgiving sin?

Romans 4.1–4   Abraham, Father of the Faithful

Some reading should be done before this chapter is studied. To understand Paul's thesis we must first know about one of the great men of the O.T. Read Gen. 12—25 over the next few days and Heb. 11.8–19.

'By faith Abraham . . .' Four thousand years ago Ur of the Chaldees was a sea-port on the Persian Gulf, where man first learned to sail the open waters. It was the London or New York of that distant age. The dhows sailed east to the Indus valley ports, and to Ceylon, and the talk of sailors in the Euphrates valley town made one, Abraham, a citizen of Ur, aware of a great world across the waters. And down the Fertile Crescent, which made a route for the caravans up the river and round into Syria and Egypt, came the traders with stories of magnificence beside the Nile, and of the ships which came from Crete, and who told of other races, other cities, other ways. It was a varied story of human activity, with one common element for the man of Ur who listened, questioned, thought. The whole world, east, west, north, south, was lamentably lost in grotesque views of God, and soul-destroying superstition. The cruel cult of human sacrifice, the slaughter of babies, or the sacred prostitution, which he saw in Ur, were the common practices of man. Or there were worse. In Egypt they worshipped the bull, the cat, the ram, the crocodile. In Crete there were sanguinary rites of bull-fighting. . . . Abraham had become aware of nobler truth, that God was one, that God cared for man, and prompted the mind of the man who reached for Him. He had heard a voice and listened.

For thus an amazing project took shape. Abraham was the first missionary, the first man with an ardent desire to share a saving truth with his fellow men. He was aware, as perhaps no other man of his day was aware, of the vastness of the world. It was obvious that one man alone could not influence the multitude of mankind from farthest east to farthest west. But a *nation*, dedicated to the truth, might do what one man could hardly do. Hence the magnificent plan which took Abraham out from his homeland to found a nation in the clean desert—by faith. Hence the call which came, to a heart concerned and prepared to hearken. 'Abraham believed . . .'

Romans 4.5–8 Not by Works

It was a bold affirmation at the end of the last chapter when Paul claimed that the Law and the Prophets contained the root of his doctrine that salvation was by faith. It was natural enough that the great father of the Hebrew people (Matt. 3.9) should be invoked as a test case. Paul is most glad to examine the great story in that context, and does so in both this passage and the letter to the Galatians. That is why, not only the story of Abraham in Genesis, but also Gal. 3, should be read in connection with these six readings.

Paul's point has been that deeds do not win a saving merit, even if those deeds be the observance of the Law. It is rather faith, a simple trust which takes God at His word, which justifies. To the Jew of Paul's day brought up on the Law, this was revolutionary. Paul replies that, on the contrary, the most honoured figure in their history is the prime and perfect illustration.

Abraham had recognized the voice of God in the mighty conviction that held him. God was one, and God must be made known. It seemed impossible, in view of his childlessness, that he could become a great nation, that he could father the twin kindred implied in the 'stars of heaven' and the 'sand which is on the sea shore' (Gen. 22.17). More, did not his trust endure as the years went by, and an heir seemed impossible, did he not continue to believe when it appeared that the heir, at last apparent, was to be removed from him by his own hand?

Some rabbinical thought had seen this rebuff to their legalism, and had argued that Abraham was chosen because he was the most righteous man available. There is no evidence for this. Abraham was fallible. He hastened ahead of God in the matter of Hagar. Earlier he had abandoned Palestine for Egypt. He had lied to Pharaoh.

It must have been faith which counted, as the great word to Abraham said (Gen. 15.6). And more than a millennium later, Paul repeats, the great king and psalmist confirmed the truth. Hence Psa. 32.1 f. which are a reaching for N.T. truth.

Romans 4.9–12 An Objection Answered

It should be understood that Paul is still imagining a debate with a keen-minded Jew such as he must often have had in the synagogues and with the rabbis (Acts 17.2; 28.23). The interlocutor concedes his point about Abraham. Very well, Abraham was justified by faith, but is he not the father of the Jews (John 8.33), and does not that suggest that the dispensation of such grace is for the privileged nation only? Paul replies with a typical rabbinical argument. In writing to the Galatians he points out that the covenant with Abraham was 430 years earlier in history than the giving of the Law, and therefore took precedence over the Mosaic code (Gal. 3.17). Similarly, here he points out that the rite of circumcision, the national 'sign in the flesh' of the Jewish people, was instituted (Gen. 17.10 ff.) *after* the covenant, in fact fourteen years later. The argument for a Jew would be cogent. The objector is brought back to the same point of refutation in a carefully constructed argument. Verses 1–8 correspond to 3.27 f. and vs. 9–12 to 3.29–31.

Two further points might have been raised. The covenant with Abraham had international reference (Gen. 12.3). Also this was the implication of the change of name (Gen. **17.**5) from Abram, which seems to mean 'exalted father', to Abraham, which means 'father of a multitude'. That multitude, too, if the dual figure of speech is to be pressed, is of earthly and heavenly progeny (Gen. **22.**17), not only the Hebrew people who have penetrated all nations, and the Semite descendants of Ishmael, but also a spiritual posterity, those who, by faith, become the children of the father of the faithful.

It is moving to see the sweep of history which began with the obedience of one man who had a God-given vision, and pursued it in faith, one man like any other man, stumbling, rising, failing but carrying on. There is no calculating the end of one act of trust, sacrifice, and godly endeavour.

Meditation: John **11.**40

Romans 4.13–16   The Law No Negation

Paul presses his point about the Law. He insists again on the global nature of the promise to Abraham (Gen. **12.**3; **18.**18; **22.**18). If Abraham's covenanted heritage was to be confined to his own nationals, then its geographical limits were closely defined (Gen. **15.**18–21 in specific terms, and in more general terms at Gen. **13.**14 f., cf. Josh. **1.**2–4). The O.T., however, contains the hint of a wider posterity, which the N.T. takes up and claims (Heb. **11.**10; and observe Paul's point at Gal. **3.**16 and 29 where he claims Christ, and therefore Christ's people, as the true posterity of the patriarch).

This covenant, he has shown, rested on faith. If the Law, given over four centuries later (Gal. **3.**17), is to be the permanent way of salvation, a covenant is annulled twice over. First, that which was universal is peremptorily confined to one nation, and secondly and more seriously, 'faith is null and void' (14). A new principle is introduced. To inherit the promise men must keep the Law, and since to keep it is impossible, the race, which had known God's grace in the promise to Abraham, and had learned from him to move out in trust, passes under the shadow of wrath.

In v. 15, Paul digresses a little to develop this argument. He is to return to it later, and it has a place in the letter to the Galatian wanderers. He is always a little anxious lest he should appear to say that the Law was an unnecessary intrusion. The debates with the rabbis had shown him how necessary it was to make this point. The Law had its place and purpose. It did not negate the promise to Abraham. It prepared the way for the consummation of that promise, by closely defining sin. It could not cure. It could not save. Grace all along had been the way.

'Not the labours of my hands
Can fulfil Thy law's demands;
Could my zeal no respite know,
Could my tears for ever flow,
All for sin could not atone:
Thou must save, and Thou alone'

(A. M. Toplady).

Romans 4.17–21 What is Faith?

A papyrus scrap from Egypt once provided a vivid translation of the word variously rendered 'substance' and 'assurance' in Heb. 11.1. Few have been bold enough to use the suggested translation, but it runs: 'Now faith is the title-deeds to the things we hope for . . .' 'Faith,' said Augustine, 'is to believe, on the word of God, what we do not see, and its reward is to see and enjoy what we believe.' Tennyson may have had Augustine's definition in mind when he wrote in the Prologue to *In Memoriam*:

'We have but faith: we cannot know;
For knowledge is of things we see;
And yet we trust it comes from Thee,
A beam in darkness: let it grow.

Abraham had God's word that he should have a vast posterity. Circumstances seemed to make such an event physically impossible. His trust was tested to the limit—and so he hoped when hope seemed against all probability (18). He believed that at the touch of the Creative Hand, the death which was creeping through his body could create life. Perhaps Paul has another 'new creation' in mind, that of which he wrote to Ephesus (Eph. 2.1,5).

Abraham weighed all these factors. His story shows his active consideration of such adverse circumstances. He must have been conscious of the tug of doubt. His mistake over Hagar reveals as much. He was tested and knew that he was being tested. But 'no distrust made him waver . . .' (20). He conquered doubt, in other words, for that phrase does not claim that no qualms beset his mind, keen in its intelligence. And in the victory thus gained, he strengthened his faith, the aim and purpose of such testing. It 'gives glory to God' (20) thus to trust Him, and the reward is sturdiness infused into one's faith—to the very point where faith becomes something near to knowledge, a blessed paradox (2 Tim. 1.12). Let Tennyson continue on that fine integration of mind and heart:

'Let knowledge grow from more to more,
But more of reverence in us dwell;
That mind and soul, according well,
May make one music as before.'

Romans 4.22–25 For Us Also

Paul sums up. James Denney may be quoted in his comment on this paragraph. He points out that it is not arbitrarily that 'faith is reckoned as righteousness'. Faith, he continues, 'is the spiritual attitude of a man who is conscious that in himself he has no strength, and no hope of a future, and who nevertheless casts himself upon, and lives by, the word of God which assures him of a future'. This is the necessarily and eternally right attitude of all souls to God. 'Now,' says Denney, 'this was the attitude of Abraham to God, and it is the attitude of all sinners who believe in God through Christ; and to him and all alike it is reckoned by God for righteousness. The gospel does not subvert the religious order under which Abraham lived; it illustrates, extends and confirms it.' (*Expositor's Greek Testament*, 2.621.)

Fittingly, the chapter ends with an affirmation of that faith in Christ which Paul was expounding (24 f.), in a rhythmical statement which may have been a credal formula for Christians, and especially Jewish Christians. It is couched in the poetic form of Hebrew parallelism, so apparent in the Psalms ('a lamp to my feet and a light to my path'). There is no theological separation between Christ's death and His resurrection, as though atonement for sin and justification for the sinner were separate divine processes. Paul always associated the death of the Lord with His rising again. He knew Christ as the Risen One who had died, and ever lived for our justification.

The RSV obscures the O.T. origins of the language in v. 25. The AV is actually closer with the rendering 'delivered for our offences.' In Isa. **53** the same verb is used twice in the Septuagint version (6,12). That chapter concludes (12): 'because of their sins he was delivered up.' This is the phrase Paul echoes, for he commonly has the Greek version of the O.T. in mind.

Let Denney conclude: 'It was the greatest display of power ever made to man when God raised Christ from the dead . . . The only right attitude of any human being in presence of this power is utter self-renunciation, utter abandonment of self to God. This is faith, and it is this which is imputed to men in all ages, and under all dispensations, for righteousness.'

A new section of the letter opens here, and runs on to 8.39. Verses 1–11 anticipate the theme of the whole section.

Peace is the first-fruit of our justification. The rebellion is over. Reconciliation (Col. 1.20) is won. The Christian is no longer at odds with the whole constitution of the universe. He has accepted God's will. He has set out to become the person God intended him to be. Peace is declared, and part of it is intended to be that peace of mind and heart which has ever been mankind's elusive quest (John 14.1,27). Such is the affirmation of v. 1.

By the same blessed process God is available to us, His power ours to claim. Nothing alienates or stands between, 'so that if He were suddenly to reveal Himself we should still know exactly where we stand, and should not have to shrink away from His presence' (1 John 2.28, Phillips). The glory of God, from which man fell disastrously short (3.23), is that held before us as a goal to reach for, a standing to be won by grace. Such is the hope of v. 2.

Hence victory over anything life can do. It was difficult to follow Christ in Rome. It is difficult today. No easy course is charted. There is persecution, unpopularity, loneliness. But if faith stands firm, there is the assurance that no experience is meaningless, that everything committed to God's creative hands can turn to good (8.28), and that the fruit of adversity is endurance. Endurance is no passive quality, no crouching under the shield as the 'slings and arrows of outrageous fortune' rain down. The shield could be a weapon of offence in the ancient armoury, and so, too, is the shield of faith. Endurance is active. It is one of the noblest of man's qualities. Such is the challenge of v. 3.

Hence character. The buffeting of the wind makes the tree strong. No sturdiness forms in the hothouse. If we would be strong we must face the storm. Christ did, and Christians are called to be like Him. Such is the prospect of v. 4.

And this is no vain hope, for God, now ours to have and to hold, fills life with His presence. His Holy Spirit indwells and sanctifies. His new-given life seeps outwards from the surrendered heart to colour thought, word and deed, and to make us like Him. Such is the consummation, the promise of v. 5.

Questions for further study and discussion on Romans chs. 4—5.5

1. What are the essential elements in 'gospel preaching'? Is there a substitute for such evangelism? Should its emphasis vary in various contexts of time and society?

2. Consider the career of Abraham in relation to faith, faithfulness, doubt, obedience and the other values and faults which Paul has mentioned.
3. What was there of similarity in Paul's and Abraham's vision of the world and its needs?
4. What is legalism? Is it found in Christian attitudes?
5. If faith and knowledge are not the same, how can Paul say: 'I know whom I have believed'?
6. What is the basis of Christian peace? By what faults or inadequacies is peace so often lost?

Romans 5.6–8 What Manner of Love?

It is after the manner of Paul to break into a lyric passage of praise. To this habit we owe some choice passages in his letters. 1 Cor. 13, the immortal poem on Christian love, is one such flight of language. These verses are in the same style.

The love of God holds the wonder of the writers of the N.T. Look at 1 John 3.1 and 1 Pet. 1.3 f. And likewise these three verses. It was 'at the right time' that Christ died, no fortuitous tragedy, no chance crime, turned by the imagination of men into theological propositions. At the proper time, determined by the Providence of God, Christ died.

'The Good Man', whom the great Plato had imagined four centuries before in Athens, appeared on earth, and men did to Him as Plato had anticipated they would in a quite uncanny prophecy. 'The Good Man,' he wrote, 'will be scourged, thrown into chains . . . and after enduring every pain he will be crucified' (Plato, *Republic* 361 E). And see Psa. 22 and Isa. 53.

In v. 7 the Greek text uses a definite article '. . . for *the* good man one will dare even to die'. It is another of those almost unconscious turns of language by which Paul demonstrates his complete familiarity with the common patterns of Greek thought. The Stoics talked of 'the Wise Man', and Greek philosophical debate was prone to such idealizations. Paul was using the language of his day. One so ideally good would be worth dying for.

But, Paul continues, it was not for such a one, but for *us*—poor specimens of the human race—that Christ chose to die. It was for 'the ungodly' (6), 'sinners' (8). Christ's death for such creatures assures us, therefore, of God's love. It went far beyond what the utmost of human love would dare to go (7). Thus, then, God reveals His love, 'presents it', as the opening verb of v. 8 literally says, in its final and unmistakable demonstration.

It is for man to choose, whether to accept or to reject, and in such choice fervently, sincerely, frankly made, lies health for the soul. The Christian does not claim perfection, but believing as he does that Christ chose to die to reveal to him the truth about his desperate evil and God's love, he personally accepts that sacrifice as his own. In this lies for him reconciliation to his God, a knowledge of forgiveness, and a spring of happiness, poise, and character.

Romans 5.9–11 Christ's Death Linked with His Resurrection

Paul is writing intensely, and on such occasions he writes in compact and heavily loaded language, difficult to translate lucidly without expansion. The AV(KJV) rendering is bold and literal, a tradition followed closely by the RSV.

It is therefore a passage in which other versions may be profitably consulted. For example, here is Phillips on v. 10: 'If, while we were His enemies, Christ reconciled us to God by *dying for us*, surely now that we are reconciled we may be perfectly certain of our salvation through His *living in us*.'

Assurance, in a word, comes from acceptance of the fact of Christ's atoning death as the basis of our salvation, and the consciousness of union with an indwelling *risen* Christ as a continuing experience.

The argument runs thus, step by step: The initial problem is the greatest. How can sinful man be reconciled to a righteous God? How can a holy God demonstrate His love for the rebel, and bestow divine righteousness on him? How that major difficulty can be overcome has been explained in 3.21–30. God has 'put forward' Christ to be an 'expiation' for our sins. His death was the demonstration, and by faith in Christ crucified, man is brought near to God.

If such grace was shown us, then, while we were yet sinners, much more, with that transaction done, can we trust the living Christ to preserve us, not only from the temptations which beset the path, but from final judgement. He died on the cross, but He rose from the dead. He lives while we live, in us, available, implicated, involved, and He will be present at the awesome encounter in another life when we meet God.

This is a thought to which Paul will return, for example in the triumphant words of ch 8. And note how intimately Christ's death is linked with His resurrection. Without a living Christ there can be no assurance, just as without the dying Christ there could be no salvation.

Verse 11 speaks of 'boasting' in God ('rejoice', RSV). Such boasting is not 'excluded' (cf. 3.27). 'To make one's boast in God is the perfection of religion' (James Denney). See Pss. 34.2; 44.8; 2 Cor. 11.17.

Romans 5.12–14 Christ and Adam

Pause now, as Paul does, to take stock. The relation of Christ to the race of man has been expounded in the tract of argument from 3.21 to 5.11. The first eleven verses of this chapter sum up the whole of this passage, and v. 11 is a summary of the rest. 'Therefore' can refer to the larger passage, or to either of the summaries. Paul might have ended v. 14 with a sharper reference to v. 12, and said: 'so also by one Man righteousness entered into the world, and life by righteousness'. This is what he virtually says. He is contrasting Adam and Christ. In the former the race finds a unity in the flesh, and in the sin and death to which sin is heir. In Christ the race could find unity again, a unity in the spirit, and in righteousness and life to which the spirit by faith can be the heir (1 Cor. 15.21 f., 45–49).

The argument is theologically less potent in modern thought than in ancient and Jewish thought. The involvement of group and family in the sin of the individual was demonstrated grimly in the tale of Achan. On the other hand there is truth which might even find genetical confirmation in the argument. As Macbeth realized too late, we cannot 'with the deed trammel up the consequences'. Adam admitted a force of death into the world of men. The fatal principle gained entry into the world, and it was impossible to exclude it save by an extraordinary act. The communicability of sin, in man's close-knit society, is demonstrable. Hear Professor Butterfield again: 'If there were no more wilfulness throughout the whole of human nature than exists in this room at the present moment, it would be sufficient to tie events into knots and to produce those deadlocks which all of us know in our little world, while on the scale of the nation-state it would be enough, with its complexities, ramifications and congealings, to bring about the greatest war in history' (*Christianity and History*, pp. 37,38.)

As John Donne said, three and a half centuries ago, 'no man is an island, entire of himself'. And have we any need to prove or to demonstrate the indissoluble link between sin and death?

Note: F. F. Bruce, in Tyndale N.T. Commentaries, *Romans*, pp. 125–131, writes lucidly on this passage.

Thought: How much do we contribute this day to the world's total of good or evil?

Romans 5.15–17 Man's Restoration

How is the image of God, in which man was originally created, restored? The Christian answer, as we have already seen, runs thus:

Man stands under condemnation, and there must be no baulking that fact in fruitless tribute to human pride. Man, too, is conscious of moral freedom, and unless the universe is a vast and incredible mockery, he *is* free and responsible. The will of God has been revealed to men, and there is not one who has wholly made that will his own. Man stands condemned. He stands condemned before God, and to deny the fact makes chaos of God's righteousness.

Nor, the doctrine continues, is divine holiness an obscure conception to be brushed aside in the name of grace. God's condemnation of sin, His wrath repelling sin and abiding upon it, are not the notions of ignorance, fear and primitive demonologies. They accompany the loftiest views of the deity, justice and righteousness. They stand or fall with the Christian conception of sin and command no less an authority than Christ Himself. They are implicit in the whole N.T., whose writers one and all insist that God's condemnation of His creatures is a serious thing dealt with in bitter seriousness by Christ.

Christianity says quite simply that God's condemnation for sinful man is removed 'in Christ'. How? The modern mind, anxious for formulae, empirical proof, and illustrative analogy, is not content with mere dogma. How can the death of 'one Christus, who was put to death in the principate of Tiberius, by the procurator Pontius Pilate', alter man's relationship to God in the twentieth century? Some, confronted with the dilemma, would answer merely with the determination of Galileo, 'Nevertheless, it does.' And, in fact, it is common human experience that the gospel works. From Paul on the Damascus Road to Augustine in the Gardens of Milan, to Bunyan, Newton, Moody and Spurgeon, dramatic conversion and the revolution of human character have been a commonplace of man's experience. To analyse the phenomenon of conversion, to unravel, as investigation well may, the psychological processes involved, neither explains the fact away nor invalidates its theology. In all history, only the Christian gospel, with its doctrine of redemption, has effected constant, widespread, and far-reaching changes in human lives.

It is demonstrable in a myriad case-histories that Christ has redeemed from fear of death and the dread of God those who in simple faith have accepted His work as being personally significant; that the power of such faith has been a deep fountain of social good and untold personal happiness; that the very image of God has been seen in clear and unmistakable lineaments in a multitude of all degrees, of all nations, who have accepted the forgiveness which the Christian gospel offers in Christ and His 'finished work'.

Note: V. 15: 'Many' is literally 'the many' (see also v. 19, where it is so translated by the NEB). This is a Hebrew idiom indicating the mass of mankind.

Romans 5.18–21 The Blessed Contrast

The conclusion, then, is: 'As through one offence the result for all men was condemnation, so also through one righteous act the result for all men is justification and life.' The comparison or contrast between Christ and Adam is thus closed, but into the situation intruded the Law (20). Sin, Paul means, preceded the Law. The condemnation which fell on sin was earlier than the Mosaic Code. The Law came to sharpen the realization of sin. See Gal. 3.19 ff. and the expansion of this concept in 7.7 ff. of this epistle. The Law made the realization of need, along with the conviction of sin, sharper, but it followed that grace was simultaneously more vividly apprehended as God's embracing and sufficient answer and remedy. Paul's own sense of triumph and gratitude rises to its climax as the chapter ends, and the close is almost a doxology.

The skill with which Paul puts the Law in its proper place should be noted. He has not lost sight of his Jewish audience, nor of the imaginary objector, who will appear again in the opening verses of the next chapter. He will not discuss the Law summarily. Nor is it his place to deal with it as sovereignly as Christ did. He merely concentrates on showing, both in the context of Adam and of Abraham, that before, and without the Law, the elements of the situation and the essentials of the problem were the same. Paul was deeply concerned with history.

He uses a vivid word in v. 20 which literally might run: 'the Law came sideways in . . .', interrupting, but interrupting with salutary purpose, a moving flow of history. Phillips is hardly correct in rendering 'the Law keeps slipping into the picture to point the vast extent of sin', for the tense is aorist. The reference can only be to the historic giving of the Law. Once it was given, sin was apparent, no longer latent, but defined, diagnosed and 'multiplied'. Grace became a dire necessity, a clamant need. Hence the vital linking of the Testaments.

Note: V. 18: '. . . condemnation for all men . . . life for all men . . .' Dr. Leslie C. Allen (*A N.T. Commentary*, Pickering and Inglis) comments that the *scope* of 'one man's trespass' and 'one man's act of righteousness' was and is 'all men'. He continues: 'The limiting phrase in v. 17 suggests that in the second case it is restricted to those who actually accept God's offer of salvation. To suppose that Paul taught the universal salvation of all individuals is to ignore the realism which years of missionary experience must have inculcated in him. "All in Adam", "All in Christ" is meant.'

Meditation: 'The last words of Mr. Honest were, Grace reigns. So he left the world' (Bunyan).

'Could my zeal no respite know . . .'

Romans 6.1–4   The New Life

Singlemindedly Paul has pursued his argument of sin and grace. The sharper the conviction of sin, the deeper the realization of grace, has been his argument. And now the imagined objector steps in subtly or perversely. 'If that is so, the more we sin, the greater the grace bestowed in forgiveness.' A temptation for the theologian is the verbal quibble. Exploring the infinite with finite words, forgetting the living, present reality of God in formulating propositions about Him, men have been reduced to strange dilemmas.

Paul knew that he would face such quibbles in Rome. He had, no doubt, already met them elsewhere. Hence this passage, the swift refutation, and the great statement about union with a living Christ. Baptism is presented as a symbol of death and burial. In the catacombs both fonts and baptistries are to be found, and the mode of baptism would appear to have been dictated by the amount of water available.

On the other hand, the Jew knew only baptism by immersion. Such was John's baptism in Jordan. At Masada a baptistry has been recently discovered, and, to the gratification of orthodox Jewry, the rock-hewn tank holds precisely the amount defined by rabbinical regulations as enough completely to cover a man. Such was the baptism a Gentile convert to Judaism knew. This is the background of Paul's use of the figure and the ritual for the Christian's 'burial with Christ', and his resurrection to a new mode of life.

Let Handley Moule conclude: 'The previous argument has made us conscious that Justification, while a definite transaction in law, is not a mere transaction; it lives and glows with the truth of connection with a Person. That Person is the Bearer for us of all Merit. But He is also and equally the Bearer for us of new Life, in which the sharers of His Merit share, for they are in Him. So that, while the Way of Justification can be isolated for study, as it has been in this Epistle, the justified man cannot be isolated from Christ, who is his life. And thus he can never *ultimately* be considered apart from his possession in Christ of a new possibility, a new power, a new and glorious call to living holiness.' (*Expositor's Bible*, 5.556.)

Meditation: '. . . so we too might rise to life on a new plane altogether' (v. 4, Phillips).

Questions for further study and discussion on Romans chs. 5.6—6.4

1. Can any form of Christianity exist withóut firm faith in the historic fact of Christ's resurrection?
2. What is meant by the phrase 'the second Adam'?
3. What is 'God's wrath'? How does human anger differ? Is there such a quality as 'righteous indignation'?
4. List three hymns which best express God's grace revealed in Christ.
5. What does Paul mean by the phrase 'a new creation' (2 Cor. 5.17), and John by 'you must be born anew' (John 3.7)?
6. Define 'eternal life'.

Romans 6.5-10 Risen with Christ

Union with Christ at one point, in His death, means union with Him in the whole sequence of events which followed—His resurrection and His exaltation. Victorious living, our very immortality, is implicit in this reality. To imagine that a sinner could accept the gift of grace, and then continue living his old life, would betray an error of so fundamental a nature as to call into doubt his whole affirmation of acceptance.

He who has 'died with Christ' is emancipated from a servitude (6); but is released, as death in all cases releases, from all bonds and obligations (7). The NEB is particularly good on this challenging and important passage. 'The man we once were has been crucified with Christ, for the destruction of the sinful self' (6). The new life in Christ will be the same life which Christ Himself lives, a life inaccessible to death. Something between thirty and forty years were to pass before John closed the canon of the N.T. with his Gospel and the first of his three letters which accompanied it. Over that period Paul's doctrine of union with Christ, which appears in more than one form and context in his writings, had been taught and experienced in the Church. Perhaps that is one reason why John so stresses 'eternal life' in his writings. 'Eternal life' is the life of this passage, that mode of living which Christ, risen from the dead, experiences, and which is shared by those 'in Him'.

The new life in Christ gripped the imagination of the early Church, and one of the commonest *graffiti* in the catacombs beneath Rome, so haunted by the early Christians of the city to which Paul addressed his words, is the phrase 'in Christ', scratched on wall and sepulchre in Latin and in Greek. 'Abide in Me', said the Lord in the last hours before His death, and that last talk with His disciples should be studied alongside the passage before us. Abiding is 'that

54

continuous act whereby we lay aside all that which we might derive from ourselves, to draw all from Christ by faith' (Godet—adapted).

On that word we can conclude this note, for it provides a commencement for the next. Inevitably Paul's theme has returned to its major note. It is all 'by faith'.

Meditation: John 3.16.

Romans 6.11–13 The Psychology of Faith

The new life in Christ is real, but must be realized. Look at each verse in turn: (*i*) *Verse 11*: 'Reckon yourselves . . .' 'Consider yourselves . . .' 'Regard yourselves . . .' The various versions strive with equal success to render a Greek present imperative. That tense implies a process, a continuing action, a repeated endeavour and obedience. The whole psychology of victorious living, of vital Christian faith, is here. We must lay hold of our potential, 'work at our salvation'. A Christian, conscious of a thrust of evil in the heart, a tug of carnal temptation, the drag and pull of old unregenerate ways of thought, speech and action, must respond by the declaration: 'In Christ I am dead to this.' So, too, seeing that the life in Christ is not repression but sublimation, when an urge to good, a movement of God's indwelling Spirit prompts to righteous action, to Christlikeness, to creative living, he must similarly respond with the declaration: 'So be it, Lord. Let me so live, so speak, so think.' The result is growth in grace, the replacement of old ways, responses, reactions, by new, godly and salutary things.

(*ii*) *Verse 12*: For, in truth, a tyranny is broken. The verse may be rendered: 'For never let sin reign as king in this mortal frame, so that you should obey sin in all its urges.' The one-time slave and subject has been liberated. He has a new Lord, and should serve Him, not the old, discredited, defeated despot. Let there be, to borrow Kipling's conclusion to *The Dawn Wind*, 'the noise of fetters breaking', when 'everyone smiles at his neighbour and tells him his soul is his own'.

(*iii*) *Verse 13*: Our bodies, in truth, are now God's temple (2 Cor. 6.16), not mere tools and weapons (the Greek word means both) of a ruthless overlord, who cares nothing for the victims of his tyranny. We become persons in Christ, real, alive, vital, not the unloved and unregarded instruments of evil.

It is a magnificent passage. It is by faith that the Christian lays hold of his privilege. It is defect of faith that leaves him serving still a tyranny that is broken. Christ died that we might be free. He lives to keep us free.

Meditation: ... *'Bringing all my burdens,*
              Sorrow, sin and care,
              At Thy feet I lay them
              AND I LEAVE THEM THERE.'

Romans 6.14–18   The New Allegiance

The passage reiterates with new urgency what has just been said.
'It is not restraint, but inspiration, which liberates from sin; not
Mount Sinai but Mount Calvary which makes saints' (James
Denney). Paul is going to expand this thought in the next two
chapters but at this point the old difficulty of 3.8 and 6.1 comes to
his mind again. It must have been a favourite objection in the
hands of legalistic Jews. Hence this final refutation:

(*i*) *Verse 14* sums up, using again the imagery of v. 12, 'For sin
shall not be your overlord. For you are under grace not under law.'

(*ii*) *Verse 15.* Are we then to sin because we are no longer ruled
by regulations, but are bound instead by our debt of love to a
pardoning and redeeming God? Banish the very thought.

(*iii*) *Verse 16.* Is it not simple and obvious truth, set in an immortal
context of words by the Lord Himself, that no man can serve two
masters (Matt. 6.24)? A slave, in ancient law, was the exclusive
property of one master, and his one essential function was simple
obedience. There are two masters for man—sin or Christ. Man is
able to choose. One servitude is a heavy burden and its end is
death. The other's yoke is easy (Matt. 11.30), and its end is life and
righteousness. The Greek word translated 'either' is an emotive
form common enough in Plato, but found only here in the N.T.
It is as though Paul says: '*of course* there can only be the *two*
alternatives'.

(*iv*) *Verses 17 f.* Now follows a turn of style which is often
characteristic of Paul. It is part of the warmth of his character,
and to be observed in such passages as Phil. 2.1–18. Paul makes
some statement of profound theological truth, as he does here, and
ends with the hearty assurance that those whom he addresses know
the truth of it all in personal experience, and have chosen obedience
and Christ. See also the severe words of 1 Cor. 6.9 f. followed by
the warm confidence of v. 11.

The practical challenge which emerges is that both God and sin
need servants and tools. God works through men, and sin curses
the world through those in whom it dwells.

Thought: *'Christ has no hands but our hands*
            To do His work today.
            He has no feet but our feet
            To lead men in His way . . .'

Of course, says Paul half apologetically, in face of the implied thought that Christian living itself is a species of slavery, 'I am simply using a human figure of speech to get my meaning across to you' (19). In fact, trained as he was in Greek rhetoric, he had been carried on by the neat contrast he was developing between the two masters, and the two allegiances. He returns to the point to forestall an objection. Christianity is true freedom, not slavery. (See 3.5 and Gal. 3.15 for other examples of Paul's apology for such a point of style. He was too good a scholar to treat an illustration of truth, or an illuminating analogy, as if it was an expression of truth itself. Preachers and expositors should note.)

Led on by his careful parallelism, a habit of Hebrew poetry, as well as a mode of Greek rhetoric, Paul proceeds to develop the thought that in all states of life there is a bondage and a liberty. Bound like slaves 'to uncleanness and lawlessness', the pagan was at liberty in relation to righteousness. That is, as Phillips rightly renders, he 'owed no duty to righteousness' (20).

What advantage lay in such a damning freedom? None, but only horrifying recompense. With a sharp contrast between 'then' (21) and 'now' (22), Paul appeals to the fruits, the results of the contrasted attitudes. Shame and death lay on the one side. Sanctification and life lay on the other. Man is quite free to choose.

'Sanctification' merits deeper study than one brief note can give it. Paul, in fact, is returning to the thought which appeared at the opening of the chapter—'reckoning oneself dead to sin and alive to righteousness'. It is the blessed process whereby the indwelling Christ takes over a life, filling, purifying and transforming it into His own likeness. There is battle enough, as Paul is to show in the closing verses of the next chapter, but the movement is begun as soon as a sinner in faith repudiates sin's tyranny, and accepts the lordship of Christ. Such is the 'free gift'—no 'wage' but a gracious donative (23).

Meditation: '*O Christ, Thou art within me like a sea,*
                 Filling me as a slowly rising tide.
                 No rock or stone or sandbar may abide
                 Safe from Thy coming and undrowned in Thee'
                                                      (E. L. Pierce).

Note: Professor G. Walters has an excellent article on Sanctification in the *New Bible Dictionary* (IVP).

The subject of the previous chapter is continued, under a new figure and illustration. In the earlier passage the bondage was that of sin. Here the bondage is that of the Law. Very boldly, in view of the fact that he is addressing the Jews who must have formed a large element in the Roman Christian congregation, Paul stresses the nature and limitations of the Law.

He points out that law of any sort is master of a person only during life. Death voids all contracts. A woman, bound by the legal contract of the marriage bond, is free to marry if that bond and contract are broken by her husband's death. The illustration is only a rough analogy, for in its application it is the bonded person who himself 'dies to the Law' in sharing mystically the death of Christ. It is a difficult passage, and it is easy to appreciate C. H. Dodd's suggestion that one should not here press too far the form of the words or the elegance of the logic. One should cut right through to the question of what Paul meant. And that seems abundantly clear. As the Christian must reckon himself dead to sin and alive to the righteousness which is his in Christ, so similarly he should consider himself emancipated from the Law by a species of death, the death he shares with Christ, just as in Christ he shares Christ's new life—and death annuls all legal obligation.

To the Gentile and to the modern Christian the argument seems unnecessarily elaborate. To the Jew it was vital. The Law, since the Captivity, had meant everything. It had been the cement of their nation. And it had bulked largely in the experience of the last two centuries, during which, growing beyond its salutary function as conservator of Jewry and Judaism, it had overwhelmed all Jewish life. Paul knew the strength of the Law in personal experience. He also knew its power to daunt and to condemn. Of that he is presently to speak in terms of theology and personal experience. He had known also a vast emancipation, and is urgent to share the liberty he had found with all who would listen to him. The Galatian church had demonstrated how difficult it was for Christians, who had truly believed in Christ, to cast off the tyranny of the outmoded Law. The Epistle to the Hebrews touched the same theme.

Meditation: Phil. 3.4–10.

Romans 7.5–10   The Purpose of the Law

Paul was vividly aware that this line of argument contained a peril. He was a 'Hebrew of the Hebrews', as he told the Philippians, and he was not ready to deny the whole heritage of his race. Moreover, the O.T., the authority of which he would not have questioned for a moment, represented the Law as a gift of God, as a part of a Covenant. And he had the authority of the Lord Himself for such an attitude. The Sermon on the Mount goes beyond the Law, and the Lord in Matt. 23, in His denunciation of Pharisaic legalism, speaks with scorn of man's elaboration of the divine code, but neither in the Sermon on the Mount, nor in any contest with the scribes, did Christ sweep the Law aside as irrelevant, faulty, man-made, or contemptible.

It was essential that Paul should integrate the Testaments, that he should assert the Christian's freedom in Christ and yet show a true and salutary function for the Law. It was a brilliant stroke of theological insight to effect this synthesis, and, for the evangelism he had before him, it was a first essential. It was to be Paul's greatest contribution to Biblical theology.

What then was the function of the Law? It defined sin. The very prohibition revealed the nature of sin. An appalling phenomenon of the present 'age of affluence' is the 'permissive society' lauded by some politicians, and 'the situation ethics' of certain 'new theologians'. It is a condition marked by the discrediting, abandonment and denigration of absolute standards, and the result is a wide failure to apprehend, to appreciate and to feel the gravity of sin. There must be Law. Without absolute demands there can be no definition of sin, no challenge to it. In this sense, as Paul says, the Law brought sin into being. It located and named it.

But Law can do no more. It can convict and condemn. It cannot save. It can quicken conscience, but cannot assuage its pangs. It is only the trusted servant, as Paul told the Galatians, who cannot educate the child but can bring him to the one who can. The Law is divinely given, essential—but halts short and provokes despair, unless it be fulfilled in Christ, unless it hand over its slain victim to His resurrecting strength.

For Reference: Acts **15**.10; *Gal.* **2**.16–21; **3**.21–29; **5**.1; *Heb.* **10**.16–20.

Romans 7.11–14 The Law is Good

The Law was a way of life. Could a man but keep it absolutely he might need no Saviour. It was the spiritual tragedy of the rich young man who came to Christ that he thought that he had actually kept the Law (Mark **10**.17–22). And yet that same enquirer was troubled in heart and felt that he lacked the 'eternal life' which is the gift of God's grace. Paul knew that fact in sharp realization.

The Law was that which exposed him to condemnation, and spelt out the sentence of death.

In v. 11 there is an acute piece of psychological insight which adds a facet of truth to this fact. Such is man's fallen nature that the very definition of sin prompts to sin. The Law, says Paul, deceived me. Gen. 3.13 provides an illustration. The prohibition becomes a challenge, provokes rebellion, suggests defiance. And always, as in Eden, there is the lurking thought of possible impunity. The Tempter turned the prohibition, intended only for Adam's good, into a force for destruction, mingling it with a lie.

It is the eternal nature of sin that it takes that which is good and transforms it into evil. Test that thought in all areas of human folly and wrongdoing and it will be seen to be true. The Law was good, but it was made by sin into a bridgehead of evil. But this raises the problem of v. 7 in a new form. Paul repels the thought that a good thing was made a source of death for him. It was part of God's intention that sin might appear sin, shown forth in its true nature, for if sin turns a good gift into a curse, could anything more sharply awaken a desire for deliverance?

To the close of v. 11 we seem to hear Paul's own testimony of his confrontation with the Law. He seems to be telling us how, in his early maturity, he had ridden smoothly along the stream of moral rectitude and reputation for piety, until he had struck the rock of the commandment: 'You shall not covet', with its implication of selfish ambition, and arrogant desire. Then, as though from an ambush, sin arose (7) and made the strong and self-reliant man aware of the ramifications of his weakness and sin (8). He discovered the Law, and with it death (9). He was struck down on the road of life (11), convicted of sin by that which he had professed with pride to follow and observe, and conscious of his desperate need. The passion of Paul's first persecution of the Christians found its deep psychological roots here. He was a desperate man battling against the urgent pressure of the devastating truth.

Romans 7.15–20   The Conflict Within

This passage has occasioned much unnecessary difficulty. To be sure, it does look like a confession of defeat, but it requires an extraordinary Christian to disclaim acquaintance with the inner strife which Paul confesses. This must be an utterance of his Christian experience, no mere recollection of unregenerate days. It requires a true Christian to acclaim the excellence of God's demands, and strive to make them real in life's experience. It is God's prompting in the heart which fires this deep desire for holiness, and this profound dissatisfaction with all achievement. It is absurd mechanically to interpret the moving words of a great and noble soul, to note that no specific reference is made in them to the Holy Spirit, and therefore to assign the confession to a section of life unblessed by the Divine Presence. It is the Holy Spirit which prompts the mood described, and the Holy Spirit which sanctions the very confession.

Paul discovered that life was a battle, and that the nature of man slips easily towards evil. Those who teach otherwise deceive those they teach. The N.T. sets no limits to our victory over sin and our baser self, but it can lead to nothing but frustration, disappointment and despair to suggest to those who accept Christ, that sinless perfection lies within easy reach and to give the impression that flawless virtue is the immediate mark and ready attainment of those who follow Him.

Two passages then for meditation: (*i*) 'The picture is true for the whole course of Christian life here on earth, for there is never an hour of that life when the man who "says he has no sin" does not "deceive himself" (1 John 1.8). And if that sin be but simple defect, a "falling short of the glory of God", if it be only that mysterious tendency which, felt or not, hourly needs a divine counteraction, still, that man "has sin", and must long for a final emancipation' (Handley Moule on this passage). (*ii*) It was said of Brother Lawrence 'that when he had failed in his duty, he only confessed his fault, saying to God: "I shall never do otherwise if You leave me to myself. It is You who must hinder my falling and mend what is amiss." After that he gave himself no more uneasiness about it.'

Questions for further study and discussion on Romans chs. 6.5—7.20

1. 'Temptation is not sin.' What does this mean? Is it so?
2. What is 'Christ's yoke'?
3. 'Christianity is a process, not a sudden attainment.' What are the implications of this statement?
4. Study 'sanctification'—its theology and its application to ordinary living.
5. Illustrate the Lord's attitude to the Law from the First Gospel.
6. 'Sin can usually be shown to be a perversion of something intended to be good.' Can you agree with this and illustrate it?
7. What is implied by the fact that the N.T. likens Christian living to the task of the soldier, the athlete, the wrestler, the charioteer, the fisherman, the farmer and the shepherd?

Bishop Handley Moule has written with deep understanding of this passage (*Expositor's Bible*, 5.563–567). All great literature renders up its meaning only to those who give mind and heart to the reading of it. The good bishop gave both, and has written penetrating words on Paul's confession. He points out that into its words 'there creeps no lying thought "that he is delivered to do these abominations" (Jer. 7.10); that it is fate; that he cannot help it. Nor is the miserable dream present here that evil is but a phase of good. . . . It is a groan of shame and pain from a man who could not be thus tortured if he were not born again. Yet it is also an avowal—as if to assure himself that deliverance is intended and is at hand—that the tyrant is an alien to him as he is a man regenerate . . .'

The exclamation of thanksgiving in v. 25 shows that the deliverance he longs for is no postponed and promised consummation, to be granted only in another life. It is part of present experience. The military metaphors of v. 23 show that the battle is on, and no battle is static. All conflict moves towards victory or defeat. The Christian, as Bunyan points out in his great allegory, is at war, but need have no doubt concerning the outcome. He is certain to win. The day will bring its test of strength and will, its wounds and toil, but each day should bring victory closer. Our Ally is at hand, involved in the conflict . . .

We should be grateful to Paul for this confession. It is too commonly our experience for us not to recognize in it the fight we daily fight. This epistle is no mere textbook of theology. It is, like the Psalms, a record of the soul. Dr. Alexander Whyte, quoted by F. F. Bruce (*Romans*, Tyndale N.T. Commentaries, p. 151), was right when he said that the recognition of the personal involvement of Paul in what he wrote was a touchstone of understanding for this epistle. Whyte said: 'As often as my attentive bookseller sends me on approval a new commentary on Romans, I immediately turn to the seventh chapter. And if the commentator sets up a man of straw in the seventh chapter, I immediately shut the book. I at once send the book back and say "No, thank you. That is not the man for my hard-earned money".'

Romans 8.1–4   No Condemnation

The chapter falls into three divisions, of which the first, which speaks of the Spirit as the principle of righteousness and life, covers the first eleven verses. The opening verses are one of the great triumphant passages to which Paul sometimes rises.

The negative in v. 1 is emphatic. 'There is therefore now no condemnation *at all* for those who are in Christ Jesus . . .' The Holy Spirit pervades the chapter. To be 'in Christ Jesus' means to be indwelt by God, to have God's power available to the outreach of faith, to be emancipated, and under no bond of broken servitude.

To 'walk . . . according to the flesh' means to live the life of the pagan world, to be the puppet and plaything of undisciplined lusts, and to know the frustrated helplessness and pain of those who know that the fruit of such living is unhappiness and defeat, but who see no hope of deliverance. The 'works of the flesh' are listed in Gal. 5.19–21. They are the base reactions to which human nature turns.

The word 'Spirit', the antithesis of 'flesh', occurs a score of times in this single chapter. To 'walk . . . according to the Spirit' is to catch the vision of God's emancipating power (2), made real and visible in Jesus Christ, God's demonstration of Himself to men (3). Christ gave the race a fresh start. In Adam all sinned. This was the contention that initiated this train of reasoning three chapters back. Christ broke the spell. Like a new Creation, a second Adam, He faced the same conditions, confronted the same temptations, but rendered up to God a perfect obedience. And so a man could be made free of Adam's corrupted race, and made one with Christ, in whom doom and defeat fell on sin. He was given a new start, the past cancelled, its servitude broken. It remained only to realize that life, and lay hold of the privilege. This is what Paul means by 'liberty' (2 Cor. 3.17; Gal. 5.13).

Meditation: The fulfilment of prophecy in Paul's doctrine. See Ezek. 36.25—37.14 and Jer. 31.33 f. (The Lord was referring to both passages in His conversation with Nicodemus—John 3.)

Romans 8.5–8   The Great Antithesis

There are two kinds of life, the life which ends in death, introverted, self-centred, seeking all its satisfaction in the pursuit and fulfilment of the passing and ephemeral desires of the body. Opposed to it, and as different as life is from death (Eph. 2.1–6), is the 'eternal life' of which John, writing thirty to forty years later, speaks, the life which seeks God's will, outward-going, free, conscious of God's presence, help, upholding, the life available to all who will lay hold of it in faith.

The Lord told the story of a fool (Luke 12.15–23). The man was a farmer, no monster of wickedness. In a difficult land, he had made farming pay. There is no suggestion that he had won wealth by any means other than hard work. But he mistook his body for his soul. He thought life needed only a heap of wheat and farm produce. He

63

thought he could control the future. He illustrates **v. 6.** He was typical of those who live according to the flesh. Such a life is, as Shakespeare made Macbeth describe it, 'a brief candle'—

> *'Life's but a walking shadow, a poor player,*
> *That struts and frets his hour upon the stage*
> *And then is heard no more; it is a tale*
> *Told by an idiot, full of sound and fury.*
> *Signifying nothing . . .'*

Such is not the life 'in Christ'. Paul exhausts metaphor in his attempt to make clear and challenging the difference. We have quoted Eph. **2.** Look at the first four verses of Col. 3 with its climax in vs. 3 f.: 'You have died, and your life is hidden with Christ in God, and when Christ, who has become our very being, shall appear, then you shall share His glory.' Or as Phillips renders: '. . . Christ, the secret centre of our lives . . .'

Look, too, at Phil. 3.12–16 where Paul makes it quite clear that the life 'in Christ', the life 'according to the Spirit', is no effortless or sudden transformation. It is attained by growing and continually exercised faith, by 'abiding'. 'He must go on increasing, and I must go on decreasing', said John the Baptist, if his words may be translated with due stress on the present infinitives in the text. They express continuity, a process, and contain a deep Christian truth (John 3.30). Our 'brief candle' merges its flicker with the unquenchable 'Light of the World'.

Romans 8.9–11   Risen with Christ

Observe how vital in Paul's teaching is the truth of the resurrection. To believe in the historic fact of the resurrection is essential for a Christian faith. The name Christian cannot properly be given to anyone denying the deep truth of that event. To be sure it is, as these verses show, a mystical experience, part of living 'in Christ'. But that experience loses all meaning if Christ be not truly risen. It is the apprehension of the fact, the realization that He did indeed conquer death, which makes possible the basic affirmation: 'My Lord and my God!'.

Thomas was the last of the apostles' band to see the risen Christ, and he was no man to hazard life on a false report, mistake, hallucination or fabrication. Remembering the census documents of the eastern provinces, where identification is often made by reference to permanent scars, he said: 'Unless I put my finger into the print of the nails, and my hand into the spear wound in His side, I will not believe.' Such were Christ's identifying scars, and such demonstration Christ offered the doubter. 'My Lord,' cried the broken man, 'and my God!' Catch, to use the words of J. B. Phillips' well-known little book, the 'ring of truth' in the breathless simplicity of that affirmation. 'Blessed,' said Christ, 'are those who have not seen and yet believe.'

'Hath He marks to lead me to Him?' asks Stephen of Saba in the hymn which he built round Thomas' experience. He has, indeed, His marks, marks on all history, marks on countless transformed lives, and He still calls for Thomas' affirmation. No despite is done to reason in making it. Once it is made, life can never be the same again. Such committal involves all life, penetrates the whole person. . . . In Greece, at Easter, the cry goes up: 'Christ is risen', and for forty days no other greeting of welcome or farewell is used, only the one triumphant proclamation. Thus the Greek Christian signifies that no activity of life, no movement of the mind, no plan of work, no project of pleasure, indeed, no pain, no joy, no sorrow, no speech, no thought, lies outside the scope of an embracing faith. And unless Christ be risen there is no Christianity, all hope is cut at the root, the foundation of all goodness sapped . . . More. The indwelling Spirit is that of Him who raised Jesus from the dead (11), and therefore immortality is also assured.

Romans 8.12–17   The Indwelling Presence

The theme continually returns to the Christian's intimations of immortality. It is because the eternal Spirit of God indwells the Christian that his survival is assured. It is because he is one with the Risen Lord that he will share in that resurrection.

Other implications follow. If God's Spirit lives in the Christian, the mind of God should be discerned by the Christian, and God's guidance should be his common experience. This guidance, be it understood, does not suspend or override his judgement and reason but informs both, leading to sanctified discernment between right and wrong. Guidance, in a thousand situations, needs no more than that clear knowledge. At that point God's way becomes obvious.

We thus return to the thought that has been implicit in much of what Paul has already written—that life for the Christian is a process of renewal, a moving towards reality. First comes by faith the knowledge that God Himself has penetrated the very person, the 'heart' of the Biblical imagery. Then comes the realization of that continuing fact, deeper daily committal to all that it implies of present wisdom, enveloping love, and increasing power—until at last we become like Him, lost in Him, and yet, paradoxically, more ourselves, our true selves, more alive than ever we could have been lost in death. Such is the redemption of the personality.

Inevitably the body dies, but the body is not all. It is the end which counts in all that has to do with man, whom God made 'in His image'. Reviewing twenty years ago Professor Butterfield's *Christianity and History*, McEwan Lawson wrote: 'There is a habit in this machine age of thinking we have explained everything when we have stated its origin . . . Long ago Aristotle pointed out that for the full explanation of anything you have to look not only at its origin but at its goal. An oak springs from an acorn, but it springs from an acorn so that it may reach air and sun . . . A man may begin humbly enough, but his explanation is only complete when you can see that the goal of his journey is festooned by stars.' Such is 'the blessed hope',

> *'with this elate*
> *Let not our souls be desolate . . .*
> *But strong in faith in patience wait*
> *Until He come.'*

Meditation: 2 Cor. 4.16.

Notes: V. 15: 'spirit of sonship' should probably read 'Spirit . . .' as in the AV(KJV), NEB. The Spirit of the Son is given to the Christians (Gal. 4.6). V. 17: Note the Christian's identification with Christ as heirs of God (cf. Matt. 21.38; 25.34) and as those who suffer (cf. 2 Tim. 2.11 f.; 2 Cor. 1.5; 4.10; Phil. 3.10 f.).

Romans 8.18–21   Ravaged World

In yesterday's note the figure of adoption was not stressed because it means less in the modern social context than it did in the ancient world. F. H. Palmer's article in the *New Bible Dictionary* provides material for those interested in the metaphor.

But we must pause here to mark the triumphant point Paul has reached in his developing argument. By adoption the child of God is made absolutely and completely a member of God's family. The sharer of its privileges, the partaker in its life.

Then abruptly he brings the subject back to earth, for man, after all, sure though his heritage may be, is here on earth, this dying planet, this polluted world. The adopted child of God must endure, in a spoiled and alien environment, all manner of testing until God claims His own.

The argument then begins to tangle with a piece of extraordinary insight. That the very planet suffered in man is implicit in the O.T.

(Gen. 3.17; Isa. 11.9). Paul pictures the ravaged globe, and the suffering of its humbler creatures finding pause and healing in God's consummation of His creative and redeeming project.

'We must make peace with nature,' said President Nixon in his 'state of the union' address in January 1970, but no peace can be made with nature, save by those who make their peace with God. How menacingly demonstrable is the truth that man involved the planet in his fall and ruin. Man's mastery of nature shares the bend and twist which sin has given to all man's other God-given qualities. In the hands of a rebellious creature it has become a force of destruction. C. S. Lewis pictured the Un-man in *Perelandra* walking through the newly-created Paradise, and tearing open the coloured frogs, ripping leaf and flower from the trees, destroying, sadistically, instinctively. In exact proportion to his 'progress', 'culture', 'civilization', man has become a devouring force before whose onslaught nature has wilted. During three to ten centuries nature can build an inch of fertile topsoil. During one reckless century man has used up, over vital areas of the world's surface, all nature's stored resources. Greedy farming and selfish exploitation have taken no thought for the morrow. Hence bared hills, choked streams, dust-bowls, famine, disaster, polluted air, fouled rivers and dead lakes, as nature answers back. 'The whole creation has been groaning in travail' because of man. Why, when all else forms a scheme harmonious, does man give the impression of disharmony? Why does he act like a brutal nomad in occupation of lands not his own? Why seek further than the penetrating explanation behind the Genesis story? Man fell, and from his fall came his pain, his toil, his exile.

Romans 8.22–25 Hope

Yesterday's note overflowed into v. 22. In Christ lies the hope for all creation. Verses 19–22 speak of the sighing of the world under the feet of its rebel occupants. In vs. 23–25 is the yearning hope of the Christians themselves. A third section follows which will form the next note, vs. 26 f., which tell the rich truth of the Spirit's intercession.

The 'first fruits of the Spirit', that earnest of God's presence, only sharpens the hope of full emancipation, makes the Christian at times feel an alien in a strange land, a citizen of heaven exiled on earth. (See 1 Cor. 15.53–58; 2 Cor. 5.2; Phil. 3.21 for the line of thought, and, for the same teaching about the Spirit under a different figure of speech, 2 Cor. 1.22; 5.5; Eph. 1.14.)

The theme of hope then takes over. Hope is inherent in our

67

salvation. At times, in the stress of circumstance, hope is all we have. Faith engenders it. The alternative is despair, and despair is rampant around us. Without Christ what hope is there for man? Without a return to Christ what solution is there for the mounting problems of society? H. G. Wells, who began life as an optimist, ended with the abandonment of his conception of a society evolving by technology and science into the glory of a millennial peace and plenty. He ended with 'Man at the End of His Tether' dying 'in the disease-soaked ruins of a slum'.

Where there is no hope there can be no endeavour, and denied hope, as some would deny men hope, the vital energies of civilization will decay. Whatever enlarges hope exalts courage and endurance (25), and nerves men to face difficulty and testing. Undermine hope by undermining faith, and the spirit of man will wither. Faith and hope infuse love (1 Cor. 13.13). Let both decay, and love dies, and if love dies the world dies, submerged in selfishness and hate. And what hope can there be if death is finally supreme—death for man, and the 'vast death of the solar system', of the late Bertrand Russell's despairing phrase?

Meditation: 'Whether we be young or old,
           Our destiny, our being's heart and home,
           Is with infinitude, and only there;
           With hope it is, hope that can never die,
           Effort and expectation and desire,
           And something evermore about to be'
                    (Wordsworth, The Prelude 6.603 ff.).

Questions for further study and discussion on Romans chs. 7.21—8.25

1. What principles of Christian preaching derive from Paul's evident personal involvement in his theme?
2. Did Nicodemus understand, from his great knowledge of the O.T., what the Lord said about rebirth?
3. What is life to you?
4. What is involved in immortality, and why does the Christian believe in it?
5. Why are faith, hope and love linked? (1 Thess, 1.3; 5.8; Gal. 5.5 f.; 1 Cor. 13.13; Heb. 6.10–12; 1 Pet. 1.21 f.).
6. What is the significance of 4.18 and 5.5 in the light of Paul's teaching on hope?

The third testimony forms one of the gems of Scripture. Prayer is the life-blood of faith. The Lord prayed, sometimes the night through in times of spiritual crisis, and no one can be truly Christian who does not, by the instinctive uplifting of the heart, seek God's aid in times of menace, stress, difficulty and temptation.

But, in the light of these verses, let two deep truths be realized. First, as Archbishop Trench said: 'Prayer is not overcoming God's reluctance, it is laying hold of God's willingness.' If the Spirit indwells the Christian, and that has been the chapter's insistent theme, then God's mind mingles with ours in our prayers. R. W. Dale has a striking comment on the passage before us which underlines this thought. It illustrates, he wrote, 'in a startling manner the truth and reality of the coming of the Holy Spirit—the extent to which, if I may venture to say it, He has separated Himself—as Christ did at His incarnation—from His eternal glory and blessedness, and entered into the life of man. His intercession for us—so intimately does He share all the evils of our condition—is a kind of *agony*'.

Secondly, note that, clear and coherent, and indeed, specific, as we should be in the framing of our prayers, we cannot, being ignorant of the future, know precisely that for which we should properly pray. God answers prayer, and that is the experience of all Christians, not always in accordance with the garbled specifications of the petitioner, but in ways infinitely more subtle, more rewarding and wise. Sometimes, in times of stress, failure and strife, there is nothing else to do but bow in surrender, commit whatever it is, or whatever has happened, to the eternal wisdom and love, and to leave God Himself to phrase petitions that we could only phrase if we knew all, and could foresee all. C. H. Dodd puts it thus: 'Prayer is the Divine in us appealing to the Divine above us', but it is more than that. It is a surge of faith born of His Presence in the heart, and confident of an answer because the uplift of the needy heart cannot be other than the prompting of God. It is such a resource and refuge, in a God whom He called Father, that Christ gave to men in the Lord's Prayer.

Meditation: 'I have been driven many times to my knees by the overwhelming conviction that I had nowhere else to go. My own wisdom, and that of all about me, seemed insufficient for the day' (Abraham Lincoln).

Two themes are here apparent: (*i*) *God's Plan*. It is logical to believe that, if our lives are committed to the guidance and government of Perfect Love, then Love, which is God (1 John 4.8), will desire our ultimate and perfect happiness. And if our lives are controlled by Perfect Wisdom, then God, who is omniscient and makes no mistakes, can plan and perfect our happiness. The only limiting factor is our will. How completely can we or do we commit our lives to the Power who, in perfect love and perfect wisdom, can secure our ultimate felicity, usefulness and content? It also follows that any experience committed to God, whether it be pain or pleasure, good or evil, can be woven into the pattern for good. Phillips' rendering: 'everything that happens fits into a pattern for good', brings out the point that nothing, even failure and sin, is exempt from God's transforming beneficence if it is, in complete faith, surrendered to His creative hands.

(*ii*) *Predestination*. Let it be realized that this solemn subject eludes our comprehension. Theologians, from Augustine to Calvin and today, have sought to reduce to logical synthesis the facts of God's foreknowledge and human freedom. It cannot be done without leaving natural questionings about ultimate love and justice which cannot be shrugged off. It is useless to say that 'in the course of justice none of us would see salvation', that 'because grace is grace none of us is entitled to it', that 'no one can demand that God should give an account of the principles on which He bestows His grace' . . . All these statements are quite true but will not satisfy those who see what Barclay calls 'a strange and terrible selectiveness' in it all. Barclay, in fact, cuts through much dangerous and baffling speculation when he refuses to take this passage as either a considered statement of theology or a piece of Christian philosophy, but rather the lyrical expression of a mature facet of Christian experience. When a Christian looks back over the course of his life, conscious though he is that he has decided of his own free will again and again at vital moments of crisis or encounter, there is all along the solemn conviction that God was at work. How the blend of human and divine is effected no one knows or will know this side of heaven, but to look at the passage as lyric testimony leaves the mind at peace and praising, not crushed and daunted by sombre thoughts of God.

Romans 8.31-34 Certain Victory

The lyric mood continues as Paul rides his wave of exultation. With a clear reference to the story of Abraham's ultimate demonstration of faithfulness (32; Gen. 22.16), Paul speaks of God's tremendous exhibition of His care for man. At the cross of Christ God finally revealed His nature. He was 'in Christ reconciling the world to Himself'. If He could suffer thus to convince and save, how true must be the opening words of the chapter! There can be 'no condemnation' in time or eternity, if God has gone to this length to redeem.

Who alone could condemn? Only Christ, who lived as man to qualify beyond all human disputation for the role of judge, and through whom in consequence, God will indeed judge 'the quick and the dead at His appearing'. But see, for those who trust Him, Christ sits not as judge but as intercessor. Phillips renders this triumphant passage well: 'Who would dare to accuse us, whom God has chosen? The judge Himself has declared us free from sin. Who is in a position to condemn? Only Christ, and Christ died for us, Christ rose for us, Christ reigns in power for us, Christ prays for us' (Acts 17.31; Heb. 9.27).

It is interesting to see Paul's mind, in the fervour of this grand passage, working within the context of Scripture and the oral tradition of the yet unwritten words of Christ. We have already pointed out the reference to Gen. 22. Observe also Matt. 6.33; Isa. 50.8 f.; 52.13-53.12; Psa. 110.1. A mind soaked in the O.T. Scriptures finds mode and framework for thought and its expression in remembered text and situation, allusion and echo.

Here then is Christian security, the last ground of assurance, that essential to peace and poise. It is Jesus Christ, 'at God's right hand', with the atoning death a fact of history, and pleading His people's cause. The imagery is, of course, that of a royal court, but the word-picture is vivid and complete—'bold we approach the eternal throne . . .' See also Heb. 7.25; 9.24; 1 John 2.1 f.

And it is all of faith, for Paul's major theme is still implicit.

Meditation: 'Faith is the root of all blessings. Believe, and you shall be saved; believe, and you must needs be satisfied; believe and you cannot but be comforted and happy' (Jeremy Taylor).

Romans 8.35-39 Triumphant Ending

The somewhat over-conservative rendering of the RSV does not do justice to the power and poetry of Paul's conclusion. Both Phillips and the NEB catch its spirit well. We shall look at each verse in turn:

Verse 35. The physical trials listed are those of Paul's own experience. Look at other autobiographical passages—2 Cor. 6.4–10; 11.24–27; 12.10.

Verse 36. The mention of the 'sword' suggests to Paul, steeped as he is in the O.T., the words of Psa. 44.22, which is quoted exactly as it stands in the Greek Bible, the Septuagint. But note the transformation. The psalmist, in bleak despair, expostulates with God. He could understand how men could suffer for sin, or for abandonment of God, but not 'for God's sake', for fidelity and truth. Paul understood. To suffer for Christ's sake was to enter into the fellowship of His sufferings, and to be honoured by the blessed partnership (5.2; 2 Cor. 1.5; Col. 1.24).

Verse 37. The word so happily rendered 'more than conquerors' was perhaps a poetic coinage of Paul's. The RSV was wise to retain it from the AV(KJV). The Christian is pictured as no battered and exhausted victor, but as a confident, triumphant conqueror.

Verse 38. The opening verb is that of 2 Tim. 1.12: 'I . . . am persuaded . . .' (AV[KJV]). Then come the powerful alternatives. Life is often more difficult to face than death. Christ conquered death. He also conquered life, and our life is hidden with Him (John 8.51; 10.28; 11.25; 2 Cor. 4.16 5.5; Heb. 2.14 f.). 'Angels . . . principalities . . . powers' are probably the spiritual forces against which the Christian wars (Eph. 6.12). These hostile powers which lie behind the material universe have already been defeated by Christ (Col. 2.15; 1 Pet. 3.22). Phillips' rendering 'neither messenger of heaven nor monarch of earth' may be correct. The remaining alternatives, 'things present . . . things to come', are understandable in the experience of everyone.

Verse 39. Summing up, Paul repeats v. 35. He has spoken of the dimensions of time (38). Rhetorically he adds the dimensions of space, and then grasps the very universe. Nothing, no, nothing, can divide the child of God from his Father.

Meditation: '*Thou wilt keep him in peace, PEACE . . .*' (Isa. 26.3—literally).

'*. . . the future all unknown—Jesus we know, and He is on the throne.*'

Romans 9.1–5 The Jews

A positive exposition of the gospel has occupied the first eight chapters of the letter, and concluded on a high note of faith. This chapter introduces a new theme. It has been reasonably suggested that chs. 9—11 form a distinct and coherent unit because they are, in fact, an address which Paul habitually gave to synagogue congregations wholly composed of Jews. Yet there is a connection with what goes before. Paul finds it necessary to answer a question which would puzzle many of his readers. How was this new message of righteousness and salvation apart from the Law consistent with the privileged position of the Jewish nation? Had God rejected them? Was He inconsistent?

Thus this section is intimately woven into the structure of the epistle. Paul had himself passed through an agonizing reappraisal of all that Judaism meant to him, and all Christians of Jewish birth and upbringing had similarly to reassess a lifetime of belief and thinking. They had to realize that their cherished heritage was not an end in itself but a means to an end, not final and complete, but a preparation destined to find consummation, completion and submersion in a fuller revelation.

The bulk of Jewry found the adjustment impossible. Hence a grim dilemma of daunting magnitude for all who treasured Judaism. Hence the passionate attempts to absorb Christianity and make it a reforming sect of Judaism. The Messiah, as was expected, came from the Jews, but, if Paul preached Christ's message aright, the Messiah brought condemnation, not redemption, to the mass of the 'chosen people'. In short, the Jew protested, if the Christian Church represented the consummation of God's plan for the world, then God appeared to deny all that He had owned and to have broken the ancient covenant with Israel.

This, to any devout Jew, would have seemed impossible. It followed that the preaching of Paul must be rejected as mistaken or perverse. Paul had passed through the stress of this dilemma. He had seen with God's own clarity that there was no contradiction. Since his first audience everywhere was Jewish, it was essential for him to speak convincingly of this difficult theme. The next three chapters are his argument.

The first five verses show how he loved his blinded compatriots. Then, from **9.6–29** Paul asserts the sovereignty of God. The Jew had no special claim on God. Next, from **9.30—10.21** Paul boldly avers that the Jews' rejection by God is the result of their own wilful stubbornness. In ch. **11** he shows how the ingathering of the Gentiles made the ancient promise real.

Romans 9.6–9 True Israel

Is then God's plan defeated, if those who, as a people, gave Christ to the world, have rejected Him? Not at all. Paul appeals to all the range of history. Embedded in the events of the earliest covenant is a principle of choice. 'Abraham's children', the race of the promise, were those of one line, that of Isaac. Ishmael was equally a son of Abraham, but had no part in the lineage of the covenant (Gen. 21.12). The real descent was not as man, but as God ordained it (Gen. 18.10–14), with the accompaniment of special overruling, and in a context of miracle.

It was therefore established, even in the time of the patriarch, that a selected line was that which should carry Abraham's name. It was not merely physical descent that should be the determining factor. The word (6) in virtue of which Isaac was born was a word of 'promise' (8 f.). He was 'born from above', and there is no other way of becoming 'a child of God' (8) save by such a process. Gal. 4.28 calls Christians 'children of promise', like Isaac. It therefore follows that the privilege of such sonship is open to Gentiles as well as to Jews. Observe the bold reasoning by which Paul attaches the right of the Gentile to salvation to the most ancient covenant of the Jew. If we are Christ's, we are also Abraham's descendants.

It had, in fact, been implicit in the whole situation. Abraham, on the great historic occasion, had been bidden to observe the sands of the surrounding desert as a picture of his posterity. He had been told to regard the stars of heaven, although it is only in the present century that man has known that their multitude is comparable with the desert's sand. Here, in poetic imagery, is the suggestion of a twin posterity—earthly and heavenly.

The climate of thought has changed. We see no difficulty in the theme of Abraham's posterity. A 'chosen people', in the narrow Jewish sense, would be *our* stumbling block. Paul's careful argument demonstrates the different historical situation in which his evangelism was cast. Those scholars who maintain that the Roman church to which Paul wrote was synagogue-based, and partially Jewish, are probably correct. Paul's argument would seem logical to them. At least it fell within the pattern of their common dialectic.

And from that thought emerges another. God is ready to meet us on the level of our preoccupations, to move within the framework of our thoughts. And that should be the endeavour of our own evangelism—to meet men and women where they think or understand, however perverse sometimes such habits of thinking may appear to us.

Questions for further study and discussion on Romans chs. 8.26—9.9

1. How does faith enter into prayer?
2. How does the great hymn: 'O Love, that wilt not let me go', illustrate the synthesis of God's action in a human life and man's freedom of will?

3. 'The pattern of fear changes from century to century, but not fear's remedy.' Discuss this.
4. Why were the Jews 'chosen'?
5. What were 'the covenants'? How did the Jews misconstrue them?
6. Can you discern reasons for God's choice of Isaac and Jacob?

Romans 9.10–13 Further Illustration

In a further movement of argument which would appear relevant to the Jews whom he addressed, Paul moves forward one generation in the story of the patriarchs. Paul pictures his Jewish opponent observing that Ishmael was discarded because it was in observance of a pagan custom that Abraham took Hagar, and that Hagar was a slave and an alien. He was therefore illegitimate, and could not rank in privilege with Sarah's son. But 'we are Abraham's seed and were never in bondage to any man' (John 8.33–39).

In answer Paul points to Isaac's children, where no distinction of paternal fault or conduct, no difference of racial background, could be alleged. The two children, Esau and Jacob, were twins. Before there could be any visible grounds of choice between them on the basis of conduct, it was pronounced that the elder by a few minutes, should serve the younger. God, in His sovereign will, rejected Esau. (Paul has in mind the opening verses of Malachi.)

Note very carefully that God is speaking of Esau and Jacob in relation to the heritage, the carrying on of the covenanted line of God's people. He is not discussing the eternal salvation or perdition of individual men and women in accordance with an absolute and pre-natal decree of God exercised without relation to their will or works, and resting solely upon an inscrutable and incomprehensible will. His object is to preclude the idea that man has claims against God, and, after his own characteristically intense fashion of argument, he pursues it singlemindedly.

He is urgent to establish the fact that the visible exclusion of a great mass of contemporary Jewry from the kingdom of their own Messiah was no breach of faith on the part of the Almighty towards the posterity of Abraham. Always, His purpose has run through an inner group—the Remnant. Paul pauses before the opaque veil of God's will. But, in Moule's phrase, 'he knows that only righteousness and love are behind it; but he knows that it *is* a veil, and that in front of it man's thought must cease and be silent'.

Note: Malachi's theme (1.2 f.) is the *nations* of Israel and Edom, not the individual ancestors of those nations, Jacob and Esau.

Israel was the elect nation, who suffered inhumanity from the hands of its 'brother' Edom. 'Hated' is a Hebraism. Edom certainly fell under judgement (Psa. **137**.7; Isa. **34**.5 ff.; Jer. **49**.7 ff.).

Romans 9.14–16 Election in its Context

We have pointed out that it was a habit of Paul in argument to pursue one end with ruthless logic. Consequently, to take a verse or a section of an argument out of its context may be to distort truth. Scripture must be taken as a whole, and statement balanced and conditioned by statement.

Now, if Paul's words are considered without these precautions, he would appear to be saying that God can do exactly what He wishes, and no man can question His justice, and secondly, that men can desire salvation with the passion and purpose of one who runs to win a race, and yet be denied it, because, without shred of explanation, God has decreed otherwise.

This cannot be true. First, although God is omnipotent, He cannot act in any way contrary to His nature. He is perfect love, and He cannot act otherwise than in love. He is ultimate justice, and cannot do other than justly. 'Shall not the Judge of all the earth do right?' said Abraham in a phrase of immortal insight. He is perfect wisdom, and cannot do other than wisely.

Secondly, consider the breadth and balance of our Lord's statements. Recognizing the work of His Father, He states a complementary truth '. . . him who comes to Me I will not (under any circumstances) reject' (John **6**.37). (The parenthesis attempts to do justice to the emphatic Greek negatives.) His invitation goes to all who will respond: 'Come to Me, all who labour . . .' (Matt. **11**.28).

Thirdly, consider F. F. Bruce's wise remarks (*Tyndale N.T. Commentary on Romans*, pp. 190, 191): 'It is a pity that in some schools of theological thought the doctrine of election has been formulated to an excessive degree on the basis of this preliminary stage in Paul's present argument, without adequate account being taken of his further exposition of God's purpose in election at the close of the argument (**11**.25–32) . . . In point of fact, as appears with blessed clarity later in the present argument, God's grace is far wider than anyone could have dared to hope . . . For centuries the Gentiles had been looked upon by the chosen people, with but a few exceptions, as "vessels of wrath fitted for destruction", and certainly God had "endured" them "with much longsuffering"; but now the purpose of His patience was made plain; what He desired was not their doom but their salvation.'

Meditation: 'See in thy choice of Him His mercy on thee. And now fall at His feet and bless Him, serve Him and trust Him. Think ill of thyself and reverently of others. And remember He "willeth not the death of a sinner", He loved the world, He bids thee tell it that He loved it, to tell it that He is Love' (Handley Moule).

Romans 9.17–20 The Case of Pharaoh

The relevant chapters of the Exodus story should be read again. Seen as human history, it was apparent that the ruler of Egypt was a tyrant, who repeatedly and capriciously changed his policy, and fought with dogged and arrogant persistence against justice and human rights, and also against fearsome natural phenomena, which he was assured demonstrated the power and urgency of God pressing upon him. He was clearly a self-willed, evil and obstinate man determined to deny justice to a race of trampled slaves.

When the Bible says that God 'hardened Pharaoh's heart', it does not mean that here was a human being who might have surrendered and done righteously, had not God deliberately frustrated his desire for good, and headed His unfortunate victim in the direction of evil. It would violate the very nature of God, and make Him like sinful man if God could be imagined forcing a human soul to do evil, or in any way blocking a desire to do good.

Pharaoh willed it all. What then does the strange phrase mean? It means that God initiated and set in motion those moral and psychological laws which Pharaoh refused to recognize. One of those laws is that, when a mind sets itself with determination to do evil, the very choice makes it more easy to do evil. When, in rebellious self-will, a man places himself in opposition to God, each moment's persistence promotes the death of conscience, and makes the road to retreat and to penitence longer and more difficult. Hebrew thought does not distinguish the intermediate steps. God created the laws of the mind. Therefore, said the Jew, God 'hardened Pharaoh's heart'.

God permitted Pharaoh, a prominent and historic example of defiant sin, to pursue his disastrous course, in order to demonstrate to Egyptian and Jew alike that God cannot be defied with impunity. Pharaoh willed it thus. God sentenced him to go on his chosen course of wickedness, and used him as a warning beacon at its ending. Grim is the fate of the man to whom God says: 'Thy will be done.'

'Pharaoh's case,' says Bishop Moule, 'was a case of concurrent phenomena. *A man* there was on the one hand, willingly, deliberately, and most guiltily battling with right, and rightly bringing ruin on his own head, wholly of himself. *God* there was on the other hand, making that man a monument, not of grace but of judgement. And that side, that line, is isolated here, and treated as if it were all.'

It is a further example of the single-mindedness of Paul's style of argument.

Romans 9.21–24 'Vessels of Wrath'

Paul took his imagery of the pot from Jer. 18.1–6. It is another example of his habit of driving the argument along one line to one specific conclusion, without care for derivative notions. He is asserting with vigour that the gulf between the intelligence of God and that of man is so vast that it is absurd to argue with Him. It is the thought of Psa. 2.2–4.

On the other hand a human being is not an insentient pot, and Paul would have been the first to stress the fact that one for whom Christ died was not dead clay. Man is born to question and to seek, and God is ready in the course of time to supply the answer. Pots are not made in their Creator's image, and it is precisely because man bears the lineaments of the divine that he does, and may, answer God. Job and Jeremiah call aloud for the justification of God's ways to man. Read the psalms, and the psalm Christ quoted (22.1).

The passage cannot mean that God creates human beings capable of suffering in order to make them suffer, and to punish them for that which eludes their control. Such a God is not the God of either O.T. or N.T. On the other hand God can reject or choose man or nation for this or that piece of work in the ordered scheme of history, and this is the thought uppermost in Paul's mind as he wrestles with the problem of Israel's rejection, and their strange hostility to their Messiah.

There is also, as F. F. Bruce points out, the defiant answering back of rebellion and disobedience, and distinct from the questioning of faithful bewilderment. Nor does this conclude the argument. In the third section of the theme Paul exhibits the will of God as exercised in such a manner that no reproach, however presumptuous, can be urged against it. Moreover, is not the fact that God withholds adverse action, asserted in vs. 22 f., sufficient indication that, even in this context of argument, Paul looks upon 'the vessels of wrath' as responsible beings who need time to repent, and that, in turn, implies the capability of repentance? 'The "wrath" of the Holy

One,' says Handley Moule, 'can fall only upon demerit, so these "vessels" have merited His displeasure of themselves . . . sin is altogether "of" the creature.'

Romans 9.25–29 The Remnant

The continuation in these verses of the austere and difficult passage which formed yesterday's study shows how completely the theme of Israel's rejection, and Israel's disobedience, dominated Paul's mind. And interwoven with that appears the thought that it was the wideness, not the narrowness of God's mercy which was prominent in his mind, for was not the fulfilment of two prophecies of Hosea visible before their eyes? The despised, and too often hated, Gentiles were the recipients of God's favour (Hos. 2.23; 1.10; 1 Pet. 2.10).

He pursues the same line of thought into the prophecy of Isaiah. The prophet foresaw dire days of tribulation falling upon his land, and such decimation of his people that 'a remnant' only would survive to carry on the national task and the divine tradition. He touched in this statement a principle of divine action, which we have already noticed, almost a principle of history—that it is 'the Few' who bring salvation (Isa. 7,8; 10.21 f.).

Historically that catastrophe, and its associated triumph, came to pass. Israel *was* ravaged. A remnant only were able to rebuild the land and rescue and preserve the national heritage. And so, Paul saw, it was happening again. A remnant only had open eyes. A few, a blessed few, recognized God's visitation in Christ. Observe the subtlety of Paul's argument, and compare it with the controversial tactics of Christ Himself in His confrontation with scribes and Pharisees. Such was the reverence paid to the text of Scripture that an oracle quoted from a prophetic authority was considered sufficient answer. Compare the form of argument in the Epistle to the Hebrews.

In neither the Lord's case, nor Paul's, of course, was this form of refutation without relevance. In the prophets, notably in Isaiah, the global nature of the Messiah's role, and the Gentile part in a world theocracy, were clearly foreseen. We have already noted the hint of a spiritual posterity for Abraham in the imagery of the stars. Note, too, the role of the N.T. in enlarging the earlier application of an O.T. passage. In both the Hosea quotations the immediate application of the words is to the restoration of the Ten Tribes to their covenanted blessing. Paul sees, and extracts, a wider significance of the principle involved, the inclusion of all the rebels of mankind in the same circle of beneficence. The Word is living, and in its interpretation (from an understanding of the Apocalypse to the use of the Bible in personal devotion) meaning is not confined to one significance, one area of truth and challenge.

Romans 9.30–33   The Stumbling-Stone

How strange the paradox! The prepared, the endowed, the children of promise and covenant, fail to grasp the consummation of all their history, the final significance of all their God had done for them, while those remote from the plan which outworked through Israel's history see, in a burst of sudden glory, the meaning of Christ, and enter into His salvation. It left Paul shocked and crushed but thrilled. But the explanation lay close to hand. Israel lacked faith. The Gentiles who accepted Christ had faith. It was as simple as that.

So this closely-woven chapter concludes. It is the attempt of a 'Hebrew of the Hebrews' to explain that which was a fearful problem for those of his race who were attracted to Christ, but who felt that the by-passing of Israel was tantamount to a breaking of ancient and sacred covenants. We have seen the main points now of Paul's solution: (*i*) The Jew thought that absolute obedience to the Law set him right with God; (*ii*) Paul, in his own living experience, had found the Law impossible to keep; (*iii*) the Law, therefore, being undoubtedly of God, had another function. It was incomplete, a preparation for Christ; (*iv*) Christ saved by faith, a gift of grace which the Law could not bestow; (*v*) and if Christ thus forgave, it followed that the Gentile who received Him, though he had lacked the preparation and advantage of the Jew, was received in Christ; (*vi*) it also followed that the Jew who rejected Christ was lost, and had no claim on God whatever. Hence the terrible dilemma.

So Christ became a stumbling-block for the Jews. He was the foundation stone of God's new structure (Matt. 21.42; Psa. 118.22; Isa. 8.14; 28.16; Acts 4.11; Eph. 2.20; 1 Pet. 2.4–8). The N.T. was fond of elaborating the image. That which was intended to be the very basis and understanding of salvation became a barrier in the path, a 'rock of offence' (33, AV[KJV]) to those who refused to place it in the proper position.

The closing words are a precious promise. Those who stand firm upon the foundation 'other than which no man can lay' will not find their confidence ill-founded. The raging flood of the Isaian passage will pass by, turbid with the world's chaos, but he will stand, and 'having done all still stand'.

Romans 10.1–4

Here begins the second section of Paul's 'Synagogue Sermon'. He has demonstrated that Israel has no claim, and right, to special treatment. Their whole history, rightly conceived, showed God acting towards man on principles quite alien from those to which they clung with such fervour. He is now about to show that this grave and fundamental error was made in self-will, but before launching this indictment he feels compelled, in anguish of heart, to cry aloud his concern and love for his people. (Read again 9.30–33, which are continued here, and might logically have been included in this chapter.)

Observe that he speaks of the Jews in the third person, an indication that he regards the Roman Christian community ('brethren') as a people apart, and not entirely Jewish in their ethnic content. The nature of his argument, so preoccupied with the imagined righteousness of the Law, and the assumption of a full and detailed knowledge of the covenants, is surely proof that the Church in Rome was not, as some contend, on the strength of this third person pronoun, completely Gentile.

But the deepest interest of these verses is their biographical content. They reveal the Christlikeness of Paul. Like his Master, he 'weeps over Jerusalem'. He has said stern things about the Jews. He is about to say more, and to press home with insistence the charge of wilful rebellion. But he does it with yearning, not anger. He pleads; he does not denounce. Read Ezek. 3.14–21. Commissioned to speak grim words to the exiles of Israel, the prophet went 'in bitterness in the heat of his spirit' to the labour camp on the great Chebar irrigation canal. And 'the hand of the Lord' fell upon him, and he 'sat where they sat' (AV[KJV]) seven days. Having shared the misery of those to whom he was to minister, he was at last allowed to speak, and did so, with no less regard for truth, but deeper understanding. Paul had already 'sat where they sat' (Phil. 3.4–6), and it is out of that fellowship of blindness, in the sharp memory of his Pharisaic sin, that he speaks the words of this epistle. It is a model for preachers. Let there be none of the denunciation which hardens and speaks of self-righteousness, no hard castigating of sinners, but rather the indictment of sin, and in all, and through all, the love of Christ constraining.

Romans 10.5–8

Paul's argument now resorts to the quotation of authoritative texts of Scripture, such as we have seen him do before, and which is surely evidence that he was addressing a congregation familiar both with this use of Scripture and the O.T. Furthermore, the clause by clause exposition of the second passage, which Paul quotes, is in the style of some of the commentaries in the Dead Sea Scrolls.

To our mind neither quotation seems, on the surface of the words, to support Paul's argument. It seems therefore to follow that the Christian Church was already familiar with the new interpretation of the verses concerned. This appears to be especially the case with the second passage, which, on the face of it, seems to bear something of the same meaning as the first. Paul turns it into an allegory of Christ, so briefly as to leave the impression that his hearers must have heard the interpretation before.

Consider the two passages: (i) Lev. 18.5. Moses was the author of the Law. He states that the man who performs its statutes shall live thereby. That is precisely what the bewildered Jew said he was doing. But Paul has been to tremendous pains to prove that such self-confidence was based on a defective view of performance, and a lamentably faulty view of sin. To keep the Law, and to 'live' by doing so, was the aim of every 'Israelite indeed'. But even before Christ came, it must have been an endeavour conscious of its inadequacy, with calling on God to aid, lift and forgive. Paul is aiming his words rather at the Pharisee and legalist, who claimed perfection, and full achievement. 'Keep the Law and live.' 'But the Law cannot be kept' (Gal. 3.10–12).

(ii) Deut. 30.11–14. Paul is not so much quoting this eloquent passage as basing upon its words a free interpretation which makes them a prophecy of Christ. The passage, in fact, meant that the Law was near and practicable, but always assuming a context of repentance and awareness of sin, and indeed, in the remote ancient setting, a remedy of ritual and sacrifice. Paul sets the passage in the context of his own argument, and his wider conviction that the Law only finds its explanation in Christ, that the Old Covenant and the New Covenant are one, and not to be separated.

Righteousness, to sum up, has not to be achieved but appropriated.

Questions for further study and discussion on Romans chs. 9.10—10.8

1. 'Some people do have better spiritual opportunities than others; and of those who have equal opportunities some profit by them others do not. Some nations have received much more gospel light than others—and are correspondingly accountable to God . . .' (F. F. Bruce). Discuss this statement.
2. 'Paul has been misunderstood and unfairly criticized through failure to recognize that it is the God-defying rebel and not the

bewildered seeker after God, whose mouth he so peremptorily shuts' (F. F. Bruce). Consider this statement.

3. 'The Lord knoweth, not only His will, but our heart, in these matters, and where He entirely declines to explain (surely because we are not yet of age to understand Him if He did) He yet shows us Jesus, and bids us meet the silence of the mystery with the silence of a personal trust in the personal Character revealed in Him' (Handley Moule). Ponder this statement.

4.
'There's a wideness in God's mercy,
Like the wideness of the sea;
There's a kindness in His justice,
Which is more than liberty.
But we make His love too narrow
By false limits of our own;
And we magnify His strictness
With a zeal He will not own.'

(F. W. Faber)   Do you agree?

5.
' "If I ask Him to receive me,
Will He say me nay?"
Not till earth, and not till heaven
Pass away.'

(Stephen of Saba)   Is this always true?

6. Are quoted texts sufficient answer in theological discussion today? What of evangelism? How 'far back' must persuasion start in the winning of this generation to Christ?

7. Sum up Israel's mistake.

Romans 10.9–11   The Gospel

The quotation from Deuteronomy contained the words 'mouth' ('lips', RSV) and 'heart'. (Glance at it again.) This suggested a great evangelical verse. 'Mouth' came first in the O.T. quotation, and that would seem to be the only reason for placing confession before belief in the passage before us.

(i) *Verse 9.* Observe the content of the confession. The Lordship of Christ, and the resurrection which established and confirmed it, are an integral part, and it is despite to language and history, not only to theology, to call anyone Christian who refuses to accept the fact of the resurrection, not as a philosophical principle or a 'salvation myth', but as an authenticated event (1 Cor. 15.1–19). Paul nowhere connects the Lordship of Christ with His incarnation only. On the basis of a mutually integrated faith and confession a believer is 'saved'. The death of Christ, and the atonement it signified, is contained in the resurrection, an event impossible without preceding death.

(*ii*) *Verse 10*. The parallelism characteristic of Hebrew is continued, but 'heart' and 'mouth' are now reversed in order. The heart, where the great transaction takes place, means the core of the personality, the true self, stripped of all those accidental accompaniments which may adhere through defect in the body which is the tool of communication; it is the person as God sees it, which shall one day stand before Him. 'Righteousness' is the gift of such faith, and righteousness, thus planted in the 'heart', must permeate the whole person, and 'work itself out' through thought and word and deed.

(*iii*) *Verse 11*. Isa. **28**.16 is quoted. Neither in the Hebrew nor in the Greek version, from which Paul commonly quoted, does the word 'everyone' occur. Paul adds it logically enough, however, and his argument about the universality of salvation turns upon it (see NEB). The verse contains no reference to the Law. He who believes, in the centre of his being, that Christ is Lord, divine and living, and believes it with sincerity and strength enough to avow it—in baptism, in public life, in the face of hostile challenge, in all life's social contexts—is a Christian. No one else is. Nor will such a faith betray him. He will know testing, experience trial, endure pain 'for the name'. If his faith is real, he will never know disillusionment with the One in whom he believed.

Romans 10.12–15   All One in Him

(*i*) *Verses 12 f*. Chapter **3** has already dealt with this truth. The world's vast problems of race find solution here. And consider the tremendous adjustment which the Jew, in Christ, was called upon to make, and which Paul had made. He was not speaking mere theory, beyond the orbit of his personal experience.

Note the natural ease with which Christ is called by the title given to Jehovah (Acts **10**.36; Phil. **2**.10 f.). For the imagery of wealth see Eph. **3**.8. It is a plain fact of common Christian experience, that Christ gives that for which multitudes would pay a price untold—*peace*. The phrase 'calls upon the name of the Lord' (cf. 1 Cor. **1**.2), is a borrowed phrase (Joel **2**.32), but, by the very fact of the lifting of such a text, it is implied that there is no distinction between Christ and God (Acts **9**.14,21; **22**.16; 2 Tim. **2**.22).

(*ii*) *Verse 14*. 'Every one' of v. 13 leads to this digression. 'Every one who calls upon the name of the Lord will be saved'—it therefore follows that the opportunity thus to invoke the name must be put in reach of everyone. It is suggested by A. S. Way in his translation of Paul's letters (a version which should be better known) that Paul frequently set out his letters in abbreviated form. He suggests that the bearer of the letter, who in some cases was the person who took it down from Paul's dictation, would be familiar beforehand with the nature of the communication, and would be sometimes entrusted with supplementary amplification. This suggestion, obviously beyond proof, could account for some of the apparent obscurities in the progress of the argument. This passage is typical. Barclay describes it as 'one of the most difficult and obscure passages in the letter', but if it could be regarded as a set of notes for amplification, rather than a finished communication, much would be explained.

(*iii*) *Verse 15.* Paul's quotation from Isa. **52.**7, produced in his own paraphrase rather than literally, suggests that the closing chapters of the prophecy, which, in their historic context speak of deliverance from exile, were already finding a place in the Christian exegesis of the O.T., as a prophecy of the liberating message of Christ. The interesting point for us is the rapidity with which the O.T. was absorbed into the thinking of the Church.

Meditation: 'No other Name.'

Romans 10.16–21   Israel's Responsibility

(*i*) *Verse 16.* Paul has quoted Isa. **52.** His mind slips to the next chapter in the prophet. His thought moved naturally within the circle of the O.T. The quotation which suggested itself also coincided with an objection which arose from his use of the Isaian oracles as a foreview of the gospel. Will all believe who hear? Is preaching the truth a guarantee of its acceptance? By no means. This, too, is prophesied. John quotes the same passage, no doubt with Paul in mind (**12.**38).

(*ii*) *Verse 17.* The same quotation caused Paul's mind to flash back to the words of v. 14. Here was 'hearing' and the proclaimed word, also in the ancient prophet. It is fascinating to watch his well-stored mind in action.

(*iii*) *Verse 18.* Similarly Paul's mind goes to Psa. **19.**4. Paul refers, of course, to the revelation of God in nature, his earlier theme in the epistle, and the natural theology he developed on different levels in his speech to the Anatolian peasants of Lystra, and to the philosophers of Athen's Areopagus. But Paul may also have had in mind the extent to which the message of Christ had been preached through the synagogues of the Dispersion. His information was complete. Ours is meagre. Were it not for the story of the ministry of Apollos, we should have no inkling of the existence of Christianity in Alexandria. Were it not for the Nazareth Decree, which is reliably dated at about A.D. 49, we would not know that Christianity probably reached Rome in Claudius' day. See Col. 1.6,23.

(*iv*) *Verse 19.* As for Jewish unbelief, there is the testimony of Moses 'in whom they trusted' (Deut. 32.21). The Church regarded this testimony as extremely significant. Observe Deut. 32.5 reflected in Phil. 2.15; the Septuagint version of Deut. 32.43 (omitted from the Hebrew and most English texts) quoted in Heb. 1.6.

(*v*) *Verses 20 f.* If this was Moses, Isaiah goes further. Paul ranges his battery of texts against the hostile Jewish opposition with devastating force. The sum of such argument is that, if God has been found and worshipped where conditions seemed so adverse, how inexcusable was Israel for not comprehending their opportunity. The very prophecies should have opened Jewish eyes to the possibility of Israel's supersession. God's arms outstretched (21) were moving testimony in Paul's mind to the tragedy of rejected love, which he, in his final enlightenment, saw historically consummated in Christ.

Romans 11.1–4 The Remnant Again

Chapter 9 stressed that God is sovereign. The next chapter underlined the fact that Israel had sinned. Both themes were pursued with Paul's habitual single-mindedness. In the present chapter he gathers up various matters by-passed in the major drive of his argument. The first is the question: 'Is Israel as a whole rejected?'

Paul first stresses the fact that he, who claims Christ's salvation, he who is the author of the indictment, is himself an Israelite, and has not repudiated his nationhood. He begins with a form of Greek interrogative which suggests a negative answer, and forthwith answers it with vigour. 'I say then, God has not rejected His people, has He? Do not let that thought cross your mind.'

Paul then proceeds to his characteristic O.T. illustration. Read again the story of Elijah in 1 Kings 18,19. The worship of the Phoenician Sun God had flooded the land. Promoted by Jezebel with drive and persecution it seemed supreme. Jezebel was the seal of a trade alliance, and there is no doubt that Ahab's Israel derived immense wealth from business conducted with the busy heathen on the coast. The oil and wheat of Israel, says Ezekiel, went down to Tyre. The wealth of the world flowed back. Ahab was rich. But prosperity is not always good for a nation. With Tyrian goods came Tyrian gods. With Jezebel came Baal. It is possible, therefore, that the choice on Carmel involved more than theology. When the people chose Jehovah they possibly precipitated an economic depression. A break with Jezebel was a break with Tyre.

Swept to decision by Elijah the people nevertheless chose

Jehovah, and streamed home with never a thought of the man who had led them back to God. It broke Elijah. How real, he must have asked, was such a reversal of loyalty? They had cast off Baal. Were they 'truly God's'? After his months of tension, disappointed beyond endurance, and under dire threat, he fled in broken-hearted despair. It was then (1 Kings 19.18) that the idea of the Remnant was born. Prophecy laid hold of it (Amos 9.8–10; Mic. 2.12; 5.3; Zeph. 3.12 f.; Jer. 23.3). Paul saw it operating again.

Romans 11.5, 6 The Chosen

From the thought that the Remnant is the true Israel, two conclusions, consistent with Paul's whole argument, emerge: (*i*) Race alone is not the basis of the choice. If the Remnant who, in prophetic times, and in Paul's own day, represent the 'Israelites indeed' of the Lord's phrase (John 1.47), it follows that to be a 'Hebrew of the Hebrews' is no final guarantee of God's acceptance. It is of faith in Christ, not the works of the Law. A man is saved, not because his parents were at peace with God, not on the basis of race, family or nation, but because of a personal and individual decision. The principle applied, to their consternation, to the Jews. It applies still. It is curious how the old heresy obtrudes. No church or nation is saved collectively. (*ii*) It also follows that, since the Jews found themselves under the same dispensation of grace as all other peoples, then members of those other races, the Gentiles, could become part of the 'chosen people' by treading the same path to salvation. The notion of a 'chosen people', in fact, has passed through a complete transformation. It is a spiritual idea, not an ethnic one.

Both of these conclusions are, as has been seen in the earlier movement of the argument, consonant with the doctrine which Paul has preached. But in the process he has answered the first question of the chapter. 'Has God cast off His people?' Not at all. A Remnant, as through all time, has accepted Him, and that remnant has become His people, reinforced, as the prophets had also foretold, by additions to their number from the mass of mankind, who found the pathway of faith to Christ's salvation.

Note a final thought emerging from the thought of the 'seven thousand'. Theirs was no aggregate salvation. There was no organism involved, no group-personality, no predetermined number. The seven thousand had not 'bowed the knee to Baal'. Their total was the sum of individual choices, each confessor was a human personality, individually choosing not to submit to the evil which flooded the land.

87

Paul cannot quench the question which breaks through again. Why, with their manifold advantages, did Israel react like this? He searches the prophets, and disturbing but illuminating oracles rise to his mind. Look at Isa. 6.9 f.; 29.10. These were words which haunted the first Jewish Christians, faced with the enormity of their compatriots' apostasy. All four evangelists quote the words (Matt. 13.14 f.; Mark 4.12; Luke 8.10; John 12.40; Acts 28.26 f.). Some visitation of God must have caused it. A numbness or a torpor has fallen upon them, not in arbitrary fashion, but as a divine judgement on their rebellion. God has said to them: 'Thy will be done', and as Pharaoh's heart was hardened, so it has tragically befallen those so blessed, so gloriously endowed, who yet persisted in denying the very purpose of their calling and wilfully continued in their sin.

Psa. 69.22 f. is quoted to similar effect. It was another O.T. passage which came with peculiar force to the early Christians (v. 21, cf. Matt. 27.48; v. 9, cf. John 2.17; v. 5, cf. 15.25). And, again from the same psalm, Paul uses the imagery of blindness which recurs in v. 10.

This, however, is not the end of the argument. 'Out of the eater came something to eat', as Samson's riddle had it, and out of Israel's tragedy comes, by God's transforming strength, the salvation of the Gentiles. Then Paul indulges a great hope. What of the glad day when a 'chosen people', Jews and Gentiles combined, the *new* Israel, should stand together 'in Christ'! He is confident that Israel's blindness cannot but be a temporary phenomenon. He was witness of the ingathering of the Gentiles. Then, surely, would come the harvest of the Jews.

A closing word from Handley Moule. The purpose of the quotation from Psa. 69.22, he says, 'is to enforce the thought that there is such a thing as positive divine action in the self-ruin of the impenitent; a fiat from the throne which "gives" a coma to the soul and beclouds its eyes, and turns its blessings into a curse. Not one word implies the thought that He who so acts meets a soul tending upwards and turns it downwards; that He ignores or rejects even the faintest inquiry after Himself, that He is the author of one particle of the sin of man . . .'

Romans 11.13–16   A Warning to the Gentiles

Almost abruptly Paul turns to the Gentiles among his hearers. It is possible to feel here the first whiff of antisemitism which has left, in some places, and at certain times, a dark stain on the Church.

Were there some in Rome who spoke with contempt of the Jews who had so misconceived their heritage and had done their Messiah to death? Paul himself has just spoken with tenderness and love of his erring people. He has just expressed the lively hope that, in the course of history, Jew and Gentile will be seen together in the fold of Christ. Perhaps he turns to the next phase of his argument because he has at times been conscious of a sense of impatience among his Gentile hearers at the 'stiff-necked' race (13).

Israel's failure, he points out, has been the Gentiles' opportunity. Frequently in Paul's own ministry of the gospel, he had turned to the Gentiles only after the Jews refused to hear him (Acts 13.46–48; 18.6; 28.25–28). And he makes the strange confession that some of the zeal which infused his own ministry was the consciousness that it might 'make his fellow Jews jealous' (14).

Besides, speaking as a devout Jew, he bids his Gentile hearers have respect for history. Alluding to the ritual consecration of the dough in the process of bread-making (Num. 15.17–21), he points out that the race was one of old renown and ancient dealings with God. They were still, for all their individual rebellion, under the glow of God's past favour. He still remembered the consecration of their beginnings. Or, does the figure imply that the first Christians were Jews, and does Paul suggest that the first-fruits were typical of wider dedication? It is difficult to be dogmatic here in the light of his earlier insistence that the race as a whole had wilfully rebelled. But does not the use of such an argument imply that, whatever the constitution of the Christian community in Rome, it was composed of people uncommonly well taught in the Jewish Scriptures?

The last word to the critical Gentiles reinforces this figure by another: what was the Gentile Christian but a twig on a tree whose roots ran deep into O.T. history?

Questions and subjects for further study and discussion on Romans chs. 10.9—11.16

1. What is the significance of confession? Why is it attached to belief?
2. Why *must* the resurrection be part of the Christian message?
3. 'Salvation depends on this: whether a sinful man will make appeal for it to Christ in prayer as to one in whom all God's saving judgement and mercy dwell bodily. It rests with Christ, so appealed to, to make a man partaker in the righteousness of God and eternal life' (James Denney on 10.12). Comment on this statement in relation to the deity of Christ.
4. How much of the O.T. can be explained only by the N.T?

5. Of Paul's quotations from Isaiah and the Psalms in **11.8–10**, Moule writes: 'The context of every citation shows abundantly that those so sentenced are no helpless victims of an adverse fate, but sinners of their own will, in a sense most definite and personal.' Check and discuss.

6. How much does the Christian Church owe to Judaism?

Romans 11.17–21 The Grafted Olive

1. The fact that grafting was believed to rejuvenate a dying olive tree explains the much misunderstood figure which Paul uses here. He speaks of Israel as a dying tree, and of the global Church as a graft upon it. When an olive tree produced badly, a slip of wild olive was grafted, and this was supposed to give new vigour to the tree. Dead branches were lopped and the ancient stock, it was thought, would find expression and new life from and through the engrafted branch, and resume its fruitfulness. Thus, rightly interpreted, Paul's figure becomes a striking picture of Israel and the Church, the succession of the covenants, and the role of Judaism.

This is the best explanation of Paul's figure, true though it may be that the practice is not followed today. Columella, the old soldier of Nero's day, who wrote safe books on agriculture in the days of Nero's Terror, is authority for the practice. It fits the scene exactly. 2. Paul has not lost sight of his warning to the Gentiles against a presumptuous attitude towards those they superseded. The Gentiles are supposed to respond to the imagery of v. 16 with the thought that, far from setting themselves against the root which nourished them, they should think rather of the dead branches stripped by the silviculturist to give them room and space to grow (18 f.). 'Fine,' says Paul ironically ('That is true' [RSV of v. 20] misses the irony). The words of v. 19 are not disputed, but let it be remembered that the arguments and reproaches levelled with some vigour against the Jews in earlier pages of the epistle can be simply reversed. The standing of the Gentiles, as of the Jews, depended on faith, and it is part of a religion which is based on faith in unmerited grace that it excludes all boasting (3.27). The Jews were native branches, proper to the tree, and yet were lopped. Shall not the Gentile graftings be at least as readily pruned?

Thought: Where boasting ends, there dignity can begin.

Romans 11.22–24 The Great Tradition

Paul has felt deeply constrained to frame a warning to the Gentile Christians. The Jews, the world over, had many enemies. Thirty years before Christ was born, Horace, the Roman poet and satirist, had a word of contempt for them. The Book of Esther tells of a threatened pogrom. Alexandria was bitterly divided between Jew and Gentile. There was a real danger, now that Jewry had done its Messiah to death, that Christians should be tempted to canalize society's dislike of the dispersed race into its own form of hostility and contempt.

Look then, Paul says, at both the kindness and severity of God. The second word picks up the metaphor of v. 17—the 'lopped' branches (RSV 'broken off'). It is a word found nowhere else in the N.T., though, in a couple of contexts, secular Greek writers similarly use it in contrast with 'kindness'. It is *apotomia*, which basically means 'cutting off'. Compare Prov. 29.1 where the metaphor is as violent—'will suddenly be broken . . .'

How complete is the coverage of the Bible! Paul warned the Gentiles out of his love and agony of mind for his own errant race. And had the Gentiles remembered, the antisemitism which has too often in history found a root in organized Christianity, would have been cut at the root. Hatred for Jews, which marred the medieval Church, would have been replaced by Paul's own yearning and pity, with incalculable results in Jewish evangelism.

There is another aspect of this theme as relevant to the problems of today. The debt of Christianity to the Judaism from which it sprang is part of the figure of the olive tree and the branches, both natural and ingrafted. Nowhere in the N.T. is the O.T. dismissed as irrelevant or disregarded. It is quoted times without number, and it is only a loose attitude towards the authority of the documents of Christianity itself, which is prepared to diminish the authority of the Jewish Scriptures. The Testaments go together and Judaism cannot but be regarded by the Christian as the seed-bed of his own faith. No book in the N.T. better illustrates this than the letter before us.

Romans 11.25–29 Paul's Last Hope

On the strength of a great word from Isaiah (59.20 f.) Paul was convinced that the present rebellious attitude of Jewry to the Christian revelation was not final. His mind sought passionately for an explanation of a situation so shocking. True, the Jews were self-willed, and had, of their own act, rejected Christ, but why had God allowed it?

The explanation came to him as a revelation from God. 'I want you,' he said, 'to understand a mystery.' The word 'mystery' occurs once only in the Gospels (Mark 4.11 and the parallel passages in Matthew and Luke); John never uses the word, but Paul uses it twenty-two times. It is used (*i*) to describe the Christian revelation as a whole (Rom. **16**.25; Eph. **1**.9; Col. **2**.2); (*ii*) to describe some special aspect of the Christian revelation (Eph. **3**.3; 1 Cor. **15**.51; and the present passage). Paul claims, in a word, that God had revealed to him that the Jews had been, of God's set purpose, permitted to go their self-willed way, in order to clear the ground for the surge of the Gentiles into the Church. At a certain point, he was sure, this would stir the Jews to divine jealousy, so that they would return to the Lord.

Enormous difficulties gather round Paul's prediction: 'all Israel shall be saved'. Perhaps this is one of the passages which illustrate A. S. Way's theory of abbreviation. Perhaps the bearer of the letter was entrusted with supplementary explanation. On the face of it 'all Israel' means all Israelites, and leaves it unstated whether that universal expression means all Israelites through all their history, or all Israelites alive at some historic moment of illumination and reconciliation. If Paul meant this he contradicted his doctrine of salvation by faith, which is the deep contention of this epistle. He has claimed, however, a special revelation from God, and therefore he could not thus contradict himself.

Difficult though the interpretation is on the face of the words, Paul must have meant the 'new Israel', the sum total of the redeemed. This is the one interpretation which conserves his consistency, safeguards his authority, and preserves the argument from the incongruous conclusion that Israel is, after all, not responsible, is a specially favoured people, and will be perforce all saved. This interpretation must be hazarded if the doctrine of the whole epistle is to hold together. Commentators, of course, who diminish Paul's inspiration and authority, dismiss the argument as emotional, and accuse the apostle of trying 'to have it both ways' (e.g. C. H. Dodd, p. 182). Let v. 26 but be regarded as a reference to a Spiritual Israel, and the pattern of argument works neatly to a conclusion.

Romans 11.30–36   The Poetry of Faith

It is with some relaxation of the mind that the reader turns to the closing verses, the epilogue of this powerful and difficult chapter. As Wm. Barclay says: 'Here theology turns to poetry. Here the seeking of the mind turns to the adoration of the heart.'

At any rate, God's last purpose for mankind has been set powerfully forth. He designs mercy for Jew and Gentile alike. Man's rebellion itself is to subserve the vast plan, for it has been shown that God has permitted all men, Jews and Gentiles, to fall into a common disobedience, in order that both, reduced to a common humility and conviction of sin, may turn in penitence to the acceptance of His grace (32).

We need not linger over the meaning of 'mercy upon all'. Paul has been accused of universalism at this point, but that reproach would again involve him in self-contradiction. His words mean no more than that God's mercy is equally available to all. It is thrust on no Pharaoh (F. F. Bruce has a lucid note on the various meanings of 'universalism' in the *Tyndale N.T. Commentary, p. 223*).

The truth more properly considered here is the fact, demonstrated in man's spiritual experience, that no situation is beyond the transforming power of God. In our personal lives, it is found true that anything, good or evil, triumph or disaster, success or failure, loss or gain, all things, committed in utter faith to God, can be transmuted into blessing. This is one of the basic truths of Calvary. And what is experimentally true in personal experience, is also true in the wider context of universal history. In this we begin to gain a glimpse of a final consummation in which sin, the fall, pain, and all the haunting inexplicable realities, all the burden of what Wordsworth called 'this unintelligible world', will be at last drawn into a final superbly satisfying pattern of blessing. And so the God who directs, also permits, and in the end commands all things to serve Him. But how important it is for the modern mind to think of both a directive and a permissive will, if God, in the context of such Providence, is to be rightly understood. For consolation in concluding the study of these difficult chapters turn to Peter's remark—2 Pet. 3.15 f.

Romans 12.1–2 The Application

Paul is always determined that conduct should not be lost in doctrine. He would have agreed with one of his perceptive commentators, F. B. Meyer, who said: 'Some weave a veil of doctrine which screens the Saviour from their eyes. It is emblazoned with creeds, definitions and orthodox statements of truth. It is not Christ, but doctrines about Christ which inspire them. The death of Christ rather than the Christ who died; the resurrection rather than the risen One; the priesthood rather than the Priest. The correctness of our notions about the Saviour may even cause us to miss the Saviour Himself.'

Verse 1. Paul has already touched on this obligation (6.12 f.). A faith which does not penetrate and enliven the activities of the body in all its actions and common tasks, was not in Paul's view a faith at all. It is a pity that the RSV did not abandon the word 'holy' (note NEB, 'dedicated'). The word has become discoloured in common use. Its basic meaning in Greek seems to be 'set apart for divine use'. The person of the Christian is 'consecrated' to God, and this, the verse concludes, is the purpose for which he was created and redeemed. 'Our heart cannot be quieted,' said Augustine, 'till it find repose in God.'

Verse 2. Here is a literal translation: 'And cease trying to adapt yourself to the age we live in, but continue the transformation which began with your mind's renewal, so that you may test out for yourselves the will of God, that, namely, which is good, well-pleasing to Him, and perfect.'

This is a crowded sentence of the sort Paul often wrote. He is eager to thrust home the truth that surrender to Christ involves rebirth, the passage from death to life. The two present tenses have been emphasized in the translation to bring out the fact that the Christian's life is not a sudden and miraculous metamorphosis, but a process aided and forwarded by the active and dedicated will. Two Greek voices merge in the two imperatives. 'Be transformed' (passive) and 'transform yourselves' (middle) are the same word. There is no need to choose one rendering and exclude the other. They blend, and in the blending underline a truth, the blessed fact that God promotes our transformation, but in active partnership with the Christian. Thus we 'work out our own salvation' (Phil. 2.12).

'The age we live in . . .' Paul was writing to Christians in Rome which shared Corinth's reputation for evil. There is a strong urge in everyone to 'do at Rome as Rome does', but the Christian must guard his response. He must never conform to the vice, the evil, the 'permissiveness' of a godless society.

Romans 12.3–5   The Body of Christ

Verse 3. The RSV misses the point in the concluding phrase. Let us translate the latter half of the verse thus: '. . . but to cultivate a balanced soundness of mind, according as God has given to every man faith as a measure.'

There is no suggestion that God metes out a varied capacity for faith. Faith may be had for the asking, and, like God's Spirit in John's phrase (3.34), is not 'given out of a measure'. Faith *is* the measure, the measuring instrument (Rev. 21.15), by which a man can assess his Christian balance, and soundness of mind. According to a man's faith, so will a man judge himself, his attitudes, testimony, and vocation. No other rendering makes sense.

Verse 4. The metaphor of the body is developed in 1 Cor. 12, and appears again in Col. 1.18 and Eph. 4.15 f. The idea is found in Plato, another indication of Paul's wide reading, and may reflect

94

conversations with Luke, the physician. The body is healthy when all its parts co-operate, each in its proper sphere. The less visible parts, as pathology demonstrates, are as vital to full health, indeed, to life, as the more visible parts. Microscopic malfunctions produce tragic diseases. So with the Church.

Verse 5. For the sake of each, and for the sake of all, it behoves us to find, by that judgement and discernment which faith can temper and control (3), the proper function allotted to us, to perform that function with zest and smooth efficiency, and not to hanker for a role and place for which we were not shaped and intended. The dependence of all is upon Christ.

'Balanced soundness of mind' is the key to such correctness of Christian conduct. It is reason, sanctified by the indwelling Christ, and co-operating with faith, which shapes the awareness of the part we are to play and helps us to play it well with no thought of envy or regret. We are equally significant. The widow of Zarephath, the child with loaves and fish, Simon of Cyrene, and the woman at the Treasury, did not realize how important was the part each played.

And note that it is equally damaging for a healthy member of the body to remain inactive, as for any member to usurp a role for which nature did not design it. Both faults cripple the body of Christ.

Romans 12.6–8 Functions Vary

Verse 6. Prophecy is that informed exposition of Christian truth which was of prime importance in the Church before the N.T. was rounded and complete. Prophecy differed from teaching by its possessing a peculiar and historically transient sense of functioning under guidance and inspiration. It consequently needed control by reason and by faith. A balanced faith could preserve a man with 'prophetic' gifts from the temptation to exaggerate or distort. Let the 'prophet', Paul says, deliver the full truth as his apprehension of Christ provides the insight. Let him keep his faith strong and whole, his personal committal to Christ complete, and in such humble integrity speak out. So he will edify.

Verse 7. 'If our gift be service, let us exercise it in its proper sphere, and likewise if our gift be teaching.' This translation leaves open, as the Greek word allows, the question which has bothered some translators (Weymouth, Moffatt, NEB, Goodspeed), whether such service is given within the sphere of the Christian community, or in society at large. Within the Church the tasks which confront those called to serve (and who is not?) are multitudinous. Problems of family, housing, the aged, the difficulties of mothers, widows, orphans, the lonely, the sick, the poor, and other tasks of mutual

95

aid, are too often neglected because too many fail to take seriously a call to a Christian function in practical service.

And what of teaching? Neglect of thought and study is a widespread source of weakness. No ministry prospers which neglects the teaching function. A well-taught congregation is a stable community. Teaching, too, functions on many levels. It demands much and too few pay the price.

Verse 8. 'Exhortation' flows from an ardent personality. It is something added to prophecy and teaching. But it must be natural, not forced. Unerringly Paul touches the fault which haunts each virtue. Let the rich be liberal, but without ulterior motives. 'Let the leader lead with zeal', runs the third phrase, never asking his followers to do what he hesitates to do himself. Let the man of mercy not spoil his ministration with mournfulness or artificial heartiness.

Observe how 'balanced soundness of mind' keeps every virtue and activity sweet. Each 'gift' can be spoiled by its own inherent exaggeration, or the spoiling infusion of self.

Questions and subjects for further study and discussion on Romans chs. 11.7—12.8

1. Name three ways in which the O.T. foreshadowed the N.T., and in which Judaism prepared the way for Christianity.
2. In what way does the Epistle to the Romans stress the debt of the Church to Judaism?
3. 'Theology is doxology or it is nothing at all' (E. Stauffer). Consider this.
4. Consider such words as 'holy', 'saint', 'saved' in the vocabulary of evangelism.
5. What disciplines aid the Christian's transformation?
6. List the 'gifts', of all sorts, necessary to the smooth and harmonious functioning of your church.

Romans 12.9–13   The Christian's Graces

Verse 9. The second and third precepts go closely with the first. True Christian love depends upon a genuine appreciation of spiritual values. In utter sincerity, it neither condones evil nor overlooks good. To 'hate that which is evil' without 'holding fast to that which is good' produces a self-righteous, censorious attitude. The reverse process produces the sentimentalist, soft, emotional, indulgent. Christian love avoids both extremes.

Verse 10. The 'honour' mentioned relates to the respect paid to each other by members of a cultivated society. Paul refers to this social grace in 13.7. The two precepts balance. Brotherly love is not intended to produce a deadening egalitarianism, in which rank is unrecognized and worth unhonoured. Rank and status, in such a society, breeds no self-esteem, and begets no servility. An eagerness in each to recognize another's worth is a surer road to communal happiness and easy fellowship than a plebeian jealousy of all who stand out from the mass.

Verse 11. The word translated 'zeal' occurs twelve times in the N.T., and is translated in the RSV and AV(KJV) in seven ways, ranging from 'haste' to 'care'. It conveys the idea of earnestness and keenness. To hold such an attitude a Christian must be ardent and dedicated. Apollos is the model (Acts 18.25).

Verse 12. The RSV incorrectly inserts 'your'. The three commands are related. Paul was no pessimist. Hope receives his blessing. Had any man a braver hope than he, who aimed to conquer an Empire for his Lord? True hope is not tense and anxious. It can only rightly claim the name when it produces patience in time of stress. And patience sustains itself by steadfast prayer. Christian optimism is no wilful blindness to grim facts. The dark side of life must be faced, but from facing it comes discipline in prayer, and waiting on God.

Verse 13. Note again Paul's striving for balanced conduct. Paul begs the Roman Christians, some of them slaves, to bear each other's needs. But he wants no closed and introverted society. The word 'hospitality' means literally 'love of strangers'. A Christian closing of the ranks can be forbidding to 'the outsider'. The corrective is an open heart to the world at large. 'Pursue hospitality', he says, implying active search for opportunity in this matter of outreaching friendliness. The verb is rendered variously as 'pursue', 'aim', and 'seek' in 9.30 f.; 14.19; 1 Cor. 14.1; 1 Thess. 5.15.

Romans 12.14–17   The Virtue of Understanding

Verse 14. The curse referred to is the formal commination, an Eastern practice. Psa. 137, for example, envisages a harassed group, meeting, as Jews did when in exile, by the river (Acts 16.13), and menaced by a hostile Babylonian crowd. Hence the too frequently misunderstood maledictions of the closing verses. The small, threatened group may have saved their lives by the act of invoking upon their foes the evil their foes had inflicted on them. The psalm is a cameo drama, and is not to be judged out of context. The precept forbids the Christian such forms of self-defence.

Verse 15. To laugh with the gay is easy. To weep in true fellowship

97

with the distressed puts a stronger strain upon love and sincerity (John **11**.35 f.). Pity is best taught by fellowship in trouble, and pity is a Christlike virtue. And nothing but Christ's pity suffices for the tragedy of self-tormented man.

Verse 16. The Christlike sympathy of the last verse calls for understanding, and understanding is never found in the self-centred, because it grows from the habit of considering another's point of view. Wand translates: 'Try and share in the common thoughts and aspirations of the rest.' Paul is asking for the 'like-mindedness' he commended to the Philippians (**2**.2; **4**.2). Personal ambition and place-seeking wreck such fellowship. Hence the second precept. There must, of course, be leadership, and Paul set some in charge of the churches he founded. Nor were they to be denied respect and deference. But that is not to promote the active quest for dignity and office in those not called to it. True eminence, however, is not self-conscious. It moves easily among all ranks. The fourth precept sums up the verse: 'Avoid conceit.' The N.T. condemns self-esteem uncompromisingly. Conceit is the child of pride, and pride is a fundamental sin.

Verse 17. 'Return no man evil for evil. Practise good before all men.' The precepts follow naturally. Paul suggests by the verb he uses that the return blow might well have been deserved. But a policy of 'tit for tat' is not Christian. Moreover, there is no time or occasion for such petty vengefulness if the preoccupation of the life is the active doing of good. Consider 1 Cor. **13**. 'Conceit may puff a man up,' said Ruskin, 'but can never prop him up.'

Romans 12.18–21   The Way to Treat Enemies

Verse 18. 'All' again ends the verse, and it is moving to remember that Paul addressed his letter to a church which numbered imperial slaves among its members. It was difficult for those who lay under the burden of servitude and its vast injustice not to harbour resentment, and resentment so often issues in acts of hostility. Live at peace, Paul says, 'as far as you can', recognizing that strife is sometimes not of the victim's own making.

Verse 19. 'Leave room for God's wrath,' says Paul. Let the wronged do nothing, only stand out of the way. God needs a clear field, uncluttered by human efforts, to accelerate the working of the moral law. 'Be still before the Lord, and wait patiently for Him' (Psa. **37**.7). Serenity is healthy, elusive though it may be. It dwells within, and not in circumstances. The key to it is a submissive will. Petrarch listed five foes to peace—anger, ambition, avarice, envy and pride. Paul has dealt with them all. Read Isa. **20** and then the closing verses of Isa. **54**.

Verse 20. Beware, none the less, of a passive attitude. Paul bids his Romans not only abstain from active retaliation, but to seek to do good to those who harm them. This, in fact, could have been an effective form of evangelism. The last words are frequently misquoted. They come from Prov. **25**.21 f., and speak of the pain of shame and self-reproach, which engender conviction of sin and a search for salvation. To see kindness to the undeserving and the hostile as a subtle form of vengeance is not to take Paul correctly. He regards such goodness as a testimony, and a mode of Christian witness.

Verse 21. The last words sum up the chapter. Paul wants no ethical vacuum. He wants constructive activity. Evil can never overcome evil. Two wrongs have never made a right. Evils only breed and perpetuate their kind. Good, on the other hand, neutralizes and replaces.

Here, then, is Christian character. Such are the men and women whom grace would make. Such is salvation in action. Salvation means quiet of mind and heart, purpose that consumes each day's reborn energy, the recovery of significance, a happiness which finds meaning in all experience, the 'abundant life' of Christ's promise (John **10**.10). 'Something lives,' as the hymn says, 'in every hue Christless eyes have never seen.' As Francis Thompson stated:

> ' 'Tis ye, 'tis your estrangéd faces,
> That miss the many-splendoured thing . . .'

Romans 13.1–5 Christian Citizenship

It is important to see Christian society in the first century in proper perspective. The Empire, running to the Rhine, the Danube, and the Black Sea, and bounded to the west by the Atlantic, and to the south and east by the great deserts, had given the Mediterranean world a stable peace. The Roman Peace was the social and political framework within which the Christian Church attained its first international form.

Roman history, written from the standpoint of the aristocratic writers of the capital, inevitably concentrated on Rome itself, on the vices and doings of the court and the prince, ignoring the proletariat, and the provinces. It is historic fact that, during the principate of the youthful Nero, whose vice and profligacy became legendary, the provinces enjoyed such quietness and stability that 'Nero's Five Years', the quinquennium during which government was largely controlled by the wise Seneca, and the soldierly Burrus, became a legend of just administration throughout the Roman world.

Paul had learned in Gallio's court, and he was to learn again in riotous Jerusalem, that Roman discipline and justice, rough though it sometimes was, and corrupt though it could be in such vicious hands as those of Felix, was a protection and a shield. Moreover, the Jews were restive throughout the world. The mood of the Empire's most difficult people was heating towards the tragic explosion of A.D. 66, and that event had world-wide repercussions. As Paul found when seeking a passage from Corinth to Jerusalem, and again in Jerusalem itself, a collaborating Jew such as he was, with his assumption of Roman citizenship, was in acute danger.

He was also hopeful that the fabric of the Empire could be Christianized, and he did not wish the Church to become branded as a dissident, rebellious group. A decade later Rome drove the Church into this position, but hope of partnership still lived when Paul was writing. The Empire, too, was sensitive about organizations within its body. Hence these wise words, repeated in 1 Tim. 2.1 f. and Tit. 3.1, and echoed in 1 Pet. 3.13–17.

Paul's own growing awareness of the power and usefulness of the Empire in his programme of evangelism may be traced in Acts. It takes first form in Cyprus, reached a climax in Philippi, and may be illustrated from Corinth, Ephesus and Jerusalem.

Romans 13.6–10   Debt of Love

The taxes levied by both imperial and local government were manifold, but generally administered and collected with greater justice under the Empire than under the earlier Republic. But whatever they were, taxes were an obligation, and it is a practical application of Paul's previous exhortation to obedient citizenship that all obligations should be met.

Christian tradition was firmly established long before the four Gospels were written. More than once Paul speaks of having handed on 'what he had received' (1 Cor. 11.23; 15.3). There was a corpus of apostolic information, carefully conserved and diligently transmitted. Mark's Gospel is the written account of what Peter gave his young convert. In this chapter it is possible to watch Paul's mind ranging over the account received, and recalling the memorable reply concerning the tribute money (Matt. 22.21).

The recollection takes his mind on to the incident recorded in Matt. 22.35–40, and he echoes the tradition yet to be recorded. Perhaps he also remembers the story of the rich youth, who professed to have kept all the commandments, for the order in which the commandments are listed reflects Luke **18**.20, and not the Exod. **20** order. It is interesting to see his thought moving over a firm, clear body of tradition. So remote was the Church from the practice alleged by one strange school of literary criticism, which imagines it reading back into the saga of Christ incidents which they created to justify practice, belief or emerging forms of worship.

There is a debt of love which each man owes to all mankind. If a man honestly endeavours to discharge this debt, he will naturally not harm his neighbour, so needs no prohibitions to hedge his path. Sexual sin, for all the vapid romanticizing which surrounds it, results not from love, but from too little love, from selfishness and introverted carnality. Love never destroys, so does not harm another's life, never deprives and so inhibits stealing. Love rejoices in another's advantage, and so does not covet. This theme was superbly expressed in the First Epistle of John. It was the preoccupation of the last of the apostles, that which he finally and most vividly remembered of the One with whom he had walked sixty years before.

Romans 13.11–14 Clothed in Christ

Verse 11. No difficulty should be felt in the apostle's expectation of Christ's coming. How could it be otherwise? We know nothing of the future, and the N.T. gives no clue to the date of history's consummation, save that it follows an age of mounting sin and accelerating apostasy. What of today? And for the first time, faced by the accumulating heritage of human sin and folly, the scientists have become frequent prophets of doom.

Verse 12. The 'works of darkness' are deeds which shun the light of day, and therefore are not Christian (John 3.20 f.). The Christian's life is not a sleep but a battle. For 'the armour of light' see the full development of the image in Eph. **6.**

Verse 13. Note the vices which Paul chooses to stress. Revelling is the unbecoming noise of the drunken and the selfish, the creation of disturbance common enough in the overcrowded environment of today's urban civilization, as it was in Paul's similarly city-ridden world. The Christian should conduct himself with dignity, quietness and thought for the tranquillity of others. Drunkenness is disgusting folly in anyone. The Christian should properly boycott alcohol, if he is to follow with any care Paul's argument in 1 Cor. **8.** Alcoholism claims from five to ten per cent of social drinkers, causes crime untold, and accidents without number. A Christian can argue for 'moderate drinking' on no grounds of sincerity. The third vice was immorality, the 'debauchery' of the odd rendering in the RSV. It has taken the world nineteen centuries to return to the 'permissiveness' of Rome's society. Chastity was scorned. It is scorned again. The fourth word is 'shamelessness'; 'licentiousness' is not a good translation. The stage has begun, for the first time since the scandalous nude theatre of Nero's day, to dare thus to flout virtue. It is uncanny how this decade has turned many a wheel full circle. 'Contention' or 'quarrelling' is the opposite of love. It is based on self-assertion. 'Jealousy' is similarly love's negation, for it thrives on self-esteem.

Verse 14. This is the famous verse of Augustine's conversion. He tells of it in his *Confessions* (8-end). The metaphor is that of clothing oneself in the moral disposition and character of Christ, taking not the armour of the earlier figure (as in the NEB) but rather garments which, after all, are the most visible feature of us. Phillips gets it well: 'Let us be Christ's men from head to foot, and give no chances to the flesh to have its fling.'

Romans 14.1–6   The Weaker Brother

The sudden raising of the matter of 'the man who is weak in faith' is a little puzzling. The unemancipated Christian was a common problem. In Colossae, in the Lycus valley, the legalism which was a mark of the type Paul has in mind, had attached itself to strange doctrines and elaborate superstitions, and called down the apostle's vigorous denunciation. In Galatia the deviant Christians had cluttered their faith with elements from a discarded Judaism. In Rome, as in Corinth, the group whose inadequacies Paul recognized seems not to have been coherent or powerful. They are 'weaker brethren', and are not addressed directly. They are mentioned because they constitute a real problem for the Christian community.

We have already quoted 1 Cor. 8. In the course of the argument of that epistle, Paul saw that his own liberty was curtailed in love because its full exercise might cause misunderstanding among those who did not share his insight into the meaning of the freedom he had found in Christ. Likewise here. He bids the community at large not argue with 'the weak in faith', but receive him, presumably in the spirit of Christian love and understanding, which has been a theme of the last two chapters. The weak, in such fellowship, could become strong.

Who were these 'weaklings'? We have suggested that the Roman church was a mixed body. There would be Jews who had recognized Christ, and with them Gentile proselytes, who had first turned to Judaism from the vice and paganism of their world, and then had moved on to Christ. Thirdly, there would be Gentile converts who had come to Christ directly. It may, indeed, have been difficult for converted Jews and proselytes to grasp in full significance that it was all of faith. No prohibitions and taboos based on law and regulation now existed. It was now a matter of faith, and after that of love. It was a weakness of faith not so to move to freedom. Hence the phrase.

Romans 14.7–12   'No Man is an Island'

As so often happens in the writings of great souls, the particular turns to universal truth. Distilled from the words doubtless directed towards a special problem reported from Rome comes this great passage which touches the very heart of our humanity, and our deep responsibility. It is a fact that we are part of a body. This is one of the slender threads which bind this chapter, and this penetrating utterance to what went before in the letter. Phillips renders: 'The truth is that we neither live nor die as self-contained units. At every turn life links us to the Lord, and when we die we come face to face with Him' (7 f.).

The translator perhaps had in mind a word of the Dean of St. Paul's, three and a half centuries old. 'No man is an Island,' wrote John Donne, 'entire of itself. Every man is a piece of the Continent, a part of the Main . . . Any man's death diminishes me, because I am involved in Mankind. And therefore never send to know for whom the bell tolls. It tolls for thee.' Thomas Hughes, author of the Victorian classic *Tom Brown's Schooldays*, wrote of Arnold, Rugby's historic headmaster: 'He taught us that, in this wonderful world, no boy can tell which of his actions is indifferent and which not. He taught us that, by a thoughtless word or look, we may lead astray a brother for whom Christ died. He taught us that a boy's only safety and only wisdom lies in bringing the whole life into obedience to Him who made us for Himself and redeemed us with His own precious blood.' Such, too, is the theme of the Bible: '. . . she took of its fruit and ate; and she also gave some to her husband, and he ate' (Gen. 3.6). And see again 1 Cor. 8.13; 9.12, and most solemn of all, Isa. 53.6. Christ was 'involved in mankind'. The Christian hermit, trying to escape such involvement, like the pagan Epicurean before him, betrays a trust.

For this we shall give account. Consider vs. 10,12. There will be a time and place where we shall face ourselves and God, where every word and action shall be seen undistorted and in its true light. We shall one day stand in the full blaze of truth, and that overwhelming fact should be part always of our thinking. In the light of it who are we to judge our brother, we who know so little of ourselves, let alone the perplexities of another? It is only 'the gold, silver, the precious stones' which we have built upon the foundation of our salvation which will survive that Scrutiny.

'Then, O my Lord, prepare my soul for that great day.'

Questions and subjects for further study and discussion on Romans chs. 12.9—14.12

1. Distinguish love from indulgence.
2. Assess the part of hospitality in winning others.
3. Why is pride a vice?
4. What guidance may the modern Christian find in Paul's attitude towards constituted civil authority?
5. How can a Christian have rules without being legalistic?
6. Should Christians ever argue over 'scruples', or is each Christian sovereign in such matters?
7. What is conscience? Is it a sure guide?

Romans 14.13–23   Our Debt of Tolerance

'We owe the world,' says an Arab proverb, 'a debt of tolerance.' Paul's continued insistence on this issue seems to indicate that he is answering a specific enquiry. In both the letters to Corinth and to Philippi there is indication that replies are being made to queries and comments sent to him. We should understand what he writes better if the letters written to him had been also preserved.

The point he makes, with some urgency, is that even when a person is right in a certain view, his conviction must not be thrust upon others without regard to their feelings. There are ways of persuasion, and gentleness is not compromise. This is not to be taken as an excuse for blurred thinking on matters of moral and ethical importance, nor to suggest that it is wrong to hold the firmest of convictions. Paul only pleads for discernment over what is vital and what is not, and for the tolerance which respects another's earnest scruples.

The reference to a 'stumbling-block' in v. 13 (cf. v. 21) reveals how deep this problem goes, and at the same time Paul's spiritual insight. Suppose the example of the 'emancipated' Christian, a powerful personality perhaps, leads a weaker man to adopt a practice which his conscience condemns? The man who so acts has suffered damage. An occasion for stumbling has been put in his path. Paul knew what Christ had said on moral defilement; it is not in things but in the heart (Mark 7.20–23). (Here is another

104

indication of the reality of the oral tradition.) He is not in any sense superseding the Lord's words but applying them in the Lord's name to a special situation. Vv. 14 and 15 continue v. 13. Align, too, v. 17 with Matt. 5.6,9 f., 12 and 6.31. It is again fairly clear that Christ's words were the common currency of Christian thought, either from records antedating the present Gospels, or from the oral tradition.

In the light of this challenging statement on Christian responsibility what would the Christian answer be to Cain's surly question: 'Am I my brother's keeper?'? It is a question to be answered before the judgement seat (10).

Romans 15.1–13 One in Christ

In this section we cover thirteen verses. They deal, in the main, with truths and counsel underlined earlier in the letter. As we read through the letter, and draw near to the mind and heart of the writer, it is possible in these two concluding chapters to sense his relaxed mood. A tense and difficult theological exposition is ended. He has written chapter after chapter of vigorous and fervent reasoning which has engaged all his powers. It was doubtless a relief to turn to simpler, if not unimportant questions, the peace of the church, its principles of fellowship, and finally the personal greetings which always closed an ancient letter.

With the notion of the Christian community as a functioning body still in his mind, Paul begs the Roman Christians to help one another. Phillips renders v. 1 in a homely but effective way: 'We who have strong faith ought to shoulder the burden of the doubts and qualms of others and not just to go our own sweet way.' A church should be marked by mutual understanding and concern. Such is the spirit of Christ (3).

Harmony was the apostle's deep concern. The plea for harmony dictated the Philippian letter. He pleads for it here, and shows that it grows round Christ. Those actively at one with Him are naturally at one with each other (5). So is God honoured before men (6). Disharmony shatters testimony.

The next two verses hint at a source of possible division. We have seen that a rift between the attitudes of Jewish and Gentile Christians could have been the occasion of the impatience deprecated in the last chapter. With some delicacy Paul now hints to the Jews that the Gentiles, who had joined them in the Christian community, merited a welcome (8). Indeed they were a fulfilment of prophecy (8–12; Psa. 18.49; Deut. 32.43; Psa. 117.1; Isa. 11.10).

From the last quotation, anxious not to press his point, but to

105

allow the ancient Scriptures to carry their own persuasion to the minds of those who revered them, he picked up the word 'hope' and bracketed a verse with it (13). It is quite exquisitely tactful, and is not, as Hilaire Belloc said, 'the grace of God in courtesy'?

Romans 15.14–21   Apostle to the Gentiles

It is often assumed, perhaps because of the altercation with Barnabas over Mark (Acts 15.39), or because of his bold confrontation of Peter (Gal. 2.11), that Paul was a stern man, intense and rigid. The impression is quite wrong. The last note ended with a reference to courtesy. Paul was indeed courteous, loving, gentle and tactful. He wrote the letter to Philippi because he felt in conscience bound to rebuke two women dissidents. He spent three chapters speaking of unity, exalting Christ, and gently exhorting the church, and only then did he mention Euodia and Syntyche, quickly following the needed rebuke with words of commendation.

The Roman church clearly needed the most careful instruction in matters vital to the Christian faith. Its Jewish element in particular required a deeper appreciation of the role and the limitations of Judaism. It is also clear that the place of the Gentiles was not secure. Paul has discharged his duty of instruction, and discharged it faithfully. He now turns with warmth and cordiality to comfort those who may have found his uncompromising doctrine daunting, and failed to see the compassion and concern with which he spoke to them.

He reminds them, too, of his God-given office. He was the apostle to the Gentiles, and purposed soon to preach in the capital of the Empire. He had long worked to that end. In a great arc of territory from Antioch of Syria and Cyprus to Illyricum, at the western end of the Egnatian Way, he had sought to plant his Christian cells in the chief cities of the Mediterranean world—Antioch of Pisidia, bastion of Roman power in central Asia Minor, Ephesus, the great religious centre and proconsular seat, Philippi, strategic key to northern Greece, Corinth, crossroads of central Mediterranean trade, Athens, intellectual capital of the world—and Rome remained. The sheer scope of such evangelism is overwhelming. Set it beside our feeble exploitation of the vast facilities for communication at the Church's disposal today, and let us pray, even as Christ commanded, that more reapers be sent forth into the ready harvest. And who, if not those who pray?

Romans 15.22–33 'Man Proposes . . .'

The passage is poignantly autobiographical. In pursuance of his audacious plan of winning the Empire to Christ, Paul had set Spain in his programme of evangelism. It was a sure instinct. Spain gave Rome much. The bulk of the meagre remains of Latin literature which have survived from the fifties and the sixties of the first century was the work of Spaniards. Seneca, Nero's tutor and prime minister, his nephew Lucan, the epic poet, and several others prominent in Rome's contemporary cultural life, came from Spain. Spain was also to provide three emperors, including Trajan and Hadrian.

Whether Paul ever did reach the great western peninsula we do not know. If he did not, the plan was wrecked by his visit to Jerusalem. In Jerusalem the intransigent Pharisaic wing of the Christian Church was domiciled. Paul, who had been a Pharisee, yearned to win them. He knew that they looked askance at his Gentile evangelism, and his scheme was to demonstrate Gentile love by carrying to Jerusalem a large sum of money, contributed by the Christians of the Empire, to relieve poverty in the Jerusalem community.

The poverty was no doubt real, and may have come about to some extent because of the short-lived experiments in Christian communism recorded in the early chapters of Acts. Jerusalem was tense amid the growing terrorism of the countryside, and the deepening opposition to Roman rule. The Empire sought to hold the turbulent province with a meagre garrison of 3,000, based at Caesarea. Procuratorial government was weak and inadequately armed. Paul knew that he risked his life (30,32). He persisted in his project, as Luke frankly narrates, against all advice. He failed to win the dissidents. The journey led to his arrest and imprisonment. God overruled and brought him none the less to Rome. Precious documents of the N.T., the 'prison epistles', no less than Luke's two books, for which the research was done while Paul was in protective custody at Caesarea, arose from what, on the face of it, was a catastrophe. Read the story and assess Paul's mood, his expectations, and his disapprovement, in Acts 21–23.

Romans 16.1–6 Greetings and Commendations

Such chapters are of more interest than might at first be thought. These verses introduce some of the personalities of the early Church, give some insight into its social structure, and reveal with what habitual facility people moved about through the Mediterranean world. People today may move in such lands with greater speed. They could hardly move with less impediment.

Phoebe was a 'deaconess' of Corinth, a rich woman probably, who lived on the seaboard of Corinth's eastern port. If deaconess is not too technical a term, Phoebe was the first on record to hold the office. Paul may have written the letter in her home, and she may have undertaken to carry it to Rome.

Prisca, or more familiarly, Priscilla, and her husband Aquila, were a much travelled pair. They were also Paul's hosts at Corinth. They had been expelled from Rome in A.D. 49 when Claudius legislated against the Jews, and opened a cloth or tent-making business in Corinth (Acts **18**.2,18,24–26; 1 Cor. **16**.19; 2 Tim. **4**.19). The references show that this earnest couple fostered churches both in Corinth and Ephesus. Now they are back in Rome. Aquila had come from Pontus. They illustrate the home-based nature of the early Church (Philem. 2), and also the vital nature of a joint testimony by a husband and wife of like mind.

Since Aquila and Priscilla were last heard of in Ephesus, the bold suggestion has been made that this chapter was a letter, or part of a letter to Ephesus which somehow became attached to the epistle to Rome. The suggestion is typical of the nonsense which sometimes invades N.T. studies. The only basis for such a theory is someone's inability to accept the mobility of ancient populations. There is no evidence to support it. Irresponsible conjecture, rashly rushed into print, has been for a century a feature of Biblical studies which would not be tolerated in any other branch of literary criticism and exegesis.

But to conclude on a more constructive note: again we see a feature of the first century which marks the twentieth—habits of travel, immigration and change of residence, all of which propagated and spread the gospel. Can this be harnessed again?

Romans 16.7–16 Honours Roll

Twenty-six Christians in Rome are mentioned by name in this chapter, several of them women. Observe the affection and generosity of Paul's reference to them. Some had known Christ before he did. Others had shared his imprisonment. Thirteen of the names occur in documents or inscriptions relating to Caesar's vast community of slaves, freedmen and clients. These names, of course, are not uncommon, and the reference may not be to the same individuals. Paul, however, does speak in Phil. **4**.22 of Christians in Caesar's household, and in v. 11 he refers to Christians in the household of Narcissus, the notorious freedman of Claudius. His household was a coherent whole, although Nero had killed him two or three years earlier. It is likely that Aristobulus was the grandson of Herod the Great. Claudius, who, in his foreign policy, imitated Augustus, had close relations with the Herodian house, and it is known that Aristobulus was educated in Rome. His household may have been absorbed into that of Claudius at Aristobulus' death, but would retain a distinctive identity. It is evident that the imperial household was deeply infiltrated by Christianity. The leaven was working upwards. It was to reach the top (see *The Archaeology of The New Testament* by E. M. Blaiklock, pp. 162–165). Tryphaena and Tryphosa mean 'dainty and delicate'. Paul jokes slyly when he speaks of how they 'laboured to exhaustion' for Christ (such is the force of this verb, 12). Is Rufus, to whom Mark, probably writing in Rome, appears to refer (Mark **15**.21), the brother of Alexander, and son of Simon, who carried the cross? Had they emigrated from Libya (see Acts **11**.20)? And was Nereus the chamberlain of Domitilla, and part of a story of aristocratic Christianity? (Barclay has several pages of reserved conjecture on the list, and the *Expositor's Greek Testament* assembles factual evidence).

> *'They lived not only in ages past,*
> *There are hundreds of thousands still,*
> *The world is bright with the joyous saints*
> *Who love to do Jesus' will.*
> *You can meet them in school, or in lanes, or at sea,*
> *In church or in trains, or in shops or at tea,*
> *For the saints of God began just like me,*
> *And I mean to be one too.'*

Romans 16.17–27   Final Warning

With some abruptness, in the midst of the final salutations, comes a warning. The perennial peril of the Church is faction, and faction so often emerges when some exhibitionist, or aspirant for power, thrusts upon the congregation, in the guise of conviction, and sometimes under the name of God, his own peculiar doctrine (17 f.). Paul had met them in his Galatian churches, at Corinth and Colossae. He feared their intrusion at Philippi (Phil. **3**.18 f.) and at Rome. A man who sets out, in selfish propagation of his own notions, to disturb the peace of the Church, bears a heavy responsibility. As heavy is the burden of guilt upon those who clutter the path to Christ (17). Those who 'by fair and flattering words deceive the hearts of the simple-minded', have been known in all ages. Paul's stern warning is relevant today. He was sure Rome could deal with this intrusion on her unanimity and peace. He hints that such abuses are best nipped in the bud. Perhaps the potential division which has emerged once or twice in this epistle was beginning to crystallize round certain personalities, and Paul may have tactfully thought it wiser to defer the warning to a context remote from his earlier reference to the doctrinal or radical division.

Paul's circle send their greetings. Perhaps they may be identified (see Acts **13.1**; **17.5–9**; **20.4**; 1 Cor. **1.14**; Phil. **2.19** f.).

Finally, the doxology (25–27). All the leading ideas of the letter may be discovered interwoven in it. This alone is sufficient to defend its authenticity against the doubts which have been raised about its place and authorship.

And so we leave one of the great documents of Christianity and the most difficult of Paul's letters. As with all Scripture which demands hard thinking and searching of the heart, its study is abundantly rewarding.

Questions and subjects for further study and discussion on Romans chs. 14.13—16.27

1. Apply Paul's directions in **14.22** f. to social situations in which Christians find themselves today.
2. Tolerance should be an active virtue. When passive it could be a vice. Discuss this statement.
3. How does the map reveal the form and scope of Paul's evangelism?
4. Can we expect God always to overrule our mistakes?
5. How could we do more to reproduce the structure of the early Church? The home 'infiltration'?

First Corinthians

The Church at Corinth

In the middle of the first century Corinth was a city of great importance. It had attained eminence at a much earlier date, owing to its commercial and maritime advantage as a sea-port on the isthmus between central Greece and the Peloponnesus, but had been destroyed by the Romans about two hundred years before Paul's first visit (Acts **18**). After lying in ruins for about a century, it was reconstructed by Julius Caesar in 44 B.C. and peopled as a Roman colony.

In the first century A.D. the city was heavily populated (200,000 freedmen, 400,000 slaves have been estimated); and its place as a political and commercial centre is gauged from the fact that the Romans made it the capital city of the senatorial province of Achaia in southern Greece.

But the reputation of Corinth for moral corruption is also well known. The 'Corinthian life' became synonymous with luxury and licentiousness. At the same time, its pretensions to philosophy and literary culture made the phrase 'Corinthian words' a token of polished and cultivated speech.

In this 'swinging city' of busy commercial life and social entertainment Paul spent a year and a half or more during his second missionary journey (Acts **18**.11,18), having arrived in the city probably in the winter of A.D. 50–51. He found a welcome in the home of Aquila and Priscilla, with whom he carried on his trade of tent-making as well as conducting some evangelistic ministry (Acts **18**.4–18).

Problems at Corinth

The converts won to Christ seem to have belonged to the lower strata of society (**1**.26–29), but not exclusively so (**1**.16; **11**.17–34; Rom. **16**.23). They were not free from the prevailing tendency to intellectual pride (**1**.18–20; **3**.18,19; **8**.1); and added to this was a proneness to sensual sin, equally characteristic of their native city (**5**.1–11; **6**.15–18; **11**.21). The most glaring defect of the church's life, however, must have been that of party divisions (**1**.12; **3**.3;

111

Photo: Corinthian Canal, linking the Aegean and the Ionian Seas, is 4 miles long and 75ft wide

Photo: Temple of Apollo at Corinth

11.18 f.) represented by their allegiance to apostolic names, and their bickering which drew them to the civil courts to settle their quarrels (6.1,6). They even carried their wrangling to the Lord's Table (11.17 ff.). And they did all this claiming as their watchwords 'knowledge' (8.1) and 'liberty' (6.12; 8.9; 10.23) but were blissfully unaware of the serious moral crisis which was blowing up (5.1 ff.). Rather, they were exulting in the largesse of spiritual gifts with which they had been endowed (1.5; 14.12), although they needed careful instruction as to their meaning and use (12.1; 14.37).

Paul and Corinth

Of all the churches that Paul founded as a 'skilled master-builder' (3.10), none caused him more concern than the community at Corinth. 'Anxiety for all the churches' (2 Cor. 11.28) was no idle phrase when he reflected on his dealings with the Corinthian saints. He claimed a special relationship to them (3.10; 4.15; 9.1,2; 2 Cor. 3.2; 12.14,15), and maintained a shepherd-like care in every situation.

Details of the precise number of letters that he wrote to them and the various visits he paid to Corinth are a complicated business which the text-books try to sort out. One of the clearest statements is presented in the IVF *New Bible Dictionary*, pp. 255–257.

The immediate occasion of *1 Corinthians* is more straightforward. Various reports had reached Paul of the troubles at Corinth (1.11). The church members themselves had written requesting guidance on specific matters of doctrine, custom and procedure, and were not loath to offer their own views at the same time (7.1; 8.1), while professing to remain loyal to Paul's earlier, oral teaching (11.2). Moreover, the coming of some of the church leaders (16.17) doubtless filled in some of the background of the tangled situation at Corinth. The letter before us is a reply to, and an inspired commentary on, just this situation. It was written at Ephesus (16.19) about A.D. 55.

Helps: The Tyndale Commentary on the epistle by Leon Morris (IVF–Eerdmans) is highly commended. Of a similar pattern is M. E. Thrall's edition of the Cambridge Bible Commentary. For more detailed study, J. Héring's commentary is now available in English translation.

1 Corinthians 1.1-9

Ancient letters which have survived, mainly as papyri, from the first-century world of Graeco-Roman civilization follow a fairly set pattern. The writer gives his name, addresses those to whom he is writing, and offers a greeting. There is also a frequent reference to thanksgiving to the gods and a prayer for the recipients' good health and safety.

The apostle Paul took over much of this stereotyped form, but filled it with a new, Christian content. Mark the distinctive Christian elements in the opening verses:

(*i*) *V. 1* reveals his privileged position, shared by only a limited number in the early Church, of apostleship—and unique in the sense that he alone was called to be God's special messenger to the Gentiles (Acts **9.**15; Rom. **15.**15–18; 1 Tim. **2.**7).

(*ii*) The addressees of v. 2 are the people of God in southern Greece, the chief city of which was Corinth. With Israel, God's elect and holy people, they are included in one covenant of grace, but distinguished as those who invoke the name of Jesus as Lord just as O.T. saints called on the name of Yahweh their God in worship (e.g. Gen. **4.**26; **21.**33). As a local outcropping of the universal Church, the church at Corinth is made to feel its spiritual kinship with all other believers (as in 1 Pet. **1.**1–2).

(*iii*) The specific Christian blessings of grace and peace are called down in the apostolic prayer. And it is not accidental that this order is preserved throughout the N.T. We may enjoy peace with God and the gift of His peace solely on the ground of His gracious act of redemption in Christ (Rom. **5.**1–2).

(*iv*) Thanksgiving for Paul takes the form of praise to God for the enrichments which the Corinthian believers have known (4,5); indeed, they are deficient in no spiritual gift-by-grace (Gk. *charisma*). But as Paul chides them later (**14.**12), with all their preoccupation with these gifts they must be sure of a right motive. What is it (**12.**31)?

In case any of them had imagined that they had received *all* that God had to offer, a gentle reminder follows (8), viz. Christians are still pilgrims *in via*—on the road to God's fullness. They await their completed redemption (Rom. **8.**23–25) at the Lord's triumph-day. Then God's faithfulness which has already called them to the state of grace will promote them to the state of glory (9).

1 Corinthians 1.10-17

Outwardly the church at Corinth seemed to be in a good healthy condition (5–7), but there was one glaring defect. What was it (10)?

Reports had reached Paul from at least two sources that there were divisions and rival groups in the church. One source is specified (11);

the other may be inferred from the arrival of certain church members who, no doubt, gave him a first-hand account (**16**.17). Later, when Paul has to speak plainly to them on a specific matter of morals (**5**.1), he will again refer to these reports.

The trouble-spot on which Paul now concentrates is the party-spirit which disfigured the life and witness of the church (12). Apparently four factions were using the authority of eminent names to engage in a competition of unholy rivalry.

Paul's reply to this situation is of great importance, both for a theological understanding of the nature of the church, and also for our present-day concern for Christian unity.

His argument is closely-knit and cogent. As there is only one Christ, there can be only one Church, composed of those who claim allegiance to Him as Lord, which in turn is confessed in baptism (13). Into His name all believers were baptized (Rom. **6**.3 ff.; Gal. **3**.27) and so called to be members of one body (Rom. **12**.5; Col. **3**.11,15). This simple fact of one Lord, one body, excludes all notions of party allegiance and selfish rivalry, which suggest that men's names are more important than the Head of the Church, and that there can be several 'bodies', all professing allegiance to the same Head. Paul will show the illogicality of this later (**3**.21; **12**.12 ff.).

Because baptism was being used in this perverse way Paul disclaims an undue emphasis on the rite (17). The supporting argument is that there is a third factor in the series—one Lord, one Church, and one gospel which binds together all those who are Christ's.

1 Corinthians 1.18-31

The missionary task assigned to Paul was not to gather converts who claimed a special attachment to *his* name. Rather, it was the Christ who encountered and summoned him that gave him a gospel to proclaim (17).

The content of that message is now powerfully expounded and its effect on those who come within earshot of it is clearly shown (18–25). *Three types of reaction* may be distinguished:

(*i*) To those 'who are being saved' (present tense) the cross represents the epitome of divine power, leading to salvation (Rom. **1**.16). The association of power with the humiliation and ignominy of death on a Roman gibbet—a death reserved for the most degraded and despised in Roman society—may seem very surprising and, at first sight, to hold together mutually contradictory ideas (cf. 2 Cor. **13**.4). But Paul goes on to explain that in the very weakness of God, suffering initial defeat at the hands of wicked men, divine *wisdom* is displayed and the heart of God revealed (25). Tacitly to be understood is the conviction that God raised Him from defeat and death, and so vindicated His own honour (Acts **2**.23,24).

As the suffering, lowly Christ portrays God's strength-in-weakness, so it is with those who belong to Him. As Christians, they are despised and written off as insignificant members of a sophisticated society (26–28). But this choice and calling of men, irrespective of their social status, also reflects the wisdom of God. To what purpose (29)? Those who have found in Christ the secret of life's purpose and God's plan realize that it is God's initiative and power which have led them to this blessedness—and so they give Him their thanks for undeserved mercies (31).

(*ii*) 'But they have not all heeded the Gospel' (Rom. **10**.16). The preaching of the cross, then as now, divides men into the stark categories of those who respond and those who reject. The Jewish people, with their insistent clamour for 'signs'—as seen in the ministry of Jesus from its beginning to its close—refuse to believe that a crucified man can be their Messiah, for Deut. **21**.23 proves that He must be under a divine curse. Paul's reply is given in Gal. **3**.13. The curse He assumed was for our sakes.

(*iii*) The Greeks find the cross a laughing-stock (22,23) because it contradicted their ideas of divine wisdom—indeed, it taught the exact opposite of their axiom that the gods cannot and do not suffer mortal pain. They remain aloof and untouched by human misery. The Christian answer lies in a God who entered our life at every level—and tasted death (Heb. **2**.9) at its bitterest (Mark **15**.34).

1 Corinthians 2.1-5

The counterpart to the Jews' insistence on credentials (e.g. Mark **11**. 27–33; John **4**.48; **6**.30; **7**.15) was the Greeks' love of oratory and impressive public-speaking. To them the acme of learning was the presentation of a well-ordered and persuasively uttered discourse on some lofty (and preferably novel) theme (Acts **17**.21).

It is not to be wondered at therefore that Paul's preaching in Athens should be dismissed as the weird pronouncements of a babbler (Acts **17**.18–20). And Paul himself possibly felt that little good had been accomplished at Athens as he moved on to Corinth. But it would be wrong to infer that he viewed his Athenian 'experiment' as a dismal failure and that vs. 1–5 were written out of a new resolve to abandon completely a more philosophical approach (see *Bible Study Book* on Acts **18**.1–4 for another, more likely, explanation).

The present paragraph must stand on its own feet as representing the avowed aim of Paul at every phase of his ministry; but at Corinth it was brought home to him with peculiar intensity that his ministry was to offer a straightforward presentation of the cross (2), decked out with no human embellishments and conveyed with no reliance on rhetorical persuasion (4).

Indeed, his bearing and public proclamation were just the opposite of the qualities which marked the accomplished Greek orator and debater. He chose no high-sounding terms (1), and resorted to no clever notions to dazzle his hearers into acceptance (4). His sole reliance was on the Spirit who gives an unaccountable authority to the Christian preacher who recognizes his own weakness and the sufficiency of God's help. But there was another motivating factor in Paul's self-chosen aim. What was it (5)? Men who can be won over *simply* by forceful rhetoric can be lost when a more persuasive pleader comes along with a glib tongue and an engaging manner. Isn't this the reason for the success of many present-day false cults, with their salesmanlike approach and easy flow of language?

1 Corinthians 2.6-16

The scriptural term 'wisdom' needs a careful definition. Paul had been at pains to show that the apostolic preaching of the cross does not look to any human philosophy or man-devised argument for its persuasiveness. Reliance of unredeemed and unilluminated man on his own supposed innate ability to know God is fore-doomed (1.21). The 'wisdom of this age' (6) is ephemeral and, in the realm of the spirit, vain. So Paul draws his confidence from the assurance that his message is based on *God's* truth, and announced in dependence on the Holy Spirit (2.4).

But there *is* a wisdom which is appropriate (6)—based on divine revelation, not human discovery (7) and communicated to men by the Spirit (10–12). And the same Spirit who imparts the true knowledge of God to the receptive mind must also be at work in conveying the gospel message in the *language* which the apostle uses (13)—a most important observation, shedding much light on the modern problems of communication.

How can unregenerate man ever appreciate the saving value of the cross and see his own need as a desperate sinner whose only hope is in Christ crucified (2.2)? This is the starting-point in all considerations of evangelism, especially sharpened in present-day concerns to reach the masses outside our Christian fellowships.

These verses lay down certain clear guide-lines:

116

(*i*) The bankruptcy of human wisdom, uninspired by divine revelation, is seen most clearly in the way Christ was rejected (8; John 1.11; Rom. 10.2–4). The cross which men prepared for the Lord of glory is the supreme example of human perversity, opposition and rejection; yet behind the evil designs of the Jewish leaders and the callousness of the Roman authorities stand the Satanic agencies of evil spirit forces, surnamed 'the rulers of this age' (8). Who was their leader (2 Cor. 4.4; John 14.30)?

(*ii*) 'Natural man' (14, RSV marg.), i.e. the person unrenewed by the Spirit and dead to God in sin (Eph. 2.1; 4.17–18) can never, left to himself, penetrate the barrier which separates him from the world of God and His truth. He is doomed to remain in ignorance and darkness—unless the awakening Spirit visits him, as v. 11b makes plain.

(*iii*) Yet there is always hope, which rests on the initiative of God (10) and the illumination that His Spirit imparts (12). What does the Spirit grant? What are 'the gifts of the Spirit of God' (14) in this passage?

Meditation: Job 28.28.

1 Corinthians 3.1-9

Humanity is apparently divided into two camps: those who do not know God (Gal. 4.8), the 'unspiritual' (i.e. lacking the Spirit's regeneration) of 2.14; and those who have received the Spirit (2.12) and who thereby appreciate the apostle's message (2.13). To them is given the inestimable gift of 'the mind of Christ' (2.16). Does Phil. 2.5 help us to understand this phrase?

There is, however, a third group, 'men of the flesh' (3.1) (Gk. *sarkinoi*). The background here is Gal. 5.16–24, which pictures the internal conflict set up by the opposing forces, Spirit *versus* flesh. *Sarkinos*, then, means a Christian in whom the 'flesh' (i.e. the old life-principle) still retains the upper hand and dominates his entire personality. Into this category the Corinthians put themselves, partly because of their spiritual immaturity ('babes in Christ'), but more culpably because they cherished some worldly notions. They were 'behaving like ordinary men' (3), not measuring up to the stature of redeemed manhood in Christ (Eph. 4.13–16). What was the mark of this stunted growth which characterized their childish and worldly ways (3,4)?

Paul returns to the earlier theme (1.10–16) and confronts a church split into rival parties and claiming allegiance to several of the apostles. They needed the reminder that these men whom they exalted were 'slaves of Christ' (5) who, if they had accomplished anything of lasting worth in their ministry, owed it to the enabling of the Lord. Certainly, they should not be held to be in competition with one another, thought of as gathering followers and so (unwittingly) promoting jealousy and a party-spirit (3).

In Christian service the key-note is *co-operative endeavour* (6–9). Paul teaches with metaphors drawn from horticulture and the building trade. Apollos and he are like farmers whose duty it is to sow and to tend the young plants—in time a harvest will be their reward (Gal. **6**.9; 2 Tim. **2**.6). But only God can make the seed germinate and grow (7). Similarly, the apostles are construction workers, giving time and energy to the erecting of a building. But as the harvest field is God's, so also is the finished building (9; Heb. **3**.4). The lesson should be obvious to this faction-ridden church: all God's servants are useful; each has a particular job; but none is indispensable.

Question: Which other Christian community was remaining at the infantile stage (Heb. 5.11–14)?

1 Corinthians 3.10-23

Paul as a townsman never seemed happy with agricultural illustrations (see Rom. **11**.17–24, where his use of the olive tree metaphor seems adapted to his own purpose contrary to nature!). It is not unexpected therefore that he prefers to drive home his point with the imagery of a *building* (10–15).

The argument is constructed in a logical fashion. Every building must have a solid foundation (11)—the Church is secure at this point at least (Matt. **16**.18; **21**.42; Eph. **2**.20, NEB; Rev. **21**.14), as Jesus had Himself emphasized (Matt. **7**.24–27) and it was the unique privilege of the apostolic ministry to lay that foundation by their preaching and confession of Christ. In that sense the Corinthian church is Paul's work (**9**.1); and he was careful not to claim more than his rightful assignment as 'a skilled master-builder' (Rom. **15**.20; 2 Cor. **10**.13–18).

The foundation has been 'well and truly laid', but he is anxious that the erecting of the building shall also be done competently and with the right materials (10b), because the final inspection will quickly show up any defect—and that Day of testing is certainly coming (13).

Various building materials are available. Some are suitable, others are not (12). The contrast is between what is durable (gold, silver, precious stones) and what is not (wood, hay, stubble), when the

118

building catches fire (13). Then, the conflagration will test the worth of the builder's effort—and if he has used useless materials, his work will be destroyed, although he doesn't forfeit his life in the fire (cf. 9.27).

One particular building next occupies the apostle's attention, viz. God's sanctuary (16,17), for this is the application of the building metaphor and its teaching. 1 Pet. 2.4–10 is the best commentary, with its reminder that the Church is God's people as a worshipping community and His witness as a holy people in a fallen world.

Vs. 18–23 bring together the varied themes of the previous discussion. Man's wisdom is of no avail—a truth buttressed by two O.T. citations (19,20); even Christians lapse into worldly patterns of thought when they pin their hope to the men who are but God's instruments (21); and so, far from claiming a party-allegiance, let the Corinthians recall the vastness of their heritage as God's people (23) in which Messiah and His people are viewed as one entity which belongs to God (12.12). No inferior subordination within the Godhead should be read into the closing phrase therefore.

Questions for further study and discussion on 1 Corinthians chs. 1–3

1. What effects do cliques in our Christian fellowships have (*a*) on us as individuals; (*b*) on the church; (*c*) on the 'outsider'?
2. Paul preached an unvarnished gospel (2.2 ff.). Use this as a criterion in assessing the value of modern methods of communication in presenting the message of Christ. Which can hinder, and which can assist, its presentation?
3. 'We have the mind of Christ' (2.16). What does this mean to you?
4. What factors today inhibit growth in Christ (3.1), in churches and in individuals?
5. Define in contemporary terms the meaning of gold, silver . . . hay, stubble. What is really worth while in your church and life?

1 Corinthians 4.1-13

The correct designation of the apostles is offered: they are stewards and servants, whose virtue lies in the way in which they fulfil their commission. The vital quality is trustworthiness, i.e. faithfulness to the commission that God assigns, whether as planters or waterers of the seed (3.6–8).

At Corinth there were those who, out of preference for Peter as an original member of the Twelve, or Apollos as an eloquent and gifted teacher of Alexandrian wisdom, disparaged Paul. In 2 Cor. 10–12 we shall be examining the specific charges that they brought against him. For the present he disclaims any concern to be brought before the tribunal of their judgement (3,4). He is content to await the final Day (3.13) when the Lord will test openly his labours and motives (5).

Paul and Apollos were evidently being set in opposition as party-leaders; but it is clear that many Corinthians were themselves setting up factions within the main parties (see 11.19). Whichever way the rivalry was being fostered, it is all reprehensible, for (Paul reiterates) no teacher or Christian has any virtue in himself, and no gift he can claim to have is his independently of God (7). It is a salutary reminder that all our more gifted brethren hold their privileged ministry as a sacred trust from God!

Vs. 8–13 are written in ironical vein, aimed at deflating the pride of the Corinthians who imagined that they didn't need any apostle! In a series of powerful contrasts Paul sets out the price which he and his colleagues were paying for the apostolic ministry exercised on the churches' behalf. 2 Cor. 6.4–10; 11.23–29 should be read as close parallels. All these texts underline the axiom of Christian service: no gain without pain; if we would bless, we must bleed (Jowett).

Notes: V. 1: 'the mysteries of God'=revelation of divine truth, once hidden, now disclosed in Christ and the Church. V. 3: cf. 1 John 3.20,21. V. 6: an exegetical *crux* which has commentators baffled. RSV is more a paraphrase; NEB translates as though a proverb were being quoted: 'learn to keep within the rules, as they say'. V. 9: the illustration is that of gladiators in the arena, and v. 13 reflects the cruel Athenian practice of killing off certain criminals and good-for-nothings if a plague struck the city. V. 10: the report had reached Paul that because he suffered so ignominiously, he couldn't be a true apostle. His reply is exactly the opposite—see 2 Cor. 12.10–13.

1 Corinthians 4.14-21

Paul turns to a direct and personal appeal, reminding us that his 'letters are real letters, not systematic theological treatises' (L. Morris). And there is a noticeable change of mood in the apostle's writing in this paragraph. Previous sections have been severe and sternly ironical (4.8–13), now he takes up a wooing note and directs this tender appeal to them as 'my beloved children' (14). There is a time for both approaches, and we need tact and wisdom to know which line is the more appropriate in any given situation.

The Corinthians are not only his harvest-field and building (3.9,14); they are his spiritual children of whom he is not ashamed to be called their father (15). Hence the call to imitation, similar to the higher summons (Matt. **5**.48; Eph. **5**.1).

So that there will be no misunderstanding of what his parental intentions and directives are, Paul is sending Timothy, his trusted lieutenant, to amplify and enforce his applied teaching (17).

Timothy's visit is also to be a preparation for Paul's own coming, of which he gives promise (18,19). He anticipates that both Timothy's mission and his own projected visit will be challenged, knowing the arrogance and indiscipline to authority which there is at Corinth. So, if they will not be persuaded by a tender appeal, they must take the consequence of a stern warning (21). The choice is theirs.

Notes: V. 14: Paul's letters often had a disturbing effect (2 Cor. **2**.9; **10**.9–11), and on at least one occasion he regretted his severe reproach (2 Cor. **7**.8). V. 15: although the church had been helped by other teachers, it would never escape its indebtedness to its human founder. The father-son relationship is drawn from Jewish teaching —'Whoever teaches the son of his friend the law (of Moses), it is as if he had begotten him'. V. 16: cf. **11**.1; Gal. **4**.12; 2 Thess. **3**.7,9; Phil. **3**.17. V. 17: 'I am sending' is the sense. V. 18: 'arrogant' is literally 'puffed up', 'swollen' (with pride)—*the* distinguishing mark of the Corinthian church (**4**.6,19; **5**.2; **13**.4). V. 20: one of the rare occurrences in Paul's writing of a term so characteristic of Jesus' preaching. The same contrast, 'talk' *versus* effective action, is found in 1 Thess. **1**.5. V. 21: a close parallel is seen in Job **37**.13: God deals with His people either in discipline or in love, but always for our real good.

1 Corinthians 5.1-5

Paul can hardly credit it, but reports have confirmed that the church at Corinth has lost all sense of moral responsibility and is actually condoning a glaring case of incest. Indeed, the matter is aggravated not only by a failure to deal with the offender (even the Gentile world condemned such) (1), but by the church's attitude of continued arrogance. This may imply that what to Paul should have been an occasion of discipline had been treated as a matter of some self-congratulation (2). This interpretation, if correct, would confirm the idea that some Corinthian Christians had accepted gnostic teaching which sat loosely to moral standards, particularly in matters of sex-relations.

At all events, Paul knows what must be done. The 'new morality' at Corinth must be strongly rejected (2b).

A church meeting is to be called when, with Paul's presence

among the members, a solemn excommunication of the offender is to be carried out—a severe judgement on a severe moral transgression (3,4). Yet the *spirit* of the church's united act is not to be vindictive, but remedial (5). Expulsion from the church, which may seem to be unduly harsh and likely to arouse resentment, will (in the end) serve the higher end of the man's spiritual good (5b).

Notes: V. 1: incest was forbidden by Roman law and the Levitical code (Lev. **18.8**). If the man's father were still living, adultery would be added to incest and so the case would be aggravated in its moral perversion. V. 2: the penalty for this immoral union, according to Jewish tradition in the Mishnah, was death by stoning. The Pauline prescription is less severe, viz. excommunication from the church's fellowship. V. 5: the plain sense is the meaning given above, viz. expulsion from the church to the domain of Satan outside, whence believers had been delivered (Col. **1.13**; Acts **26.18**). But as this expelling was treated as serious, the shock may well have led to physical death: hence 'destruction of the flesh', or at least to the suffering of physical consequences (as in Acts **5.1–11**; **13.11**; 1 Tim. **1.20**).

To think over: 'This proceeding may seem to have little compatibility with the spirit of the incident in John 8.1–11.' But is there not a vital difference between a penitent and an arrogant sinner?

1 Corinthians 5.6-8

This portion gives important insight into the *nature of the Christian life* in Paul's teaching.

The setting has already been fixed by the preceding incident; and Paul's rebuke (6) is well made. Not only had the church dealt in a lax way with a moral crime; by its attitude it showed a grave ignorance of the real meaning of the Christian life.

The illustration Paul makes use of is drawn from the Passover ritual in which unleavened bread played a significant role. Before the days of the feast, a ceremony was—and still is in the homes of faithful Jews—performed to search out and destroy all traces of yeast or any kind of fermenting material. In old editions of the Passover service-book a picture of an old man with a candle is sometimes placed as a frontispiece; and at the close of the search, on the eve of Passover, a solemn declaration is made that if any leaven has been inadvertently overlooked in the kitchen or house, it is pronounced null and void!

When Passover begins, in the Jewish calendar on Nisan 14, the use of leaven is forbidden and unleavened bread is the diet. A symbolic value was attached to this, as Lev Gillet has described in his book *Communion in the Messiah,* for the rising of the dough is an apt picture of the swelling of pride, and the Jews must be reminded that they were a poor and servile people when the Lord redeemed them from Egypt (Deut. 7.6–11; 26.5–9; two important passages!).

Against this background the Corinthians are called to (*i*) clear out every trace of (moral) evil (7) by dealing with the presence of arrogant sin in their midst (13); (*ii*) recall that they are the New Israel of God, summoned to be a holy people to the Lord and redeemed by the Paschal Lamb Himself (typified by the lambs of Exod. 12.3–7); (*iii*) celebrate the Christian Passover (8) which lasts, not for seven to eight days as in the Jewish rite, but for a life-time; for the entire Christian life is a festival of joy and gladness as we are continually reminded of the new life of freedom from sin's tyranny, to which God in Christ has called us (1 Pet. 1.14–19). It is to a reaffirmation of this high calling that we are bidden every time we gather at the Lord's table and commemorate the new Exodus and take the Passover 'dishes' of bread and wine (11.23–26).

1 Corinthians 5.9-13

We are still considering the theme of discipline and the treatment of evil practices. Some of the Corinthians were immoderately lax (5.2); others had misunderstood an earlier letter and had become inordinately rigid (10) by refusing *any* contact with the outside world.

Obviously Paul's earlier instruction had been misapplied; and what was intended as a call to discipline *within* the church had been taken as an invitation to the life of a recluse by severing all association with men of the world (10). Paul shows how impossible this is— except, perhaps, by setting up a monastic, self-contained community like the people of the Dead Sea scrolls. But this withdrawal from society is never countenanced in the N.T. The Church is the light of the world, the salt of the earth (Matt. 5.13–16)—not a shut-off community, practising a world-denying ethic and living only to itself.

The withdrawal that Paul did stress was in the matter of *church discipline* (11). Members of the church who try to profess the faith *and* to adopt pagan ways of life are to be severely dealt with (11–13). Even to welcome them at the Lord's table, in their unrepentant frame of mind and manners, or possibly to any meal-table, is an act of encouragement to them (2 John 10,11; 2 Thess. 3.14,15). Rather, they must be 'judged', i.e. shown their folly and firmly reminded of the high moral standards demanded by the New Covenant. Even one immoral man can spoil the fellowship by his influence (6) unless he is checked. The point is clinched by a reference to Deut. 13.5. What is the relevance of this text?

1 Corinthians 6.1-11

Paul's discussion about judgement and its exercise within the Christian fellowship leads him to consider another misdemeanour at Corinth. When there is a dispute between fellow-believers—and Paul accepts that the Christian society will contain members who get at loggerheads with one another—the issue should be settled in a way far from what was being adopted at Corinth. There the Christians had the audacity (1: the verb 'dare' is a strong word) to have the case taken to litigation and tried by non-Christian magistrates.

The apostle had some plain words to speak about this procedure:

(*i*) It is wrong in itself (6,7), because it shows on the one hand a lack of spiritual competence when a church cannot order its own life without recourse to pagan legal tribunals (5); and, on the other, a spirit of contentiousness and standing up for one's rights, which quickly degenerates into actual injustice and a perverting of the right, so that a man with a grievance seeks for more compensation than that to which strict justice entitles him (so v. 8). And all this involves fellow-Christians.

(*ii*) Another reason for this improper method's condemnation is that it exhibits a worldly attitude. Christians will one day be the arbiters of the world's destiny (2), and this will require great spiritual discernment (3). On the present showing the church at Corinth does not appear to be well qualified for this grand judicial office!

The final assize (2,3) leads him to consider those who exclude themselves from God's realm (9,10)—a throw-back to 5.11, and a solemn reminder that whatever the Corinthians' character may have been in immoral society, now by rebirth and baptism and the sanctifying agency of the Spirit (11) they are new creatures in Christ (2 Cor. 5.17; Eph. 4.17–24), with old habits passed away.

Notes: V. 1: Rom. 13.1–8 certifies that the Roman law system was good—for its prescribed purpose. The trouble came when believers called in the authorities to settle *internal* frictions. V. 4: 'If therefore you have everyday questions to decide, do you set those for whom the church has no respect upon the bench?' (Anderson Scott). Or the tone may be ironical, and the verse refer to inferior people in the church. Verse 5 probably supports the second idea. V. 7: Matt. 5.39 ff., cf. 1 Pet. 2.23. V. 9: sexual perversity is a sign of fallen nature in every age. V. 11: Acts 22.16 shows that baptism into Christ marked a clean break and a new start.

1 Corinthians 6.12-20

The prevailing ethos in the city of Corinth, infamous for its moral laxity and inimical to the Christian standards of purity and self-control, had infiltrated into the church-life and given rise to an ugly situation which required the reiteration of the basic Christian moral prescription: 'shun immorality' (18).

Not only had some church members begun to indulge in immoral practices by a misuse of their bodily functions (leading to gluttony and fornication), they were claiming justification for their actions in the name of Christian liberty (12: the first part of each sentence should be in quotation-marks, cited from the Corinthians' letter to Paul). The apostle responds with a crystal-clear statement of Christian ethics and with some principles which are as apposite today as when he first enunciated them.

The first point to be explained is the meaning in Paul's letters of 'body'. To us it is used of our physical frame, but Paul's usage is much more complex. 'The body . . . is not only the material body . . . but the imperishable form of the personality' (Weiss). It stands for the real self, the whole person. This specific sense which Paul gives explains v. 18: union with a prostitute is an offence against the whole person—indeed against two persons, the man and the woman (15), and so is a betrayal of Christian profession as well as a degradation of womanhood.

These verses give a *locus classicus* of Paul's teaching on the body:

(*i*) The body has been redeemed, with a price paid for its purchase (20). The Christian is therefore in a very real sense not his own, to please himself. His whole being exists for God's glory whose image he reflects (11.7).

(*ii*) The body is sanctified by the Holy Spirit who indwells the believer as the Presence of God (the *Shekinah*) filled the Jerusalem Temple (1 Kings 8.11); it is to be treated with respect and dignity, never defiled or abused, since it is the Spirit's shrine (19).

(*iii*) The body is a member of Christ (15), i.e. it forms a part of His body, the Church, of which He is the Head, and is to be used in His service (Eph. 1.23; 4.16; 5.30). Sexual irregularities cause damage to the integrity of the persons involved, and so deform the body of Christ by perverting this union between Christ and His bride (16).

(*iv*) The body will be raised (14), which means that God has a purpose for the body, albeit as a spiritual body (15.44) but with some connection with the human life here in this world, in eternity—and we shall be judged *then* for what we do *now* (2 Cor. 5.10).

Meditation: Rom. 12.1–2.

1. Consider in ch. 4 the implications of becoming a 'father' in Christ, and assess your ability to assume this responsibility.
2. Church discipline is a live problem today. What has ch. 5 to teach us on (a) the responsibility of leaders to deal with offenders; (b) the spirit which should motivate their actions? See 2 Thess. 3.15.
3. 5.11 is an astonishing list of vices which professing Christians were practising. They are mainly 'sins of the flesh'. What other sins disfigure our lives today?
4. 'It is no part of the Church's function (5.13) to discipline those who are not members' (Morris). What is the bearing of this on (a) Sunday observance; (b) divorce laws?
5. What does the N.T. teach (in addition to ch. 6) concerning the way in which Christians should settle their personal differences and grievances?

1 Corinthians 7.1-16

Of all human relationships the association of man and woman in marriage is the closest and most personal. It is not surprising that (i) Paul should go on from his earlier discussion (6.15,16) to expound some of the deeper implications of Christian marriage; and (ii) that the Corinthians themselves should have raised these fundamental questions in a letter of inquiry to him (1). The replies he gives fall into well-defined sections.

(i) *Vs. 1–7.* It makes much better sense if we read 'It is a good thing for a man to have nothing to do with women' (NEB) as a statement quoted from the Corinthians' letter; then v. 2 is a Pauline comment. The apostle who wrote Eph. 5.21–33 is not likely to have expressed a stark condemnation of conjugal union, implied in v. 1. The rest of the paragraph covers the same ground as the *Ephesians* passage, with mutual regard and responsibility in sex relations spelled out in some detail. 1 Pet. 3.7 completes the full Christian picture of God's intention for the married state.

It is important to try to read between the lines here. Evidently some Corinthians had taken the (gnostic) view—later expressed in 1 Tim. 4.3—that marriage and marital unions were inherently evil and were abandoning all conjugal connections. Paul goes to the root of the matter by his assertion that marriage is part of God's will for the race, and like all His creation pronounced 'very good' (Gen. 1.31).

(*ii*) *Vs. 8–9* consider the case of those who do not or cannot marry. Celibacy is approved, whether for those who were unmarried or for those who had been married and had lost their partner by death. If, however, the celibate state imposes too great a mental and psychological strain, and marriage is possible, the latter course is preferable.

(*iii*) *Vs. 10,11* contemplate a situation in which one partner is faced with the problem of a disagreement within Christian marriage. Jesus' teaching on the indissolubility of marriage (Mark 10.9–12) is invoked as a directive. Divorce, on this ground, is not permitted.

(*iv*) *Vs. 12–16* give apostolic commentary on the Lord's teaching, by way of application to specific instances of situations which Jesus' words never envisaged, viz. one partner, who becomes converted, has to face the prospect of life with an unbelieving partner. Again, divorce is only contemplated if the non-Christian spouse desires it. Otherwise let the marriage continue, with the prospect of conversion always in view and a wholesome inheritance into which the children may enter (14). 'Holy'=brought within the sphere of God's grace.

1 Corinthians 7.17-24

The apostle's ruling direction in the delicate concerns of husband-wife relationships, where one partner is a Christian and the other is not, is given in v. 15: 'God's call is a call to live in peace' (NEB), i.e. wholeness of life in which our personalities can, under His good will, develop and mature.

The same ruling applies in the next section (17–24). The discussion, however, has shifted, if momentarily, from marriage to social and racial distinctions.

Circumcision was a mark to which the Jewish people attached great importance (Rom. 3.1). Paul's attitude was that which he adopted to all religious ceremonial: it is useful if practised with sincere motive and as a spiritual aid within the overall context of salvation by faith alone, by grace alone. So he can confess 'Circumcision has value, if you obey the law' (Rom. 2.25); and obedience implies another 'circumcision' (Rom. 2.29, already anticipated in Jer. 4.4; Phil. 3.3). In the light of this a physical sign in the flesh is of little value (19; Gal. 6.15)—but is a positive spiritual menace if trusted as an article of salvation. Hence his controversy with the Judaizers in Galatia, on which see the Notes on Gal. 5.2, etc.

Social status presents a more complex issue. Slavery was a commonplace part of the Graeco-Roman society in which the

Church was born. Paul raised no standard of revolt against this inhuman institution. We may ask why he did not—and find part of our answer in his letter to *Philemon*.

There were opportunities for a slave to gain freedom, chiefly by the payment of a sum of money deposited in a temple and transferred to the slave's owner. Paul encourages this process (21)—and moves on to remind all, whether slaves or freed men, that they are under the yoke of Christ and are His purchased property (23). Use your present lot—and hope for the best. This is his practical advice (24); and he himself exemplified it (Phil. 4.11–13).

Thought: 'A Christian man is a perfectly free lord of all, subject to none. A Christian man is a perfectly dutiful servant, subject to all' (*Luther*).

1 Corinthians 7.25-40

Celibacy is again to the forefront of the discussion, and Paul, with some apparent reluctance, offers the advice which he has been requested to give as an apostle who possesses the Spirit (40), although he concedes that he has no oracle of the Lord to which he may appeal (25).

Certain governing principles are set out which make it expedient not to enter upon marriage. It is a moot point how far these conditions obtain today—and we must always remember Paul's own qualifications (28). Can you detect the principles?

(*i*) The acute 'time of stress' in which apostolic Christianity was being established (26, NEB), with no clear future, mainly because a clash with State (leading to persecution and death by martyrdom) could be discerned by any with eyes to see.

(*ii*) The uncertainty of society's continued existence, bounded (as the Church has always believed) by the prospect of the Lord's return and the winding up of history (29,31).

(*iii*) The need to live as those who knew themselves to be pilgrims and strangers in the world (26–31; Heb. 11.13; 1 Pet. 2.11), and so to be set free from the anxiety which comes with the ownership of property—and the domestic responsibility of a wife, children and home-life (32–34). Again, Paul inserts a proviso, in no way wishing to hold his converts 'on a tight rein' (35, NEB), but solicitous only that they may 'wait upon the Lord without distraction'. A missionary situation required a stringent ethic; the question is how far, with the advent of Christian civilization and culture, these prescriptions still obtain.

We have assumed that normal marriage opportunities and arrangements are in Paul's mind (as, e.g. in v. 27). The next section (36–38), however, has been variously interpreted. The AV (KJV) presents the problem of whether or not a father should allow his virgin daughter to marry. The RSV envisages the problem confronting an engaged couple; while the NEB has in view an unusual practice, found in the later Church, of a couple who lived together in an unmarried state and without sexual intercourse. The risks involved in such a 'Platonic' friendship of spiritual marriage are obvious, and there is no evidence of any such practice in N.T. times. What Cyprian later condemned, Paul, knowing human nature as he did, is not likely to have condoned. Two facts are clear: celibacy and marriage are both natural, and a person must make his or her choice.

1 Corinthians 8.1-13

The introductory phrase poses another query on which the church sought Paul's mind. And he opens his reply with quoting a statement from the Corinthians' letter. The Christians were evidently asking which spiritual gift ranked highest. They preferred 'knowledge'; Paul retorts that it is 'love' which takes precedence, and later chapters will amplify vs. 1–3.

The real issue before the Christians at Corinth with their confidence in knowledge had to do with idol-meats (on the background, consult *New Bible Dictionary*, 'Idols, Meats offered to').

The church was obviously in two minds over the propriety of eating food which had been formerly used in temple-worship, only a portion of which was actually consumed in sacrifice, and which later was offered for sale in the butchers' shops. Was the Christian housewife at liberty to use this meat, because, after all, idols were non-existent and couldn't contaminate the food? Or, should she refrain because idolatry *did* cast a spell over food, thus making it 'unclean' and unfit for consumption by believers?

The apostle's answer is detailed and spread over two chapters (8,10). He begins by agreeing with the maxim that (*i*) there is only one God, and (*ii*) so no idol has any real existence (4–6). But this, to Paul, is not the whole story. Other factors enter in and modify this initial judgement: in these verses the considerations to be borne in mind are (*a*) we should respect the conscience of 'weaker brethren' for whom idolatry was a very real problem and who did not share the enlightenment of the 'knowledgeable' of v. 1; (*b*) liberty must be balanced by our concern for others (9), for it was a serious offence to cause any fellow-Christian to stumble; in fact, it was like striking a blow at Christ Himself (12); (c) the whole business of eating idol foods, or refraining, is a matter of personal indifference to Paul (8), and he is interested only in securing the well-being of other Christians who *may* be impeded in their spiritual growth (13).

Notes: V. 5: reflects the polytheism of the ancient religious world. V. 12: Christ is affected by an offence against His people (Acts 9.4f.).

Question: Which other church had 'strong' and 'weak' brethren (Rom. 14.15)?

1 Corinthians 9.1-18

The connection of this section with the foregoing is not easy to see, and a suggestion has been made that ch. 9 is part of a separate letter. But this proposal is unrequired once we recall the two themes now taken up. First, in ch. 8 Paul has been showing the need of considerateness of other people's needs; now he states that this has been the policy of his ministry, even to the point of refusing a right which properly belonged to him (12). Secondly, he is sensitive of the criticism which has been passed on him (1), for his conduct has evidently been questioned or misunderstood by his detractors. The argument against him would run: Paul doesn't claim his right of maintenance as an apostle because he is unsure of his true apostleship. He replies by asserting the qualifications that he has (1,2). What are they?

Vs. 3–7. As an apostle whose labours have been fruitful in establishing the Corinthian community under God, he goes on to say that the privilege of financial support from the churches is his too (4); and for a married man, like Peter, an apostle may rightfully expect the help of the churches to enable his wife to accompany him in his itineraries (5). There is Old Testament precedent for the rule that the Lord's servants do not look in vain to the Lord's people for their upkeep and support.

Vs. 8–14. That Old Testament rubric extends to cover maintenance in the actual work of the ministry (9–11, 14), and if the other apostolic leaders at Corinth had been given their rights, why should Paul's rights be called in question (12)?

Now comes the important turning-point in his treatment. He has chosen voluntarily to renounce these rights (12). Why? At all costs he wishes to avoid the charge of unscrupulous dealing—a theme treated at length in 2 Cor. 10–12.

Vs. 15–18. Preaching the gospel is for Paul akin to the effect of fire in Jeremiah's bones (Jer. 20.9); he preaches because he cannot help himself; a divine compulsion rests upon him (16), even if he wanted to quit (17). The conclusion is plain therefore. The work of God is its own reward, found in the joy of service to Christ and the privilege of being usable in His hands (18).

Thought: Paul's reasoning in this section does not absolve us today from our responsibility for the worthy upkeep of the ministry (Luke 10.7; 1 Tim. 5.18).

1 Corinthians 9.19-27

As Paul had cleared himself of the charge of uncertain motives in not securing financial support, so he moves on to show his deep concern always to make himself available to others, even to the point of adopting certain courses of action which would be unnatural to him. Again, we may ask, What is his motivation in all these renunciations and acceptances (22b, 23)?

He offers two explanations. First in vs. 19–23, he makes it clear that in his missionary service his aim is to gain the greatest possible number of converts: 'by all means [to] save some' (22). The reason for this passage (20–22a) is probably to be sought in some criticism which had been levelled against him. His opponents—justifiably enough from their viewpoint—accused him of a confused attitude to the relation between Jews and Gentiles. Sometimes he observed the Law (Acts 21.24) as though he were a pious Jew; at other times he identified himself with the Gentiles to such an extent that a rumour could circulate that he had abandoned all his ancestral heritage (Acts 21.21). Understandably Paul was under a cloud of suspicion from all quarters: did he really know his own mind? Or had he no fixed principles?

The paragraph (20 ff.) offers a *rationale* of his missionary conduct. He felt himself genuinely freed from Mosaic obligations—but if nevertheless he sometimes observed the commandments of the Law it was for the particular purpose of not offending Jews who were likely to become Christians, in conformity with the principle stated in 8.13 (so Héring).

Vs. 24–27. In the second place, so conscientious was his evangelistic passion that he knew that, when he had striven to make the gospel presentable to all, he was still left with his greatest problem—*himself.* The Christian worker and evangelist must keep a watchful eye on his own inner life, taking spiritual self-discipline as seriously as the athlete observes strict rules of training, diet and self-control. Otherwise his hopes of being successful in the gospel's service are as futile as those of the unprepared entrant for the Isthmian Games held at Corinth. His great fear (27) is that after doing the preaching

131

(as an art to be learned!), in God's eyes he should be disallowed, like a runner or boxer who gets disqualified and sees his efforts wasted.

Meditation: 2 Tim. 2.5; 4.7,8: two passages which go together.

Questions for further study and discussion on 1 Corinthians chs. 7-9

1. Is divorce ever the answer to a marriage problem? Discuss the social responsibilities Christians have in joining marriage counselling groups. What is the Christian view of marriage?
2. Food sacrificed to idols is not a burning issue with us. What current situations should be guided by the principles which Paul lays down here?
3. How far should 'strong' Christians allow themselves to be controlled by the scruples of the 'weak'?
4. What 'rights' can we as Christians forgo in order to present the gospel more effectively?

1 Corinthians 10.1-13

The Christian life, according to the N.T., holds in tension a restful assurance and a healthy fear. On the one side, we have the confidence of Rom. 8.28-39; Phil. 1.6, with a pledge of eternal security; but lest this assurance should dull our moral senses and breed a careless attitude, we must recall the warnings of Heb. 2.1; 10.4-9; 10.26-39; 12.25; 2 Pet. 1.10 and 1 Cor. 9.27.

It is this salutary reflection on the need of personal discipline in his own life that prompts Paul to deal with the prevailing mood at Corinth. The pith of his admonition is that religious profession, expressed in the use of the sacraments, is 'no safeguard for a careless life which takes liberties with itself' (J. Moffatt).

The quiet reminder which Paul gives is that the Old Testament people of God had their special 'moments of revelation' when God came uniquely near; they enjoyed their 'sacraments', as they were 'baptized into Moses' (2) and sustained by the life-giving water out of the rock (4). But, as they turned aside to idolatry and became apostate from the true God, they quickly met their fate (5-10).

O.T. incidents of 'judgement in spite of privilege' (e.g. Amos 3.1,2) do not belong simply to the story-book of the ancient past, Paul warns (11); through them we are admonished today (Heb. 3.7-19). The call is one of self-examination (12) and a turning away from all presumption and blind trust in religious ceremonial or any supposed 'once for all' status, which makes the professor insensitive to the moral standards set by the gospel and demanded of God's people in every age. Temptation to slackness will come, but no trial has power to overwhelm us while there is provided a way out (13). But it is easier to find the 'way out' if we refuse, in the first place, to pass through the 'way in' to a compromising situation. Hence v. 14 (cf. 1 Tim. 6.11).

Notes: Vs. 1–5: 'it looks as though the Corinthians expected salvation to be automatically guaranteed to them because they had been baptized and because they shared in the Lord's Supper' (Thrall)— an offer, *mutatis mutandis*, made by pagan cults of Paul's day, and today. Vs. 6–10: five examples of Israelite lapses are given. Can you spot them? (Num. **11**.4–6; Exod. **32**.6; Num. **25**.1–9; **21**.4–9; **16**). The numerical discrepancy between Num. **25**.9 and v. 8 is not serious; both are round figures and we may mark Paul's addition 'in a single day'.

1 Corinthians 10.14-22

Idol-worship was another common feature of daily life in Corinth; and no Corinthian believer could close his eyes to what was going on all around him. The dilemma facing the Church in pagan society is well portrayed by Godet. 'On the one hand, they could not absolutely give up their family and friendly relations; the interests of the gospel did not allow them to do so. On the other hand, these relations were full of temptations . . . Among the most thorny points in this order of questions were invitations to take part in idolatrous banquets . . . Now various questions might be raised on this subject. And first of all, Is it allowable for a Christian to be present at a feast offered in the temple of an idol? Some, in the name of Christian liberty, answered: 'Yes! . . . All things are lawful for me' (**6.12**; **10.23**). Others said: 'No! for in such a region one subjects himself to the danger of malign and even diabolical influences.'

At an earlier place in the correspondence (8.4–13), Paul assented to the truth of Christian liberty on the ground that idols are non-existent and products of the human imagination (Rom. **1.21–23** comes to a similar conclusion). Now, he presents another aspect of the case by asserting that behind the idol lurks a demonic influence (19, 20), and it is this demonic power which is capable of contaminating, not food, but *persons*. The awful consequence is that a Christian, by entering into liaison with the idolater at a temple feast, may open the door to demonic influence upon his life; and this would lead to a compromise in the believer's discipleship as he enters into communion with Christ and His rival—a course which, in any case, is doomed to failure for the reason given in Matt. 6.24

(v. 21: 'cannot' here means that a consistency of profession is lost the moment the Corinthian acknowledges the claim of the demon on him).

The Lord's table is not a pious act in memory of a past figure of history. The Christian worships no dead Christ, but discovers, as he commemorates the Supper, that the elements of bread and wine are 'bearers of the presence of Christ' (16), communicated to a living faith which receives Christ at His table. There is, moreover, a horizontal reference in the Church's fellowship meal (17), for in sharing in Christ's body and blood, believers realize their focus of unity as His body in the world—and this vocation commits them to His sole Lordship, unshared by rival gods. 'Communion', rendered in the RSV 'participation' (16), 'partners' (20), is a key New Testament word (see *New Bible Dictionary*, pp. 245 f.).

1 Corinthians 10.23—11.1

The burning question raised by the Corinthian correspondents still required further treatment. At the earlier place (8.10) the situation envisaged is an invitation to share a meal with an unbeliever at his god's temple. The worship of Serapis included a meal at the temple as the devotees gathered, and in a surviving papyrus letter an invitation to such an occasion is recorded: 'Chaeremon invites you to dinner at the table of our lord Serapis in the Serapeum tomorrow the 15th at nine o'clock'. Paul's answer to this problem is that eating such a sacrificial meal is tantamount to idolatry, and is forbidden.

But two other practical issues still remained. The practice of shopping in the market (25) and a social occasion of a meal in a private house (27) presented cases on which Paul's ruling was sought. His answers follow:

(*i*) In the case of the housewife doing her shopping in a butcher's shop, she is not required to be anxious over the food's 'past history', i.e. whether or not it has been formerly offered in a temple. Paul allows the Christian to accept it, because it is covered by the ordinance of Psa. 24.1, which declares all God's gifts to be good (1 Tim. 4.4,5).

(*ii*) In the case of an invitation to a non-sacrificial meal, the same allowance is granted, and Paul is sympathetic with the Corinthians who had evidently made the point that such occasions were part and parcel of the social and business life of their city (on a par with the lunch engagements of the modern executive). The only proviso is the action to be followed if attention is drawn to where the meat has come from. If this happens (28), the 'eating is prohibited, not as *per se* idolatrous, but because it places the eater in a false position, and confuses the conscience of others' (Robertson-Plummer). Notice again Paul's delicate concern for another's well-being (24,29,32,33).

The last word on the subject is a final one in every sense (31), setting the highest standard possible, viz. to live to the greater glory of God.

Notes: V. 23: observe the quotation-marks. Paul is citing from the Corinthians' letter to him. V. 28: 'offered in sacrifice'—the Greek term denotes part of pagan ritual (unlike the term in **8.1**, which is capable of carrying a good or bad sense).

To think over: On v. 32: 'Christianity demands that your right shall not lead others astray, that it shall not do violence to that most sacred and delicate thing—a human conscience' (*F. W. Robertson*).

1 Corinthians 11.2-16

Two further complications in the assembled congregation at Corinth needed a ruling which this section provides: (*i*) the sense of proper order to be observed at public worship was much in debate; and (*ii*) the emancipation of women at Corinth created its own difficulty once it became customary for Christian women to share vocally in the congregational service. As a loyal Jew Paul takes his stand on the divine ordering laid down in Genesis (cf. 3,7; 1 Tim. **2.**13,14); but as a Christian, priority in creation and in society is tempered by the reminders of mutual honour and interdependence (8,11,12). Eph. **5.**21–33 represents the full flowering of this teaching which the Christian Church has been painfully slow to receive and act upon.

Paul has no qualms about the part which women may play in Christian worship. The functions of prayer and prophecy (defined in **14.**3 as a rough equivalent of preaching) are fully granted; the sole proviso is the adopting of a proper head attire (5—the alternative of v. 6 is not always remembered!) But that alternative, offered in v. 6 is apparently withdrawn in v. 15, where a woman's hair is part of her femininity, and the possibility of her being shaven in order to avoid wearing a covering (6) is regarded as contrary to nature (15). Paul cuts short any extended discussion (16).

A note should be added to relate this passage to 1 Tim. **2.**11,12, which seems to take away any feminine participation in public worship (cf. **14.**34,35). The present writer (in *Worship in the Early Church*) has argued that the prophetic gift may have included speaking in tongues (cf. Acts **21.**9) and that Corinthian women were abusing the gift; Paul is therefore warning against unseemly

135

behaviour in an assembly where public worship would quickly get out of hand—and the same restriction is imposed on the Ephesian community in 1 Tim. **2.8** ff. There it is also a question of women taking *office* in the church as distinct from exercising a *function* (as in 1 Cor. **11**). The former is forbidden, while the latter is permitted (with due safeguards of good order).

Notes: V. 10 has been an unsolved mystery. Miss Thrall seems to shed some light in her suggestion that the angels are the guardians of the moral order of God's world. 'If a woman without a veil should lead the congregation in prayer, or if she should deliver some prophetic message . . . and should do this *bare-headed*, then she *brings shame on her head*', viz. by showing disrespect to her husband, the head of the family. Conversely, with men, if they cover their head, they forfeit their God-appointed place.

1 Corinthians 11.17-22

The trouble within the Corinthian church was not that the believers were avoiding congregational meetings for service and sacrament, but that they failed to understand and apply some elementary principles of Christian worship (17). Hence Paul's word of reproof.

Two criticisms are raised in this section. First, the lack of unity in the church had become most obvious at the very place where that unity should be most powerfully demonstrated (18). Paul can't put his finger exactly on the trouble-spot but fears the worst: 'I believe there is some truth in it' (NEB); verse 19 is ironical, and looks back to earlier references (in **1.10** ff.; **3.3;21**) which clearly indicate that the church was sharply divided into groups, and a jealous spirit prevailed. The rebuke of the apostle is the corollary of the truth (**10.17**) of the oneness of the church, which shows a single loaf at the fellowship meal; and by this quarrelsome and divisive attitude the Corinthians were denying the unity of the Church at the precise point at which its oneness as the body of Christ should be displayed and realized to the full.

The second feature of the Lord's Supper observance was no less serious. Verse 20 must mean: 'When you meet as a congregation, it is not possible to eat the Lord's Supper in the conditions desired by the Lord' (so Héring). The outward form may be observed and the members may go through the motions associated with the cup of blessing and the breaking of the bread (**10.16**), but solemn worship employing holy things is in vain unless the *spirit* of the worshippers is right. Psa. **51.6–19** is a classic statement of this requirement; and can you recall some of the prophets' condemnation of 'wickedness and worship' (as Ewald characterized Isa. 1.10–31; cf. Amos 5.21–24; Mic. 6.6–8)?

The grievous fault at Corinth was a sin of selfishness and greed (21). The rich members arrived early at the assembly (in a house, no doubt, 22) and began their meal; the poorer members, probably slaves whose duties detained them, came late only to find all the food consumed. The early arrivals had had a royal time—to the point of intoxication. No wonder Paul lampoons this situation in tones of astonished disgust (22)!

Notes: V. 20: 'the Lord's Supper' is a comprehensive term, embracing a fellowship-meal (the *Agape* or love-feast) in the framework of which a communion service was held.

1 Corinthians 11.23-26

The setting of the Lord's table service was (as vs. 21,22 indicate) that of an ordinary meal; and this custom is found elsewhere, e.g. in the document known as the *Teaching of the Twelve Apostles* or *Didache* which describes the Church in Syria in the decades A.D. 80–100. But gradually (for reasons not unrelated to the consequences which followed the procedure at Corinth) this combination of a meal and a sacrament was abandoned; and the solemn observance of the communion came to be practised on its own.

These familiar words should be read alongside the Gospel accounts (Matt. 26.26–28; Mark 14.22–24; Luke 22.17–19) and the differences noted.

Substantially the sense is the same in all the accounts; it is the emphasis which varies. In Paul's account the chief emphases are:

(*i*) Verse 23 makes it plain that Paul was no innovator, but that he is transmitting to the Corinthians the substance of the holy rite which he himself received.

(*ii*) Both 'bread' and 'cup' form the main elements of the service, and are tokens of something greater, viz. the body and blood of Christ. The sacrament consists not simply in bread, but *broken* bread (RSV marg.); not in wine, but *poured out* wine (10.16). The stress falls not on the elements (as though they held some magical virtue) but on the actions. Jesus' words are interpretative of His actions; and these acts are parabolic and symbolic in line with the tradition of the O.T. prophets' symbolic actions (e.g. Jer. 27,28). Paul's statement further stresses the individual response needed ('for *you*', 24; 'you drink it', 25).

(*iii*) His reference to the *new* covenant recalls Jeremiah 31.31 ff., and is characteristically part of his inspired understanding of the gospel (see Notes on 2 Cor. 3 and *New Bible Dictionary*, 'Lord's Supper').

(*iv*) 'In remembrance of Me' is again Pauline; it is absent from the Markan tradition and the shorter text in Luke. Passover analogies help us to understand the phrase, as they throw light on the function of the elements. As the annual Paschal feast brought a re-living of Israel's redemption, so the Christian 're-lives' (in a most dynamic way) the events of his redeeming experience. He is there—in the upper room, at the cross and empty tomb. And with joyous expectancy, he awaits the Lord's return (26).

1 Corinthians 11.27-34

The vital phrase in this passage which is the practical application of Paul's recital of the words of Institution (23–26) is found in verse 29; 'without discerning the body'. Some fearful consequences are the result of a failure to heed this warning (27,30,32).

Some interpreters take the phrase to refer to the elements which represent the crucified body of the Lord; then the sin will be one of profanation or an ill-considered approach to the holy ordinance (so M. E. Thrall: 'to treat the bread and the wine as means of appeasing hunger and thirst is an act of desecration').

Alternatively and preferably, 'the body' may be a description of the Church (as in 10.17; 12.12) which is closely linked with Christ. Then, Paul's criticism fastens on the Corinthians' lamentable disregard of their oneness in Christ, giving rise to the practices which so disfigured their fellowship meal: selfish interests (21); gluttony and drunkenness (21); and snobbery (22). By these malpractices, unworthy of their Christian profession and allegiance, the Christians were despising the Church of God (22) by failing to discern the true nature of Christ's body in which there is no room for proud display and ill-tempered inconsideration of others. This attitude, so rife at Corinth, implies such an insensitive concern at the table that the meal was celebrated 'in an unworthy manner' (27) and in a high-minded spirit on which God's judgement was visited (30–32). Paul's answer matches the need (33,34), viz. be considerate by making the occasion a true action of the brotherhood, and let the demands of hunger be satisfied *before* you come to the assembly in order not to show up the poorer church members who brought only a little food or even nothing at all (22)!

Thought: How should we prepare for the communion service?

Questions for further study and discussion on 1 Corinthians chs. 10 and 11

1. Do you take the warning of **10.12** seriously? Can you fall? In what ways?
2. What situations in your own environment would correspond to the idolatrous association at Corinth?
3. How, in reading Paul's epistles, are we to distinguish between their permanent principles and their local and temporary applications?
4. Are there times when, as Christians, we should refrain from partaking of the Lord's Supper (**11.27–32**)? What factors are involved here?

1 Corinthians 12.1-3

The Corinthian body of believers were not slow in representing to Paul the special endowments they had received. He acknowledges this fact (**1.4,5,7**) and calls attention to the church's eager desire to excel in the gifts of the Spirit (**12.31; 14.1,12**).

To possess the Holy Spirit's gifts (*charismata* is the Greek term) is one thing; to set them in a right order of priority and to use them worthily is another. It is to this second matter that Paul now addresses his words (**12.1**).

The opening paragraph of vs. 1–3 is important because it is the apostle's reminder that not every claim to religious ecstasy is necessarily Christian. There are good spirits—the Holy Spirit *par excellence* is the gracious indwelling power of God in His children (Eph. **1.13,14**; 2 Cor. **5.5**; Rom. **8.9–16**) as he had already taught them in this epistle (**3.16; 6.19**); and there are demonic spirits (again earlier references may be in his mind, **10.20,21**). Where is this distinction most sharply drawn (1 John **4.1–6**)? And what test of discrimination is there to be applied?

Paul recalls the pre-Christian life of his readers (2). They were led into error and practised the worship of dumb deities—'dumb', that is, in the sense of Psa. **115.4–8**; but often pagan divinities induced in their devotees a state of trance and religious rapture. 'Mystical experience' in every age may be explained in various ways—from the sublime transport of the Christian mystic (cf. 2 Cor. **12.2–4**) to the victim of the witch-doctor's art in West Africa, the practitioner of psychological auto-suggestion, or the addict of LSD. Clearly some criterion of genuineness is needed.

That this need was not an imaginary one is clear from verse 3. In a religious ecstasy some member of the congregation had uttered the oath 'Jesus be damned!'—a cry which must have sounded as offensive to Paul as to us today. Worse still, he attributed it to the Spirit; but, Paul sharply retorts, this cannot be the case, for the Holy Spirit leads no one to utter an uncontrolled blasphemous remark. Rather, it is His ministry to inspire the earliest Christian confession of faith 'Jesus is Lord', by which alone salvation is known (Rom. **10.**9; Phil. **2.**9–11).

> *Meditation:* '*No man can truly say*
> *That Jesus is the Lord,*
> *Unless Thou take the veil away,*
> *And breathe the living word.*'

1 Corinthians 12.4-11

'Gifts of the Spirit' (1, NEB) are now treated in some detail; and the passage focuses our attention on the four principles which Paul is concerned to underline and drive home.

(*i*) The inclusive scope of His gifts-of-grace (*charismata*) is made clear at the outset. Notice the terms which run like a thread through Paul's treatment: 'in every one' (6); 'to each' (7); 'all these' (believers who exercise some spiritual gift, 11). As every Christian *qua* believer and member of Christ's body is indwelt, baptized and watered by the Holy Spirit (12,13), so he is the receiver of some endowment which fits him for useful service within the fellowship. It is this feature which stamps the Christian Church as a unique social institution in the world; it is a society in which, ideally, every member has a part to play and a task to perform. Everyone in the Church is important—irrespective of what social scientists call stratification (and the church at Corinth *was* socially stratified—see those passages which speak of division, rivalries and snobbery based on wealth)—although no one is indispensable.

(*ii*) The rich variety of the Spirit's gifts is displayed by the phrase 'varieties of gifts' (4), all of which are attributed to the same Spirit. All Christians have some gift; but not the same gift. Vs. 8–10 enumerate nine specimen 'workings' (6), some of which are perpetually in demand in the Church's life in every age, and, by the same token, some of which may have been needed only in the first century. Do you accept this distinction between gifts of permanent validity and value, and gifts of temporary and apostolic usage, now withdrawn? The danger in refusing this distinction is seen in attempts made to recapture 'apostolic Christianity', which are (*a*) forgetful that the Spirit is our contemporary and fashions *new* gifts for the needs of

140

the twentieth century and (*b*) guilty of theological anachronism, harking back to a past which is beyond recall.

(*iii*) Lest the Corinthians imagined that the lack of some spectacular gift (tongues, healings, miracle-working?) was a sign of disfavour, the apostle reminds them that the Spirit's sovereign disposing (11) is the final rule. 'As He wills' should sound the death-knell to jealousy and envy as Christians were evidently in fierce competition in desiring the more remarkable phenomena in their church life. The lesson is not lost today. It is tragic when we try to serve the Lord in a job for which we have no spiritual ability or aptitude.

(*iv*) The invariable purpose of the gifts is clearly spelled out: 'for the common good' (7), i.e. for the well-being and growth of the entire community. See **14**.12 and especially Ephesians 4.12–16.

Question: Do we need the gentle prodding which Paul gives to Timothy (2 Tim. 1.6)?

1 Corinthians 12.12,13

'Paul's discussion of this subject is epoch-making' (L. Morris)—a verdict which commands our assent, especially as we go on to appreciate the masterly way in which he dealt with this faction-ridden, proud and independent church. The two verses before us sum up the body of Paul's doctrine of the Church.

(*i*) The unity of the Church is a unity with diversity, as the analogy of the human body illustrates. The physical frame is composed of many parts, all with necessary functions, but we speak of *a* body as a single entity. So it is with the Church which is made up of many individuals, all with varying temperaments, personality and gifts, and yet in a very real sense they are not many but 'one body in Christ' (Rom. **12**.4,5). Diversity of gifts (**12**.4 ff.; Rom. **12**.6) does not destroy the oneness of the Church; rather it transforms a drab entity into a living organism which pulsates with life—'the common life in the Body of Christ'.

(*ii*) The regenerative work of the Holy Spirit in conviction of sin and the imparting of new life, leading to the saving confession of **12**.3, includes the forming of this one body which is one in another sense. For the Christian Church, by definition of its nature and calling as the body of the Lord, can tolerate no divisions caused by accidents of race and social position (13). Which passages does this verse call to mind (Gal. 3.28; Col. 3.11)? The gospel sacraments are a perpetual witness to this breaking down of barriers which divided the ancient world: baptism is into the one Name (1 Cor. **1**.13 ff.) and at the table of the Lord it is from one cup which is shared that all drink.

141

(*iii*) The most striking thought lies embedded in this most important section. 'He calls the Church Christ', commented Calvin, and so agrees here with ancient tradition which asserts such a closeness of bond between Christ and His people that they form 'as it were one mystical person' (Aquinas), *totus Christus*, the 'whole Christ', which is a corporate title embracing Jesus as the Head and His ransomed people as necessary members. As a shepherd requires a flock, so Messiah must have a Messianic community; and it was this thought which arrested Saul of Tarsus on the Damascus road (Acts **9**.4,5: 'Why do you persecute *Me*?, not simply My people)— and this conviction of Christ-in-His-Church never left him (1 Cor. **8**.12).

Question: Is it possible to be 'in Christ' and not in the Church?

1 Corinthians 12.14-26

Four salient items stand out in this portion:

(*i*) *Vs. 14–16*. Every Christian is a necessary member of the community. The use of analogy drawn from the inter-dependence of the human body is not new. Already in the Stoic philosopher Epictetus we meet the saying: 'You are a citizen of the world and one of its limbs'. Paul's treatment, however, is far more insistent on the impossibility of one member becoming amputated from the rest of the whole body—even if that organ, now personified, wanted to cut itself off. And certainly—and this is the apostle's point driven home to the Corinthians' predicament of mutual rivalries and jealousies—it is foolish for one member (the foot or the ear) to want to detach itself from the corporate whole because it is not some other member. Every part plays a necessary part in the harmonious functioning of the whole.

(*ii*) *Vs. 17–22*. Every Christian needs the help of every other Christian. Again, the Pauline insistence is double-edged. As in the human body, each part cannot function on its own and, at the same time, if it fails to do its job, the whole body feels the effect of this break-down. Exactly so in the Church. Individual believers are likened to 'a single organ' (19) with a specific part to play, but not in splendid isolation from the rest of the fellowship. And if that one member fails in his responsibilities, the entire family of God is affected. Rom. **14**.7 well illustrates the inter-relation and reciprocal dependence which makes a 'solo performance' type of Christian living unthinkable according to N.T. standards (Eph. **4**.25b, which may well be a motto to be held in constant review, both in our local congregations and ecumenical relationships).

142

(*iii*) *Vs. 23–25.* Particular respect should be shown to those members of the community who appear to be less important than the rest. The key thought is: 'that there may be no discord in the body' (25), applied here to a situation in which social haughtiness and spiritual superiority were a prevalent malaise. Proud Corinthians, richly endowed with spiritual gifts and material possessions, were looking down their noses at the poorer brethren as 'inferior' (24)—a word Paul picks up and throws back at these snobs with devastating effect!

(*iv*) *Vs. 25,26.* Every Christian is sympathetically involved in the prosperity or misfortune of his fellow-Christians. Perhaps this is the one place in Scripture where 'care' or 'anxiety' (Greek *merimnan:* the same term is used negatively in Matt. 6.34; Phil. 4.6) is positively commanded as our duty: be anxious—about your fellow-Christian; when he is afflicted, sympathize, and when he flourishes, rejoice in the honour he has received (26).

1 Corinthians 12.27-31

The maximum content having been extracted from the analogy of the human body, a final verse (27) sums up. There is one body, into which all believers are baptized at conversion as they utter the Spirit-inspired confession (12.3,13). Of this body Christ is the Head (Eph. 1.22,23; Col. 1.18), and gathers the members into a true unity as His limbs and organs. So individual Christians are likened to the several parts of the body which, under the control of the Head, represents 'the whole Christ', i.e. Christ's agents in the world of men. A body's health consists in its organs and cells functioning properly and in unison, so, with 'each part ... working properly' (Eph. 4.16), Christ's body grows and matures. What is the pervasive atmosphere in which this development takes place (Eph. 4.16c)? Paul will turn to this theme as to 'a still more excellent way' (31).

The N.T. Church, from its inception, was an ordered society. It was, however, *not* hierarchical and institutional in the later sense of possessing rigid orders of a priesthood of ministry; but equally it was *not* a shapeless and loose association of freely consenting individuals who decided to form a church as a convenient social unit. There was, from the beginning, an ordered life and a rudimentary ministerial pattern, indicated in verse 28. Much controversy has centred on the exact nature of the apostolic office and other various ministerial functions in the early Church; and the interested student is recommended to consult E. M. B. Green's *Called to Serve* for an admirable survey of the N.T. and early Christian data.

'Apostles' rank as the first in Paul's list, for the reason supplied in Eph. 2.20 (cf. Rev. 21.14). They were the original founder-members of the Christian society, with certain additional persons (notably Paul) who claimed to have met the requirements of Acts 1.22 (cf. 1 Cor. 9.1; Gal. 1.1). The order of 'prophets' (e.g. Agabus in Acts 11.27 f.; 21.10) was concerned with a revelation of the divine will for the congregation (Acts 13.1), a function shared with 'teachers'—and mainly of an itinerant character (Eph. 4.11). The other persons referred to (in v. 28) possessed a functional gift, exercised in the assembled worship of the church.

The point of the rhetorical questions (29,30) is that in each case the expected answer (clearly stated in the Greek) is No. Not all Christians can claim to possess the full range of the gifts: and there are some gifts (e.g. apostleship) which are unique and unrepeatable. But one 'way' in which any gift is to be exercised is open to all.

1 Corinthians 13.1-3

The purpose of this great chapter, Paul's 'hymn of love', is often not fully appreciated. This purpose is to show that, while the Corinthians were to be commended for their seeking the greatest gifts of the Spirit (12.31, 14.12), any gift is valueless unless it is accompanied by love. Love (Greek, *agape*) is *not* one of the gifts which a person may or may not have; it is the indispensable disposition or attitude without which all the gifts combined are misdirected and in vain. It is a question, therefore, of love *plus* whatever endowment of the Holy Spirit we may have received. The *charisma* is to be exercised always under the control and directive of love.

Vs. 1–3 are intended to demonstrate the priority of love over all its rivals, and to enforce the lesson of 'a still more excellent way'. Five possibilities are considered; each makes a claim to be the hall-mark of a devoted Christian life—and each is rejected as spurious and ineffectual, if love be absent.

(*i*) The gift of moving eloquence and ecstatic speech (1), granting the ability to stir men like a fanfare of trumpets, or the crashing of cymbals. There is here a possible side-glance at the Apollos party (1.12) who took as their guide the eloquent preacher of Acts 18.24. Paul, by contrast, set his face against the misuse of rhetoric (1 Cor. 2.1; cf. 2 Cor. 10.10).

(*ii*) The gift of intellectual prowess (2a) suggests the facility of persuasive and logical presentation ('prophecy' is defined in 14.3), along with a claim to possess some secret lore. Some Corinthians were not reluctant to place this intellectual ability at the top of their list (1 Cor. **8.**1)—but Paul quickly deflates the pride to which this gift can so easily lead (**8.**2).

(*iii*) The gift of a practical, working faith (2b) is, on the surface, most desirable (cf. Mark **11.**23), for by faith in God great things are attempted and achieved. Yet the danger is one of exhibitionism and showmanship by which 'faith' is paraded and publicly 'demonstrated'. The warning of Matthew **7.**22,23 is always needed.

(*iv*) The gift of a concern for humanity seems praiseworthy enough (3); and the philanthropist who gives his money and even his life (RSV marg. may be correct: some early Christians sold themselves into slavery in order to relieve the needy with the money their slavemasters paid for them) is often a rebuke to professing believers. But the vital issue is always *motive* (hence RSV marg. again). Why do we respond to the claim of 1 John **3.**17,18? Have we ever searched our motives in Christian Aid Week? Or when money and clothes are needed in some city stricken by earthquake?

(*v*) Accepting the RSV of verse 3, we may find a characterization of religion as asceticism which leads to martyrdom. Again, we applaud the sacrifice of the martyr—not a uniquely Christian trait, as Buddhist monks who died in the petrol fires in Saigon, Vietnam exemplify. But the motive is once more the chief consideration—and some early Christian martyrs didn't always face the arena out of a pure love for Christ and His truth.

To Ponder: 'The Church of Christ was for them (the Corinthians) a stage on which they aspired to be conspicuous figures' (Denney). Do we ever so regard our membership of Christ's body?

1 Corinthians 13.4-7

After establishing the indispensable qualification of love in all our religious and humanitarian acts, Paul turns to set out the pattern of Christian *agape*, and describes its features.

There are two reasons why these verses should be read often: Henry Drummond counsels us to read the chapter every day for a month and to note its effect on our life.

First, love is a term in need of careful definition. Today it is a rag-bag of a word, containing all manner of meanings. But as a Christian term, a fruit of the Spirit (Gal. **5.**22) and an incentive to our daily living (Gal. **5.**6), here is the inspired characterization.

Secondly, these verses give a pen-portrait of the Lord Himself (1 Pet. **2.**21 tells us of the example of Christ), and what more vital spiritual exercise could there be than a contemplation of the Lord of love.

The paragraph falls into three divisions.

(*i*) Positively, what love does (4a). Patience and kindness are natural partners, as elsewhere (Gal. **5.**22; Col. **3.**12; 2 Cor. **6.**6), where the combined forces of these virtues are equally a fruit of the Spirit, a sign of election and a method of evangelism.

(*ii*) Negatively, what love does not do (4b–6). Christian *agape* as the basis of ethics contains a salutary abstinence-motif, warning the believer away from certain danger-points. It is not afraid of pin-pointing certain vices as elements in the moral life to be shunned (against the notion of current 'situation ethics' for which there are no absolutes of right and wrong). Paul lists eight undesirable quali-ties in these verses: jealousy, conceit (literally 'gives itself no airs', is no 'wind-bag', Arndt-Gingrich), pride (the damning sin at Corinth; so **4.**6,18,19; **5.**2; **8.**1), rudeness (whether as lack of good manners or indecency), selfishness, irritation (Acts **15.**39 gives the same word), the unforgiving spirit (a commercial term is used: hence 'keeps no register of wrongs') and unrighteousness.

(*iii*) Inclusively, what love does all the time (7). The Greek word (*panta*) is translated as the object of the verbs in RSV, but it is better taken as an adverb of time: 'continually'. So there is no limit to love's endurance, no end to its trust, no fading of its hope; and love can outlast anything.

Who can scale the heights set by this lyric? The secret is discovered in the indwelling Christ whose life shines out in the Christian's attitudes and actions (Eph. **3.**17), as Samuel Rutherford once quaintly put it: 'When Christ comes to live in a man's heart, His face is often seen at the windows.'

1 Corinthians 13.8-13

The third part of this N.T. 'song of songs' stresses love's permanence. The scene is set in the future: 'When that which is perfect comes' (10) and the present order gives place to the life of the Age to come. At present in 'this age'—references to this phrase are worth tracking down (Gal. **1.**4; 2 Tim. **4.**10; 1 John **5.**19; 2 Cor. **4.**4)—nothing can strictly be called perfect by reason of sin, sorrow and human finitude. Hence our experience, in all its facets, is 'in part' (12) and is a pointer to a more complete state in the consummation (cf. Matt. **28.**20).

Two points are made by the apostle as he bids us reflect on love's continuance beyond this life into the new Age.

(*i*) Love is in contrast with transient qualities (8). The gifts of prophecy, tongues, knowledge are all related to, because relevant to, this Age. They have a value, and need to be cultivated. Hence the admonitions of **14.**1,20 (answering v. 11 of this chapter); but *their value is conditioned by their need* (see the earlier discussion on **12.**8–10 on 'tongues', the need for which in congregational worship has passed with the composing of N.T. Scripture and the fixing of the canon). And in the coming era, prophecy (=preaching, **14.**3) and knowledge will also be displaced, giving way to an encounter with God in Christ and a perfect face-to-face communion (12a) which will render the mediation of preaching and knowledge superfluous (12b). But love, because it is akin to God's own nature (1 John **4.**7–12)—and is indeed an expression of it—will remain.

(*ii*) Love is the climax of the permanent qualities. Other Christian virtues will remain in conjunction with love. What are they (13)? Yet love takes the first place. In what sense is love the greatest? Reviewing the chapter, we may answer: (*a*) because it is the very soul of the other gifts (1–3): (*b*) because it is supreme by its own excellence and shines in its own light: (*c*) because it is of the very essence of Deity (1 John **4.**16).

The three virtues of v. 13 are mentioned together elsewhere (1 Thess. **1.**3; **5.**8; Col. **1.**4,5; Eph. **4.**2–5; Rom. **5.**1–5; Gal. **5.**5,6); and evidently formed a well-known triad. The present writer is inclined to offer his own interpretation of v. 13b in view of the definite article before *agape* and the presence of a comparative ('greater') which is normally taken as superlative. 'Faith, hope, love abide—the well-known trio; but greater than these is the love (of God)' shed in our hearts (Rom. **5.**5).

Questions for further study and discussion on 1 Corinthians chs. 12 and 13

1. Do we really appreciate the work of the Holy Spirit in leading us to Christ (**12.**3)? Outline this aspect of N.T. doctrine.
2. What is the bearing of ch. **12.**12,13 on (*a*) church unity proposals and objections today; (*b*) issues of segregation and the urbanization of the churches?
3. Discuss, in the light of ch. **12.**12–31, our relationships as different members of Christ's body—to God, to one another, to the world. To what extent is this being worked out in our individual lives?
4. Why is love described as a 'still more excellent way' (**12.**31)?

1 Corinthians 14.1-5

'Put love first' epitomizes the apostolic counsel at the conclusion of his discussions on love's pre-eminence and permanence. Once this is understood and done, the believers should not be slothful or lacking in spiritual ambition, but seek to be the very best for God by using to the full whatever enduement the Spirit has granted. Which gift does Paul place at the head of the list (1)?

In fact, there must have been some controversy within the church over the relative value of two types of public utterance: prophecy, and speaking in an ecstasy. These are clearly distinguished in vs. 2,3; and pride of place is given to prophetic speech on the ground that 'the prophet, although inspired, speaks a comprehensible language and, without interpretation, can have a beneficial effect on the meeting' (Héring). The exact nature of this type of public speaking is spelled out in v. 3: it is a ministry which builds up (a favourite Pauline idea, as we have seen), and exhorts (cf. Rom. 12 as a good example of this kind of utterance, known as *paraklesis*) and comforts (the term is *paramuthia*=consolation, and a specimen of this ministry is found in 1 Thess. 4.13,14 and Rev. 3.7–13). Would it be fair to say that this nuance of N.T. ministry is represented by the modern term 'preaching' or the 'ministry of the Word'?

Glossolalia—speaking in a tongue—on the other hand, is a language phenomenon in which the speaker is caught up in rapture, utters words which are not immediately intelligible, and thus exercises a ministry which needs a complementary gift of interpretation (4).

Some modern interpreters of this passage make the helpful distinction also between the use of a 'tongue' as an exercise of private devotion (so 2,4) in which the communion of the soul with God is so intimate and profound that no earthly language can be the vehicle of its expressions (cf. Rom. 8.26,27; 2 Cor. 12.2–4), and Paul had known this experience (18); and the use of *glossolalia* as a part of public congregational worship. In the latter instance, the key-phrase is 'in church' (19,28), with its variants, 'if the whole church assembles' (23), 'when you come together' (26).

If we accept this distinction based on the place where 'the tongues' are exercised, the opening verses deal with their value in private intercourse with God. In the secret place of communion, such a practice has value and the believer is 'built up' (4) as he fathoms the depths of spiritual experience (1 Cor. 2.10–12). But the corporate value is only made possible if the man who utters ecstatic speech can give an intelligible sense (13), whereas prophecy, which requires no translation, is more highly commended (5).

1 Corinthians 14.6-12

In Paul's consideration of spiritual gifts, which extends over three chapters (12–14), the most important directive he gives is contained in today's reading. At v. 12 he clearly indicates (*a*) that there was some dispute and uncertainty within the Corinthian assembly over the relative importance of the gifts in their diversity (**12.**4), and this lack of understanding had engendered a rivalry and zeal to lay claim to 'best gifts'; and (*b*) that his rubric is an insistence that all shall be done for the 'building up (of) the church'. This healthy reminder harks back to **12.**7 where the manifestation of the Spirit is given 'for the common good', i.e. for the benefit of the whole community of believers. The societary nature of the Christian life and spiritual experience is a principle written into Pauline ecclesiology, and we neglect it today at our peril.

The gift of 'tongues' is a test-case. Apparently this was a spiritual enduement on which the Corinthians (or, some of them) placed great score, and the whole church was rent over the use of this gift. Ecstatic speech was uttered in the public gatherings for worship and Paul's ruling on this matter was sought.

With characteristic generosity he puts himself in the place of the man who gives expression to this gift (6). Notice how he regards as most vital the need to *benefit* others by the various components of Christian worship. Any benefit from the exercise of 'tongues' can only come if there is accompanying interpretation; otherwise the gift has no value whatever (9)—a clear indication that (*a*) this *glossolalia* is practised in public assembly, in contrast with the situation of vs. 2–4; and (*b*) the phenomenon at Corinth is not the same as the Pentecostal gift of 'tongues' (Acts 2.4–11) when 'the apostles' form of speech, whatever it may have been, was intelligible to the whole audience' (Thrall: see too Vol. 3, p. 361).

Paul's commonsense attitude runs through this section, with illustrations drawn from ancient musical practices (7), military parades (8) and the art of communication by speech which is only effective if the language is understandable. Has this passage, as we review it, anything to teach us on the great need of our Christian generation—to master the art of the communication of the gospel to an uncomprehending world?

1 Corinthians 14.13-19

In earlier passages Paul has made the distinction between intelligible and ecstatic utterances; now he further defines the contrast as that between a practice in which the mind is alert and active (obviously implied in the prophetic ministry of 14.3 and negatively in v. 14) and

149

the use of a tongue which is the product of a spiritual upsurge requiring no mental effort. The inference which Paul doesn't draw out, but which may surely be gleaned from these verses, is that emotional experience, uncontrolled by the mind and inducing a trance-like state, needs careful safeguard: so we should interpret v. 15 which places no dichotomy between spirit and mind, but rather requires that both should be in full operation and harmony when the believer is at prayer.

There is a further reason why ecstatic speech needs control, when it is used in congregational worship. Unless some intelligible interpretation is given (13), an immature Christian, lacking this gift and the accompanying gifts of interpretation and discernment (for such gifts were not universally shared as 12.30 makes clear), will not be able to enter helpfully into the worship. In a specific instance, if he listens to what seems to him to be gibberish with no sensible meaning, he will not be able to confirm the truth of the prayer by his audible Amen (16) and he will not be built up in his Christian life (17). Therefore, Paul concludes, the usefulness of the gift of tongues in public assembly is strictly limited, and is set over against the ministry of prophecy in which even five words which are readily intelligible to the catechumen are far more profitable than two thousand times that number of words which fall meaninglessly on uncomprehending ears.

V. 18 refers to the earlier portion of the chapter when Paul is relating the gift to its private exercise. With this practice he finds no fault, because no interpretation is required; but 'in church' a restraint must be placed on *glossolalia* and 'to regard it as the gift supremely to be desired is a form of selfishness' (Thrall), because it forgets the chief end of worship. What is that (v. 26b)?

1 Corinthians 14.20-25

There is still another factor to be borne in mind. The exercise of 'tongues' in an open service, to which not simply immature Christians are welcomed as novitiates, but also rank outsiders who attend out of curiosity or concern, may have a detrimental effect. Paul calls for some serious consideration to be given to the subject (20) as interested non-Christians visit the Corinthians at their worship.

He recalls to them an O.T. passage (Isa. 28.11,12) in which God threatens to punish His rebellious people by foreign invaders (the Assyrians) whose strange language will mystify the Jewish nation (cf. Isa. 36.11 ff.). Because the Jewish kingdom remained obstinate to the prophet's pleading in God's name, they would be judged by

150

(*a*) suffering a foreign invasion and (*b*) being hardened in their unbelief (Isa. **6.**9–13). In the O.T. context these 'strange tongues', spoken by Israel's enemies, confirmed unbelieving Israel in their unbelief and so acted detrimentally.

Paul now takes over this reference to Isa. **28** (given in v. 22 as well as v. 21), and expresses the fear that the same effect may very well follow if an unbeliever (23) enters a Christian assembly in which there is an unrestrained use of tongues. Then, as upon ancient Israel, the effect will be deleterious, and the impression created will lead to the conclusion, You are mad! (23b). On the contrary, if the gift of prophecy is being exercised, the words spoken will not only be intelligible but a powerful convicting and converting agency (24,25), moving the non-Christian visitor to repentance by the manifest tokens of the Divine presence in the midst of His people. It is obvious where Paul's sympathies lie when it comes to setting the gifts of the Spirit in any order of priority and importance.

Notes: V. 22 presents a problem, the Gordian knot of which is swiftly cut by J. B. Phillips by his expedient of reversing the affirmatives and negatives of Paul's statements, without any textual warrant. M. E. Thrall offers a better view: 'Ecstatic utterance is not intended to be something which produces belief in Christianity. It is a phenomenon which leaves non-Christians in their unbelieving state. Prophecy, on the other hand, is intended not to confirm unbelievers in their unbelief, but to encourage conversion to the Christian faith.' As an alternative interpretation, v. 22 may be a Pauline comment on the Isaiah passage and 'tongues' and 'prophecy' may be taken in their O.T. sense of Assyrian foreign languages which confirmed (by God's judgement) Israel's apostasy, whereas Isaiah's prophetic ministry was beneficial to the remnant which believed (Isa. **8.**16). There is precedent for this Pauline use of O.T. in 2 Cor. **3.**16,17.

1 Corinthians 14.26-33

The Church which meets us in the pages of the N.T. is a worshipping community of believing men and women. No one, in the light of such texts as Acts **1.**14; **2.**42,46; **4.**31; **5.**12,42; **13.**1–3; **20.**7–12, is likely to dispute this statement, but two caveats need to be entered. First, we know less about N.T. worship than we would like to know, and it is temptingly easy to fill in the gaps of our knowledge by reading back into the period from the later history of the Church. Secondly, we are almost exclusively dependent on *1 Corinthians* for the data, and it may well be an unwarrantable assumption to believe that what was true at Corinth held good for the rest of Christendom in the early period or, even, for the other Pauline churches. Where else in the N.T. have we references to 'tongues', or such explicit detail about the Lord's Supper procedure?

Vs. 26–33 give insight into the type of public worship which was practised at Corinth. Clearly informality and a sharing of spiritual gifts were the chief features, with a movement to a more formal and stylized pattern of worship (which meets us in the later epistles) already peeping through. This section may well represent a mid-way landmark between the spontaneity of *1 Thessalonians* and the more structured developments in *Ephesians*, as the present writer has argued in his book *Worship in the Early Church*, ch. 12.

A comparison of these texts (1 Thess. 5.16–22 and Eph. 5.19 ff. with its parallel in Col. 3.16 ff.) is instructive; and throws some light on the problematic verses in today's reading. Praise and 'hymning' (14.14,15,26) stand at the head of the list of church practices. Some reading of Scripture and its exposition is implied (as in Acts 20.7 ff. and Col. 3.16=1 Thess. 5.20,21). At Corinth there was *glossolalia* (possibly hinted at in 1 Thess. 5.19) and its necessary adjunct, interpretation (27,28). Prophecy is encouraged, for reasons which run like a thread through these Corinthian chapters (31b)—can you fasten a label to them? And a final cautionary word is added (corresponding to 1 Thess. 5.21) that prophetic utterances must be tested (29), and the welfare of the whole church kept well to the forefront. Hence the need to have some understanding about speaking in turn lest a babble of voices distract from and destroy the real intention, viz. intelligible communication and responsible reception of God's word to the congregation (31).

1 Corinthians 14.34-40

V. 33b, which places the rubric of general church custom on the ban imposing a silence on women members, is taken with v. 34 in RSV. The phrase could very well go with v. 33a, of course.

The precise phrase 'keep silence in the church(es)' in v. 34 looks back to v. 28; and provides us with a necessary exegetical clue. In the light of 11.5 ff. (interpreted by 14.3), Paul cannot mean that the women church worshippers are to take no vocal part in the service; and the prohibition on 'speaking' (34b) must be seen in context.

Some commentators give to the verb the sense of 'chatter', as though the women were becoming a nuisance by their whispered or disturbing conversation; and Paul, in the interests of good order and discipline, counsels their silence with the counter-suggestion

152

that if they have questions to ask they should reserve their conversation until they get home (35).

Alternatively we may interpret 'speak' as a reference to *glossolalia;* and the Pauline check is on the Corinthian women, who (in their city life) whilst enjoying a considerable measure of freedom according to the pre-suffragette standards of the ancient world, were taking the further unwarranted liberty of speaking in tongues. It is to this silence (i.e. not to exercise the gift of tongues) that they are bidden in our verses, for Paul can quickly perceive the danger of public worship getting out of hand (as in 11.17 ff.), and especially where the women were concerned. The same may have been true later at Ephesus in view of 1 Tim. 2.8 ff., especially v. 11 of that chapter which uses the same term as the present passage (34: they 'should be subordinate'). Cf. Eph. 5.22 which, in one manuscript tradition, has the same verb in a passage which may again have a similar situation in mind. As a small point in support of the above view is Paul's use of the verb to speak (*lalein*) which is constantly employed in the phrase 'to speak in a tongue', not the alternative verb 'to say something' (*legein*, found in v. 34: 'the law *says.*') And a final, clinching argument is supplied by the rhetorical question of v. 36. Evidently Corinthian believers—both men and women—were claiming possession of a private revelation conveyed doubtless in a 'tongue' as though God had exclusively spoken to them. He has to remind them that apostolic truth is shared throughout the Church—and no claim to a 'secret doctrine' (a later gnostic speciality!) can be entertained. Let them receive this as the Lord's command (37) and lay his teaching to heart (39,40).

Questions for further study and discussion on 1 Corinthians ch. 14

1. This chapter is concerned with clear. communication. How, in contemporary society, can we make God's Word intelligible, and show it to be relevant to non-Christians?
2. If the desire to speak in tongues was evidence of spiritual pride and a desire for the spectacular in Corinth, and thus drew Paul's censure, what would we find has taken its place in our local church situations?
3. Look up references in the N.T. to the ministry of women in the life of the Church and society, and define their function. Is this being fulfilled today?
4. What was the chief fault Paul found with the Corinthian church, and how does he deal with it?

1 Corinthians 15.1-11

The Church of the N.T. era was a confessing Church as well as a worshipping community. By 'confessing' we mean the possessing of a body of authoritative doctrine which was the given, acknowledged, and shared heritage of those who formed the early Christian Church in the world of the Roman empire. Only on the assumption of a corpus of doctrine which was accepted as binding and authoritative can we explain (*a*) the Christian consciousness of the Church's being a distinct entity in the world over against the Jews and Gentiles (1 Cor. **10.**32); and (*b*) the Church's missionary zeal in proclaiming the gospel which was *not* offered as a tentative suggestion to be entertained along with other attractive possibilities, but as God's unique truth, demanding a full and unreserved commitment (Gal. **1.**8,9; 1 Thess. **2.**13; 2 Cor. **11.**4 f.). It is with this background that we should approach verses 1,2.

The main tenets of the apostolic creed are clearly spelled out in what many scholars today recognize as a crystallization of the Church's teaching on the Person and work of Christ (3–5). Certain tell-tale marks in this passage stamp it as a credal formulary: (*i*) the four-fold 'that' introduces each line of the creed (3,4,5): (*ii*) the vocabulary is unusual, containing some rare words and expressions which Paul never again employs (e.g. 'in accordance with the scriptures'): (*iii*) and that we are in touch with a Christian confession of faith which takes us back to the earliest period is confirmed by Paul's preface (3). What he had received as part of the instruction he had learned in the first days of his discipleship, that he now transmits as a sacred tradition which is in line with general apostolic practice (11).

What were the chief points of their belief? The cross as an atonement for sins; the reality of His death, attested by the burial; the veritable resurrection on the third day; and the appearances of the living Lord as conqueror of death—these were the facts on which faith and salvation rested (1,2). And all these events, rooted in history and confirmed by experience, were seen to be grounded in O.T. Scripture (Rom. **1.**2–4). Which passages would be used?

The Lord's appearing to His disciples included a revelation to Paul (8), thus calling him to the apostolic office. Paul is here defending his position, and warding off an insinuation (made at Corinth) that he was a 'monstrosity' (see 8, NEB) and not truly qualified. He admits the unlikelihood (from a human point of view) of his ever becoming a believer, but sees in God's grace the only explanation possible for such a transformed life (1 Tim. **1.**12–17). And in that sense we can all share his conviction: by the grace of God we are what we are.

1 Corinthians 15.12-19

Paul's citation of the creed had a purpose in view. He is leading up to the theme which the remainder of the chapter will deal with: the resurrection of Christ and of His people.

Again, we may reconstruct a little of the setting. Evidently there were those in the Corinthian assembly who held strange views about the life after death (12). This denial of the resurrection may have taken one of two forms. The current Greek notion (e.g. stated by the Athenians, Acts 17.18,32) was that man's immortality depended on his divine soul which survived death by being released from its imprisoning receptacle, the body. After the dissolution of the body from which the real self escaped at death, that soul was either absorbed into the divine or lived on in a shadowy existence of the underworld, Hades. But any hope of *resurrection* was to the Greek mind unthinkable.

The other possibility (of which there is evidence in 2 Tim. 2.18 and later gnostic literature) which some Corinthians may have espoused was the view that the resurrection had already taken place, and that no future hope awaited the Church.

Paul faces the heresy at Corinth head-on. He recalls the basic conviction of Christ's own resurrection as the true starting-point (13); and proceeds to show that unless this particular resurrection really happened, no vital assertion of Christian truth can be certainly made—with the corollary that *one* resurrection (viz. Christ's) proves that His people may confidently expect their resurrection in like manner (Phil. 3.20,21).

'The Archimedean point on which all else turns'—so Künneth in *The Theology of the Resurrection* describes Jesus' triumph over death. What is at stake if this assertion of a real resurrection (over against spiritual survival or a demythologized version) is denied? Paul gives three fateful consequences: (*i*) Christian faith, awakened by the preaching of the *kerygma* of vs. 3 ff., is empty, for its content has evaporated (14,17): (*ii*) moreover, our experience of sin's forgiveness is shown up as a piece of self-deception (17b), for we believe that His death did remove our guilt, but lack the vital proof that God accepted Him as our substitute and Saviour. Only the resurrection can offer such a guarantee: (*iii*) the future hope is seriously imperilled both personally (19) as well as for those who have died 'in sure and certain hope of the resurrection to eternal life' (18).

155

1 Corinthians 15.20-28

V. 20 rings out a stirring affirmation in contradiction of the hypothetical 'if's' (six of them in the preceding paragraph). Christ *has been raised* (a perfect tense, denoting a past-event with continuing consequences), and logically this one fact overthrows all the doubts and denials previously entertained. Christian faith is solidly based and has definite content; Christian forgiveness is no will-o'-the-wisp of auto-suggestion (as Bernard Shaw once described it: 'a beggar's refuge'), but a real experience, confirmed by God's vindication of His Son; and Christian hope for the future takes on an anchor-like assurance (so Heb. 6.19,20), for His victory includes the ultimate home-gathering of those who are His (John 14.19), just as the first sheaf reaped from the harvest-field and brought as an offering (Lev. 23.10 f.) betokened the full ingathering and the completed Harvest-home celebration.

Paul's continuing discussion elaborates the third of the affirmations included in v. 20. He is concerned to demonstrate that the resurrection of Jesus is bound up with the resurrection of all those who belong to Him. If this understanding of the apostle's purview is remembered, it will help us to interpret aright the problematic 'all' in vs. 22,28. No universalism is intended in this passage for the simple reason that Paul's thought here is concerned to show the relation between Christ and those who formerly were 'in Adam' (and so liable to Adam's just deserts of death and separation from God) but who now are found 'in Christ' (and, as such, beneficiaries of His redeeming work, which includes their union with Him in His death and victory). The notion is that of the corporate Christ (as at 12.12), i.e. Christ and 'those who belong to Christ' (23) viewed as a single entity. He is their representative; they are part of His personality.

So far Paul's thought has looked backwards to what happened to Christ when He was raised (20). Present and future are now taken up into his scheme, for His Easter triumph was the beginning of a present reign (25) to be consummated at His final acclamation when all His foes are put under His feet in actuality as they are now subject to Him by right. The test-case is death; once conquered by His victory (2 Tim. 1.10), death still is at work in the world but will at the last be itself destroyed (Rev. 20.14). But Christ's universal rule sets up no rivalry to God's sovereignty (28). His mediatorial reign now will be fulfilled in the perfected kingdom when God's will, to which the Son is Himself obedient (Heb. 10.7; John 5.30; 6.38; 8.29), shall be universally acknowledged—and that will includes the

156

acclamation 'Jesus Christ is Lord' (Phil. **2.11**) and the summing up of all in Christ (Eph. **1.10**).

1 Corinthians 15.29-34

Truth is always related to life, and Christian belief must have its counterpart in the influence it exerts on a Christian's behaviour.

Paul moves on, therefore, to point out some of the practical implications of what the denial of resurrection entails. (*i*) If there is no resurrection, the practice of baptism for the dead has no meaning (29). Precisely what that meaning was in the mind of both apostle and church is still a matter of some doubt; and a bewildering variety of interpretations has been forthcoming. The most likely view is that members of the church at Corinth were receiving baptism on behalf of friends or relatives who had died before they could pass from the status of interested inquirers to that of full members of Christ's body. The baptism was thus a proxy-baptism. An alternative view sees in baptism a reference to martyrdom (cf. Mark **10.38** ff.) and it is undeniable that a Christian's death for Christ's sake in the arena was in later history taken to be the equivalent of his baptism, if he had not been able to enter the fellowship by the regular procedure of initiation. In either case, the inference is pointed: why practise a custom or risk the possibility of martyrdom if either the deceased friends have no hope in death or the martyrs die in vain? And in no case does Paul, as G. R. Beasley-Murray makes clear in his full discussion of the verse, give positive approval to this Corinthian practice which may well have been an excrescence in their church life.

(*ii*) If there is no resurrection, Paul's apostolic hazards which exposed him to mortal peril are foolhardy acts (30,32)—a charge which his enemies in 2 Cor. **11,12** (see notes on these chapters) brought against him. His entire life was a facing of risks for Christ's sake; one notable instance at Ephesus (the reference may be metaphorical of the violence of human opposition) is again the subject of his correspondence in 2 Cor. **1.8–11** and is a commentary on this allusion to 'fighting with wild beasts' (Acts **19.23–40** seems to belong to another occasion).

(*iii*) If there is no resurrection—and so no final judgement—Christians may as well adopt the pagan philosophy of 'live for today' (although taken from Isa. **22.13**). But Paul would counter this with the solemn reminder of Rom. **14.10–12** and 2 Cor. **5.10**.

157

1 Corinthians 15.35-41

In a sense the discussion up to this stage has been preliminary, although most needful. Against those who denied a resurrection hope, Paul argues (*i*) by asserting the pivotal event of the Lord's resurrection in which His people are included, and (*ii*) by showing the baneful consequences on Christian life and service of such a denial. But evidently there were Corinthians who, as converts to Christ from the Greek world, preferred a denial because they misunderstood what the term resurrection meant. They imagined it stood for a resuscitation of dead corpses and in a grossly materialistic fashion thought simply of resurrection-life as a prolongation of earthly conditions. Some clarification was needed; and Paul now gives it (35).

Two issues are involved. How is life out of death possible? What are the nature and qualities of the resurrection body?

The first question is answered simply by taking an illustration from the world of nature (36). A seed is planted in the earth where it 'dies'—but its 'death' is in order to germination and new life which in time produces growth, full development and fruitage.

The second question is more elaborately discussed and is carried over into verse 49.

(*i*) Still using the analogy of nature, Paul points to the obvious, viz. that the fruit which is grown is not identical with the seed that is sown (37). It is the acorn which goes into the ground, but it is the oak tree which appears. No identity is envisaged, although the oak springs out of the acorn, and in that sense is related to it.

(*ii*) Every seed has its own special form, according to the divine will (38)—a principle which goes back to Gen. 1.11. Moreover, in the kingdoms of animate matter as distinct from the world of vegetation, there are different types of body corresponding to the habitat of men, animals, fish and birds (39). Each species has a body suited to its environment.

The foundation of Paul's argument is firm. God is a God of order and purpose, with resources of infinite adaptability. 'How great Thou art' is the creature's fitting response (Rev. 4.11).

1 Corinthians 15.42-50

The hinge in Paul's argument is v. 42, for its purpose is to link the foregoing analogy with the subsequent reply which the question of v. 35 had evoked.

The body, as we have seen from ch. 6.12–20, is a key-term in Paul's thought. Based on clear O.T. teaching, he assumes that the body as part of God's created order is good; it is the vehicle of the human spirit, indeed it *is* the spirit in visible expression as representing a man's true self ('everybody'=everyone); but it is beset by natural limitations. Some of these restrictions are part of God's ordering of life (e.g. the body is weak, mortal and subject to decay, because like Adam's it will return as dust to the earth: Gen. 3.19 lies behind vs. 47,48a). More seriously, it becomes an 'instrument of unrighteousness' (Rom. 6.13) because man, as a sinner, uses his body as the vehicle of his transgression of God's command. This teaching lies in the background of vs. 42 ff. with its vivid portrayals of finite and unredeemed man's 'natural body': it is perishable, capable of dishonour (when man abuses his body), weak, physical (i.e. liable to dissolution in the grave)—and all because it is stamped with Adam's likeness (49a). Made in God's image, he chose to live independently of his Creator, suffered the defacing of that image and passed on a twisted nature to his posterity (Gen. 1.26,27 which goes with Gen. 2.7, in turn quoted in v. 45; Gen. 3.17–24; 5.3).

But with Christ's coming a new beginning was made. Sin's rule and its fateful chain of consequences were broken. As Paul expounds this new chapter in humanity's story in this passage, the spiritual era has arrived (46) and those who are 'in Christ' share all the benefits which His advent, obedience (reversing Adam's primal disobedience), death and triumph have secured. Christians receive the blessings bestowed by the last Adam as a life-giving spirit (45) and are partakers of the nature of the heavenly Man (48,49, RSV marg.). And not least, in their final inheritance they receive a spiritual body like His (50), whose qualities form the counterpart of the first halves of vs. 42–44. Phil. 3.21 sums it up; but the process of renewal has already begun (2 Cor. 3.18; Gal. 4.19; Eph. 4.24), and at Christ's coming the transformation will be complete.

1 Corinthians 15.51-58

'Conformed to the image of His Son' (Rom. 8.29) is the ultimate goal of God's electing and saving purpose, so surely and securely to be accomplished that Paul can speak of it in a past tense as something already made good (Rom. 8.30, cf. 8.17 which adds a proviso, however). The details of this final working out of divine plans for the Church are given in our passage.

(*i*) The *time* of it is related to Christ's return and glorification

159

(2 Thess. 1.10), placed at some future date when the events of 1 Thess. 4.13–18 will occur. This matches the Pauline reference in Phil. 3.21. His appearing is described as instantaneous (52) with the trumpet-call of Matt. 24.31 denoting the calling together of God's elect people; the holy dead will be raised and glorified; and the Church of the end-time on earth will be transformed and united with the Church triumphant in the Lord's presence.

(*ii*) Paul's immediate interest in our portion concentrates on the surviving Christian generation of that time, and is expressed in the phrase 'we shall . . . be changed' (51), i.e. transformed by the assumption of a spiritual body (44). V. 53 amplifies this change by the thought of the 'putting on' of immortality as a covering, so transmuting the believer's earthly form. Where else does Paul use this imagery (2 Cor. 5.2–4)? And that new life marks the transition from the old Adamic order of sin and death to the new Age of which prophecy (Isa. 25.8; Hos. 13.14) had spoken. Both texts are adapted, however, to Paul's purpose. How?

(*iii*) The link between sin–law–death in Rom. 5.12 ff. explains the presence of these terms in vs. 56,57. The logic in both passages is clear and incisive. A broken law requires the exaction of a penalty; this penalty is death; and death assumes its awful character, not as a biological necessity (Heb. 9.27), but as the 'sacrament of sin' (Denney). It is the outward and visible sign of a spiritual dis-grace.

In a significant turning-point, however, characterized by the Pauline 'but' (57; Rom. 5.15), a new hope is heralded and a fresh start is offered to men by the announcement of God's redeeming act in Christ. Hence, the last word is one of victory (three times repeated in three neighbouring verses).

Another typically Pauline section completes the thought. In the light of God's deed and the Church's new life in the risen Christ, a call to perseverance and service rings out (58). Soteriology, in Paul, always carries an ethical appeal; indeed without the presupposition of our standing in Christ, any summons to ethical endeavour would be a counsel of despair and a call to barren moralism (Phil. 2.5–11 is followed by 2.12,13).

1 Corinthians.16.1-4

A dominating influence on Paul's missionary life and service was the redeeming of a promise he had made at Jerusalem (Gal. 2.10). He recalls the promise, offering some guidance as to the way in which the money was to be gathered in lest there should be any 'last-minute rush to get subscriptions in' when he visits Corinth (as

Moffatt phrases it). Why did Paul attach so much importance to this fund by which Gentile churches promised financial help to the 'saints' at Jerusalem?

Once the money is brought in, plans are afoot to send it to Jerusalem (3,4); and we know from Acts **24.**17 that Paul did accompany these messengers whom the churches appointed to carry the gifts (2 Cor. **8.**23). The apostle has in mind the claim laid upon Jews of the Dispersion. Every male Jew over the age of twenty years was required to contribute towards the maintenance of the Temple and its services. The money as a Temple tax was collected at various centres and taken by responsible agents to the Holy City.

Set in this context is v. 2 which sheds a welcome light on the early Christian attitude to stewardship. Three principles may be detected.

(*i*) There is clear evidence of Christian concern for those in distress, as we have seen in reference to the Jerusalem community (see notes on Acts **4.**32–37 in Volume 3, p. 370f.); and the allusion to the churches of Galatia is best understood in the light of Gal. **6.**10, where the admonition to generous concern for the needy is given a sharper point and added practicality by the words, 'especially to those who are of the household of faith' (i.e. the Jerusalem believers). Where else does this concern and aid for fellow-believers become a test of our profession (1 John 3.17,18)?

(*ii*) Giving is advocated as a systematic and regular exercise by the setting aside of a part of one's income 'in proportion to his gains' (NEB). Some Christians adopt a principle of tithing, but the apostolic Church knows little of this type of giving which belongs more to the O.T. order.

(*iii*) What may seem to be a very mundane business—the duty of allocating a sum of money from the weekly budget—is set in a noble frame by the reference to 'the first day of the week' (2). This is the Church's holy day, a day of fellowship in commemoration of the resurrection (Rev. **1.**10) and of the Supper-meal (Acts **20.**7).

1 Corinthians 16.5-12

Travel-plans and *personalia* are the chief items in this passage.

Vs. 5–9 give Paul's notice of intention to come to Corinth via Macedonia and his promise to stay with the church there for some time (7). This reads like a small detail of little consequence. In point of fact, it turned out to be a major issue between the apostle and the Corinthians and a cause of great distress to both parties. For Paul had to revise his plans—and the opponents of Paul capitalized on this change by treating it as a breach of good faith and a token of his instability of character (cf. 2 Cor. 1.15 ff.).

He plans to stay on in Asia Minor until Whitsuntide, however, for a reason specially dear to his heart (8,9). What was it (cf. Col. 4.3; 2 Cor. 2.12; Rev. 3.8 for the imagery of an open door to mean an evangelistic opportunity)?

Vs. 10,11 give a commendation of his coadjutor, Timothy, who is elsewhere associated with Paul and his mission almost as his 'second self' (see 4.17; 1 Thess. 3.2). When Paul couldn't come himself, he sent Timothy as an extension of his own person (Phil. 2.19–24); and at Corinth he anticipates and fends off some criticism by this paragraph of warm approval and commendation. 'Some of the Corinthians were inclined to disregard the authority of Paul himself. They might well show even less respect to *Timothy*, who was younger in age and junior in status' (Thrall). The same idea underlies 1 Tim. 4.12 when Timothy had to stand on his own feet.

V. 12 is an indication that, whatever the Apollos party at Corinth (1.12) might think, their leader and Paul were on cordial terms (4.6); and conversely if there were those at Corinth who labelled themselves 'Paul's men', this notice that Apollos is encouraged to visit the church with their leader's approval is a blow to their undue exaltation of the apostle. Whatever rivalries existed at Corinth, there was none between the Christian leaders whose names were being bandied about in this way (3.21,22).

Question: Shall we ever learn that in the Church of God preachers and leaders are 'servants through whom you came to believe' (3.5); and that it is a small matter who is second so long as Jesus is first?

1 Corinthians 16.13-24

Vs. 13,14 ought not to be passed over for these injunctions are of timeless application, and the call, 'let all you do be done in love' recapitulates some of the leading themes of Paul's earlier discussion (8.1; 13; 14.1).

Vs. 15–18 introduce us to some of the church members who had visited Paul and brought news of their church's life and problems. Stephanas has already been referred to as the head of a believing household, baptized by Paul (1.16), and who had given a praise-worthy lead in laying themselves out to serve God's people (NEB). He and his colleagues were evidently leaders in the church, and are commended as worthy of respect for the good order of the con-gregational life. Which other Christian communities needed to honour their leaders (1 Thess. 5.12,13; Heb. 13.17)?

162

Greetings are sent from the Asian churches—Paul is writing from Ephesus (8)—with special mention made of two prominent workers, husband and wife, who played an important role in early Christianity (Acts 18.2,3,26). Their home was Rome, but they were driven out by the imperial edict of A.D. 49 and had settled at Corinth and Ephesus. Paul owed much to them (Rom. 16.3,4; 2 Tim. 4.19).

The description of 'the church in their house' (19) puts us back into the first century and into the worshipping life of small companies of men and women who made up God's Church in its earliest days (cf. Philem. 2). Unusual customs were practised, viz. the holy kiss (of peace) (20) as a sign of mutual affection among the worshippers (Rom. 16.16; 2 Cor. 13.12; 1 Thess. 5.26; 1 Pet. 5.14). In its context, the practice is mentioned as a call to a breaking down of all barriers within the divided Corinthian church.

Recent study of the N.T. has made much of the final paragraph (22–24), and related it to the assembling of the church for public worship during which Paul's letter would be read aloud (as in Col. 4.16; 1 Thess. 5.27). The verses may be arranged in lines (so NEB) as a dialogue-pattern between the leader at the Lord's table and the congregation; and characteristic notes of a communion service are sounded: fraternal love having been established (20), the table is 'fenced' by the dismissal of any who are not committed believers (22). The cry *Marana tha* ('Our Lord, come') is an invocation and prayer for the risen Lord's presence with His people at the meal; and the concluding grace is pronounced, to which Paul adds his own affectionate greeting (24).

Questions for further study and discussion on 1 Corinthians chs. 15 and 16

1. Are creeds today a help or a hindrance in (*a*) worship and (*b*) church unity discussions?
2. The resurrection of Christ: what is its relation to (*a*) faith, (*b*) preaching, (*c*) living? Does it figure sufficiently in our presentation of the gospel?
3. Paul does not use the argument of a familiar chorus—'He lives within my heart'—why not?
4. Some of the topics in the letter are a cause of agitation and debate today, e.g. spiritual gifts, matters of worship, and church discipline. What have you learned about these questions at Corinth, and what is their relevance to the modern church?
5. What principles regulate *your* stewardship?

Second Corinthians

INTRODUCTION

This epistle was written shortly after *1 Corinthians*; and it seems clear that it was composed in Macedonia after Paul had left Ephesus. If we seek a more precise dating and a more certain knowledge of the relation between the two Corinthian epistles, we shall soon find that we have entered a most difficult field of New Testament chronology.

A good starting-place is 1 Cor. **16.**1,2. There Paul implies that the collection at Corinth for the poor believers in Jerusalem had not yet been started. But in 2 Cor. **8.**10; **9.**2, he writes that the Corinthians began the collection 'last year'. As McNeile-Williams in their *Introduction* say, 'The relation between the dates of the two epistles depends upon this phrase'.

Paul had sent Titus to Corinth while he himself proceeded to Troas (2 Cor. **7.**6; **12.**18). Titus had gone to enforce the apostle's views and bring back word to Paul concerning the effect produced by a letter which Paul had written in view of the crisis in the Corinthian church (2 Cor. **2.**4 f.; **7.**8–13).

These were days of anxious strain (2 Cor. **2.**13; **7.**5), and not finding Titus, Paul had left for Macedonia (**2.**13). There Titus met him and brought good news. He intimated that Paul's 'severe letter' (**2.**4) had done its work well, although Paul feared earlier that he might have written too severely (**7.**8). He rejoiced, however, that the crisis was over and the estrangement between him and the church occasioned by one prominent man's opposition to him at Corinth (**2.**5 ff.) had passed. The occasion of *2 Corinthians* is to be sought at this point.

'His relief was unbounded . . . It was not a moment for dealing with Christian doctrine or church practice; the letter is simply a pouring out of the man himself' (McNeile-Williams).

Yet there are important sections of the epistle which deal with doctrinal matters (e.g. **5.**1–10, on the resurrection; **5.**15–21, on reconciliation), and church practices (e.g. chs. **8,9** on Christian stewardship). But, with this proviso, the judgement of McNeile-Williams may stand; and we shall best appreciate the letter if we read it as Paul's *apologia* or spirited defence against his attackers.

2 Corinthians is therefore a very human (though inspired)

document, and opens a window into the inner life of the apostle. R. H. Strachan's words are a tribute to this feature: 'The letter is an artless and unconsciously autobiographical description of the ways in which Paul was accustomed to meet slander and calumny, physical danger and bodily suffering, disloyalty and ingratitude, from those for whom he had given of his best, and disillusionment and disappointment that invaded his spirit from time to time.'

Helps: There are some excellent commentaries, suited to all types of readership. R. V. G. Tasker in the Tyndale series is the best all-purpose volume, with P. E. Hughes in the New London/International Commentary (Marshall, Morgan & Scott–Eerdmans), an invaluable aid to the advanced student.

2 Corinthians 1.1-7

Letters in the first century usually began with a mention of the writer's name and then that of the addressee. The normal practice was to follow this with a line of greeting (as in Acts **15.23**; **23.25,26**). Paul follows this customary pattern, but inserts some *extra* items by (*i*) linking Timothy's name with his own; (*ii*) addressing the church of God (note the singular expression) in the district of southern Greece, and (*iii*) turning the colourless 'greeting' (*Gk. chairein*) into a rich Christian salutation, calling down on his readers God's grace (*charis*) and peace.

The opening section breaks out into jubilant thanksgiving to God (3,4). What are the chief themes of praise? Two reasons are supplied for the apostle's outburst. The first (in 3–7) is our reading for today; the second falls in tomorrow's passage (8–11).

Paul is glad that, in spite of the many troubles which have weighed upon him, he has known the special strength of God (4). Suffering was ever his destiny as the apostle of the Gentiles (Eph. **3.13**; Col. **1.24**), and this was made known to him at the commencement of his Christian life (Acts **9.15,16**).

There is a divine purpose in human suffering which is borne for the gospel's sake. Thereby the cause of Christ is advanced—so Acts **14.22** and Col. **1.24** ff. And His afflicted servants are qualified to enter sympathetically into the experience of others whose pathway leads them through a vale of tears (4,6,7). So Paul the apostle is no man who lives a detached existence, untroubled by hard knocks in life; and by the same token he is no aloof pastor, remote from the people to whom he ministers.

Notes: V. 3: 'Father of mercies'=the Father who bestows mercy, who delights to hear His children's cry (Psa. **145.18,19**). Mark the

165

oft-repeated word for 'comfort' (*lit.* encouragement, strengthening) here—ten references in five verses.

Thought: 'Patiently endure . . . sufferings.' Not easy advice, but there are great rewards (1 Pet. 2.19–21).

2 Corinthians 1.8-11

A second reason for Paul's thankfulness of spirit is given in this section: he had been rescued from the jaws of death!

In relating the experience of a crisis in Asia which exposed him to mortal danger he makes it plain that it was only by God's mercy that he and his fellow-missionaries had been saved (10); yet God works by the prayers of His people, and Paul does not forget this side of the story as well (11). Those who prayed for him are invited to share his gladness; and there is no finer stimulus to our prayers than when we hear from some friend at home or abroad that he is rejoicing in an answer to *our* praying on *his* behalf.

The precise nature of 'the affliction we experienced in Asia' is not easy to pinpoint. Some suggest that the phrase alludes to the riot in the Ephesian theatre (Acts **19**.23–41: see *Bible Study Book* on this passage, with the suggestion made there that there was a time of social anarchy which followed the assassination of the proconsul). 1 Cor. **15**.32, the famous description of 'fighting with beasts at Ephesus', may refer to the same incident, or more likely to some other hazard to which his life was exposed. Other scholars (such as Deissmann) found a clue in the phrase 'the sentence of death' (9), which may be a technical term for a death-sentence in a civil court. If this is the meaning here, does it imply that Paul was arrested, tried, and faced with the prospect of death? A hint of this may underlie certain verses in Phil. (**1**.20 ff.; **1**.30; **2**.17; **3**.11), if that letter belongs to the middle period of Paul's ministry, i.e. the time of his Ephesian ministry. Alternatively, it may be more simply believed that Paul suffered an acute illness which threatened his life. At all events, it was extremely serious ('so terrible a death', 10, Moffatt), and he was marvellously delivered by divine assistance and human prayer.

Notes: V. 11: a Greek word of fifteen letters is translated 'you must help by prayer'. There are three notions in the verb, (*i*) prayer as *work* (Col. 4.12,13); (*ii*) prayer as *co-operation*, a ministry of assistance along with other Christians; and (*iii*) prayer as undergirding *support* by which our weaker brethren are sustained in their service.

Meditation: Paul's deadly affliction is unknown to us; but no extremity is too great for the God of resurrection (9)—so Eph. 1.19 ff.

166

2 Corinthians 1.12-18

The key-phrase is in v. 17, which is somewhat obscured in the RSV. The literal translation is 'When I therefore was thus intending (to change my plans), did I act with *the* fickleness (of which I am accused)?' The definite article here and before the 'Yes' and 'No' in the same verse 'probably indicates that Paul is quoting what is being said about him at Corinth' (Tasker). The allegation of vacillation—blowing hot and cold at the same time—arose directly out of a change of Paul's travel plans (15,16). In 1 Cor. 16.5 he expressed the hope of visiting Corinth after he had passed through Macedonia. He hints now that this original idea will have to be modified; and a second visit, bringing a 'double pleasure' (15) will not be possible in view of the atmosphere in the Corinthian church (see 2.1). Hence the revised itinerary, which he explains in order to rebut the criticism of indecision and a failure to keep his first promise brought by his opponents at Corinth. All this background is necessary to understand Paul's indignant protest, 'Do I make my plans like a worldly man?' (17).

The same background helps us to make sense of the earlier section (12–14), for Paul is leading up to a frank statement of his change of mind by declaring the *motives* which inspired all his dealings, his words and his letter-writing habits. Read over these three verses and see how carefully Paul goes down the list of activities which have presumably been misinterpreted at Corinth; and pick out the terms he uses to show that his motives and actions have always been beyond reproach.

Notes: V. 12: 'the testimony of our conscience'. What other references to 'conscience' can you trace in Paul's speeches in *Acts* (e.g. 24.16) and the epistles (e.g. 1 Tim. 1.19; 4.2)? V. 13: a subtle play on the Greek words 'You don't have to read between the lines (*anaginoskein*) in my letters: you can understand (*epiginoskein*) them'. *Our* problem in reading Paul's letters today is that we know far less than we would like to know about the immediate circumstances which called them forth.

Thought: 'As surely as God is faithful . . .' (18). The character of God as altogether faithful (1 Cor. 10.13) was an unshakable rock on which Paul's whole appeal and ministry rested (Rom. 3.4). Is He not trustworthy for you today?

2 Corinthians 1.19-22

It was bad enough that Paul's enemies at Corinth had attacked his character as unreliable and shifty (17); it was worse when they go on to insinuate that his gospel is just as unreliable and unsure. The purpose of today's passage is to answer that serious charge. How does Paul do it?

First, he defines clearly the person of Jesus Christ as the Son of God whom the early missionaries proclaimed. They offered no dialectic (yes/no type of preaching, which leaves the hearer in doubt as to His authority and ability to save, or else confuses him to the point of thinking of the gospel as irrelevant: how modern all this is!), but boldly declared that Christ is the answer to all human need (19).

Then, He has placed His seal of endorsement and fulfilment on the O.T. prophecies and promises by declaring them to be valid and available to the believer (20). The only appropriate response which the Christian can make is a confident Amen, by which he accepts God's promises for what they are worth—utterly confirmed by Christ Jesus.

Finally, the message of the apostle is no sham and fraud, because he has been specially appointed and endowed by God for his work. There is a seal upon his ministry, placed there by the Holy Spirit. What is it (1 Cor. **9.1**,2)? And the Christians at Corinth who too are men and women sealed by the Spirit (Eph. **1.**13,14) should be able to recognize a spiritual affinity with Paul and his party; and certainly ought never to doubt their integrity. 'Are we then the men to say one thing and mean another?' (Phillips) sums it up.

Meditation: Think of some of the promises of God in the O.T. which are given a fuller content in Christ; and of those promises which you have proved in your experience.

2 Corinthians 1.23—2.4

V. 23 tells us the real reason for Paul's change of travel arrangements and non-appearance at Corinth. He comes clean—even by uttering a mild oath in the spirit of Ruth **1.**17; 1 Sam. **14.**44; 2 Sam. **3.**35; 1 Kings **2.**23. He would not inflict upon them 'another painful visit' (2.1). The plain sense of this text is that Paul had already paid a visit to Corinth which *did* cause him pain. This visit is not recorded in *Acts*, and is known only by inference.

Moreover, on the previous occasion to which he now looks back with sorrow, there was *one* person who was the ringleader of the opposition and who personally resisted him and made things very unhappy (2). We shall learn more about this man (now truly sorry for his misdemeanour) in vs. 5–11.

Besides a painful visit which the apostle had paid, there was also a tearful letter he had written (3,4). Once more we are in the realm of conjecture and inference. Three possibilities are open to us as we try to locate the identity of this letter.

It may refer to the former epistle, known as our *1 Corinthians* (so Denney and P. E. Hughes), but this is unlikely, as that letter hardly fits the vivid description which Paul gives. A second possibility, which most modern critics hold, is that a portion of this 'tearful letter' has been preserved in 2 Cor. **10–13**. There are objections to this suggestion, not least that the *character* of the hypothetical fragment is more warmly indignant and polemical than sorrowful. The most probable possibility is that the letter in question has not survived.

The letter whose tenor and tone we can guess from the descriptiveness of v. 4 *had* caused pain to the writer, but was intended for the Corinthians' good. This deeply-moving passage 'reveals . . . the essential qualification of the Christian minister—a heart pledged to his brethren in the love of Christ. Depend upon it, we shall not make others weep for that for which we have not wept' (Denney).

2 Corinthians 2.5-11

Still in reflective mood Paul remarks upon the outcome of the visit he previously made and the insult he had to bear. Vs. 5–11 deal with his attitude to the one who caused him pain, i.e. the man who had insulted him and fomented the trouble at Corinth. Once more we are faced with a problem of detection: who was this man, and was the insult directed against Paul personally?

We may dismiss the view that it was not Paul himself whose character was aspersed but one of his associates (e.g. Timothy) as most improbable. Paul's use of the personal pronoun in v. 10 clinches the point.

Many older scholars (supported by P. E. Hughes) find here an allusion to the case of the immoral man in 1 Cor. **5.1** ff., but we have no proof that this man, although severely reproved for his sinful ways, ever bore animosity to Paul himself; and once the supposition of an intermediate visit to Corinth is granted, it becomes a natural consequence that the cause of the painful visit should be traced to the actions of this offender on that occasion.

Whatever the immediate outburst of feeling against Paul may have been caused by, there is no doubt what the outcome was. Following the 'severe letter' (cf. **7.8**), the church had condemned the behaviour of this man and imposed a disciplinary penalty. The stern measure adopted by the church had moved the miserable man to penitence, and Paul's purpose now in writing is to advocate a forgiving spirit and the restoration of the punished man, lest he is driven to despair (7). If this undesired effect did follow, it would serve only Satan's interest, whose designs are ever to set Christians against Christians (so Rev. **12.10**). Forgiveness is now the order of the day: Paul has forgiven and holds no grudge. He calls upon the Corinthians to do likewise (10). Paul catches the spirit of Christ whose magnanimity he will later extol (**10.1**)

Thought: On v. 11, 'the greatest ruse of Satan is to make us believe that he does not exist' (Oberlin). Are we alive to what Calvin called his 'machinations', sometimes (as here) devised in unusual ways?

2 Corinthians 2.12-17

Vs. 12 and 13 look back to Paul's travels after the uproar in Ephesus (Acts **19–20.1**). He turned north-westward from that city and came to the seaport of Troas (Acts **20.5**) where an evangelistic opportunity awaited him.

The agitation which troubled his spirit at Troas and which impelled him to cross over the Aegean Sea into Macedonia in search of Titus is simply reported, with no further explanation. In fact, at this point, the story-telling breaks off, and will not be resumed until **7.5**. The intervening verses form one large digression on the theme of the gospel ministry, its methods and its men. V. 14 is an ejaculation which prefaces the whole.

The ministry of Paul is distinguished in two ways: (*i*) it calls forth a double reaction from the hearers. As we have seen time after time in the *Acts*, a fence-sitting neutrality was impossible once a man had been confronted with Paul's presentation of the message of Christ. Now he explains to us something of the nature of this 'rejection or response' which he had known. To those who are destined to salvation the 'word of the cross' (1 Cor. **1.18**) is a perfume of Christ, offering life in Him (16); but to the obdurate and Christ-refuser it smells only of death and doom. Thus an awful responsibility rests on the hearer: 'Take heed then how you hear' (Luke **8.18**), as well as on the preacher. The rhetorical question (16) will be answered in **3.5**. (*ii*) The ministry of God's servant is marked by sincerity (17; cf. **1.12**) in contrast to 'many' who 'made merchandise of the word'—a strange phrase, probably referring to certain prevalent religious teachers who put their preaching on a commercial basis by the constant flourish of the collection-box. Paul will have none of this (1 Cor. **9.15–18**), and mentions the only sort of accrediting worth having (17b).

Notes: V. 16: there is an interesting use by the rabbis of **the**

170

term 'aroma' in reference to the law. They spoke of the Mosaic law as a medicine, either fatal (to the ungodly) or life-giving (to the righteous). In the case of the Israelites, the law as a vitalizing power counteracted the baneful effect of the 'evil impulse'—what Paul calls 'the flesh', but *his* secret of victory is discovered elsewhere (Gal. **5.**16 ff.). An extension of this background is offered by W. D. Davies, who notes that Jewish traders sometimes became missionaries by holding out the offer of a 'medicine of life' (based on Psalm **34**). Paul perhaps is using the very term (in 17: pedlars) which they employed.

Question: Am I living today 'in the train of His triumph' (*14*)?

Questions for further study and discussion on 2 Corinthians chs. 1 and 2

1. As a Christian, how should I endeavour to deal with depression and moods of anxiety—in myself and in others?
2. 'The testimony of our conscience' (**1.**12). Look up the N.T. occurrences of the word 'conscience' and consider its function in the non-Christian's and Christian's experience.
3. What 'promises of God' (**1.**20) yet await fulfilment?
4. How is the 'fragrance . . . of Him' best spread? Consider the areas of speech, action and attitude in which it can be released.

2 Corinthians 3.1-3

It is a helpful clue to notice that Paul's thought in **2.**17 is not only enlarged later in the epistle (in chs. **11,12**, where again he denies any mercenary motives in his gospel work), but follows on directly in **4.**2. Ch. **3** is therefore likened to a separate exposition, tucked in between two links in Paul's thought; and has a theme all of its own. He expounds, with tremendous verve, the *greatness of the gospel* and its superiority to the Mosaic-Judaic order.

The introductory lead-in to the topic is found in today's verses. Paul, having stated the sincerity of his motives (**2.**17b), back-tracks a little, for he finds this assertion something of a distasteful business (**3.**1). It is not easy for him continually to harp on the openness of his behaviour and the purity of his motives, but the situation at Corinth required it (**1.**12). If any proof is needed of the truth of his apostleship (he is saying, 2,3) let it be found, not in letters of commendation such as his enemies were in the habit of using, but in the lives of those whom his preaching had influenced. Such an 'epistle' existed in the case of the Corinthians themselves. Their new life in

Christ is written upon 'our hearts' (see Notes), but is really evident for all to see.

Christ is the author of this life-transforming work of grace. Paul as His minister has led the converts to Him; and the marks of genuineness are not characters written on parchment with ink, but the fruit of the Spirit (Gal. **5.**22,23); not letters chiselled out of stone, but engraven upon the human heart.

This latter thought is drawn from the contrast between the law of God written by Him upon stone tablets and delivered to Moses (Exod. **31.**18), and the promise in Jer. **31.**33 that God would, in the future, put His law in the inward parts and write it on men's hearts. The day of *that* fulfilment, Paul declares, has now dawned.

We may pause to ask, Why was this promise given? Was not the law sufficient? The answer lies in Jer. **31.**32: 'My covenant they broke' (cf. Heb. **8.**9). The covenant-engagement entered into by Israel at God's behest and initiative had proved a failure because of Israel's defection (see Isa. **1.**2; Hos. **6.**7,8; Jer. **3.**20)—hence the need for, and promise of, a *new* covenant. To this subject Paul turns.

Notes: V. 1: 'letters of introduction' were given to travelling Christians to certify their good standing as they visited the churches and sought hospitality (Acts **18.**27). V. 2: RSV reads '*your* hearts', but the margin 'our' is better attested and makes happier sense.

Thought: '*You are a letter from Christ*' (*3*). *What message do others read in your life?*

2 Corinthians 3.4-6

To follow the rest of the chapter some preface is needed, and we must come to grips with a startling phrase 'ministers of a new covenant' (6), claimed by Paul, and no doubt giving a shock to Jewish-Christians who would interpret this as a bold claim on the apostle's part to supersede Moses, the founder of O.T. covenant-religion. Indeed, *that* was precisely the claim that Paul made in this phrase.

If Paul were called upon to justify his vocation, he would (*i*) disclaim all personal worthiness (5), while (*ii*) at the same time refusing to undervalue the high office and great qualifications that *God* had given to him and his fellow-missionaries to the Gentiles (6).

The 'new covenant' stands in direct contrast to 'the old covenant' (14), the religion of Moses as interpreted by the Jewish rabbis. As Heb. **8** concludes (v. 13), the mention of a *new* covenant renders obsolete what it replaces, and this means that a new dispensation has been inaugurated by the coming of Christ, in fulfilment of Jer. **31.**31 ff.

172

Three features marked out this promised 'new covenant' from the old: (*i*) *inwardness;* no longer would God's law be inscribed on stone, but it would be inwardly impressed on men's hearts (=minds, consciences, affections); (*ii*) *individualism;* in contrast to the old order in which the priestly tribe acted representatively for the nation, and God was approached only indirectly, 'they shall all know Me' with no restriction imposed; (*iii*) *a full forgiveness;* under the Levitical system, forgiveness was provided for a limited number of offences only. There was simply no provision made for sins committed 'with a high hand' (i.e. deliberately). Only the gospel of the cross promises an adequate assurance that *all* sin is pardoned (1 John 1.9).

Of this *new* covenant, symbolized and signified in the cup at the Last Supper (Matt. 26.27,28) and ratified in the blood of Calvary (Heb. 13.20), Paul was made a minister (6). The 'old covenant' as a way of salvation is branded as out-of-date on account of its 'weakness and uselessness' (Heb. 7.18)—features which by their inadequacies helped to prepare the way for a new order which offers men what they need most of all—life in the Spirit.

Thought: 'The life of God in the souls of men'; does this sum up the faith of the N.T. gospel?

2 Corinthians 3.7-11

We are now prepared for a series of contrasts in which the old and the new covenant are discussed together. There are three lines of approach which the apostle takes; vs. 7–11 take two of them.

First, the law set the standard, but offered no power to reach it. For that reason Paul does not mince his words: the law 'kills' (6); it is 'the dispensation of death' (7) which, in turn, leads to 'condemnation' (9). These strong terms can only mean that the law set the target of a perfect standard; but men, who are sinfully weak, are unable to attain it.

Paul finds no fault with the law in itself (Rom. 7.12,14), but discovers that the law mocked and taunted by calling him to an impossibly high level, but offering him no assistance or dynamic of attainment. In this way, what God intended as good is turned into a death-dealing instrument (Rom. 7.13)—and the reason? Turn up Rom. 8.3a.

Secondly, Paul goes on to teach that the law had an honourable purpose, but it was only temporary. The illustration of the law's 'parenthetic character' (as Gal. 3.16 ff. describe it) is seen in the way in which the glory of both the law (7,11) and the lawgiver, Moses (7),

173

was only a passing one. The background reference is clearly Exod. 34.29–35, which describes the splendour which shone from Moses' face when he returned from communion with God. That radiance, however, faded in time and at length disappeared. From the lawgiver, Paul argues to that which he represents, viz. Judaism whose glory, once historically a reality, is now fading away; indeed, its day is over, and its impermanence has given way to that which has come to stay, viz. the gospel (10,11).

All of this contrast adds up to one firm conclusion: the Christian ministry is meant, by Divine intention, to supersede the old Judaic ceremonial order. The glory of God is to be sought now, not in the law or the Temple or the priesthood, but in the face of Jesus Christ (2 Cor. 4.6; Tit. 2.13). John's prologue says the same thing exactly (John 1.17).

2 Corinthians 3.12-18

Having taken his readers thus far, Paul is now ready for a third element in the distinction between the two covenants. The law betokened a barrier between God and the people of Israel, both in Moses' day and in Paul's. Why did the lawgiver place a veil over his radiant face (13; Exod. 34.33)? Part of the reason was to prevent the people's disappointment when they saw the glory fading; but Exod. 34.30 tells that 'they were afraid to come near him', partly because of the 'radiation' of his face (Exod. 34.29 reads literally that 'the skin of his face sent forth beams').

Paul finds in this circumstance a profound explanation, for the veil which Moses wore is no mere historical detail. It speaks of a barrier which still hides the truth from the Jewish reader of the O.T.

When the Jews of Antioch, Ephesus or Corinth hear the law read in the Sabbath worship of the synagogue (14,15), they fail to perceive its true significance. They imagine that it is the final revelation of God, not (as Paul has shown) a preparatory agency making them ready to receive the Christ (Gal. 3.24). Therefore they remain hardened and blinded (4.3,4; Rom. 11.25) in spite of their inestimable privileges as God's ancient people to whom the law was first entrusted (Rom. 3.1,2; 9.4,5).

But whenever a Jew turns to the Lord, how different is the result as the veil is lifted and 'Christ in all the Scriptures' is made known! The two on the Emmaus road show what *can* happen (Luke 24.27, 32; cf. v. 44).

Vs. 17,18 require a comment. The crux is the sentence 'the Lord is the Spirit'. If we recall that the preceding verse is taken originally

174

from Exod. 34.34, though Paul is novel in the way he applies it, we are on the right track. Then v. 17 is a comment on the reference to Moses' turning in to God's presence: 'Now in the verse mentioned, the Lord whom Moses approached means *for us* the Spirit who leads a man to turn to Christ and confess His lordship' (1 Cor. 12.3)—this is Paul's meaning.

The office of the Holy Spirit is further described in vs. 17b,18; He brings the Jewish believer out of bondage to liberty, and transforms all believers, Gentiles as well as Jews, into God's pattern, viz. the perfect man, Christ Jesus, as a progressive experience and by communion with the living God (Rom. 8.29; Gal. 4.19; Phil. 3.21; 1 John 3.2). So 'every Christian becomes a Moses' (Héring), reflecting (RSV marg.) the Divine glory in this life in anticipation of our perfect conformity to Christ in the next.

2 Corinthians 4.1-6

'This ministry' looks back to the contrast with the Mosaic order which is superseded in Christ. It is committed to men—notice the link in thought with 2.17b—in the amazing mercy of God, as the writer had proved in his own case (1 Tim. 1.12–14). As a consequence, the apostle can exercise the work God entrusted to him with *confidence*, never losing heart. What would tempt Paul to grow discouraged? If he relied solely on human resources or was foolhardy enough to practise 'disgraceful, underhanded ways' in order to gain some cheap victories, and secure some quick conversions which evaporate as soon as they are gained (2)? Opposition from his Judaizing enemies who accused him of trying to do exactly this (Gal. 5.11)? The hardness of the human heart which remains strangely obdurate and resistant (3), in spite of Love's appeal?

Paul's unbounded confidence rests on the following grounds: (*i*) the sincerity of the messengers should be obvious to all (2); (*ii*) the gospel itself which is *God's* truth shines in its own light, but with an appeal enforced by the character of the messengers who convey it (2b); (*iii*) the failure of many to respond is not due to any lack of adequacy or relevance of the message (3,4). Rather, the reason lies in the Satanic grip on the human mind and heart (4); and (*iv*) the sublime message is 'Jesus Christ as Lord' (cf. Rom. 10.9; 1 Cor. 12.3), by which it pleases God to illumine the spiritually responsive and bring men out of the darkness as impenetrable as primaeval chaos (Gen. 1.2; Jer. 4.23) into the marvellous light of reconciled fellowship with Himself by the same authoritative, sovereign power which dispelled the world's darkness and said, 'Let there be light' (Gen. **1**.3; see 1 Pet. **2**.9).

Paul himself had known that 'dark night of the soul' suddenly lifted by the radiant presence of God's glory in Jesus' face in his conversion experience (Gal. **1**.15,16; Acts **9**.3; **22**.6,11; **26**.13) and knew it as a reality in the lives of his Christian friends (cf. Phil. **1**.6, where 'good work' looks back to Gen. **1**.31). Who else caught sight of the divine radiance in the person of Jesus (Acts **7**.55)?

Meditation: Pick out some of the verses which speak of Christ as Lord of glory (1 Cor. 2.8; Col. 1.15–20; Phil. 2.6–11; Heb. 1.1–4). 'Thou art the King of glory, O Christ.'

2 Corinthians 4.7-12

Such a message as vs. 5,6 describe may well, without exaggeration, be called a 'treasure' whose value is in no way diminished by the cheap and disposable pots which carry it. This is how Paul saw himself—having no inherent worth save as a messenger and transmitter, or to use his metaphor, as an earthenware jar in which some precious commodity was carried. Let us recall the vocation given him at his call (Acts **9**.15, using the same word).

The purpose of the arrangement whereby the truth of God is deposited in frail vessels is now made plain (7b). What is it? So far from being protected and preserved unharmed from 'the slings and arrows of outrageous fortune'—as the Greek cults believed their 'divine men' as the herald of the gods to be specially favoured—Christ's messengers are consigned to a life of humiliation and danger. And it is all in order to leave the unmistakable impression that the power of the message does not derive from the ingenuity and skill of the pleaders but comes solely from the inherent truth of the message as God's word.

'I die every day' (1 Cor. **15**.31) may be dismissed, at first glance, as a piece of Pauline rhetoric. But the passage, in a series of eloquent contrasts (8–10) and memorable phrases, leads to the identical conclusion (11,12). Put in simple language, it requires that the disciple should share in the humiliation of his Lord in the confidence that he will also share in His triumphant risen life (14).

Notes: V. 7: 'earthen vessels'—lit. *ostraca*; many of these pottery lamps have been found in archaeological diggings. V. 10: 'the dying of the Lord Jesus' is better, i.e. His attitude of self-renouncing, self-giving sympathy for, and help to, others—even to the death of the cross (Mark **10**.45; Luke **22**.27). But for Him death (uniquely sin-bearing, to be sure) became the gateway to life; and so it will be for His faithful servants, even if a martyr's death is entailed (2 Tim. 2.11–13; 4.6–8).

2 Corinthians 4.13-18

The apostle and his fellow-believers are closely knit in many ways; and Paul viewed his sufferings as directly beneficial to the churches (see Eph. 3.1; Col. 1.24; 2 Tim. 2.10). By his life of hardship and exposure to mortal peril (1 Cor. 15.30) he was securing the maintenance of the faith and so consolidating their Christian standing (12).

But the hope of a final vindication, when death will lead through resurrection to the last home-gathering of the Church, is not the apostle's exclusively. When the apostle is introduced to his Lord's presence (14), those who are with him in Christ will share the victory too. That was his eager longing (Phil. 1.21–23; 3.10,11), although it was no escapist death-wish which had settled upon him. If God willed the continuance of his apostolic trials and labours, as he tells the Philippians (1.24), the result must be that 'as the abounding grace of God is shared by more and more, the greater may be the chorus of thanksgiving that ascends to the glory of God' (15, NEB).

Meanwhile, no other proof of the 'earthiness' of the apostle's physical frame is needed than the reminder of v. 16. His body, in its finitude and weakness, is constantly in the process of decay in the normal course of 'growing old'. Added to this is the exposure he has known to all the hazards and dangers described in vs. 8–12, now euphemistically seen as 'this slight momentary affliction' (17)! But, parallel with that process and the endurance of ceaseless risks, the real life of the spirit is being renewed and revitalized by the power of God.

Paul's horizon is bounded by an eternal prospect (18), and spiritual insight enables him to see beyond the visible and tangible to the eternal realities of that world where God's presence is the most real of realities. From such a perspective he will go on, in ch. 5, to consider the Christian hope.

Thought: 'We faint not . . . while we look not' (16,18). Where are our eyes fixed today?

Questions for further study and discussion on 2 Corinthians chs. 3 and 4

1. To what extent is 3.6 a guide in the interpretation of Scripture?
2. Being changed . . . from one degree of glory to another (3.18). How would you explain this to a new convert?

3. 'We do not lose heart' (**4.1**). What factors threatened to discourage Paul? What advice does he give in this chapter which is of practical use to us in facing adverse circumstances?
4. Does ch. 4 make the Christian faith appear 'reasonable'? At what point must faith supersede reason?

2 Corinthians 5.1-5

The immediate occasion for this treatment of the resurrection hope is to be found in the apostle's experience of mortal peril at Ephesus (see notes on **1.8**–11). But it links on admirably with the previous discussion in **4.16**–18. The frailty of the human body reminds him of the believer's prospect of what lies beyond death, and that before long 'the earthly tent we live in', i.e. his body, will be taken down in death and dissolution. Two parallel passages should be read in conjunction with these verses—1 Cor. **15.42**–57, and Phil. **3.20**,21. These five verses contain some important teaching on a difficult and (admittedly) mysterious subject, viz.:

(*i*) The threefold contrast between the Christian's present body and his future 'spiritual body' (1 Cor. **15.44**) is made: (*a*) the present is likened to a tent; the new body will be a building, which implies permanence and stability (see this contrast in Heb. **11.9**,10); (*b*) the old is 'of the earth' (1 Cor. **15.47**) with all the association of human weakness and defects (so Gen. **3.19**); the new body will be God's work in sovereign power, called into existence directly (contrast Gen. **2.7**; Psa. **139.15**); (*c*) the present body is perishable, while the new will be 'eternal in the heavens' (1).

(*ii*) In v. 2, Paul's 'groaning' is related to his desire to receive his new body. But it is no death-wish, as we observe earlier (see on **4.13**–18). He is really yearning for the Lord's return, when the body of his future existence will be given (1 Cor. **15.51** ff.; Phil. **3.20**,21).

(*iii*) The verb of vs. 2,3 is a double compound which suggests that he longs to put on the resurrection form *over* the old body. On this view, the 'groaning' is lest he should undergo death from which he naturally shrinks, i.e. to enter by death into the intermediate state, described as 'being unclothed' (3,4), although consciously with Christ (Phil. **1.23**).

(*iv*) The Holy Spirit is the divine assurance that what God has promised to do will be accomplished because He has *already* begun to do it. The first instalment (**1.22**) guarantees the later, full consignment.

Notes: V. 1: The metaphor of a tent is drawn from Lev. **23.42**

(Feast of Tabernacles). Living in tents ('booths') was to remind the Israelites of their pilgrim life *en route* to Canaan.

2 Corinthians 5.6-10

Let us continue our notes on the nature of the resurrection hope:

(*v*) The intense aspiration of the apostle is expressed in the term 'to be clothed upon' (2,4) which is later spelled out for us in the phrase 'at home with the Lord' (8). Included in this eager longing (notice the terms of preference in v. 8) is the prospect of receiving a glorified body, like his Lord's (Phil. 3.20,21).

(*vi*) From comparable Scriptures we know that the bestowing of the new, spiritual body is timed at the Lord's return in glory, and this is implied in Rom 8.17.

(*vii*) There is a down-to-earth, practical application of this teaching, e.g. v. 9, where the Christian's ambition is stated in a memorable phrase; and Paul can never forget that our present life with all its practicalities and opportunities for service will one day be tested at the tribunal of Christ (10; Rom. 14.10–12).

What phrase in today's portion is twice repeated? See vs. 6,8, and notice the solid foundation on which Paul's confidence is set. Encouragement in Christian living and service came to him as no emotional upsurge requiring some artificial stimulus, but as a logical deduction from a God-given *fact* which he received in *faith*. It is vitally important to get our priorities right from this passage, and v. 7 will be a most useful guide to any who are confused. *Feelings* are no spiritual barometer; they fluctuate and vary according to all manner of circumstances—even the weather affects them, or our relation with other people (e.g. our employer, or our mother-in-law). We rest upon God's promised word—what He has spoken and given —as unchangeably sure; and on this fact of revelation faith is content to rest and therefrom to draw its strength and stability. John Fletcher of Madeley helpfully comments: 'I build my faith not on my experience, though this increases it, but upon the revealed truth of God.'

Question: Think of the O.T. saints who 'walked by faith, not by sight' (Heb. 11.8,11,27). Can you add to this list?

2 Corinthians 5.11-15

Two motives of Paul's ministry are suggested in these verses. What are they (vs. 11,14)? Is there any conflict between them?

The apostle exercises his God-entrusted tasks of preaching and teaching in no off-handed manner. He marvels at the high dignity and privilege of the work committed to him (11). The term 'persuade' has a double flavour; we try to win men for Christ (as Luke 5.10), and we try to convince them of our own purity of motive. As Denney comments, 'The first (significance) is suggested by the general tenor of the passage, and the second seems to be demanded by what follows.' The second view—complementary to the first—is the point of the appeal in vs. 12,13.

He is turning to the allegations which had been brought against him that his intentions were insincere—and, indeed, that he was out of his mind! The apostle's rejoinder to this insinuation—brought against his Lord also (Mark 3.21)—is to admit that he has known times and experiences of spiritual elation and ecstasy (cf. ch. **12**) but he has never sought his own glory in these things, and all that has happened to him has ever been 'for God', i.e. redounding to His glory. Can you think of Jesus' teaching which follows the same line (John 7.18 f.)? Equally, in calm and 'ordinary' moments of life he has always had the pastoral welfare of the Corinthians in view (13).

The basis of Paul's doctrine of reconciliation is laid in v. 14. The bedrock is the conviction which places a certain evaluation upon the death of the Lord Jesus. This conviction may be spelled out in certain propositions: 'One died for all, i.e. His people; and in Him they all died—to sin and self; now they must all live for Him.' The key-terms are substitution, representation and renewal. 'Christ's death was the death of all, in the sense that He died the death they should have died; the penalty of their sins was borne by Him; He died in their place; and that is why His love has such a compelling power over the believer, and engenders in him such undying gratitude' (Tasker). This sense of obligation leads to a new life in which self is dethroned and Christ becomes the new focal point (15).

2 Corinthians 5.16,17

The life of the Christian who has received the benefit of the reconciliation wrought by Christ crucified is above all a life of *newness*.

First, for Paul, there came a new estimate placed on the person of the Lord Himself (16). Modern theology has placed a great deal of weight on this verse, and drawn some far-reaching conclusions. For example, it has been suggested that Paul no longer had any interest in the human Jesus of history, but fastened all his attention on, and pinned all his preaching to, the risen, exalted Christ; and in this way a wedge is driven between the Jesus of the Gospels and the

Christ of Pauline faith—an axiom accepted by many preachers today who have come under Bultmann's influence and the new radicals. Obviously we cannot discuss the issue in full, but it is a matter of great importance, and N.T. Christianity as the evangelical sees it stands or falls by the continuity between the Jesus of the Gospels and the exalted Lord. Carl Henry's editing of essays by evangelical writers on this theme and published as *Jesus of Nazareth: Saviour and Lord* (Tyndale–Eerdmans) performs a most useful service in spotlighting the critical nature of Christianity's anchorage in history.

More likely, what Paul meant was that formerly he, as a Pharisee, saw in Jesus only a Messianic pretender 'from a human point of view'; now, as a Christian, he worships Him as the Christ of God and Lord of the universe. This is the difference that the resurrection has made (Rom. 1.3,4; Phil. 2.6–11; 2 Tim. 2.8).

Secondly, there is the newness which conversion to Christ brings (17). Notice Paul's favourite expression for being a Christian; he is a man 'in Christ' (12.2) who enjoys a faith-union with the living Lord and whose whole life is intertwined with that of his Saviour, so that there is no real difference between 'in Christ' and 'Christ in you' (Col. 1.27). 1 Cor. 6.17 is a fine statement of the close inter-relationship. And by this union we are introduced to a new Age, foretold by prophets and yearned for as Israel's hope of Messianic blessedness. So the old order has gone; the new era has dawned, with its attendant blessings. What are they? Sermons in Acts 2 and 3 will give the answer.

Thought: 'A new face has been put upon life by the blessed thing that God did when He offered up His only begotten Son' (J. Gresham Machen).

2 Corinthians 5.18-21

Here are the heart-centre and pulse-beat of the Pauline gospel with its notes of man's estrangement from God by reason of sin, and the accomplishment of God 'when in the death of Christ He put away everything that on His side meant estrangement, so that He might come and preach peace' (Denney) to guilty sinners.

To His servants God entrusts 'the ministry of reconciliation' (18), centred in the reconciling 'word', or message (19). They are His ambassadors (20), calling on men to accept what God in Christ has done for their salvation. The nub of the gospel is in v. 21: 'a divine deed wherein, by God's appointing, our condemnation came upon the sinless Christ, that for us there might be condemnation no more'

(A. M. Hunter). The same writer adds a further elucidation: 'Christ's suffering was "penal" in the sense that He had to realize to the full the divine reaction against sin in the human race in which He was incorporated, and to which He had betrothed Himself for better for worse.'

This is the doctrinal content of Paul's preaching of the cross (1 Cor. 1.18); but the objective work of God in Christ needs a subjective application to sinners; the intermediate link is the ministry of the Word, and what is contained in v. 20 is the hinge.

It is important to grasp the sense of this verse. It is not so much that God calls on us to lay aside our hostility to Him and be at peace; rather the accent falls on objective atonement. He invites us to enter into the peace with Himself that He has made by the sacrifice of His Son. The reconciliation, on His side, is complete, for Christ's work is an accomplished work. The gospel call therefore is 'Receive the reconciliation; believe that God has at tremendous cost, through the death of His sinless Son who took the sinner's place and died under His curse, put away all that on His part stood between you and peace' (Rom. 5.6–11).

> Meditation: 'A mind at perfect peace with God,
> Oh, what a word is this!
> A sinner reconciled through blood,
> This, this indeed, is peace.'

2 Corinthians 6.1,2

Having given a clear statement of reconciliation, Paul now proceeds to offer a practical and positive *application* (1,2). This is a timely reminder to us today, whether as preachers or hearers, that it is not enough to hold correct doctrine, or even to preach it in a detached and objective fashion: the gospel must be applied, i.e. brought home to men and women and so presented that they realize that they have a personal choice to make and a personal responsibility which may not be evaded.

Earlier (5.20) the apostle had spoken of his entreaty, offered as though it were God Himself who was making the appeal. The verses in ch. 6 inform us what the content of this entreaty was: it was that 'you have received the grace of God; do not let it go for nothing' (NEB). In this appeal Paul is conscious of co-operating with God who entrusts the task of evangelism to His servants (see 1 Cor. 3.9). He is concerned lest his Corinthian friends should fail to grasp the full import of salvation by grace alone. How could this possibly happen? Which other congregation gave Paul concern because of this very danger?

The answer to the first question is along the following line: If they imagined that they could make any contribution to their salvation (as the Galatian Christians were fondly supposing, egged on by the Judaizers), then grace loses its distinctive character as a gift offered *gratis* (as Augustine was later to say), and so would be received 'in vain', i.e. to no purpose. For if man can be his own saviour, or can put forward a claim of merit in the hope that on that ground God will be favourably disposed to him, he has no real desperate need of God's grace; and Paul's readers and all who read these Notes must lay to heart James Denney's salutary words: 'The kingdom of heaven is not for the well-meaning; it is for the desperate!' Any other attitude to the gospel's provision smacks of pride and self-sufficiency.

Moreover, this is no speculative issue. There is urgency about it, as Paul clinches his point by a citation from the O.T. We, like the N.T. Church, live in the gospel age of privilege: 'the acceptable time, the day of salvation' is the present hour which will soon pass away (1 Cor. 7.29). What are the termini—death (Heb. 9.27)? The end of the age (Matt. 13.24–50)? The recession of God's saving influence upon a human soul (Heb. 3.12–19; 4.6,7; 12.17)? Remember Bunyan's picture of the man in the iron cage?

2 Corinthians 6.3-10

These verses are a remarkable 'apology' (in the sense of a spirited defence) as he lets us see the nature of his service for Christ and his fellows. No accusing finger may be justly pointed at him, charging him with insincerity or wrong motive (3,4a).

Nine trials are enumerated in three groups; and they are all hardships to which he has been exposed in fidelity to his calling:

(*i*) The first group are trials of a general character ('afflictions, hardships, calamities'—how were these borne?).

(*ii*) Particular sufferings are next described ('stripes' [AV] caused by the whip, imprisonments, tumults, i.e. result of mob violence. Can you recall some incidents in *Acts*?).

(*iii*) Self-imposed duties are then mentioned, as these were required in the service of the gospel ('labours'—NEB has 'overworked' —a modern malaise in the Church, where too few are attempting too much; 'watching' is not a reference to religious vigil, but to sleepless nights; 'fasting' in AV may again be a general expression for 'hunger' [RSV], 'starving' [NEB]).

183

Paul goes on to describe the spirit or disposition in which he faced these bitter experiences (6–8a). His character was often attacked and aspersed unmercifully; he was even branded as a 'deceiver' (8). Yet he insists that all about his character is 'above board' in spite of the inevitable 'dishonour' and 'ill repute' which his opponents raked up as material to discredit him.

We can only guess at what they said, but it must have been something like this: 'This Paul' (as Demetrius, Acts **19**.26, scornfully called him; and Tertullus said even worse things, Acts **24**.5) 'is really a nobody and may be safely ignored (9); he is a foolhardy person who runs unnecessary risks which make him as good as dead already, and so of little value in the eyes and esteem of men (9b). His sufferings are a mark of God's displeasure (9c). He is of melancholy disposition (10), has no influence in the world where money talks and possessions count' (10).

In a series of expressive phrases Paul negatives the scurrilous verdicts of his enemies, and returns an affirmation to every objection levelled at him. There is a place for a rebuttal of false allegation, we learn; but we must be as prepared as Paul was to face the close scrutiny of our motives and the worth of our Christian service.

2 Corinthians 6.11—7.1

From a passionate statement of the apostolic ministry in **6**.3–10 we go on to read of a still more intense expression of Paul's yearning over the Corinthian congregation. Read vs. 11–13 and then **7**.2, and you will see why many scholars hold that the intervening section, **6**.14–**7**.1, forms a separate block, either as a digression in Paul's thought or an interpolation of a fragment of another Pauline letter. The latter suggestion 'can neither be conclusively proved, nor emphatically denied' (Guthrie).

Vs. 11–13 are indeed an impressive revelation of Paul's inner feelings, which are continued in the same vein in 7.2. 'Our mouth is open to you' sounds a trifle old-world for the simple and frank confession 'We've let ourselves go', in speaking without reserve or restraint. This is then matched by 7.2: 'Open your hearts to us', i.e. don't be reserved, but let me know exactly how you feel, because of the mutual trust and regard we have for one another. There must have been a happy bond of understanding formerly existing between Paul and the Corinthians, and he doesn't want to lose it. In fact, this is something of an ideal which we should cherish today; and happy is that Christian fellowship in which mutual respect and trust make

it possible for a free, uninhibited exchange of views and convictions
—and criticisms!

The digression of vs. 14–18 turns on the contrast between Christian
and pagan morality, with analogies drawn from the O.T. Paul
establishes in this way the need that God's people should not
compromise their high ethical standards, but maintain 'the ideal of the
Christian life. There is something to be overcome and put away;
there is something to be wrought out and completed; and there is
a spiritual element or atmosphere—the fear of God—in which alone
these tasks can be accomplished' (Denney).

Notes: V. 15: Belial=the Hebrew form of an Aramaic word=
'worthlessness, good-for-nothing', used in inter-testamental literature for Satan. V. 16: cf. 1 Cor. 3.16. Vs. 16–18 contain six O.T.
references. To RSV add Exod. 4.22 and Jer. 31.9.

Questions for further study and discussion on 2 Corinthians chs. 5–7.1

1. 'The pilgrim Church' (5.1–5) is a vivid N.T. picture (Heb. 11.13;
   1 Pet. 1.1; Jas. 1.1). What influences tend to make us 'settle down'?
   How can we best combat them?
2. There are two ruling considerations in Paul's service for Christ:
   today and 'that day' of His Return (5.6–10). Are they ours? What
   do they imply?
3. Would you agree that 'endurance' and 'forbearance' are the chief
   qualities in 6.4–10? What qualities are most required in contemporary circumstances?
4. What inhibitions (6.12) sometimes destroy true Christian
   fellowship?

2 Corinthians 7.2-8

A renewed impassioned plea for a restoring of amicable relationships between the apostle and his people at Corinth is the subject
of the first verses of our passage. On his part there is no strangeness
or bitterness; and he has every confidence that they will be fully
reconciled to him. 'I have great confidence in you' is a phrase found
elsewhere in Paul's correspondence with the churches, as he appeals
to their best intentions; and he does so with a directness of speech
by using a Greek term (*parrhesia*) normally reserved for the forthright public proclamation of the gospel (e.g. Phil. 1.20; Eph. 6.19,
etc.). His character and conduct have been always for their good,
and now he is rejoicing that they have acted upon his advice; so he is
filled with consolation and joy (4).

The mention of his present jubilation leads Paul to review the past and share further with his readers the record of events which have caused his gladness of spirit. 7.5 then looks back to 2.13 and relates to the historical sequence from Troas to Macedonia where eventually he was joined by Titus. In what state of mind was he then (5)? And how was he relieved (6)?

Titus came with uplifting news that the 'severe letter' (2.4 f.) had done its work (8–12). This, perhaps, was the chief cause of joy. Paul had had second thoughts on the severe tone he had been compelled to adopt in his writing (8). Now, in retrospect, he realizes that the momentary pang of conscience had been worth it, for the sudden, sharp shock of that letter had called the church to repentance and moved it to take action in dissociating itself from the action of the wrongdoer and censuring him (7; cf. 2.6–11).

Titus had been the messenger of this news; and so the weight resting on Paul's spirit was lifted (6). How often has this been true in Christian experience: a kindly word of encouragement, a sympathetic look, an understanding letter, or even a meaningful grip in a handshake—and our spirits have been revived by some Christian's thoughtful concern for us!

2 Corinthians 7.9-16

More reasons follow for Paul's uplift when Titus met him in Macedonia (5,6). Not only had the church taken positive and courageous action, Paul's own estimate of the Corinthians themselves had been vindicated, as vs. 4,14 make clear. He had confessed to Titus that he believed, deep in his heart, that all would be well, and now he has not been put to shame, but rather what he said is 'found to be true' (14).

Titus also rejoiced (13), and his joy infects the apostle. The way in which Paul's delegate (commended in 8.23) had been received, and the prompt obedience the Corinthians had rendered to his words as the apostle's representative, had endeared them to Titus (15); and so both apostle and delegate rejoice together. The crisis at Corinth is over, and Paul is confident that all is well (16).

Two difficulties call for comment. One is a minor point to do with translation. The AV gives (12) what is perhaps the more literal rendering, but we are then faced with the problem that, on that showing, Paul wrote the 'severe letter' not in order to deal with the offender or to recall the Corinthians to obedience, but to elicit their zeal. We may clear up the difficulty if the clause, 'although I wrote unto you' is completed in the main verb of v. 13, '(nevertheless) we have been comforted'. Then the rest of v. 12 is a parenthesis with the sense that the apostle is reassured not only because of the changed attitude of the repentant offender, but also because of the revelation of the Corinthians' zeal for himself before God.

The other matter is the distinction drawn in vs. 9,10 between two kinds of sorrow. The first type, although short-lived and occasioned by the 'severe letter', was effectual in leading to a true repentance which brought no regret (cf. Heb. 12.4–13). The other kind of sorrow is that which takes no account of God's disciplinary chastisement and is more akin to remorse and self-recrimination. Judas' action (Matt. 27.3) may be given as an illustration of a sorrow which produces only despair and death. One effect of the former 'godly grief' is that. as far as the Corinthians were concerned, they did not 'suffer loss' (9). Probably this means that Paul would not have visited the church if it had remained obdurate, and *that* would have been to their detriment.

2 Corinthians 8.1-7

At this point the second major part of the epistle is begun as Paul turns to consider the collection which he was raising in all the Gentile churches for the impoverished Jewish Christians in the mother church at Jerusalem. It is important to see the place of this collection in the life of the apostle's missionary work, for such an enterprise was (*i*) a fulfilment of his promise, made to Peter and James, to remember the poor at Jerusalem (Gal. 2.10); and (*ii*) a testimony and practical evidence to the 'saints' in Palestine of the love of the Gentile churches, expressed in a most realistic way. There was no finer way of demonstrating the unity of both Jewish and Gentile elements in the one Church than this, and at the same time, no more powerful refutation of the Judaizers who tried to insinuate that Paul was out of sympathy with the Jewish Christians and their leaders. See Rom. 15.25–27.

The noble example of the Macedonian churches would be a well-chosen incentive to the Corinthians to 'excel in this gracious work also' (7), which in turn is prompted by the divine grace (1).

The churches in Macedonia, of which Philippi is the best known, were renowned for their 'wealth of liberality' (2)—and it is good that we have independent witness to their generosity in the way in which they supported Paul's ministry as well as the fund (Phil. 1.5; 4.10–19). Nor was such generous giving made lightly, for the churches of Macedonia were, at that time, in the grip of a financial squeeze (2), but this state of their economy did not stint their sacrificial giving (3), even to the point of their imploring Paul to take the money! Does this attitude remind you of an O.T. parallel, when God's people gave *too much* (Exod. **36**.2–7)?

Paul had commissioned Titus (6) to act as his agent for the collection. He had already made some arrangement to collect the money, but with the trouble at Corinth, no doubt the matter was put in abeyance. Now that the air had cleared, and good relations were restored, Titus will be encouraged to complete the matter.

To think over: V. 4 contains the N.T. key-term koinonia, *normally translated 'fellowship'. The word means 'sharing'—but not simply of experiences and the gospel truths, but, in a most down-to-earth way, of material resources with others. Study Acts **2.43–47**; **4.34–37**; **6.1**; Rom. **12.8**; Gal. **6.10**. Have we sufficient social concern for the needy today?*

2 Corinthians 8.8-15

By following the Macedonian believers' splendid example, Paul's readers would prove the authentic nature of their love (8)—an arresting thought which can bring us up sharp. We *say* that we love the Lord and His work; are we prepared to *show* it by what we give?

But an even higher encouragement is invoked in the next verse, tacked on almost as an aside, yet so compelling in the picture it gives. It tells of the pre-existent Lord of glory, who became poor by choosing to accept our earthly life (Luke **9**.58) and at length to give His all (Mark **10**.45) for His people's everlasting good. Let this example inspire the Corinthians, and all Christian folk, especially when they recall that by that self-chosen poverty of the Lord they have entered into an inheritance of spiritual wealth. 'For your sake' and 'you' are emphatic by design. It was *for them* He laid His glory aside and gave Himself to the awful consequences of humiliation. Small wonder, then, that Paul with Phil. **2**.5–11 in mind, will round off the discussion on Christian response in stewardship with **9**.15!

Some principles of Christian giving follow (10–15). Three points should be underlined and taken to heart:

(*i*) A willingness both to promise help and then to give it (11). Here is a prime requisite in Christian responsibility, viz. not only to begin a good work, but also to finish it.

(*ii*) Opportunity, expressed in the phrase 'according to what a man has' (12). This is obviously the determining factor in the matter of the *amount* of our giving, which is not to be measured by the quantity of the gift alone, but by the extent of the sacrifice involved (Mark **12**.43,44).

(*iii*) The quotation from Exod. **16**.18 exposes the law of reciprocity (15). Paul does not intend that the Jerusalem saints should be relieved by causing the Corinthians to be burdened (13). The golden rule is 'equality', i.e. fair shares for all. Let those who have share with those who have not, so that both may be provided for.

Question: Notice how Paul goes to the O.T. for an authoritative ruling or illustration, notably to the events of the exodus and redemption from Egypt (1 Cor. 5.7,8; 10.1–13). He sees the Church as the New Israel, redeemed from bondage and sustained on her pilgrim journey. Where else do you find this thought in the N.T.?

2 Corinthians 8.16-24

As compensation for a life of tireless journeyings (2 Cor. **11**.26) and little opportunity to settle down in a particular place for any length of time (1 Cor. **4**.11), God gave His servant a great army of Christian co-workers and Christian friends who, like the Philippians, became his partners in the work of the gospel (Phil. **1**.5,7). William Barclay has counted sixty persons whom Paul mentions by name in his letters, and twenty names referred to in Luke's *Acts.*

Today's reading tells of one familiar name, Titus (16); but it also makes allusion to two other persons whose names are concealed from us (18,22). This is perhaps a salutary reminder that we know less about the *personalia* of the N.T. than we think we do. After all, there were Christians *before* Paul's arrival on the scene— a fact to which he pays grateful tribute (Rom. **16**.7)—and doubtless fine Christians contemporary with him.

The two colleagues are both attractively described and warmly commended (18,19 for the one; 22,23 for the other). They are mentioned for the reason that they, along with Titus, are to be sent to Corinth as the churches' delegates for the administration of the relief fund. Paul has a particular purpose in view in selecting these three men. What is it (20,21)? And it is important that these brethren should be of sterling character and probity (22). Indeed, what higher accreditation could they have than in v. 23: 'they are delegates of our congregations (presumably in Macedonia); they reflect Christ' (NEB marg.)?

Notes: V. 18: many guesses have been made: Luke's name as a suggested identity goes back to Origen and Jerome. A likely choice is Aristarchus (so Zahn and Windisch) who is called a Macedonian and a companion of Paul (so v. 19) in Acts **19**.29; cf. Acts **20**.4; **27**.2. But perhaps we should seek a more prominent figure. Then Apollos would be an admirable candidate in view of v. 18 (cf. Acts **18**.24–28). V. 22: the second 'brother' is even more obscurely referred to; and no guess as to his identity is profitable.

Thought: Let us thank God for countless 'unnamed saints', particularly ministers of the Word who labour in obscurity.

2 Corinthians 9.1-5

This chapter which still continues the theme of 'the offering for the saints' (1) falls into two parts. Vs. 1–5 appeal to two motives in order to reinforce the spirit of love in the matter of the collection. Can you name them? Then, vs. 6–15 go on further to urge Christian liberality, and Paul quotes the blessings which accompany such a disposition.

V. 1 does, however, present something of a problem. Either, with R. V. G. Tasker, we ignore the chapter division which in any case was artificially added and was never intended in Paul's correspondence, and so read on as though the apostle were continuing his subject; then, the introductory phrase of v. 1 is a literary device used to resume the writer's counsel; or, with Héring and others, we think of ch. **9** as a separate note from Paul, written at an earlier time than ch. **8** and taken by Titus whose (hypothetical) mission as the bearer of ch. **9** is referred to in **8**.6. Most scholars prefer the first and simpler solution.

In the opening section (1–5) the thought is governed by the contrast between the churches of Macedonia and the church at Corinth. Paul's honour is at stake because he has set forth the Corinthian community as a model of readiness to contribute; but their tardiness in completing the matter (caused, doubtless, by the upset within the church) seems to belie this honour Paul has set upon them. So now he calls upon them to fulfil their task, and in so doing, to confirm the confidence he has in them. Above all, he wants the money to be forthcoming freely, and he picks out a number of expressive ways of getting home this truth (2,5)—the last reference is particularly telling and incisive: 'I want it to be forthcoming as a generous gift, not as money wrung out of you' (Moffatt).

Notes: Vs. 2–4: the two ways in which Paul drives home his appeal are given. They are *emulation*, with the Macedonians setting the standard; and *shame*, lest the Corinthians' slackness should in any way reflect adversely upon Paul's confidence in them or their own self-respect.

Thought: Consider Paul as a spiritual director and pastor, armed with that most necessary quality—tact and the right approach to a delicate situation.

2 Corinthians 9.6-15

'To give', says one ancient commentator, 'is not to lose, but to sow seed.' And so it is the natural metaphor (6), drawn from horticulture, which is employed to apply the principle of generosity in giving. The key-phrase lies in v. 7: God loves a cheerful giver. The Greek term, translated 'cheerful', gives us our English 'hilarious'— a new slant on the spirit which should actuate us as we bring our gifts to God or take on some responsibility in stewardship. The type of giving which Paul recommends is opposed to that suggested by the adverbs 'reluctantly' (lit. 'out of sorrow', sorry to part with the money!) and 'under compulsion' (lit. 'because of stern duty or necessity').

True stewardship implies that we give because of love, and not simply because we cannot avoid it—for various social reasons. Love by its very definition cannot help but give, for 'this is love's prerogative, to give, and give, and give'. The highest expression of such love is found in the N.T. teaching on God's grace (8), and the consummate proof and demonstration of that 'love-in-action' is focused in the Gift beyond words of v. 15, the Lord Jesus Himself (Rom. 5.6–11).

Notice the outworking of Christian giving in the intervening verses (9–14): (*i*) it yields a rich harvest of thanksgiving to God (12) who is honoured when His people take their discipleship seriously; (*ii*) the almsgiving of the Corinthians bore spiritual fruit—it convincingly showed the Jerusalem church the true Christian standing of the Gentile brethren (13); (*iii*) this recognition called forth from the Jewish Christians a spirit of intercessory prayer and a longing to be drawn to them because the grace of God so evidently rested on the Gentile groups (14).

Paul sets forth here a picture which so often filled his vision—a united, world-wide Church of Christ, composed of believing Jews and Gentiles, 'all one in Christ Jesus' (Gal. 3.28; Eph. 2.11–18), and discovered in this kinship, which broke down one of the toughest barriers in the ancient world (Col. 3.11), a cogent confession of the reconciling gospel (13). For if the gospel does not unite Christians, how dare we expect that its message of reconciliation will be believed by the world?

1. God often encourages His harassed servants through a human voice (7.6). Can you name other occasions when Paul was so cheered and guided?
2. Which O.T. characters illustrate 'worldly grief' (7.10), e.g. Esau, Saul? How would you try to bring such a person to an experience of 'godly grief'?
3. What has Paul to teach us today in our 'Christian stewardship' campaigns and ventures?
4. On money, consider John Wesley's advice: 'Gain all you can; save all you can; give all you can.' What is the place of the collection in Christian worship?

2 Corinthians 10.1-6

To everyone who reads through *2 Corinthians* as a continuous piece of writing—as distinct from those who take only a small portion at a time—it becomes immediately clear that **10.1** opens a new section altogether. There is a distinct break at this point, which has been explained in a number of ways. The usual 'critical' opinion is that chs. **10–13** form a separate letter and are to be identified with the 'severe letter' of **2.4; 7.8**, sent earlier to Corinth. But it should also be noted that there is a considerable body of scholarly opinion, both conservative and otherwise, that supports the integrity of the last four chapters in the sequence in which they fall in the epistle as we have it.

On the latter view (championed, e.g. by Prof. Tasker), Paul turns now to deal with the still recalcitrant and factious minority in the church. The whole section of four chapters may be called *a statement of his apostolic authority* which was the point at issue between himself and his traducers who were upsetting the Corinthians. The great majority of believers in the church had been won back by his past visit and previous letter, but there was still a pocket of resistance; it is to them that these chapters are addressed.

Vs. 1–6 are an impassioned appeal to the Corinthians themselves. Paul states his own clear motives and sincerity by defending himself against the suspicion that he was acting 'in worldly fashion' (2). He rebuts this charge with a military metaphor (3–5).

He is still a human being, living in the world (3), and encumbered with human infirmities, but he resolutely denies any false methods which he calls 'weapons . . . of the flesh'. His chosen weapons are of divine power, and demolish all arguments and plans which are simply human fantasies (4,5, see NEB). This is a side-glance at the Judaizers who appear to have taught that the 'elements' (see notes on Gal. 4.8 ff.) or the heavenly bodies should be worshipped (as in Col. 2.16–18), as part of their attempt to re-introduce the Jewish legalistic system and impose it on the Corinthian converts. Paul knows of no rightful place for any ceremonial which comes between God and His people; and reliance on 'knowledge' (Gk. *gnosis*) has already (1 Cor. 8) been branded as a mark of false teaching.

2 Corinthians 10.7-11

'Look facts in the face' (7, NEB) is Paul's head-on appeal, and answer to his critics' charge implied in v. 1: 'My critics have said that I am feeble when I'm with you in person.'

The counter-argument is directed against his opponents who claimed a special position as Christ's men (7), and did not hesitate to criticize the apostle on the ground that he was inferior to them (10). *They* made out that they enjoyed a special place in the church as authoritative teachers and possessed a commanding presence. Moreover, they had one great advantage in their favour; they were at Corinth and able to influence the church there at first-hand.

It seems too that they turned their presence at Corinth to their own designs, for implicit in Paul's paragraph is the thought that he was under fire because of his absence. The point on which they had fastened was that he preferred to stay at a safe distance and to conduct his defence by correspondence (9,10). This policy, they were suggesting, is a coward's refuge, for it seemed to imply that Paul was a strong personality when he wrote his letters, but when he appeared on the scene, his personal presence was nowhere near as impressive. Perhaps too his opponents were harking back to his supposed indecisiveness of action (1.17) and failure to come to Corinth as he had promised (2.1). Now (they would explain to the Corinthians and so capitalize on Paul's non-appearance) we know the real reason; he was afraid to come, and can only terrify people by letters written from a comfortable distance (9). How does he reply to this charge (11)?

Notes: V. 7: no allusion to the 'Christ party' of 1 Cor. 1.12 should be read into this mention of 'being Christ's'. V. 10: Paul's letters were (and are) exactly this: cf. 2 Pet. 3.16. The second part of the statement is what Paul stoutly denies, if duplicity and 'double-talk' are insinuated. But we have it on his own confession that he was no eloquent preacher or captivating orator (1 Cor. 2.3,4; 2 Cor. 11.6), like Apollos (Acts **18**.24). His message, however, was charged with a power no human rhetoric can command. To what source does he trace it?

Thought: Think of all the Church owes to Paul's letters. 'The words of St. Paul are not dead words, but are living creatures that have hands and feet to carry away a man' (Luther).

2 Corinthians 10.12-18

The apostle now takes the offensive, and opens his defence by charging his enemies with a false set of values (12). At the same time, he makes it clear that he has not trespassed on the limits which God has set for his missionary service. He is, *par excellence*, the apostle to the Gentiles, a vocation spelled out to him at his conversion and call (Acts **9**.15; **22**.21) and accepted by the pillar-apostles as part of the gentleman's agreement at Jerusalem (Gal. **2**.9). Indeed, the mission to the Gentiles is his peculiar province which God Himself apportioned him (13)—and Corinth falls in that category as a non-Jewish community.

This reference is clearly intended as a side-look at the Jewish Christian proselytizers who were molesting a Gentile church and endeavouring to impose the yoke of Judaism and certain extraneous beliefs upon them. Paul replies that if any preacher is 'out of bounds' at Corinth, it is not he himself, but the Judaizer who had gone beyond the limit assigned to him.

Paul most carefully justifies his integrity here (14), insisting that when he first came to Corinth he did so with clear conscience and intended in no way to 'poach' on the missionary territory of other Christians (15,16; cf. Rom. **15**.20).

At Corinth he may justifiably claim to be the human founder of the church (1 Cor. **3**.6: 'I planted'). What right have the Judaizers to encroach on *his* work (1 Cor. **9**.1; 2 Cor. **3**.2)? Their mandate does not operate at Corinth.

Yet the final arbiter in this matter of evangelistic 'division of labour' and territorial comity is no human committee, nor does an agreement, made between Christians, mean much unless it is the Lord who directs. True—and herein is the relevance for modern missionary service—He expects His servants to honour their arrangements and not to act irresponsibly in defiance of agreements as to mission fields; but it is *His* work and whatever success is given comes from Him to whom alone the credit and glory belong (17,18, quoting Jer. **9**.24).

2 Corinthians 11.1-6

One of the difficulties we face as we read Paul's correspondence with the churches of his day is that of not knowing precisely the background to the turns of phrase he employs. It is true that we have a good picture of the overall scene at Corinth, but some smaller details remain—and perhaps must always remain—obscure to us. The present chapter, along with ch. **12**, is a good illustration.

Obviously, at places Paul is ironical (1,8,11). He finds it necessary, if distasteful, to explain why he is required to justify himself and put his actions in the clear. But it is needful because of the close link that he claims with the church (2), likened here to the Bride of Christ. Which other passages concerning the nuptial dignity of the Church spring to mind?

Because he cares so much for Christ's people, he is most solicitous lest they should be led astray (3). How could this happen?

Some important verses sketch in the character of the men who are later severely reprimanded (13-15). Three descriptions of their work are given in today's portion:

(*i*) Their most dangerous work was that of enticing the believers away from a single-hearted devotion to Christ, and in attempting this (cf. Mark **13.22**) they were doing the devil's work for him, as the serpent did in Eden (3,14: both texts are based on Gen. **3.4,13**). If this seems a staggering thought, let us recall Mark **8.33**!

(*ii*) These men—Paul's antagonists—are heretics, preaching a different gospel which centred in a different Jesus from the Person of the apostolic message (4). It is true that Paul prefaces his statement with an 'if', but 'he is not likely to cherish real fears on the ground of imaginary suppositions' (Strachan); so 'if' (4) really means 'as is the case'. It is difficult to be sure what this warning is intended to refer to. Was it a purely human Jesus whom the false teachers presented, or an heretical picture altogether, like the later gnostics, who turned Him into a sort of demi-god? We cannot tell.

(*iii*) These men claimed the authority of the Jerusalem apostles, surnamed ironically 'extra-special messengers' (Phillips). They bolstered their opposition to Paul by appealing (perhaps on their own initiative) to Peter, James and John against him. But Paul knows of no such rivalry or inferiority (5,6).

2 Corinthians 11.7-11

The 'little foolishness' of v. 1 is now explained. What agitates Paul's mind and caused him a certain reluctance was his self-justification of policy. He had refused to accept maintenance from the churches (7).

The implication of this is that he had been taken to task on this score, with the innuendo that he did not claim his (rightful) due because he knew in his heart that he had no apostolic standing and so no entitlement to it.

But Paul takes pains to go into the matter in some detail, although he has already made his position clear in 1 Cor. **9**. In effect, he is reiterating the same disinterested concern to offer his services freely (7: 'without cost to you'). He does this, not because of any inferiority complex or unwillingness to receive financial help. Indeed, he had already received and gratefully acknowledged help from the Macedonian churches (9), notably the Philippians who had sent regularly a gift (Phil. **4.**15–19) to relieve his need.

The issue at Corinth—as at Thessalonica—turned on the construction which his enemies placed on his receiving money. Both at Corinth and in other places (1 Thess. **2.**9; 2 Thess. **3.**8,9) Paul intentionally refrained from exercising his prerogative—and not always for the same reason. Can you see the difference in this chapter from what he says to the Thessalonians?

A further point emerges in v. 11. Paul's refusal to accept sustenance at Corinth was being used in another way. His enemies were accusing him of being spurious and so honestly refusing the support; his friends were professing to be grieved that he took this line of action, which they interpreted as a sign that he had no regard for them and that they had fallen into disfavour. Hence the heart's cry, 'God knows I do (love you)!'

For further study: Paul claimed two privileges as a servant of Christ: (*i*) the right of maintenance by the churches (1 Cor. **9.**3–14), and (*ii*) the right to refuse this (1 Cor. **9.**12,15; cf. Acts **18.**3; **20.**34). But what does he claim for *others* (Gal. **6.**6; 1 Tim. **5.**17,18; 2 Tim. **2.**6)? And what is the bearing of this on (*a*) lay ministry, and (*b*) full-time pastoral ministry? If a church calls a minister, does it not thereby pledge to him freedom from financial strain?

2 Corinthians 11.12-15

Reverting to the dispute which had called forth this explanation of his attitude to maintenance, Paul hits out at the false teachers who were trouble-makers at Corinth. If they simply attacked him and sought to discredit his work, that would have been one thing; far more serious was their advocacy of a false gospel, by which they placed themselves under the judgement of Gal. **1.**6–9.

They professed to be able to draw upon apostolic authority for their credentials. Paul warmly retorts: ' "Apostles"? They are spurious apostles, false workmen—they are masquerading as "apostles of Christ" ' (13, Moffatt). For in so doing they are emulating their leader, Satan, who himself masquerades as a messenger of God.

The lesson is clear: appearances are deceptive; and we should not be too readily impressed by the superficial attractiveness of teachers who claim to be heaven-sent messengers. The test is more rigorous and vital: what do they teach, and does their character conform to the message they bring—and do both doctrine and manner of life square with God's revelation? Do you recall Jesus' teaching here (Matt. 7.15-23)? And the apostle's no less stringent criteria (2 Tim. 3.10-17)? And the serious admonitions of John (1 John 4.1-5; 2 John 7-11)?

V. 14 raises an interesting point. Gen. 3 tells of the devil's use of the serpent who in turn enticed Eve by a specious promise and a piece of trickery (1 Tim. 2.14), but no mention is made of the devil's transformation into an angel of light. Paul here is evidently drawing upon a Jewish tradition which related how Satan once took the form of 'an angel' and joined the other angels in praising God.

Paul again does not mince his words about those who practise a deceit which Satan has inspired. They are his agents at Corinth, and will share his fate (15; cf. Matt. 25.41,46).

Question: How would you react to the suggestion that Paul is here unduly harsh in the judgement he metes out to the Jewish teachers?

2 Corinthians 11.16-21a

More irony peeps through at v. 16. Possibly, as on previous occasions in his running debate with the Judaizers, the term 'fool' was one which formed the substance of a charge brought against him. And when we remember that he includes the little term 'too' (16), it seems that the pattern of boasting had already been set by the Judaizing teachers themselves; why shouldn't Paul then have his turn?

V. 17 is rightly enclosed in parentheses; it is a qualification which the writer feels he must insert lest his readers should fail to catch the spirit in which he is writing. He is not 'boasting' 'after the Lord', which means here 'as a Christian' (so NEB), but as a man who deliberately puts himself in the place of those whose pretensions he wants to expose; Paul is arguing *ad homines*, to use the technical term.

The Judaizers have been conspicuously successful in the inroads they have made into the Corinthian assembly, and v. 20 is a surprising statement of the way in which they have been accorded hospitality. The Corinthians have shown a singular lack of discernment, almost naïvety, in welcoming the false prophets with their grandiose claims and pretensions; will they (Paul is asking) extend the same attitude to him as he plays the role of a fool?

They have tolerated these men, allowing themselves to be ordered about, robbed of their money (cf. 2.17) and duped by these false teachers—even to the point of being insulted by them in a way which any Jew would regard as a most humiliating experience—a blow on the face. Paul, in this tremendously sarcastic passage, now simply asks for a hearing as he will present *his* case. 'What a pity *we* are not like that—you seem to prefer bullies' is his final thrust (21).

Notes: V. 18: lit. 'since many (of these men) make a proud claim of their flesh', i.e. the marks of circumcision. Paul's only hope lay in the exactly opposite direction (Gal. 6.12–15). V. 20: the Judaizers had brought them into slavery—a verb found elsewhere only at Gal. 2.4. On the contrary, Paul owned another bondage (4.5). The second verb is rendered 'exploits you' by NEB, i.e. squeezes you dry by getting rich at your expense.

2 Corinthians 11.21b-33

Having taken up his assumed position of foolishly boasting, Paul goes on to give a record of his past life of service for Christ's sake and the gospel's.

The true tests of apostleship, he avers, are not in loud claims and unsupported pretensions. The acid test is found in the appellant's record of suffering, service and sympathy with others for their good. So Rom. 15.15–19; 2 Tim. 2.10; 3.10–12.

Paul has a notable record of his trials, and in retailing them, he tells us many things that we should never otherwise have known.

He begins by claiming a pure descent as a true Jew (22). Then he proceeds to show that he is a true 'minister of Christ' (23) by reciting a catalogue of privations and sufferings. Added to the physical strain of a life of hardship (23–27) there was a mental and spiritual liability also to be carried: 'my anxiety for all the churches' (28); and no church gave him more anxiety than Corinth! Finally, he adds the ever-pressing and exacting responsibility of the 'care of souls', watching for the opportunity to help another in distress, entering sympathetically into his deep need, and sharing something of his travail (29).

As a postscript he rounds off with a personal account of the

Damascus episode of Acts **9.25**. Why is this event, in itself, trivial in contrast with the hair-raising experiences and hazards of vs. 23–27, put last? One possible solution is that Paul's objectors had fastened on this incident, distorted it and turned it into an accusation of a cowardly escape from Damascus. More likely, however, is the view adopted by Calvin that Paul singles out this experience for mention because it left upon his mind an ineffaceable impression as the first trial after his conversion that he knew for the sake of his loyalty to Christ.

Notes: V. 22: cf. Phil. **3.5**. V. 23: Clement of Rome (A.D. 96) says that Paul was imprisoned seven times. V. 24: cf. Deut. **25.3**. V. 25: Acts **14.19**; **16.22**. V. 26: 'danger from false brethren'—a particularly distressing experience (2 Tim. **4.10,14–16**). Vs. 32,33: see *Bible Study Book* on Acts **9.24,25**.

Meditation: 'If anyone is made to stumble, does my heart not blaze with indignation?' (29, NEB). Is it compassion for the wayward, or indignation at any who causes another to stumble, that motivates Paul in this exclamation?

Questions for further study and discussion on 2 Corinthians chs. 10 and 11

1. 'The knowledge of God' (**10.5**) is *the* big issue in every age. How is He known—by human discovery (cf. Job **11.7**), or humble submission to His self-revelation (Jer. **9.23,24**; 1 Cor. **2.9–14**)? How can this be explained in today's world?
2. What are the problems which missionary society leaders face in South America, S.E. Asia and Japan because Paul's principles of **10.12–18** have been *either* overlooked *or* forgotten?
3. Héring says of Paul, 'Always to be the first to plant the flag, that is his ideal' (**10.16**). What problems do pioneer missionaries face?
4. Who are present-day counterparts of those described in **11.13–15**?

2 Corinthians 12.1-6

There was one more charge which his accusers at Corinth had to level against his right to be called an apostle; and correspondingly one further need to 'boast' (1) by way of self-justification. Paul's defamers, no doubt, taxed him with a deficient spiritual experience, insinuating that he was lacking in experiences of a 'mystical' nature, 'visions and revelations of the Lord'. By contrast, he was a plain, prosaic man, they would assert.

Paul therefore further unburdens his secret soul and permits himself to reveal his inner heart. The 'man in Christ' (2) is Paul himself, although the whole narrative is written in a roundabout way. Why does he express himself like this?

He relates a datable experience in which he was transported in an ecstasy to the presence of God. There he 'heard' the indescribable words, which are his secret (4), for no human language can be adequate to convey the impression which such an immediacy of the divine presence meant to him. Such an elation of spiritual experience may very well have proved an invaluable and unanswerable debating point, giving evidence that his apostleship carried a credential which none of his rivals could challenge; but strangely Paul goes on straightaway to renounce any confidence which he may have placed in this type of authorization (5,6). He never makes mystical experience a ground of claiming apostolic authority. To his opponents such experiences would have been remarkable accomplishments, giving to their status and teaching an added authority and impressive kudos. Paul places no such value on ecstasy, nor does he imply that he was nearer to God then—when caught up into Paradise—than at other times under normal conditions. This is an important observation, which should set us on our guard against all forms of 'mysticism' and exceptional experiences which are made the basis for some claim in a matter of Christian doctrine or practice. We do not deny that God may visit us or other believers in special ways; but all subjective experience must be tested by fixed objective standards. What are they?

Notes: V. 2: 'The third heaven'=a Jewish expression for the immediate presence of God.

2 Corinthians 12.7-10

If Paul will not boast of his rapturous fellowship with the Eternal, he will speak freely of his 'weaknesses' (5); and the two are closely related.

The 'thorn in the flesh' (7, AV, KJV) is a curious phrase admitting of at least two meanings. It is clear that (*i*) it was inherently evil as Satan's emissary; and (*ii*) it came to him as an affliction. Some definite handicap which restricted Paul's missionary service is evidently in view, so much so that he prayed repeatedly for its removal. The answer which came was a paradoxical one: the thorn remained, but its sting was drawn, and its limiting purpose (so designed by Satan) was turned to good effect. The bane became a blessing; and, as one writer comments, through God's 'No' Paul learned God's 'Yes'.

The positive value of the burden he was compelled still to carry was threefold:

(*i*) By this Satanically-inspired attack (cf. **2.**11), God's purpose was achieved in keeping His servant in a humble dependence on Him. 'Lest I should be exalted above measure' (7, AV, KJV) is perhaps the key-phrase; and Paul learned humility by enduring a crippling weakness which reminded him always of his frailty and finitude.

(*ii*) V. 9 teaches that by this denial he came to experience Christ's presence and power in a new way; in a hard school of discipline and suffering he learned lessons of trust and dependence on God's strength which presumably he could never have known without the restricting presence of some weakness. As only the self-confessed ignorant can really be taught, so only those who know their need find in Christ the supply and fulness of God.

(*iii*) Many scholars, led by Sir William Ramsay, have found in this reference an indication that Paul was a sick man, attacked often by malarial fever; and so have explained his short stay in the lowlands and unhealthy climate of Pamphylia (Acts **13.**13) and his swift journey, beyond the Taurus mountains, to the more bracing regions of Galatia. Gal. **4.**13,14 would confirm this view, and illustrate the truth that illness, instead of closing a door on service for Christ, actually prompted Paul to venture forth and to claim the Galatian towns for the gospel.

What exactly, then, was this 'stake' in the flesh (an O.T. expression, Num. **33.**55)? Apart from malaria, epilepsy or defective eyesight have been suggested, while Tasker interprets the phrase (as NEB marg.) as a thorn '*for* the flesh', i.e. to prick the apostle's pride. No one knows for sure—a providential concealment, so that all who suffer for Christ may find in Paul their companion.

2 Corinthians 12.11-18

Vs. 11–13. Again Paul reminds his readers that all he is writing has a distinct purpose in view—and the mood he is adopting as much as the contents of the letter are both dictated by the immediate situation at Corinth. *They* have compelled him to play the part of a braggadocio, and to parade himself as though he were out of his mind with conceit and self-importance (11). He has bragged without restraint—and all to show that the accusations levelled at him by those who were undermining the Corinthian community are without substance.

These three verses (11–13) really give a resumé of his case against the Judaizers.

(*i*) 'He is nobody', they say; very well, Paul replies, but I am not,

201

on any showing, a bit inferior to the so-called 'super apostles' whose authority his enemies were laying claim to (11).

(*ii*) 'He is a plain, ordinary man, ungifted and undistinguished'; but Paul has a ready answer: I have the signs to accredit me as an apostle—miracles, wonders and deeds of power; and even something more convincing still, the patience to cope with fractious people (12)!

(*iii*) 'He doesn't really care for you Corinthians. He has neglected the church'; and Paul can say that this insult is without foundation, and cannot be substantiated. Yet, ironically, only in one matter is it true—'I did not make myself a burden to *you* by taking your money (cf. **11**.20). Please forgive me for failing to sponge on you!' (13).

Vs. 14–18. Paul turns to consider future relations with the Corinthian church (14), holding out the promise of a third visit. This implies, as we saw earlier, an intermediate visit, referred to in **2.1**. Now, as he contemplates the visit ahead, he makes it clear that what he wants is not money but the wholehearted acceptance by the church of his authority, a submission to Christ and a confidence in himself, with a clearing of the air of all suspicious and mutual recriminations.

But perhaps the Corinthians still believe that he has deceived them with clever tricks (16). This insinuation maintains that Paul was astute enough not to take any money directly from them; but he shared in the proceeds for the collection which they gave to his agents, notably Titus. The answer to this is a reminder of the facts which relate to the mission of Titus and the unnamed brother of v. 18 (the same man as in **8.22**?). This latter person would be a man well known to the Corinthians and who would be able to testify to Titus' honesty—and incidentally to Paul's too. His presence would guarantee the integrity of the other Christians involved in the collection scheme (cf. **8.6**).

To ponder: Paul's earlier teaching (8.21) expressed his own conviction to act always in a way above suspicion, especially in money matters. Can we say the same?

2 Corinthians 12.19-21

Yesterday we took our guide from what Paul writes at **8.21**: 'Our aims are entirely honourable, not only in the Lord's eyes, but also in the eyes of men' (NEB). Both elements in this statement are important, but if it came to a question of priority, Paul makes it clear that so long as his motives are pure in the sight of God, that is the main concern (2 Tim. **2.15**)—and in the end it is the approval of

God which counts, even if men misconstrue and misrepresent (19). After all, the apostle has nothing personally to gain as he seeks, above all, the well-being of the Corinthians.

This thought of the church's growth in grace leads him to express the fear of its sorry state at the time of his writing his earlier letter (2.3,4; 7.8,12). Vs. 20,21, as R. H. Strachan comments, are the fullest description we have of the state of affairs that called for the 'severe letter'. We have here a picture of a Christian congregation which contained men who have retained worldly ambition, and have not been purged from motives of self-seeking and moral laxity. Indeed, the word-pictures conjured up by these verses make us think of professed Christians who practised a sub-Christian morality, as sins of the spirit (20) and sins of the flesh (21) are regrettably joined to form a composite whole. Which group of sins is more heinous in the sight of God?

It is small wonder therefore that Paul has to write so severely to them, castigating such unchristian moods and practices as are listed. A large part of his concern for the 'upbuilding' (19; cf. 13.10) of the church requires the eliminating of these malpractices, and the rooting out of every wrong spirit which prompts them. His great fear (21) is that his stern words will be misunderstood, and his authority further defied, so that again he may be humiliated before them; and in place of a legitimate pride in his converts' growth in holy living he will have only a cause of deep sorrow. One feels that Paul would have had little sympathy with 'situation-ethics', in view of the way he deals with the Corinthians' sins.

Notes: Vs. 20,21: for this list of vices cf. Gal. 5.20 f.; Rom. 1.29 ff. AV, KJV has 'lasciviousness', which is an ugly word for an equally ugly moral symptom (Gk. *aselgeia*=licentiousness, sensuality). Corinth was infamous for such moral loose living, especially due to the cult of Aphrodite practised there. Which other Pauline church is exhorted—in a contrary way—to catch the spirit of the city in which it flourished and witnessed for Christ (Phil. 1.27; 3.20)?

2 Corinthians 13.1-4

The promise and prospect of a third impending visit (12.14) are renewed in v. 1. Paul has already issued a direct and strong warning, as an authoritative spokesman of Christ (3), about the ethical laxity of the members who had sinned. He reiterates that warning (2) and tells them plainly that he will deal firmly with any repeated indiscipline and trifling with Christian moral standards. He is clearly an advocate of *prescriptive* ethics!

There is a veiled threat of some discipline (in 2,3) which he will exercise, not in his own right or name, but simply and solely because he is the genuine messenger of Christ, who seeks, as an overriding consideration, the highest welfare of the church (v. 9).

Yet Paul's threat of a severe reprimand is tempered by some paradoxical thoughts (3b). He is weak in himself and seemingly powerless to remedy the menacing situation at Corinth; but clothed with an authority which derives from his status as Christ's apostle—almost His personal representative—Paul has the ability to cope firmly with this ugly problem and to bring to bear upon it Christ's own power as Head of His people. 'The Church is subject to Christ' (Eph. 5.24), and to the apostle who represents Christ to the congregation. Yet (if we recall 1.24) this authority is exercised in no dictatorial or authoritarian fashion, as though Paul were simply imposing his own personal whims and wishes on the church. It is an authority, exercised in the spirit of the Crucified (4), which will bring the Corinthians to see the folly of their ways. In other words, it is love which subdues—by turning disobedience and hostility into a glad acceptance of God's will and a willing alignment of our selfish ends to His nobler purposes for our lives. It is the message of the cross applied to a difficult and delicate situation, created by a still rebellious minority at Corinth.

Notes: V. 1: Paul is still under fire from a small group of malcontents who maintain their resistance to him. But can they agree on the accusation they bring? asks Paul, reminding them of Deut. **19.**15 (cf. Matt. **18.**16). V. 2: a clear allusion to the second ('painful') visit; see NEB.

Meditation: 'Crucified in weakness.' Consider Bonhoeffer's comment on this phrase: 'God in human form, not, as in other religions, in animal form—the monstrous, chaotic, remote, and terrifying—nor yet in abstract form—the absolute, metaphysical, infinite, etc.— nor yet in the Greek divine-human or autonomous man, but man existing for others, and hence the Crucified.'

2 Corinthians 13.5-10

We are left in no doubt that Paul cherishes the church's highest good—their 'improvement' (9), their 'building up' (10), their stability as a Christian community with the Lord at the centre (5). What are the ways to achieve these exemplary ends?

(*i*) Self-examination (5), which *may* be a painful process of self-analysis, dealing ruthlessly with the present condition and not refusing to face the unpleasant sight of our own sins and failures. But this leads to

(*ii*) Repentance, i.e. a confession of our past evil ways as deserving of God's judgement and a turning from them (12.21). Paul had no room for cheap grace or any easy way back to favour. Penitence—and all that is involved in a forsaking of sinful practices and tempers —is an indispensable condition to restoration and renewed fellowship.

(*iii*) The apostle's prayers are also a force to be reckoned with (7,8), for he carries the burden of the church's good on his pastoral heart, and yearns to see them in right relationship with the Lord and himself.

(*iv*) Threat, which Paul is not afraid to use (10), reminding his readers that he may have to deal severely with the offenders if they do not, in his absence, set matters right. And he will have no compunction in claiming the God-given authority which he has, as apostle to the Gentiles, to ensure the church's highest well-being.

(*v*) Optimism is a final factor, for Paul was irrepressibly hopeful for his churches. He has confidence that as the truth is mighty and it prevails (8) so, once the Corinthians perceive the truth of the appeal he makes, they will accept it and act upon it. So he expects that all will be put right in the end (9).

Notes: V. 5: 'Jesus Christ is *in* you'—better, 'among' you (as in Mark 10.43, which uses the same phrase). It is the Church as a whole which is called to the test, not individuals, though, of course, the Church is made up of individual members. Vs. 5–7: the repeated 'reprobates' (in AV, KJV) means 'those who fail the test' (cf. the same word in 1 Cor. 9.27).

2 Corinthians 13.11-14

Two final sections round off Paul's appeal and contain his 'adieu'; perhaps we should also add, in view of 12.14 and 13.1,2,10, the note of 'au revoir'.

Vs. 11–13 assure the Corinthian believers of his continuing interest, and call for harmony within a divided congregation. This reference to 'agree with one another' and 'live in peace' confirms the view taken earlier that chs. 10–13 are written to a minority group within the church, which still remained unconvinced by Paul's earlier correspondence; hence this final appeal for a coming-together in mutual consent and unity within their ranks.

The divine blessing is promised (11b) to a fellowship whose reconciliation Paul fervently anticipates; the outward token of this is expressed in the practice of the 'holy kiss'. Associated with early Christian worship as a mark of true brotherhood (Rom. **16**.16; 1 Cor. **16**.20; 1 Thess. **5**.26; 1 Pet. **5**.14), this practice persisted into the later liturgical life of the Church, and the references to it at the close of the N.T. epistles give extra support to the belief that these epistles were intended to be read out in public worship services (clearly in 1 Thess. **5**.27; Col. **4**.16 and probably Rev. **1**.3), and the reading was to be followed by the Lord's Supper. Then, the practice of the kiss would be an act of mutual affection and confidence, implying a putting away of all disagreements between the church members, in anticipation of a fresh realization of unity as they shared in a common loaf and cup (so Matt. **5**.23,24; 1 Cor. **10**.16,17). But Acts **20**.37 reminds us that this practice was simply a current demonstration of fraternal greeting.

The closing verse is the familiar apostolic benediction, and a clear statement of N.T. Trinitarianism which is 'economic', i.e. the relationships of the Persons are described in connection with the world of men. Hence the order is that of Christian experience, and 'the grace of the Lord Jesus Christ' stands first. For it is by Him, incarnate, crucified and triumphant, that we come to know the Father's love (John **1**.14–18; Rom. **5**.8–11; Heb. **9**.14) and to rejoice in the fellowship of the Divine Spirit. The last phrase may mean *either* that fellowship which He promotes between believers (Eph. **4**.3) *or* the Christian's fellowship with Him as a Person (John **14**.17). The second view is preferable: see *New Bible Dictionary*, 'Communion'.

To ponder: Read 1 Pet. 1.2, and trace the themes there described in 2 Corinthians.

Questions for further study and discussion on 2 Corinthians chs. 12 and 13

1. Ought we to *seek* an enraptured communion with God (**12**.1–4)? If so, by what means—and to what effect?
2. 'I will most gladly spend and be spent for your souls' (**12**.15). Why did Paul feel like this? List the characteristics of a true pastor. Who is called to this task?
3. Paul's great pastoral ambition was the Church's upbuilding (**12**.19). Trace it in Rom. **14**.19; **15**.2; 1 Cor. **14**.3,5,12,26; 2 Cor. **10**.8; **13**.10; Eph. **4**.12,16,29. What implications can you draw from this?
4. Why must evil in the church be firmly dealt with (ch. **13**)? On whom does the duty fall?

Galatians

INTRODUCTION

'The Epistle to the Galatians is spiritual dynamite, and it is therefore almost impossible to handle it without explosions.' History has confirmed this striking judgement of R. A. Cole, who goes on to illustrate the part this letter played in Luther's spiritual awakening and John Wesley's assurance of faith. There are three questions on which some guidance may be given.

I. *Who were the Galatians?* This is no easy question to answer, because Galatia was a wide area of Asia Minor, embracing the modern country of Turkey.

The term, as used in Acts 16.6; 18.23, refers to the southern part of the territory and included such place-names as Antioch and Iconium, where Paul preached during his first missionary journey and where churches were then formed, according to Acts 14.

Another possibility is that the Galatians inhabited the northern area as inhabitants of the imperial Roman province which was established in 25 B.C. This 'Northern Galatia' view was the general opinion of the early Church fathers, but leaves us in complete ignorance as to who the Galatian Christians were, because *Acts* contains no record of Paul's penetration so far north.

A number of good reasons have persuaded scholars in this century (led notably by Sir William Ramsay) to locate the first readers in Southern Galatia; and it is this view that we have accepted, although the matter is still under debate. One apparently small point, I think, tips the scale. Barnabas is spoken of (at 2.9,13) as though he were well known to these churches; and this fact ties in with the view that 4.13 refers to Paul's South Galatian mission when Barnabas was with him.

II. *When was the letter written?* Here again there is no complete certainty; and how we answer the question of the Galatians' identity in part affects our fixing a date to the letter.

Once a 'South Galatian' destination is entertained, it becomes possible to suggest a dating as soon as possible after the first missionary journey (Acts 14; see the *Bible Study Book* on *Acts*) and *before* the Apostolic Council of A.D. 49 (Acts 15).

The alternative proposal, on the view that the events of Gal. 2 are *the same* as those recorded in Acts **15**, is that the letter must then be dated at a later period of Paul's ministry, and the usually accepted view, on the ground of a community of ideas and a common terminology, is to put *Galatians* in the period of *2 Corinthians*, i.e. between Acts **19.1–20.2**.

The first-mentioned and earlier dating is, however, most attractive, and has the supreme merit of harmonizing the history of *Acts* and the chronological data which Paul supplies. And it is most persuasively argued for by such scholars as F. F. Bruce and, most recently, William Neil.

On this earlier dating, which makes the epistle the earliest Pauline composition in the N.T. canon, the following identifications may be suggested: Ch. **1.2** refers to the churches founded on the first missionary tour (Acts **13.14–14.21**). Paul's second visit to the area is that of Acts **14.21b–23** and the mention of a preaching of the gospel 'at first' (Gal. **4.13**) looks back to the early days of his evangelization.

The visit to Jerusalem, spoken of in **1.18**, is that of Acts **9.26**, and the consultation in **2.1** ff. is the same as his visit in Acts **11.30**. Ch. **2.2** speaks of a private visit (hence there is no explicit allusion in *Acts*), but the mention of a coming to the city in response to a 'revelation' (**2.2**) chimes in with Agabus' prophecy (Acts **11.28**).

On this endeavour to harmonize the cross-references, the letter is dated *c.* A.D. 48 and was probably written from Syrian Antioch, *en route* to the Apostolic Conference of Acts **15**.

III. *Who were the troublers of the Galatians?* The traditional view— and the most satisfactory—is that Paul's opponents were Jewish-Christian emissaries from Jerusalem (**2.12**) who arrived on the scene, insisting that 'by faith alone' was insufficient for full salvation. Paul's gospel, they maintained, was only half the truth, and circumcision—*the* badge of a full Jew's relationship within the covenant and a necessity for all male converts to Judaism from the pagan world— was needful. Acts **15.1** gives a succinct statement of their dogma and so the implication was clearly made, once Paul had moved on, that he had left behind only 'half Christians' who still lacked a full status within God's covenant.

Alongside this doctrinal controversy—and indeed as part of it— they conducted a 'smear' campaign against Paul, alleging that he was no true apostle, was dependent on (and so inferior to) the Twelve. Moreover, he spoke with a double voice over circumcision, not requiring it in Galatia, but permitting it on occasion (Acts **16.3** may have had an earlier precedent) because he wanted some easy converts and so wished to avoid persecution (**1.10**; **5.11**).

Paul's response to these insinuations is warmly written around the twin themes of *faith* and *freedom*. With forthright indignation, because so much is at stake (1.7–9; 2.5; 4.11; 5.4,7), he rebuts all charge of dependence on human authority, presses home the need of justification by grace alone without human merit-seeking or religious ceremonial and through faith as a sinner's simple acceptance of all that God offers in Christ, and sets the law in its right perspective as a preparation for the gospel. Moreover, he declares, not only is the law's régime over as a way to salvation; its prescriptions as obedience to an external code and the mechanical observance of religious institutions (4.10) are powerless to enable a man to gain the victory over sin's dominion. The Holy Spirit's grace and power are needed for this—and He too is God's gracious gift (3.5; 5.18,25).

The sufficiency of Christ and His atoning work; and the dynamic of the Spirit—these are the leading themes of the epistle and give it a timeless relevance as much needed in the twentieth century as in first-century Galatia.

Helps: Smaller commentaries on the epistle are those of R. A. Cole (Tyndale New Testament Commentaries) and W. Neil (Cambridge Bible Commentary), and both are highly to be commended. On a larger scale, H. N. Ridderbos has contributed in the New London–International series. An occasional reference to Bishop H. C. G. Moule recalls his small but most searching little book *The Cross and the Spirit* (Pickering & Inglis).

Galatians 1.1-9

Right at the beginning of his letter, Paul strikes the characteristic note. He is, by God's own appointment, an apostle, charged with an authority which none can dispute. This appointment came to him on the Damascus road as he both encountered and was commissioned by the living Christ (Acts 9.5,15; 22.14; 26.16); hence the reference to God 'who raised Him from the dead'.

The gospel which Paul is charged to proclaim has a uniqueness which means that it can tolerate no rival (6,7), even though such a spurious 'gospel' claimed a special revelation (8,9; cf. 2 Cor. 11.4).

Two matters are important in this section. First, the *content* of Paul's gospel is clearly stated in vs. 3–5. It begins with God's grace—and ends in His glory; and at every intermediate point the initiative rests with Him, and the sole human response required is faith in the accomplished fact of God's redemption in Jesus Christ. 'Peace' may be ours because of what He did on the cross, viz. He freely gave

Himself because of our sins and so made possible a deliverance from the old order ('the present evil age') of sin and death, and an entrance into that new world of fellowship with God in the Church (Col. **1**.13), in which the powers of evil are broken (1 John **3**.8).

Secondly, the background is the false teaching of the Judaizers who sought to impose Jewish ceremonial practices upon the new converts as part of God's requirement for salvation. This 'extra' (Acts **15**.1) is strenuously rejected by Paul, and branded as 'a different gospel, which is not an alternative one' (6,7). He writes urgently because of his amazement that the Galatians have been so easily impressed by these false teachers (6). They have received them with favour; he puts on them a fearful verdict (9), viz. excommunication.

Galatians 1.10-17

V. 10 is the first of the many personal interjections which punctuate this letter. Paul is on the defensive. He has been accused of offering a gospel which is incomplete and unheard-of. Now he repels the attack by taking his stand on the sincerity of his motives. Where else does he do this? (see 2 Cor. **2**.17).

Vs. 11–17 are perhaps the clearest statement of where Paul's gospel came from; and it is set in the framework of his autobiography in miniature. His message is not earth-born, or man-made, or the product of his own fertile imagination (11,12). Who gave it to him? Why, the same Person who changed his life, and set it on a new course.

So Paul re-tells the story of his conversion (literally, a turning round). First, what he was *before* Christ met him, summed up in the phrase 'my former life in Judaism' (13). Keep an eye, as you read, on Phil. **3**.3–16, and 1 Tim. **1**.13–16. That old life was marked by bigotry (13) which made him the Church's enemy number one; singlemindedness to succeed as a Jew by really trying hard (14a), a zeal which made him an excellent pupil in rabbinical school, marked out for promotion (Acts **22**.3).

This re-telling of his pre-Christian ambition is checked by one of Scripture's tremendous 'buts' (15). Paul's life was henceforth re-oriented in a new direction as a result of God's pre-natal choice (15), Christ's appearing to him (notice the RSV here, 'to me', 16), and appointing him to His service (16). Thereafter he was a changed man—a new man in Christ (2 Cor. **5**.17). Saul had died; Paul was alive unto God through Christ (Gal. **2**.20; Rom. **7**.9; **8**.13).

Notes: V. 13: see Acts **8**.3. V. 14: 'traditions of my fathers'—these were the rabbis' additions to the explanations of the Mosaic law, making life so hard for the average Jew, who gave up in despair. Saul accepted the challenge and was determined to excel. V. 15: Israel's prophets traced God's hand in their early preparation (Isa. **49.**1; Jer. **1.**5). V. 16: Paul's mission in life was to preach (Eph. **3.**7–9) and to carry the gospel to the Gentiles (1 Tim. **2.**7).

Thought: Christians are 'men who have been brought from death to life' (Rom. 6.13).

Galatians 1.18-24

Begin today's reading with v. 17. The entire paragraph has one ruling purpose: to show that his ministry did not derive from any human authority; and (as an equally important consideration) that Paul did not act in opposition to the leaders of the Jerusalem churches. His conversion and his mission were, in fact, special cases and supreme instances of God's sovereignty in choosing whom He wills, and appointing men to His service as He pleases.

So the recently-converted Paul didn't ask permission to preach by going to Jerusalem (17) nor, at a later time, did he seek authorization for his ministry from the original apostles (19). Yet his early ministry was becoming widely known and appreciated, gladdening the hearts of Christians who saw in him a magnificent trophy of divine grace (23,24).

There were two exceptions, however. Following on his trip to 'Arabia', a region inhabited by Nabatean Arabs, he came to Jerusalem via Damascus. At the capital he met Peter, from whom he gained certain information; and during these two weeks he doubtless learned much of Jesus' ministry which is reflected in his letters to the churches.

There is no conflict with what he had just written. Paul maintains his independence as to Christ's personal call and authorization as an apostle; but he was ready to receive further enlightenment from those who had known the Lord 'in the days of His flesh' (Heb. **5.**7; Acts **1.**21). And who was better qualified to help him than Peter?

James the Lord's brother was his second contact. Formerly an unbeliever (Mark **3.**21; John **7.**5), James had been convinced by Jesus' risen authority (1 Cor. **15.**7) and, during Peter's incarceration, had assumed leadership in the Jerusalem church (Acts **12.**17; see *Bible Study Book* on this incident).

Notes: The record of the apostle's movements is compressed, and needs to be filled out from *Acts*, especially **9.**19–25 and 2 Cor.

11.32,33. In particular, note the part played by Barnabas (Acts 9.26–30) in vouching for Paul as a genuine believer and gaining for him an introduction to the church leaders.

Meditation: Believers were thrilled at the news of Saul's new-found salvation (24). Who will presume to refuse any whom the Lord welcomes (Rom. 15.7)?

Galatians 2.1-5

Paul continues to recount the story of his dealings with the Jerusalem church. There are some difficult problems of identification posed by v. 1, for the natural question to ask is, which visit to Jerusalem in *Acts* matches the description given here? And, 'after fourteen years' from when?

The most likely solution to what has been called 'one of the most complicated problems of N.T. criticism' is: (*i*) that this paragraph refers to the visit of Acts 11.30; and (*ii*) that Paul is counting from the time of his conversion, which probably occurred in A.D. 33. This would bring us to the date A.D. 46 for the second Jerusalem visit.

But perhaps these are minor matters in comparison with the chief point that Paul is wishing to establish. Two short visits to the Jerusalem apostles could hardly have meant that he was seeking their permission to evangelize; and when the second interview took place, Paul had already gained considerable experience as an evangelist in Syria and Cilicia (1.21) and at Tarsus in particular (Acts 9.30; 11.25).

So far from being at odds with Peter and James—as his enemies had insinuated to the Galatians—Paul received their blessing. He brought with him a test-case in the person of Titus (3). The latter's presence clearly sharpened the issue which lay at the heart of the debate: ought Gentile Christians to be received into the church on equal terms with Jewish Christians, without the imposition of the rite of circumcision?

A careful reading of vs. 3–5 does nothing to clear up an obvious ambiguity: was Titus circumcised, or not? If he was, the wording is at least clear that the surgical operation was not carried out due to 'submission' (5), but rather out of deference to the tender susceptibilities of Jewish Christians in the capital city. Otherwise—and the view that Titus was *not* circumcised is to be preferred—Paul stood firm under pressure, refused to concede the need for Titus' circumcision, and did so on the supremely vital ground that (*i*) advocates of circumcision were insincere men (4), and (*ii*) the truth of the gospel should be maintained at all costs (5). Only on this conclusion can we make sense of his later insistence in **4.8–5.12** that circumcision is an invitation to spiritual ruin.

Galatians 2.6-10

More light on the *entente cordiale* at Jerusalem. Paul received approval from the church leaders there, who endorsed his commission as apostle to the Gentiles—not that he placed much importance upon that approbation; hence his rather ironical allusions to the pillar apostles of v. 9, although he does grant that they (Peter, in particular) were 'men of high reputation' (NEB), on account of their membership of the original apostolic band.

The certificate of approval he received was then all the more reason for the Galatians' refusal to hearken to the specious lies which the Judaizers were putting out. Paul's apostleship bore all the marks of a God-given authority; Peter and the others had accepted it; a division of missionary territory had been agreed to, and Galatia fell within the province of Paul, as one 'entrusted with the gospel to the uncircumcised'; and finally there had been a hand-shake all round, so sealing the agreement (9).

The only insistence which the Jerusalem leaders required was a matter on which Paul had no qualms (10), in fact he welcomed every opportunity to do the very thing which they were keen to press on him—to accept some measure of financial responsibility for the poverty-stricken Jewish believers at Jerusalem. Paul remained faithful to this vow right up to the end: see 1 Cor. **16.1** ff.; 2 Cor. **8–9**; Rom. **15.25** ff.; Acts **24.17**; and saw in this 'collection for the saints' an admirable way of cementing Jewish and Gentile elements in the churches.

Comment: '*There are varieties of service, but the same Lord*' (*1 Cor. 12.5*). *It is a happy Christian who has found his niche and serves the Lord faithfully—and who recognizes the gifts and opportunities which God grants to others.*

Galatians 2.11-13

Three verses comprise our reading, but they will bear close examination. The earlier section closed on what was, to all intent, a happy note of general agreement and mutual acceptance. 'Parity of ministers' is the modern phrase, with the sense that in the Church of God some have a specific vocation (Peter to preach to Jews; Paul to carry the good news to the Gentiles) and no one should refuse recognition of another's God-entrusted work. Unhappily then (as now) this simple solution broke down.

The issue came to a head at Antioch; and we have the sad picture of 'Paul *versus* Peter' (as William Neil sub-titles the section). The change of location, from Jerusalem to Antioch, may well explain the confrontation and the debate which followed, just as Christian co-operation in certain missionary areas (e.g. South India) is often sadly absent in situations where denominational loyalties are historically deep-seated (e.g. in some cathedral cities in England).

The place of Antioch in early Christianity is important. It was 'a bastion of Hellenism in the Syriac lands . . . the inevitable meeting point of the two worlds' (Dix); and in the time of the Maccabees many of the Jews of Jerusalem showed their adoption of Greek ways by becoming honorary citizens of Antioch. It is easy to imagine, then, how a liberal, tolerant spirit prevailed there; and Peter (called here by his Aramaic name Cephas) at first fell in with the practice of sharing a common table with Christian Gentiles.

The arrival of a party of Judaizers, whose 'platform' is succinctly stated in Acts **15.1**, soon changed this happy comity. Peter, motivated by fear and unsure of his convictions, gave up table-fellowship with his fellow-believers on the ground that they were Gentiles and so (from the official rabbinic standpoint) 'unclean' in themselves and 'contaminating' to others. Nor did this action go unnoticed by others (13).

Notes: V. 11: Paul took the initiative in openly rebuking Peter. The reason for this forthright decision will be seen later. V. 12: lit. 'he cut himself off'—a possible pun='he played the Pharisee', who were self-styled 'separated ones', anxious to preserve their ritual purity. Paul may later (**5.12**) revert to this play on words.

Galatians 2.14-17

The reason for Paul's head-on collision with Peter is now given. The charge is clear: it was that his 'conduct did not square with the truth of the gospel' (NEB, cf. v. 5 for the same ruling principle).

The first part of Paul's remonstrance is clear, and it is aimed at showing up the shallowness of Peter's vacillation. He had claimed to accept the equality of *all* believers in Christ—and his presence at table with uncircumcised Christians proved it. Why a sudden *volte-face?* Why give in to pressure from the party whom James had sent (12)? Where were Peter's convictions now?

Paul's answer shades off into a statement of the gospel of justification by faith in Christ (16), defined negatively as 'not by human

214

achievement'. In this context, 'works' implies an acceptance of Jewish circumcision which is made the basis for a proud claim upon God, as Eph. 2.8–10 amplifies. The Pauline argument rules out of court this attitude to God and His law, because (*i*) no one has ever perfectly kept the law, not even the Jews to whom it was given (16); and (*ii*) God has provided a way of acceptance with Himself in Jesus Christ. The only hope therefore is an acceptance with God 'by faith in Christ' (16).

V. 17 presents something of a conundrum, until we remember that its line of argument is directed against a false insinuation (stated emphatically in Rom. 3.8; 6.1 ff.) that Paul's gospel was an invitation to licence and immoral living. The Jewish opponents were saying: Let circumcision be adopted and enforced on Gentile believers as a proof of their break with old pagan ways of life. Paul counters this suggestion. Justification by faith without the law means union with Christ (2.20). *If* this means an antinomian attitude, which throws off all moral restraint, then Christ is the responsible agent. *But* this is a caricature, and a complete perversion of what new life in Christ means (so Rom. 6.6–23, which should be read as Paul's devastatingly logical rebuttal of any attitude which leads to careless living and trifling with the moral demands of the gospel because [it is said] we are 'not under law, but under grace').

Galatians 2.18-21

Notice Paul's courtesy in his polemic against Peter's wavering and insincerity which had the baneful effect of leading others (notably Barnabas, 13) astray. For, clearly, when he says, 'If I build up again those things which I tore down' (18), it is Peter who should be the speaker. The description fits Peter's action like a glove. It was he who had turned round completely, under pressure from the 'false brethren' (4) who represented James' party (12).

Paul places the capstone on his previous argument against these men. With the coming of Christ and the provision of God to meet the desperate human situation created by a sinner's inability to keep the law, the latter's régime as an instrument of salvation is over (19).

A new basis is laid for the divine-human relationship. The old self-life is condemned and put on the cross; yet there is no annulment of personality, no call to asceticism and self-punishment. The dying of self is an invitation to a glorious new possibility: life in union by faith with a living Lord who henceforth controls the believer and lives out His resurrection life in him (20). Only from the vantage-point of this 'dead to self—alive to God' experience can the cross be seen in its true light. Only as sinners cast themselves upon the mercy of God therein as the *sole* ground of their hope, does the cross assume its real importance; for if there is any merit in human achievement, if there is any second way to God or side-door entrance into God's awesome presence, then Christ's death is 'to no purpose' (21). He 'died for nothing' (Phillips).

Notes: Vs. 19,20: the *tenses* of the verbs are important—'I died to the law' is aorist, looking back to the grand renunciation of Paul's Damascus road experience when he gave up all hope of self-justification (so Phil. 3.7). 'I have been crucified' is perfect, denoting a past action which has a continuing effect. 'I live'—a present tense, for life in Christ is a moment-by-moment fellowship.

Meditation: Paul doesn't cast away his personal pronoun, but he inflects it. 'I', in a deep sense, is annulled; but what a glory comes to 'me'.

Questions for further study and discussion on Galatians chs. 1 and 2

1. They 'want to pervert the gospel of Christ' (**1.7**). What are the modern counterparts of this attempt to tamper with God's good news?
2. On what doctrinal and ethical issues today would you not yield (**2.5**)?
3. '*Free from the law, oh, happy condition.*' In what sense is this line (*i*) true, and (*ii*) false?
4. Psa. **143.2** is quoted in **2.16**. Study the place of the law as a 'preparation for the gospel' here and in Rom. **3.19–31**.

Galatians 3.1-5

The discussion now turns from the past episode at Antioch to the present situation in Galatia. Paul's clear-demonstration that (*i*) there is no hope or value in seeking to get right with God by observance of the law, and (*ii*) in any case, God has Himself made full provision in the gospel, has come between, and so prepares for his impassioned appeal (1).

The issue of the Galatians' ready acceptance of a 'different gospel' (**1.6**) is squarely set before them, and they are invited to draw their own conclusion. But Paul can only marvel that they have been so easily swayed. It was as though an evil spell had been put upon them, and they had been mesmerized into a tame acceptance of the Judaizers' false message. If they had been in a 'neutral' position of unconverted Gentiles, it would be hard to understand their ready acceptance of such a message; but in their most privileged case of having already had 'Jesus Christ . . . publicly portrayed as crucified' before their very eyes, Paul can only recoil in horror before their unaccountable and insensible behaviour! He challenges his readers to consider their past Christian experience, and does so along three lines:

First (2–5), how did they become Christians in the beginning? Was it because of an acceptance of what the law *demanded* or what the grace of God *gave* to responsive faith? Paul touches here on the vital point of N.T. Christianity: salvation is ours, not by achieving, but by receiving (John 1.12).

At their conversion, did they become only partial Christians, needing some supplement (3)? This is an obvious tilt at the Judaizers' innuendo that their experience, while good and satisfying up to a point, needed the addition of obedience to the law.

Still pressing his hearers to consider what conversion means, Paul goes on (5): God who has given His Spirit in response to trustful acceptance (so Eph. 1.13,14) and who shows His manifest presence in the Church's life, works at every point as His people believe, irrespective of their being circumcised or not.

So, on every ground, religion based on law cannot explain Christian experience, both at its commencement and during its course.

Question: Where had the Galatian Christians seen the crucified Christ placarded before their eyes? In the preaching of the Word? In the reading of the Passion narratives? In the gospel sacraments?

Galatians 3.6-9

Paul switches to a second line of attack. It is aimed directly at the Galatians, but the real opponents are those Jewish-Christians who have unsettled them (1.7; 5.12) and are therefore the more blameworthy. A cautionary reminder to any who aspire to become Christian teachers, as James' epistle (3.1) recalls!

The Jewish teachers had evidently made much of Abraham in their propaganda methods, offering the plausible argument: You Gentiles wish to inherit the blessings of righteousness which our forefather received; why then do you hesitate to follow his example and get circumcised? Paul meets this argument from Scripture by encountering the Judaizers on their own ground.

Abraham (he retorts) did indeed receive divine approbation, and God put him 'in the right' with Himself. But on what basis? The patriarch was, above all, a man of *faith* (6), and it is those who tread this pathway who find acceptance with God (7). Besides, as Paul elsewhere is at pains to elucidate (Rom. 4.9–12), Abraham was set right with God *before* he practised circumcision, so the Judaizers have given away their case by an appeal to the great founder of O.T. theocracy and the grand exemplar of O.T. piety.

One further Scriptural citation is needed to drive the last nail into the Judaizers' argument, already riddled with massive objections. Scripture itself is appealed to in God's first promise to Abraham (Gen. 12.3; 18.18) who was to be the ancestor, not of the Jews only, but of 'all the nations'. The gospel promise, universal in its scope and trans-national in its embrace, was already given in the call of Abraham, the first Jew and the founder of the race. How, then, could the Judaizers' claim that the Gentiles must become Jews in order to be complete Christians ever be entertained? Paul's logic must have been irresistible (9).

Further study: Consider Abraham in N.T. thought. James Denney once described him as the 'pattern Christian': 'All the New Testament writers who wish to prove anything about true religion say, "Look at Abraham".' Read Rom. 4.1–25; Heb. 6.13–15; 7.1 ff.; 11.8–19; Jas. 2.21, and the saying of the rabbis that 'with ten temptations was Abraham our father tempted, and he stood steadfast in them all'.

Galatians 3.10-14

A third, clinching argument is introduced as a final rebuttal of the claim that the gospel of grace is deficient and needs the 'extra' observance of the law. Again from Scripture, Paul proceeds to show that legalistic religion, so far from being a required extra, lies under the judgement of God Himself. The only exception to this verdict of condemnation would be if a man could be found who perfectly kept the law. But this possibility is excluded by the facts of sinful human nature and society, and endorses the solemn verdict of Deut. 27.26 (quoted in v. 10). A later part of this letter (notably 5.2–4; 6.13) will add in a further consideration, viz. that anyone who embarks on the road to God by law-keeping and ritual observance is on a slippery slope which (like unregenerate human nature) leads only and inevitably downwards and away from God.

So right relationship with God can never be attained by legalism which is virtually self-trust. So much is 'evident' (11) negatively. Positively, the same conclusion is reached from Hab. 2.4 (cited in v. 11) which declares that a man receives acceptance with God and a righteousness 'from God' (Phil. 3.9) on the exercise of faith. Not that faith *per se* saves; rather faith is the human attitude of receptivity which takes what God in His grace holds out. And the end-product is 'life', i.e. communion with God, made possible by our being accepted by Him.

The law, in its original intention by God, served the same end, namely, to lead men to life (12, quoting Lev. **18.**5). The fault—or better, the breakdown—in this plan does not lie with the law (see Rom. **7.**10,12,14,16), but with fallen human nature which is not amenable to the law's discipline and finds, in its perversity, obedience to be impossible. The result is clear: 'the written code kills' (2 Cor. **3.**6), and puts human nature under the curse of a broken law.

Here is a knot which God alone must untie, as Luther remarked. And the divine way of unravelling the tangle is classically set forth in v. 13 (cf. 2 Cor. **5.**21). The curse which rightfully belongs to a guilty race was voluntarily assumed by One who, although He stood outside it and was therefore blameless, chose to identify Himself with our human misery and need—even to the point of God-forsakenness on the cross. He died a sinner's death; He became a sinner by substitution, and so exhausted the claim of a broken law for those who, in faith-union with Him, enter into the blessedness which Abraham enjoyed by anticipation: favour with God (14).

Galatians 3.15-18

V. 14 has brought the apostle's counter-argument to triumphant conclusion. Jesus Christ, by God's appointment, has taken the sinner's place and, having borne his sentence of condemnation, has secured the promise of his acquittal in the new Age, which the early Church knew to have begun already (2 Cor. **5.**17). What was the great sign that the era of Messianic blessedness had arrived? See Acts **2.**16 ff., 33; **3.**25,26; **5.**31,32. The unanimous answer was the work of the Holy Spirit in the Church, so fulfilling Ezek. **36.**26,27.

At this stage Paul faces another objection. To be sure (it was argued by his opponents) God gave Abraham a promise which included his 'offspring' (16), but we know that this refers to the Jewish people exclusively by the historical fact that God some centuries later than Abraham's time made a covenant by law with *them*; so (in a way) the Mosaic law supersedes the Abrahamic promise.

Paul's stout 'No' to this line of discussion resounds in our paragraph. We may pick out his various counter-replies:

(*i*) The allusion to Abraham's 'offspring' turns on the fact that the word is singular in number (in Gen. **12.**7), and so must be taken in a collective sense (16). It is not a conglomeration of people (i.e. the

219

Jews) who are in view, but the Messiah and His people, seen as a single entity (as in 1 Cor. **12**.12). What is being contradicted here is both the Jewish claim to be the true 'sons of Abraham' and the view that Christ has innumerable 'churches' which 'are not on speaking terms and cannot eat together' (Grayston).

(*ii*) The giving of the law at a *later* period does not invalidate the earlier promise made to Abraham (17), no more than a codicil added to a human will destroys the terms of the original testament once it has been ratified and sworn to (15). On a higher plane, God's unconditional pledge to Abraham cannot be disturbed or nullified by any later and temporary economy, i.e. the law. *That* covenant stands and cannot be invalidated; and it is God's promise to Abraham which the Gentile Christians have inherited, thereby by-passing the law's requirements.

(*iii*) V. 18 contains a hint of something Paul will elaborate at greater length in other places. Law and promise are not opposed to each other, but if it is claimed that the law outmodes the promise or that the promise has been cancelled, *then* the element of God's grace in *both* dispensations has been denied and the gospel has been subverted (clearly in Rom. **9**.6).

Meditation: Ponder Heb. 6.13–18. What are the 'two unchangeable things' mentioned there?

Galatians 3.19-22

A discussion in this argument over the promise and the law is bound to raise an obvious query: Why then the law? (19). If, as Paul says, the promise stands and all that God purposed for Abraham and his posterity has been fulfilled in the Church, why was the law given? And if you grant that *God* gave it, did He make a mistake in so doing?

Paul's theological discussion so far has apparently driven him to the point of denying any value to the venerable law; and the Judaizers who are lurking in the shadows are ready to pounce on him for a kill. Now is their chance to discredit him to the Galatians as a false teacher!

But Paul is ready with an answer. Three reasons for the law's importance are supplied, and they are all intended to show that it had a place in the divine scheme, but that now its day is over.

First, the law came to give the definition of legal offence to human wrongdoing (19). The law sets up a landmark between right and wrong in God's eyes: when a person deliberately passes beyond the marker, he trans-gresses, i.e. he is shown to be an offender against

God's law, and so his action takes on the character of *sin*. In Rom. 7.7 ff. Paul takes this description of the law's function a step further. How?

Then, the historical circumstances of the giving of the law to Israel proved its inferiority. Various intermediaries were needed as the law was given from God via Moses via the angels to the people (19b,20: see too Acts 7.38,53; Heb. 2.2, based on Deut. 33.2), whereas the promise to Abraham was directly from God Himself.

Thirdly, the success of the law as an agent of justification is vitiated by human nature which is sinful in itself (Luther's phrase is worth recalling: 'turned in upon itself' and turned away from obedience to God's will) and so impotent. Law *would* be enough to save, if only human beings *could* keep it. But that's precisely the trouble—Rom. 8.2–4; 2 Cor. 3.6–11. No wonder then that 'Scripture (probably Deut. 27.26, mentioned in v. 10) has declared the whole world to be prisoners in subjection to sin' (22, NEB). Law, in these circumstances, is like a railway ticket to a soldier in a prisoner-of-war camp. He *would* use it if he *could.* The help we need must come from outside—from God.

Galatians 3.23-29

One more observation about the law is to be made. Paul had earlier stressed that its function was a provisional one 'till the offspring should come' (19), who is Christ and His reign of grace. The discussion now considers a further task of the old economy. The law played the part of a custodian, keeping men in ward as a stern disciplinarian (23,24). But the custodian's job lasted only until the child reached the age of maturity; then his responsibility was at an end. So 'faith has come'; and we are called to live as mature members of God's family (25).

Mention of God's family leads on to some exceedingly vital statements whose relevance is as important today as in the time of the Galatian situation.

(*i*) *V. 26*: we become God's children in the fullest sense, that is, 'in Christ Jesus', through *faith*. His Fatherhood extends to all in the limited sense that He created all men (Acts 17.28) and sustains the world by His providence and care (Jas. 1.17). But entrance into His family is by adoption and grace; and on its human side by faith in the Son of God (John 1.12) who is the firstborn of many brethren (Rom. 8.29).

(*ii*) *V. 27*. Entrance upon the experience of adoption is by faith made articulate in confession (Rom. 10.9). Hence baptism became for the early Church the rite of initiation into a new society of those who shared a common parentage—with a family likeness (Rom. **8.** 29; 1 Cor. **15.**49; 2 Cor. **3.**18).

(*iii*) *V. 28.* In that new society the inveterate barriers which kept the ancient world apart are overcome. Divisions of race, social position and sex are all transcended in Christ who unites all men and women in His Church into an unbroken fellowship. Application of this teaching to the modern world problems of racial prejudice, social snobbery and sex inequality is too obvious to require further comment.

Questions for further study and discussion on Galatians ch. 3

1. Paul's appeal is to the Scripture (6,8,10,11,13), to spiritual experience (2–5), to logical reasoning (11). Are these the emphases of a valid ministry today?
2. Faith in Christ for salvation was not an expedient on account of the failures of the Law, but His purpose from the beginning. How does Paul demonstrate this?

Galatians 4.1-7

The closing verse of ch. 3 is a summing-up of Paul's earlier discussion. He has shown that God's unconditional promise to Abraham has found its realization in the coming of Christ, the true 'seed of Abraham' (Matt. **1.**1); but Christ is not a solitary person; rather He is an inclusive personality who as 'the corporate Christ' possesses a people who also are the rightful heirs of the promise (3.29).

The next paragraph naturally considers what heirship means. The contrast is a direct one between 'slaves' and 'sons' (**4.**7). The former word aptly describes the restrictions placed on a child in his minority, although it doesn't say anything about the cruelty and finality which the slave-class in the first-century world endured. Rather, Paul fastens on the single point of comparison: both a slave and a child are under the will of another person (4.1–2). In the case of men and women before their conversion, this lordship imposed a very real bondage (3).

Christ came to be a liberator (4). In God's good time He took our nature and shared our human experiences, voluntarily placing Himself in subjection to those alien forces which tyrannized over man in the first-century religious world ('the elemental spirits of the universe', 3). But the effect of this identification, made for *our* good, was a happy one; for by it we are set free and welcomed into God's family (5) as His mature children, no longer in tutelage and in the grip of fear.

Some of the characteristics of the new liberty that Jesus Christ brought are given in vs. 5–7. Adoption as His sons; the witness of the Holy Spirit in our hearts; and our entry upon an inheritance—those are the great benefits secured to us by Christ's coming into the world as its Redeemer.

Notes: V. 3: Paul's term means either first or 'basic moral principles' (Phillips)—a meaning paralleled in Heb. 5.12 and denoting the imperfect apprehension of divine truth before Christ's coming, or 'spiritual forces of the universe', cosmic powers in astrology which were identified with the stars and were thought to rule and enslave men's lives (Col. 2.8,20). V. 9 tips the scales in favour of the latter view, and 'if the Galatians had been pagans before conversion (as v. 8 makes obvious), then such astrological speculation would have formed part of their religious system' (Cole). V. 6: 'Abba'—lit. 'dear father'—a child's name for his parent which Jesus both used and taught His disciples to use (Mark 14.32–39; Luke 11.2–4).

Galatians 4.8-10

The Galatians are now forcefully reminded of their 'state by nature' (8). It was a religious plight characterized partly by fear and partly by ignorance. And the two traits go together. Ignorance of the true God, who is self-revealed in nature and supremely in Christ (Acts 17.22–31; John 17.3), delivers men over to all manner of superstitious dread and uncertainty.

The Graeco-Roman world in which the Galatians lived was filled with forebodings and fears, chiefly on the ground that the stars were believed to be hostile powers and to hold human life in the clutches of determinism and fate—a popular belief that is with us today.

But Paul roundly condemns all such vain illusions: the elemental spirits which they tried to propitiate by various religious ceremonies (10, a reference to astronomical calculations which decided which 'days' were 'good' days for business or travel or marriage, and which 'seasons' were favoured by the gods as likely to produce fertile ground and bountiful harvests) are trounced as 'weak and beggarly'. They are as senseless and ineffectual as modern-day predictions of the horoscope, palmistry, occultism and all the mumbo-jumbo of newspaper fortune-telling.

The decisive break with the old life came at the point of coming to know God (9), or rather (Paul qualifies) becoming recognized by God, which in turn leads us to know Him personally as Father (6) and to receive the seal of the Spirit as His inner witness (cf. Rom. 8.14–16). No longer is there cause for fear; ignorance is dispelled; and the Christian enters upon his inheritance as a person whose life in this world enjoyed the apostolic benediction of 2 Cor. 13.14. We may notice the Trinitarian reference in vs. 4–7. Cf. Heb. 10.29; 1 Pet. 1.2.

Paul can again only stand back in amazement that these Galatian believers should ever *want* to return to a bondage from which they have been so graciously set free!

Thought: 'If I'm not what I ought to be, thank God, I'm not what I used to be.' Read and then ponder the sorry state of those outside of Christ—1 Cor. 12.2; Col. 1.21; Eph. 2.1 ff.; 4.22; 5.8; Tit. 3.3. 'Such were some of you' (1 Cor. 6.11).

Galatians 4.11-16

'I am afraid I have laboured over you in vain'—these words come straight from Paul's pastoral heart as he grieves over his wayward children and is solicitous for their highest welfare (1 Cor. 4.15). We should observe that the earlier part of his discussion was general in character and tone (4.1–7); then, he turned directly to confront his readers with a change to a second person plural (8 ff., *you*); now, he ends up by speaking to them at point-blank range (12).

This impassioned plea recalls his first contact with the Galatian churches (13,14, which look back probably to Acts 14.1 ff.). It was on that occasion that (*i*) they received him so warmly as a divine messenger, surnaming him Hermes, the messenger of the gods among the Greeks (Acts 14.12); and (*ii*) they did not despise him on account of some bodily disfigurement from which he suffered (13,14). If v. 15 is connected with this bodily ailment, it would suggest that Paul was afflicted with some eye complaint or severe head pain (perhaps migraine) which upset his vision. 2 Cor. 12.7–9 is often taken as another description of this 'thorn in the flesh'.

But the enthusiastic welcome the Galatians gave the apostle (15: see NEB) and the way they received him as an inspired messenger of his Lord (14) reflect only the strangeness of their subsequent *volte face*. Paul is anxious over them; he seeks to win them back to the apostolic gospel; but he fears that some plain-speaking will be needed, and so runs the risk of turning them away from himself as their pastor and father-in-God (16). But it is a price that must be paid if the truth of the gospel is to continue (2.5,14).

'They who first break a destructive custom must bear the brunt of their (the people's) indignation'. So wrote Richard Baxter in *The Reformed Pastor*. And Paul knew something of this misunderstanding at Galatia.

Galatians 4.17-25

Vs. 17–20 continue the personal plea by interposing at least one explanatory circumstance. The reason for the Galatians' reversal is found in the trouble-makers who have infiltrated the churches, spread poisonous doctrine for ignoble ends (17), quenched the Galatians 'conquering newborn joy' in Christ (15) and arrested their growth in Christ-likeness (19). No wonder Paul is saddened (11) and bewildered (20)!

Every element in the Judaizers' malevolent work claimed a reply and a counter-measure. It is one thing to deplore false teaching in the church, but simply to express regret and sorrow that things have come to a pretty pass is not enough. Action must be taken— and that commits Christian teachers and leaders to preparing a case for the defence of the faith.

Vs. 21–31 form (along with 5.1) a self-contained section in which Paul exposes the hollowness of much of the false doctrine and insinuations which the Judaizing preachers have brought with them, and most likely meets them on their own ground, viz. that of Scriptural exegesis (21).

Vs. 22–25 invite us to consider the familiar passage of Abraham's household in which two women, Hagar (Gen. **16.**15) and Sarah (Gen. **21.**2), lived uneasily together.

Paul's chief interest is with the two mothers and their children, Ishmael and Isaac (22,23). The plain sense is given in *Genesis*, but Paul finds a deeper meaning by treating the account allegorically (24). Where else does he use this method of interpreting Scripture (cf. 1 Cor. **9.**8–10; **10.**1 ff.)?

The general pattern of identification is clear, although some details are obscure, hence the early variations in the text of v. 25a. Today's portion takes up the one line of the story, viz. that which runs from Abraham by way of Hagar, a slave woman, through Ishmael her son to Sinai, with its law-giving and consequent condemnation of the sinner. From that point it is a short step to the Jerusalem of the (unbelieving) Jews and the Judaizers (24,25). The conclusion that Paul has established is exactly relevant to the situation: there is *bondage* at every level.

Notes: V. 23: cf. Rom. **9.**7–9. Vs. 24,25: the meaning is: These

225

women represent two covenants; one is made at Mount Sinai, and produces only bondage for the offending law-breaker. Now Sinai is a mountain in Arabia (RSV marg., NEB)—whence the Arabs originated, the inveterate enemies of the Jews—and it stands for the present Jerusalem, for she is in slavery with her children, i.e. the slavery of legalism.

Galatians 4.26—5.1

If the line from Ishmael produces only slavery and misery, how different is the ancestral chain which begins with Isaac whose name is associated with the laughter of rejoicing (Gen. **18.**12–15; **21.**1–7). Hence the appropriateness of the citation of Isa. **54.**1 in v. 27.

The reason for such gladness is now explained. From the same patriarch runs also the line of Messianic promise (23), via Sarah and Isaac to 'the Jerusalem above', i.e. the heavenly Zion of Heb. **12.**22; Rev. **3.**12; **21.**2, which is now a present reality in the Church. The primary reference in this term is to the kingdom of God, inaugurated by Christ and proclaimed by the Church, but not to be identified with it. Rather, it is in the Church now that the powers of the Age to come are already being felt (so Heb. **6.**5) and Christians receive an 'antedonation' (Jeremias' expressive word) of what will be the final blessedness of the fully established and perfected Rule of God.

The line which Isaac began is one of liberty, which must not be surrendered (**5.**1), even though there are pressures to yield.

Paul's conclusion has been reached by way of an intermediate stage in which he shows from the mutual disagreement and eventual hostility between Ishmael and Isaac that the two lines are irreconcilable (30). And by the same token those who are 'children of promise' (28,31) must expect to be misunderstood and persecuted by those who cling to Jewish legalism. The hint should be obvious for the first readers to see and act upon: 'The Galatians are to drive away Judaizing suggestions' (Grayston).

The long section (**4.**21–**5.**1) is a piece of sustained typology and its application, demonstrating the tension between freedom and slavery. Such a discussion was needful in view of earlier references to what the Galatians were *before* conversion (**4.**3,8) and what is their present status as free children of God. Nothing can alter that; but liberty can be easily lost (Paul warns) by a false acceptance of the suggestibilities of those who wished to recall them to a state no better than the paganism they had been grateful to leave—the Judaizers' insistence on the law which meant nothing short of a submission to a 'yoke of slavery' (**5.**1; contrast Matt. **11.**28–30; John **8.**36).

Discussion point: 'The New Testament does not say, "You shall know the rules, and by them you shall be bound", but "You shall know the truth, and the truth shall make you free" ' (J. Baillie).

Galatians 5.2-6

The mention of 'circumcision' (2) focuses on the chief issue between Paul and the false brethren of the Jewish-Christian party. Their slogan could be epitomized in the same word, according to Acts 15.1, and the ugly rumour according to Acts 21.21 was later to need some firm handling.

Paul makes the position crystal-clear in language which will remind the reader of an earlier verse (2.21). In fact, in these verses of today's reading much of the preceding argument is summed up. It may be helpful if we can reduce it into a series of statements:

(*i*) If there is any saving value in religious ordinances (e.g. circumcision) apart from the cross of Christ, then Christ's death has been superfluous. But if Christ's atonement is all that the unique value of His person and His worth makes it, then it follows that no 'extra' is required to make our salvation complete.

(*ii*) The moment we introduce the notion of independent ceremonies and give them a status (3), we have shut and bolted the door to God's kingdom *on our side*. For there is no possibility of sinners ever gaining merit in their own strength, and the implication, 'he is bound to keep the whole law', means that he is committed to an impossible standard. Cf. 3.10; 6.13, and see the note on v. 4.

(*iii*) Righteousness, if ever we are to gain an acceptance with the Most High, must come to us as a gift, received by faith which in turn is inspired by the Spirit (1 Cor. 12.3), and never to be striven for (5); and with that gift is the promise of final vindication at God's tribunal.

(*iv*) Outward ceremonials are largely irrelevant—indeed, a positive hindrance if we trust them as saving agencies. What matters most (6b)?

Notes: V. 4: lit. 'you are made impotent', i.e. your relation with Christ is completely severed (so NEB against Phillips). For the verb, see 3.17; 5.11; 1 Cor. 1.28; 2 Tim. 1.10. The second verb is conative: 'you who try to be justified by the law'. They are attempting the impossible, in any case. The third verb has nothing to say on the vexed issue 'once saved, always saved'. It means that salvation by grace is utterly opposed to self-justification, and if a man attempts the latter course he has fallen out of the domain of God's grace (NEB).

Galatians 5.7-12

The quintessence of Pauline Christianity is found in v. 6b: faith made operative by love. 'All that matters in the life of a Christian is to be *in union with Christ Jesus,* committed to Him in loyalty and obedience, in trust and gratitude' (Neil)—and the evidence of such a relationship in faith is the way in which our fellowship with Christ works itself out in love—to God supremely, and to our neighbour no less importantly (Matt. **22.**37–39; Luke **10.**25–37). Which passage in *Romans* is Paul's commentary on the Lord's teaching (Rom. **13.**8–10)?

The argument merges, as before, into a personal appeal, which alternates between rank pessimism (7–9) and unbounded optimism (10). Only on the evangelical principles which have been enunciated can (*i*) Paul's ministry with its incessant conflicts as the Judaizers dog his footsteps, and (*ii*) the meaning of the cross of Christ be understood (11). If these mean anything worth while in the eyes of God and men, the Judaizers are like 'troublers of Israel' (12)—see 1 Kings **18.**17,18—and deserve the fate accorded to the prophets of the false god, Baal (1 Kings **18.**40).

Notes: V. 7: cf. **2.**2; Phil. **2.**16; 1 Cor. **9.**24–26: Heb. **12.**1. The N.T. often uses this metaphor taken from Greek games. V. 8: there was evidently one particular trouble-maker whom Paul had in mind (so in v. 10); and the use of the metaphor of yeast in a lump of dough is a reminder that one man's wrong influence spreads far beyond himself and his own circle, as at Corinth (1 Cor. **5.**6) and in other churches (Tit. **1.**10,11; Heb. **12.**15). V. 11 qualifies v. 6. Circumcision for the Jew was part of his ancestral heritage (Rom. **3.**1,2; 1 Cor. **7.**18–20), but it could be dangerous if a Jew clung to the rite as a hope of securing salvation (Rom. **2.**25–29). But Paul was missionary to the Gentile peoples, and it was a travesty of the grace of God to insist on the rite *for them.* Hence the report that Paul's preaching was anti-circumcision, and hence the virulence of the Jewish attack on him. But the stumbling-block of the cross, i.e. that salvation is offered grace-wise, faith-wise, still had been insisted on (1 Cor. **1.**23). V. 12 'suggests that those who are so fond of surgical operations for religious motives should imitate the eunuch priests of Cybele' (J. N. Sanders) and get themselves castrated. Paul doesn't mince his words.

Question: Is there a modern counterpart to circumcision as a stumbling-block of the cross?

1. 'In bondage' to idolatry (4.8, cf. 1 Cor. 10.20). What forms of idolatry are seen in the world of western culture today and in primitive societies?
2. Consider 4.19. What did Paul's 'travail' involve?
3. 'Faith working through love' (5.6). How may my faith show itself in action?

Galatians 5.13-15

Once again our reading is a short paragraph of three verses. But again, as on previous occasions in our reading of *Galatians*, almost every word gives room for pause, reflection and comment—and application, as we seek to lay up God's Word in our hearts (Psa. 119.11).

Up to this point in his running debate with the impressionable Galatian Christians Paul has been making plain the danger of bad religion. He has done it by a series of contrasts: law *versus* promise; merit *versus* grace; and slavery *versus* liberty. But now it is time for him to say more exactly what Christian liberty really is; for it may be that, as in other places of early Christianity, there was a tendency to misunderstand and misapply the slogan 'saved by grace alone'— see Rom. 6.1 ff.

Christian freedom is not licence, and does not give us free rein to please ourselves (13). There is a salutary safeguard to prevent such a degeneration. What is it? V. 13b supplies the all-important directive, and the writer picks up the same word as he has used in earlier discussion and gives it a new twist: 'Be slaves'—not to any legalistic code or supposedly meritorious ceremonial, like circumcision—'to one another in the love you show in your mutual relationships'. Through love be in *bondage* to others.

In this way the spirit of the law is honoured (14) as Christians put other people (especially those who have a claim upon us) first in their consideration and care. Evidently there was need to underline this teaching in a Christian assembly where all was far from harmony and brotherly love (15).

Notes: V. 13: 'occasion' (AV, KJV), 'opportunity' (RSV), is literally 'a base of operations', used in the military sense. The 'flesh' in this verse means the self-life, still present in the believer and which struggles to re-assert itself—or, to continue the military metaphor, provides a launching-pad from which sin (as a missile) may be let loose, to the hurt of others. V. 14 quotes Lev. 19.18 (cf. Rom.

13.8–10) and poses the deceptively simple questions, Who is my neighbour? What does it mean to 'love'? The answer to the first question is supplied in Luke 10.25–37: my neighbour is anyone in need, who lies across my path, or whom my helping hand can reach. A good substitute for 'love'—a modern term with a range of meanings whose poles are as distant from each other as 'heaven' and 'Hollywood'—would be 'care'. 'You shall *care for* your neighbour as *you care for* yourself.'

Galatians 5.16-21

The self-life, called in v. 13 'the flesh', must not be allowed to dominate, but isn't this a counsel of despair? How can we resist the pull of the old nature, which often feels as irresistible and relentless as the force of gravity?

Paul faces the issue squarely and offers no easy solution. Notice (*i*) he does not deny the seductive power of the fallen nature in the Christian, nor does he teach that conversion automatically transfers us to some spiritual *nirvana* beyond the reach of temptation. The flesh is real, and provokes a very bitter conflict within the Christian's life (17).

Then (*ii*) the 'opposite number' in the conflict with the flesh is the Holy Spirit whose grace and power are the believer's resources (16,18). Drawing upon those resources will give us strength to counteract the downward pull of the flesh; submission to the leadership of the Spirit will provide reserves of spiritual energy by which the flesh can be curbed. Paul has a side-glance here (18) at the Judaizers' claim that the only way to moral victory was to put oneself under the restraint of the law—a prescription which Paul had tried for himself and found illusory and ineffective (Rom. 7.13–23). The only hope offered to the 'wretched man' (Rom. 7.24) who cries out for deliverance is that which bids him call in the resources of the Holy Spirit.

The 'works of the flesh' present a fearsome catalogue of vices, only too common in human society, whether ancient or modern. They may be sub-divided: (*i*) inordinate human appetites given unbridled sway (19); (*ii*) perverted religion (20, idolatry, sorcery); (*iii*) antisocial behaviour (20); followed by (*iv*) some personal lapses (21, envy, drunkenness, orgies and the like). They all spring from our lower nature which expresses itself sometimes in blatant crime (in 21, some MSS add 'murder'), sometimes in a perversion and abuse of a God-given instinct (sex misused in pornography, indecency and immorality; thirst getting out of hand in drunken bouts); and often in some deadly forms which we treat only too lightly (quarrels, fits of rage, selfishness).

Galatians 5.22-26

'The fruits of the Spirit are the virtues of Jesus.' This is an appropriate comment on the verses which describe the quality of Christian life which is produced by a practised 'walking in the Spirit'.

The metaphor of 'walking' (in 16,25) is drawn from the O.T. (e.g. Gen. 17.1; Psa. 1) and comes to mean the practical application in daily conduct of a person's communion with God. Can you think of the O.T. 'hero of faith' whose life-story is summed up in such a sentence? See Gen. 5.24.

It is not surprising therefore that victory in the moral battle is shown by the growth of the Christlike qualities named in vs. 22,23. The Holy Spirit's activity produces such a harvest of ethical characteristics which cover a person's threefold relationship. In his relationship with God there are the members of the first group (love, joy, peace; cf. 2 Cor. 13.14). In manward relations, the second triad of patience, kindness and goodness marks out the man whose public life before his fellows is a commendation of what he professes to be. His personal life is a happy blend of fidelity, gentleness and self-control. Here is a threefold scope of human activity which may well set the standard for our lives—and one which is attained by those whose conduct is shaped by the Spirit (25).

V. 24 is a solemn reminder, however, that this ethical harvest may only be expected if the ground is well ploughed over, weeds removed and the soil cleared of impurities. Hence the call to a process of self-denial, which puts the lower nature on the cross with Christ (2.20) and leaves no room for the gratifying of unseemly desires, aspirations and ambitions which would usurp the kingly control of Jesus in our lives. And what is true in our personal life (24) will soon have its effect on our social relationships (26). 'No man liveth unto himself' is a fundamental principle which works both helpfully and harmfully.

Galatians 6.1-6

The life of the Christian is never to be in splendid isolation. 'The New Testament knows nothing of solitary religion' was advice given to John Wesley, and well heeded by him. Our verses today have some pertinent comment and criticism to offer as they pose a number of searching questions.

231

(*i*) How do we deal with a lapsed brother? Leaders in a church clearly have a responsibility in discipline not to be shirked; but let them deal with the offender gently and without censoriousness (cf. 1 Cor. **10.**12, which also picks up the Lord's teaching of Matt. **7.**1–5). Above all, the responsible Christian should seek to understand a delicate situation with sympathy and personal interest (2).

(*ii*) How do Christian leaders exercise authority, without being open to the charge of an overbearing manner? When does authority become authoritarianism? The safeguards are found in vs. 3–5. V. 4 is a call to self-examination, but no suggestion of pride in one's own achievement is implied. The spirit is rather that of 1 Cor. **10.**24; Rom. **14.**13 f.

(*iii*) Are we shouldering responsibility which God intended us to assume (5)? Note that the 'load' of this verse represents a different Greek word from that in v. 2, and here is probably a military expression. 'Every man must "shoulder his own pack" ' (Phillips).

(*iv*) Are those fully engaged in the Lord's service being adequately supported by Christians who derive benefit from their ministry (6)? The first application is that of the duty which a catechumen has to repay his teacher; but the relevance to ministerial stipends today is obvious. The circumstances which made it unwise for Paul to accept money from certain churches and to prefer to maintain himself (Acts **18.**1–3) must always be seen *in context*. At Thessalonica (1 Thess. **2.**8–9) and at Corinth (1 Cor. **9.**12–18) he intentionally forwent his claim to maintenance because of the need to refute the charge that his motives were insincere; but he had no scruple about receiving gifts from Philippi (Phil. **4.**10–19) and endorsed the principle of Luke **10.**7 (cf. 1 Cor. **9.**14; 1 Tim. **5.**18) for the elders appointed in the Galatian congregations (Acts **14.**23).

Galatians 6.7-10

The mention of 'the harvest of the Spirit' (**5.**22) prompts Paul to continue this thought, prefaced by a stern warning that the order and constancy which we observe in God's world of nature, with its law of seedtime and harvest (Gen. **8.**22), are also part of God's moral world. Jesus said the same, you will remember (Matt. **7.**16–20). And earlier still, Hosea had warned the people of his day that sowing and reaping belong together (Hos. **8.**7).

Another pair of contrasts which we have met in a previous passage recur too: the flesh and the Spirit (**5.**13–26). The background here is probably the rabbis' teaching that human behaviour is governed by two impulses, one good, the other evil. These were found in a man's inner life, setting up a conflict (as in **5.**17). Paul, the ex-rabbi, had discovered, however, the secret of victory in Christ (2 Cor. **2.**14; Rom. **5.**17; **7.**25; **8.**2–13) and the confidence which stems from that moral conquest, viz. that to sow in the field of the Spirit is to be assured of a harvest of eternal life (NEB). The thought of Rom. **8.**12,13 is closely paralleled.

'Sowing' stands not only for moral endeavour and pre-occupation with those things which please God (Rom. **8.**6); it is equally a picture-word for Christian service (as in 2 Cor. **9.**6–10) in which the great malaise is a tendency to grow fainthearted. Paul himself perhaps knew that discouragement at first-hand (2 Cor. **4.**1,16— how does he fight off this despondency?). Having known something of the temptation and the way through, he writes an encouragement to the Galatian workers (9).

There are many calls on our interest, energy and pockets. 'Let us do good' (10) is an incentive which no Christian will fail to respond to, once a worthy cause is presented to him. But there has to be a priority. Who has first call on our stewardship of time and money?

Notes: V. 7: the strong admonition, 'Make no mistake about this: God is not to be fooled' (NEB), looks back to the proposal that the Christian may treat the high standards of morality with impunity (**5.**21). Possibly some Galatians had gone to the opposite extreme, and argued that as they were free from the (Jewish) law, they were free to cast off *all* moral restraint.

Galatians 6.11-18

The apostle now takes over from his amanuensis, a professional scribe whom he employed to write what he dictated, according to ancient letter-writing procedures (see Rom. **16.**22 for the name of one such writer). Sometimes Paul added only a final greeting and his signature (2 Thess. **3.**17), but to these readers at Galatia what William Neil terms 'a final salvo' is fired. The apostle wishes his errant church to be in no doubt as to the issues involved in their danger of 'deserting Him who called you . . . and turning to a different gospel' (**1.**6).

These closing verses then are by way of summary and reminder. The futility of any blind trust in religious ceremonial is reiterated; especially the Judaizers' insistence upon circumcision (12,13) comes in for a final condemnation. There is a subtle play on words here, chiefly on the term 'flesh'. The Jewish-Christians were harping on circumcision, i.e. a surgical operation to remove a piece of human flesh (12). Paul retorts, by inference, that this is something of deeper significance; it is a confidence in one's own religious achievements which are to be renounced once and for all, at the foot of the cross (14; cf. Phil. 3.2–11 for a full statement of this theme).

In any case, two things are clear: (*i*) the important item in the spiritual life is not an outward form or display, but a new spirit which derives from sharing in the risen life of Christ (15; 1 Cor. 7.19; 2 Cor. 5.17; 1 Cor. 6.17). And (*ii*) the only bodily marks which interest Paul are those scars obtained in suffering for the gospel's sake (17). Memories of his treatment at Lystra (Acts 14.19) would no doubt be in his mind; indeed, they were as permanently impressed on him as the scars themselves, as his witness in later life recalled (2 Tim. 3.11).

Notes: V. 17: this verse has given rise to the notion of the *stigmata* (brands), thereby turning Paul into a mystic. But the plain sense is against this. The 'marks of Jesus' are signs of his courageous service for Christ and the gospel (1 Cor. 15.30–32; 2 Cor. 4.8–12; 11.23–30). A slave was usually tattooed as a sign of his belonging to his master; and Paul is a slave (Rom. 1.1, etc.) of Christ—whose service is perfect freedom.

Meditation: 'My glory all the cross' (14). But are we prepared for the cost of this sacrifice, with its death to self (2.20) and to the world?

Questions for further study and discussion on Galatians chs. 5.13–6.18

1. How can we avoid this freedom (5.13) becoming an excuse merely to please ourselves?
2. 'A true Christian is one who has not only peace of conscience, but war within' (J. C. Ryle). Do you find it so? And what is the secret of victory?
3. What does Paul mean by 'well-doing' (6.9)? What relation has this to 'reaping'?

Ephesians

In spite of the traditional heading, relatively little is known about the recipients of the letter designated 'Ephesians'. The letter was delivered to its destination by Tychicus, who in Eph. 6.21 and Col. 4.7 is named as Paul's emissary. Presumably the Colossian epistle was delivered at the same time since in both letters Paul states in similar language that Tychicus will inform the readers concerning his current situation. Paul has had no personal contact with the community addressed in *Ephesians*; the tone of the letter is impersonal. He knows of his readers' faith in the Lord Jesus and of their love toward other Christians (1.15; 4.21). He assumes they have heard of the special work God has given him to do for their sake (3.2). The community appears to have been exclusively Gentile (cf. 2.11 f.; 3.1; 4.17 ff., 25 ff.).

The following reconstruction of the life situation which gave rise to this letter is based on the total evidence of *Ephesians* and *Colossians*. While Paul was in prison in Rome the need became acute for new materials with which to instruct converts in Asia Minor. It is likely that the apostle had already gathered portions of the tradition in anticipation of this need. An impetus to bring together the material was provided by the arrival of Epaphras, who informed Paul of the threat to Christian truth in the Lycus Valley. In response, the apostle penned *Colossians*. At the same time the epistle that we know as *Ephesians* may have been sent to Laodicea and an extra copy left at Ephesus, the metropolis of Asia Minor. This would explain a reference to the Laodicean letter in Col. 4.16. If this assumption is correct, *Ephesians* (like *Colossians*) is a letter addressed to the Lycus Valley region. Its specific destination is Laodicea and its purpose is to foster Christian maturity. The apostle intends that '*Ephesians*' will be read at Colossae as well; the copy left at Ephesus provides assurance that Paul's directive will reach the greater part of the province. The letter was written in response to the newer religious philosophies sweeping the area; the mystery religions and incipient gnosticism, which threatened to obscure the nature of salvation; the significance of the Church, and the cosmic dimensions of the sovereign plan of God.

*Ephesians 1.1,2   The Apostle to the Gentiles

Paul introduces himself as an apostle (1). The background to the term is provided by the Jewish and Christian concept of the ambassador who speaks and acts with the authority of the one who commissioned him. Paul was commissioned by God to represent Jesus Christ. Like those who were apostles before him, he has seen the risen Lord (Gal. **1**.16; I Cor. **9**.1; **15**.8) and has received a specific appointment to go to the Gentiles (Gal. **1**.15 f.; **2**.7–9). As the 'apostle to the Gentiles' having Christ's authority, he does not hesitate to instruct people with whom he has had no previous contact.

It is generally agreed by textual critics that the words 'in Ephesus' in the initial greeting are not original. They were added to later manuscripts by one who failed to see that this letter could not have been addressed to the community which Paul founded in the metropolis of Asia (cf. **1**.15; **3**.2; **4**.21). The absence of a specific place-name gives to the letter a universal quality. What Paul has to say has relevance to all the people of God who show loyalty to Jesus Christ. The apostle prays that they may experience the unfailing grace and dynamic peace of God which is able to sustain them in the turmoil and tension of life. Already in the salutation of the letter Paul points to the resources which encourage growth toward maturity in the individual and in the church.

*Ephesians 1.3-10   God's Glorious Purpose

Ephesians may be regarded as a word of wisdom to the mature (cf. **4**.12–14; I Cor. **2**.6–7). More extensively than any other N.T. letter it has been given the form of prayer. The entire first half of the epistle (**1**.3—**3**.21) and much of the plea for worthy conduct in the second half is presented in the language of prayer. Within a framework of prayer (cf. **1**.3,16; **3**.14,21; **5**.20; **6**.18,23 f.) Christ's achievement on behalf of the Church is confessed before God and men. When *Ephesians* is recognized as a word of wisdom couched in the form of prayer, its language and style are intelligible. The pastoral concern, the formal liturgical style and the involved sequence of thoughts which are such marked characteristics of this letter find their exact parallel in other letters where Paul gives himself to prayer of adoration, confession and supplication (e.g. Rom. **8**.31–39; **11**.33–36; **16**.25–27; Phil. **1**.6–11).

These qualities are evident throughout **1**.3–14, which Paul wrote as a single sentence of carefully balanced clauses. This expanded benediction presents a solemn review of the redemptive activity of the Triune God. It is possible to read this paragraph as a hymn in three stanzas of uneven length, each stanza being rounded off with a reference to the praise of God's glorious grace (vs. 3–6,7–12,13–14). The theme of the 'hymn' is God's eternal purpose in history (cf. v. 9). The vertical or ultimate phase of God's plan is presented in vs. 9 f.; the horizontal or historical phase is summarized in vs. 3–8 (cf. 3.4–6); the resultant phase, the creation of a fellowship of love, is expressed in vs. 11–14 (cf. 3.9–11).

When Paul thinks about what God has done for the Church, he breaks forth in joyful praise. Before God spoke the creative word which brought the world into being, He chose us to be a holy and blameless people (3 f.). He determined that we should be His sons and that the Church should be like a family (6). He made provision for the removal of our guilt and the enrichment of our lives through abundant grace (7 f.). That provision is conceived historically by Paul: God sent Jesus Christ into the world to overcome the distance between Himself and the world through His death on the cross (7). It is also conceived cosmically: the ultimate secret of God's will is that His Son should be the Head of all things, the earthly and the heavenly (9 f.). Christ is seen in relationship to God's total purpose for the universe: He reintegrates all elements of the universe to God. There is in Paul's statement a broad possibility of interpretation, but the immediate context indicates that what is primarily in view is the overcoming of the alienation between men and God.

Thought: When you consider that when God purposed to fashion the universe you were so important to Him that He determined to send His Son into the world to die for you, the only appropriate response is prayer of adoration and confession.

Ephesians 1.11–14 The Seal of God

One of the distinctive characteristics of *Ephesians* is the trinitarian structure of its thought. More emphatically than elsewhere in his letters Paul is conscious of the participation of the Persons of the Godhead in the work of redemption. In the initial benediction, the determination to reconcile men to Himself is the function of the Father (3–6); the accomplishment of redemption is the achievement of the Son (7–12); the application of redemption is the work of the Spirit (13 f.). Although the order in which Paul refers to the three Persons differs, his emphasis falls repeatedly on their mutual co-operation in reconciling men to God (cf. 2.4–10,13–18; 3.1–6; 3.14–19; 4.1–6; 4.30—5.2; 5.15–20; 6.10–18).

Vs. 11–14 continue the remarkable sentence in which Paul reviews the redemptive activity of the Triune God (1.3–14). His careful formulation is appropriate to a baptismal context. Until the end of v. 12 Paul consistently uses the first person plural ('we'/'us'); with v. 13 he abruptly introduces the second person plural ('in Him you also'). This change is intelligible when the entire passage is seen as a fragment of a baptismal charge to Gentile Christians. 'We' who first hoped in the Messiah (12) are Jewish Christians like Paul who have come to faith; 'you also' (13) refers to Gentiles who have responded to the word of preaching. Thus he introduces a key theme of *Ephesians*; that God has reconciled both Jews and Gentiles through the cross of Christ (cf. 2.1–7,11–22; 3.6).

Paul speaks of the Holy Spirit as the 'pledge' or 'guarantee' of our heritage (14; 2 Cor. 1.22; 5.5). The term is familiar from the old Greek manuscripts where it denotes the first portion of a payment which is finally to be made in full. The Spirit's presence with the believer thus constitutes God's promise that He will perfect His work in him. The Spirit sets a seal upon the true child of God which assures him that he belongs to God and that he is entitled to personal fellowship with Him (cf. 2 Tim. 2.19). Even now he enjoys a rich foretaste of what he will experience fully in God's presence when the Holy Spirit has completed His work the Christian.

Thought: Since in baptism you acknowledged a Lord, there remains no pretext for disobedience.

Ephesians 1.15-23 The Headship of Christ

Paul was dependent upon others for his knowledge of Christianity in the Lycus Valley. It is natural to think of the report that Epaphras had given to him (see on Col. 1.8). The fidelity of his readers to Jesus Christ and to one another moves Paul to pray that they may have the spiritual insight to perceive the truth that is hidden in God and which can be unlocked only in the experience of life and fellowship with Him. One by one the apostle introduces the themes he will develop in the first half of the letter: the hope inspired by God's call (cf. 2.1–10,12–18), the glory which belongs to the divine inheritance (cf. 2.19–22; 3.1–6), and the surpassing magnitude of God's power (cf. 3.7–21). Paul recognized that all that the Gentiles possess in Christ depends upon the initiative of God.

The extent of the power which God has made available to men is the resurrection of Christ and His exaltation to a place of sovereign authority over every dignity reverenced by man. The sphere in which Christ's lordship over cosmic and earthly powers is made visible is the Church. Already in this first reference to the Church it is evident that Paul is not speaking of local churches but of the universal Church seen in an idealized perspective (cf. 3.10; 4.16). While in *Colossians* Paul develops the concept of the headship of Christ, in

Ephesians the Church as the full expression of Jesus Christ is more prominently in view. In his letters the apostle uses the metaphor of the body on three different levels: (*i*) the Church is like any human body (Rom. **12.**3–8; I Cor. **12.**12–27); (*ii*) the Church is like the body of Christ offered up for us upon the cross (I Cor. **10.**16 f.; **11.**23–27); (*iii*) the Church is like the body of Christ risen (Eph. **1.**19–23). At each level a metaphorical use of the statement, 'the Church is like a body', is sustained, but the metaphor does not mean the same thing in every case. Only in *Ephesians* does Paul reflect upon the Church as the body of Christ risen and exalted over all things (20–23). The exaltation of Christ is described in the highest terms (cf. **1.**4 f., 9 f., 20–23; **3.**11 ff.). Christians are assured that God has given to the Church a Sovereign who is also Head over all things. The Church has authority to confront the powers which oppose God because her Head is the Lord of all.

Ephesians 2.1-7   The Rich Mercy of God

Between *Ephesians* and *Colossians* there are closer contacts in content, language and style than exist between any other N.T. letters. About 70% of *Colossians* is shared by *Ephesians*, while approximately 50% of *Ephesians* finds its parallel in *Colossians*. It is a striking fact that when the content of *Ephesians* which is common to *Colossians* is removed, there remain units of tradition which are complete in themselves and distinctive:

1.3–14—an expanded benediction consisting of a single sentence.
2.1–10—a confessional summary of the new life, consisting of a single sentence.
3.14–21—a prayer that the readers may understand the mystery of Christ.
4.1–16—an elaborate exhortation to unity supported by confession and the interpretation of Scripture.
5.8–14—an exhortation to walk in the light, concluding with a fragment of a hymn.
5.23–32—a theological expansion of one section of the household code, developing the mystical marriage of Christ.
6.10–17—an expanded exhortation to the armour of God.

These seven units show careful preparation. So well have they been integrated with the remaining portions of the letter that they are recognizable as independent units of tradition only because we possess *Colossians*. It has been suggested that Paul had prepared these units for instructing converts either prior to, or following, baptism. In their present context they recall the readers to the

239

instruction they received and the liturgy in which they participated in order to encourage growth toward maturity.

The fruitfulness of this suggestion is evident in the second unit, 2.1–10. If this section is understood as a summary of the elementary facts of conversion which was taught in connection with baptism, its meaning can be unfolded in terms of the state of men before their conversion (1–3), the means and results of salvation (4–7) and the intention of the Christian life (8–10).

Paul has spoken of the divine power which brought life to God's people (1.19). He now returns to that point in order to emphasize the contrast between the condition of death in which they had formerly lived and the life which they now enjoyed. The evil character of the past, both of Gentiles and Jews, is set forth categorically (1–3). That Jews as well as Gentiles are included Paul signifies by the variation between 'you' and 'us' (2,5) and by the strong expression 'we all' (3). The past was marked by a condition of death which can be expressed by the hyphenated term 'life-of-death'. What is meant is life in a realm where the powers of death constantly have access to you. The term further implies a total insensitivity to the claim of God, and a willing adoption of a course of life inspired by a spiritual power opposed to God (2; cf. 5.6).

The hopelessness of the past serves to thrust into sharper focus the rich mercy of God's intervention. The contrast between vs. 1–3 and 4–7 is caught in Paul's expression, 'But God. . . .' For no other reason than His infinite love, God rescued us from spiritual death and gave us life. The appropriate figure for this change in condition is resurrection. In v. 5 Paul finally introduces the verb on which the whole sentence depends: He 'made us alive together with Christ'. (In the RSV, 'and you He made alive', in 2.1, is introduced from v. 5.) Paul's statement combines two thoughts: (*i*) Jews and Gentiles, who were previously separated, have become united in this new experience of life. (*ii*) As they rise together they are united with Christ in His experience of resurrection (5,6). The apostle's main emphasis, however, is not on the nature of the new life experienced in Christ but on the immeasurable richness of God's mercy and kindness in bestowing life on us (4,5,7).

Thought: By God's undeserved favour you stand rescued from your wrong doings and evil nature.

Ephesians 2.8-10　　　　　　　　The Grace of God

While reflecting on the magnitude of God's love Paul declares in an emphatic parenthesis, 'by grace you have been saved' (6). These words, which are repeated in v. 8, express a central idea in Paul's theology. They declare that the nature of God is to give freely because of His own love. God does not deal with men on the level of human achievement but on the level of their deepest needs. He brings salvation as His gift to men and then creates a disposition of trust and receptivity within them, that they may receive what He gives. Salvation is wholly God's achievement. All attempts to help ourselves by misguided efforts at human achievement merely foster a false sense of security in our own merit (9). Because salvation comes as the pure gift of God, nothing is required of us but the willingness to receive what He has given. Where that willingness does not exist, God brings it into existence by His gracious disposition toward us. (This assumes that the statement in v. 8b qualifies its nearest antecedent, '. . . through *faith*; and this [faith] is not your own doing, it is the gift of God'.)

The Christian is never a self-made man. Paul emphatically declares that we are God's 'workmanship', using a term from which we derive the English word 'poem' (10). Just as in Rom. 1.20 the universe is described as God's creative poem, the Christian is now presented as God's redemptive poem. In each instance the poem is to point beyond itself to the Master Poet whose eternal power, deity and grace are displayed through His craftsmanship. The work of new creation (cf. 2.15; 4.24) crowns the creative activity of God and indicates that what He intends is the achievement of good works. Once he has experienced the grace of God the Christian finds that he devotes himself to good actions because they express the essence of his very nature. Even then all occasion for boasting is removed. The good works which he finds to do are his because God has placed them there for him to discover. The grace of God, the gift of God and the good works of God—these are the elements which distinguish the new life in Christ from the realm of death in which Paul's readers had previously existed.

Thought: You are what God has made you; give Him the glory.

Questions for further study and discussion in Ephesians chs. 1.1—2.10

1. Review the commitments you made at the time of your baptism together with the charge you received. Are there features of your devotion which need to be rekindled?
2. What are the implications of saying that the Church is like the risen body of Christ? Can this be said of a local congregation?
3. What is involved in growth toward maturity? How is growth best achieved?
4. What thoughts are most important in Paul's concept of grace? Write a short definition, avoiding religious cliches.

5. Why are the works which a Christian performs for God 'good' works? In what does their 'goodness' consist?

Ephesians 2.11,12   Exclusion from Privilege

The plight of the Gentiles in the ancient world was twofold: their moral degradation invited the wrath of God (2.1–3; 5.6); their exclusion from the privileges which God gave to Israel removed them from a direct confrontation with God. This second feature of their existence Paul exposes in vs. 11 f. Resuming the train of thought with which he had begun the chapter, Paul calls his Gentile readers to reflect on the contrast between their present experience in the Church and their recent past. A deep hostility had separated them from the people of the synagogue. Accidents of birth and training were made the basis for mutual disparagement. The Jews, priding themselves on the outward sign of the covenant which declared them to be the people of God, had expressed their contempt for the Gentiles in the name, 'the uncircumcision' (11). This superficial and unspiritual way of regarding men was a sufficient indication that circumcision could be little more than a mark made by human hands, a work of the flesh.

The prejudice which separated men pointed to the deeper problem of the actual religious condition of the Gentiles. Prior to their experience of the grace of God they were without Christ, in whom God's grace found its most pointed expression (12). As a consequence of their separation from Him, they were like men living outside of the gates of a city-state. Not only did they lack the civic rights of the free citizen; they were not even resident aliens within the city. Paul describes the former condition of his readers as alienated from the commonwealth and strangers to its charters. They possessed no hope of engaging the attention of its Sovereign to permit their entry within the city. In fact, they possessed no real knowledge of Him. The picture is one of utter abandonment to life in the world without the meaning that only a knowledge of God can supply.

Question: What prejudices remain within you, separating you from men who need to be graciously approached for Christ?

Ephesians 2.13-18   Reconciliation

It is frequently asserted in modern theology that God has acted in Christ to reconcile all the world to Himself. Consequently, our primary concern is not to seek to effect the reconciliation of all men to Christ, but to proclaim that all men have been reconciled already. This entails a form of universalism which has had a great impact on contemporary thinking about evangelism and missions. Paul stands emphatically opposed to this kind of reasoning. He knows nothing of universal reconciliation. The one circumstance in which Paul knows that peace exists horizontally between men and vertically between men and God is the circumstance in which men stand before the cross of Christ. The gospel which centres in the death of Christ creates the situation in which men experience God's peace. Eph. 2.13–18 furnishes a graphic description of the new thing which God does in reconciling Jew and Gentile in the one Church (cf. Col. 2.13 f.).

The contrast between the plight of the Gentiles and God's generosity which is expressed in v. 4 with the emphatic, 'But God . . .', finds an echo in v. 13, 'But now in Christ Jesus . . .'. What follows is an account of the radical change of relationship for Gentiles which was achieved through the cross of Christ. The basic cause of hostility and alienation is sin. The divisions between men and God may be overcome because Christ offered Himself as a sacrifice for the sins of the world. Because of His death the sins of both Jews and Gentiles may be forgiven (1.7). As both are brought near to God, they are brought near to each other.

The hostility between Jews and Gentiles and the exclusion of the Gentiles from the presence of God found a tangible symbol in the stone barrier erected between the Court of the Gentiles and the Temple. An inscription in Greek and Latin prohibited the presence of any foreigner beyond the barrier on penalty of death (cf. Acts 21.29 f.). By His death Christ in effect tore down that barrier which separated men from each other (14 f.), just as His death was marked by the tearing of the Temple veil which symbolized the separation of men from God (Mark 15.38). The verses which follow (15–18) are built around an exposition of Isa. 57.19, 'Peace, peace, to the far and to the near, says the Lord; and I will heal him'. The terms 'far' and 'near' designate the Gentiles and Israel respectively (cf. Acts 2.38 f.). 'The Lord' who by His declaration of peace effects the creation of a third race of men—neither Jew nor Gentile but Christian—is Jesus.

Ephesians 2.19-22 The New Temple

The result of Christ's reconciling action was the radical alteration of the status and position of the Gentiles. Paul brings his thoughts to a head by reverting to the civic terminology of v. 12. He assures his readers that the Church is a commonwealth in which all possess the rank of free citizens (19). The terms 'strangers' and 'sojourners' are to be read in the light of v. 12: Paul means, specifically, strangers to the promises expressed in the divine covenants, and sojourners in the commonwealth made up of God's people. While the civic metaphor expressed the quality of privilege Gentiles share with Jews in Christ, the figure of the household permits a more intimate touch. Both Jews and Gentiles have access to the Father (18); both were marked out as God's sons (1.5). Thus both together constitute the members of the divine household, which Paul elsewhere designates 'the household of faith' (Gal. 6.10).

The transition from the figure of a household built upon a strong foundation to the thought of the temple in which God dwells appears at first sight to be abrupt. But in the ancient world a temple was not a place for public worship, like a church building, but the actual dwelling place of the deity. God's own household is thus the place where He dwells. Paul describes the Church as such a holy temple on earth. The foundation of the New Temple is the word of God entrusted in a special way to the apostles and prophets in the Church (cf. 3.5; 4.11; 1 Cor. 12.28). As men commissioned to proclaim and interpret God's word, they have primary responsibility for building up the community of faith. The chief cornerstone binds the parts of the building together and gives to the walls their lines. Upon Christ the whole structure rests (cf. Psa. 118.22; Isa. 28.16; 1 Pet. 2.5); His power shapes the building and guarantees its growth toward completeness. The Gentiles have their place in the holy structure. They are like new tiers of stone which are constantly rising upon the foundation as the building continues to be erected. Finally, the building is defined, not by the general term for temple, but as the inner shrine where God manifests His glory. Paul's point is that the living God displays His presence in the world through a living household created by the Holy Spirit.

Ephesians 3. 1-6   God's Surprise

To judge from the vocabulary of *Ephesians*, Paul's readers were keenly alert to the new religious philosophy sweeping the Roman Empire; the eastern mysteries and incipient gnosticism. The apostle, recognizing that the Church must prepare itself to meet a syncretistic philosophy bidding for the allegiance of men, found himself challenged to crystallize his own thinking over against this threat. In *Colossians* he uses the language of religious syncretism against syncretism, but in *Ephesians* the same vocabulary is used to express a distinctly Christian point of view. Paul was open to new ways of understanding and explaining the person and work of Christ; in the vocabulary and thought of some of the newer movements he found a fresh vehicle for addressing the Church of Asia Minor (cf. 1.20–23;

2.2,15; **3**.2–6,9 f., 15,18; **5**.32). The description of the gospel as the hidden mystery of God in ch. **3** has its background in the search for a more adequate presentation of the Christian message.

The mystery is God's secret which He has finally revealed through the apostles and prophets (3,5; cf. **2**.20). Men must stand before it as young children who need to be instructed, for its meaning must be spiritually discerned (cf. v. 5, 'by the Spirit'). There were hints of God's gracious intention toward the Gentiles in the O.T. The promises concerning their salvation were always understood, however, as if the Gentiles had to come to the Jews (cf. Isa. **2**.2 f.). The promised Messiah and the redemption He brought belonged to Israel (Rom. **9**.5). The thought that Messiah was for the Gentiles (cf. 8; Col. **1**.26 f.) was something unimagined. It is the unexpected surprise that Gentiles share the inheritance, the commonwealth and the covenant promises which had belonged exclusively to Israel, that Paul has been commissioned to proclaim among the nations (6).

The Christian mystery was different from all other mysteries in two important respects. (*i*) The mystery of Christ must be publicly exposed so that it penetrates the world. All other mysteries are in their deepest sense alien to any public proclamation; the initiate was pledged to guard the secret revealed. (*ii*) In pagan mysteries 're-conciliation' between a man and deity occurs by some cultic act, an ecstatic experience and the adoption of a particular ethic. In Christianity reconciliation is accomplished through the word of preaching, faith and active love. Paul points his readers to the Church as the fellowship of those who have been surprised by joy as they have come to share in God's open secret.

Ephesians 3.7-13   The Function of the Church

Paul was a task-theologian. His total approach to life and mission was controlled by his commission to be the 'Apostle to the Gentiles'. He never lost a deep sense of privilege that God had allowed him to preach 'the unsearchable riches' of the gospel. His protest that he was 'the very least of all the saints' (8) must be understood in the specific context of his persecution of the Church prior to his conversion (see 1 Cor. **15**.9 f.; 1 Tim. **1**.12–16).

Paul's task is to make all men understand the nature of God's plan to gather all things together in the Church, which is the fellowship of those who share His secret (9–11). The shift of emphasis from the person of Christ to the Church when speaking of 'the mystery' in this context is only an apparent one. Because the Church is the body of Christ, the mystery of Christ is incorporated and made visible in the Church. The Church does not exist as an end in itself but to be the show-case where God displays His wisdom to the world, and particularly to those powers of destruction which are opposed to His purposes. Already in its historical existence the Church makes an impact upon the realm of the hostile powers. This extremely high concept of the Church is consistent with God's eternal purpose which found its expression in the cross of Christ. Through the cross believers are made alive (1.7; 2.13–18), but the principalities are disarmed (Col. 2.15). These are two effects of reconciliation which must be mirrored in the Church. Paul's language implies an entirely new concept of mission in which the Church regards seriously its cosmic significance and finds in its access to Christ the resources sufficient for its task.

Thought: If the Church is to be a mirror of God's intention to reconcile men, self-assertiveness and petty individualism can have no place in its ranks.

Ephesians 3.14-19 The Love of Christ

Reflection upon what God has done for the Gentiles always had the effect of driving Paul to prayer (cf. 1.3–14, followed by 15–19; 2.11–22, followed by 3.1,14–19). He intended to begin his prayer in 3.1, but was diverted by contemplation of the grace which God had given to him. His interrupted thought is resumed in v. 14 with great intensity because of the intervening consideration of God's magnificent plan. Paul's posture and his designation of God are unusual (14 f.). In Judaism, where it was customary to stand for prayer (cf. Matt. 6.5; Luke 18.11,13), kneeling was a sign of deep emotion and earnestness (cf. I Kings 8.54; Luke 22.41; Acts 7.60; 9.40; 20.36; 21.5). Paul regularly addressed his prayer to the Father (cf. 1.17; 2.18), but in this instance he reflects on what the designation 'Father' means in the context of God's open secret. God is the Father of the whole universe. In the same manner that the clans of Asia Minor called themselves by the name of their supposed ancestor, all races, earthly and heavenly, may trace their lineage to the Creator in whom the concept of fatherhood is seen in its perfection.

The content of Paul's prayer repeats in another form the concerns which had informed the prayer of 1.17–19, that the inward life of his readers may be transformed and strengthened. The new element is the stress upon an intimate knowledge of the love of Christ made possible through His presence in and with believers (18 f.). A true knowledge of God is unattainable without the experience of love in the fellowship of the Church (the position of 'with all the saints' is emphatic). The love of which Paul is speaking is intensely practical.

246

It comes to expression in the love you show to Christ and to other men for His sake in their experience of sorrow, trial and suffering. To the extent that his readers know the love of Christ Paul is confident they will attain the fulfilment which God intends for them and will find themselves in harmony with God's eternal purpose.

Thought: No good thing does the Lord withhold from those who walk uprightly in love.

Ephesians 3.20,21 — A Shout of Glory

Consistent with his practice in *Romans* and elsewhere, Paul brings the first main section of his letter to a close with an ascription of praise to God. What prompts him to break forth into a doxology is reflection on the divine power which is operative in the lives of believers. The apostle was concerned that his readers should know the immeasurable greatness of that power, and his initial prayer was directed specifically to this desire. The dynamic which energizes the Church was there defined as the power which raised Christ from the dead and exalted Him to a place of sovereign authority at the Father's side and which is active in subduing every force which is hostile to God (1.19-23). In the second prayer Paul has asked God to give his readers a blessing which transcends human understanding or expression (3.16-19). His confidence that his prayers will be answered in a manner which far exceeds his own expectations has its source in the vision of the incomprehensible majesty of God. The God whom Paul served filled him with a sense of awe and wonder. His own inability to exhaust the inexhaustible resources of God is emphasized by terms deliberately chosen: 'immeasurable greatness' (1.19), 'surpasses knowledge' (3.19), 'far more abundantly than all that we ask or think' (20). Glory belongs to such a God, whose reality had so deeply impressed itself upon His servant.

Paul has spoken clearly about the work of reconciliation which God has determined to accomplish through Christ. He has developed a high concept of the Church as the pledge of that ultimate and perfect unity which God will achieve. His vision of what God shall yet accomplish embraces the whole universe. The closing words of the doxology sound these themes once more: to God be glory, not only in the Church where He has displayed His intention but in that infinite realm of being of which Christ is the centre (21). The conception of a thunderous peal of glory unfragmented by space and uninterrupted by time is breath-taking.

Question: How majestic is the God whom you serve?

1. Does what Paul says in 2.11 f. about the attitude of Jews to Gentiles have any bearing on a Christian approach to racial prejudice? What is the root of prejudice?
2. Why is universalism, in its several forms, an example of human wisdom rather than an expression of Biblical truth?
3. What are the factors which separate men from each other today? How can Christ's reconciling action be brought to bear on them?
4. How would you explain the character of reconciliation to a neighbour who knew little about Christ or the Bible?
5. A variety of figures describe the character of the Church (e.g. family, city, temple). Make a list of the metaphors used in *Ephesians* and decide what Paul wishes to say by each one.

Ephesians 4.1-6   The Unity of the Church

The primary theme of *Ephesians* is that all things are moving toward unity, by which Paul means perfection (cf. 1.9 f.). In developing this conception Paul gave an exposition of God as Father over the whole universe (3.14 f.) and of the reconciliation of the cosmos (1.19–23; 2.20–22). A secondary theme clarifies how the Church relates to God's eternal purpose. Paul establishes two points: (*i*) The Church is an expression of the future, a pledge of that ultimate and perfect unity which God will achieve. Therefore, it is imperative for there to be oneness within the Church (4.1–6). (*ii*) The Church is the means by which God confronts those hostile powers of existence which stand opposed to unity (3.10,20 f.; 6.11 f.). The Christian is one who experiences in history what reconciliation to God means. The Church must therefore be a dynamic expression of the significance of Christ's death and resurrection. It must be the place where the alienation and hostility of the world are broken down. The fact that within the Church the walls of partition which separated Jew and Gentile have been removed already (2.14–16) indicates that God is bringing His sovereign purpose to fruition. It is in the light of this fulfilment that Paul pleads with his readers to demonstrate humility, patience, and love in their relationships with one another. Unity is the creation of the Spirit of God (cf. 2.18; 2 Cor. 13.14; Phil. 2.1), but it must be realized and guarded by believers (1–3).

Confession belongs to the heart of worship. The confession of the synagogue is reduced to capsule form in the ancient words of the *Shema*: 'Hear, O Israel: the Lord our God is one Lord' (Deut. 6.4). The confession of the Church, which forms an exact counterpart to Israel's acknowledgement, expands the *Shema* to speak of the one

Spirit, the one Lord, the one Father (4–6). The repeated emphasis upon the word 'one' in the credal confession strengthens the emotional impact of Paul's plea for unity in the Church.

Thought: Your confession of faith in 'the Holy Catholic Church' affirms your pledge to work for its realization in the local churches where you worship.

Ephesians 4.7-16   Corporate Maturity

As he contemplates the unity of the Church Paul never loses sight of the individuals of which it is composed (7, 'to each of us'; 13, 'until we all'). Each believer receives a particular measure of grace as Christ's gift. To emphasize his point that Christ is the giver of gifts to the Church Paul introduces a citation from Psa. **68.**18 which depicts the victorious king ascending the mountain of the Lord attended by a long line of captives. Both the Hebrew and Greek text of the passage state that the king *receives* gifts from men, but Paul goes back to an older form of the text which has survived in the Targum, the Aramaic translation of the Hebrew Scripture which was used in the synagogue, and in the Old Syriac translation. Vs. 9 f. furnish an example of early Christian *midrash*, an exposition of the O.T. in terms of the life of the Church, in which Paul interprets the meaning of the words 'He ascended on high' and 'He gave gifts to men'. The king is Christ, whose ascension (cf. **1.**20–23) implies the necessity of His incarnation and death on the cross, where He disarmed the principalities (cf. 1 Cor. **2.**7–10; Col. **2.**15). The gifts which He bestows upon the Church are individual men who are dedicated to the tasks of ministry. Within the unity of the Church there is a necessity for the diversity of gifts in order to achieve the corporate maturity which God intends.

The purpose of Christ's gifts is that all believers may be equipped to fulfil some aspect of ministry. (V. 12 should be read without a comma after the first phrase: 'for the equipment of the saints to do the work of the ministry'.) Paul does not envisage that any member of the Church will be a mere spectator to its worship and involvement with mission. It is the corporate maturity of the whole body, in which every believer is to participate, which is the goal that he holds before his readers (13). What Paul pleads for is a living and vibrant unity of the Church with Christ whose life provides the dynamic for growth and harmony among the diverse members of His body. The marks of Christ's presence will be a forbearance of one another in love (2), truthful speech with love (15) and mutual growth in love (16).

Thought: When God gives gifts to the Church, He usually wraps them within a man.

Ephesians 4.17-24 The New Creation

Paul began the second half of the letter by calling upon his readers to lead a life consistent with the fact that God had called them to experience His grace. The implications of what a 'worthy' life entails are drawn out in 4.17 ff. There must be a sharp break with the pagan past. With deft strokes Paul paints a sobering portrait of the futility and depravity of life without God. We grasp its confusion, alienation and callousness expressed in the reckless exploitation of persons in an endless and empty quest for meaning to life, a quest which finds its echo in the lamentable secular existentialism in contemporary literature and drama. The emptiness which Paul describes formed the recent past of his readers (cf. 2.1–3; 5.8). They must not act as if they were still trapped in an existence where total abandonment to the sensual element in life reduced them to obsession with the realm of the sordid in a world estranged from God.

Christians cannot act like they did before their conversion because they have come to understand the true meaning of life (20 f.). To 'learn' Christ is to listen to Him until you become possessed by His mind and will, and learn to regard life through His eyes (cf. 1 Cor. 2.16; 2 Cor. 10.5). This involves a radical renewal of your personality by the Holy Spirit, so that the whole direction of your will is controlled by Christ. God created man to be like Him in righteousness and holiness (Gen. 1.26) but man desired to be 'like God' in knowledge and freedom. The result was the debasement which Paul found displayed in the licentiousness of Gentile life. The apostle calls his readers to 'live out' the true humanity which the new creation makes possible.

Ephesians 4.25-29 Mutual Responsibilities

Paul does not content himself with a general presentation of the sharp contrast between the old life of pagan futility and the new life of purposefulness in Christ. A series of admonitions clarifies specific areas of conduct in which believers have an obligation to behave responsibly toward one another. The context for what Paul has to say in this section is furnished by life in the Church (see especially 25b and 29b). The sins of falsehood, anger, theft, and inappropriate speech are those which disrupt the fellowship which believers share and obscure the unity which God intends to accomplish through Christ.

The warning to abandon falsehood as a way of life is reinforced by

250

a quotation from Zech. **8.16.** Like the parts of the human body, Christians are related to each other and must be able to depend upon one another. Earlier 'speaking the truth' had been qualified by the words 'in love' as the condition for attaining maturity in Christ (15). The prolongation of anger is always dangerous and must be restrained. When quarrels are allowed to continue beyond a day, the devil has an opportunity to embitter men against each other and to destroy the signs of reconciliation effected by Christ. The third exhortation does not imply the existence of professional thieves within the local congregation but concerns parasites who were attempting to live at the expense of their neighbours. Such men are to devote themselves to honest work in order to be able to assume their responsibility to support members of the fellowship in times of crisis. The avoidance of 'worthless' speech is to be accompanied by the cultivation of subjects which contribute to the spiritual development of other Christians.

Each of the admonitions of this section may be understood as a commentary on **4.3.** They clarify what is entailed in an eagerness 'to maintain the unity of the Spirit in the bond of peace'.

Thought: An index to your Christian maturity is provided by the way in which you express your anger.

Ephesians 4.30—5.2   The Imitation of God

Throughout this letter Paul has stressed the person and work of the Holy Spirit (cf. **1.**13 f.; **2.**18; 3.5,16; **4.**3). He now cautions his readers not to 'grieve' the Spirit of God (30). The background to his plea is provided by Isa. **63.**7–10 which recalls Israel's failure to appreciate the intimate way in which God had identified Himself with them. They 'rebelled and grieved His Holy Spirit', and God became their enemy. Paul warns that Israel's experience could be repeated among his readers if they refuse the leading of the Spirit. The specific context in which Paul's plea is intelligible is the concern of the Spirit to achieve unity within the Church (3). The verses both before and after v. 30 focus upon sins of speech, expressing attitudes that set men against each other. Expressions of 'bitterness', which Aristotle defined as a resentful spirit that refuses reconciliation, vex the Spirit of God.

What is required of men who have experienced God's kindness (**2.7**) is a demonstration of qualities which owe their existence to the Spirit (Gal. **5.**22 f.). Harshness and an unwillingness to forgive an individual who has offended you are inconsistent with the experience of forgiveness by God (cf. **1.7**). As children of God who have experienced adoption into His family (**1.6**), Christians are to take

251

their example from Him. Because He was kind (2.7), they must be kind; because He was tender-hearted (2.4), they must be as well (32). The bold command to imitate God (5.1) occurs only here in the whole N.T. You are most like the Father when you translate His love into practical action. The kind of love for which Paul pleads finds its supreme expression in the cross of Christ (2).

Thought: When you are thoughtless and hurt another Christian you break the heart of God.

Ephesians 5.3-14   The Life of Moral Obedience

In defining dispositions and actions which offend the Spirit of God, Paul moves from sins which promote discord to those which corrupt and degrade human character. Reckless abandonment to sensuality was common in Hellenistic society. While it was impossible to shield his readers from the grosser side of life the apostle urges them not to dignify baseness by making it a topic for conversation. Impurity, lust and flippant speech have the effect of dulling your sensitivity to the leading of the Spirit, whose nature is holiness. The appropriate mood of the Christian life is one of thanksgiving which sees and acknowledges the beauty in human love and the rightful enjoyment of sex as the gift of God (cf. 22–33). Paul solemnly warns that those who are guilty of sexual vice are no better than men who serve idols rather than God. The immoral and amoral man is not only excluded from the realm where God is sovereign but is consigned to wrath (3–6).

In order to reinforce the absolute difference between the community of faith and the pagan environment in which they live Paul resorts to the image of light and darkness. Men who have fellowship with God are committed to the moral life. Elsewhere Paul speaks of 'the fruit of the Spirit' to define this character (Gal. 5.22 f.). Here he sustains the image of light in order to contrast the fruitfulness of life in fellowship with God (light) with the barrenness of the sensual life (darkness). The same point is sustained in the contrast between exposure and secrecy. The life of unquestionable purity and integrity, by its very existence, exposes the shallowness and ugliness of the life which must be carefully masked (7–13). The section is brought to a close with an excerpt from an early Christian hymn (cf. v. 19) which refers to the Christian's experience of death and resurrection and the bestowal of light through Christ, shattering the darkness of the pagan past (14).

Thought: The joy of the Christian life is to discover God's will by doing it.

1. What gifts of the Spirit have you seen exercised in the Church? How have these gifts contributed to the maturity of the Church?
2. How can more Christians be encouraged to take an active role in the mission and worship of the Church? Why is a spectator-role unacceptable?
3. What signs of the emptiness of human life without Christ have you noticed in the past week? How can you approach 'empty' people with the 'fullness' of life in Christ?
4. What attitudes and actions disrupt the fellowship of believers today? What dispositions reinforce the unity of the Church?
5. Collect all the references in *Ephesians* to the Holy Spirit. In what ways will your life be enriched by a greater awareness of the specific ministries stressed in this letter?

Ephesians 5.15-21 Disciplined Maturity

Paul rounds off his exhortation to the whole congregation by returning to the demand for disciplined maturity. Since they have received wisdom from God (1.8), they should be able to discern that a secular society imposes pressures which can erode Christian standards. God-given opportunities to expose the sham of life without Christ are to be seized; in this way time will be brought into relationship with God's redemptive purposes (15 f.). The crisis of belief and unbelief heightens the demand for sound moral judgement (17). A high amount of Christian intelligence is required to discern on every occasion what God would have you to do. Paul, therefore, cautions the believers to give first priority to the perception and performance of the will of God.

The apostle recognizes that it is legitimate to desire the keener life in which thought and expression are quickened, but insists that only the Spirit of God can satisfy this desire (18). Drunkenness leads only to the folly of uncontrolled actions, dissipation and the progressive mastery of the will by drugs. In contrast, the control of the Holy Spirit, affirmed constantly and repeatedly, results in His progressive mastery of your life so that you become adjusted to the will of God. Vs. 19–21 clarify Paul's admonition in v. 18 and provide three evidences of the life controlled by the Spirit of God: joyful fellowship, sustained thanksgiving and mutual consideration. The life of the Spirit shared by the fellowship of believers is exhilarating and releases them to the freedom which exists wherever Christ is Lord.

Thought: Every new movement of the Spirit has brought to the Church a fresh outburst of song.

Paul had set forth as the presupposition of *all* Christian relationships the necessity to maintain unity (4.3), to walk in love (5.2) and to be subject to the claims of one another (5.21). He now repeats these emphases under the subject of Christian marriage, where these principles become very specific. The apostle was a strong supporter of marriage as a form of Christian obedience (note how v. 22 echoes v. 21). The foundation for his teaching was Gen. 2.18–24, where marriage is disclosed as God's intention for man (cf. v. 31). What is distinctive of Eph. 5 is that Paul treats extensively the significance for the married pair of the relationship of Christ to the Church. Elsewhere reverence for Christ provides the sole motivation for wives to respect their husbands as the head of the home (Col. 3.18). The same appeal is sounded in *Ephesians*, but is undergirded by a further appeal to the submission of the Church to Christ, her Head (22–24).

As the union of Christ and the Church is derived from the cross, so the husband must renounce himself in order to benefit his wife. In this act of renunciation he is consecrated. Because he consecrates his wife by bringing her to her true destiny, he may be regarded as her 'saviour' (23,25–27). Thus the Christian pair reflects to the world the intimate relationship of Christ the Head, and the Church which is His body. With profound insight Paul describes the woman as her husband's body (28 f.) through which she reveals him. This in turn sheds light on the meaning of the Church as the body of Christ. The privilege of the Church as the body of Christ is to meet her Lord and to reveal Him to the world by making Him visible. For that reason Paul sees a deeper implication in Gen. 2.24 than a counsel having to do with marriage. He suggests that in their marital union the Christian couple is to come to a deeper understanding of the relationship of Christ and the Church, and to declare that understanding to the world by their obedience one to the other (31–33). For the pagan world, in its sexual confusion (cf. 4.17–19; 5.3–6), the Christian pair is both a judgement and a promise. They represent a judgement, because their presence in the world in the fulfilment of the will of God calls into question all merely human solutions of man's sexual nature. They are a promise, for their existence is a pledge in this age of the fulfilment of God's purposes for man in the age to come.

Ephesians 6.1-4   Children and Parents

A remarkable quality of Scripture is its simplicity of expression.

Its essential commands are intended to be understood by those to whom they are addressed. When God speaks to children, He seems to stoop down in order to be heard and He speaks in simple words they can understand: 'Obey your parents in the Lord' (1). Although Hebrew and Greek, the languages of the Bible, belong to different linguistic families, in both the word 'to obey' is an intensified form of the verb 'to hear'. Obedience is a consequence of listening intently to the voice of God. Paul emphasizes the fact when he grounds his admonition in the Fifth Commandment, which concerns filial duty to parents (2 f.). The 'rightness' of obedience lies in the fact that God has commanded it and a Christian home commends it. Of all the commandments the fifth is the first to which a promise is attached; obedience to parents is rewarded by God's approval and long life. Disobedience to parents is a mark of a reckless indifference to divine authority and invites the judgement of God (Rom. 1.30; 2 Tim. 3.2).

The obligations of parents to one another extends to their children as well. The response to obedience is to be understanding and instruction (4). Paul assumes that it is the father who has primary responsibility for discipline in the home, but he warns against the exercise of an authority which is void of the sympathy and love which Christ inspires. Paul's own conduct with a young church indicated that exhortation, encouragement and command were legitimate elements in 'the discipline of the Lord' (cf. 1 Thess. 2.11). When the education of children is based on the admonition of the Lord they can perceive that the obedience they give to their parents shows the respect they have for God.

Ephesians 6.5-9   Slaves of Christ

The presence of converted slaves within the household motivated Paul to place the relationship of slaves and their masters in a distinctively Christian perspective (cf. 1 Cor. 7.20-24; Col. 3.22—4.1; Philem.; Tit. 2.9 f.). A particular necessity to do so at the time he wrote his letters to the Lycus Valley was provided by the presence of Onesimus, the fugitive slave from Colossae (cf. Col. 3.18—4.1, 7-9).

Paul restores a sense of dignity to the work of believing slaves when he instructs them to obey their masters as an act of reverence for Christ. They are to regard themselves, not as men from whom every vestige of individuality has been taken by servitude, but as 'servants of Christ' who do the will of God. In the O.T. the designation 'servant of the Lord' is a title of honour reserved for men like the Patriarchs, Moses or David, who stand in a unique relationship to God. Paul instructs Christian slaves to recognize that they belong to that distinguished company when they perform their tasks as a service rendered to God, and not because they are constrained to do so. Their attitude is to be characterized by a basic humility which stems from a keen sense of shortcoming (for 'fear and trembling' cf. 1 Cor. **2.3**; 2 Cor. **7.15**; Phil. **2.12**) and by a determination to serve Christ willingly. When men stand before the exalted Christ what counts is not whether they laboured under conditions of bondage or freedom but the spirit in which they accomplished their tasks.

Christian masters are to reflect the generous attitude of their Lord. They are to recognize the intrinsic worth of good work and to reward it with fairness. Fair treatment will secure ready obedience. The warning that the Lord will be impartial in His judgement is intended for both parties; slaves and masters stand on the same footing in the Judgement.

Ephesians 6.10-17 Warriors of God

Spiritual conflict belongs to the nature of Christian life. The demonic has ceased to be a real element in the world-view of many Christians, but Paul's awesome description of the spiritual forces against which the Church contends must be taken seriously. The apostle insists that our conflict is ultimately not with men, but with Satan and his hosts (11–13). Christ alone has subdued the demonic (cf. **1**.20–23). Consequently, the Christian must draw his strength for conflict from his union with Christ (10).

Paul urges the believers to put on the whole armour of God (11,13), and proceeds to describe its parts. While his description may owe something to what he observed in the military quarters where he was confined, its primary inspiration is drawn from Isa. **59.**17, which describes God as arming Himself in order to rescue His oppressed people (cf. also Isa. **11.**4; **52.**7). This influence is evident in vs. 14, 15 and 17. The purpose of the girdle was to hold the clothes in place and to prevent their interference with movement. Truthfulness or sincerity constitutes the girdle of the Christian warrior which holds together the other qualities of his life. The breastplate or coat of chain mail protected the vital parts of the body. Like the divine Warrior described by Isaiah, the believer protects himself by his integrity (14). An important part of the soldier's equipment to which Rome paid much attention were the military boots designed for long marches over terrain of every description. God's warrior must be prepared to carry the gospel everywhere in response to the command of Christ (15).

After describing the normal dress of the soldier, Paul speaks of his implements for battle. Faith is compared to an oblong shield, which was designed to offer protection to the whole body. Paul's unusual term denotes a shield constructed of wood and covered over with a thick hide. Arrows stuck in the hide, but could not set it on fire even when they were loaded with flaming pitch. Faith in the presence of Christ in the experience of conflict is like that kind of shield, because it offers a total protection against all the insidious attacks of the demonic hosts (16). The helmet of salvation identifies the Christian as a warrior of God who bears the divine crest. He has the assurance of his salvation which permits him to focus all of his energies on the course of the battle. His weapon is as spiritual as the warfare in which he is engaged (cf. 2 Cor. 10.3–6). He trusts in the written Word of God which he possesses and in every form of Christian utterance which is prompted by the Spirit of God (cf. Mark 13.11). Because he is equipped in this manner, he may fight valiantly for Christ even against spiritual forces greater than himself.

Thought: It is tactical suicide to underestimate the strength of the Enemy.

Ephesians 6.18-20 Prayer in the Spirit

Extensive exposure to the Word of God and to prayer was Paul's formula for the attainment of Christian maturity. The reference to the Sword of the Spirit (17) finds an echo in the exhortation to pray in the Spirit (18). Paul urges his readers to pray for one another and for himself. To pray 'in the Spirit' is to be aware of the presence of the Holy Spirit, who provides direction, assurance, and comfort in the experience of prayer. Paul acknowledged that frequently we do not know how to pray appropriately, but the Spirit prays as we pray, conforming our prayers to the will of God (Rom. 8.26 f.). Earnest intercession for others is an arena experience, involving conflict with the demonic (12 f.).

The apostle was conscious of his own need to be supported by prayer at this time. In a parallel passage (Col. 4.2–4) he urged the Colossians to pray specifically that a significant opportunity for ministry may develop. Here he asks that his own mouth should be opened to expound fully and boldly the open secret of the gospel. His description of the gospel as a 'mystery' resumes one of the main themes of the letter; the hidden purpose of God for the Gentiles which He has graciously revealed through the apostles and prophets of Christ. Paul designates himself an ambassador, commissioned to proclaim this message (cf. 2 Cor. 5.20). In Rome he could have seen envoys sent to the imperial city from all nations of the Graeco-Roman world, vested with the honours and dignity of their sovereigns. He too is an envoy, but an envoy in chains, true to the character of an apostle as one who is laden with gifts and with suffering in the world (2 Cor. **4.**7–12; **6.**3–10; **11.**23–29). He has come to Rome not to his own personal glory, but to exalt Jesus Christ as his Lord and King.

Thought: The secret of power with God and with men is discovered only through intense involvement with prayer.

Ephesians 6.21-24   An Undying Love for Christ

Paul closes all his letters with a personal section. In the present instance he is writing to a church he has never visited and about which he has learned only through others (**1.**15). He is unable to identify any of his readers by name but contents himself with conveying a general benediction upon the entire congregation. The first two verses are nearly identical with Col. **4.**7–9, where Paul assures the Colossians that Tychicus will augment their letter with an oral report on the apostle's present circumstances. He extends the same courtesy to the other churches of the Lycus Valley because he sees in his situation a ground for encouragement to other Christians. God has not abandoned him but has given him a ministry in spite of adversities. His readers must know the realities of God's faithfulness to them as well.

The letter had opened with a prayer for grace and peace (**1.**2). It is brought to a close with a benediction which sounds again the note of peace. 'Peace be with you' was a customary word of farewell. Paul expands this parting greeting to include 'love with faith'. His prayer is that the love of God may inform faith, and that faith may give direction to the expression of that love. The appropriate response to God's love is an undying love for Jesus Christ. Paul's qualifying term could be translated 'incorruptible', suggesting a love which was exempt from change and decay. This quality of love is never a human achievement but owes its existence to the life of Christ within the believer. It belongs to that heavenly sphere in which God has blessed us (**1.**3). Christians live upon the earth, but they experience a quality of life and emotion which transcends the possibilities of unredeemed human nature. Paul prays that God's favour may remain with all who demonstrate a sustained love for the Lord who loved us and died for us.

Thought: An undying love for Jesus Christ is the appropriate response to Christ's love and death for you.

Questions for further study and discussion on Ephesians chs. 5.15— 6.24

1. What distinguishes the mere passing of time from significant

258

Photo: By the river at Philippi

Photo: Traditional site of Paul's imprisonment at Philippi

time? How can you bring your time into relationship with God's purposes?
2. How can home-life and marriage make Christ known to neighbours for whom the Church has had no meaning?
3. How can relationships between parents and children be improved? Why do young people from Christian homes frequently rebel against their parents?
4. What attitudes should the Christian cultivate toward his employer, and the Christian employer toward his employees?
5. Why has the demonic element in life been regarded so lightly by secular culture and by many churchmen as well? How can the reality of Satan as the adversary of men be conveyed once more?

Philippians

INTRODUCTION

The Roman colony of Philippi was evangelized on the second missionary journey in response to a divine vision summoning Paul and his party into Macedonia (Acts **16**.6–40). Vigorous public efforts to propagate the gospel throughout the city, and specifically among citizens of the colony, provoked hostility. Paul and Silas were beaten and imprisoned (cf. I Thess. **2**.2). Nevertheless, there was a positive response to the gospel on the part of resident aliens like Lydia and her household and by enfranchised citizens like the local jailer. The work was sufficiently advanced to merit leaving Luke at Philippi to provide leadership for the new church when Paul left the city. (Note that the first 'we' section in *Acts* ends at **16**.17 with Luke at Philippi; the next one is introduced at **20**.5–6 where Paul has rejoined Luke at Philippi.)

Paul revisited Philippi twice before his imprisonments in Jerusalem, Caesarea and Rome (Acts **20**.1–6; 2 Cor. **2**.12 f.; **7**.5 f.). It is probable that when he returned to Macedonia in the last years of his life (cf. Tit. **3**.12) he again made his way to Philippi, fulfilling his intention to visit the church once more (Phil. **1**.26; **2**.24). Between these two points may be located Paul's letter to the Philippians.

Philippians is a deeply personal letter, written out of mature affection for a company of believers who had repeatedly encouraged Paul in his labours for Christ. It is essentially the apostle's word of thanksgiving, not merely for a gift received and services rendered, but for the warm concern which the members of the church continued to show for him. Paul recognized that the church was anxious concerning two specific matters: they had heard that his circumstances as a prisoner had changed, and they had learned of the severe illness of Epaphroditus, the messenger by whom they had delivered their gift to Paul. To relieve their anxiety Paul determined to send Epaphroditus back to Philippi, fully recovered, with a letter of commendation and assurance (2.25–30).

Paul felt a closer emotional bond with the Philippians than with any of his other churches. This is evident from the opening lines of the letter where, instead of asserting his apostleship, Paul contents himself with the designation 'bondslave of Christ Jesus' (1). The term translated 'bishops in v. 1 refers to those having over-all responsibility for the church—'overseers'. It commonly designates financial officers for townships and guilds in Hellenistic texts, and the Philippian bishops had exercised this function in arranging for gifts to be sent both to Paul and to the poor in Jerusalem. The 'deacons' are the pastoral leaders of the congregation who are designated by a title which stresses the idea of service. From other churches Paul had been unwilling to accept for himself even the bare necessities of life (2 Cor. 11.8–11), but he was confident that his integrity was unquestioned at Philippi. The prayer for grace and peace (2) springs from the gospel of reconciliation in which both he and the Philippians rejoiced.

Philippians 1.3-11   Joyful Thanksgiving

These verses reveal the depth of the personal relationship which existed between Paul and the believers at Philippi. The apostle warmly acknowledges his readers' earnest participation in his work (3–5). As he thinks back upon the early days of the mission he thanks God continually for every member of the church. Among the first members were Lydia and her household, and the burly Roman jailer who had fastened Paul's feet in the stocks (Acts 16.14–24). Paul refused to think long about the scars incurred from the beating with rods. God had brought deliverance to himself and to the jailer (Acts 16.25–34). How could he exclude this man from his prayer of thanksgiving and joy? It is evident that Paul was far more sensitive to the mercies of God than to the antagonisms of men.

The apostle's thanksgiving is couched in intimate terms: 'I hold you in my heart . . . I yearn for you all with the affection of Christ Jesus' (4,7 f.). The language is striking precisely because Philippi was almost exclusively Gentile in character. In a city of a quarter of a million inhabitants there could not be found ten Jewish men who were heads of families, the minimum for the establishment of a synagogue. In Phil. 3.5 Paul reminds the church of his Pharisaic background. No Pharisee would have embraced a Gentile with the affection Paul here expresses for his converts. In this radical change of attitude there is reflected the transformation of character and perspective which Paul experienced when confronted by Christ.

While Paul's confidence for the steadfastness of the believers rested upon God (6), he prayed regularly that their love—for himself and for each other—might increase yet more, equipping them to participate in the full harvest of righteousness which God calls forth through Jesus Christ (9–11). One by one Paul touches upon the themes developed throughout the letter: his thanksgiving and affection for the Philippians, his confidence in God's control of all circumstances, the necessity for an increase in love, and Jesus Christ as the source of life and fruitfulness.

Thought: The 'affection of Christ Jesus' in your life makes possible warm relationships which would be impossible otherwise.

Philippians 1.12-14   Anxiety and Prayer

The anxiety of the Philippians for Paul's welfare is understandable. His circumstances had changed. No longer was he allowed the relative freedom of living within his own hired house in Rome (Acts 28.16,23,30 f.). He had recently come to trial in connection with his appeal to Caesar and was currently in prison awaiting the verdict. The decision, once reached, was beyond appeal; he would either be released or sentenced to death (1.7,13,16,19–26; 2.17). Paul was not deceived about the seriousness of the moment, nor was he unappreciative of his friends' concern (cf. 4.14). Yet the appropriate response to anxiety was—and remains—a quiet reliance upon God expressed through prayer (1.19; 4.6).

Paul has peace of mind, for behind the troubles that have befallen him he can discern the hand and purpose of God. His altered circumstances had actually served to advance the gospel (12). During the course of his trial it had become known to the whole praetorium guard (Caesar's *élite* troops) and to all associated with his case that his imprisonment was due to his bold witness for Christ, not for a criminal offence (13). Moreover, as a direct result of his defence of the gospel, local believers were proclaiming Christ with greater boldness (14). Their number included slaves and freedmen attached to the emperor's residence (4.22). In this turn of events Paul saw the affirmation of the principle he had expressed earlier in a Letter to Rome: 'In everything God works for good with those who love Him, who are called according to His purpose' (Rom. 8.28). He knew from his experience that the Christian does not live 'under the circumstances' but above them!

Question: What good can you find in the most trying circumstances of your life today?

Philippians 1.15-18 The Pauline Superiority

It is always difficult for the Christian to face rebuff and meanness of attitude prompted by jealousy and envy on the part of those who belong to the family of faith. Paul was not spared this experience. He was aware that by giving a public account of his ministry in Rome he was entering upon the decisive phase of his apostolate (Acts 19.21; 23.11; 27.24). His trek across Asia and Europe was like the path of a bleeding rabbit across new-fallen snow. He might have surmised that his imprisonment in the imperial city would win for him enthusiastic support and sympathy from the brethren in Rome. If this was his expectation, he was keenly disappointed.

Paul has just stated that his imprisonment has encouraged a great boldness for public testimony on the part of the believers (14). He now acknowledges that there was a diversity of motives behind this new fervour for evangelistic outreach. Some saw in his imprisonment an opportunity to rub salt into his wounds. Paul traces their motivation to a spirit of envy and rivalry (15). His language suggests that these brethren had worshipped at the shrine of Eris, the goddess of discord, rather than at the altar of Christ. There was in their manner a crass selfishness which sought to direct glory to themselves, in the supposition that this would afflict the apostle (17). In others, who had increased their concern to bear public witness to their faith, Paul saw good will (15) and a spirit of love which affirmed their partnership with him (16; cf. vs. 5,7). Paul refused to be depressed by this evidence of disunity and immaturity in the church at Rome (18). This attitude of Christ-centredness and detachment from attacks upon his own person may be defined as 'the Pauline superiority'.

Thought: It is as easy to work for yourself in 'Christian service' as in any other vocation.

Paul's thought reverts to the anxious concern of the Philippians as they contemplate what it means for him to stand before Caesar's tribunal. What if the verdict should be the sentence of death? Paul answers forthrightly, 'I shall rejoice' (19). With a supreme confidence in God he affirms his trial will result in his vindication (cf. Job 13.18). It was natural for Paul to think of vindication at this time. He had exercised his right as a citizen to have his case heard in Rome and for two years had undergone house arrest while waiting for his trial (Acts 25.9–12; 26.32; 28.16–19,30 f.). Nero's tribunal could exonerate him, confirming that Paul had not offended the Temple or Caesar (Acts 25.8). Paul's confidence did not rest in the wisdom or the clemency of the emperor, but in God. For this reason he can speak of *vindication* (19) even when contemplating a sentence of death. The faithful intercession of his friends and the unfailing presence of the Spirit of Jesus Christ assure the apostle that he will face the court unashamed and present his witness for God with all openness (cf. v. 7). Paul has no way of knowing how his trial will turn out (see 2.23). His one concern is that Christ shall be magnified through his bodily life (20). Paul is convinced that whether he is acquitted and enters upon a new phase of ministry (22,25 f.), or falls a prey to the executioner's axe, there will be a new advance of the gospel.

The ground of such apparent 'reckless abandon' is expressed in Paul's triumphant affirmation that he lives his life only in Christ (cf. Gal. 2.20). When seen in the perspective of union with Christ, death can only mean the gain of a life of completed fellowship with Him (21). Paul was a profound thinker, whose thought provides the foundation for much of Christian theology. But in this context he appears primarily as the fervent disciple of the crucified and risen Christ. For Paul, as for the Philippians, Christ is the giver and sustainer of life and the object of all his hopes. If he were given his own preference, he would collapse his earthly tent and seek the immediate presence of Christ (23). However, the fact that he was yet alive was sufficient indication that his apostolic labours were not yet complete. Paul, therefore, anticipates a reunion with the church which shall give them ample cause 'to glory in Christ Jesus' (26). Then, too, Christ shall be magnified.

Thought: The line between physical life and death loses significance when you live 'in Christ'.

Philippians 1.27-30   A Call for Steadfastness

Deeply sensitive to the power of language to stir deep feelings, Paul addresses the Philippians first as Roman citizens and then as Macedonians. Only to Philippi, proud of its colonial status which conferred Roman citizenship on large segments of the population, does the apostle write, *'Discharge your obligations as citizens* who are worthy of the gospel of Christ' (27). The italicized words render a verb which occurs infrequently in secular or Biblical documents, but always signifies conduct regulated by a law of life. In this context Paul envisages the entire church as citizens of heaven whose responsibilities are dictated by the central concerns of the gospel (cf. 3.20 f.). What follows is a call for steadfastness in the face of conflict. This may have been associated with emperor worship, for it is known that Philippi was one of the few Greek cities that possessed an order of Roman citizens pledged to the worship of the divine Augustus—the *Augustales*—while an inscription at the nearby port of Neapolis refers to a municipal magistrate from Philippi who functioned as a high priest of 'the divine Claudius'. A flourishing imperial cult would bid for the allegiance of all members of the colony. In the face of such pressures, the Philippians must stand firm with an uncompromising loyalty to Jesus Christ.

The company of men striving side by side, refusing to be frightened by their opponents (27,28), evokes the image of the phalanx, the most formidable military device in antiquity. It consisted of a corps of highly disciplined spearmen who were formed into ranks which were close and deep. As long as the men of the phalanx did not break rank they were virtually invincible and struck terror into their enemies. With the phalanx Philip of Macedon had united the city-states of Greece, while his son Alexander the Great had brought to its knees the mighty Persian Empire. Philip had founded the city of Philippi, giving it his name. It is unlikely that the Philippians missed Paul's allusion to their glorious past. The same spirit of unity and valour which had infused the phalanx sent forth for world conquest must now be evidenced by the members of the Church as they contend for the faith of the gospel. Appealing to their pride as Macedonians and Romans, Paul calls for steadfastness as Christians that they may be vindicated by God in a trial of faith similar in character to his own (29,30).

Question: Steadfastness in conflict demands discipline of life. Are you constantly training to fight the enemy?

Philippians 2.1-4 Minding 'the One Thing'

Paul has just appealed for unity on the ground that conflict makes harmony of purpose imperative (1.27–30). He now sustains that appeal, urging unity for its own sake as a distinctive mark of the

Church of Jesus Christ. V. 1 indicates the reasonableness of Paul's plea; v. 2 expresses the idea of unity in four different phrases; vs. 3,4 illustrate the appeal concretely.

The apostle was confident of his access to the Philippians. He has already spoken of the encouragement he has experienced from Christ through them and of the mutual affection and esteem which binds him and his friends (1.3–5,7 f., 19 f., 25 f.). Now he appeals to the Church to reconsider their relationship with him and to affirm that he has not misjudged them (1). If they are really open to him and have shared with him the realities of Christian experience, let them now crown his joy by sharing a common disposition (2). The believers had not sufficiently grasped the character of church fellowship. The proud individualism of the Greek spirit had been brought into the assembly of faith and each one took with utmost seriousness 'his own interests' (4). Paul summons the believers to climb down from their thrones and to mind 'the one thing'. What is meant by this unusual expression becomes clear in v. 21, where Paul speaks of men who regard their own interests with greater seriousness than they do the interests of Jesus Christ. This was the situation at Philippi which detracted from Paul's joy. To mind 'the one thing' is to bring every thought into captivity to Jesus Christ (5; 2 Cor. 10.5); it is to put the seriousness of 'the one thing' above the seriousness with which we regard ourselves (3 f.). This demands a life of love prompted by Jesus Christ and directed toward Jesus Christ, but exhibited in the relationships we sustain with one another. That is why Paul speaks of the hindrances to Christian love: self-assertiveness, conceit and crass selfishness. He calls for a practical demonstration of humility which recognizes another man as a recipient of grace. Christian humility takes another brother intensely seriously and listens to his point of view as one listens to a superior. Only when men stand on the level ground of mutual respect do they stand together; only then do they recognize in their midst the one Lord to whom each bows his knee.

Thought: We do not know how to care about ourselves properly until we begin caring about others.

Questions for further study and discussion on Philippians 1.1—2.4

1. What considerations assist a man to be more sensitive to God's mercies than to the antagonism he encounters from men?
2. Why are jealousy and envy found even among Christians? How can these dispositions be overcome?
3. What signs of immaturity do you find in local churches with

265

which you are familiar? How can individuals be helped to a greater maturity?

4. What forces in modern society oppose the Church and its standard? Is conflict with culture inevitable wherever the Church exists?

5. What are the implications of minding 'the one thing' (2.2)?

Philippians 2.5-11   The Lordship of Christ

Paul finds in the humility demonstrated by Jesus Christ the supreme illustration of what he has been urging. 'Let this disposition be yours which is appropriate to those who are in Christ Jesus' (5). What follows is a six-strophe hymn in honour of Christ. Its relevance to what Paul has just been saying lies in the willingness of the Lord to climb down from *His* throne and to assume the position of a *slave* who placed the interests of others above His own (cf. v. 4).

The language of the hymn must have had a great emotional impact on men proud to belong to a Roman colony and to possess Roman citizenship. It describes in vivid terms the humiliation of Jesus who assumed the form of a slave and in obedience to God suffered crucifixion, one of the forms of death reserved by Roman law for slaves condemned to die (6–8). Though executed in a manner which filled every citizen with horror, He was vindicated by God (9–11). The last strophes of the hymn depict an enthronement scene in which the Church is caught up to share in the Lord's triumph. The confession forced from all of the cosmic powers which tyrannize life is none other than that made by the believer in his baptism, 'Jesus Christ is Lord'. Urged to acknowledge that Caesar is Lord by the officials of the imperial cult, the Church is called by God to live and suffer under the lordship of Christ.

The hymn rehearses in dramatic form the redemptive facts upon which Paul's ethical injunction ultimately depends. The confession, 'Jesus Christ is Lord', leads the believer back to his baptism and calls upon him to affirm the submission to Christ and to the others in the fellowship he acknowledged on that occasion. Humility and obedience have meaning if Christ is Lord.

Philippians 2.12,13   Fear and Trembling

Paul has just reminded the Church that the foundation for all that he has been saying to them about responsible relationships is the humility and obedience to God exhibited by Jesus (6–8). He now resumes the urgent solicitation of vs. 1–5. He does so in the firm confidence that his readers are 'in Christ Jesus' (5) and that they acknowledge the lordship of Christ (11). This is made amply clear in the term of address, 'beloved'. The apostle now shows the consequences of their being 'in Christ Jesus'. They are to strive for their vindication with 'fear and trembling'. Though Paul is absent from the flock (12; 1.27), God is present, achieving the fulfilment of His good pleasure (13; 1.6). The contrast in the passage, then, is not between man who works (12) and God who works (13), but between Paul who is absent (12) and God who is present (13).

By his word order, Paul indicates that the emphatic words in v. 12 are 'fear and trembling'. On each occasion that Paul has brought these words together they are decisive (1 Cor. 2.3; 2 Cor. 7.15; Eph. 6.5). From the parallel contexts it is clear that this expression denotes a basic humility in relationship to other men. What Paul here demands of the Church is the same humility he called for in v. 3, the same willingness to see something from another's point of view. All who are in Christ Jesus stand in that vital relationship through grace. The humbling of one man in the presence of another is the work of God who plants within the believer the disposition to approach another man in humility (13). The man who approaches another within the congregation with fear and trembling acknowledges that he has submitted his own life to the power of God and that all vindication proceeds from God alone (1.28).

Question: How willing are you to look at another person's point of view?

Philippians 2.14-18 Children of God

A sustained concern for humility (cf. vs. 3 f., 7 f., 12) leads Paul to instruct the believers concerning their responsibility to exist in the world as those who have acknowledged the lordship of Christ. The dispositions against which he cautions—grumbling and questioning (14)—are those which arise from a failure to exhibit the humility appropriate to those who are in Christ. Grumbling or murmuring was the scandal of the wilderness generation (cf. Exod. 15.24; 16.2; 17.3; Num. 14.2,29; 16.41). Of Israel Moses had to say, '. . . they are a perverse and crooked generation' (Deut. 32.5). Paul now turns this around. The Gentile church at Philippi can be blameless and innocent children of God because they follow the path of humility marked out by Jesus Christ (15; cf. 1.10; 2.7 f.). This news constitutes 'the word of life' to which the believers are to hold fast (16). The world is filled with self-centred men who seek their own glory; this is the character of a 'crooked and perverse generation'. If the Philippians will order their lives in accordance with Jesus' humility, Paul will be proud to present them as his 'joy and crown' (cf. 4.1) when he appears before his Sovereign on the Day of Christ.

The thought of appearing before Christ brings the apostle back to the real possibility that he will be sentenced to death. He does not shrink from this prospect. He places his death vividly before the eyes of his readers by alluding to a pagan practice which could be observed in Philippi and elsewhere, the custom of pouring a cup of red wine over the sacrifice upon the altar (17). The Philippians, as priests, offer their faith to God in the midst of a crooked and perverse generation which had shed Paul's blood at Philippi and imprisoned him at Rome. Should he be put to death his blood would be the libation, consecrating the service of his friends to God. The thought of crowning his service to God through his death was meaningful to Paul (the same figure recurs in 2 Tim. 4.6), and provides for him a new ground of rejoicing.

Thought: The Christian's acceptance and affirmation of life stand in opposition to complaining and questioning about the circumstances that come along.

Philippians 2.19-24   Oriented to the Interests of Christ

Paul deeply appreciated the concern which the Philippians had expressed over the outcome of his trial. While he has found an appropriate ground for rejoicing, whether the result be acquittal or the sentence of death (1.19–26; 2.17 f.), he is sensitive to the extent with which his friends have shared his sufferings. To put them at ease he announces that he will send Timothy to Philippi as soon as a verdict is forthcoming (23). He adds affectionately that he will be as cheered by news of them as they will be by Timothy's report (19).

Timothy had been associated with Paul from the beginning of the second missionary journey (Acts 16.1–3). He had been commended to the apostle by the Christians both in Lystra and Iconium, and perhaps by prophetic utterance as well (cf. 1 Tim. 4.14). With the possible exception of Luke, he proved to be Paul's closest companion, working with him in Macedonia, Achaia, Asia and Rome. In several of the Pauline letters his name is associated with Paul's in the salutation (2 *Cor.*, *Phil.*, 1–2 *Thess.*, *Philem.*). While Paul was thoroughly aware of a certain timidity and reticence in Timothy's nature (1 Cor. 16.11; 1 Tim. 4.12; 2 Tim. 1.7 f.), he did not hesitate to entrust to him important missions to Macedonia, Corinth, Ephesus and elsewhere. The apostle's references to his younger companion are laden with affection (cf. 1 Cor. 4.17; Phil. 2.19–22; 2 Tim. 1.4 f.; 4.9,11,13,21).

While Paul is not yet ready to send Timothy, it is clear that he has no other associate in Rome to whom he is willing to entrust this mission (20 f.). All of the other men about him lack the essential quality of a genuine concern for the welfare of the churches. The problem is that they suffer from the same short-sightedness which afflicted many of the Philippians; they allowed their own interests to overshadow the concerns of Jesus Christ (cf. v. 21 with v. 4). Paul had no such misgivings concerning Timothy. The readers had first-hand knowledge of the quality of his service for Christ, for he had been actively engaged in the mission to Philippi. Paul would send him as soon as he could see his own situation more clearly—and if it please the Lord, he himself will come before long (24 f.; cf. 1.25 f.).

Question: Am I allowing my own interests to overshadow the interests of Jesus Christ?

Philippians 2.25-30   God's Gambler

The Christians at Philippi prepared generous gifts for the apostle Paul and commissioned one member of the congregation, Epaphroditus, to deliver them to Rome. The description of him as 'your messenger and minister to my need' (25) suggests that the church expected their delegate to remain in Rome, caring for the apostle's personal needs. Now that he was returning to Philippi Paul is careful to commend him highly for his labour, and to preclude any suspicion that he had failed to fulfil the expectations of the church. From Epaphroditus Paul had learned of the anxious concern of the Philippians for his welfare, and of the state of affairs within the congregation. He readily acknowledges Epaphroditus' faithfulness in delivering the gifts (4.18), and in sustaining through his presence the partnership which the Philippians shared with the apostle (1.5,7; 2.25,30). Paul assumes personal responsibility for sending the messenger to Philippi. The church is solemnly instructed to receive him with all joy and honour. He returns to the congregation not as a shirker from duty but as a wounded soldier who has been honourably discharged after meritorious service (29,30).

Paul makes a delicate play on the name 'Epaphroditus' in v. 30. The name suggests that pagan parents had devoted their son to the service of Aphrodite, the goddess of love. But she was also the patroness of gamblers. Appian and Plutarch inform us that Roman soldiers and the Greeks generally called the highest cast of the dice 'epaphroditus'. The term spoke of one blessed with gambler's luck in the throw of the dice because the divine hand was behind it. Alert to this background, Paul says Epaphroditus gambled with his life, but won because God was with him and merciful to him. The term 'risking' in v. 30 is very rare, but occurs in an inscription from the Black Sea: 'to the ends of the earth witness was borne to him that in the interest of friendship *he exposed himself to dangers* by his aid in (legal) strife, (taking his client's cases) even up to the emperors'. The inscription reminds us of this little-known servant of God who assisted Paul and gambled his life to complete what was lacking in the service of the Philippians to the apostle.

Question: Commitment to Christ is a risk. Are you willing to gamble your life for Him?

Philippians 3.1-7   A New Disruption

The somewhat turbulent opening of ch. 3 comes as an unexpected surprise. An abrupt change in tone and subject is apparent in the lack of transition between vs. 1 and 2. The probable explanation for the rupture in thought is that Paul was interrupted in the course of dictating his letter. Before returning to this task he received reports of the renewed activity of the Judaizers—men who were attempting to put Christians back under the law as a prerequisite to salvation and who were boasting in their Jewish pedigree. With biting sarcasm Paul applies to them the epithet they applied to all Gentiles, 'the dogs'. They are evil-workers whose goal is the mutilation of the flesh, contrary to the Roman laws governing the colony of Philippi (2; cf. Acts 16.21). In contrast, the Gentile Christians of Philippi constitute the true circumcision which God desires (cf. Deut. 10.16), since they acknowledge that the ground of their confidence is God alone (3).

Paul shows that 'according to the flesh' he has more of which to boast than any Judaizer—though to him this is 'foolishness' (cf. 2 Cor. 11.19,21,23). Among his inherited advantages Paul lists circumcision (the seal of the covenant), direct Israelite descent, a rich tribal heritage and parents who were concerned to maintain the language and traditions of Judaism. For his part, he had demonstrated an earnest piety and a fanatical zeal, patterning his life after the patriarch Phinehas (cf. Num. 25.6–13; Psa. 106.30 f.). By choice he joined the Pharisees, and his strict observance of the law would demand the verdict 'blameless' in any human court.

But if Paul had once regarded these advantages as 'gain' he now categorized them as 'loss' (7). He does not look upon them as something indifferent or unimportant but sees them as *detriment*, as impediments which stood in the way of his coming to faith in Christ. They had given to him a false sense of security and had prevented him from sensing God's indictment on his *goodness* (cf. Isa. 64.6). This is what Paul—and every Christian who contemplates the former objects of his devotion and the conduct of his life—is forced to recognize for the sake of Christ.

Question: What gains in your life must be counted as loss, so that your true security is in Christ alone?

Philippians 3.8-11 Vital Union with Christ

The union of the Christian with Christ lies at the heart of Paul's piety. What this entails is clarified by the present section. Paul has experienced a radical change of values. He now realizes, not merely the worthlessness of what he used to value, but the loss which he suffered through a false sense of security. For him the knowledge of Christ surpasses all other things, and for the love of Christ he has suffered the loss of 'all things'—specifically, his 'goodness' in which he had boasted (4–6). This radical reassessment of his values was a direct result of the irresistible intervention of Christ in his life when the Lord attached Paul to Himself. From that moment Paul was aware of being entirely bound to Christ. The fanatical persecutor of the Church (6) became the devoted disciple and apostle of Jesus Christ who now acknowledges that the one thing worth possessing is the knowledge of Christ (8–10).

The knowledge to which Paul refers is not intellectual but personal, intimate and practical. It flows from the vital union of the believer with Christ in which the life of Christ is mediated to the Christian through the Holy Spirit. Paul can speak of Christ in the believer or of the believer's life in Christ to express this reality. Two consequences which flow from this union are brought home to the Philippians. First, one who knows Christ in this manner has abandoned all efforts to establish his own righteousness or to *achieve* the status of 'blamelessness' (cf. v. 6). He is content to *receive* a righteousness which God bestows only upon the man who has surrendered to God's judgement on his goodness (9). This collapse of self-confidence is the essence of faith from a human point of view; it is an expression of confidence in the achievement of Jesus Christ alone. Secondly, the intense desire to know Christ which flows from this union demands an identification with Christ in His resurrection and sufferings (10). The order in which Paul states these aspects of Christ's experience is remarkable. We are to experience the power of His resurrection in order to be enabled to participate in the sufferings which were laid upon Christ (cf. 1 Cor. **15**.30 f.; 2 Cor. **4**.10,16). Paradoxically, this preparation for sharing the experience of Christ's death, which is achieved through the infusion of the power of His resurrection, leads full circle back to the experience of

271

resurrection power itself (11). This is the mystery and the glory of life in Christ.

Thought: At its heart, Christianity is not intellectual; it is a warm, personal friendship between each believer and Jesus.

Philippians 3.12-16   The Dedication of a Racer

This section continues to develop the line of thought set forth in vs. 7–11. The apostle thinks of himself as a contestant in the stadium (cf. 2.16; 1 Cor. 9.24; 2 Tim. 4.7 f.). He is a 'runner' who speeds toward the goal with outstretched, but empty, hands. Although he knows himself to be thoroughly committed to the race, he has not yet attained *anything*. He therefore strains every muscle to the demands of the course and sprints toward the prize which is yet before him. What sustains the apostle in a life of unbroken 'running' is the divine constraint in the call of Christ (12). On the road to Damascus the exalted Lord laid hold of Paul and made Himself known to His athlete as 'Lord' (Acts 9.3–6,17). He filled Paul with the power of His resurrection and enrolled him within the fellowship of His sufferings (cf. Acts 9.15 f.). With that Paul is content. He finds within himself a new kind of zeal. Formerly he had persecuted the Church (6); now he pursues the fulfilment of God's plan for his life (12) and the prize of the resurrection, 'the upward call of God in Christ Jesus' (14; cf. 10).

The suggestion that Paul had not yet attained *anything* provokes in his readers (and us) a protest. Is he not *the* Apostle of Christ to the Gentiles? Do not his knowledge, his work, his evident successes, indicate he has already reached many goals? Paul remains firm: 'I judge that I have *not* already apprehended.' With resolute will Paul refuses to look back upon the part of the course which now lies behind him (13). To speak now of achievements would be to return to the attitude of vs. 4–6, which Paul has renounced. He will rely on a new surge of strength, and race toward the goal in the confidence that response to the summons of Christ carries its own prize (14). Jesus Christ is not only the beginning of his life, but its present reality and its future goal.

Having begun with a threefold 'beware' (2), Paul now urges the Philippians to consider the relevance for their lives of what he has said in vs. 4–14. In the conditions of existence under which Paul lives and labours they are to see the conditions which govern their own existence (15). A man becomes conformed to Christ, not as in Hellenism by a dedication ceremony, but by work, struggle and suffering. While there may be divergence of opinion regarding the

272

details of what this involves, Paul is confident that both he and his readers are on a path which has, in principle, taken the direction marked out in vs. 4–14. He urges them to continue in that same direction.

Question: Are you running straight toward the goal—or are you still looking back?

Questions for further study and discussion on Philippians 2.5—3.16

1. List the implications of the lordship of Christ for your life.
2. Is an attitude of 'fear and trembling' acceptable in current society? Does Paul's exhortation in 2.12 imply that the Christian must allow others to take advantage of him?
3. What is the fundamental difference between complaint and constructive criticism?
4. Read an article on the Pharisees in a good Bible encyclopaedia. What attracted Paul to this group? What attitudes toward commitment did he bring with him from his background when he became a Christian?
5. How can you effectively tell a non-Christian what life in Christ entails? Reduce your thoughts to a two-minute statement!

Philippians 3.17-21   A Heavenward Perspective

Having set forth Jesus Christ as the supreme object of Christian desire, Paul can now make himself a secondary example to the church (17; cf. **4**.9). He summons the church to follow him in considering as loss all that the flesh finds as a ground of boasting (4–7), in refusing a righteousness of their own (9), in forgetting what is behind and racing on toward the goal (13 f.). In pointing to what the believers may see in him Paul is in fact pointing toward Christ, toward the evidence of the power of His resurrection and the fellowship of His sufferings (9 f.). There is no presumptuousness in commending such an example to the church.

The urgency which attaches itself to Paul's plea arises from the threat to faith posed by those who pretend to march under the banner of faith (18,19). Paul is referring once again to the Judaizers who prompted his heated outburst in v. 2. The cross of Christ stands radically opposed to all religious and ethical presumption which seeks to achieve by works what can only be given through faith. The enemies of the cross of Christ are all those who resist the grace of God and refuse to walk the way of 'loss' described in vs. 4–14. Paul sees in the insistence upon circumcision a frontal attack upon the sufficiency of the cross of Christ, and an affront to the wisdom of God. Despising the cross, despising faith and its righteousness, they shall experience destruction (19). The phrases which follow in v. 19 allude to circumcision and a reliance upon the flesh (cf. vs. 2 f.).

In contrast to the 'enemies of the cross' who set their minds on 'earthly things' Christians have been constituted a 'commonwealth', and the object of their hope is 'in heaven' (20 f.). The term 'commonwealth' was used technically to designate self-sufficient and self-governing communities of non-citizens who formed a city within a city. The metaphor came readily to Paul's mind since he had seen Jewish commonwealths in many of the larger cities of Asia. His point is that Christians are not citizens, but resident aliens, in the world, and their confidence rests, not in the world's wisdom, but in the wisdom of God. With patience they await the triumphant return of their Sovereign, the Lord Jesus Christ, who will radically transform the body—not by the marks of circumcision but by 'the power of His resurrection' (cf. vs. 10 f.).

Thought: There is power available in Christ to live a life worthy of imitation.

Philippians 4.1-3 — A Delicate Pastoral Problem

While conflict makes unity imperative, it is important for its own sake as evidence of a common disposition binding the church together in Christ. This was much upon Paul's mind. He had experienced disunity in the church at Rome (1.15–17). Now a flagrant instance of disaffection threatened the unity of the church at Philippi. With this in view Paul prayed for an increase of love and the approval of what is excellent, that the church may be found blameless at Christ's coming (1.9 f.). He expected Christians to 'stand firm in one spirit . . . contending side by side' for the gospel (1.27). He urged a demonstration of 'the same disposition' (2.2). This precise language recurs in 4.1–3, where the apostle makes a pointed personal appeal to Euodia and Syntyche. With the warmest affection Paul salutes the church and urges them to 'stand firm thus in the Lord' (1). He appeals to the two women to share 'the same disposition in the Lord' (2).

Paul's method in dealing with this delicate congregational problem is worthy of notice. Delaying until the last moment to name the two women, the apostle prepared for this exhortation by a sensitive use of language in ch. 2. His admonition to avoid selfishness or conceit, but to esteem others in genuine humility (2.3), finds supreme illustration in Christ Jesus who refused to grasp equality with God, but assumed the form of a slave, and in deep humility became obedient to death (2.6–8). The plea to extend one's concern

274

beyond one's own interests to those of others (2.4) finds support in the example of Timothy, a man 'genuinely anxious for your welfare' (2.20–23), and Epaphroditus, who risked his life to serve Paul on behalf of the Philippians (2.29 f.). Paul's point is clear: selfish vying for personal rights and honours is inconsistent with advancing the cause of Christ. Finally, Paul requests a close friend to reconcile the two women (3). At each point the ground of the admonition is the rightness of such conduct 'in the Lord' (4.1 f.). Paul could not ignore the breach of unity within the congregation, but his manner of confronting those involved exhibits Christian concern and tactfulness.

Question: How are you contributing to the unity of your church?

Philippians 4.4-7 — Joy, Gentleness, Thanksgiving

Paul was growing old. The sufferings he had endured had certainly taken their toll (cf. 2 Cor. 4.8 ff.; 6.4 f.; 11.23 ff.). Yet, for all that, he had not lost his sense of the vibrancy of life. As he dictates this letter the words 'joy' and 'rejoice' come to his lips repeatedly (cf. 1.4,18; 2.17 f.; 3.1; 4.4,10). They express a defiant 'nevertheless' to all of the disappointments and hardships of the Christian life. The command, 'Rejoice in the Lord always' (4) sounds a keynote to the entire epistle. The Christian can rejoice at all times and under all circumstances precisely because the source of his joy is 'the Lord'.

'Forbearance' or 'moderation' (5) was a virtue esteemed by many in the imperial period, as shown by the inscriptions. It speaks of a gentleness which arises out of strength rather than weakness, a fair-mindedness which refuses to harbour resentment but extends love and understanding toward another. In the Greek Psalter used at Philippi the term was used to express God's readiness to forgive (Psa. 86.5). We can have this kind of gentleness, Paul states, because 'the Lord is at hand'. The words constituted a greeting which Christians exchanged with one another. Here they are a sober reminder that this was no time to quarrel because someone had failed to recognize one's worth. Euodia and Syntyche needed to understand this!

The final two verses resume the theme of 1.12–26 and 2.17—3.1. The anxiety to which Paul refers (6) is specifically the concern for Paul in the face of trouble and uncertainty which the Philippians had expressed through Epaphroditus. The appropriate response to anxiety is a quiet reliance on God expressed through prayer *with thanksgiving.* The ground of thanksgiving is the certain knowledge that God is aware of our needs even before we express them (cf. 4.19). He knows that the song of praise will push anxiety from the heart. The anxious heart is the unguarded heart, but the divine

275

response to thanksgiving is the peace which God possesses, which anchors the heart securely in Christ Jesus.

Thought: Gentleness is strength held back.

Philippians 4.8,9   The Christian in the World

If the Philippians belonged to a commonwealth in heaven (3.20), it was also true that they were resident aliens in the world. Since their conversion to Christ they had found the world to be an arena of conflict and suffering (1.29). It posed a threat to life and provoked anxiety (2.27,30; 4.6). Its people warranted the epithet 'crooked and perverse' (2.15). There was another side to reality in the world, however, to which Paul directs their attention in v. 8. The term 'whatever' must not be watered down or limited to aspects of thought and life which are distinctively Christian. Paul commands the believers to recognize everything that is humanly true and good in contemporary society as a focal point for thoughtful consideration. Elements of truth, purity, beauty and moral excellence in culture provide control and direction even for the pagan. They are to be appreciated as expressions of God's common grace by which He restrains chaos and enriches the life of men. When the world knows what is good, the Christian must know it as well. Paul therefore commands, '. . . think about these things'.

Complementing God's common grace is the deposit of Christian truth bestowed on the Church as an expression of His special grace. Paul defines this deposit in terms of the tradition which the Philippians had received from his teaching ministry and had seen embodied in his personal ministry (9). The world frequently *knows* what is good but fails to *do* what is good. What the Philippians have learned from Paul is that, knowledge of the good demands performance of the good—for only then is this a knowledge of God. When the apostle commands, 'Do these things', he is echoing his earlier summons to 'hold true to what we have attained' (3.16) and to imitate his example (3.17). These constitute the conditions under which a man may walk with the God of peace in the world.

Thought: The understanding of goodness must not be confused with the doing of it.

Philippians 4.10-13   Sufficiency through Christ

The letter draws to a conclusion as it had opened, with a further acknowledgement of the gifts he has received from Epaphroditus (18 f.), and an expression of deep affection for the believers at Philippi. Here, perhaps more than elsewhere, the letter abounds in small touches which convey Paul's involvement with the life of this church and his meaningful use of language drawn from a pagan environment but bridled for the service of Christ.

Paul has great joy that the deep feelings of the Philippians for him have 'blossomed' once more (10). The reason for his joy is that they had found an opportunity to help *him* make an offering to God (18)! He cannot regard their gifts as supplying something necessary which he lacked because he has not been aware of any need (11,12). Employing language which his readers would appreciate, Paul states that he has attained what the philosophers have been seeking. He is 'self-sufficient', refusing to be led astray either by wealth or by poverty. Changing the figure, Paul asserts he has been 'initiated into the mystery' of facing every condition of existence—to be full or to be hungry, to have abundance or nothing. These appeals to familiar figures in any great Hellenistic city have a certain playfulness to them. But the apostle quickly qualifies his affirmations by a reference to Christ which has no parallel among the philosophers or the initiants to the mysteries: 'I can do everything through Him who gives me strength' (13). Paul's self-sufficiency is not Stoic apathy or cynical resolution to the realities of human life but a firm reliance upon the Lord who always takes thought for his needs (cf. v. 19). The joy, confidence and sufficiency which he experiences flow from his vital union with Jesus Christ and give to the apostle a superiority to all outward circumstances.

Philippians 4.14-20   A Generous Offering to God

From the narrative in Acts **16** one might judge that the church in Philippi consisted of a few women, the Roman jailer and his family, and some few others. This initial impression is undoubtedly mistaken. The work had been sufficiently advanced to warrant leaving Luke at Philippi to provide pastoral leadership to the young church. Continued hostility on the part of significant elements in the city failed to intimidate the believers. In the weeks which followed they twice contributed to the support of Paul and his companions in Thessalonica (15 f.). When the apostle moved on to Corinth they sent aid to him again (2 Cor. **11**.8–9). While Paul commends all the churches of Macedonia for their eager support of the collection on behalf of the impoverished believers in Jerusalem, what he says of them to the Corinthians was true pre-eminently of the Christians at Philippi (2 Cor. 8.2–5). Their generosity repeatedly refreshed Paul and sealed their participation in his labours for the gospel (15, cf. **1**.5). Paul can rejoice in their partnership with him precisely because a gift brings superabundant blessing to the giver (10,14–17,19).

Paul again introduces the language of accounting ('partnership

... giving and receiving', 15), as in 3.7. Now with respect to their latest contribution he exclaims, '*I have received full payment*, and more' (18). The italicized words translate a single Greek term found hundreds of times on commercial papyri and ostraca to indicate that an obligation has been met in full. The commercial language is quickly overshadowed, however, by the adoption of the vocabulary of sacrifice. Paul has lifted up before God the gifts bestowed on him as a peace offering intended for the Lord. He recognized that the affection directed toward him was ultimately directed toward God. The acceptance of the offering will be verified in the gracious response of God, who will meet every need of the Christians in that same generous manner that Paul's needs have always been met (19).

Paul has not once used the word 'thanks' in expressing his thanksgiving. Rather he treats the gifts as something especially gratifying because they represent an offering well-pleasing to God. In spite of the restraint, Paul emerges as a man of affection who was able to win and hold the affection of others.

Philippians 4.21-23   Christian Greetings

The letter draws to a close with the conveyance of greetings and a final benediction. Paul requests that his greeting be extended to each member of the community (21). His use of the term 'saint' in the singular is unique. Elsewhere in the N.T. it is customary to use the plural, as does Paul in v. 22 ('all the saints'). What is even more striking is Paul's command to greet each Christian 'in Christ Jesus'. Even greetings must reflect the sphere of life in which Christians move; they should breathe the spirit of Christ. The affection for one another expressed in the exchange of greetings between Paul and his friends is rooted in the vital union which they share in Christ. The implication is that strained relationships, like those between Euodia and Syntyche, can be improved only as the relationship between each believer and his Lord is strengthened.

To his own greeting Paul adds the salutation of certain 'brethren' who are with him. Presumably this designates those who were associated with leadership in the church at Rome, including Timothy, Aristarchus, Mark, Jesus surnamed Justus, Luke and Demas (cf. Col. 4.10 f., 14). Finally, the entire church at Rome sends its greetings as well, including members of 'Caesar's household'. One of the certain tokens of the advance of the gospel of which Paul had assured the Philippians (1.12) was that a number of slaves and freedmen attached to the imperial residence had come to faith. Whether their conversion was a direct result of the removal of Paul from the house he rented to a cell in the praetorium is uncertain, but

278

the apostle has had contact with them and takes special pleasure in conveying their greeting. He then adds in his own hand the prayer for grace (23).

Questions for further study and discussion on Philippians chs. 3.17—4.23

1. A 'heavenward perspective' has been caricatured as a desire for 'pie in the sky by and by'. What does it really entail?
2. What are the most effective ways of dealing with ungraciousness on the part of distinguished members of the Church?
3. Why is thanksgiving to accompany prayer and petition (4.6 f.)? How can one always be thankful?
4. List some illustrations of truth, purity, beauty and moral excellence in contemporary culture. Can these be used to point men beyond culture to God?
5. What is the relationship of the sufficiency we experience through Christ, and genuine self-sufficiency?

Colossians

INTRODUCTION

The first century A.D. was an age of syncretism. The essence of syncretism is the tendency to identify deities, rites, observances and interpretations of one people or region with those of another. Men did not hesitate to alter or modify their religious orientation by adopting elements of belief or expressions of piety originally quite foreign or distinct from their own. Judged from the religious and social perspective of the Roman world, Christianity represented merely another new cult. Particularly in Asia Minor attempts were made to accommodate its truth to Hellenistic religious philosophy. Faced with this threat of syncretism, a primary concern of the apostle Paul became the integrity of the gospel. This is expressed pointedly in *Colossians*, which was written at a time of crisis when the nature of salvation was being obscured by false teaching.

*Colossians 1.1,2   Christianity in the Lycus Valley

The letter to the *Colossians* was sent from Rome to the Lycus Valley in the old Phrygian region of Asia Minor. To speak of the Lycus

279

Valley is to think of three centres whose fortunes were largely intertwined: Laodicea and Hierapolis, both important and wealthy cities, and the more ancient town of Colossae whose former glory was now eclipsed by its neighbours (cf. 2.1; 4.13,16). Probably Colossae was the smallest centre to which Paul wrote a letter.

The apostle's earlier epistles are addressed formally 'to the church . . .' or 'to the churches' (cf. 1 and 2 Thess.; Gal.). In *Romans*, *Ephesians*, and *Colossians*, the address is to the saints and brethren. This can hardly be accidental. In each instance Paul is writing to churches where he was personally unknown (cf. 2.1). The designation of the addressees as 'saints and faithful brethren' permits a more personal and less official greeting to a people with whom Paul had become acquainted only through oral report (1.4,9). The absence of personal contact between Paul and the church also explains the qualification of the term 'apostle' with the important phrase 'by the will of God'. Paul intends to instruct the believers concerning the character of Christian truth and the salvation they enjoy. The opening lines establish both his authority to do so and his openness to his readers.

*Colossians 1.3-8   The Ministry of Epaphras

The man responsible for bringing Christianity to the Lycus Valley was Epaphras, a native of Colossae (4.12). Not only had the Colossians first heard the gospel from him (6,7), but he had laboured diligently at Laodicea and Hierapolis as well (4.13). His own initial contact with the Christian message probably can be traced to the time of Paul's extended Ephesian ministry. As a direct result of his daily teaching in the lecture hall of Tyrannus, Luke reports, 'all the residents of Asia heard the word of the Lord' (Acts 19.10). This wide extension of the gospel may have taken place as Paul's disciples were instructed by him and then returned to evangelize their own native towns. This supposition explains why Paul writes of Epaphras that 'he is a faithful minister of Christ *on our behalf*' (7). Epaphras had preached the gospel at Colossae as Paul's emissary. It also explains Paul's dependence upon Epaphras for his information concerning the Christians of the Lycus Valley (cf. vs. 4,8 f.; 2.1) and the apostle's assumption of authority over a church with which he had little personal acquaintance. While Paul was unable to visit all the congregations established during the course of his Ephesian ministry he had a vital interest in them. On this understanding the church at Colossae was established in the period A.D. 52–55.

Perhaps five years after the founding of the church, Epaphras sought out Paul in Rome to inform him of developments within the congregation. Although the work had advanced (6), a type of teaching had been introduced which, if unchecked, could only obscure the character of salvation and reduce Christianity to an unwholesome asceticism. To judge from the relative mildness of Paul's response (in contrast to the tone assumed in *Galatians*), the error had not yet subverted the gospel.

Apart from the letter written in anguish to the Galatians, all Paul's epistles begin with a word of thanksgiving (3–5). Here the specific ground of thanksgiving is the triad of Christian virtues: faith, love and hope. Paul had been informed by Epaphras concerning the faith of the Colossians and the love they had for other believers. The third element is introduced by Paul himself because it has direct bearing on what he wishes to say to the church. An adequate basis for hope is found in the gospel, which Paul defines as 'the word of truth' (5), anticipating his characterization of the false teaching as 'human tradition' and 'empty deceit' (2.8). The growth of the gospel among those who have received it, and its penetration into the whole world (6), offer proof of its truth and sufficiency to satisfy the deepest yearning of the human heart.

Thought: When a Christian proclaims the good news of Christ without reserve, who can say how far that proclamation will spread?

Colossians 1.9-14 Entrance Already

The burden of Paul's prayer was that his readers might know the riches they possessed through the gospel, and might wait with patience and joy until their life which is hidden with Christ appears with Him (cf. 3.1). One by one the apostle touches upon the shibboleths which the false teachers had used as a goad toward rigorism in the life of the believer: 'filled with the knowledge of His will', 'all spiritual wisdom and understanding' (9), 'a life worthy of the Lord', 'fully pleasing to Him', 'increasing in the knowledge of God' (10). Paul's desire for the church is not less, but he also prayed that they might experience *joy* and *thanksgiving* (11,12), two emphases which were conspicuously absent from the negative restrictions the congregation had begun to accept. In contrast to submission to ascetic practices in order to qualify for visions (cf. 2.18), Paul urges joyful thanksgiving to the Father 'who has qualified us to share in the inheritance of the saints in light' (12; cf. v. 5). In contrast to rigid self-discipline as the means of attaining perfection during one's lifetime (cf. 2.17), Paul exults in the God who has already 'transferred us to the kingdom of His beloved Son' (13). The apostle's image is a satisfying one, for in the classical writers the verb signifies the removal of whole communities from one district to another.

Formerly the Colossians were enslaved in the land of darkness. But God rescued them and transplanted them into a kingdom which is flooded with light. The king is God's dear Son who forgave their sins and confirmed their freedom (14). In this manner, prior to any explicit reference to the Colossian error, Paul indicates that Christians have already experienced what the false teachers had argued was available only through a life of rigorous self-denial. Believers do not have to struggle to gain entrance to their inheritance; God has graciously provided that entrance through His Son.

Thought: When you live in a kingdom flooded with light, in which God's own Son is Ruler, joy and thankfulness are always possible.

Colossians 1.15-20   The Primacy of Christ

To introduce the heart of his teaching about Jesus Christ, Paul employs the language of worship. He draws upon the fragments of a hymn that may have been familiar to Christians of the Lycus Valley. The hymn consists of two stanzas or strophes, built in a parallel way:

Strophe 1 (**1.15–18a**)	*Strophe* 2 (**1.18b–20**)
He is the image of the invisible God,	*He is the beginning,*
the first-born of all creation;	*the first-born* from the dead . . .
for in Him all things were created.	*for in Him* all the fullness of God was pleased to dwell.

The first strophe reflects upon Jesus' relationship to God and the world; the second reflects upon His relationship to salvation.

The parallel statements cited may be viewed as propositions acknowledged in the worship of the Church, to which Paul adds his own commentary. First, Christ is the image of God before men, the Revealer of the Father. The contrast is between Christ who is seen and God who is unseen, even in the visions of the false teachers. The opening line of the hymn thus anticipates Paul's strong statement on the Incarnation (2.9). Second, He is described as the Lord of all creation. The term 'first-born' stresses uniqueness rather than priority in time (cf. Psa. 89.27). Jesus is the 'first-born' because He is the agent of creation and the heir of creation. The relationship of the Son to all created existence is that of the Lord to subjects. The stress in the first strophe thus falls on the sovereignty of Christ.

In the second strophe Paul is concerned to establish the relationship of the Son to the Church. The relationship is that of Head over the Body (18). In 2.19, where Paul is developing a physiological metaphor, Christ is described as the head which sends down life into the whole body. In v. 18 and 2.10 the thought is more political. 'Head' means properly 'leader'. The statements which follow also have a political tone, speaking of Christ's pre-eminence and of His sovereign act of reconciliation (18,20). Paul sets before the Colossians the primacy of Christ over the whole Church. The false teachers, by joining to the gospel an insistence upon human devices for attaining an advanced spirituality, have failed to submit to Christ as Head. They have substituted their wisdom for His. As a result they were in danger of becoming truncated, 'not holding fast to the Head', and so losing the life that He supplies. What is required is a return to worship in which the Church, in humble adoration, acknowledges that Jesus Christ is pre-eminent 'in everything' (18).

Colossians 1.21-23   Christ the Reconciler

Paul has just affirmed that Jesus Christ is the agent of God's magnificent work of creation. The very orders of angels of which the false teachers spoke—thrones, dominions, principalities, authorities —owed their existence to Him (16). As the keystone to all created existence, Christ alone prevents the return of all things to a state of chaos (17). From this archimedean point the apostle then directed the gaze of his readers to a moment beyond time when Christ will have achieved the reconciliation of all things to Himself (20). But Paul does not allow his readers to become lost in the depths of reflection. He points them concretely to Golgotha and the shed blood of Jesus, the Lord of life. Nothing less than this is the cost of the reconciliation He has achieved.

In the verses which immediately follow, Paul moves from the language of worship to the worshipping community itself (21 f.). The cosmic achievement of Christ found its practical outworking in the Lycus Valley in the reconciliation of the Colossians. The object of Christ's reconciling action 'on earth' (20) were men who knew within themselves a profound sense of alienation from God and from each other (21). Their evil deeds merely intensified the hostility they expressed through their style of life. Modern 'existential' man feels himself penetrated by Paul's language precisely because this is his experience. The violence of the language which follows, locating the moment and point of reconciliation in 'His body of flesh by His death' (22), is calculated to point beyond doctrine to the reality of death upon the cross (20).

The purpose of Christ's reconciling action is to achieve a new creation (cf. 3.10), in which men who were 'estranged' may know the bold approach to God of those who are 'holy'; those who were 'hostile in mind' may know in their relationships to others a blamelessness, and those who practised 'evil deeds' may be scrutinized by God and men and pronounced 'irreproachable'. All of this, Paul affirms, *Christ* will achieve. But it is the responsibility of the Colossians to be rooted in faith, not shifting from that hope of the gospel for which Paul had thanked God (3,5) to some lesser hope offered by local teachers (23).

Question: Do you believe that Christ can meet the estranged and lonely parts of your personality, and link them with a holy God in joyful reconciliation?

Colossians 1.24-28 Ministerial Sufferings

When Paul dictated the letter to the Colossians he was in chains (4.10,18). Yet he found an occasion of joy in the sufferings he endured since he was bearing in his flesh the 'afflictions of Christ' (24). The apostle took seriously that the afflictions were really Christ's because they were ultimately directed against Him. Every time he had scourged a Christian it was as if he had laid the lash on the back of Christ (Acts 9.4). Now he is whipped, imprisoned and exhibited as a spectacle, and Paul rejoices that he may bear these indignities on behalf of his Lord. He completes what is lacking in the suffering to which he has been appointed as an apostle (Acts 9.16). He participates in 'the beginning of sufferings' (Matt. 24.8) which must precede the triumphant return of the Lord. Since the entire local church will share in this triumph, Paul's sufferings are 'for your sake' and for the benefit of the Church at large. The term 'afflictions of Christ' is never associated with the redemptive suffering of Jesus upon the cross. It speaks, rather, of those ministerial sufferings which Paul bears because he represents Jesus Christ.

Paul was specifically the Apostle to the Gentiles (Gal. 1.15 f.; 2.7–9). He rejoiced that the message with which he was entrusted was one which centred in hope—'Christ in you, *the hope* of glory' (27; cf. vs. 5,23). He labels this news a 'mystery', aware that the false teachers were offering mysteries of their own to those who would listen. But Paul quickly qualifies this term as a secret which has been revealed by God to the *entire* Church. It is the open secret that God has chosen to dwell in the hearts of Gentiles, who had no claim upon Him, through Jesus Christ, the source and goal of all hope. In contrast to spiritual advance for the few urged by the false teachers (2.16–18), the intention of Christ and of His minister is that *every man* may be presented to God irreproachable and mature (28; cf. 4.12).

Thought: Suffering endured for Jesus is the easiest kind to bear, since He shares the burden with you.

The Greek term from which the word 'asceticism' comes denotes primarily training or exercise appropriate to an athlete. The derived meaning is discipline necessary for engagement in a spiritual contest (cf. Acts 24.16). In contrast to the false asceticism promoted by slogans at Colossae (2.21), Paul displays the true 'asceticism' of the athlete of God. Though confined to a cell, he engages in an arena existence (1.24,29; 2.1; cf. 4.12 f.). Prayer, thought and wrestling with issues consume his energies on behalf of all the churches, but particularly those in which he has not been directly involved. The specific mention of Laodicea (2.1) anticipates the apostle's command to send his letter to that community (4.16). Apparently the errors at Colossae had penetrated the church at Laodicea.

The purposes which move Paul to his prodigious labours are expressed in terms which echo the prayer of 1.9 f. (2,3). The condition for realizing this goal is the unity of the Church. It is as believers are 'knit together in love' that God is pleased to unveil yet more of His open secret. In 1.27 Paul had defined 'the mystery of God' as Christ in the midst of the Gentiles achieving the fruit of His reconciling action on the cross. Here he defines that mystery as 'Christ', the embodiment of 'the Wisdom of God'. In the Wisdom literature of the O.T. (especially Prov. 8.22 ff.) God's wisdom was personified and four predicates were ascribed to it: 1. Wisdom was with God in the beginning and functioned as Creator (cf. Col. 1.16). 2. Wisdom sustains the creation, acting in God's behalf upon the earth (cf. 1.17). 3. Wisdom reveals God to men (cf. 1.15). 4. Wisdom reconciles men and makes them friends to God (cf. 1.20). Paul did not hesitate to designate Jesus as 'the Wisdom of God' (1 Cor. 1.24,30) and to interpret His functions in these categories (Col. 1.15–20). Now, with a view to the speculations of the Colossian teachers, he reminds his readers that the true source of wisdom and knowledge is a deeper personal knowledge of Jesus Christ. If there is a secret to be known, it will be known only through a knowledge of Him.

Questions for further study and discussion on Colossians chs. 1.1—2.3

1. How is the gospel threatened by religious syncretism today?
2. What is the distinctive character of Christian hope?
3. What does it mean to affirm the sovereignty of Christ in every sphere of existence?
4. What implication does the primacy of Christ over the whole Church have for current ecumenical dialogue?

5. What examples of alienation and hostility between men do you find in your newspaper, contemporary literature and drama? What does Christ the Reconciler mean to these situations?

Colossians 2.4-7   Growth in Christ

The apostle had just pointed to the infinite treasures of the truth of God available to the believer in Christ (3). His purpose in doing so was to prevent anyone from deceiving the Colossians into thinking that something beyond their life in Christ was necessary to complete their salvation. For the first time in the letter Paul makes a direct allusion to the false teaching. He labels it a delusion couched in 'beguiling speech' (4). The new doctrine was supported by appeals to its plausibility; the apostle exposes it as specious. They would be led astray from the truth by false reasoning.

What prompts Paul to warn the believers of deception is his own feeling for them. He is with them 'in spirit' and rejoices in the steadfastness of their faith in Christ (5). If the military terminology may be pressed, the apostle envisages the Christians as soldiers arranged in orderly formation prepared to support an unbroken front of faith. They had received Christ Jesus as Lord through the apostolic teaching which Epaphras had faithfully proclaimed. Now Paul pleads for them to live their lives as men who were united with Christ through faith and who derive their own life from His (6). This thought is expanded by means of the mixed metaphors of a living organism sending down its roots into the subsoil, and a building nearing completion as it rises from an indestructible foundation (7). The first figure suggests that faith must be living, sustained by the life of Christ Himself; the second, that faith must experience growth toward perfection. Faith is thought of as an active principle which establishes the Christian in his relationship to Christ. Paul's response to 'beguiling speech' is an appeal for continued growth in the Christian life experienced through the word of truth conveyed in the apostolic tradition (cf. 1.5 f.), and abundant thanksgiving.

Thought: There is an immense difference between a passive faith and an active rest in Christ.

Colossians 2.8-15   The Triumph of Christ's Death

This paragraph, which consists of a single compact sentence, is one of the most important in the entire letter. After a warning not to be captured by false tradition (8), it offers to the readers an incisive statement of the importance of Christ's death for them (9-14), and affirms the cosmic extent of His triumph (15).

Paul's warning resumes the interrupted thought of v. 4 and vividly depicts the danger which imperils the church; the false teachers are slave-raiders who would carry the believers off bodily (8). 'Philosophy' is probably the designation used by the proponents of the new teaching to commend their distinctive emphases. In the first century the term denotes a mode of life rather than intellectual pursuit, and frequently approximates the term 'salvation'. Paul uses the word derogatorily, describing the teaching it embraced as 'empty deceit', the product of human cleverness and demonic inspiration (cf. v. 20; Gal. 6.3,9). It reflected of cosmic powers hostile to Christ and entailed enslavement rather than freedom.

What was promised in the offer of 'philosophy' was 'fullness of life' (cf. v. 10). The Colossians already enjoyed this in Christ (9,10)! What the believers needed was not new teaching but a return to the tradition (cf. vs. 6,7). Paul therefore echoes the great hymn in honour to Christ which he had introduced in 1.15 ff. Because the totality of deity lives in Christ as it was embodied in Him at the Incarnation (9), there is no reason to seek God or power of life elsewhere. The completion sought by the Colossians is already their possession 'in Him' (10). It is probable that the local teachers urged circumcision as a preliminary rite to the visions which constituted perfection (2.11,17 f.). Paul insists that believers have already experienced enrolment within the covenant fellowship through the circumcision of Christ, a bold figure for Christ's death (with v. 11 cf. 1.22; 2.15). He lists three benefits which accrue to believers from Christ's death: the removal of spiritual alienation (symbolized by literal uncircumcision, cf. Eph. 2.11 f.); the enjoyment of the resurrection life of Christ; the forgiveness of all trespasses (13). What this forgiveness entailed for Christ the apostle makes vividly clear through the image of a statement of indebtedness personally signed by the debtor (for example of the form, see Philem. 19). We had manifestly failed to discharge our obligation to God and merited the death which forfeiture imposed. But Christ assumed our debt and discharged it by His death; He smeared out our signature on the bond by nailing it to His cross (14), and triumphed utterly. Participation with Christ in His triumph is incompatible with submission to a teaching which owes its inspiration to the defeated cosmic powers (15 cf. v. 8).

Question: Have you participated in both Christ's death and His triumph?

Colossians 2.16-19 The False Teaching

The sole source for reconstructing the false teaching found at

Colossae is Paul's letter. Certain aspects of the error may be readily identified. From Judaism came an insistence on circumcision (11), legal ordinances (14), food and drink regulations, and observances of the festival calendar (16). The rigorous asceticism which found expression in the regulations of v. 21 may or may not be Jewish in origin. The designation 'philosophy' (8) and the use of catch-words like 'knowledge' (*gnosis*), 'wisdom' and 'mystery' suggest a syncretistic religious outlook. There were important colonies of Jews both at Laodicea and Hierapolis. That they had been penetrated by religious syncretism is suggested by inscriptions and rabbinic statements calling into question the character of Phrygian Judaism.

The key to understanding the precise nature of what was being taught at Colossae lies in the interpretation of Paul's difficult reference to 'self-abasement' (humility), 'the worship of angels' and 'visions' (18). In early Christian literature the term 'humility' could have special reference to *fasting;* this is appropriate to vs. 16–23 where there is reference to food and drink. Understood in a comprehensive sense, the word designates all the elements of rigorous self-discipline implied in vs. 16–23. Visionary exaltation, encouraged by fasting and severity to the body, was widely known in the Hellenistic world. Fasting and the heavenly journey by which the seer is given entrance into the sphere of the angels is a common theme in Jewish apocryphal literature and in the Gnostic texts of the Hermetic Corpus. That which was seen upon entrance into heaven was *the worship performed by the angels*. Without exception, the works which speak of visionary entrance into the heavenly sphere describe the highest office of angels and men as the adoration of God. Accordingly, v. 18 speaks of fasting and rigorous self-discipline in order to experience a vision of the heavenly sphere. 'The worship of angels' does not mean the veneration of angelic creatures by men but rather the worship directed toward God *by the angels*. This vision of the heavenly liturgy and its attendant glory was designated 'a shadow of what is to come' (17). By rigorous asceticism, the false teachers contended, men could receive in their lifetime a vision of the angelic service into which they would enter—a vision others would behold only after death. It was this prospect which appeared so attractive.

At the heart of the Colossian error was ignorance of the redemption Christ had achieved. It was felt that the Christian could enter into the inheritance of the saints only by a grim struggle. As Christ put off the body (1.22; 2.11), the Colossians sought to subdue their bodies with severity. As He assumed His place far above all rule and authority (1.16–18; 2.10), they sought to enter the heavenly sphere.

In short, they lacked assurance that in and with Christ *they themselves* had experienced a full deliverance and were being renewed in knowledge after the image of God (cf. **1**.13; **2**.10–12; **3**.1,10). Instead, they had to *earn* the divine vision through ascetic discipline. The error did not spring from a false view of the person of Christ but from a false estimate of the present salvation provided through Him. But it led to a truncated existence, cutting an individual off from the life-giving presence of Christ (19).

Question: Are there contemporary substitutes for a genuine renewal in Christ by which you are tempted?

Colossians 2.20-23 The New Legalism

Having exposed the worship and doctrines of the false teachers, the apostle now turns to their practical demands. These resulted in a new type of legalism, against which Paul directs the same basic criticisms urged against legalism in *Galatians*. In Christ we have died to legalism. The Christian is to be controlled by Christ as He expresses His will within the life of the believer, not by regulations imposed from without.

Paul's argument begins with the foundation truth that believers have been identified with the Christ who in His death triumphed over the powers hostile to God (20; cf. v. 15). Why, then, should they seek to live as if they were yet in bondage to these powers? Rules and regulations belong to the structure of the world. So long as a man has no life beyond this structure he is subjected to rules prescribed for him. But in Christ the Church has been transferred to a sphere of freedom (cf. **1**.13) in which the old restrictions are recognized to be useless. Paul mockingly repeats the slogans of the local teachers (21). These counsels were offered as the means of attaining a higher condition of holiness. Yet they all refer to things which waste away through use (22) and bind the thoughts of men to the sphere of quite ordinary existence. Paul levels three telling criticisms against the new legalism: (*i*) the ascetic practices urged to attain entrance into heaven were mere human devices arbitrarily imposed (22; cf. Isa. **29**.13); (*ii*) it entails a loss of liberty in so far as those who accept the regulations submit to bondage to their fellowmen; (*iii*) it amounts to little more than a solemn pretence (23).

Approaches like fasting and rigorous discipline of the body had the appearance of wisdom, but involved submission to a piety which had its origin in the human will. The proud claim of visions (**2**.18) indicates that these practices encouraged conceit, blinding the Colossians to the truth that God alone must redeem *and mature* them. In this light, the prohibitions and spiritual disciplines adopted at Colossae were in actuality a subtle form of fleshly indulgence (23). The Christian is free to use the world precisely because Christ has freed him from the world.

Colossians 3.1-4 Life in a Risen Lord

Paul had sufficiently exposed the fallacies of the new teaching at Colossae (2.4–23). The task now before him is to display the character of the hope set before the believers (cf. 1.5), and the obligations which such a prospect imposes. In contrast to the negative approach to Christian existence urged by the rigourists, Paul points to the reality of life in a risen Lord. He had earlier said that in baptism a man is united with Christ in His death and His resurrection (2.12). He now returns to that affirmation as an encouragement for believers to act in accordance with the position they enjoy. Since you have experienced resurrection life, he writes, let your concerns be those of the risen and exalted Christ (3.1). Paul's point is supported by spatial imagery. The false teachers, in spite of their concern for heavenly visions (2.18), were really concerned with the lower sphere of the world (2.20). Christians, on the other hand, through their union with Christ belong already to that heavenly sphere where the Lord now lives and reigns. When Paul says, 'Seek the things that are above' (1 f.), it is probable that he again echoes a catch-phrase of the false teachers. But here it is an exhortation for believers to conform their whole will and disposition to that heavenly world to which they now belong through Christ.

Consistent with his emphasis on baptism as a death to the old style of life, Paul now speaks of the new heavenly life which is hidden 'with Christ in God'. The life of Christ which distinguishes the Christian from other men is a profound reality (cf. Gal. 2.20). Its full character has not yet been unveiled, but Paul's language in vs. 3 f. suggests that it is a 'concentric' life. It is a life which draws its existence from the very centre of all reality as opposed to the 'eccentric' life of the man who has no vital relationship with Christ. When Christ returns to celebrate His triumph (cf. 2.19), His people will share His glory (4). They will appear in their true character as those whose life has become one with Christ's life (cf. Phil. 3.20 f.; 1 John 3.2). Throughout this section, and the admonitions which follow, the perspective is controlled by the thought of the full life which belongs to all who are in Christ.

Question: Are you appropriating the privileges of the position you already have in Christ?

Baptism marked a critical moment in the life of the Christian in which he affirmed that he had died with respect to his former manner of life. Since he had received a Lord, all pretext for disobedience was removed. Paul now builds on this understanding. The action of Christ in removing us from the sphere of death into life (1.13 f.; 2.9–14) demands a response in the believer. He must consign to the sphere of death the marks of the old life (5, 8 f.). The Pauline indicative, 'You have died' to the old style of life (2.11 f.; Rom. 6.3–11), finds its counterpart in the imperative, 'Put to death' those signs of the old life which attempt to reassert themselves. The enumeration of two series of five vices, climaxed by one more (5,8,9, [to which correspond five virtues crowned by love, 12–14]), may reflect an early catechism which converts were expected to learn.

Immorality and crude self-centredness indicate that the governing motive of life is pleasure and a pampering of the flesh. The equation of this disposition with idolatry (5) stems from the enthronement of self in the place of authority which belongs to God alone. Self-deification inevitably dulls ethical sensitivity and always invites the wrath of God (6; Rom. 1.18 ff.). The rescue of men from this degraded condition was the remarkable accomplishment of the Christian mission.

The second list of vices (8 f.) are those which find expression through speech. Because they display an attitude of bitterness toward others, they are expressions of that self-centredness which Paul has just denounced.

The basis for Paul's appeal is the radical transformation of character experienced by every believer. The apostle compares it to the changing of a garment. When the Christian enthrones Jesus Christ as Lord of his life, he exchanges the rags of unrighteousness for the robes of Christ's righteousness (9 f.; cf: Rom. 13.14; Gal. 3.27). The knowledge which he now needs is not some secret insight like that offered by the false teachers, but a knowledge which depends solely upon the inward renewal of his nature by God. This drastic renewal Paul sees as a new creation in which arbitrary distinctions of a racial, religious, cultural or social nature, which set one man over against another, are done away (11). According to a Latin proverb, 'Man is a wolf to his fellow man!' When Christ is given pre-eminence (1.18) men must recognize that no basis exists for anyone to exalt himself above another or to exploit another for his own advantage.

Thought: The renewal of your nature must be reaffirmed every day by an act of renewed commitment to the Lordship of Jesus Christ, if the freshness of your devotion is to be preserved.

Colossians 3.12-17   The Marks of the New Life

The removal of the marks of the old life leaves a vacuum which must be filled. Paul urges that his readers display the tokens of their new life in Christ. He had just said that in Christ there exists no distinction between Greek and Jew (11). Now the apostle applies to the Colossians terms which in the O.T. were reserved for Israel alone (cf. Exod. 19.5 f.); through Christ they have been set apart from the world as God's beloved children (12). They are to demonstrate by their lives that they belong to the new family of faith. Having shed the rags of pagan bondage, they are to put on the robes of splendour which belong to sons alone (cf. Luke 15.15,21 f.). The qualities which Paul commends are the opposites to the signs of bitterness enumerated in v. 8. They reflect Christ's life within us by which our attitude toward others is conformed to His own. If the Christian is to make Jesus Christ visible in the world he must treat other men as Christ treated him (13). What the Colossians had been forgiven is sufficiently indicated by vs. 5–7. The qualities of generosity which Paul lists are to be crowned by a love which knows what it is to say 'No' to oneself in order to be able to say 'Yes' to another. Paul depicts love as the girdle which holds in place the garments of the new life (14). Love makes it possible for men to share genuine fellowship in Christ.

The achievement of unity within the larger fellowship of the church is the concern of vs. 15–17. Paul was a realist who knew that occasions of friction arise inevitably whenever men meet in close fellowship, whether in families, places of work or in churches. God's provision for harmony in the Church is the grace of Christ experienced, first in reconciliation to God, but reaffirmed as Christ is allowed to arbitrate all disputes and differences (15). A keen awareness of the presence of Christ tends to reduce personal bias to the small dimensions it deserves. The presence of Christ becomes vocal in the word of Christ expressed through the tradition (2.6 f.) and the worship of the community (16). When Christ's word controls one's thinking, dependence upon the Lord Jesus will be reflected in all that is said and done (17). The result of an intimate union with Christ is the possession of His mind and outlook prompting a sustained spirit of thanksgiving.

Thought: A forgiving spirit is the finest indicator that you have experienced Christ's forgiveness.

1. What are the elements of the 'full life' which Christians enjoy through Christ (**2.9 f.**)? What is suggested to you by the expression 'the concentric life' (cf. **3.1–3**)?
2. What was entailed when Christ assumed your indebtedness to God and discharged it by His death?
3. Are there signs of an unwholesome asceticism in the Church today? A new legalism? A piety which has its originates in the human will?
4. Are rules and regulations always inconsistent with Christian freedom?
5. What arbitrary distinctions of a racial, religious, cultural and social nature exist in local churches and denominations today?

Colossians 3.18-21   The Ordering of the Household

At the time Paul dictated *Colossians* he had with him Onesimus, the fugitive Colossian slave. He had been wrestling with the whole question of the relationship of Christian masters and slaves. Now he turns abruptly to what has been called aptly the 'household code' (3.18—4.1; cf. Eph. 5.22 ff.; 1 Pet. 2.18 ff.); a set of instructions concerning the ordering of life in the family as a whole. The first section of the code treats the relationship of husbands and wives and of parents and children, since these are foundational to family life. The distinctly Christian contribution to the ordering of family life was the stress on reciprocal responsibilities. Even in Judaism, where family relationships were given a significance not found elsewhere in antiquity, it tended to be assumed that husbands and fathers had rights to be exercised, while wives and children had duties to be performed. In emphasizing that all members of the household had rights and duties, Paul develops a conception of family life which is implicit in Jesus' teaching concerning marriage (cf. Mark **10**.2–16).

Wives are instructed to fulfil their appropriate duties in the Christian home. The new freedom in Christ did not permit the neglect of household tasks or responsibilities toward their husbands. Husbands are commanded to provide that climate of loving support which makes it possible for their wives to fulfil their obligations happily. Aware of the conventions of Hellenistic marriage, Paul warns against surliness and discontent, which can ruin Christian marriage, and turns husbands and wives against each other (18 f.).

The reciprocal relationship of husbands and wives finds its complement in parents and children. God set before Israel the commandment to honour father and mother; He now reaffirms that this is His will in the new life (20). The responsibility of Christian fathers is understanding in the use of their authority. Paul's statement recognizes that firm discipline is necessary, but cautions against nagging and fault-finding. The purpose of discipline is not to irritate but to encourage willing obedience on the part of sons and daughters. Children must know they live in a home where they are recognized to be persons in their own right whom God loves and cares for.

Thought: God holds the Christian father responsible for the regulation of his household and the spiritual training of his children.

Colossians 3.22—4.1   Responsible Freedom

The economy of the Roman Empire was sustained on slavery. Not merely the lowest, most degrading tasks, but all forms of manual labour were considered beneath the dignity of a citizen and proper only to slaves. Moreover, by Roman law, and in the common view, slaves were accorded no recognized existence. They were not persons, but property, possessing neither rights nor legal recourse against harsh and brutal treatment.

Since many of the early converts to Christianity were slaves, and others owned slaves, it was necessary for Paul to clarify his position on slavery. The apostle deals with the situation as it then existed. He argues that a Christian may serve God in any social status. External circumstances are a matter of indifference. While a Christian slave should avail himself of the opportunity for release, even if he remains unliberated he may know the dignity of being the Lord's freedman (I Cor. 7.20–24).

In the second section of the household code nearly twice the amount of space is assigned to the relationship of slaves and masters as compared with the directives to the free members of the household. The reason for this is not merely the immediate problem of Onesimus but the greater complexity of the issues involved. The apostle is aware of the sense of injustice which the condition of slavery provoked. What he does is to set the relationship of slaves and masters in a Christian perspective which shatters traditional conceptions. Though conscious of the inequities between slaves and their masters, Paul orders the slaves to obey wholeheartedly as an act of reverence to the Lord. When it is love for Christ which impels slaves to work heartily, Paul offers the encouragement that they share in the inheritance of the saints (cf. 1.13), and are citizens of a kingdom which refuses to distinguish between men in terms of bondage and freedom (3.11,22–24). He also cautions that a condition of slavery offers no excuse for disobedience. Moral responsibility extends to slaves as well as to all other men (25). By insisting on this fact, Paul succeeds in restoring a sense of stature to those who were degraded in their own eyes by their condition.

The responsibility of masters is to treat all their slaves with equal fairness. No room is allowed for favouritism or for action based on a mere whim or a flare of temper. The reminder that they also have a Master is a sober warning that God will hold them responsible for the way they have treated their slaves. The acknowledgment of a Master in heaven provides a safeguard against dishonest service from slaves, and against abuse of power by their owners.

Colossians 4.2-6   An Approach to Maturity

There is an intimate connection between 3.16 f. and 4.2–6 in the structure of Paul's thought. In v. 16 the apostle began to instruct the Colossians concerning their responsibility to one another and to Christ in worship and daily experience. The thought of mutual responsibility, however, provided an appropriate context for Paul to digress on the household code (3.18—4.1). He then returns abruptly to his interrupted exhortation to the Church as a whole (4.2–6). When 3.16 f. and 4.2–6 are read together, it is clear that the apostle is speaking about an approach to Christian maturity. The centrality of the word of Christ in worship (3.16); a dependence upon Christ in word and deed (3.17); a constant reliance upon earnest prayer (4.2–4), and a wise conduct in the world (4.4 f.): these are the dispositions which must be cultivated. What binds the points of this programme together is the stress upon thanksgiving as the keynote of the Christian life (note 3.16,17; 4.2; cf. 1.12; 2.7; 3.15).

Paul did not hesitate to appeal for prayer for himself and for those with him (especially Timothy and Epaphras, 1.1,7; 4.12,13). He does not request deliverance from danger or hardship but a significant advancement for the truth of Christ (3 f.). At the time the churches of the Lycus Valley were founded, Paul had used the image of the open door (1 Cor. 16.9). He now returns to that figure, aware that even in prison God has already opened doors before him (Phil. 1.12–14; 4.22; Philem. 10). To share the good news was of such crucial importance to Paul that he refused to trust in his own ability to speak clearly and incisively. The church is to pray that God will assist him to proclaim the truth in an appropriate manner.

Paul expected all believers to share a sense of obligation to those not yet reached by Christ. His plea for wise Christian behaviour (5) arises from an awareness that the life-witness of Christians can be attractive and effective in winning men for Christ. Employing a common Greek metaphor for sparkling conversation (6), Paul

Colossians 4.10-14

At the conclusion of a letter, Paul often conveys the greetings of friends who are with him. The names mentioned here may have become familiar in the Lycus Valley during the period of Paul's extended stay at Ephesus (about 100 miles away). Aristarchus was from Thessalonica; like Tychicus, he had accompanied the apostle to Jerusalem with the collection and then, apparently, had voluntarily shared house-arrest in Rome (Acts **19**.29; **20**.4; **28**.30 f.). The reference to John Mark of Jerusalem is surprising since Paul's unwillingness to take Mark on his second missionary journey had caused a serious rupture with Barnabas (Acts **15**.36–40). This is the first indication that Paul had become fully reconciled to the younger man (cf. 2 Tim. **4**.11). Jesus, surnamed Justus, is mentioned only here. His Aramaic name was actually Joshua, but in Hellenistic society he would be called by his surname. The complaint that these three are the only Jewish Christians who have been a comfort to the apostle echoes Paul's report of a factious spirit on the part of many in the church at Rome (Phil. **1**.15 f.).

Among his Gentile friends the place of honour is given to Epaphras. Paul stresses his fidelity to Christ and his earnest concern for the Colossians, that the church would stand firmly against false teaching. The reference to the efforts he had exerted for the Christians of the Lycus Valley is obscure. A plausible suggestion is that he had come to Rome to raise money for the churches in a time of crisis. If Paul is alluding to the great earthquake which did so much damage in Asia Minor at just about this time, Epaphras had come to Rome to enlist the support of wealthy Christians for families who had lost everything in that disaster.

Luke was one of Paul's most constant associates from the time of the second missionary journey (see the 'we' sections in Acts **16**.10–16; **20**.6—**21**.17; **27**.1—**28**.16) until the time of his death (2 Tim. **4**.11). That he was a physician explains this long and close relationship. The apostle's ill health was aggravated by the conditions of imprisonment. The company of a doctor whom he could trust, and with whom he shared deep fellowship, was a great encouragement to Paul. With Luke, Paul mentions Demas (cf. Philem. 24; 2 Tim. **4**.10), who later proved faithless when association with Paul endangered his life.

Colossians 4.15-18

Paul now greets those whom he knew in Colossae and the neighbouring towns. His contacts in the Valley may date to the period of 'generation-gap' between parents and children? What relationships must be established in order to bridge the gap?

3. What are the implications for labour relations in what Paul has to say about slaves and masters?
4. What is involved in a distinctively Christian concept of work?
5. What can an individual or a small group of Christians do to improve the effectiveness of their conversation for Christ (4.6)?

1 and 2 Thessalonians

INTRODUCTION

The dynamics of the Gentile mission to a cosmopolitan centre and the problems which emerged with the establishment of a church are illustrated by the two letters to the Thessalonians. The first letter clarifies the meaning of commitment to Jesus Christ for men among whom idolatry had been common and to whom immorality had been a way of life. The second letter deals with a misunderstanding that had created a crisis in the church. With these documents—possibly our earliest Pauline correspondence—the use of letters emerges as an invaluable support in the mission to the Gentiles.

1 Thessalonians 1.1-3   Thankful Remembrance

Thessalonica was the most important and populous centre in Macedonia in the first century. Situated on the inmost bay of the Thermaic Gulf, it was the chief seaport of the district and the seat of the provincial government. It was a free city, boasting a popular assembly for the transaction of public business and civil magistrates elected by the people (Acts 17.6,8). The presence of an established Jewish community with a synagogue was especially attractive to Paul, who arrived in Thessalonica in A.D. 49 or 50. During his stay in the city he made the synagogue the focus of his mission but met with only moderate success (Acts 17.1–4). The real thrust of the mission occurred in the market and on the streets where a number of Gentiles unreached by the synagogue were persuaded to abandon idolatry and to acknowledge the lordship of Jesus (1 Thess. 1.9 f.).

In 1 *Thessalonians* the writer is clearly Paul (note the emphatic use of the first person singular in 2.18; 3.5; 5.27; cf. 3.1, 'alone').

299

Photo: Thessalonica from the Acropolis

Photo: Old city walls of Thessalonica

Yet he associates with himself, as the senders of the letter, Silvanus (the Roman form of Silas; cf Acts 17.4,10) and Timothy, and makes use of the first person plural ('we', 'our', 'us') throughout. More is involved in this than the mere acknowledgment of the part played by Paul's companions in the evangelization of Macedonia and the establishment of the church at Thessalonica. The apostle is acting upon the ancient law of testimony which demanded that the truthfulness of a statement be established by the agreement of two or three witnesses (Deut. 17.6; 19.15). Silas and Timothy stand with Paul as witnesses to the truth-content of what he has written both in the first and second letters to the church. Both epistles were addressed from Corinth where the three missionaries had found a good reception of the gospel.

The association of grace and peace in the initial greeting (1) reflects the core of the ancient high priestly blessing (Num. 6.24–26). Paul thanks God that the Thessalonians have displayed a triad of Christian virtues in their lives: faith, love and hope (3; cf. 5.8). They had rightly seen that a personal relationship of trust and loyalty to Christ was inseparable from action. The result was an active faith in ordinary affairs, an involvement in the more costly service of love in missionary labour and an endurance of hardship inspired by Christian hope. With Calvin we may see in v. 3 'a short definition of true Christianity'.

Thought: Commitment to Christ must be demonstrated every day.

1 Thessalonians 1.4-10   The Power of the Word

Paul addresses the Thessalonians warmly as 'brethren beloved by God' (4). He found in the fruitfulness of their lives an adequate proof that God loved them. The heart of divine election is God's sovereign decision to choose a people, making them peculiarly His own. Formerly this had meant Israel almost exclusively (see Deut. 7.6–11; Amos 3.1 f.). A startling consequence of the obedience of Christ was the inclusion of the Gentiles within the community of God's chosen ones. Paul was called to proclaim this profound news among the nations (Acts 9.4–6,15 f.; Gal. 1.11–16; Rom. 15.8–22; Eph. 3.1–13). The response to the word proclaimed at Thessalonica provided clear evidence that God had chosen them. Wherever Paul proclaimed the gospel he knew God would prepare a people to receive it as the word of truth. He regarded preaching, therefore, with utmost seriousness.

The power of the gospel to compel conviction and transform disrupted lives deeply impressed the apostle (5,7). He recognized that the Holy Spirit, who convinced men that what they were hearing was 'the gospel of God' (2.2,8 f.), was the source of that power. Preachers were common in the ancient world. Stoic and Cynic philosophers grappled with the basic questions of life and ethics. Sophists of many schools proclaimed eloquently the way to wealth, fame and happiness. There were many competitors for the allegiance of men. Paul constantly thanked God that his message was received at Thessalonica not as 'the word of men but . . . the word of God' (2.13). Both in proclamation and in the daily life of the community God's word was characterized by a power which distinguished it from all human cleverness and deception. That power explains the joy of believers in spite of affliction (6) and their radiant testimony to their experience with the gospel (8). Although they were newly converted, they had already caught the vision of evangelism and missionary outreach (7,8).

Their testimony echoes the preaching which had undergirded the mission to Thessalonica. Paul had urged 'faith in God' (8). The futility of serving dead idols was exposed in the presentation of the 'living and true God' (9; cf. Acts 14.15–17; 17.24–29). The heart of Paul's message was Jesus as Son of God and Saviour (10). That He was Son of God was demonstrated with power through His resurrection (cf. Acts 17.30 f.; Rom. 1.4). Though now in heaven, He will return in sovereign triumph. That He was the sole Saviour from the wrath invited by the idolatry and immorality of pagan society the Thessalonians firmly believed. Their commitment was not to a principle or to a system of thought but to the person of Jesus in whom God's gracious favour found its most pointed expression.

Thought: When Jesus Christ is given a central place in contemporary preaching, God still displays His power to transform lives.

1 Thessalonians 2.1-8   Approved by God

In 1.5 Paul writes, 'You know what kind of men we proved to be among you for your sake'. These next paragraphs furnish a commentary on this verse. They recall the circumstances under which the Thessalonians first heard the gospel and the treatment they had received from the evangelists. A note of protest may be detected in much that occurs here. Paul, apparently, is responding to slanderous charges impugning his integrity, urged by the same Jewish leaders who had earlier disrupted his work (Acts 17.5–8,13). His defence is an appeal to what the Thessalonians themselves can verify ('you yourselves know', 1; 'as you know', 2,5; 'you remember', 9; 'you are witnesses', 10; 'for you know', 11, etc.). They know that he was no imposter.

The success of the mission (1.8; 2.1), in spite of sustained opposition, was due in large part to the apostle's sheer courage inspired by God. The beating and imprisonment suffered at Philippi (Acts **16.**12 ff.) and the violence with which the Jews of Thessalonica attacked him (Acts **17.**5–8) were sufficient to dissuade a man of merely human resolution (2). Paul persisted in the mission for one reason: God had entrusted him with the gospel and he must please God (4). The approval of God was more important to Paul than the success of the mission, but the success of the mission offered the necessary proof that the apostle's message was true, his motives pure and his approach sincere. His appeal cannot spring from 'error', for what he proclaims is the gospel of God; he cannot be guilty of 'uncleanness', for he has been approved by God; he cannot present his message 'with guile', for he speaks to please God who sifts the heart (3,4). Paul had refused to resort to flattery, like some sophist, or to seek his own gain or glory (5,6). On the contrary, he had exhibited that quality of tender affection experienced by a mother as she nourishes her child at her breast. It was an act of obedience to God to share the gospel with the Thessalonians. It became an act of love when the apostle and his company gave themselves completely to the young church (7,8). Paul was a disciplined man of authority. He was also a man of deep affection (8). In this paragraph you see a pastor who has found sufficient reason to endure suffering (2) and the impugning of his integrity (3,5 f.).

Question: Is God's approval of your life more important to you than any other consideration?

1 Thessalonians 2.9-12 An Honest Conscience

Although there were many itinerant preachers and soothsayers in the ancient world who found market-place 'evangelism' a lucrative trade, Paul and his party could not be numbered among them. He had refused support from the new converts and had paid for the food consumed by himself and those with him (2 Thess. **3.**8). During his stay in the city the Philippians twice sent gifts of money to him (Phil. **4.**16), but his needs were met primarily by his own work as a skilled craftsman (cf. Acts **18.**3). The wisdom of this course of action became apparent when the charge of greed was rumoured about (5). Paul could remind the Thessalonians that he had toiled arduously throughout the period he had preached the gospel (9).

The suggestion that the enthusiastic gospel of the Spirit which Paul proclaimed had led to impurity is met with a forthright appeal to the twofold testimony of the Thessalonians and God (10). The conduct of the evangelists had been irreproachable before God and men. Any standard lower than this would have been inconsistent with their own solemn charge to live a life worthy of God (12). When Paul had wished to express the affection he had shown for the believers he spoke of a mother with her children (7). He now appeals to the image of a father with his children to express the moral earnestness with which he had instructed them (11). He had been sensitive to the particular needs of individuals and had adjusted his approach accordingly. With the hesitant he employed a word of urging; with the faint-hearted he resorted to encouragement; with the weak he did not hesitate to command. His ministry undoubtedly entailed both public and private instruction (cf. Acts 20.20), for Paul knows that he has worked with 'each one of you'. His concern was to help each convert see what was implied by 'a life worthy of God' (12)—the very God who now summoned former idolators to be citizens of His kingdom and participants in His glory. The motive for obedience which Paul planted in the mind of the Thessalonians was thanksgiving to God for His grace and an eager desire to experience fully what God has prepared for those who love Him.

Thought: Your credentials as a Christian should include a vibrant faith in Christ and irreproachable conduct before God and men.

1 Thessalonians 2.13-16 The Effective Word

Paul was filled with a sense of thanksgiving whenever he thought of the way in which the gospel had been received in Thessalonica. It would have been possible for the crowds that milled through the streets and bazaars to regard him as just one more peddler of popular religious philosophy or morality. His readers, however, had listened to his message and welcomed it as the word of God. They saw plainly that while the manner of expression was his own, God was uttering His own powerful, creative word through him (13). What distinguished the apostolic word from what was proclaimed by a sophist was its ability to impart life. The word had taken root in the hearts of believers and showed its power in daily experience.

That effectiveness was particularly evident in the endurance of the church under the pressure of disruption and persecution from other residents in the city. The apostles saw in this perseverance proof that they were being faithful to Jesus Christ. Jewish-Christian and Gentile-Christian congregations were united in a common bond of fidelity to Jesus Christ and a common experience of suffering because they were Christians (14).

The words which follow (15,16) should be recognized as an expression of heart-break and exasperation on the part of one who had suffered much from his own countrymen. From the time he became a Christian in Damascus (cf. Acts 9.24) to his present experience in Corinth (Acts **18**.5 ff.) Paul had been the object of repeated attack by zealous Jews who saw in him a threat to true piety. At Thessalonica it was Jewish leaders who instigated the riot which made necessary Paul's sudden departure from the city (Acts **17**.5 ff.); not content with this achievement they had pursued him to Beroea as well (Acts **17**.13). The mention of suffering inflicted by the Jews (14) was like pulling a plug from the dike; with a rush of emotion the apostle spills forth his grief that his own people should be so insensitive to the purposes of God. The catalogue of sins reaches its most poignant expression when Paul speaks of the road-blocks raised by the synagogue to the preaching of salvation to the Gentiles. It is the rejection of the gospel which moves Paul to bitter denunciation reminiscent of the prophets of God.

Thought: God has allowed you not only to believe in Christ but also to suffer for His sake.

1 Thessalonians 2.17-20   Presence and Absence

Paul had been forced to leave Thessalonica abruptly (Acts **17**.5-10). He had moved on to Beroea, Athens and finally Corinth. The mission to Thessalonica had been initially successful. Yet he remained anxious about his converts. When it became impossible to satisfy a strong desire to return to Thessalonica ('Satan hindered us', 18) the apostle while yet in Athens dispatched Timothy, who afterwards rejoined him in Corinth (3.1–6). Timothy's report greatly encouraged Paul, but there was also sobering news. Taking advantage of the apostle's absence, opponents had maligned his character and misconstrued his failure to return to the city as a proof that he cared nothing for his converts. They compared Paul to the roving charlatans who could be found in any Hellenistic city, preying upon the gullibility of the people. Such imposters moved from town to town, working solely for their own advantage, with no real concern for those who flocked to them.

Paul answers these insinuations in 2.17—3.13. Was his failure to return to Thessalonica a proof that he cared nothing for his converts? When he had been separated from them ('in person not in heart'), even for a short time, he had eagerly desired to return and see them face to face. The degree of eagerness the apostle experienced is apparent as he abandons the first person plural used in the letter to this point ('*we* were bereft . . . *we* endeavoured . . . *we* wanted to come to you') and he thrusts himself before his readers ('*I, Paul*, again and again'). With a rush of emotion he demands of his converts, 'What is our hope or joy or *crown of boasting before our Lord Jesus at His coming?* Is it not you?' (19). The apostle's language could not help but evoke deep feelings among his listeners since the italicized words exhibit his alertness to the conventions of the society in which they live. When a ruling monarch officially visited a Hellenistic city the populace would form a triumphal procession to escort him into the city. Citizens knew when a state visit was planned because taxes were levied or contributions solicited in order to prepare an appropriate gift for the royal guest. A papyrus from the third century B.C. speaks of contributions for a crown of gold to be presented to the king. While the monarchs of this world at their coming expect a costly crown, the Thessalonians themselves constitute the crown which Paul will joyfully present to Jesus at His coming (20).

Question: When speaking about the gospel, are you as sensitive to the conventions of contemporary society as Paul was in his day?

Questions for further study and discussion on 1 Thessalonians chs. 1.1—2.20

1. What evidences exist that the preaching of God's Word is still accompanied by a display of power?
2. In the Christian mission must success reward faithfulness to God? What is meant by 'success'?
3. Should a minister involve himself in secular employment to support himself and his family?
4. What pressures does a secular society impose upon the Church today? How may these pressures be effectively nullified?
5. What images and metaphors based on contemporary life and culture will assist us to present the gospel intelligibly.

1 Thessalonians 3.1-5   Apostolic Anguish

From the time of the second missionary journey Paul adopted the policy of delegating important tasks to members of his company. When he was forced to withdraw from Philippi, Luke was left behind to organize and nurture the believers. Under similar circumstances Silas and Timothy remained at Beroea to consolidate the gains of the mission (Acts 17.14). When Timothy rejoined Paul at Athens he found the apostle exceedingly restless concerning the welfare of the believers at Thessalonica. While Paul writes in v. 1 '*we* could bear it no longer', he says clearly in v. 5, '*I* could bear it no longer'. When it became apparent that Paul could not leave the city he sent Timothy north once more to learn how his people were faring.

Timothy had undoubtedly earned the respect of the Christians during the weeks he had laboured at Paul's side. Paul's esteem for this younger man is expressed often (cf. 1 Cor. 4.17; Phil. 2.19-22).

Here he designates his delegate 'our brother and God's servant' (2), a man fully qualified to assist the oppressed young church. Timothy's ministry was a reinforcement of teaching Paul had already committed to the church. The experience of the Thessalonians from the first days of the mission confirmed that suffering is an integral element in Christian experience (3; 1.7; 2.2). The statement that 'through many tribulations we must enter the kingdom of God' (Acts 14.22) was an established item in the catechetical instruction Paul shared with all his churches (4). Subsequent experience had served only to confirm the importance of that insight.

Paul was fully aware of the dynamics at work in Thessalonica and the eagerness of the Tempter (cf. 2.18) to unravel the fabric of faith. Continued opposition by neighbours and kinsmen, aggravated by the reports that Paul actually cared nothing for the believers, would provide fertile ground in which to plant the suggestion that the commitment to faith was not worth its cost. Behind that suggestion Paul saw clearly the devices of Satan. Out of deep concern for his converts Paul had extended himself through the person of Timothy.

Thought: Your deep concern for the welfare of other Christians is a reflection of God's yet deeper concern.

1 Thessalonians 3.6-10 Inexpressible Joy

In the transition from v. 5 to 6 there is a change of tone from anxious concern to joyful relief. Timothy has just returned to Corinth with a report which exceeds the apostle's highest expectations, and his delight is apparent in every line. Paul had sent Timothy to Thessalonica to learn the condition of their faith (5). Timothy had returned with the news that their faith in Christ was virile, their love toward one another earnest, and their affection for the apostle deep (6; cf. 1.3; 4.9 f.; 2 Thess. 1.3). They had not forgotten Paul and were as eager to see him as he was to be in Thessalonica once again (2.17–20; 3.6,10 f.). So overwhelmed was Paul that he speaks of Timothy's report as 'the receiving of a gospel' through which he was comforted and made to know a new surge of life. Only here in all the N.T. does this non-technical use of the term 'gospel' ('good news') occur. What encouraged Paul most of all was the steadfastness of the Thessalonians on the matter of *faith* (7). When he speaks of his life depending on the firm stand of the believers (8), he is not resorting to hyperbole. The one thing that made life worth living was the experience of introducing men to the Saviour, and the privilege of watching them grow in grace and knowledge.

Paul had laid a sound foundation for faith at Thessalonica. But he recognizes at once that to God alone belonged the glory for the faithfulness of his converts (9). He finds himself inadequate to express the thanksgiving which wells up in him as he presents the Thessalonians to God in prayer. At the same time he is not blind to the realities under which his converts live. They are subject to many pressures and still young in the faith. While their faith in Christ is strong it lacks moral depth and doctrinal certainty. Paul, therefore, continues to pray earnestly and unceasingly that God may yet permit him to return to his friends, that he may bring them to a greater maturity in the Lord (10).

Question: Is your stand for Jesus Christ so firm that it furnishes a source of encouragement to your pastor?

1 Thessalonians 3.11-13   A Spontaneous Prayer

As Paul records his transition from the depths of anguish to the heights of exhilaration he is overwhelmed with emotion and breaks into spontaneous prayer. The lines he has just dictated suggest the direction of his thoughts: v. 11 resumes v. 10a, while vs. 12,13 are prompted by v. 10b. The prayer serves to round off the larger section, 2.1—3.10, and prepares for what Paul has to say in the second half of the letter.

On repeated occasions Paul had experienced the desire to return to Thessalonica but Satan had hindered him (2.17 f.). Recognizing that only God can remove the obstacles that Satan has erected, Paul prays earnestly that God may yet enable him to visit his friends. That no sharp distinction is entertained in Paul's mind between 'our God and Father' and 'our Lord Jesus' when he bows to pray is suggested by the fact that the word 'direct' is singular. Paul senses a unity of action between Father and Son in the response to prayer.

Paul's second petition is that the Lord may perfect the love which the Thessalonians have already displayed toward one another until it overflows to the enrichment of 'all men'—stubborn Jews, calloused pagans, those who slander them or persecute them (cf. Matt. 5.44–48). God alone is able to bestow love of this quality. Conversely, only love of this quality will direct the attention of men beyond the believers to God Himself. The presence of love in ever-increasing measure is the certain pledge that the church is being prepared for presentation to the Father on the day when the Lord Jesus comes with all His saints. What God will demand is blamelessness in holiness. Love toward God and love toward one's neighbour turn one away from selfish concerns and open the way to that moral perfection which is the condition of holiness. It is this radical transformation of character that Paul desires for his con-

307

verts, that they may face the awesome event of Christ's return without fear or shame.

Thought: Spontaneous prayer is the response of the sensitive Christian to the clear evidence of God's involvement with his life.

1 Thessalonians 4.1-8   A Call to Personal Purity

Paul's desire to return to Thessalonica reflects a concern to supply something lacking in the faith of the believers (3.10). Even under the most favourable circumstances difficulties could be expected among converts from paganism. While yet in the city Paul had anticipated the need for practical instruction in such important areas as personal morality and holiness (4.1-8), love and mutual respect (4.9), social conduct and work (4.11,12; 2 Thess. 3.10). He now supplements his oral instruction by devoting the final two chapters of the letter to specific areas of shortcomings and uncertainty in the congregation. The key to this material is provided in 5.14: what Paul has written was prompted by the temptations of 'the weak', the discouragements of 'the faint-hearted', and the unbrotherly conduct of 'the idle'. The apostle's ultimate concern is that his converts may 'please' or satisfy God (4.1; cf. 2.4,15).

By 'the weak', Paul means those who are weak with respect to some aspect of faith. Apparently moral weakness was the particular problem of this group (4.3-8). It is understandable that the attitudes of some Christians living in a cosmopolitan seaport had been shaped by the conventions of pagan society. In Hellenistic society, generally, sexual morality was treated as a matter of relative indifference. Moreover, religious sanctions had become attached to forms of immorality, since fertility rites were an accepted form of consecration to the deity in certain of the mystery religions and cults. Believers needed careful and repeated instruction concerning the type of life which God demanded; specifically, that consecration to the living God was both religious and moral in character.

Paul's explicit instruction is based on the fact that personal sanctification is the will of God for every Christian (3). This means that the primary demand upon the Christian is to live his life in all respects as one who is set apart for devoted service to God. This requires the discipline of one's body and thoughts and the cultivation of a purity of life. Immorality is incompatible with commitment to Jesus Christ—then and now. To be enslaved to the passions of lust, to enter marriage merely for sexual convenience, or to commit adultery, is to imitate 'the heathen who do not know God' and to invite divine judgement (5,6). The apostle marshals forceful reasons why the Christian cannot confuse his freedom with pagan licence:

308

there is a fearful judgement upon sin (6); purity of life alone is consistent with the character of the Christian's call 'in holiness' (7); impurity expresses a contempt for God who has given His *Holy* Spirit to the believer (8). These considerations demand a fresh hearing in contemporary society where promiscuity, the exploitation of persons, and the flouting of divine authority are commonplace and find their champions even within the Church.

Thought: Formerly men loved persons and used things; now they love things and use persons.

1 Thessalonians 4.9-12   The Dimensions of Love

A second group within the church Paul designates 'the idle' (5.14). These were men whose refusal to work had disrupted the life of the Christian community and incurred the disrespect of those who were not Christians. While the Roman world tended to despise manual and even supervisory labour as beneath the dignity of the citizen, the command to work drew its sanctions from the cultural mandate to 'subdue the earth' and from the Law of God (Gen. 1.28; 2.15; 3.17-19; Exod. 20.9). It was the responsibility of every Jewish father to teach his son a trade by which he could support himself. While in Thessalonica Paul had worked night and day to meet his needs (2.9). When idlers joined the young church he laid down the rule, 'If any one will not work, let him not eat' (2 Thess. 3.10). In disregard of this explicit instruction some within the assembly had not only refused to work but had sought to be supported by other Christians. When support was denied on the ground of Paul's dictum, the idle made their plea on the basis of 'love of the brethren'. This is the background presupposed in vs. 9–12.

That God had taught the Thessalonians to love one another was clear to the apostle (9,10). Nevertheless, he exhorts them to demonstrate yet more love, and introduces a series of specific responsibilities which define the depth of love for others which God demands. It is the practical orientation of communal love which is the startling element in this section. Who had considered that to live quietly, to mind one's own affairs and to work with one's hand were actually a consequence of the love which God teaches? Yet further reflection attests that each of these actions springs from a selflessness which has its source in divine love. A basic consideration for others moves the Christian to avoid unnecessary conflict and the uninvited intrusion of himself in the affairs of another. This same considerateness moves him to the honest labour which commands the respect of outsiders and frees the labourer from dependence upon others for support. The idle needed to recognize the practical dimensions of Christian love.

Thought: Both Christians and non-Christians will evaluate the sincerity of your love for God by the way you treat others.

1 Thessalonians 4.13-18 Christian Hope

Even though only a few months had elapsed since Paul left Thessalonica, some from the fellowship had died. Death was an awesome reality in the ancient world. Grim inscriptions along the roads reminded travellers that it was the common experience of all men. The anxiety of 'the faint-hearted' concerning those who had died is understandable. Paul had proclaimed the death and resurrection of Jesus (1.10); yet he may have neglected to instruct the Thessalonians that they would participate in the resurrection. The apostle had spoken much about the glorious event of Jesus' coming with all His saints. Did the death of Christians exclude them from sharing in the triumphant climax to history?

The encouragement furnished by Paul's response to these concerns can be appreciated when his words are contrasted with a pagan letter of consolation dating from the second century:

> 'Irene to Taonnophris and Philo, good comfort. I am as sorry and weep over the departed one as I wept for Didymas. And all things which were fitting I have done, . . . But, nevertheless, against such things one can do nothing. Therefore, comfort one another. Fare ye well' (Oxyrhynchus Papyrus No. 115).

While this letter both opens and closes on the note of comfort, its most striking feature is a frank recognition that no real basis for comfort has been provided. After the expression of sincere sympathy and the appropriate memorials, after the grief and tears, the fact of utter helplessness remains.

How different is the encouragement Paul offers to the faint-hearted. The reason they are not to 'grieve as others who have no hope' is that God who raised Jesus from the dead will also raise believers who have 'fallen asleep' (13 f.). For them, death is no ultimate catastrophe. Not even Jesus, the Lord of life, had been spared the experience of death. But He rose again! Because of His resurrection 'sleep' is no longer a euphemism for the finality of the grave, but a description of a rest which is followed by an awakening. The fourth-century preacher, John Chrysostom, helps us to sense the majesty of v. 17: 'When a king made his entrance into a city, certain ones among the dignitaries, the chief officials and those who were in the good graces of the sovereign, would go forth from the city in order to meet him, while the guilty and the criminals are kept within the city where they await the sentence which the king will pronounce. In the same manner, when the Lord will come, the first group will go forth to meet Him with assurance in the midst of the air, while the guilty and those who are conscious of having committed many sins will await below their Judge' (*In Thess.* Hom. VIII). For Paul's readers, who were familiar with the Hellenistic ceremony described by Chrysostom, the language evoked deep feelings and was readily understood. The final admonition to 'comfort one another' thus rings with confidence and joy based on the character of Christian hope.

Thought: Death remains an enemy to the Christian, but one who has been vanquished by the Lord of Life.

1 Thessalonians 5.1-11   Sons of the Day

The second concern of the faint-hearted was their unpreparedness for the Day of the Lord, when God comes to judge all men and unleash His wrath (cf. Amos **5.**18; Isa. **13.**6–8; Ezek. **13.**10; Jer. **6.**14; **8.**11, etc.). Paul had instructed them that the Day of the Lord will come with an unexpected suddenness 'like a thief in the night', catching the wicked unaware (2 f.; cf. Luke **12.**39; 2 Pet. **3.**10). Without a blameless life men cannot enter into eternal fellowship with the Lord (**3.**13; **5.**22 f.). Who is sufficient for such a demand? The faint-hearted were fearful for their own salvation.

At the beginning of the letter Paul had anticipated his present words of encouragement when he expressed his assurance that God had chosen the Thessalonian Christians (**1.**4). Now he takes up their concern in earnest, perhaps in response to a specific request for further information concerning 'times and seasons' (**5.**1). The Thessalonians were asking, 'How long will it be before the Lord comes?' and 'What guide posts will help us to recognize the nearness of His coming?' The apostle assures his readers that they do not need additional instruction concerning the Day of the Lord (cf. 2–5), but a fresh determination to demonstrate the vigilance and sobriety characteristic of the 'day' (6–8). 'Night', 'darkness', 'sleep', 'drunkenness' describe those who are insensitive to the divine purpose and for whom there will be no escape when the Day of the Lord exposes their deeds to the judgement of God. 'Day', 'light', 'wakefulness', 'sobriety' evoke the image of the Church vigilant, waiting expectantly for the coming of Christ. The church knows all that it needs to know—that the Day of the Lord will come, that God will bring to fulfilment His sovereign purposes, and that God demands a life consistent with the character of Christian calling (**4.**7). The antidote to anxiety and fear is

311

engagement in a spiritual warfare, for which God has provided an adequate armour in faith, love and hope (8; cf. Eph. 6.10–20). To dispel unwarranted fears once for all, Paul reassures his readers, 'God has not destined us for wrath, but to obtain salvation through our Lord Jesus Christ' (9, cf. 1.10). He reminds the Thessalonians of Christ's death on our behalf and His ultimate intention that we shall 'live with Him' (10; cf. 4.16 f.). The Day of the Lord *is* a day of wrath, but not for God's redeemed people. In this assurance there may be found a sufficient reason for mutual encouragement and edification (11).

Thought: God calls the Church to be vigilant in order that He may display it as the Church Triumphant.

1 Thessalonians 5.12-22 The Conduct of Church Life

The call for mutual encouragement and edification with which the previous section ends (5.11) prompts the apostle to set forth some guidelines for regulating the conduct of church life. He casts them in the form of admonitions addressed to the congregation as a whole: vs. 12,13 concern the leadership of the congregation, vs. 14–18 the relationships between members of the fellowship as a whole, and vs. 19–22 the response to prophecy and other charismatic manifestations in the public gatherings of the believers.

The church is charged to respect those who were appointed elders in the congregation (cf. Acts 14.23). In view are men like Jason (Acts 17.5), Secundus (Acts 20.4) and Demas (2 Tim. 4.10). It was their task to work diligently among the membership of the church, preside over its meetings and maintain discipline. Paul's language implies an appreciation for those who exercise the gifts of leadership based on close observation of the quality of their personal lives and labour. A consideration of their Christian service should dissolve any resentment toward their assumption of authority and move the congregation to hold them in special esteem and affection. It is the responsibility of the fellowship to provide a climate which will enable the elders to do their work. Conflict is always distracting. Paul, therefore, counsels, 'Be at peace among yourselves' (12,13).

The exhortations to the 'brethren' which follow clarify the responsibility of the entire congregation to engage in the tasks of ministry. The admonition of the idle, the encouragement of the faint-hearted, the assistance of the weak (14) are precisely the ministries Paul has fulfilled among the Thessalonians. Now they are assigned to all with the added admonition to be patient in dealing with weakness of any kind. Christian love will refuse to keep a tally-sheet of injuries received but will find its fulfilment in services which may be rendered to all—without discrimination (15). Unbroken joy, prayer and thanksgiving afford sufficient proof of the out-working of the will of God within the fellowship (16–18).

The concluding admonitions consist of five crisp sentences which recognize the legitimacy of the exercise of spiritual gifts within the congregation as well as the necessity of testing their origin (19–22). The test is simple: what is good is to be received, while every form of evil must be rejected. Paul finds in the presence of the Spirit the pledge of the discernment required from all believers.

1 Thessalonians 5.23-28   The God of Peace

Paul's concluding word to the congregation is a prayer that they may be completely and utterly God-possessed men. It will become the apostle's frequent habit when bringing a letter to its close to think upon 'the God of peace', as he does here (23; cf. 2 Thess. 3.16; Rom. 15.33; 2 Cor. 13.11; Phil. 4.9). The reference is to the divine peace of restored relationship with God which the Thessalonians enjoyed through the reconciling work of Jesus Christ. The fellowship enjoyed with God on earth is the prelude to unbroken fellowship throughout eternity. For that reason Paul prays that the work of sanctification, by which believers are prepared for God's presence, may be brought to a point of maturity. The words 'spirit and soul and body' are not to be understood as providing some insight into the constituent 'parts' of man, but should be understood rhetorically as further emphasizing the term 'wholly'. In a contemporary context Paul might well pray in terms of 'heart and soul', by which he would mean simply 'your whole person' (cf. Mark 12.30). In praying that believers may be kept 'sound and blameless' for their presentation to Christ at His coming the apostle echoes a theme introduced first in the prayer of 3.13. Paul's own experience of the faithfulness of God assures him that his prayer will be wonderfully answered (24).

The letter closes with three brief requests and a benediction. The request for prayer (25) is a reminder that Paul, Silas and Timothy also labour in a context of trial, and can be sustained only through the intercession of the believers and the strength which God supplies. The kiss of peace which men shared with men, and women with women—presumably on the cheek—was the sign that God had constituted the Church one family in Christ (26). None was to be excluded from this token of affection. The letter—to be read publicly —must serve to compensate for the visit he cannot undertake at this time; in it Paul has said what he would wish to say were he present with his people. The final benediction (28) replaces the single word

313

'farewell' in papyrus letters with the blessing of Christ upon the congregation.

Questions for further study and discussion on 1 Thessalonians chs. 3.1—5.28

1. Why must suffering be an integral part of Christian experience?
2. In what ways can Satan hinder a pastor or a church? What resources has a Christian when 'hindered' by Satan (cf. **2.17 f.**)?
3. How may the character of Christian love be communicated to a secular world which has used the word 'love' in a cheap and degraded sense?
4. What bearing does Paul's word to the weak (**4.3–8**) have upon the so-called 'new morality'?
5. What attitudes displayed at a modern funeral and in connection with death illustrate the need for Paul's instruction in **4.13–18**?

2 Thessalonians

2 Thessalonians 1.1-4   Growth in Spite of Adversity

Only a tentative reconstruction can be offered of the events between the reception of Paul's first letter by the church and the composition of the second. The outward situation at Thessalonica appears little changed. Persecution has continued (**1.4**; cf. **2.17**; **3.3 ff.**). Paul, Silas and Timothy are still together, evidently at Corinth, where opposition to the gospel also persists (**1.1,7**; **3.1 f.**). Our scanty evidence suggests that the second letter was addressed to Thessalonica in A.D. 50, perhaps no more than two months after the first.

Its immediate occasion was the emergence of a new crisis within the congregation. Some individuals were convinced that Paul had said that the Day of the Lord was actually present (**2.2**). This furnished a new argument for the idle and rekindled all the fears of the faint-hearted. If the Day of the Lord had come, what time remained to acquire the holiness or the faith, hope and love upon which Paul had insisted (1 Thess. **3.13**; **5.8**)? The wrath reserved for unbelievers would certainly overtake the Christians as well! When the elders saw that the crisis was more than they could cope with effectively, they sent word to Paul by the first of their number who had occasion to journey to Corinth (cf. **3.11**). *2 Thessalonians* was written in response to this urgent request for help. It is a simple, tactful, pastoral letter, devoted almost entirely to encouraging the same faint-hearted Christians previously addressed (**1.3—3.5**), and to admonishing the idle (**3.6–15**).

The opening lines of Paul's two letters to the church are almost

314

identical. The addition of 'our' before 'Father' in the address indicates that Paul is contemplating the relationship of sonship which the Thessalonians have come to enjoy with God the Father in common with all those who have experienced faith through Christ (1). The prayer for grace and peace (2) is repeated from the earlier epistle, but now the apostle reminds his readers of the divine origin of these gifts. In both the address and the initial greeting God the Father and Christ the Lord are intimately associated. The existence of the church and the bestowal of the qualities which sustain its new life are the gifts of God as we know Him in Jesus Christ.

The ground of the apostle's continued thanksgiving for the Thessalonians is located in the vigorous growth of their faith, the increase of their love for one another and their steadfast endurance in the face of persecution and affliction (3,4). Adversity had prompted a depth of Christian experience to which Paul could appeal when instructing the churches of Achaia. In spite of a misinterpretation of hope, in spite of severe suffering, the church of the Thessalonians was characterized by a dynamic faith and a devoted love inspired by Jesus Christ.

2 Thessalonians 1.5-10 The Last Judgement

Paul urges the Thessalonians to penetrate beneath the opposition they are encountering and to perceive the righteous judgement of God (5). The fact that their faith has increased rather than diminished under adversity (3), and that they have been sustained in much affliction (4) are sufficient evidence that God is just and cares for His own. God's nearness to them in their suffering is the pledge that He will judge between believers and their persecutors. Until the time of that judgement, suffering has meaning precisely because it is endured for sake of the kingdom of God.

But there must be no mistake; there *is* a retributive judgement of God (6). Retribution for sin is a necessary consequence of life in a moral universe over which God rules as Sovereign. With deft strokes Paul paints a canvas on which is sketched the Last Judgement (7–10). The colours he chooses are dictated by the language and thought-forms of the O.T. when it speaks of the Day of the Lord (cf. Isa. 2.10,19,21). Jesus Christ, the righteous Judge, is given central prominence. Before Him are assembled two companies of men. The first consists of those who have recklessly disregarded God's laws and have refused obedience to the gospel (8). Their rejection of God is further expressed in their affliction of the weak and their persecution of the righteous. Having refused the fellowship of the Lord during their earthly life they now experience exclusion

315

from His presence and His glory forever (9). This is the just and inescapable consequence of a deliberate defiance of God. The second company is comprised of those who have served Christ faithfully and have enjoyed His fellowship. Their reward is to experience relief from the affliction of the world (7) and to enjoy in the fullest measure the immediate presence of God in Christ for ever. The reality defies the ability of language to describe all that is meant; the apostle depicts the company of the redeemed as open-mouthed, filled with marvel at the glory of Christ. Paul's point is clear. To be a son of the Kingdom now, faithfully following Jesus the Christ, is to be with Him always (cf. 1 Thess. **4.**17). To reject Christ, and stubbornly align oneself with the company of the disobedient, is to suffer eternal loss.

Question: How significant is the judgement of God in your thinking?

2 Thessalonians 1.11,12   The Goal of God's Call

Throughout the Thessalonian correspondence Paul emerges as a man of prayer (1 Thess. **1.**2 f.; **3.**11–13; **5.**17,23,25,28; 2 Thess. **1.**3,11 f.; **2.**16 f.; **3.**1,5,16,18). He assures the believers that he thanks God for them *always* (3). He now adds that he prays for them *always* (11). His prayer is prompted by reflection on the triumph of Christ in which the Thessalonians will participate. He asks God to count them worthy of his honour and to mature the qualities of life they possess, so that they may add glory to Christ at his coming.

Later in the letter Paul reflects on the origin of God's call in its eternal character and the issuance of the divine summons through missionary proclamation (**2.**13 f.). Here the call is viewed from the perspective of its culmination. God alone can equip His people to fulfil their destiny as Christian men at the Lord's coming. God brings to birth within us 'good resolves' and only He can enable us to translate these holy impulses into action. He bestowed the gift of faith and only through the consecrating work of the Holy Spirit does faith find its fruit in works of love.

The fulfilment of 'every good resolve' and 'work of faith' has as its one purpose the glorification of Jesus Christ (12). Paul's formulation reflects the Greek text of Isa. **66.**5, 'That the name of the Lord may be glorified'. In the O.T. the 'name' involves the character of the person designated; the son who is named 'Immanuel' has the character of 'God-with-us' (Isa. **7.**14). In Paul's prayer 'the Lord' is identified as 'the Lord Jesus', and 'the name of our Lord' is His person as revealed through His word and works. The person of the Lord Jesus is to be glorified by the magnificent witness to His grace which the Thessalonians give when Jesus is revealed at His coming.

In that high and holy moment every knee will bow before Him and every tongue will confess that He is indeed Lord (Phil. 2.9–11). What will move men most to marvel will be the radical transformation achieved in those who formerly served idols (cf. 1 Thess. 1.9), but who now evidence the fulfilment of good resolve and the perfection of works of faith. On that occasion the Thessalonians will share in Christ's triumph. They have shared His sufferings; they will also share His glory. This is the final outcome of 'the grace of our God and the Lord Jesus Christ'.

Thought: The sufferings we have endured for Christ are not worthy to be compared with the glory which shall be revealed in us.

2 Thessalonians 2.1,2   Rumour and Unrest

At this point Paul speaks about the excitement and unrest in the congregation. In his earlier letter he had spoken of the coming of the Lord and of the gathering of believers to Him (1 Thess. 4.16 f.; 5.10; cf. Mark 13.26 f.). He had made it clear that while the Day of the Lord comes suddenly, its arrival will pose no surprise to 'the sons of the day'. The finest preparation for its appearance is a life of vigilance, sobriety and prayer (1 Thess. 5.2–10). In spite of this instruction, a rumour of the imminent appearance of the exalted Lord appears to have unsettled completely the thought and action of a number within the fellowship. They were behaving irrationally and irresponsibly. If the end of the world were already upon them, what time remained for getting ready to meet the Lord? If the Lord were at hand, what necessity remained for working?

The rumour, which circulated as certain truth, was that the Day of the Lord would come before the end of the year. (In the papyri, Paul's term 'has come' is used with reference to the current year.) It is difficult to trace its source. What Paul had said in the first letter allowed the interpretation that the Lord would come during their generation (1 Thess. 4.17). It is possible that they misconstrued what he had said about the awesome suddenness of His appearing (cf. 1 Thess. 5.2 f.). What is clear is that Paul's authorization was claimed for the statement that the Day of the Lord had come. The apostle emphatically denies the report and categorically dismisses any allegation that in prophetic ecstasy, in ordinary conversation or in a letter, he had proclaimed that the crisis of consummation was at hand. The ease with which the congregation had been disrupted was particularly disturbing, since Paul had given them specific instructions concerning the conditions which must prevail before it would be meaningful to talk about the end of the world (2.5). The apostle had the right to expect a degree of maturity on the part of believers,

317

whose responsibility was to pass all rumours and reports through the grid of truth committed to them in the apostolic instruction.

Thought: A broad exposure to God's Word and quiet reflection upon its meaning is the best preventative for panic in a time of crisis.

2 Thessalonians 2.3-12 God's Sovereign Control

In this letter there is a vivid reference to the final judgement (1.6–10), a brief sketch of the events which precede the consummation (2.3–8), and a characterization of 'the lawless one', whose coming counterfeits the coming of the Lord (2.9–12). But precisely in these passages Paul emerges as a pastor who offers these descriptions not for their own sake but for the practical encouragement of his converts. Thus nothing is said about the events surrounding the manifestation of 'the lawless one' (9–12) until Paul has spoken of his destruction (8). The intention is not to introduce new truths but to remind the Thessalonians of the oral instruction the apostle had given while still with them (5). There is a theology of history and judgement implied in the letter, but it is subordinated to a distinctly pastoral concern. Accordingly, it is a mistake to turn to *2 Thessalonians* for a blueprint by which to read the 'signs of the time' and to plot the course of the unveiling of the Antichrist. Much that Paul wrote in this section—for example, the identity of the power or person who restrains the Lawless One (6,7)—remains obscure to the modern reader. Nevertheless, the affirmation that all things take place by God's sovereign will is transparent. This truth, together with the corollary that God has destined believers to life and fellowship with Himself (1.5 ff., 11 f.; 2.1,13 ff.; 3.1–5), was the message that the faint-hearted needed to hear.

The pattern of truth envisaged by Paul is sufficiently clear. He had instructed the believers to look for a general rebellion against God before the end arrived. There is no reason to suppose that he had in his mind a clear picture regarding the form that the rebellion would assume. He now reminds his readers that it has not yet occurred. A divine restraint of lawlessness yet provides time for rescuing men who are perishing (3–7).

The Lawless One is the embodiment of wickedness in human form. The description of his coming, power and self-deification amounts to a blasphemous caricature of Christ. He is swept into prominence on the crest of a wave of rebellion prompted by the activity of Satan. Yet he too is subject to the sovereign control of God who will destroy him and introduce the consummation of history through Jesus Christ (3,8–10).

Paul's thought is related to a practical situation: the end has not

318

yet arrived. The Thessalonians must carry on in a sober and disciplined fashion in spite of deception and persecution. Positively, they must love the truth and find their pleasure in righteousness, confident that God alone is sovereign.

Thought: When you are confronted by lawlessness and rebellion everywhere it is time to make certain that God is enthroned at the centre of your life.

Questions for further study and discussion on 2 Thessalonians chs. 1.1—2.12

1. Are persecution and adversity necessary for the Church to experience marked growth?
2. How can the Christian community help their neighbours to take seriously the reality of the coming Judgement?
3. Why do men defy God? Is there anything Christians can do to lead them to faith and obedience to God?
4. What are the conditions of the world today that frequently cause Christians to think that the Day of the Lord is imminent?
5. Collect the passages from *Daniel*, the Gospels, *1 John* and elsewhere, which shed light on the character and purpose of the Anti-Christ or the Lawless One. Should Christians fear his coming.

2 Thessalonians 2.13-15 Chosen and Instructed

A consideration of the deception of many who are to perish because of their refusal to receive the truth of God (10–12) confirms the apostle's thankfulness for the Thessalonians who so warmly received the gospel (13). His people were afflicted and perplexed. Paul assures them that they have nothing to fear in life or death. Like Benjamin, whose blessing was to dwell in safety with God (Deut. 33.12), they are 'brethren beloved by the Lord'. Like Israel, God loves them and chose them because of that love (Deut. 7.6–8). Before the world began God had taken thought for them. The certainty of their deliverance from sin, death and condemnation lies in the timeless will of God that they should experience salvation. This had become clear when they responded joyfully to God's call through the gospel proclaimed by the apostle (14). Their response to the God who committed Himself to men was the commitment of themselves to God. The prospect Paul now holds before the congregation is the enjoyment of the full perfection of Christ's glory. With this vision before them the Thessalonians are to stand firm, conscious of the sanctifying work of the Holy Spirit and the undergirding of the everlasting arms of a loving Father.

To assist them to stand firm, Paul commends to the church the importance of apostolic tradition (15). Under this category he includes both oral and written instruction. Much is said in *2 Thessalonians* about the establishment, preservation and authority of the apostolic tradition (cf. **2.**1 f., 5,15; 3.6,10,14,17), and it is clear that Paul regards his letter as a depository of tradition (3.14). The tradition of teaching delivered to the church remains normative for the testing of doctrine and the regulation of conduct. If the Thessalonians will remember this there will be no recurrence of an atmosphere of crisis in the congregation based on misinformation or deliberate deception (2.1 f., 5).

2 Thessalonians 2.16,17   The Benediction of God

Throughout ch. 2 Paul has been concerned to quieten the frantic excitement of believers who were convinced that the Lord would come before the year was completed. His pointed appeal not to be torn from their moorings like ships poorly anchored in a storm (2.1 f.) was buttressed by a patient and clear rehearsal of the parade of events which must precede the Day of the Lord (2.3–12). A word of thanksgiving to God for the unmistakable tokens of His choice of the Thessalonian believers prepares the church for a calm and reflective consideration of the pattern of truth set forth in the oral and written instruction which they have received (2.13–15). Paul then crowns his response to the crisis with a prayer (16 f.).

The source of encouragement for the ruffled believers is 'our Lord Jesus Christ' and 'God our Father', whom Paul sees as one in bestowing love, comfort and hope upon the congregation. The mention of the Son before the Father is due to the fact that the apostle has just been contemplating what it will mean to share 'the glory of our Lord Jesus Christ' (14). But of both Father and Son it may be said that 'He loved us and gave us eternal comfort and good hope through grace' (16). This language echoes the strong assurance Paul has just given to the believers in vs. 14 f., where he spoke of God's loving favour, His eternal choice, and of the hope of glory set before the believers. He now adds a fervent petition that they may appropriate that comfort and strength which God has made available to them from eternity, and that He will enable them to reflect stability in all that they do and say (17). One can sense the peace of this benediction upon the congregation.

Thought: God's comfort is the assurance that He is concerned with all that exposes you to hurt and suffering.

2 Thessalonians 3.1-5   A Request for Intercession

Before introducing the second main theme of the letter (3.6 ff.),

Paul draws attention to his own perilous circumstances on the Isthmus, and invites the believers to pray specifically that the word of the Lord may 'speed on and triumph' (1). The word of preaching is regarded as a spiritual force which is capable of sweeping through the land under its own power. While Corinth was well known for its vice and violence, Paul was far less concerned for his own safety than for the success of the mission. He coveted for the province of Achaia the same enthusiastic response to the gospel that he had witnessed in Macedonia. What he actually encountered, however, was the concerted effort of men dedicated to halt the advance of the mission. The allusion to 'wicked and evil men' has in view certain Jewish leaders in Corinth who were at this time making Paul's work as difficult as possible (Acts **18**.6,12–17). The sad word that 'not all have faith' (2) refers almost certainly to the stubborn refusal of the synagogue to acknowledge Jesus as the promised Messiah. Was the vision through which God strengthened Paul (Acts **18**.9–11) the answer to the prayers of the Thessalonians?

The apostle's attention moves quickly from his own encounter with evil men to the plight of the Thessalonians, who also experience harassment (cf. 1 Thess. **2**.14; 2 Thess. **1**.4–7). The lack of faith in men sharpens his appreciation of the faithfulness of Christ, who will strengthen the believers and protect them from evil (3). Whether Paul has in view evil men (cf. v. 2) or the Evil One (cf. **2**.9) is unclear; the ambiguity may be deliberate, since the evil which men do is inspired by Satan. Confronted with powers greater than their own, the Thessalonians were to flee to Christ for refuge.

Paul's confidence that the Thessalonians would carry out the instructions he is about to give is based upon their common allegiance to Christ (4). Before turning to the matter immediately at hand—the discipline of the idle—he prays that the Lord may direct their hearts to the love of God and the patience of Christ, which are to find a response in the obedience of believers (5).

Thought: As you pray for the advancement of the gospel through pastors, teachers and missionaries, your confidence can rest in the faithfulness of God.

2 Thessalonians 3.6-13 Persistent Idleness

The remainder of the letter is addressed to the persistent problem of idleness. The offence of those in the congregation who refused to work was twofold: they were living irresponsibly, and their conduct indicated a rejection of explicit teaching which Paul had given. Paul had first confronted the problem of idleness in the early days of the mission (10). He had supplemented his command enjoining the necessity of work with exhortation in his first letter (1 Thess. **4.**11 f.; **5.**14). He now imposes a more severe injunction upon the congregation, to place the idle under the discipline of separation (6). Paul's appeal drew its support from his own example of toil and labour while in Thessalonica (7–9; cf. 1 Thess. **2.**9). He had applied himself to his trade as a tent-maker (cf. Acts **18.**2 f.), and with the money he earned he had paid for the food eaten by his company (8). The motive which prompted this course of action was the necessity to establish a pattern of responsible self-support which could be imitated by his converts (7,9). In any great cosmopolitan centre idlers and beggars could be found in great number. When these men came to faith it was necessary to demand of them a reformation of manners. Persistence in the professional loafing which suited their disposition would burden the church unduly and detract from the seriousness with which the gospel was advanced. To set them an example, Paul had refrained from accepting hospitality or support; he would not make the gospel a spade with which to dig, in spite of his right to do so (cf. Matt. **10.**9–10; 1 Tim. **5.**17 f.).

Throughout this section Paul is writing to the majority in the congregation. He now speaks directly to those unwilling to work. Moffatt's translation succeeds in reproducing Paul's word-play in v. 11: '. . . some of your numbers are loafing, *busy-bodies* instead of *busy.*' On the authority of Jesus Christ Paul commands them to cease their interference and to earn their own living (12). The final word is addressed to the whole congregation. They are not to be distracted from the central concerns of the Lord by the hysteria of the faint-hearted or the demands of the idle for community support (13). The prayer of v. 5, pointing to the steadfast patience of Christ, is the apostle's provision for a people who, understandably, are growing weary with exasperation.

2 Thessalonians 3.14-16   Enforcing Discipline

Paul's final provision for dealing with the idle implies a public reading of his letter (cf. 1 Thess. **5.**27). Once the letter has been publicized no excuse remained for an unwillingness to comply with its instructions. If tactful exhortation failed to solicit obedience, and the apostle's strong injunctions were disregarded, social pressure must be brought to bear upon the recalcitrant individual. He can no longer be regarded as a person in good standing within the church. He is to be 'noted', which may mean that he is to be publicly named in a meeting of the church. Close fellowship is to be withdrawn from the offender in order to drive him to his senses. No action less radical could hope to penetrate a heart hardened by the persistent refusal to heed the apostolic teaching—delivered first orally at Thessalonica (3.10), and then in written form in the two letters to the church. Discipline is imposed to shame the man into thoughtful reflection and repentance in order that he may be brought back into the fellowship of the obedient.

Basic to Paul's approach in the discipline of the idle is the assumption that the social relationships of individual Christians are a matter of concern for the whole congregation. Society judges the church by the public actions of those who profess to belong to the church. The man who becomes a Christian, therefore, is responsible to God and to his brothers in Christ. If he breaks faith and brings dishonour to the name of Christ it becomes necessary for all within the fellowship to exercise moral courage and deal with his offence. Yet the heart of Christian discipline is love. This moves the apostle to caution against tactlessness or unnecessary harshness in the application of discipline: the offender is not to be regarded as an enemy who must be purged, but is to be warned as one would warn his own brother of imminent danger (15).

The purpose of discipline is to restore sound life to the congregation. Paul recognizes, however, that only 'the Lord of peace' can mediate that quality of dynamic relationship and understanding within the church which will assure a climate of peace in which the tensions of the fellowship may be resolved (16). The peace of which the apostle speaks is a reality which asserts itself over against the threat of conflict and misunderstanding. Paul is himself a mediator of this peace when he adds to the traditional greeting, 'The Lord be with you', the significant word 'all'. Within the 'all' are included the troublesome idle as well as the pillars of the congregation. The presence of the Lord with 'all' will guarantee both the administration of the quality of discipline demanded and the restoration of the disciplined to the fellowship of the obedient.

2 Thessalonians 3.17,18   A Prayer for Grace

The penning of the final greeting in Paul's own hand was very important, for it guaranteed the authenticity of the document. Our practice of signing our personal name at the conclusion of a letter was unknown in the ancient world; the place of the signature was taken by the final greeting written by the sender himself. In many original papyrus letters the final greeting is clearly in a hand different from the rest of the text. In such cases the sender dictated the letter to a professional scribe and then endorsed it on his own by appending the final greeting himself. On three occasions Paul says explicitly that he has written the final greeting 'with my own hand' (1 Cor.

16.21; Col. **4.**18; 2 Thess. **3.**17). He also refers to his writing in Gal. **6.**11 and Philem. 19. This suggests that while Paul may have written the brief letter to Philemon, he dictated the other four except for the final greeting (which in the case of *Galatians* extends from **6.**11 to the end). The importance of the caution that 'this is the mark of authenticity in every letter of mine' (17) lies in the fact that some people were attributing to the apostle statements which he had not made and had succeeded in creating confusion and disturbance (cf. **2.**1 f.). Paul assures his readers that they will be able to distinguish between the false and the true by applying this test to letters purporting to have come from him (cf. 1 Thess. **5.**21).

The burden of the final greeting is 'the grace of our Lord Jesus Christ' (18). It is significant that the letter both opens and closes with a prayer for grace. This should not be understood as a mere formality, for Paul's prayers are intimately related to the crisis at Thessalonica. The gracious favour and steadfast love of God expressed in Jesus Christ provide the centre of stability for Christians hard pressed by persecution and slander from without (**1.**4), and by fears and disturbances within, the congregation (**2.**1 ff.). The final greeting is identical with the conclusion to *1 Thessalonians* (**5.**28), with the significant addition of the inclusive word 'all'. As in v. 16, Paul's pastoral concern reaches out to the entire congregation in an expression of tenderness which would not exclude the troublesome or the disorderly. While it had been necessary to speak harshly concerning those who caused disruptions in the church, the magnanimous 'all' demonstrates the reality of the grace of our Lord Jesus Christ, and lends to the prayer the character of a blessing.

Questions for further study and discussion on 2 Thessalonians chs. 2.13—3.18

1. Does church tradition have a legitimate place alongside Scripture for governing the Christian life? What distinguishes apostolic tradition from later ecclesiastical tradition?
2. Do Paul's words about the idle have any bearing on modern attitudes toward employment?
3. Frequently discipline is no longer exercised in a local congregation. What factors led it to be discontinued? Should it be reintroduced? What will guarantee a right use of church discipline?
4. It is not easy to be magnanimous toward troublesome people in the church. How may such a disposition be cultivated?

1 Timothy, 2 Timothy, Titus

INTRODUCTION

These three writings are known in modern times by the collective title the 'Pastoral Epistles'. They contain material of use to pastors, and are concerned with the immediate practical problems confronting the Christian in a pastoral situation. As they stand they give guidance to Timothy and Titus, two of Paul's assistants, as to how they should handle the problems involved in their oversight of churches. These men were, of course, not pastors of individual groups of Christians, but rather superintendents of pastors whose sphere was much wider.

Nowhere in antiquity is there any indication that the general character of these letters was doubted. It was accepted that they were genuine letters of Paul and that they were written to the two recipients mentioned. But in modern times both conclusions are often doubted. It is held that the letters were written, probably early in the second century, by some orthodox believer, anxious to perpetuate Paul's teaching as he understood it, and only conventionally addressed to Timothy and Titus. The principal reasons for holding such views are first, linguistic (the language of these three letters is held to be so different from that of the ten 'genuine' Pauline letters that they must come from a different author) and secondly, doctrinal (the Pastorals are said to be concerned with doctrines which were of no concern to Paul while, conversely, characteristic Pauline doctrines are passed over).

It may be significant that few critics care to commit themselves to the view that there is nothing Pauline about our three letters. They usually hold that there are some genuine Pauline fragments which a later writer has taken and written up. It may be accepted that there is something Pauline about them. And a number of competent critics are convinced that the objections to Pauline authorship of the whole will not stand up to critical examination. For the view that the letters are late and non-Pauline see the Introductions to the commentaries by C. K. Barrett and A. T. Hanson, and for the Pauline view those by J. N. D. Kelly and D. Guthrie.

In these studies we will treat the letters as genuine Pauline products, written with a desire to convey to Paul's younger assistants guidance for the oversight of the churches.

As to their date, the biographical details which emerge incidentally make it impossible in the judgement of most scholars to fit them into the period covered by *Acts*. It seems that Paul was released

Photo: Ephesus Plain where the Temple of Artemis stood

Photo: Temple of Artemis

from the imprisonment mentioned at the end of that book and engaged in further missionary activity. The Pastorals belong to this late period.

1 Timothy 1.1-11 The Lawful Use of the Law

A first-century letter usually began with the name of the writer, a short description of him, the name of the recipient(s) with a similar brief description, and a little prayer. Paul breathes life into this conventional framework by making it the means of bringing out important Christian teaching. Here we see something of the nature of apostleship (a man does not say, 'I think I'll be an apostle'; he must first be commanded by God and Christ), the close relationship between God and Christ (none else could be joined together as they are), the tender relationship between Paul and his convert Timothy, and the primacy of qualities like grace, mercy, and peace. Paul usually has grace and peace in his greetings, but in his two letters to Timothy 'mercy' is included as well.

In the letter proper, the first thing emphasized is the importance of sound doctrine issuing in upright living. 'The law is good,' Paul says, 'if any one uses it lawfully' (8). It is for the restraint of wickedness of all kinds (9 f.). This might be put in another way, as when Paul speaks of the aim of his charge to Timothy as love (5). The use of both ideas shows that he is not arguing for the kind of 'situational ethics' dear to some modern thinkers. He agrees that love is the important attitude for a Christian, and that it proceeds 'from a pure heart and a good conscience and sincere faith' (5). But this does not mean that the law can be disregarded. Elsewhere Paul tells us that 'love is the fulfilling of the law' (Rom. 13.10) and this is much the thought here. This is not in contradiction of the gospel, but in accordance with it (11). And it is something given, something entrusted, to Paul (11) and indeed to all Christians.

But it is always easier to get into an argument than to live the Christian life. It is human nature to prefer vigorous discussion to sacrificial living. 'Certain persons' (3) whom Timothy confronted were using the law the wrong way. Evidently they were using some form of allegorical interpretation which made the Bible yield 'myths and endless genealogies' (4); they had 'wandered away into vain discussion' (6). It is still quite possible to use the Bible not as the source of 'the divine training that is in faith' (4), but as the starting point for the exposition of our own pet theories. Calling these 'Christian' or 'orthodox' or 'sound doctrine' does not make them so. For that there must be a real subjection to what God has revealed.

Wonder at the miracle of grace which changed Saul the persecutor of the Church into Paul the apostle of Jesus Christ never left this transformed sinner. The mention of the gospel with which he has been entrusted (11) immediately recalls to his mind what that gospel meant in his own experience. He had 'blasphemed and persecuted and insulted' Christ. His conversion did not represent a minor change in a man who was fairly well disposed to things Christian. It represented God's miracle in the heart of a deeply guilty man. Both the guilt and the miracle were real. There is always a tendency for Christ's followers to limit the power of God. Without ever putting it into words we frequently act as though we expect conversions only among those who have the right background and upbringing. While we should never undervalue the importance of good early training nor the way God so often uses this to bring about spiritual depth, we should not regard it as the indispensable preliminary to a real conversion. The miracle of Paul has been repeated many times in the history of the Church, not least in our own day.

Out of this two important lessons emerge. The first is that the salvation of sinners was the purpose of the coming of Jesus into the world (15). 'He did not only come to seek; it was to save He came.' The second is that God uses whatever experiences a man has before his conversion as well as those afterwards. Paul received mercy 'for this reason', that Christ's work in him might be an example. Every converted sinner has that in his background which now redounds to the glory of God no matter how little credit it was to the sinner when he did it.

Notes: V. 13: 'blasphemed and persecuted and insulted' translates three nouns, 'blasphemer and persecutor and insolent man'. That he acted 'ignorantly in unbelief' is not the reason for Paul's being saved, but it is a mitigating circumstance. He had even then acted 'with a clear conscience' (2 Tim. 1.3). Notice that he does not exaggerate his sinfulness. V. 14: 'overflowed' translates a strong term giving the thought of lavish and abundant supply. V. 15: 'The saying is sure and worthy' renders a Greek expression (*pistos ho logos*) found only in the Pastorals (1 Tim. 3.1; 4.9; 2 Tim. 2.11; Tit. 3.8). It marks the saying as both important and reliable. Paul's humility comes out at the end of the verse. V. 17: typically Paul's gratitude finds expression in a little outburst of praise. 'The King of the ages' (RV margin) is found only here in the N.T. (unless it be read in Rev. 15.3). It is a strong affirmation of God's eternity.

Paul's testimony to God's grace at work in him is not an idle tale. He means Timothy to be inspired by what God has done in him, so that he too may go on to fulfil all God's purpose in his own life. God has important work for Timothy to do and it is important that he should not fail to accomplish it. There is dispute about the meaning of 'the prophetic utterances which pointed to you' (18), and some see a reference to Timothy's ordination, calling attention to 4.14. But perhaps more relevant is Acts 13.1–3, which speaks of the work of the Holy Spirit in initiating the travels of Barnabas and Paul which were to lead the apostles to Timothy. Cf. NEB, 'that prophetic utterance which first pointed you out to me.' Either way Paul is stressing the divine initiative in calling men to any work of ministry. Timothy should obey the charge not because on the purely human level he has started a work and ought to finish it (true though that might be), but because God has designated him for a piece of service which he dare not fail to accomplish. Paul is able to point to a certain Hymenaeus and Alexander who have rejected the leading of their conscience and who accordingly have 'made shipwreck of their faith' (19).

After this build-up it is perhaps surprising that the very first duty Paul lays upon Timothy is that of prayer, particularly prayer for rulers and all in positions of authority. But prayer is not the tepid, insipid thing that modern Christians have so often made it. It is an adventure with God. It is a powerful weapon for the waging of our warfare in the world. It is the believer's one effectual means of bringing about mighty results. And this is not to be confined to what we would call 'spiritual' things. The issues of community life concern the Christian as much as they concern any member of the community. But whereas his unbelieving brother usually does no more than complain about those set over him, the Christian can, and must, pray for them. In his prayers he is a partner with them and sets forward right purposes.

Notes: V. 20: The meaning of 'delivered to Satan' (cf. 1 Cor. 5.5) is not clear, but it involves disciplinary action and probably supernatural punishment. 2.4: God's will is for salvation, not that men be lost. V. 6: 'ransom' (*antilutron*) points to the substitutionary nature of Christ's offering of Himself.

Meditation: Three key doctrines of the Christian faith are found in vs. 5,6—the unity of the Godhead, the mediatorship of Christ, the atoning sacrifice of the cross.

1 Timothy 2.8-15

The respective places of the sexes have been a problem from the very beginning. It is clear that in the early Church there were some women who felt that the fact that 'there is neither male nor female; for you are all one in Christ Jesus' (Gal. 3.28) abolished all distinctions between the sexes. They were emancipated, and could do anything at all that men could do. Paul deals with the topic more than once. He maintains that before God there is no room for a superior sex. All are equal in His sight. But that does not mean that the functions to be discharged by the two are identical. The sexes are cast for different roles, and, while full allowance should be made for exceptional cases, neither should try to usurp the functions of the other.

On this occasion his subject is public worship. Men should pray everywhere, he says. 'Lifting holy hands' reminds us that posture for prayer is not without significance. The Bible does not prescribe any one posture, but as we pray we should be aware that our attitude of body is not without influence on our attitude of mind. 'Without anger or quarrelling' spells out the importance of right inward attitudes. We cannot pray effectively when filled with concern for our own petty vindication. It is likely that we should take the sense of v. 9 from the previous verse, 'that women likewise should pray, dressed in seemly apparel'. Paul's first point is that women should set more store by their manner of life than their manner of dress (9 f.; this does not mean that they should not dress attractively, it is an insistence that the priorities be right). His second is that a woman should not take a place of superiority over her husband (12; 'men' [RSV] is singular, and it is the usual word for 'husband', though it can on occasion mean 'man'). He drives this home by an appeal to the case of Adam who was 'not deceived' by Satan in the way Eve was. He simply followed her, but her fall came about through assuming an unwarranted place of leadership. V. 15 might mean that women will be 'brought safely through childbirth' (NEB margin), or 'saved' in the sense of finding fulfilment and a proper place in life through bearing children. The man who has just written vs. 5 f. cannot be held to mean that eternal salvation is won by childbirth.

Thought: The conditions of effectual praying are purity (selfward), peace (manward), faith (Godward). (A. M. Stibbs on v. 8.)

1 Timothy 3.1-7

Paul's second 'sure saying' (cf. 1.15) emphasizes the nobility of Christian service. He is speaking specifically about the 'bishop', who, most competent scholars agree, is to be equated with 'presbyter' (cf. Tit. 1.5-9). 'Bishop' stresses the thought of oversight, as 'presbyter' that of seniority. These officials exercised leadership in the early Church, and from their functions there emerged in due course the offices of presbyter and bishop as we know them in the later Church (I have discussed this more fully in *Ministers of God*, ch. V). At this early stage in the Church's history, Paul's prime concern is that those who so exercise leadership should be men whose lives agree with their teaching. Notice the importance attached to home life (2,4 f.). It is an interesting provision that the bishop must not be a recent convert (6): maturity in faith is important for all who exercise any function of leadership. Paul also attaches importance to the way the Church's leadership is seen from outside (7). If the bishop does not have a good reputation there is danger. The devil will catch him and that will be greatly to the disadvantage of all that he stands for. He himself will be harmed and so will the Church.

Study: In view of conditions created by contemporary society, list in order of immediate importance the bishop's qualifications and duties found in these verses. To what extent are these demands met in your local church? Should church officers be appointed if no one fulfils these high standards exactly?

1 Timothy 3.8-13

It appears that in the early Church the staple of the local ministry was bishops and deacons (apostles, prophets, and others exercised wider ministries and cannot be thought part of the local organization). So after speaking of the bishop Paul turns his attention to the deacons. Between two sets of instructions specifically addressed to deacons (8–10, 12 f.) there is another for 'the women' (11). Some hold this to refer to the wives of the deacons, others to deaconesses. The principal point in favour of the former is that there is little clear evidence in the N.T. of a specific order of deaconess, or for that matter in the early Church. In favour of the latter is the difficulty of seeing why Paul should take two bites at the deacon's duties interspersed with an instruction that does not concern a church official. On the whole it seems more likely that he does refer to deaconesses. As in the case of bishops, deacons must be people of good character. They must have a sense of serious purpose, be careful of their speech and indulge themselves neither in wine nor in gain. A firm hold on the faith is important (9) and it is important that they be tested before being admitted to office. Unfortunately Paul does not tell us in what the test consisted, nor for that matter in what the office consisted. We are left to guess at both. We do not know what deacons did in those early days. There is a reference to the deacon's home life (12) and to the result of serving well (13).

Notes: V. 8: Deacons are to be 'serious' (*semnos*) as are the women (11); and for that matter the bishops, (4); the same root is there rendered 'respectful'. The term denotes a sense of high and serious purpose, the opposite of frivolity. V. 9: 'mystery' means something that men cannot possibly work out for themselves (not simply that which is difficult to work out), and usually, as here, there is the added thought that it has now been revealed. Men would never have guessed that the way of salvation has nothing to do with their good living, prayers, offerings, etc., but that it depended on God's sending His Son to die for us. That had to be revealed. V. 11: 'slanderers' is literally 'devils'. Let us not take slanderous gossip lightly as though it were a normal part of human life. It is not. It is devilish.

1 Timothy 3.14—4.5   The Faith—and its Perversion

At the end of ch. 3 we have a poetic expression which may well have formed part of a Christian hymn. The arrangement in the RSV brings out the rhythmical structure, though it is not certain that this precise form should be followed (it could be three couplets or simply six lines). 'He' (16) at the beginning is properly 'who' or 'He who' (see margin; some manuscripts read 'God' but 'He who' seems correct). This is not explained but there is no doubt but that Jesus Christ is meant. The hymn then refers to His incarnation, then apparently to His resurrection. It was this that the Spirit used to bring about His vindication (cf. Rom. 1.4). 'Seen by angels' may refer to the same thing, for angels saw Him at the resurrection. But it may well be the ascension that is primarily in mind at this point. There is uncertainty about the last line. This may be another reference to the ascension, but it makes good sense to see it as used prophetically of the final triumph. Then the six lines of the hymn would represent six stages arranged chronologically. This is a magnificent statement of the sweep of Christ's saving work.

But some are not content with it, and Paul moves immediately to those who 'will depart from the faith' (4.1). That the Spirit 'expressly says' this indicates that what is to take place is not beyond God's control. He is supreme despite the ragings of men and their

331

preference for 'deceitful spirits and doctrines of demons' (4.1). The heretics in mind are wrong in three ways: (i) Their doctrine is astray as we have seen. (*ii*) Their conscience is also astray (2). (*iii*) Their attitude to the things God has created is astray (3). In the ancient world as in the modern men sometimes advocated celibacy for religious reasons. Some also drew up curious food laws. Paul insists that both are completely wrong, for there is nothing God has created which is to be rejected if it is received in the proper way (4.4 f.).

Notes: V. 15: Note the dignity of the Church and its place in God's scheme of things. V. 16: 'mystery' again, the essence of 'our religion' is not of human origin but has been revealed by God. 4.4 f.: control of diet for proper reasons is not in question. Paul is opposing the erection of food laws for religious reasons. The Christian knows no such taboos. V. 3: Paul is not saying that none is called to serve God in the unmarried state (cf. 1 Cor. 7.7), but that celibacy is not in principle to be exalted above marriage.

Questions for further study and discussion on 1 Timothy 1.1—4.5
1. What is the place of the O.T. in the life of the Christian?
2. Bearing in mind 1.12–16 and 4.1–5 discuss the relationship between a right faith and right conduct.
3. What place should the believer be taking in the life of his community?
4. How can Paul's teaching on women be applied to the modern situation, especially in situations like the mission field?
5. How do Paul's criteria for bishops and deacons apply to the ministry of the modern church and to the service of lay people?

1 Timothy 4.6-11   Training in Godliness

That we simply grow in the Christian faith by doing nothing about it is a crazy notion. Paul has already pointed out that the devil is active and eager to trip up even Christian leaders (3.7). Now he develops the theme that it is important for the servants of God to train themselves in godliness (7). There is always the temptation to erect any rules that may be devised by Christians into a system which must at any cost be complied with. It is even easy to slip into the error of thinking that our systems enable us to acquire merit before God. When such attitudes occur our systems are a snare. But that does not mean that we should go to the opposite extreme and simply drift through life. We must be nourished (6). We must be trained (7). We must toil and strive (10). It is very helpful for the believer to work out a rule of life whereby he engages in the kind of reading, prayer, worship, and the like, which will build him up in the faith. There is no one way of doing this. To lay down rules binding on all Christians would be a calamitous error. But, human nature being what it is, for the average Christian settled habits, especially of prayer and Bible study, are tremendously important.

The Christian is nourished on 'the words of the faith' and of 'good doctrine' (6). This means that study of the Bible and of Christian doctrine are a necessity. The fact that we do this will in itself put us off 'godless and silly myths' (7). Perversions of the faith abound. But the Christian who is nourished in the Word of God and in sound doctrine will not readily fall a prey to them. We are familiar with the value of physical exercise for the development of physical fitness. Paul brings out the point that there is a spiritual analogy (8). He goes further, for he points out that training in godliness is of value not only in the here and now, but also 'for the life to come'. What folly accordingly to neglect it! He solemnly assures Timothy of the importance of this (9) and rounds off the section with the reminder that all this is worth doing because our hope is set on God. When Paul speaks of God as 'the Saviour of all men, especially of those who believe' he is not saying that all men will be saved ultimately and that believers will be specially saved. He is saying that God watches over all men, delivering them from evils and showering His blessings on them. He makes His sun shine on all and sends rain on just and unjust alike (Matt. 5.45). But 'Saviour' has a fuller, richer, and deeper meaning for men who believe. They are saved in a way other men are not.

1 Timothy 4.12-16   An Example to Follow

Student unrest, protests, and even riots, in many lands mean that modern youth is in no danger of over-submissiveness. 'Let no one despise your youth' (12) is scarcely a necessary injunction for our generation, no matter how much Timothy needed it. Young people as a whole are very confident, at least in their criticism of the 'establishment'.

But even modern youth may well ask itself 'Exactly what am I trying to do? What kind of life am I seeking to establish?' Paul reminds Timothy that men do not live unto themselves. Inevitably their lives form some sort of example. What sort is the important thing. Both 'speech and conduct' are important, and Paul looks for a lead 'in love, in faith, in purity'. All three are important in a world like ours and doubly so among rebellious youth. Timothy was a public figure in the Church and Paul goes on to consider how he should discharge his responsibilities. It is interesting that in the conduct of worship he singles out public reading of Scripture, preaching, and teaching (13). It is still the case that these are the significant elements in worship. Christian worship must centre on the reading of Scripture, for it is rooted in what God has revealed in Christ. And the preaching which sets forth the teachings of Scripture is a necessary consequence. 'Teaching' is not so very different from preaching, but it puts some emphasis on instruction in sound doctrine. It is not a matter of indifference what is taught in the name of Christ. A little later Paul stresses this again: 'Take heed to yourself and to your teaching' (16). In a day when many conflicting views are put forward as authentic Christianity it is well to give attention once more to the content of teaching. Scripture affords our standard, and that which does not agree with the revelation is not accepted.

Paul further exhorts his young friend, 'Do not neglect the gift you have' (14). It is easy to sigh for gifts we do not possess and in the process neglect the one God has given us. In Timothy's case Paul is apparently referring to ordination, for that is the natural interpretation of the laying on of the hands of the elders. Fulfilment of any ministry is not automatic, but requires diligent effort.

Notes: V. 16: 'save' is used in a wide sense of realizing to the full what is implicit in the Christian salvation.

1 Timothy 5.1-8   Honour where Honour is Due

Paul turns to classes of people in the church and instructs Timothy in the proper attitudes to be taken up towards them. He begins with the 'older man' or perhaps the 'elder' (it is not always certain whether the term is being used of age or of official position; but the official appears in v. 17, so that here we probably have senior citizens). It is not proper for a youth to rebuke his elders. Timothy should therefore treat older men as he would his father. This gives the clue to the way the Christian should interpret all his relationships within the community of believers. He should treat fellow Christians as brothers, mothers or sisters (1 f.).

It seems clear that in the early Church there was a sustained attempt to relieve the needs of widows (cf. Acts 6.1 for the early origin of the practice). Due to the social customs of the day they were in a particularly vulnerable position and the church saw their care as something important. But the financial resources of the church were very limited, and it was important that they be used wisely. This appears to be behind vs. 3 ff., with the distinction between 'real widows' and others. Paul enjoins family piety. People should make provision for their own where they can (4; cf. v. 16). It seems not unlikely that when the church began to help the needy widows some who were far from worthy tried to get on the list. So Paul speaks of the kind of life that a 'real widow' will live. He contrasts her dependence on God and her constant prayers with the self-indulgence of one who 'is dead even while she lives' (5 f.). And Paul can use very strong language when he comes to the importance of making proper provision for one's own immediate family (8). This is not the kind of thing to be left to the collective efforts of the church where one can well do it oneself. Even unbelievers will often perform this duty and in so doing show up the professing Christian who does not. 'He has disowned the faith' is a strong statement and should provoke serious reflection.

1 Timothy 5.9-16 Young Widows

Paul continues with the problem of widows. First he speaks of enrolling mature widows whose lives commend the faith. Presumably this means putting them on an official list of people who would be given financial or other assistance, and who apparently would be expected to do something to forward the work of the church. The widow who qualifies is over sixty years of age, has been 'faithful in marriage to one man' (9, NEB; this cannot mean 'having been the wife of one husband' [RSV], for Paul goes on to commend second marriage, v. 14), and has lived an exemplary life.

Younger widows are a different proposition. From v. 12 it seems that being 'enrolled' meant pledging oneself to some form of service which involved continuance in the unmarried state. Young widows naturally looked forward to remarriage in due course, and this made it difficult for them to fulfil their pledge. While they were doing service it would be with a divided mind, for some of their attention would be concentrated on their own future marriage. And if they did marry, the pledge to continue in that service would be broken. Paul is not blaming them for a desire for remarriage. On the contrary, he expressly encourages it (14). But he is realistic enough to see the effect of their natural desires on their performance of the duties expected of those on the roll. Moreover, lack of maturity may lead them to indulge in gossip when they think they are engaged in visiting (13). Paul was a very practical person! On all counts it was better that they be not enrolled.

Over against this Paul sets the desirable procedure. These young widows should by all means remarry (14). This would give each a proper place in a household and an important task to perform. Instead of being the targets for legitimate criticism they would then give no occasion for 'the enemy' to gain an entrance. Paul makes it clear that he is speaking out of experience. Some had already made the most grievous error by straying after Satan (15). The reference in the concluding verse to 'any believing woman' is somewhat puzzling as one would have thought the duty of providing for one's own family rested on male Christians as well as on women. Probably Paul means that if there are widows in a household they will come under the immediate care of the housewife. Thus she should 'assist them'. The church can then concentrate its aid on those who are really destitute.

Thought: V. 14: 'The greatest gift of Christianity to the social fabric is the development of the idea of home' (G. Matheson).

1 Timothy 5.17-25   The Ministry of Elders

The exact functions of the elders are not set out in the N.T. But we may assume that they were not dissimilar to those exercised by the synagogue elders, in which case the elders were the responsible local officials. Here we learn that they (or at least some of them) 'ruled' and that some laboured 'in preaching and teaching'. The implication from the latter statement is that some did not preach or teach. They were to be remunerated for their work (18), and esteemed as reverend personages, not lightly to be accused (19). But this does not mean that they were not to be accused under any circumstances. They might on occasion do wrong, and the persistent sinner must be rebuked publicly (20). Precisely because they were leaders and very much in the public eye, wrongdoing on their part must not be condoned. So Timothy is warned against respect of persons (21).

In its context the reference to 'the laying on of hands' (22) must refer to ordination (cf. 4.14). This is a very important act, and must be exercised with due care. To ordain a man who is not worthy is to be responsible for the harm that will follow; it means participating in the sins of another. At the end of our passage another aspect of sin is emphasized, namely, that in the end sin will out. Sometimes sin appears hidden, sometimes obvious. But nothing can prevent final disclosure. It is comforting to reflect that the same is true of goodness (25).

336

There is a little health note (23). The ancients did not know that germs in the water supply could cause disease, and they were ignorant of the fact that the alcohol in wine killed them. But they normally drank nothing but water or wine, and they observed that people who drank water only, sometimes got diseases that those who used wine did not. It is this which is behind Paul's injunction. In our day, when there is a multiplicity of beverages and when the causes of sickness are better known, it is possible to get the required result without resorting to the use of wine.

Notes: V. 17: 'honour' is usually taken to mean or at least include the thought of remuneration ('stipend', NEB). V. 18: Note the linking as 'Scripture' of verses from Deut. 25.4 and Matt. 10.10 (or Luke 10.7).

Thought: The ministry especially worthy of 'double honour' (17) is that of preaching and teaching. Consider the implications of this fact.

1 Timothy 6.1-2   Slaves

Slaves presented a problem to the early Church. On the one hand slavery was an institution accepted throughout the world, and probably no one envisaged a society in which there could be no slaves at all. But on the other, there was that in Christianity which was incompatible with slavery and which meant that in time those who took their faith seriously must do away with this monstrous system. Believing slaves were regarded by Christians from the very first as brothers in Christ. They were men for whom Christ died, and they were redeemed just as truly as any free man. So Paul can understand the unity of believers in Christ to mean among other things that 'there is neither slave nor free' (Gal. 3.28). He can speak of a slave as 'a beloved brother' of his owner (Philem. 16).

Now to some slaves this must have been heady teaching. Accustomed all their lives to being treated as no better than cattle, to being bought and sold in the market place, to being chattels for their masters' use, it was an intoxicating thought that they were their masters' equals in God's sight. It was only to be expected that some in this new-found faith were inclined to presume on their new relationship. Especially when their masters were Christians they found it difficult to retain their ordinary station. And this in turn must have been something of a hindrance to the gospel. If becoming a Christian meant putting up with disrespect from slaves and finding them less ready to work than where the owners were heathen, some-slave owners would not even consider the claims of the gospel.

337

Thus in the N.T. from time to time there are warnings to slaves not to presume on their new relationship to their masters. In our present passage Paul is pointing out that slaves should give their owners due respect. Indeed they should serve all the more willingly in that those who receive the benefit of their labours are themselves believers.

1 Timothy 6.3-10 Misinterpreting the Faith

Paul comes back to the thought of false teaching which he has already opposed (**4.1** ff.). It is important that we take Christianity for what it is and not impose our own pattern on it, making it what we wish it to be. That is the way of pride (4), the way which in effect means (whatever its exponents may say) that those who put it forth know better than Christ and His apostles. A concern for orthodox teaching does not come simply from an innate conservatism. It comes from a firm conviction that there is a finality about God's sending of His Son. Men cannot improve on the teaching of the Son of God or on that which He committed to His apostles. The apostles bore the definitive witness to Jesus and to reject this is to walk the way of pride and self-sufficiency. The false teachers Paul has in mind also had a love for controversy. Discussion of issues can be a useful way of clearing up the points involved. But it can degenerate into 'disputes about words' and result in angry wrangling (4 f.).

Mixed in with the heretical teaching was a concern for material profit. Regrettably throughout the centuries there have been those who have used religion as a means of personal profit, and the sorry story is not yet over. Paul points out that to imagine that 'godliness is a means of gain' is to be 'depraved in mind and bereft of the truth' (5). But this enables him to make the point that godliness does indeed bring gain, though of a very different sort than money. The end of our passage is a discussion of the way in which the love of money can harm spiritual life. This should be closely studied in an age as materialistic as our own. It is the case that men will often retain their faith in the face of difficulties and even persecutions, but surrender it in the piping days of peace and prosperity. The love of money and all it brings is an insidious thing. It can and does corrupt the most unlikely people, and bring in its train all kinds of evils (10).

Notes: V. 9: 'desire to be rich' means 'set their will on being rich'. V. 10: 'all evils' means 'every kind of evil' not 'all the evil there is'.

For self-examination: 'Content' (8). Does this describe my inner feelings today in regard to what I possess, what I have achieved, and what I want? How far should it?

1 Timothy 6.11-21   The Good Fight of Faith

Paul concludes his letter with a renewed call to Timothy to engage in strenuous Christian service, and with special warnings for the rich and the knowledgeable. It is never easy to be a Christian, and believers must always be alert against temptation to think that they will grow in spiritual maturity and judgement by the simple device of sitting still. There are some things that can be learned only in quietness and waiting on the Lord. There is 'a time to keep silence' as well as 'a time to speak' (Eccl. 3.7). But it is also the case that God has called His servants to work for Him in a busy world, a world where evil abounds and where it is easy to find excuses for avoiding difficult courses of action. So Paul can exhort Timothy, 'Fight the good fight of the faith' (12). The devil is often likened to an enemy, one who takes hostile action against the people of God. It is important to be clear that our battle is a real one and that it calls for our best endeavour in the strength of Christ. Paul appeals to Timothy's call and to 'the good confession' he made before many (12). Some understood this to refer to his baptism, but it seems more likely to refer to ordination. Paul reminds Timothy that his solemn confession had been made before God and Christ (who Himself made 'the good confession'), so it is not to be regarded lightly.

The apostle has some words for the rich (17–19). They are tempted above most men to rely on what is at best temporary and uncertain, and need help in getting their priorities right. They still need help, as do those who put their confidence in 'what is falsely called knowledge' (20). Undue preoccupation with what appears to be knowledge can be damaging to faith.

Question: What are the marks of a 'man of God' indicated in vs. 11,12?

Questions for further study and discussion on 1 Timothy 4.6—6.21
1. How can Paul's injunction to Timothy to set an example (4.12) be applied to your own situation?
2. What relevance has Paul's teaching on widows to the modern church?
3. In the light of Paul's teaching on slavery (6.1 f.) discuss the role of the Christian in social change.

4. What does Paul teach us in these chapters about the right use of material possessions?
5. Paul says a good deal about false teaching and about knowledge (e.g. **4.6 f., 6.3 ff., 20 f.**). In days when men know so much and esteem knowledge so highly, how may we apply his words?

2 Timothy 1.1-5   Thanksgiving

As with *1 Timothy*, Paul opens this letter in the conventional way, but he adapts the conventional framework in order to bring out Christian teaching. He speaks of his apostolate as 'by the will of God' and also as 'according to the promise of the life which is in Christ Jesus' (1). God does not send His apostles aimlessly. He has a definite plan, and they move according to that plan, a plan which concerns the bringing of life to sinful man. The word 'promise' is a reminder that life comes as God's gift. It is not earned by human merit. Paul strikes a note of tenderness when he refers to Timothy as 'my beloved child' (2). Clearly Timothy was very dear to him.

As we turn to Paul's opening thanksgiving we may profitably reflect that this is a necessary part of the Christian life. The ungrateful Christian is a contradiction in terms. All that is necessary in order to come up with matter for thanksgiving is a good memory. So Paul now remembers that his ancestors had served God 'with a clear conscience' (3) and he is following in their steps. The Christian faith he professed was not a recent invention but the fulfilment of all that was involved in the religion of his forefathers. He worshipped the same God as they, and did it with complete sincerity. Paul is able to recall also that Timothy had cause for similar thanksgiving, for his mother and his grandmother had been women of faith, that faith which Timothy himself now possessed (5). While we cannot trust to the merits of our predecessors in the faith, it is always good to recall them and to thank God for them.

The tears of which Paul writes (4) were evidently tears shed by Timothy when they parted. There were not the same inhibitions in those days about men weeping as in the modern western world. This is evidence not of weakness but of affection.

A point to ponder: Paul uses three different expressions for remembering in vs. 3,4,5 (and another in v. 6). Memory is important and many-sided.

2 Timothy 1.6-14   The Pattern of the Sound Words

Arising out of the goodly heritage in which Timothy stood, Paul proceeds to exhort him to faithfulness in his ministry. It is usual to take the gift given by the laying on of Paul's hands (6) as the divine enablement given at Timothy's ordination (cf. 1 Tim. 4.14), though some prefer a reference to an equivalent of confirmation. The point in either case is that God's gifts do not operate automatically and quite irrespective of men's spiritual states and inclinations. Such gifts must be 'stirred up' if they are to be effective.

Much of our passage is concerned with the necessity for boldness in Christian witness and ministry (7,8,12). In every age it has been easier to be timid than to stand up and be counted for Christ. And in every age men have needed the uncompromising message of what God has done in Christ for their salvation. It is still important that Christians be ashamed neither of the gospel by which they stand nor of their fellow Christians with whom they stand (cf. v.8). This will often involve a measure of suffering, but then that is inseparable from the life of the Christian (3.12), and especially from that of the preacher (11 f.).

The other great thought before us is that of the given nature of the Christian message. Notice the way the thought of what God has given runs through our passage (6,7,9,12,14). God gave the gift of salvation, in all its many sidedness. But He has entrusted the proclamation of that full and rich salvation to men. They are not to try to improve on it. They are to proclaim it.

Notes: V. 7: notice the importance of self-control and the company it keeps. V. 12: 'my deposit' might be 'that which I have committed unto Him,' but the RSV is probably correct. The same word 'deposit' is found in v. 14.

Meditation: Trace in vs. 9–11 our past salvation, our future hope, our present duty.

2 Timothy 1.15—2.13   Endurance for Christ

The theme running through this passage is the importance of being single-minded in our service of Christ. It is not easy to be a Christian and never has been. So active is the opposition that it comes naturally to a man like Paul to use military terms for Christian service. Thus here he speaks of being 'a good soldier of Christ Jesus' (2.3). The metaphor has point.

Paul first brings this out by drawing attention to a couple of citizens who fell short (1.15) and to one who did not (1.16 ff.). The time of testing sifts men. It is not to be taken for granted that a man who starts out hopefully on the path of service will continue. These two did not. From this Paul turns to direct exhortation to Timothy to 'be strong in the grace that is in Christ Jesus' (2.1).

Then he borrows illustrations from three different spheres of human endeavour to drive home his point that endurance to the end is a necessity. The soldier does not entangle himself in civilian affairs. The athlete must strive lawfully (which involves strict training). The farmer must work hard before partaking of the fruits of his labour.

Paul is qualified to exhort his young friend, for he is practising what he preaches. He is no arm-chair strategist, giving good advice in the knowledge that he himself will not be hurt. He writes from prison (2.9) and speaks from a wealth of experience, much of it painful, which gave him full and accurate knowledge of what being a good soldier of Christ means.

It is generally held that 2.11–13 is part of an early Christian hymn, and that the words 'The saying is sure' refer to the following, not the preceding. The point of the hymn in this context is that it forms an encouragement to troubled Christians. It speaks of the certainty of ultimate vindication for those who serve Christ faithfully (11,12a). It reminds us of the grim certainty that will follow a denial of Christ (cf. Matt. 10.33). But the hymn ends on a note of assurance. God is faithful, and His faithfulness will persist. This is not a charter for laxity of service, but an encouragement to troubled souls, despairing of their ability to do what they should. Their security rests not on their abilities but on God's faithfulness.

Meditation: The believer's strength is unmerited, since it is 'in . . . grace'; but it is also unlimited, since it is 'in Christ Jesus'.

2 Timothy 2.14-19 God's Workman

Paul is fond of contrasting mere words with real power (e.g. 1 Cor. 2.4; 4.19 f.; 1 Thess. 1.5). When a man becomes a Christian this means more than mere outward profession. It is true that what the Christian says is important. He is to bear his witness to Jesus. But it is even more important that he should have a witness to bear, that he should be manifesting in his life the power of the Spirit of God. It is in this spirit that Paul urges Timothy to do his best to be 'a workman who has no need to be ashamed' (15). There is nothing high-faluting about 'workman'. It is a down-to-earth word (used often of agricultural labourers), and points to the fact that honest toil is a prime requisite for Christian service. It does not matter if we have no mystic visions. It does matter if we do not produce hard work in the service of our Lord. So Paul warns Timothy once more against 'disputing about words' (14), and 'godless chatter' (16). The false teachers with whom Timothy was confronted were evidently long on talk but short on performance. It is a temptation in the way of every Christian.

Paul singles out one specific error, namely, that of holding 'that the resurrection is past already' (18). This could doubtless be made to look superficially attractive, for there is a sense in which it is true (Col. 2.12; 3.1). But clearly these teachers were affirming it in a different sense. They were interpreting it in a 'spiritual' sense which precluded any future resurrection of the body. This is the kind of error which Paul combats so magnificently in 1 Cor. 15. It must always be opposed because 'Christianity without a resurrection ceases to be a living faith' (Guthrie). The consequence of such teaching was that some were unsettled. But Paul is not dismayed. He knows that 'God's firm foundation stands' (19), and he sees this in two O.T. passages, Num. 16.5,26. His confidence is in God.

Notes: V. 14: For 'disputing about words' cf. 1 Tim. 1.4,7; 6.4,20; 2 Tim. 2.16; 3.7 f.; 4.4, Tit. 1.10; 3.9. V.1 5: 'rightly handling' (*orthotomounta*) means literally 'cutting straight' but whether the imagery is from cutting a road (Prov. 3.6, 11.5), or cutting stones, or cutting a furrow (so NEB), is not clear. In any case the stress is on 'straight' rather than 'cutting'. V. 17: Hymenaeus is probably the one mentioned in 1 Tim. 1.20.

2 Timothy 2.20-26 — Vessels for Noble Use

Upright living and the proper exercise of godly discipline in the church are the topics before us. The general bearing of the illustration from the vessels in a house is clear, but the detailed application is not. In a great house vessels of wood and earthenware have their uses, and Paul would certainly not have held that the humble and ill-equipped have no place in God's scheme of things. The thought is not so much the native qualities of believers as what they do about themselves. It is as though the vessels were able to determine for themselves something of their quality. Paul is saying something rather like the metaphor of costly or shoddy materials in building, which he uses in 1 Cor. 3. So if a man 'purifies himself' he will be 'for noble use' not ignoble.

Paul develops the theme that Timothy (and others) should aim at uprightness of living and disposition (22), but this brings him to the further thought that this means refusing to associate with 'stupid, senseless controversies' (23). The proper attitude towards those in error is a matter of some difficulty. On the one hand the Lord's servant must not do or say anything to countenance the error. On the other, he is not so much concerned to win an argument as to win men for Christ. He must resist the error but in such a way that he does not repel those who hold it. He must correct his opponents indeed, but 'with gentleness' (25). The aim is to deliver them from 'the snare of the devil' (26). The RSV goes on, 'after being captured by him to do his will', taking both 'him' and 'his' to refer to the devil. Both, however, might refer to God, who would then be described as He who delivers. Perhaps better is the RSV margin, which sees 'captured by him' as the devil's work, but takes 'to do his will' with 'come to know the truth', i.e. they escape the devil to do God's will.

2 Timothy 3.1-9   False Teachers Again

It is clear throughout these epistles that Paul is greatly concerned for both purity of life and purity of doctrine. He does not regard the way a Christian lives as unimportant, nor does he dismiss the opinions he holds as of no significance. It matters that he hold the true faith and that he show this by his manner of life. At this point Paul informs Timothy that 'in the last days' there will be false teaching. To the very end we must expect that there will be some who will pervert the faith. Paul is not speaking simply of men who live badly. He is talking of professing believers, men 'holding the form of religion but denying the power of it' (5). These people are characterized in the first place as 'lovers of self' (1), and much of what follows stems from that. The unhappy list in vs. 2–4 is made up of qualities which are natural enough for those dominated by selfishness.

At the beginning Paul speaks of 'the last days.' But the evils he mentions are not confined to the End, and we may suspect that he was troubled by people of this kind in his own day. Certainly this is the case in v. 6 (notice the present tense). He appears to be speaking of religious leaders, perhaps ministers, who used their influence wrongly. They captivated credulous ladies of the type who never reach a firm knowledge of the truth (6 f.). But Paul is confident that this will not get out of hand. He likens the work of the false teachers to that of Jannes and Jambres. These names do not appear in the O.T., but in a number of early writings they are the names of the Egyptian magicians who opposed Moses. It is possible that the teachers Paul opposed practised magic (someone has remarked that superstition and heresy are often connected). But his 'as (the magicians) so (the heretics)' requires no more than that they opposed the truth. Paul concludes with an assurance that 'their folly will be plain to all' (9). Their success will not last.

Notes: V. 6: 'weak women' is a contemptuous diminutive, 'little women'; 'silly' might be a better translation. 'Burdened' is 'heaped up,' a descriptive word. V. 8: 'counterfeit' = 'that has not passed the test.'

> *Conviction:* *But this I know, all flesh shall see His glory,*
> *And He shall reap the harvest He has sown,*
> *And some glad day His sun shall shine in splendour*
> *When He, the Saviour, Saviour of the world, is known.*

Questions for further study and discussion on 2 Timothy 1.1—3.9
1. In the light of 1.3 ff. discuss the place of home training in the faith.
2. How far is military imagery applicable to Christian service today?
3. Discuss the relationship between the effort of man (2.1 ff.) and the faithfulness of God (2.13).
4. In what ways can we use the imagery of the ordinary to illuminate the path of Christian service (cf. 2.20 f.; 1 Cor. 1.26 ff.).
5. How far can we apply 3.1 ff. to conditions in our own day?

2 Timothy 3.10-13   Paul's Example

One of the interesting features of the Pauline correspondence is the way the apostle so confidently appeals to his own example. He can call the Thessalonians to witness 'how holy and righteous and blameless was our behaviour to you believers' (1 Thess. 2.10), and he can even say, 'you became imitators of us and of the Lord' (1 Thess. 1.6). The whole thrust of his letters is such that he cannot have meant that he was without any sin. He is too insistent on universal sinfulness for that. But he knew very well that no believer can commend the gospel he preaches unless his life agrees with his words. And Paul was wholehearted in his living out of the faith. He had given himself unreservedly to the service of Jesus Christ and he knew that he had done so. Therefore he could and did point men to his own example. In the very different circumstances under which we live we cannot use the same language about our own lives. And in any case few of us would claim that our lives meet Paul's standard. But unless we are living in such a way that if men did follow our example they would be brought closer to Christ we cannot expect to commend the gospel. The importance of upright living cannot be overestimated.

All this lies behind this section of Paul's letter. He knows that Timothy has observed his teachings and his life. He singles out his aim, his faith, patience, love and steadfastness, before coming to

345

persecutions. It is perhaps worth pointing out that the mention of love is specially frequent in Paul's writings. We usually think of John as the apostle of love, but Paul uses the noun more than anyone else (seventy-five times out of its one hundred and sixteen N.T. occurrences). Paul is such a controversial figure that we sometimes see him as a doughty fighter, but overlook the fact that he is gripped with the importance of love.

Nor did this come from a sheltered existence, for he had to contend with tremendous difficulties. So he goes on to encourage Timothy in his troubles by pointing out that he himself had been through bitter persecutions and God had delivered him from them all (11). He goes on to make the extremely important point that this is the common lot of Christians (12). We must not expect that in an age like ours we shall escape. If our commitment to Christ is wholehearted, we must expect persecution of some kind.

Notes: V. 11: Antioch, Iconium, and Lystra were all places Paul visited early in his ministry. Was he turning Timothy's attention to what had first attracted him to Paul? V. 12: 'desire'—the word denotes an effort of will.

2 Timothy 3.14-17   The Complete Man of God

Paul goes on from his own example to what he trusts Timothy will make of it. He is very anxious to see his protégé firmly established in the faith. He draws his attention in particular to two things, his mentors in the faith and the place of holy Scripture. Paul has already alluded to the faith of Lois and Eunice (1.5), the grandmother and mother who had been Timothy's instructors in his earliest years. In view of what he has just said we cannot doubt but that he includes himself under this heading also. He had been the means of Timothy's conversion and he had started him along the Christian way. As Timothy esteemed his predecessors in the faith, so he must take with the utmost seriousness what they told him of the way.

But Paul's most important counsel concerns Scripture. From his earliest days Timothy had known the O.T., and Paul speaks of Scripture as 'able to instruct you for salvation through faith in Christ Jesus' (15). Christ is the key to all Scripture and one cannot come to salvation apart from Him. But clearly Paul regards the place of the Bible as supremely significant. He goes on to speak of it as 'inspired by God', an expression which appears to mean 'God-breathed', i.e. it is the utterance of God. Some have suggested that we should translate in some such way as 'Every inspired scripture has its use' (NEB). The objection to this is that it may be held to mean that Paul is distinguishing between inspired and non-inspired Scripture, which would be an impossible thought for him. He is saying that Scripture comes from God and that therefore it is thoroughly reliable. It is profitable in a variety of ways. In the area of doctrine it is of value positively for teaching, negatively for reproof. It is just as useful in matters of conduct, negatively for correction, and positively for training in righteousness. Thus Paul can speak of the man of God as 'complete, equipped for every good work' (17). It is still the case that no servant of God can expect to be fully equipped for the service of God unless he is well grounded in the truth of the Bible.

Question: What 'sacred writings' of the O.T. can you recall which are able to 'instruct you for salvation through faith in Christ Jesus'?

2 Timothy 4.1-5   Preach the Word

It arises out of what Paul has been saying that Timothy should be active in God's service. There is no point in having a man of God complete and equipped for every good work if he sits down and does nothing. So having pointed to that use of Scripture which will enable Timothy to become the sort of person he ought to be, Paul immediately goes on to urge him to make the utmost use of the training he has had. This is no light matter and Paul introduces it with a solemn charge before God and Christ. He characterizes Christ as Judge, which will remind Timothy that he is a responsible man. He will one day give account of himself to this Jesus before whom Paul charges him.

The content of the exhortation boils down to one pithy command: 'preach the word' (2). All else is but commentary. Today men are often filled with the importance of modern knowledge and with the necessity for Christians to be aware of the contributions of science, philosophy, and the like, to our understanding of life and of the universe in which we live. It is well in such times to remember whence the essential Christian message is derived. We must not be obscurantist, and we certainly cannot hope to preach the gospel with any prospect of success if we ignore the world in which we live or insist on using the categories of a bygone age. But it is still the case that the essence of the gospel is a given message. We are not at liberty to manipulate its terms (cf. Gal. **1**.6 f.).

Paul points out that Timothy will face a time when people will prefer another message. In every age faithful preachers of the gospel have found that this is the case. There is that about the gospel which puts down men's pride, and leaves them utterly dependent on the grace of God. This does not appeal to the natural man and his ears 'itch' for someone who will flatter his ego a little more. In this frame of mind he will listen to any myth rather than the gospel. But this does not mean that the man of God is to go along with the demand. He is to be constant in following what he knows to be right. It means steadiness, and it means the enduring of suffering (cf. **3.**12). But it means also that the man of God fulfils his ministry (5). And there is no greater satisfaction on earth than that.

2 Timothy 4.6-22 The Good Fight

We should not overlook the importance of the 'For' which begins this section of the letter. The reason Paul has now urged Timothy to be urgent as an evangelist and to fulfil his ministry is that he, Paul, has finished his work. He describes this first in terms of sacrifice ('already I am being poured out as a libation', i.e. a sacrificial drink offering; he uses the same metaphor in Phil. **2.**17). Then he speaks of departing, after which come three further ways of looking at his life, probably all taken from the Games. The word rendered 'fight' is a technical term for competing in an event at the Games; 'the race,' of course, means a running contest (notice that Paul does not speak of having beaten others, but only of having completed the course); 'the faith' will for Paul mean the whole content of the Christian faith, but there is probably also a glance at the Games where the competing athlete must pledge himself to compete lawfully. Paul has kept the rules, so to speak, and lived out the faith for which he stood. So there awaits him 'the crown of righteousness' (8), which reminds us of the crown awarded to the successful athlete. We could understand this to mean the crown consisting in righteousness, but this is scarcely in harmony with Paul's thought that the believer is already justified or righteous in God's sight. More probably it refers to the reward to be given at the last day to the man whose righteousness has been manifested in his living, a reward which goes not to outstanding men like Paul only, but also to 'all who have loved His appearing' (8).

Notes: V. 8: 'that Day', i.e. the day of judgement; 'His appearing', probably the second advent which was longed for ('loved'), not feared. V. 10: Demas had been a trusted fellow worker (Col. **4.**14; Philem. 24). V. 13: 'the books' were evidently papyri, perhaps in roll form, 'the parchments', i.e. the 'vellums', were more costly writing material. Paul does not say what was written on either, but it seems probable that Scripture was included. Some think citizenship papers or other important personal papers may also be meant. V. 16: Apparently Paul had already had a preliminary stage in his trial, but none of his friends stood by him. Despite this the Lord delivered him at that stage (v. 17), which gives the Apostle confidence that the Lord will continue to watch over him and bring him to 'His heavenly kingdom' (18).

Meditation: 'Luke alone is with me'—the earthly friend. 'The Lord stood by me'—the divine Companion.

Titus 1.1-4 God Never Lies

We have already seen in both the letters to Timothy how Paul delights to take the conventional epistolary opening and make that the means of bringing out important Christian teaching. He does it again here, with an emphasis on the reliability of God. God never lies and thus we may and must believe Him implicitly.

But as the convention demanded, Paul begins with himself. Nowhere else does he describe himself as 'a servant of God', though he does use the phrase 'a servant of Jesus Christ' (Rom 1.1, cf. Phil. 1.1). The following expression is far from straightforward. Literally it means something like 'according to the faith of God's elect . . .', which the RSV understands as 'to further the faith . . .' and the NEB, 'marked as such by faith and knowledge and hope— the faith of God's chosen people. . . .' The words appear to mean not so much the purpose or the mark of his apostleship as that it is this which is the very essence of it, the characteristic of it. His apostleship is grounded in and determined by the qualities named.

'The faith of God's elect' preserves a due balance between the divine initiative and the human response. 'Their knowledge of the truth' draws attention to the importance of apostleship in promoting advance in the knowledge of what God has revealed.

But the main part of this opening is concerned with 'eternal life'. This is spoken of as the object of hope. But this hope, as is usual in the N.T., is not a vague optimism, but the present conviction of something which is not yet but which surely will come. There is, of course, a sense in which eternal life is the Christian's present possession. But there is another sense in which its full realization is yet future, and it is this which is before us here. Though we do not yet see it, there is no doubt about it, for it rests on the promise of God and God 'never lies' (2). The promise goes back 'ages ago'. The manifestation is up to date, in the preaching of the Word as it has been entrusted to Paul. There may possibly be a glance at Jesus as the Word (as in John 1.1), but this is not the main thought. That is rather that God is pleased to manifest Himself in the preaching

349

He commits to His apostle Paul. Notice that Titus, like Timothy (1 Tim. 1.2), was a convert of Paul's (4).

Meditation: 'The truth which accords with godliness' (1). The truth of God is not intended merely to be admired, or apprehended, or approved; it is meant to be translated into action.

Titus 1.5-16 — God's Stewards

Clearly Titus was a man of ability and one in whom Paul placed a good deal of trust. He had left him in Crete, he says, 'that you might amend what was defective' (5). This is a fairly tall order, but Paul appears confident that Titus would be successful. In the present passage Paul's concern is chiefly with the ministry. First he speaks of the qualifications to be looked for, and then of the opposite kind of teaching ministers would meet.

Paul says much the same to Titus as he said to Timothy on the qualifications required in ministers (1 Tim. 3). He speaks first of 'elders' and then of 'a bishop,' but this should not be understood in the sense that there were many elders in a church and but one bishop. As Barrett puts it, 'The elders you appoint must have certain qualifications, for a man who exercises oversight must be. . . .' Paul insists on the necessity of an upright life, a good home and family, and a firm hold on sound doctrine so that he can deal with false teachers (9).

Interestingly, the men of Crete were troubled by teaching with a Jewish flavour (10,14). Apparently it had something to do with food laws, for Paul cites a Cretan poet among other things for the expression, 'lazy gluttons'. But the main thrust of the quotation is that the Cretans 'are always liars'. This incidentally is written into the Greek language with the verb *cretizo*, 'to lie'. The poet also speaks of Cretans as 'evil beasts' ('vicious brutes', NEB). It adds up to a grim situation where very firm action is necessary. So he calls on Titus to 'rebuke them sharply' (13). There are occasions when the servant of God must take a very strong line. These people were thoroughly corrupt (15 f.). They required the firmest of firm hands.

Notes: V. 10: The worst heretics were Jewish, but these were not the only ones. V. 12: The poet is Epimenides (6th–5th century B.C.), though some think Paul takes the quotation immediately from Callimachus (3rd century B.C.). Epimenides was widely held to be a prophet and Paul evidently uses the general title. V. 16: This is surely the ultimate condemnation of the merely professing Christian.

Questions: (1) What other Scriptures than v. 16 distinguish between words and works? (2) How far does this fit your life?

350

Titus 2.1-10

Once again we have an emphasis on sound doctrine. Whatever be the case with the false teachers Titus is to teach what is correct. Throughout the Pastorals this concern for teaching what is right is constant. But it is also the case that these same Epistles stress the importance of lives that commend the sound doctrine that is taught. Paul insists that right teaching and right living must go together. At the end of the passage under consideration he urges slaves so to live that 'in everything they may adorn the doctrine of God our Saviour' (10), and this might well be held to apply to all. Paul looks for Christians who will show by their lives what manner of faith it is that they profess. As in *1 Timothy* he has instructions for various classes in the church. The older men, who were in that distant age looked up to as leaders and revered for their experience and wisdom. are to show a due appreciation of the seriousness of life (2). The older women are likewise to act becomingly and to train up the younger. The injunction tells us a good deal about both age groups. The younger women are to be specially careful of their home and family duties (4 f.). It is, of course, still the case that the effectiveness of their husbands' work and the future of their children depend to a large degree on their making the home what it should be. When he gets to young men, Paul singles out the importance of self-control, an exhortation far from being out of date in view of the undisciplined lives common in some quarters. Titus himself is not excluded, and indeed the exhortation to him personally is much more detailed than that for young men in general (7 f.). To whom much is given of him shall much be required. As elsewhere in the N.T. slaves get a special mention. As we saw when dealing with 1 Tim. 6.1 f., Christian slaves, especially if their masters were also Christian, were strongly tempted to presume on their relationship, and Paul is very anxious that they should commend the Christian faith.   *Notes:* V. 2: Notice 'love'; Paul always sees it as important. V. 3: 'reverent' has a meaning like 'suited to a sacred character'. For the Christian all of life is sacred.

Titus 2.11-15

Having dealt with the kind of conduct he looks for in believers Paul goes back to the basis of it all. The 'For' which introduces v. 11 should not be overlooked. Men should live in the way outlined because God has acted for salvation. 'The grace of God' is viewed dynamically. It 'appeared'. In Christ the very grace of God was seen. Grace is one of the great Pauline words (Paul uses it 100 times out of 155 times in the N.T.), and it emphasizes the freeness of God's gift of salvation. This is universal in its scope (Lock sees 'all men' as meaning 'all classes of men, even slaves'). It is in keeping with the characteristic emphasis of these Epistles that this grace 'trains us' in right living (12), and that both negatively and positively. It is reinforced by an appeal to the 'blessed hope,' the second coming of our Lord Jesus. This is distinguished from the first advent by the explicit reference to His 'glory'. Notice that Jesus is expressly called 'God'. The deity of our Saviour meant a good deal to the men of the N.T. and those moderns who have rejected the doctrine have cut themselves off from a considerable part of the riches of Christianity. It matters immensely that the salvation we proclaim is not one which proceeds·from any created being but from none less than God Himself.

Christ's saving work is described in terms of redemption (14). This means the setting free from slavery or a death sentence by the payment of a price (called the 'ransom', cf. 1 Tim. 2.6). Here redemption is 'from all iniquity'. Left to ourselves we could not break free from our sins, but Christ's redemptive act frees us from both their consequences and their power. The result is 'a people of His own who are zealous for good deeds' (14). Nothing less is adequate as the fruits of our redemption.

This is a grand message. A grander has never been committed to men. So Paul confidently calls on Titus to proclaim it 'with all authority' (15). In this he speaks directly to the need of our day.

Notes: V. 13: Some favour the AV, 'the great God and our Saviour Jesus Christ', but this is not the most natural meaning of the Greek (there is but one article; 'appearing' is never used of God; 'God and Saviour' is a recognized combination). The RSV is better.

Titus 3.1-15 The Life of Faith

The duty of Christians to the State comes in for brief mention. They are to be submissive and obedient, for the State is performing a necessary function and one which would be impossible without the co-operation of citizens. In the same breath Paul mentions the necessity of being kind and courteous to all men (2). The believer has obligations to those who are outside the faith.

We should treat all men well, for we recall from what we ourselves were saved (3). In 2.11 Paul almost personified grace, and here God's goodness and loving kindness are treated similarly. They 'appeared'. That is to say they were made manifest, became visible in Jesus Christ. Paul proceeds to speak of our salvation through the mercy of God, a salvation which comes 'by the washing of regeneration and renewal in the Holy Spirit' (5). Most today see a reference to baptism. This is possible, though it is also possible that Paul is using 'washing' symbolically and defining it as regeneration and renewal. If a reference to baptism is held to be present it is not in the sense that the rite of itself conveys spiritual blessings, for in this context Paul is stressing the very opposite of ritualism. It is the activity of the Holy Spirit which is important. This is not to be separated from the work of Christ (6) but is its necessary completion. He goes on to speak of this salvation in terms of justification, grace, hope, and eternal life (7), a rich collection of significant terms.

Before he finishes Paul has yet another warning against false teachers (8–11). A significant feature of this section is the reference to repeated admonition (10). For a man to be rejected as a heretic there must be persistence in error in the face of repeated warnings.

Notes: V. 1: 'Remind them' shows that this is not a new instruction. They already knew it. V. 4: 'God our Saviour'; cf. 2.13. V. 5: 'the washing of regeneration and renewal in the Holy Spirit' is seen by some to be two operations (as NEB, 'the water of rebirth and the renewing power of the Holy Spirit'). The RSV is to be preferred. V. 14: To the end Paul insists on 'good deeds'.

Meditation: 'The saying is sure' (8). *Collect and reflect upon these sure 'sayings' of the Pastoral Epistles (1 Tim 1.15; 3.1; 4.8,9; 2 Tim. 2.11; Tit. 3.8).*

Questions for further study and discussion on 2 Timothy 3.10—Titus 3.15

1. Discuss the ways in which Scripture can profit modern man and train him in righteousness.
2. How should we apply the words 'be urgent in season and out of season' (2 Tim. 4.2) to our own situation?
3. What can we learn from the *Epistle to Titus* about the Person of our Lord Jesus Christ?
4. Gather the references to the attitude Titus should adopt towards the Cretans. How far are they applicable to our own situation?
5. How does Paul bring out the change made in men's lives when they are saved by Christ?

Philemon

INTRODUCTION

This is a purely private letter from Paul to his friend Philemon about a runaway slave named Onesimus. It seems that Philemon lived at Colossae, and that this letter was sent to him at the same time as Paul's letter to the Colossian church (cf. the references to Onesimus, Col. **4.**8 f., and Archippus, Col. **4.**17). Paul was in prison somewhere (1), and he had evidently been the means of the conversion of Onesimus (10). Now he is sending the slave back to his owner, but this letter is evidence that he is taking every care to ensure that Onesimus be properly received. It is a delightful letter, giving us a revealing glimpse into first-century life and showing us from a new angle the way Christians lived out their faith.

Most scholars hold that the imprisonment in question was in Rome, and that it came toward the end of Paul's ministry. It is possible that it was during another of Paul's imprisonments (2 Cor. **11.**23). There is no way of deciding the point.

Nothing is known of Onesimus other than what we learn here, though there was a tradition in the early Church that he became a bishop. Similarly, nothing is known of Philemon other than what we glean from this letter.

Philemon 1-7 — Refreshing the Hearts of the Saints

Once again we have the typical beginning to a first-century letter. Paul characterizes himself by his current imprisonment, which he sees as 'for Christ Jesus'. He links Timothy with him in sending the letter, but there seems no reason for thinking that Timothy had any real part in its composition. The recipients are Philemon, Paul's 'beloved fellow worker', Apphia (apparently Philemon's wife) and Archippus (who may well have been the son of the house; a little message is sent to him in Col. 4.17). 'The church in your house' appears to mean that a local group of Christians assembled for worship in the home of Philemon. What relationship such a house church had to the church of the city we have no means of knowing.

Paul goes on to say that he gives thanks for his friends. It is characteristic that the two qualities he specially notes are love and faith (5). There is no substitute for love in living out the Christian life. And, of course, unless there is a genuine faith in Jesus Christ there is no Christian life at all. It is likely that we should link love with faith as directed towards Christ and all the saints (rather than thinking of this as referring to faith only). Paul goes on to speak

of the way he himself had derived 'much joy and comfort' from the
same love, and he explains that 'the hearts of the saints have been
refreshed through you' (7). An outgoing love (which ought to be
characteristic of the way all Christians live) has far-reaching effects.
Obviously it makes an impression on its immediate objects. But it
does not stop there. Philemon's kindnesses to the saints at large
brought joy and comfort to Paul and doubtless to many others as
well. And, though Paul does not mention it, such love has its
effects on those outside the circle of believers. 'Behold, how these
Christians love one another!' was a verdict which brought the heathen
world to take seriously the faith that could produce such results.
It may well be that many of the troubles besetting the contemporary
Church would be solved or at least considerably lessened if the whole
Church structure were permeated by a spirit of love.

But we must not go on from there to conclude that the Church's
business is simply to show love. Paul commends Philemon for
sharing his faith (6). There is no substitute for believing on the Lord
Jesus Christ and we should be quite clear about this. It is only by
faith that we may obtain 'all the good that is ours in Christ'.

Philemon 8-25 That Useful Man Onesimus

From this section of the letter we are able to gather what had
happened. Onesimus had been a slave of Philemon's (16), but
had run away, possibly robbing his master before he left (18).
He did what many other escaping slaves did, and went to the big
city where it would be almost impossible to find him. But somehow
he had been brought into contact with Paul the prisoner and Paul
had been the means of his conversion (10). Now questions arose:
What is the place of a runaway slave who has become a Christian?
What should be done about the fact that legally he is still the
property of his owner?

Paul is clear on the matter. Onesimus must go back. He is a
Christian, and a Christian respects the rights of others no matter
at what inconvenience to himself. So Paul sends him back to his
master. It must have been difficult for him but he does it. And it
must have been difficult for Onesimus. After all he had made good
his escape and was presumably safe from recapture. Voluntarily
to go back to the slavery from which he had broken free could not
have been easy, quite apart from the fact that he must face whatever
penalties were involved in his having escaped in the first instance.
He might feel that Philemon would not be hard on him, but he

could not be sure. But he was a Christian. And that meant that he must do what was right even if it meant hardship.

This letter, then, is Paul's attempt to ensure that Onesimus is well treated when he returns. It has been held up as a model of tact, as the Apostle gently but persistently pleads for one who quite plainly had become very dear to him (12). He could command (8), but prefers that Philemon should act of his own free will (14). But he does remind his friend of what he owes to Paul (19), and of the value Onesimus the Christian would be to his master (16).

Paul makes something of the meaning of the name Onesimus, 'profitable' or 'useful.' Formerly this man had done anything but live up to his name. Now he is a valued helper of Paul's (13); he is 'the faithful and beloved brother' (Col. 4.9). So had Christ transformed this most unpromising piece of humanity.

Hebrews

This writing is anonymous. The ascription to Paul is fairly early, but by no means early enough to be decisive, and the style of the Epistle is against it. It is very different from Paul's normal style. A number of possible authors have been suggested, such as Barnabas, Apollos, and Prisca. But these are no more than guesses and we must accept the fact of our ignorance.

The recipients of the writings have traditionally been seen as Jewish Christians, tempted to relapse into Judaism. In recent times this view has been challenged by scholars who maintain that there is no way of knowing whether the writing was meant for Jews or Gentiles. They point out that the appeal to the O.T. as sacred Scripture was accepted by Christian Gentiles as well as Jews, and that the author nowhere says that he is writing to Jews. This view cannot be ruled out as impossible. But it is to be doubted whether it explains those many parts of the writing which insist on the superiority of some aspect of Christianity to something Jewish. It still remains the most likely view that Jews are in mind. But it is not written to Jewish Christians as a whole. It is clear that the recipients are a small group who might have been expected to be teachers but who had not made the progress in the faith expected of them (5.12).

It is not easy to date the Epistle. Perhaps it is relevant that there is nothing in it which indicates that Jerusalem had fallen, for in view of the line of argument adopted we might well have anticipated a reference to that event if it had taken place. On the other hand, there has been time for the gospel to spread to some degree and a certain amount of development both of doctrine and Christian maturity are presupposed. Perhaps we will not be far wrong in dating it in the 60's.

We have spoken of the writing as an 'Epistle', but this may be going too far. It certainly does not have the normal epistolary framework and it reads more like a theological treatise than a letter. We may retain the name 'Epistle' owing to its long use. But we should bear in mind that it is not by any means an exact description of the writing's literary genre.

Hebrews 1.1-4 The Revelation of God

This little paragraph forms an introduction to the Epistle as a whole. It concentrates on the revelation God has made of Himself (do not overlook the implication that men of their own selves do

357

not come to know God). He has revealed Himself in many different ways from times of old, as the prophets witness (1). But the culmination of the revelation has been reserved until recent times when He spoke 'by a Son' (2). The contrast is between the prophet who knows God externally and can say only the things that are given him from outside, and the Son who shares in the nature of deity and can speak of what God is in Himself, and for that matter show what God is in His deeds as well as His words.

Our author proceeds to bring this out by insisting on the high place Christ occupies. 'Whom He appointed the heir of all things' (2) should not be understood as if God adopted Christ into His family. Rather it is a way of saying that Christ stands to God in the relation of heir. It is a way of emphasizing His excellence, not of bringing Him down to the level of created beings. Far from being Himself created He was the means of the world's creation. He 'reflects the glory of God and bears the very stamp of His nature'. He upholds the whole universe. He 'made purification' for men's sins. He sits at God's right hand. It is difficult to see how words could more clearly convey the thought that He belongs with God and not with man, that in Him we see the very revelation of God Himself.

Notes: V. 3: 'reflects' really represents a noun with a meaning like 'effulgence'; it is not so much that He reflects glory from elsewhere as that the divine glory shines from Him. 'Very stamp' (*character*) means exact representation. He shows us exactly what God is. 'When He had made' is an aorist tense which points to a completed work. This is brought out also with the reference to sitting at God's right hand.

Question: Is Christ in your affections?

Hebrews 1.5-14   Christ is Superior to Angels

The whole of the opening phase of the argument is directed towards showing the surpassing excellence of the Christ from whom the readers were tempted to fall away. First our author shows that He is far greater than the angels. His method is to assemble an interesting collection of passages from the O.T. which combine to prove his point. He cites Psa. 2.7 to show that God does not speak to any angel in the way He speaks to His Son. It is this Father–Son relationship which is seen also in 2 Sam. 7.14, originally spoken with reference to Solomon, but here interpreted of the Messiah, the very Son of God. Next we turn to the function of the angels, which is to worship God's Son and thus definitely to take the lower place (the quotation might be from the Septuagint of Deut. 32.43 or

Psa. **97**.7). Psa. **104**.4 follows with its definite placing of the angels in the category of 'winds' (or 'spirits') and among the 'servants'. In strong contrast Psa. **45**.6 f. addresses the Son in terms of everlasting sovereignty. This puts Him outside the class of the angels. But it is significant that the quotation is continued in terms of moral uprightness. We miss the Son's true greatness if we concentrate on power and glory. His sceptre is a righteous one (8). His love is for righteousness (9). It is this which the psalmist sees as the reason for the Son's superior exaltation (9).

With this our author links Psa. **102**.25–27, with which he combines an expression from Isa. **34**.4. Again he uses the Septuagint, for the Hebrew does not contain the word 'Lord'. But the revealing thing is that he has taken words which in the original apply to Jehovah and has used them of Christ. This shows as nothing else could the very high place he assigns Him. The quotation sees the Son as having a part in creation and as remaining unchanged while the creation grows old. His eternity is not to be overlooked.

The final quotation is from Psa. **110**.1, a passage which is often cited of Christ. The words speak of God as giving Him a place at His right hand (the place of highest honour), and as overcoming all His enemies. Over against all this the angels appear as no more than 'ministering spirits', and indeed spirits whose task is to serve for the sake of saved men (14). Clearly Christ is pre-eminent over them all.

Meditation: 'Salvation' (14), like 'eternal life', is at once present and future (Westcott).

Hebrews 2.1-4 So Great Salvation

The stature of the Saviour shows the quality of the salvation. Since Christians have a Saviour so infinitely superior to the highest of created beings they must regard the salvation He wrought for them as no common thing. It is a salvation to be prized highly and sought out diligently. Yet it is easy to miss it, for this requires not a deliberate rejection but simply a drifting away from it (1). 'We are all continuously exposed to the action of currents of opinion, habit, action, which tend to carry us away insensibly from the position which we ought to maintain' (Westcott). It is the case that we may fail to attain salvation simply by neglecting it (3). God has made ample provision for the needs of all men. But if we neglect the means He has provided for our deliverance, then indeed 'how shall we escape?'

The greatness of the salvation is brought out by a comparison of the Christ, who procured it, with the angels. Elsewhere in the N.T. we read that angels played a part in the giving of the Law on Mt. Sinai (Acts 7.53; Gal. 3.19). This is not mentioned in the O.T. but our writer sees it as a way of stressing the dignity and importance of the old Law. This Law (here called 'the message', Gr. *logos*) was fully established (RSV, 'valid') and every failure to keep it brought retribution. This opens up the way for the 'how much more?' type of argument of v. 3.

The Christian salvation is thoroughly attested. Appeal is made to three different witnesses to establish this. It was in the first instance 'declared' by Christ Himself. This will refer to His preaching, but also to His actions. He set it forth by what He said and was and did. Secondly, it was 'attested to us by those who heard Him' (3). That is to say, the recipients of this letter had good grounds for accepting it. The gospel had been preached to them by people who had heard Christ. And finally, God bore witness by unusual happenings which attended the preaching. The Holy Spirit had done wonderful things. The final 'according to His own will' (4) is a reminder that these miraculous happenings are not under men's control. God acts as it pleases Him, not as men may demand, a truth which is not yet out of date.

Thought: You need not do anything to drift!

Hebrews 2.5-9   'Jesus . . . crowned with glory and honour'

The wonder of the salvation of which he has been speaking now causes our author to bring before us the further surprising truth that 'the world to come' of which he is speaking, that world which is relevant to the salvation in question, was not subjected to angels but, as vs. 6 ff. show, to man. God has for men in Christ this high destiny. The quotation from Psa. 8.4 ff. brings out the high dignity of man. The RSV renders in the Psalm 'Thou hast made him little less than God', which is a fair translation of the Hebrew. But *elohim* can also be used of created beings (e.g. Pss. 29.1; 82.1,6), so our author's translation can be defended. But in any case, however the Psalm be translated, his main point stands: God has provided for man a great destiny.

Now comes a quite different thought. From the fact that we do not yet see everything in subjection to man, as the Psalm prophesies, our author turns to what we do see. And what we see is Jesus. The human name draws attention to Jesus the man, and we may fairly reason that the writer sees in Him the fulfilment of the prophetic word. He is the Man made lower than the angels. But He is also the recipient of the highest honour because of what He did when made lower in this way. It was 'so that . . . He might taste death', and not death simply, but death for every man. Thus early in the Epistle is the point made that the death of Jesus is necessary if we are to be saved. Paul tells us that death is 'the wages of sin' (Rom. 6.23), and we cannot doubt that this is the thought here too. Since men's sin involved them in death Jesus came where men are and died their death.

'By the grace of God' stresses the freeness of it all. It implies that salvation could not be accomplished by man's own efforts. But where man could not prevail God's grace could and did. The death of Jesus then was not an accident, nor the result of the malice of His opponents simply. It was the out-working of the divine grace so that the salvation of men might be accomplished.

Hebrews 2.10-18 True Man for Man's Salvation

Life was not easy for the little group of discouraged believers to whom this Epistle was written. Almost certainly they faced the possibility of suffering for their Christianity and they must have wondered whether it was worth suffering for. Why not give the whole thing away and enter into peace?

For one reason, says our author, because Jesus suffered. And was this a dreadful accident that could not be guarded against? Not a bit of it. It was the way He saved men. To bring about our salvation He came where we are, even though this necessarily involved Him in cruel suffering and, in fact, death. But since men had sinned and brought the penalty of death upon themselves it was inevitable that their Saviour should enter their lot, and die their death. It was through death that He destroyed 'him who has the power of death, that is, the devil' (14).

To do this He had to become man. But this was the point of everything. His business on earth was not with angels. He did not come to save them (16). It was men who sinned. It was men who needed salvation. Therefore He became man and died and saved them. His genuine community of nature with us shows God's passionate concern that we be saved.

Our author speaks of Christ's being made 'perfect through suffering' (10). This does not, of course, mean that before suffering He was not perfect. But there are different kinds of perfection. The perfection of the bud is one thing and that of the flower another. There is a perfection involved in actually having suffered which

361

does not exist apart from the experience of having suffered. Christ does not merely love us enough to suffer for us. He loved us so much that He *did* suffer for us.

A series of quotations brings out His community of nature with us. These come from Psa. **22**.22 (where the key word is 'brethren'), Isa. **8**.17 (Septuagint; if He trusted in God He was certainly man), and Isa. **8**.18 ('the children'). The real humanity of Jesus was a necessity if He was to be our Saviour. Only by becoming man could He take man's death and remove man's condemnation. Our passage concludes with some other aspects of this saving work. Christ became 'a merciful and faithful high priest' (17). This concept is found in *Hebrews* only in the N.T., but, as this writing shows, it is a powerful way of bringing out what Christ has done for us. And arising out of this is the thought, full of solace to the tempted, that Christ can indeed help them, for He Himself knows suffering and temptation and that from experience (18).

Notes: V. 10: 'pioneer' (Gr. *archēgos*), like Eng. 'leader', can mean first along the way or first in importance, and in addition it can mean originator. Christ was all these. V. 17: 'to make expiation' is rather 'to make propitiation' (RV); it is the personal process of removing wrath and not the impersonal removal of sin that the word denotes.

Question: Have you ever thought of suffering as something that may make you more like Christ?

Hebrews 3.1-6   Christ Superior to Moses

Moses was revered throughout the Jewish nation as the really significant man in the history of the nation. He it was whom God had appointed to lead the nation out of its bondage in Egypt and bring it to the promised land. And he it was through whom God had given the law to His people. The great miracle of the Exodus, with the plagues in Egypt and the crossing of the Red Sea, followed by the wanderings in the wilderness, with God's providential care over His people, and Moses as the mediator of God's commands and the leader of the nation, all combined to leave Moses with such an aura as set him apart from all the great men that followed. He was incomparable. There never could be another Moses.

To say that Jesus was superior to Moses, then, was to put Him out of the class of ordinary men. If these words are indeed written to Jews it is difficult to see how the point of Jesus' excellence could have been made more strongly. This is brought out first by speaking of Him as 'the apostle (i.e. the sent one; God sent Him for our salvation) and high priest of our confession' (1). This puts Him in a unique place as regards the Christian way. Only one person could have such attributes assigned to Him. And in fulfilling His task He was faithful. This is not unique, for men have been and are faithful in their generation (the degree of His faithfulness was unique, but that is not to the point here, so it is not mentioned). Specifically, Moses was faithful. But here there is a difference. Moses was faithful as a servant is faithful, i.e. in a subordinate position. Jesus' faithfulness was that of a Son (5 f.). Moses' faithfulness pointed, indeed, beyond itself ('to testify to the things that were to be spoken later'). But this fuller meaning was realized in Christ. Moses was a faithful subordinate, but he was a subordinate. Christ was not. The point is further made with the illustration of the house (3 f.). Moses was faithful in the house, but there is One with a higher glory than that. The illustration passes over to the builder as more worthy than what he builds. God, being the builder of all, is worthy of highest honour. Christ shares this honour, for He has already been associated with God in the work of creation (1.2). There is yet another shift in the house illustration when believers are spoken of as the house (6). This is a high privilege. But notice the importance of perseverance.

Meditation: Consider Luke 16.10–12

Questions for further study and discussion on Philemon and Hebrews 1.1—3.6
1. Discuss the light shed by *Philemon* on the resolution of modern social problems.
2. What can we learn from *Philemon* about life in the early Church?
3. Discuss the way the *Epistle to the Hebrews* brings out the greatness of Christ.
4. What do we learn in this opening part of *Hebrews* about Christ's atoning work?
5. Discuss the importance of the real manhood of Christ.

Hebrews 3.7-11   Disobedience

It follows from what has been said that it is most important that due heed be given to the gospel. Failure to respond to God's gracious invitation will have calamitous consequences, precisely because it is God's gracious invitation, and because it concerns the salvation wrought out for men by none less than Christ. Our author drives home his point by an appeal to Psa. 95.7 ff. Notice that the Psalm is ascribed to the Holy Spirit, the writer preferring to draw attention to the divine origin of Scripture rather than to the human author through whom the message was mediated. The quotation follows the Septuagint in substituting 'the rebellion' and 'the day of testing' (8) for the place names given in the Hebrew.

The point of the quotation is that during the wilderness wanderings the people did not heed the voice of God. Throughout the forty years they persisted in hardening their hearts, in rebelling against God and in putting Him to the test (this means something like seeing how far they could go). But failure to obey God is never finally successful. The full weight of the divine punishment does not necessarily fall at once, but the sinner is deluded if he thinks he can escape. The psalmist stresses the fact that God is never passive in such a situation. He is 'provoked' by those sinners, He recognizes that they always go astray and that they have not known His ways. The consequence is that they must experience the divine wrath. That this is certain is emphasized by the reference to the divine oath, the oath that they will 'never enter My rest' (11). In the context this must refer to the Promised Land. But it will also have the deeper meaning of fellowship with God.

Life is a serious business and it is well for us to bear in mind that failure to heed God's voice carries inevitable consequences. These days we do not like the thought of 'the wrath of God' and many have decided that there is no such thing. Granted that it is possible to interpret it in too human a fashion, the term yet draws attention to a grim reality. If a man persists in sin he must ultimately experience the divine opposition and rejection. And that is a frightening prospect whether we call it the wrath of God or whether we prefer some softer name.

Hebrews 3.12-19 — An Evil, Unbelieving Heart

Following on from the quotation from Psa. 95 we come to the application. This example from Scripture shows that God is no respecter of persons. Even the people for whom He had performed the miracles in Egypt and whom He had brought to the very borders of the Promised Land were not spared when they persisted in unbelief and sin. The 'evil, unbelieving heart' that was in them could not but produce evil consequences. So the readers of the Epistle are warned against such a heart. It will surely lead to a falling away from the living God (12). There is an interesting combination of the individual and the community. The exhortation is addressed to them all. But they are to take care lest there be 'in any of you' unbelief, they are to exhort 'one another' and that constantly ('every day'). The community of believers has a concern for its individual members. It is difficult to preserve the highest standards of conduct and purity of belief unless there is a concern throughout the whole membership for the good of the individual.

A warning about 'the deceitfulness of sin' follows (13). Sin always comes in an attractive guise. For the original readers of the Epistle it was apparently in that of being faithful to the glorious heritage of the past. There are circumstances when such an attitude is eminently praiseworthy. But there are also times when it means the betrayal of what is highest and best. Here it signifies going back from the living Christ to that which was dead and gone. The readers are warned that to share in Christ it is necessary to persevere (14). It is not very hard to make a profession of faith in Him. But to continue as His servant through the difficulties of life is another thing again. There is paradox here. 'We share' is a perfect tense, indicating permanence. But the writer immediately goes on to say, 'if only we hold. . . .' This paradox is to be found throughout the N.T. Our salvation is given. It is all of God. We should never lose sight of this. But this does not excuse us from the obligation to persevere, and the N.T. writings contain many exhortations to constancy.

In vs. 16–19 we return to the Israelites who perished. Those who rebelled in the wilderness were not heathen men, men who had no knowledge of God. They were men who came out from Egypt under Moses' leadership. They had had such signal examples of God's power before their eyes and still had perished. Nothing external, but only continuing faith sees final salvation.

Hebrews 4.1-13 God's Rest

We now take up an expression in the Psalm, 'They shall never enter My rest'. Actually this has probably been behind the argument for some time, but the writer now openly concentrates on it. As the people wandered through the wilderness the 'rest' stood for the end of their troubles when they entered their Promised Land. But there is a deeper meaning than merely the cessation from external hostilities. Our writer recalls that the Bible speaks of God as resting on the seventh day from His work of creation (4). This indicates that there is a blessed state in which God is, and into which God's people might come. But when God swears that certain people will never enter it, then obviously the entering has not yet been accomplished. It is not these people, but some others, who will enter.

But perhaps the words apply strictly to the entering of Israel into Canaan? This possibility is ruled out by the date of the Psalm. Long after Joshua's generation had entered Canaan it was recorded that God swore they would not enter His rest. Clearly the 'rest' in question was something other than the uncertain rest of living in Canaan. The true rest still remains for the people of God (9). It is explained as resting from our labours as God did from His. This refers to the work of salvation. It is not obtained by strenuous striving. It is a good gift of God. And we do not enter into it until we cease from our own ineffectual efforts to obtain it and rest quietly on the promises of God. It is only then that we are really found resting in and with God.

It is then important that we concentrate on this rest and do not fall away by the kind of disobedience that ruined the Exodus-generation of Israelites (11). This leads to the reflection that God's Word is not to be taken lightly. It is conceived dynamically. It is not a static thing waiting for us to handle it as we will. It is 'living and active' and it stands in judgement on us. It is sharper than a sword, for it penetrates to the innermost recesses of the human personality (12). Nothing is hid from God (13). It is impossible to bluff our way through. The Word is always adequate, always revealing. We stand before God as we are, stripped of all pretensions and shams. This is a solemn warning still.

Hebrews 4.14-16   A Great High Priest

In the ancient world priesthood was accepted as a necessary part of religion. Everywhere men took it for granted that the gods are too holy for ordinary men to approach them. Worshippers need the help of a professional religious man, someone who knows the way and can intercede on their behalf. So the priesthoods performed their function on a thousand altars, for sacrifice was as universal as priesthood. Indeed a primary function of the priest was to offer sacrifices (cf. 5.1). The priesthood of the O.T. meant that the idea was just as much at home in Israel as anywhere else. It was, of course, axiomatic that some priesthoods were more efficacious than others. Like those engaged in any branch of human endeavour, priests differed in expertise, in local knowledge and in other ways. Thus all priesthoods were not put on the same level.

Our author makes use of all this to bring out important aspects of the Person and the work of Christ. Each of the N.T. writers has his own way of doing this, and in *Hebrews* we have the profound concept that Jesus is our great High Priest. He is the One who offers the sacrifice that really puts away sin and brings men to God. This can be seen as a process of redemption, of reconciliation, of justification, and much more. Seen as the work of a Priest certain aspects are emphasized in a way they are not when other metaphors are used. As the Epistle proceeds these truths will be unfolded.

In the passage now before us two significant thoughts about Christ are stressed. The one is His greatness. He is not simply a priest at home in a particular earthly sanctuary. He has 'passed through the heavens' (14), something that can be said of no earthly priest. But this does not leave Him remote from us, for the second point to be stressed is His sympathy. He came right where we are, was tempted with the same things with which we are tempted, without sinning. This may mean that He kept Himself from sin, or it may mean that He does not know those temptations which arise out of having sinned (as we, alas, do). But the main point is His community with us. He knows what we go through. Knowing then what kind of High Priest we have, let us 'with confidence draw near to the throne of grace'.

Question: How far have I really shared my weakness with Christ?

Hebrews 5.1-11 Christ our High Priest

The thought of high priesthood is carried on. First we are reminded of the things that characterize earthly high priests (the high priests of the O.T. are chiefly in mind). The principal thing is the offering of sacrifice (1), but there is an important qualification before a priest can do this. He must himself experience the weakness of those on whose behalf he ministers (2). It is this that enables him to 'deal gently' with those who fail. Of course, in earthly priests this means moral weakness, too, and such priests must offer sacrifice for themselves as well as for others (3). Presently our writer will bring out the point that this is not the case with Jesus, but for the moment it is the community of nature, the ability to understand, that he stresses. To this he adds the necessity of the divine call (4). It is not possible to have an Aaronic high priest without these qualifications.

With Christ our author takes up the two points in the reverse order. Our Lord did not take the initiative in order to make Himself a high priest, but was called of God (5 f.). The first Scripture quoted to demonstrate the point does not however mention priesthood. We must bear in mind that it is our author's basic concepts which control his manner of speech, not strict conformity to the illustrations he is using. It matters to him immensely that Christ is God's

Son, so he reverts to a passage he has already used (**1.5**) to bring out once more that Christ stands to God in the relation of Son. We must never lose sight of the fact that Christ transcends all that is meant by 'priest'. He is God's Son, and that comes first. But to this is added a further quotation which does see Him as a priest, a priest 'after the order of Melchizedek' (Psa. **110**.4, cf. Gen. **14**.18). Though Christ's priesthood resembles the Aaronic in some respects, it is Melchizedek and not Aaron who gives the significant model.

Next our author turns to Christ's earthly experiences which show Him to be one with us. The 'loud cries and tears' (7) presumably refer to Gethsemane. They certainly show that He understands our weakness. He 'learned obedience', which must be taken in the sense of His being made perfect (**2**.10). The meaning is not that He was once disobedient and became obedient, but that there is a quality of obedience known only through actually undergoing the costly act of obedience. It was in this way that He procured salvation for His people (9).

Question: What light do these verses shed on the problem of suffering?

Hebrews 5.12—6.3   Spiritual Immaturity

It is this passage above all which gives us a glimpse of the spiritual state of those for whom this Epistle was originally written. The writer expected them to have been teachers (12), which indicates that they had been Christians for some time, and that they were people of some ability. But they had not made the most of their opportunities. The result was that they were still in the kindergarten stage. Our author uses a variety of metaphors to bring this out. He does not think that the teaching he is giving is necessarily obscure. But it is so to them since they have become 'dull of hearing' (11). 'Dull' is literally 'sluggish' (the word is so translated in **6**.12). Since they were sluggish in hearing, the explanations tended to be difficult. Their position is further brought out by a comparison of the food used by the child with the 'solid food' of mature men. Milk is, of course, proper food. But it is proper only at a certain stage of development. If the physical body is to be built up to its full stature it must have the solid food it requires. The spiritual parallel is not difficult. The immature Christian lacks skill in the teachings about righteousness (which might mean righteousness of life, but more probably has to do with the righteousness that comes by faith). By contrast, the mature have trained faculties and discern good from evil (14).

It is interesting to notice what our author counts as 'elementary doctrines' when he goes on to exhort friends to go forward in the faith (6.1). Repentance and faith come first, for they are basic. A man must repent of his evil ways and really have faith, else he is not a Christian at all. It seems that 'ablutions' is a way of referring to rites with water practised by religions in general. It is elementary that the Christian should know what his religion teaches about baptism in distinction from the lustrations practised by others. The laying on of hands may point to something like confirmation or ordination, or it may point to a general rite for separation to a particular work. We are handicapped by not knowing as much about the practice of the early Church as the recipients of the Epistle. Resurrection and judgement (2) are doctrines to be learned early, as being fundamental to the faith. All this is a foundation and a necessary one. But it does not represent the last word. There is more to Christianity than that. And like the recipients of the Epistle we should go on to them.

Thought: It is possible so to concentrate on the sinner as to hold back the saint.

Hebrews 6.4-8   The Horror of Apostasy

For many Christians this is one of the most difficult passages in the Epistle and indeed in all Scripture. They see it as coming in conflict with the eternal perseverance of the saints and they find it difficult to think that no matter what sin a man has committed God should refuse to receive him back.

We should notice first of all that the state described here comes short of the full Christian experience. The Greek rendered 'the word of God' (*theou rhema;* v. 5) does not elsewhere stand for the full gospel message. And quite a number of important, even essential, Christian teachings are missing. For example, nothing is said about love. Can a man be said to have a full Christian experience if he is not practising love, love to God and to his fellow man? The passage appears to be describing the experience of a man who has enough experience of Christianity to know what is meant by it and what its demands are and who in the light of this full knowledge rejects it. Perhaps Simon Magus is an example of the kind of thing that is in mind (Acts **8**, especially vs. 13,20 f.).

The biggest difficulty to many is, however, the suggestion that those who fall away cannot come back. It is not easy in the light of

N.T. teaching in general to hold that God will refuse any sinner who calls upon Him, no matter how grievously he has sinned. But that is not what this passage is saying. Rather, it says that when a man really understands and really rejects Christianity he puts himself beyond the possibility of real repentance. He hardens himself in his chosen way. The passage does not say that God will refuse him. It says he cannot repent. The present participles rendered 'since they crucify . . . and hold Him up to contempt' (6) are significant, for they point to continuing attitudes: 'There is an active, continuous hostility to Christ in the souls of such men' (Westcott). It is not an occasional sin of which our author writes but a persistent attitude. Some indeed suggest that we should translate 'while they crucify. . . .' (so RV margin). Whether we do or not our, author is not referring to a time when these men have ceased to crucify Christ by their manner of living.

But in our concern for such difficulties of interpretation we should not overlook the fact that the passage is giving us all a clear warning of the dangers of going back on the knowledge of Christ that we have. There should be progress in the faith. To slip back is disaster, as even nature teaches (7 f.).

Question: What is the basis of true Christian 'assurance'?

Hebrews 6.9-12   Encouragement to Perseverance

The last section contained a very stern warning. There is no mistaking the seriousness of the writer, nor the unpleasant nature of the fate that he sees awaiting the apostate. It is comforting now to come upon this section which makes it clear that, while he has found it necessary to give warning to his friends, his confidence is that they will not go back. He is sure of 'better things that belong to salvation' (9), i.e. there are things about the readers which connect them with salvation (the Greek is a little obscure, but this seems to be the sense of it).

The basic reason for this is the faithfulness of God. God is not unjust. He takes notice of the realities of the situation and included among these is the fact that our author's correspondents are manifesting the truly Christian quality of love. If men who call themselves Christians are manifesting a warm love to their fellow men then the inference is that God is at work in them. And the further inference is that they are not on the way to apostasy. The love spoken of was shown in the past and still continues. It is no ephemeral thing, but something which carries on, and this strengthens the conviction that these men are in fact right with God.

But the end is not yet. Further, the love shown by the group is not necessarily shown by each and every member of it, and it is this to which the writer now directs his attention. It is important that 'each one of you' persist in the right way. Merely to be members of a group who are on the whole doing the right thing is not enough. There is a necessary element of personal participation. In encouraging them to persevere right to the end the writer draws attention to the examples of those who had gone before. He warns against sluggishness, and looks for 'faith and patience', an interesting combination. There is the combination of a reliance on God and a readiness to endure. And it is in this way that they (and we) inherit the promises.

Hebrews 6.13-20   God's Promise is Sure

The thought of promise is continued. Believers are not seeking some paradise of their own creating. They are servants of a God who has made provision for their salvation and who holds out before them certain promises. It is important to realize that these promises are thoroughly reliable. If we put our trust in God we are not following some will-o'-the-wisp. We have entered on a path that cannot but lead to the goal.

We see this in the case of Abraham, to whom God made a promise which He confirmed with an oath (13). In due course Abraham obtained what God had promised, though not without exercising patient endurance (15). God swore to Abraham and He performed His oath.

Among men an oath is the ultimate way of confirming what they have to say (16). So when God wished to convey to men the unalterable character of His promise, His unswerving determination to do as He had said, He confirmed His promise with an oath. The oath in question appears to be the one already spoken of; that to Abraham. It is relevant to a wide circle, for it includes Abraham's descendants, and indeed 'all the families of the earth' (Gen. 22.17 f.; Acts 3.25). It is not impossible that there is a side glance at the oath mentioned in Psa.110.4 which concerns the priesthood of Christ and which our author will quote in 7.21. But the main thought here is that God's faithfulness to Abraham is an encouragement to believers still. Now they have 'two unchangeable things', the promise and the oath, on which to rely.

This leads to the thought of the hope set before us (18), that hope which is 'a sure and steadfast anchor of the soul' (19). Hope in the N.T. is not a vague optimism about the future. Rather it denotes something which is certain, though as yet unrealized. The certainty is one which is attained by faith, and there can be no other way of attaining it, else hope would not be hope. Our hope is one which reaches right out into that holy place where Jesus now is. That is to say, it gives us assurance that we will one day be where He is. And this will be not through any merit of our own, but because of the high priestly work He has performed on our behalf (20).

Thought: Hope, like the Anchor, is fixed on the Unseen.

Questions for further study and discussion on Hebrews 3.7—6.20

1. How does the concept of rest help our understanding of the Christian life?
2. In what respects does the concept of priesthood help us understand Christ's work for men?
3. What do you understand by the 'elementary doctrines' of the Christian faith?
4. How may we guard against a failure to persevere?
5. What can we learn from these chapters about the importance of (a) love, and (b) hope?

Hebrews 7.1-10 Melchizedek's Priesthood

Melchizedek, the king of Salem and a priest of God, comes before us only in one incident, that in which he met Abraham as the patriarch returned from the slaughter of certain kings. He brought him bread and wine and blessed him. Abraham gave him a tenth of the spoil (Gen. 14.17–20). There is one further reference to this mysterious figure, namely in the Psalm already quoted and to which our author will refer again, Psa. 110.4, 'You are a priest for ever after the order of Melchizedek.' And that is all. Jewish thinkers on the whole neglected Melchizedek. For them priesthood came from Aaron and any other was ignored.

But the great contribution the writer of *Hebrews* makes to our understanding of the meaning of priesthood is an unfolding of the significance of this priest-king. He finds many things about Melchizedek which help us to understand what Christ has done for us. He enumerates some of them here. The name Melchizedek means 'king of righteousness' and the title 'king of Salem', 'king of peace'. It is also the case that no genealogy of this man is listed, though priests were usually very careful about such matters. Nor is there recorded anything about his birth or death. All this gives a fine picture of a priest who 'has neither beginning of days nor end of life' (3). But notice that he is said to resemble the Son; it is not the

372

Son who resembles Melchizedek. In other words it is Christ's priesthood that is the standard, not that of Melchizedek. All that the latter does is to provide a useful illustration which brings out certain aspects of Christ's priesthood.

The greatness of Melchizedek next occupies attention (4-10). This is brought out mainly by the facts that Abraham paid tithes to Melchizedek and that he received the priest's blessing. The former fact helps us see that the Aaronic priesthood is inferior. Its progenitor, Levi, 'was still in the loins' of Abraham when the tithe was paid, and thus there is a sense in which Levi paid the tithe (and thus took up the place of inferiority). This is involved also in the blessing, for the less is blessed by the greater (7). All in all, Melchizedek has much to teach us about the kind of priesthood Christ exercised.

Meditation: V. 2. There can be no real peace without righteousness.

Hebrews 7.11-14 A Change of Priesthood

Another aspect of the subject of priesthood is implied in the very existence in Scripture of a reference to the priesthood after the order of Melchizedek. If the Aaronic priesthood had done all that was required, men's priestly needs would have been fully met. There would have been no need and no place for another priesthood. The reference in the Psalm should thus have made thinking Israelites realize that the Levitical priesthood was inadequate. It is not that that priesthood did nothing. Under it the people received the Law (11) which was a great good (and would have been a greater had they realized the true function of the Law and the way it could point them to Christ; cf. John 5.46 f.; Gal. 3.19,24).

But Psa. 110 does speak of a priesthood after the order of Melchizedek. It sees this as persisting for ever. This obviously means a change in priesthood. But it also means 'necessarily a change in the law as well' (12). The Law cannot remain unaffected when the Aaronic priesthood is replaced by another. The Law, and the priesthood which offered the sacrifices prescribed by the Law, are closely bound up together. The one cannot be done away with without serious modifications in the other. Paul can speak of Christ as 'the end of the law' (Rom. 10.4), and our writer is making the same essential point in his own way.

The particular point which receives stress is that our Lord came from a tribe which was never by the Law connected with priesthood. Judah is the royal tribe, and the fact that Jesus came of this tribe accords with the fact that Melchizedek was king as well as priest. The new priesthood in Christ is a royal priesthood.

Question: What are the benefits we gain from the priesthood of Christ?

Hebrews 7.15-19 A Better Hope

The superiority of Christ's priesthood is before us again. It is not quite certain to what the 'This' which opens v. 15 refers, whether to the 'change in the law' (12) or the inferiority of the Aaronic priesthood. These are closely connected and perhaps we should not make too sharp a distinction. But it does seem that it is priesthood which is primarily in mind here.

The point of high importance that is singled out is that Christ's priesthood is 'not according to a legal requirement concerning bodily descent but by the power of an indestructible life' (16). Set thus in sharp contrast the constitutive principles of the two priesthoods show the marked inferiority of the Aaronic. It was, of course, the case that to be a priest of Aaron's line it was necessary only to be born into a particular family. And it is obvious that this confers no special efficacy on the priest so born. But with Christ it is different. It is the quality of His life that makes Him the kind of priest He is. The word translated 'indestructible' (*akatalutou*) is important. It signifies 'that cannot be dissolved' and not simply 'endless'. It is the quality of the life and not its duration that is in mind. The term is set in contrast 'bodily', which is more exactly 'fleshy', 'expressed in flesh'. That which cannot be dissolved is in the strongest contrast to that which is merely of flesh. There is also a contrast between 'legal requirement' and 'power'. We should not see these two priesthoods as on the whole similar. They are strikingly different and that in the essentials. The thought of the quality of life is reinforced with another quotation of Psa. 110.4, the important words on this occasion being 'for ever'. Christ's priesthood will never be superseded. There is that in its very nature which makes it the final priesthood.

The other point which is stressed here is the contrast between the ineffectiveness of Aaron's priests and the effectiveness of Christ's priestly work. The former line of priests and the law which went with them were set aside because they could not effect that to which they pointed. But Christ has brought us 'a better hope . . . through which we draw near to God' (19).

Hebrews 7.20-25
The Surety of a Better Covenant

The idea of permanence in Christ's priesthood is tremendously important. In the last passage we saw that the quality of indissolubility that characterizes the life of Christ is the really significant thing. It is this which is the basis of His priesthood. It makes it what it is. Now we find that there are important consequences to be drawn from it. Just as earlier Abraham's position was secured by a divine oath so is it with this priesthood. The indissoluble life would make it permanent even if it stood alone. But it does not stand alone. There is a divine oath to support it, and again we are referred to Psa. 110, this time to the words which refer to God's having sworn 'Thou art a priest for ever'. Thus both from the inherent nature of the life and the oath which God has sworn this priesthood is perpetual. The Aaronic priesthood was in due time superseded. Christ's priesthood will never be superseded. And this makes the covenant which Jesus establishes 'a better covenant' (22). The covenant stands for the whole way of approach to God. That which was associated with Aaron involved the offering of animal sacrifices and it was hedged around with a variety of requirements laid on the worshipper. If he failed to perform these the sacrifices were of no avail. Later in this Epistle the point will be brought out that in any case animal sacrifices are of no avail for the saving of men. They cannot put away sin (10.4). The way of approach which Jesus makes possible is from every point of view a 'better' way.

But the one thing which is being hammered home at this point in the argument is the quality of permanence. Clearly a covenant which depended on priests who could not continue was inferior to one which featured a priest whose life is eternal. Our author goes on to notice that those priests were limited in their ministry because from time to time they died. Death has an inhibiting effect on a man's work! But Christ is in sharp contrast. His priesthood is permanent. He continues for ever (24). Therefore He is *always* able to save those who come to God through Him. His intercession for them never ceases (25). This does not mean that He is a suppliant, but rather that His very presence before the Father in His capacity as crucified, risen and ascended is in itself an intercession which never ceases.

Thought: V. 25. 'I have prayed for you' (Luke 22.32).

This part of the argument is rounded off with a little summary drawing attention to the principal points brought out by the Melchizedekian concept of priesthood. There are three sections.

In the first it is the personal qualities of Jesus that receive emphasis. Moffatt remarks that 'it is generally misleading to parse a rhapsody' but there is a sequence of thought here which is worth noticing. Jesus is 'holy', a positive word denoting the ethical perfection associated with God, which is further described with two negative terms (forming an alliteration in the Greek), 'blameless' and 'unstained'. Then 'separated from sinners' is explained as 'exalted above the heavens'. Our author has been at pains to show that Jesus came right where we sinners are and took upon Him the weakness of our mortal nature. But He offered one perfect sacrifice to deal with our sins and now He is 'separated' from all that that involves. It is a favourite thought in this Epistle that sin has been dealt with once and for all.

The thought moves on to the sacrifice Christ offered. There is a small problem about the daily offering of sacrifices attributed to the Aaronic high priests (27), for the principal sacrifice which the high priest (in distinction from other priests) offered was the Day of Atonement sacrifice. This was an annual not a daily offering, and it is this with which our author deals principally. But there was a daily need for cleansing, and there were daily sacrifices. The high priest, of course, might offer these, and in fact Jewish writers like Philo speak of the high priest as offering daily. The expression thus accords with the office as understood at the time. In any case the contrast is between the repeated offerings under the Aaronic system (daily or yearly, the principle is the same) and the offering of Christ 'once for all'. There is a perfection in His offering lacking in theirs.

Finally, there is a contrast between the high priests in their weakness and the Son 'made perfect for ever' (28). We have before had references both to the Law (12) and to the oath (20). Now we read that the oath 'came later than the law', which means that it was the definitive thing, replacing what went before it. There is also contrast between the weak nature of the priests (they were no more than sinful men) and the Son. His relationship to God was very different from theirs, and this is rammed home with the 'made perfect for ever'. He has suffered for sin and in this way accomplished what is permanent in its effects (for 'made perfect' see note on **2.**10).

Thought: 'It is I; have no fear' (*Matt. 14.27*).

Hebrews 8.1-7 The Shadow and the Substance

Throughout the ancient world there turns up from time to time a distinction between what is real and fundamental, and what is merely a copy or shadow of the real. Plato's distinction between the ideal 'forms' which are in heaven, and the imperfect copies which are all we see on earth at best, is well known. Our author has some such idea which he brings out at intervals during the following chapters. It is not the Platonic distinction (though it may derive ultimately from it), and is probably more indebted to Exod. 25.40 (quoted in v. 5). But it would have a wide appeal. The point which our author is concerned to drive home is that in the Levitical priesthood and sacrifices we see something resembling true priesthood and sacrifices. But the true to which the shadows point are found in Christ alone.

As he begins to bring this out our author outlines the chief points in his argument so far. First, he insists that Christ's is the true priesthood because offered in 'the true tent' (2), 'the heavenly sanctuary' (5). The fact that if He were on earth He would have no priestly ministry (4) is not significant It is what happens in 'the heavenly sanctuary' which matters, and the service rendered in what is no more than 'a copy and shadow' of that sanctuary is of comparative unimportance. There is a clear warning here for those who were tempted to go back from the Priest in the true sanctuary to the priests in the copy of the true. And we should not overlook the fact in our eagerness to condemn the recipients of this letter that in our age as well as any other it is easy to prefer the shadow to the substance. 'Christians' can still go through the motions, but without getting to grips with the reality or really reckoning with the wholehearted demands Christ makes.

The final thought leads us into the new covenant which dominates the next couple of chapters. The point made here is that it is 'enacted on better promises' (6). It is a covenant of pure grace, with Christ's atoning sacrifice at its basis. It offers men the promise of full and free forgiveness. Could this have been given by the first covenant, our author reasons, there would have been no need for a second (7). The very existence of the second shows the inadequacy of the first.

Meditation: Christ serves though He reigns, and reigns in serving.

Hebrews 8.8-13 The New and the Old

One of the most perplexing problems to the student of the Bible revolves round the expression 'the new covenant'. The Bible teaches that God does not need to work by the method of trial and error, as though He had to try one covenant and when it did not work, substitute another. He sees the end perfectly from the beginning. Accordingly, when He makes a covenant, we expect it to be binding for eternity. Yet Scripture speaks clearly of a new covenant and our passage tells us unambiguously that the first is obsolete (13).

The answer appears to be that there is a sense in which any covenant God makes is unchanging and unchangeable. Nowhere in the Bible, for example, is there any indication that the covenant with Abraham is abrogated. It still stands. God's way is the way of grace and this is abundantly clear in the covenant with Abraham. It is implied, in fact, in the covenant with the people in Exod. 24 (cf. Exod. 19.4 where God's action in grace precedes anything the people do). But spontaneously the people offered to obey God (Exod. 24.3,7). Indeed, while the covenant is initiated by God's grace there is the clear implication that the people will live as the people of God (cf. Exod. 19.5 f.). Increasingly the people came to understand this in a legalistic way. And increasingly they failed to live up to their obligations to God.

Since then they were unable or unwilling (or both) to respond to the grace of God shown in the covenant, the promise of a new covenant is spelled out for us in Jer. 31.31 ff., quoted in today's passage. There is a sense in which this covenant is the same one. It is still the expression of God's grace. But there is also a sense in which it is radically new. It involves an action of the very Spirit of God within men (10). It involves their having a real and personal knowledge of God (11). And it involves their sins being really put away (12), something which happened and could happen only in Christ's atoning work. Since Christ has made all these things possible it is clear that any previous arrangement is out of date. The old is obsolete and ready to vanish (13).

Question: Can you quote any passage of St. Paul's in support of this chapter?

Questions for further study and discussion on Hebrews 7.1—8.13

1. In what respects does Melchizedek form a model for our understanding of the priesthood of Christ?
2. Discuss the meaning and implications of the 'change in the law' (7.12).
3. How does the quality of Christ's life (7.16, etc.) help us understand the effectiveness of His priesthood?
4. In what ways does the shadow-substance idea illuminate Christ's work for us?

5. What implications do you see behind the expression 'the new covenant'?

Hebrews 9.1-5 The Tabernacle Furniture

The main interest of the author was in what Christ had done for men. But he clearly loved and had a profound interest in the Jewish institutions which foreshadowed the work of Christ. In a way without parallel in the N.T. he now dwells on the place and the manner of worship under the old covenant. Though now superseded neither was without significance.

It might have been expected that he would speak of the Temple, which would have been much more familiar to the men of his day. But he prefers to concentrate on the Tabernacle which had been used in the wilderness in the formative days of Israel. The essentials were, of course, the same as those in the Temple, so not a great deal hinges on the choice. But there was something about that first Tabernacle set up under Moses which might be expected to make a special appeal to those who loved the old way of worship.

The first covenant, he says, 'had' its regulations and sanctuary. The past tense may point us back to the days of Moses when it was instituted, or, perhaps more probably, may spring from the conviction that it had now been superseded by Christ's saving work. He speaks of two tents, the first being the Holy Place, the second the Holy of Holies. The word he uses for 'the Holy Place' (*hagia*, 'holy things') does not appear to be used in this way elsewhere, but is quite intelligible. He goes on to refer to 'the second curtain' (the first would have been that at the entrance to the Holy Place). This screened the Holy of Holies, the furnishings of which are detailed. There is a difficulty about 'the golden altar of incense' (4). In the first instance the word rendered 'altar' might mean 'censer' and some understand it this way. But the RSV is almost certainly correct. The term can have this meaning and it is this that is required. In the second instance the altar of incense was not in the Holy of Holies, but in the Holy Place. It had to be, on account of the use to which it was put. But in fact our author does not say that it was 'in' the Holy of Holies at all. He speaks of the Holy of Holies as 'having' it, i.e. it belonged to the service of the Holy of Holies (cf. 1 Kings 6.22). The offering of incense was an integral part of the ceremony of entrance into the Holy of Holies. The threefold reference to gold (4) stresses the glory of Tabernacle, as in another way do the references to the cherubim and to the mercy seat (5).

379

Clearly the old way had its values, even though not the ones attributed to it by the Jews of his day.

Question: How far is it right to deduce Christian doctrine from the design and furnishing of the Tabernacle?

Hebrews 9.6-10 The Tabernacle Worship

From the furnishings of the Tabernacle we turn to the nature of the worship that was carried on in it. While he notices the daily worship performed by the priests (6), our author's real interest is in the ceremonies on the Day of Atonement. He stresses the limitations on access to the Holy of Holies. Ordinary priests could never enter, and even the High Priest 'but once a year' (7). Nor did he have the right to enter as he pleased on that day. He must first offer 'blood' both for himself and the people. Our author does not see this as merely a piece of antiquarian ritual. It has meaning. It is unthinkable that God would bring about the setting up of a complete system of worship like this without there being profound meaning in what is thus established. In subsequent chapters a number of points in this meaning will be unfolded. Here our author's concern is with the fact that the careful hedging about of approach to the Holy of Holies is in itself significant. It showed that the way into the very presence of God was not open to sinful man. The people had no way into it. The priests had no way into it. The High Priest had no way into it for every day of the year except one. And on that one day his access was severely restricted. Could it be more plainly shown that the way to God was not open? Incidentally this is a truth which still needs to be learned. In our democratic days we are apt to take it for granted that we have the right to approach God whenever we will. The meaning of the Tabernacle furniture has an important message still.

The readers of the Epistle are reminded in conclusion that the ritual regulations were concerned with the purely external. They could deal with the body (10), but they could not deal with the problems of conscience (9). Ritual is not unimportant and it has lessons to teach us. But it has in-built limitations. It should never be regarded as effecting that to which it can do no more than point.

Meditation: How much better is the Christian Order, brought in at the 'time of reformation' (10)! Its institutions are spiritual, and its blessings universal.

Hebrews 9.11-17 Christ's Effective Sacrifice

From the ineffective our author turns to the effective, from the ritual to that to which the ritual points. He reminds us of the character in which Christ appears, 'a high priest of the good things that have come' (or 'to come'; the manuscripts are divided). Some understand 'the greater and more perfect tent' to be an imaginative description of Christ as passing through a heavenly sanctuary on the way to the Holy of Holies where He would perform His priestly duties, others see it as a symbolic description of the incarnation. What is most important is not the resolution of such points but the shedding of the blood of Christ on which our author puts his stress. All else leads up to this. He has already made the point that there is no more than a limited and purely external purpose achieved by the performance of ritual (9 f.) and he repeats this (13).

But in contrast to any limited effect secured in such ways the perfect sacrifice of Christ is efficacious. It secures 'an eternal redemption' (12). Redemption in the ancient world signified release from such a plight as slavery or a sentence of death, and release by payment of a price. Christ then paid the price which secured the release of sinners from their slavery to sin (Rom. 7.14), from the sentence of death that hung over them (Rom. 6.23). And this release is not temporary but 'eternal'.

Next we have Christ's work viewed as the mediation of a new covenant. Once again there is the thought of eternal worth (15), this being linked to the redemption which deals with transgressions even under the first covenant. The old sacrifices could not really take away sin. But Christ's death can and does. The Greek word *diathēkē* means both 'covenant' and 'will', which is the point of vs. 16 f. Our author plays on the double meaning of the term to bring out his point that the death of Christ was necessary. Death brings a will into effect and the death of Christ brought the new covenant into effect, just as if it had been a will.

Hebrews 9.18-22 The Shedding of Blood

We move back in thought to the old covenant, that described in Exod. 24. Its establishment illustrates the principle that blood must be shed to effect a covenant, for Moses sprinkled blood when that covenant was brought into effect. Our author gives us some information not found in Exod. 24, for example, the mention of the offering of goats, and the use of water, scarlet wool, and hyssop, and the sprinkling of the blood. In *Exodus* we are simply told that

Moses threw half the blood against the altar and half on the people (**24.**6,8).

Our author also goes beyond the O.T. when he speaks of Moses as sprinkling with blood the Tabernacle and the vessels used in worship (21; the historian Josephus also gives this information). This of course refers to a later event, for the Tabernacle did not exist when the covenant was made. In Exod. **40.**9 ff. Moses was commanded to anoint the Tabernacle and its furniture, and presumably he obeyed this command. Nothing is said, however, about any use of blood at this time.

From this our author moves to the thought that the Law prescribed the shedding of blood on a number of occasions. Practically everything 'is purified with blood' (22). An occasional exception is allowed (cf. Lev. **5.**11), but this merely highlights the rule. The teaching of the Levitical law is plainly that 'without the shedding of blood there is no forgiveness of sins' (22). Among many of the peoples of antiquity sin was taken very lightly and regarded as of little consequence. Nobody who took the sacrificial system of ancient Israel with full seriousness could make that mistake. The solemn ritual underlined two points: the seriousness of sin, and the necessity for the offering of a pure victim if sin is to be forgiven. In this way the people of God were prepared for the coming of Him who would offer the one sacrifice that really takes away sin. The sacrifices could not remove sin, but they had an important educational function. In the modern world where the pagan view of sin is so widespread there is still the need to learn the seriousness of sin and the necessity for the shedding of blood if it is to be put away.

Meditation: E'er since, by faith, I saw the stream
Thy flowing wounds supply,
Redeeming love has been my theme,
And shall be till I die. (Wm. Cowper).

Hebrews 9.23-28 The Perfect Sacrifice

Again we have the shadow and substance concept, this time to drive home the point that Christ has offered the perfect sacrifice. The sacrifices of the Law were of limited efficacy (13; cf. **10.**1,4). They could 'purify' the 'copies of the heavenly things' (23) which is all that an earthly sanctuary can provide at best. But we need more than this if our eternal need is to be met. And that need has been met, because Christ has provided the sacrifice that perfectly meets our need. The writer sees Him as doing perfectly all that the ancient ritual foreshadowed. Thus the Holy of Holies, which was hedged about with such elaborate safeguards, and into which the high priest might enter and he alone, once only in a year, is no more than a 'sanctuary made with hands, a copy of the true one' (24). That which to the Jews appeared the very place of manifestation of the divine presence is now seen to be no more than a pointer to what really is true. But Christ ministers where it counts. He appears in God's presence for us (24). Our sin is dealt with at the highest level.

The second point that is stressed is the uniqueness of Christ's sacrifice. Our author comes back several times to the thought that the continuing nature of the ministry of the high priest is itself evidence of its ineffectiveness. But Christ did not offer Himself repeatedly. He made but one sacrifice. He offered Himself once for all (26). Intertwined on this occasion is the other thought that He offers His own blood. There is a quality about His sacrifice that could not possibly be seen in any other. The high priest necessarily entered the Holy of Holies with the blood of an animal, 'blood not his own' (25). There is a qualitative difference when Christ offers Himself.

The chapter concludes with a forward look. This must always be taken with seriousness, knowing that before all men is death and then judgement. Judgement is as certain as death. Indeed judgement is more certain than death, for some will still be alive at the end of the age and will be changed, not die (1 Cor. **15.**51). But all will stand before Christ's judgement seat (2 Cor. **5.**10). We should never take death other than very seriously. Yet the really important thing is not this. It is that when Christ appears again it will be for the consummation of salvation. Then He will not deal with sin but take His own into salvation. It will be a fearful thing not to be ready for Him when He comes.

Hebrews 10.1-10 The Will of God

There is a sense in which in this passage we come to the heart of the whole matter. Some misinterpret it by a wrong insistence on the doing of the will of God. They point out that our author quotes Psa. 40.6–8 in bringing out the truth that God does not delight in animal sacrifices. Prophetically the Psalm goes on to speak of Messiah as doing the will of God. Christ, then, the reasoning goes, has come, not like brute beasts who have no say in their being offered, but as man to make a perfect surrender of His will to God. The essence of His offering is the offering of a will completely subservient to that of the Father. In a day when many find sacrifice and substitution unacceptable such a view of the Psalm, of the teaching of this Epistle and of the nature of the atonement, finds many supporters.

But it is not what our author is saying. It overlooks his express declaration that 'by that will we have been sanctified through the offering of the body of Jesus Christ once for all' (10). Christ does indeed do the will of God. But that will is not expressed in vague generalities. It is the offering of Christ's body that is the will of God.

Our author introduces the thought by repeating that the sacrifices of the old covenant are ineffective (1–4). The Law has but the shadow, not the substance. It offers the very same sacrifices over and over in mute testimony to the fact that they cannot really cleanse (1 f.). They remind of sin each year (the Day of Atonement sacrifices are clearly in mind). But it is quite impossible for them to take away sins. Verse 4 is the definitive statement of the ineffectiveness of all animal sacrifices. Animals move on a different level from men. Their worth is infinitely less. They cannot possibly be accepted on behalf of men. It is this that makes the Psalm applicable. It categorically rejects animal sacrifices as the way, and puts the will of God in the supreme place. This means the abolition of the old way altogether and the substitution of something altogether new (9). The offering of the body of Christ is the one prevailing sacrifice. It is that which brings about the sanctification of believers. And our passage finishes with the characteristic 'once for all'. There is an air of finality about this sacrifice. It cannot be repeated. Nothing can be added to its perfection.

Thought: 'Present your bodies a living sacrifice . . . which is your spiritual worship' (Rom. 12.1).

Hebrews 10.11-18   Once for All

On a number of occasions our author has insisted that Christ suffered once and for all, and this is the central point in the passage we now study. Once again we are reminded that the Levitical priests offered repeatedly and that their sacrifices were totally unable to deal with sin (11). In contrast, Christ offered 'for all time a single sacrifice for sins' (12). Since His sacrifice really deals with sins there is no need and no place for a repetition.

The same point is brought out in a different way when our author speaks of Christ as sitting down at God's right hand. This imagery is repeated a number of times in the N.T. It is, of course, a metaphor, for we cannot conceive of spirits as having literal right hands or of adopting a sitting posture. But the meaning of the metaphor is important. Sitting is the posture of rest. It indicates that the One sitting has completed His work. That Christ is seated means that the work of salvation is accomplished. Nothing can be added to its perfection. That He is at the right hand of God means that He is in the place of highest honour. No longer is He despised and rejected of men. He is in the chief place in all of heaven.

Our author's interest in forgiveness is seen in the way he quotes Jer. 31. In ch. 8 he has quoted fully. Now he has the opening words about the new covenant, but omits a considerable section as he goes straight on to those about forgiveness. The new covenant is that which really brings forgiveness. The same point is brought out in another way when he speaks of Christ as having 'perfected for all time those who are sanctified' (14). The sanctified are those set apart for God by Christ's one offering. They are perfected because their sins are put away and they see them no more. This is for all time, for nothing more is needed. And we come back to this thought at the end with the reminder that where sins are forgiven there is no more offering for sin (18). Nothing can be added to perfection.

Hebrews 10.19-25 A True Heart

From the Saviour attention is turned to the saved. Since Christ has done so much for us there must be consequences in our attitude both to God and to men. Godwards the believer should have confidence. Because of what Christ has done for him the way into the very holiest is open to him. The curtain was rent in literal fashion to make open the way into the Holiest (Mark 15.38). And in a metaphorical way what had to be rent to make open that way was the flesh of Christ. The expression is poetic and vivid. Some prefer to take 'His flesh' rather with 'way'. The way through the curtain was His flesh, His human nature with all that this means. But the interpretation of the rending of His flesh seems more in accordance with the reference to His blood (19). What is clear is that we are being reminded of the access into the very presence of God which Christ's death brought to sinners, and we are exhorted to make the utmost use of that access. We should come with true heart, with faith, with assurance, and with our hearts purified inwardly just as water (the water of baptism) cleans our bodies outwardly (22).

For those tempted to go back there is point in the exhortation to hold fast and not to waver (23), as also in the reminder of what is involved in 'confession' and 'hope'. They should not try to stand on their own. Basic is the faithfulness of Him 'who promised'. God will not go back on His promises.

Believers can help one another. They can stir one another up to produce deeds of love and other good works. Notice how love is thought of as the most important thing in keeping men steadfast in the Christian life. And the assembling of Christians together is something not to be neglected (25). The assembly for worship, when all criticisms have been allowed their full weight, is still a source of strength to those who come with a true heart.

Questions for further study and discussion on Hebrews 9.1—10.25
1. What values do you see in the ritual and furnishings of the Tabernacle?
2. How does the concept of 'the new covenant' help our understanding of the Christian way?
3. Gather the references to Christ's sacrifice as being 'once for all'. What implications do these have for our understanding of the faith today?
4. Discuss our author's use of 'the blood'.
5. How does our understanding of Christ's sacrifice affect our daily living?

Hebrews 10.26-31 A Fearful Thing

We return now to the thought of the danger of apostasy. In mind is the man who has come to understand what the truth is, but who nevertheless has chosen to sin deliberately (26). He has rejected Christ, profaned the covenant blood and insulted the Holy Spirit (29). It is idle for this man to think that there stands before him anything other than certain and fearful judgement.

It is one of the besetting heresies of our day that this truth is not only rejected but regarded as sub-Christian. Men have so well learned the truth that 'God is love' that they have forgotten complementary truths like 'God is light' (1 John 1.5) and 'our God is a consuming fire' (Heb. 12.29). In the process they have distorted even that to which they hold, for they have confused love and sentimentality. The God of modern man is a morally flabby god, a little god who does not greatly mind if his worshippers go astray.

But the God of the Bible is a great God and One who loves, really loves, His people. He is infinitely concerned for their welfare and hates everything that makes them less than the best that they can be. True love opposes every evil in the beloved. It is this which is in mind throughout our passage when the writer speaks in terms of 'a fearful prospect of judgement', of 'a fury of fire' (27), and of what 'a fearful thing' (31) it is to fall into the hands of the living God. The fact is that we are not irresponsible children playing at life. We are responsible men, given each of us one life to live. We are to live it as those who will one day be called upon to give account of themselves. This is not meant to strike terror into us, but we are fools and more unless we see that life is too serious a business for trifling. Flippancy will not be enough when we stand before God and give an account of what we have done with His good gift.

Hebrews 10.32-39   A Call to Persevere

This passage yields a glimpse of the kind of trouble into which the early Christians constantly fell, all the more revealing in that it is incidental. Our author is not setting out to detail the troubles which Christians might be expected to face. He is exhorting his friends to remain constant in their adherence to Jesus Christ. In the process he reminds them of what they have already endured for Christ, and suggests that they should not let all this be in vain. Being a Christian in those days meant no token pain, but 'a hard struggle with sufferings' (32). It meant public abuse and it meant being linked with others so abused (33). It meant forfeiture of goods (34). There are Christians in modern times, as there have been in every age, who have such hardships to endure. Those of us whose sufferings are comparatively minor should have a lively sense of gratitude to Him who has shielded us from the worst. And when we do suffer, as suffer we must in some way, we should regard this as being in the true apostolic succession.

But our author is not dwelling on the sufferings of his friends. He recalls them, but he does not stress them. Rather his emphasis is on their being constant in their service of God. 'Do not throw away your confidence', he says (35). The implication is that confidence will normally remain. It is a wilful thing to discard it. Since God has done such a wonderful thing in us when He brought us salvation we have every reason for being confident. And we will remain so unless we give way to evil. For our confidence is not in any thing that we ourselves do, but in what God has done and will do. This does not mean that life is ever easy for the Christian. He must not expect that God will smooth out all his difficulties. That is not the path God's servants must tread. But if we cannot expect a smooth path we can expect help to get us over the difficult places. So our author exhorts to constancy. He recognizes that there are those who shrink back (38). But he does not think that his readers are included in the number. He links them with himself in the fine affirmation of v. 39.

Question: Can you imagine v. 34 being said of you?

Hebrews 11.1-7 Faith

The linkage of faith and constancy at the end of our last passage leads the writer to a more extended treatment of the subject. He begins by speaking of faith as 'the assurance of things hoped for' where 'assurance' translates *hypostasis*, 'that which stands under', and thus is the 'essence' or perhaps 'basis'. He is saying that faith is all that we now have of the things yet to be. It is faith that gives reality to those things (though not in the sense of creating them; faith simply apprehends them; cf. NEB, 'Faith gives substance to our hopes'). So with the following, 'the conviction of things not seen'. We do not yet see the realities to come. But by faith we know that they will come. It is faith which gives us the conviction of their certainty.

Faith is thus a very important quality for Christians. Without it they lack spiritual perception. With it they enter in some measure into an apprehension of what God has done and will do. The chapter goes on to bring this out, with illustrations from the lives of some of God's outstanding servants. First our writer deals with the theme in a general way. It was by faith that the ancients received God's approval (2). It was by faith that he and the men of his day recognized that creation had taken place and that 'what is seen' is not the last word (3), a judgement which is far from being out of date.

Today's passage contains references to three specific personages. Abel's offering was preferred to that of Cain because it was offered in faith. Enoch's being 'taken up' to heaven was due to faith, which elicits the important comment that 'without faith it is impossible to please' God (6). A man cannot reason himself or work himself into a place of acceptance of and acceptance by God. That is always a matter of faith. And Noah's faith was a condemnation of the world of his day as he acted on his profound spiritual convictions. Faith always shows up unbelief for the shallow thing it is.

Questions: Does reason have any place in Christian experience? If so, what?

Hebrews 11.8-12 The Faith of Abraham

Throughout the N.T. Abraham is regarded as the prototype of faith. And faith, for him, was not a conventional piety. The point first brought out here is his willingness to act with nothing to go on but his faith in God. He knew himself called by God and he knew nothing else. He could not have justified to unbelieving men a journey which meant leaving his country, his kindred and his father's house (Gen. 12.1). But his faith in God was such that he acted on God's word. He did leave his home, his family, and indeed his whole way of life.

Nor was that the end of it. He had been promised the land of Canaan, but he lived in it not as possessor but as a visitor. Isaac and Jacob shared the promise with him, but they all lived in tents, obviously temporary dwellers in the land. But Abraham's vision was fixed, not on the things that any man could see, but on 'the city which has foundations, whose builder and maker is God' (10). It is still the case that faith does not fix its attention on the same things as does the world. It is of the essence of faith that it gives the prime place to the leading of God.

Others were associated with Abraham. We have already noticed that Isaac and Jacob are said to have shared in his life. So also did Sarah, who was able to conceive only 'by faith' (11). It is worth noticing that her initial reaction was anything but one of faith (Gen. 18.12 ff.). But God did not judge her by her worst moment (as He does not judge us by ours). Sarah's settled attitude was one of faith, not doubt. She trusted God and 'considered Him faithful' (11). Thus God honoured the faith of His servants, and from one man 'as good as dead' in time there descended a great nation (12).

Hebrews 11.13-22   The Faith of the Patriarchs

This passage divides into two sections, the first a general consideration of what is implied in the faith of the men spoken of, and a second in which individual patriarchs are mentioned. The outstanding character of the faith of people like those just mentioned is shown by the fact that to the very end of their lives they never did see the realization of the promises of God. This happened, of course, because these promises are bound up with the saving work of Christ. Until He came there could be no complete fulfilment of God's promises whatever partial anticipations might be granted the men of old. But if they did not see the fulfilment there was nothing wrong with their vision. They saw themselves for what they were, 'strangers and exiles on the earth' (13). Had their interest been in earthly possessions they would have been able to go back to the land from which they came (15). But their vision was fixed on something far better, on that spiritual possession that God had for them. They were giants in faith. And it is a wonderful thing that is said of them when our writer reports that 'God is not ashamed to be called their God' (16). It calls for heartsearching on our own account as to whether God could in any meaningful sense be called 'our' God. Would He be ashamed of being called the God of people like us?

When he gets down to cases our author thinks first of Abraham's readiness to offer up Isaac, that son in whom God had said the promises would be fulfilled. The patriarch trusted God, and trusted that God can even bring men back from the dead. Indeed, our author sees a figurative resurrection in the way Abraham received his son again. Again, Isaac looked forward to a future he would not see as he invoked blessing on Jacob and Esau. And Jacob and Joseph followed in the same way by looking forward in faith to what they knew God would bring to pass after their lives had ended. Thus each of the patriarchs sets us an example. They all trusted God against the present indications. And in each case their faith was vindicated.

> Truth: *Faith, mighty faith, the promise sees,*
> *And looks to that alone:*
> *Laughs at impossibilities,*
> *And cries 'It shall be done!'* (C. Wesley).

Hebrews 11.23-31   The Faith of Moses

Abraham and Moses were regarded as the two really great men in the early history of the people. So when our author cites them as his outstanding examples of faith he is making a strong appeal to all who revered Jewish institutions and personages. In the case of Moses, faith was manifested even in his babyhood, for his parents needed faith to defy the edict of Pharaoh (23).

The point which receives special stress is Moses' readiness to put up with ill-treatment which he could have avoided by deserting the divine call. He could have lived as a royal prince, 'the son of Pharaoh's daughter' (24). Instead he chose to be one of the despised nation of slaves. Faith gave him clarity of perspective so that he could estimate aright the true significance of both. It is not being realistic, but suffering from a distorted sense of values, when a man prefers the 'security' of worldly safety to the 'uncertainties' of faith in God. On the long view it is faith that matters, faith that emerges triumphant.

This is brought out by saying that Moses 'looked to the reward' (26). He understood what the reward was if he cast in his lot with Pharaoh and his court. And he understood what the reward was if he joined himself to 'the people of God'. In both cases the lasting spiritual result and the immediate material result were in sharp contrast. So Moses endured steadfastly the present trial, his faith assuring him that this was of no consequence alongside the greater evil of abandoning the life to which God had called him. So it was the vision of 'Him who is invisible' (27) that sustained him when he left Egypt, having chosen the wrath of the ruler instead of his favour. And it was faith again which guided his actions in instituting the Passover. He had nothing but faith to guide him in keeping that feast himself and in persuading his fellow Israelites to do the same. But that faith was vindicated, as was that of the people when they crossed the Red Sea and when they captured Jericho. It is interesting to see Rahab among those who showed faith, a faith which led her to welcome the spies (31). In each case faith was triumphantly vindicated.

Hebrews 11.32-40   The Triumph of Faith

Our author has not exhausted the catalogue of the heroes of faith. There are many more and he lists some of their names (32). But for lack of time he does not go into detail in their exploits. Instead he has a quick summary. First he speaks of the broad, general results achieved by the men of faith: they had success in conflict, success in the area of government, and the spiritual reward covenanted by God (33). They also experienced forms of personal deliverance. Some were saved from wild animals, others from fire (which may stand for physical forces in general), and others again from men who would have destroyed them (33 f.). The third group of successes rings the changes on human strength: they won it, they used it in war, and they triumphed with it by putting armies to flight (34).

We may wonder why women are singled out as receiving their dead by resurrection (35). But most raisings recorded in Scripture were in fact for women (e.g. 1 Kings 17.17 ff.; 2 Kings 4.17 ff.; Luke 7. 11 ff.; John 11; Acts 9. 36 ff.), so there is point in the comment. But in rejoicing over such victories we must not think that faith is always triumphant on the human level. Sometimes it must undergo hardship and even apparent defeat. That was the way of the cross, and the Christian is to follow in the steps of the Master. So we are told of those who suffered in a variety of ways, some accepting death well knowing that their faithfulness would have its effects

391

in the resurrection (35). Some endured only insults, some accepted torture, some imprisonment, some destitution and the loss of homes and the like.

But the climax to all this comes with the surprising information that, giants of the faith though they were, and examples to believers as they continue to be, these 'did not receive what was promised' (39). This does not mean that God let them down in any way. It is our author's way of making the telling point that in the providence of God the consummation of the promises was not in the days of old, but would include his readers. God's plan is that all His people will be perfected together. Christ's saving act has consequences for the whole people of God.

Thought: 'Out of weakness . . . became mighty' (34).

Questions for further study and discussion on Hebrews 10.26—11.40

1. How may we relate the Epistle's teaching on perseverance to the modern situation?
2. What value do you see for your own situation in the way our author relates faith to the unseen world (**11.1** ff.)?
3. Our author links Abel, Enoch, and Noah (**11.4–7**). What common pattern do you discern in the experiences of these three?
4. In what ways is Abraham a model for later believers?
5. How does the example of Moses speak to an age which emphasizes material culture?

Hebrews 12.1-3   Christ our Example

There is dispute as to whether we should understand the 'cloud of witnesses' (1) as witnessing us as we live out the Christian life, or whether they are witnesses to the truth of the things of God from whose example we can learn much as we serve our Lord. In favour of the latter view it is pointed out that the word for 'witnesses' (*martyrōn*) seems never to be used of mere spectators. It is characteristically applied to those who have witnessed for the faith, and in time came to be applied specifically to those who witnessed by a martyr's death. In favour of the former is 'we are surrounded', which is not naturally interpreted of our looking to them, all the more so since the writer immediately goes on to say that we should have our attention fastened on Jesus (2). Perhaps there is a bit of both meanings. On the one hand the heroes of the past watch to see how we acquit ourselves. But on the other they do not do this as mere spectators. They are those who have borne witness in their day, as they look to us to do the same in ours.

But the important thing is that we have a race to run. We should therefore strip ourselves of everything which may hinder us (the distinction between 'weight' and 'sin' indicates that there are some things which, though not sins, the Christian should avoid, since they are hindrances to his Christian advance). And especially we should fix our gaze on Jesus. He is our perfect example and inspiration. He is the 'pioneer' (*archēgos* is connected with the root denoting 'first'; it may be first in time or first in importance; Jesus is both; He is the one who shows us the way and He is our leader as we seek to follow). He is also the 'perfecter'. He both initiates and brings to completion the faith by which we live.

Especially important is the cross. This is, of course, the way our salvation was wrought out. But it is also our supreme example. Christ accepted it despite all the shame it involved (2) and now is in the place of highest honour. When we are confronted with open hostility it is a strength to consider that we serve a Master who knows it exactly. For our salvation He put up with the worst that sinful men could do.

Hebrews 12.4-10   Sons receive Chastening

It is one of the facts of life that we do not like suffering. Nobody does. But it is also one of the facts of Christian life that suffering has been transformed by the sufferings of Christ. When we look at the cross we see that suffering can be meaningful, and that it can accomplish great good. No one who has experienced in his own soul the saving benefits of the sufferings of Christ can ever look on suffering in quite the same way again. This is not to say that we simply utter the words 'the cross' and all our problems concerning suffering vanish. They do not. But the cross means that they must be viewed in a new light. They cannot be seen now simply as misfortunes which a God who does not greatly care allows to afflict us. The cross shows us that God cares passionately for us and our best good. And since God is all-powerful He must see meaning in the sufferings that come to us. Otherwise He would not allow them to come. In a number of places in the N.T. various aspects of the problem of suffering are brought out.

Here the thought that is stressed is that the sufferings of the Christian are evidence of his status in the heavenly family. They mark him out as a son, as one for whom God cares, and cares enough to discipline. Many today thoughtlessly maintain that suffering is evidence that there is no God, or that if there is one, then He is a God who does not care about His people. Our writer draws exactly the opposite conclusion. After pointing out that his readers should not exaggerate the problem, for they had not yet suffered 'to the point of shedding your blood' (as Christ did), he goes on to the important point that sons are disciplined. A father may not worry overmuch about people with whom he has no close connection, but he is very concerned indeed for the son whom he loves. The very fact that God allows Christians to undergo trials is evidence that He is acting as a father and that He loves them. He treats them as sons and disciplines them for their profit (10). Their sufferings are evidence, not that He does not care for them, but that He does, not that He regards them as outsiders, but that He sees them as sons.

Hebrews 12.11-17   The Right Attitude to Suffering

Suffering, rightly endured, can be the means of great blessing, both to the sufferer and to those with whom he comes in contact. That was made plain in the last passage we studied. Nothing, it is true, can make it pleasant (11). But a right attitude can make it profitable. It is this with which our author proceeds to concern himself. He points to 'the peaceful fruit of righteousness', i.e. the fruit which consists in righteousness. Notice his adjective, for 'peaceful' is not a description which would spontaneously occur to most of us. But when discipline is accepted the soul is at peace. It is rid of the tensions and divisions which make life difficult for the undisciplined. It is at one with God. This is real peace.

Because of this the writer can exhort his readers to lift their drooping hands and strengthen their weak knees (12; cf. Isa. 35.3), a vivid picture of men who are not realizing their full potential. In language reminiscent of Prov. 4.26 he urges that they make the paths straight (i.e. take away awkward bends and roughnesses). The lame will then not be hurt but healed. It is easy to live in such a way as to neglect the needs of the spiritually lame, but the man who heeds the discipline God sends him will not make that mistake.

'Strive' is perhaps better 'pursue'. There is the thought of diligent and eager pursuit. This is directed towards peace, here 'peace with all men'. This follows naturally enough from that peace with God which we have just noticed (11). With this is linked 'the holiness without which no one will see the Lord'. This does not, of course, mean that men must by their own effort produce such qualities of character as fit them for the vision of God. Such an idea cannot be fitted into the N.T. Rather the writer is speaking of earnestness in living out the gospel. If a man does not yield himself to God in response to Christ's atoning act he will not see God. This is something to be sought after from the depths of one's being.

Our passage ends with the reminder that some have had a certain acquaintance with the things of God but have failed to profit thereby. It is the thought of 6.4 ff. in another form. If men nourish a 'root of bitterness' they will surely fail to obtain the blessing of God. Esau is the example of the kind of thing that is in mind. We learn here that, subsequent to his rejection of his birthright, he wanted back the blessing he had once treated so lightly. But his renunciation was a solemn act which could not be undone by tears.

Hebrews 12.18-24   The City of God

The seriousness of the issues involved is now brought out with a reminder of the inauguration of the old covenant. At Mount Sinai there were various fearful phenomena which are listed for us (18 f.). The people who heard it all entreated that they receive no more such messages (19), and even Moses, the man of God, could say, 'I tremble with fear' (21). It is clear that the scene was one of terrifying grandeur. It emphasized the truth that God is not to be taken lightly.

But the purpose of drawing attention to Mount Sinai is not that we may concentrate on the terrors. They are there, but in the background. The emphasis is rather on the graciousness which is the characteristic of the new covenant. Not Mount Sinai but Mount Zion is the place to which Christians have come, and this is described as 'the city of the living God, the heavenly Jerusalem' (22). There is grandeur about this concept (as is strikingly brought out in *Revelation*, for example). We see this in brief compass in the references to the angels, the inhabitants of heaven, and especially to God, now characterized as 'a judge who is God of all' (23). While our author is stressing the graciousness of the new covenant he does not lose sight of the fact that it includes elements of seriousness, and even severity. The issues involved are of deep and lasting consequence. When we preach the gospel we should not think that we are playing a kind of game in which it does not greatly matter who wins. We are offering men salvation from a lost eternity. And as every man must stand before the 'judge who is God of all', none can evade the challenge.

But the climax is reached in the reference to Jesus Christ (24). There is one reference to Him as the mediator of the new covenant, and one to His blood (which, as it brings blessing and cleansing, 'speaks more graciously' than that blood that pleaded for revenge, Gen. 4.10). But in this short compass our author has managed to pack a world of meaning about the graciousness of Christ. His way is a way of full salvation for us and that a salvation by free grace.

Hebrews 12.25-29   'Our God is a Consuming Fire'

The previous passage has put emphasis on the graciousness which characterizes the Christian approach. It centres on the atoning work of Christ who shed His blood that our sins might be put away completely. Salvation is thus a great and free reality. But this does not mean that we can regard the issues involved as unimportant. To reject the grace of God is to invite certain damnation.

The comparison has been made of Mount Zion and Mount Sinai (12.18–24). But this is not to be understood as though one God was responsible for the former arrangement and another for the latter. There is one God behind the O.T. and the N.T. We should not mistake His grace for weakness. Indeed, if it was a fearful thing to refuse the God who was manifested in the thunders of Sinai, it is, when we get to thinking seriously about it, a more solemn thing by far to refuse the God who speaks so graciously in Christ. Or, as our author puts it, as they did not escape who rejected the warning on earth much less will they who refuse Him who warns from heaven (25). God did indeed shake the earth at Sinai, but another shaking is envisaged, a final one, from the same God (26). This turns our attention to the importance of a sense of values. There are some things that can be shaken and destroyed and there are others which are permanent. They cannot be shaken. They will remain throughout the time of this world's existence and beyond. This is one of the things from this Epistle which need emphasis in the world of today. Men are apt to regard all human achievements as no more than relative and to go on from there to think not only that human grasp of the truth is relative, but that truth itself is relative. They deny the absolutes.

Perhaps Christians have sometimes been too prone to cling to things that are temporary and to confuse what is merely cultural with what is essential to the faith. But when full allowance has been made for that, it is still the case that there is 'a kingdom that cannot be shaken' (28). It is that with which we have to do. To reject what it stands for is calamitous, for God is implacably opposed to every evil thing. He is a consuming fire (29), a N.T. truth with enormous practical consequences.

Hebrews 13.1-6 Christian Service

The readers of the Epistle are now exhorted to fulfil some practical Christian duties. We should never be so taken up with intricate questions of the bearing of Christian truth on philosophical difficulties or on the social problems of the day that we neglect the duties that lie ready to our hands. So Christians are to manifest brotherly love. This incidentally was apparently a new virtue; the expression 'brotherly love' appears in pre-Christian times always to have been used in the literal sense of love within a family. To have such love for fellow believers is striking. And it is something which formed a potent weapon of evangelism in the early Church, for the heathen were immensely impressed when they had to confess, 'Behold how these Christians love one another!' Hospitality is another virtue to be stressed. It was important to the early Christians, for as they travelled in the service of the gospel they experienced difficulties in securing lodging places. Inns were expensive and often of dubious reputation. Hospitality in Christian homes was important.

Prisoners were usually badly treated, so that compassion towards them was not out of place. The attitude looked for here is an advance on hospitality. Strangers seek one out and bring the opportunity for hospitality, but prisoners must be sought out. Probably Christians in prison for the faith are primarily in mind. The readers are to remember them 'as though in prison with them', as in fact in due course they well might be. For the attitude which these readers in fact practised, cf. **10.34**.

In a day of sexual laxity the Christian attitude to marriage stood out. Sex is a good gift of God, and it is to be used in the way God intends, not as a mere gratification of the lusts. For the Christian there must always be the two thoughts that (*a*) marriage is indeed an honourable estate, and sex something that can be exercised 'undefiled', but also that (*b*) a severe judgement of God is against the immoral (4).

The last vice our author mentions is the love of money, which can be a fruitful cause of all kinds of evil. But when a man resists the temptation and is content with God's provision he will rejoice in a well founded confidence (6). Where God is Lord and guard we need not fear what man can do.

Hebrews 13.7-16 Christ our Sin Offering

We are reminded that Christians have a duty to their leaders, a thought to which our author will return (17). The leaders' manner of life is to be imitated (7). Perhaps it is the consideration that even the manner of life of the best men is subject to change which leads to the abrupt introduction of the thought that Jesus Christ does not change (8). Look back or forward it makes no difference. He is always constant. 'Diverse and strange teachings' (9) might lead astray. But the constancy of our Lord is an encouragement to us to be constant in our place.

The main part of our passage is taken up with a consideration of Christ's work for us viewed from the aspect of the sin offering. The 'altar' (10) should not, of course, be misconstrued as though it referred to any material earthly object. It is a way of referring to Christ's sacrifice for us, and if any material object is in view it is the cross. The interesting thing about the subsequent reference to the sin offering is that the part singled out for mention is not the manipulation of blood or the burning on the altar or the like. It is the burning of the bodies of the victims 'outside the camp' (11). These bodies were so identified with sin that they could not be offered on the altar. They were simply thrown outside the city and burned. This is a vivid way of saying that Christ in His death became one with sinners and bore their sin (cf. 2 Cor. 5.21).

This is made the basis for an appeal to the readers to be ready likewise to go 'outside the camp', not, of course, in any sense that they might be doing an atoning act, but in the sense that they are identifying themselves with Jesus, even at the cost of breaking valued earthly ties. All the more is this the case in that Christians have their citizenship not in any earthly place but in heaven (cf. 11.16). They should in accordance with their calling offer up sacrifices, but sacrifices of a spiritual character (15 f.). In the light of what Christ has done there are no others we can offer.

Meditation: Scripture everywhere recognizes the living power of a great example (7).

Hebrews 13.17-25 Final Exhortations

As he comes to the close of his letter our author has some final advice for his readers. He begins with a further reference to the place of Christian leaders. All too often church members are harshly critical of their pastors and other ministers, and their attitude may do harm to the cause of Christ. We should not, of course, suggest that ministers are above criticism. They are imperfect men and just as liable as anybody else to make mistakes. But they have important work to do and it will be hindered and not helped if they are the objects of constant attacks and criticism. Moreover, typically, they are men who have a deep concern for the wellbeing of their people. They 'are keeping watch over your souls, as men who will have to give account' (17). It is well, accordingly, that those who are committed to their care so act that these leaders can render their account 'joyfully, and not sadly'. Even if a church member disagrees with his leaders it is of no advantage to him if they have to render a sad account of him (17).

These same leaders are always in need of the help their followers can give by their prayers. So is the writer of the Epistle, and he puts in his personal request for his friends to help him by their intercessions (18 f.). This leads him into a magnificent benediction which has been a help to Christians throughout the centuries. It characterizes God as 'the God of peace' and reminds us of His part in bringing about the resurrection of our Lord. Our Lord's care for us comes out in the description of Him as 'the great Shepherd of the sheep'. Then we revert to the thought of God's constancy. He has done all this 'by the blood of the eternal covenant', i.e. the blood that Christ shed is the means of bringing about a covenant which will never be replaced. Since the Son of God Himself mediated this covenant it is final. Then we come back to the thought of what God will do in His people, equipping them for service, and the benediction is rounded off with an ascription of glory for ever. There are some personal notes, one of which speaks warmly of Timothy (23), and the Epistle is completed with 'the grace'.

Thought: If He became our High Priest by laying down His life, what can He not do with what we lay down?

Questions for further discussion and meditation on Hebrews 12,13

1. In what ways is Christ our example?
2. Relate the teaching of ch. 12 on discipline as a mark of sonship to your own circumstances.
3. Discuss the hindrances modern life presents to attaining that 'holiness without which no one will see the Lord' (12.14). How can they be overcome?
4. What conditions must we fulfil if we are to offer to God 'acceptable worship' (12.28)?
5. How far are the directions of ch. 13 applicable to modern life?

James

INTRODUCTION

Not a great deal can be said about this little writing. Its original readers are quite unknown. It is in the form of a letter, but it is not certain whether it should be taken as a real letter meant for a certain definite circle of recipients. There are no personal details such as would be expected in a writing of that sort, and the address is general. It reads much like a sermon, a little exhortation to fulfil the duties of Christian men, and to remember the essence of Christian teaching.

And if nothing definite is known of the original readers the same must be said of the author. He tells us that his name is James, and he describes himself only as 'a servant of God and of the Lord Jesus Christ', a description that would fit all of God's servants. As James was a fairly common name among the early Christians this makes it difficult for us to be precise in our ascription of authorship. It is often held that the James in question was James the Lord's brother, and that he is identical with the James who is so prominent in *Acts*. This may well be so, and it would explain the authoritative tone in which the letter is written. But it must be recognized that there is a good deal that is speculative here. In the end our verdict will probably have to be that we do not know for certain who wrote the letter, though James the Lord's brother is a possibility.

Just as there is uncertainty as to writer and readers, so there is doubt as to the date of the writing. Nothing dates it with any exactness and we are not likely to get beyond the position that it is undoubtedly early. No advanced stage of ecclesiastical development seems indicated, and the section on faith and works looks early. After Paul's writings had become widely accepted it is not easy to see a writer producing something which might be construed as opposing the great Apostle.

But if there are many uncertainties one thing is plain—we would be greatly impoverished without this little writing. Zahn speaks of the author as 'a preacher who speaks like a prophet . . . in language which for forcibleness is without parallel in early Christian literature, excepting the discourses of Jesus.' Moffatt cites this and goes on to point out that in 108 verses there are no less than 54 imperatives. This is a forthright writing stressing the importance of practical Christian action.

James is content to see himself as occupying a very lowly place, for he speaks of himself as a servant (or slave) of God. Notice that he links God and 'the Lord Jesus Christ'. He had come to see Jesus as occupying the very highest place of all. He addresses his Epistle to 'the twelve tribes in the Dispersion', which raises more than one problem. There do not appear to have been twelve tribes in existence at the time, or if there were, they were not in evidence. Again, the 'Dispersion' was a technical term for the Jews dispersed throughout the ancient world, the Jews outside Palestine, but it seems very unlikely that James was writing to the Jews as such. It thus seems likely that we should take 'the twelve tribes' as a reference to Israel indeed, but the spiritual Israel, the Church regarded as the people of God. The reference to the Dispersion will then indicate that it is the Church at large, the Church throughout the world, that is in mind and not Christians in any specific area.

To Christians at large, then, James writes on the necessity for constancy. We do not like difficulties and trials. We regard them as unfortunate necessities to be borne with as good a grace as possible. James sees them as occasions for joy (2). His point is that it is only through trials that we are able to develop the quality of steadfastness. The N.T. has a number of such exhortations to remind us that in the piping days of peace we do not really develop spiritual fibre. That comes about rather in the process of grappling with difficulties. Trials are not pleasant but the Christian should never face them in the same spirit as does the non-Christian. For the Christian, suffering has been transformed by the suffering of Christ. It is seen now as the means through which God can bring about great good. It is accordingly not to be regarded as an occasion for rebellion, but of progress in the faith. So, too, the Christian must be constant in the face of lack of wisdom and of doubt. He can look to God for all that is needed, knowing that nothing needful will be held back. But the blessing is not for the double-minded (7 f.). Steadfastness is a necessity if we are to go forward in the Christian life.

Thought: If you are wise you will ask for wisdom.

James 1.9-18 God's Good Gifts

We are always tempted to use a wrong set of values. It is natural for men to think of wealth as of great importance, and indeed there are few among mankind who do not make a serious effort to acquire a generous slice of this world's goods. James reminds us that riches will fail (11), and he goes so far as to say that it is 'the lowly brother' who should 'boast in his exaltation' (9). When a poor man receives the gospel he becomes rich in the things that really matter. He is exalted, and, though he lacks earthly wealth, he may well rejoice. Likewise the rich man who becomes a Christian has matter for rejoicing, but this time in his 'humiliation'. Like the poor man's exaltation this will refer to a spiritual condition. It is not that the rich man loses any of his wealth (though it is quite possible that his becoming a Christian will mean the loss of certain sources of gain). Rather, he has learned the true place of riches (and the place of true riches) and no longer thinks of himself in the same way. He has learned real lowliness.

A similar lesson lies behind James' next section (12-15). He counsels his readers to regard times of testing in the right way. It is a blessed thing, not a disaster, to undergo testing. The man who enjoys this experience is also learning a sense of values. To survive testing is the way to 'the crown of life' (12). This includes an understanding of the meaning of temptation, namely, that it does not come from God, but from a man's own desire. And the end result of giving way to it is death (15).

Thus both poverty and a right attitude to wealth are gifts of God. So, too, in another way, are trials. God never sends temptations, but He uses them for the upbuilding of His people. So James goes on to notice that every good gift really comes from God. Our attention may be fixed on some intermediary through whom the gift comes. But it is God who is the author. And He is not subject to change. Thus whether what comes to us seems pleasant or the reverse we can take it as from the hand of a God who never ceases to give good gifts to His children.

James 1.19-27 Deeds, not Words

Most of us like to hear ourselves talking, and in any conversation enjoy getting our view point across. And most of us like to be sure that our own interests are properly safeguarded. We all too easily become angry when we are thwarted. James reminds us that both attitudes can imperil our spiritual development. It is a much sounder policy to listen first. The Christian should be slow both to speech and to anger (19). He should make the effort to put away all evil decisively and to receive that word from God which brings salvation (21). In view of the way some have misinterpreted this Epistle, as though it were giving expression to a doctrine of salvation by works, it is well to notice this clear expression of the truth that salvation comes from 'the implanted word', not from anything that men do.

But this does not mean that our manner of life is unimportant. James is always ready to remind his readers of the importance of living out their faith. Now he uses the illustration of a man looking in a mirror, a casual glance which means very little. The man looks into the mirror and goes on his way forgetting even what it was he saw. Not in this light-hearted way should a man face his Christian obligations. For that, perseverance in well-doing is needed.

To show us the kind of thing he has in mind James turns attention to contrasting religions (26 f.). That which is not characterized by control of the tongue (cf. v. 19) is 'vain', i.e. empty. There is nothing in it. The man is self-deceived. Real religion, by contrast, comes out in a man's attitude to the defenceless. The orphans and widows were proverbial in the ancient world for poverty and defencelessness. They had no man to act as their protector and were easy prey for the unscrupulous. They normally found it very difficult to earn their living and had little redress if exploited. So it is a mark of a genuine religion to look out for such in their affliction and help them. They could make no return.

James 2.1-7 The Rich and the Poor

Clearly the problem of the right attitude to rich men exercised James greatly. Paul tells us that there were not many men of family and position in the Corinthian church (1 Cor. 1.26 ff.), and this would no doubt have been true fairly universally. There is no reason for doubting that the first converts to Christianity came largely from the depressed classes. They were poor men, or even slaves. According to the accepted standards of their day, they had been used to giving deference to the wealthy and the well placed. When they became Christians they quite naturally carried the attitude over into their new life. This natural human tendency must have been strengthened by the equally natural human tendency to be very solicitous of the few rich men who were converted. They would tend to be highly esteemed in the little Christian assemblies and to be given especial consideration, even deference.

This kind of treatment is not easy to reconcile with a proper Christian understanding of life. If all men are sinners, and all stand in need of divine salvation, then no man, no matter how wealthy, is anything other than a suppliant for the divine mercy. James reminds his readers that the kind of conduct which singles out the rich for special consideration is contrary to important Christian teachings. It means that the men who do this have set themselves up as judges, as they make distinctions between one believer and another, and, moreover, 'judges with evil thoughts' (4).

It is also the case that the poor more commonly than the rich are 'rich in faith' (5). This does not mean that God rejects the rich. Rather it arises from the fact that all too often those who have great material possessions give way to the temptation to put their trust in them. They cut themselves off from humble, dependent faith. James adds one practical point. It was the rich and not the poor who were usually responsible for the oppression which overtook the Christians from time to time. As a class it was the rich rather than the poor who blasphemed the name of God by their conduct (7). In an affluent society such warnings are very much in point.

James 2.8-13   The Royal Law

It might have been objected that James was making too much of this one point. After all, it is a natural tendency, and it is only a small thing. James' reply is twofold: in the first place it is not a small thing, and in the second it is a sin and all sin is serious.

It is not a small thing, for the supremely important thing in living the Christian life is to practise love. James calls the injunction, 'You shall love your neighbour as yourself', the 'royal law'. That is to say, it is the supreme law, that law which matters above all others. It accords with the words of our Lord Himself when He summed up the obligations resting on His followers to love both God and man (Mark 12.29–31). It is not without its interest that the command to love one's neighbour as oneself is taken from Lev. 19.18, and that in the immediate context we read, 'you shall not be partial to the poor or defer to the great' (Lev. 19.15). Thus to give special consideration to the rich, while putting the poor in a place of low esteem, means to go contrary to what is laid down in the law of God. It is to commit sin. Those who do this are transgressors (9).

Nor is there a defence that it is only a minor commandment that has been broken. To break any commandment is to become a law-breaker. This is often lost sight of. Almost everybody in our society thinks he is living, on the whole, a fairly good life (it is the other people who do the really bad things). He is usually ready to admit that there are some things he does which he ought not and that there are some things he does not do which he should. But it always seems to work out that the really serious sins are never those he commits. In the face of this very common and very natural human attitude James still has something to say. To break a law of God, any law, is to become a law-breaker. Nobody who thinks seriously about it can regard any sin as unimportant. We are responsible people. One day we must give account of ourselves to God. Judgement is a serious business. But James' last word is on mercy (13).

James 2.14-26 Faith and Works

Nowhere does James' strong emphasis on practical Christianity come out more clearly than here. Indeed, so prominent is it that some have felt that James is contradicting Paul. Paul, they say, teaches that a man is justified by faith, not works (Gal. 2.16), whereas here James is teaching the opposite and indeed goes so far as to say that 'a man is justified by works and not by faith alone' (24).

It is important not to be hypnotized by words, but to ask what James means. And it is quite plain when we try to answer this question that James does not mean by works what Paul means. Paul is speaking of those works done in obedience to the law whereby a man tries to merit his salvation. Unweariedly Paul combats this error. Men cannot acquire their salvation by works of law. But James is not talking about this at all when he looks for works. The works of which he speaks are the outworking of a living faith. Indeed he says specifically, 'I by my works will show you my faith' (18). Works are the evidence that faith is present. For James faith is undoubtedly important (see 1.6; 2.1,5; 5.15). He assumes that faith is necessary. But he denies that a right faith can exist without works. The kind of faith that lacks works is dead (17).

The faith James has in mind in this section of the Epistle is something very different indeed from what Paul means by faith (or for that matter what James means elsewhere). We are not left to guess at this, for he tells us plainly what this kind of faith is like: 'You believe that God is one; you do well. Even the demons believe— and shudder' (19). This is not the warm personal trust in a living Saviour which is what Paul means by faith. James then is opposing something which Paul is not advocating. There is no contradiction.

Finally, let us notice that James' point is important. It is always easier to make a profession of faith than it is to make good that profession in a life lived in the service of God. But it is that to which we are called. James calls attention to Abraham and Rahab as people who lived out their faith. Saving faith is a faith that works by love (as Paul puts it, Gal. 5.6).

Questions for further study and discussion on James 1,2
1. What may we learn from this part of James about constancy?
2. How is James' emphasis on an active faith relevant to your situation?
3. Discuss James' treatment of riches and poverty.
4. How does James bring out the seriousness of sin?
5. What tendencies do you discern in the modern church toward the kind of error that James opposes in 2.14–26?

James 3.1-5 — Teachers and the Judgement

It appears from the opening verse that there was a tendency in some parts of the Church to seek the teaching office. Some men always find the limelight attractive, and there were not many opportunities for finding it in the early Church. Christians seem to have been fairly closely knit as a band of brothers in Christ. There was not much opportunity for showing off before others. But teaching did put a man in a position of prominence, and men of a certain temperament sought the position in consequence. While a man should not avoid any responsibility that God lays upon him, he should not seek a post of which this could not be said. So James begins by pointing out that those who teach will be judged very strictly. It is still a principle to be carefully observed that greater privilege means greater responsibility.

The danger involved in this is that men are apt to make mistakes (2), and more particularly in the things they say. A slip of the tongue with serious consequences is always a possibility. And it is more of a possibility for the teacher than for other people. Words are his tools of trade. He uses them of necessity to convey his meaning. So to rush into a position of teaching means to thrust oneself into a situation where a dangerous error is an ever-present possibility.

This leads James to the reflection that the tongue, though small in size, is great in achievement. He finds three illustrations of this: the small bit that guides a large horse, the small rudder that steers a huge ship, and the little fire that kindles a whole forest. We should not be misled by the tongue's small size. Small though it is, it is powerful. It is the tongue that enables the teacher or the preacher to make his point. It is by the tongue that the ordinary Christian can witness to others and so win them for Christ. So James' warning on the responsibility of using aright a weapon with great potential is of wider application than simply to teachers.

Having shown that the tongue is able to accomplish great results and should not be underestimated because of its small size James goes on to the further point that it is fraught with great possibilities for evil as well as for good. Rightly used, our words accomplish much in the service of God. Wrongly used they bring about incalculable damage. In a vigorous verse James speaks of the tongue as 'an unrighteous world' (which indicates the extent of its influence as well as its bias toward evil), as 'staining the whole body' (I am wholly defiled when I misuse my tongue; it is not only a part of me that is affected), and as setting on fire the whole of 'the round circle of existence' (Moffatt). This last expression is a very unusual one, but Moffatt probably gives us the sense of it. James is carrying on the metaphor of the forest fire and indicating that the tongue can start an evil which will spread throughout the world. And its origin? It is 'set on fire by hell'. There is something satanic about the wrong use of the tongue.

James further notes that man has shown great skill as a tamer of beasts, and he uses this as yet another way of bringing out the evil caused by wrong speech. In strong contrast with his ability to handle the wildest of beasts is man's inability to control his tongue. James speaks of it as 'a restless evil, full of deadly poison', the last expression being probably suggested by his reference to reptiles (7). The poisonous tongues of snakes are often referred to in antiquity.

James' final point under this heading is that this is all unnatural. It is incongruous to use the same mouth for blessing as cursing. This is quite contrary to what we see in nature, for example in springs where the water is either fresh or brackish but not both, or in trees where the fruit is consistent. The moral is obvious. It is clear to all God's servants that they should bless and praise Him. All their other speech should be consistent with this. This sets the tone for their words to men.

Thought: 'Silence may be a sign of sanctification' (G. Scroggie).

James 3.13-18   True Wisdom

From the tongue James moves to the life as a whole and he contrasts the wise man with the unwise, though he does not use the latter term. Rather he speaks of a 'wisdom' not of heavenly origin. Just as earlier he has spoken of every good gift as coming from God (1.17), so now he thinks of all true wisdom as 'from above'. The main point which concerns him is the self-assertion of the wicked, which he finds in sharp contrast to the meekness of God's own.

Meekness, incidentally, was not universally regarded as a virtue in the Greek world. It was held that a real man would stand up for his rights and not allow himself to be trampled on. It was humiliating not to be accorded one's full rights and one's proper place. Rivals must not be allowed to usurp one's proper privileges and the like. Thus what James is castigating as 'bitter jealousy and selfish ambition' (14) was usually regarded as a proper concern for one's rightful position. The point, and it is important, is that the Christian does not take his standards from the world.

There is a reversal of values when a man knows himself to have been saved by Christ. He himself can contribute nothing to the process. His sins have been put away not by his own best effort, but by Christ's atoning death. He sees that he has sinned against God, but that God has refused to damn him. Instead, in the person of His Son, He has suffered to save him. When the significance of this has sunk in, a man cannot be selfish and self-assertive. In his measure he reacts to others as God has acted towards him, that is, in forgiving love. So he looks for that wisdom which is from above. He looks now for purity in his own life, and for an attitude of peaceableness and mercy to other men (17). He rejects jealousy and ambition as devilish (15). The connection between righteousness and peace (18) is noteworthy. The world has not yet realized, in its deep yearning for peace, that peace and righteousness are intimately connected. It is still not possible to have real peace if in our self-seeking we reject real righteousness.

James 4.1-4 The Cause of War

It is possible that James is not speaking in the first instance about wars in the military sense. He may well be using military imagery to castigate quarrels among church members. But what he says has relevance to a wider circle than quarrelsome Christians. To an age as eager for peace and as much given to war as ours these words about the root causes of wars come home with force and relevance. For the fact is that if we promote a warlike spirit it is only to be expected that we will have wars, and this whether on the grand scale between nations or on the small scale between church members. We must get down to the basic issues.

James is stressing the extremely important point that the cause of hostility is basically human passion. Men desire. Men covet. And their passions are so strong that they take into their own hands the gratification of their desires. This is the spirit that leads nations to wars and individuals to quarrels. Wherever men or nations act on the assumption that they themselves are the guardians of their own rights and that they are quite entitled to take whatever steps they deem necessary to safeguard those rights, then enmity is inevitable. For the attitude is certain to be met by a similar attitude on the side of the other party. So hostility results and this may well result in open warfare on a grand or minor scale.

For the Christian there is a further reflection that the reason he does not have what he needs is that he does not ask (2). Prayer is a mighty force. And when some of his readers are prepared to retort that they *have* prayed, James replies that they have prayed wrongly. They have tried to use prayer for the gratification of those same passions! Instead of renouncing the worldly way, they have thought they could enlist God on their side. Even in what they take to be a proper religious activity they have been manifesting a worldly spirit. They (and we) must learn that the world's friendship means enmity with God (4). There is a fundamental incompatibility here, and as long as we gloss over it with words, while retaining the worldly spirit of self-aggrandizement, we must expect strife.

James 4.5-10 God's Yearning

In rejecting the way of the world James does not want it thought that he is advocating in God's name a course which would mean anything less than the very best for God's people. God calls on men to reject the way of self-aggrandizement, but not because He wants to cramp them into a narrow and unsatisfying existence. Rather, the reverse is the case. In bold anthropomorphic language James pictures God as yearning jealously over us, as longing for us so that He may bring us into that perfect fellowship with Him, which is our best good. The exact source of the quotation in v. 5 is not clear. It seems to be a free and somewhat poetic rendering of the thought of Exod. 20.5. And its exact meaning is not plain either. The RSV takes 'spirit' to mean the human spirit over which God yearns. But it might refer to the Holy Spirit with the meaning, 'the Spirit which dwells within us yearns jealously over us'. Either way the thought is that God longs for us to find our rest in Him.

Quite in this spirit He gives us grace (6), a thought which accords with Prov. 3.34, for the proud do not look for God's grace, whereas the humble gratefully accept it. James launches into a series of exhortations, the burden of which is 'Follow the right way, and you will certainly receive the blessing of God'. James is making with some emphasis the point that God is always ready to give His blessing, but that it is quite possible for men to adopt a self-seeking way of life that cuts them off from God's help. So we should resist the devil, not yield to him (7). We should submit to God (7), and draw near to Him (8), when we will find that He will draw near to us. But our attitude must be wholehearted. This means a thoroughgoing purification (8) and a genuine sorrow for sin (9). But the man who really humbles himself before God will surely find that God will not abandon him. God will exalt him (10).

James 4.11-17 The Will of God

One of the commonest human frailties is that of setting oneself up over the law. Often it is in a comparatively minor matter, as when Christian motorists determine their own speed limits instead of abiding by those laid down by authority. Sometimes it is in a matter of great importance and the climax is reached with the criminal who defies all authority and acts according to his own desires and his conception of his own profit. A proper regard for the law is a necessity if men are to live in community. James is concerned, however, not simply with community life but with the attitude of the Christian to law. He is concerned at the way Christians sometimes act as though they are superior to law. The particular manifestation of it with which he deals is that of speaking evil of others. Gossip and slander are more than the social pastime they appear to be. They proceed from an attitude of mind which presumes to sit in judgement on others, and which is thus arrogating to itself a function that belongs to God alone. This is a dangerous practice as well as a wicked one, for the God whose place the slanderer usurps is One who is able to destroy as well as to save (12). None of us is so great (or so safe!) that he can engage in criticism of his fellow servants.

Men sometimes ignore the will of God in other matters, as when they plan without taking God into account. James does not mean that we should not exercise reasonable forethought in planning our affairs. That is only a correct use of our God-given intelligence. He is opposing the attitude whereby a Christian plans as though he were a worldly man, completely ignoring God. All our plans should include 'If the Lord wills', a provision which is not met by making up our minds and simply adding D.V.

The final verse in this chapter is notable. We usually think of sins of commission as the important ones and tend to overlook altogether the good we might have done. James reminds us that it is important to make use of every opportunity of doing good.

Failure to do good is not simply a matter for mild regret. It is sin. *Question: Link the principle in v. 17 with that in Rom. 14.23; do these represent a complete rule of conduct for the believer?*

James 5.1-6 The Perils of Riches

It is clear that in the church with which James was concerned there were problems posed by the activities of the wealthy. He has had occasion earlier in the Epistle to rebuke a wrong use of riches. As he returns to the theme we should not think that this is an obsession with something that does not matter or does not matter greatly. Through all the centuries of the Church's existence it has been the case that many whose faith stood firm in the days of doubt and difficulty have not been able to withstand affluence. The Christian life is always a battle and to the poor this is very plain. But for the rich some of the struggle has been taken out of life and it is easy for them to lose their grip on spiritual realities. The possession of a degree of affluence all too often leads to a strong desire for greater affluence and so to that love of money which is the root of every kind of evil (1 Tim. 6.10).

James clearly has in mind at this point some rich men who had engaged in oppressing the poor. He is not talking about riches in general, but about men known to him and his readers who had defrauded their labourers (4). This is a good example of the kind of temptation to which the rich are exposed and which does not confront the poor to anything like the same degree. The rich in their desire to be richer may press on without regard to the rights of others. When this happens their riches may be said to have 'rotted' and the like (2 f.). Incidentally, when James speaks of gold and silver as having 'rusted' (3) this should not be taken as evidence of ignorance of the properties of precious metals. James is not speaking of physical and chemical properties. He is referring to the fact that wealth obtained by improper means is not ultimately lasting. The rich, like all men, will stand before God's judgement, and their riches will then be found of no avail. There may also be the thought that these riches are tarnished. James is giving a serious and very vigorous warning. No man can use his wealth to the detriment of others and expect to get away with it when he stands before God. An affluent generation does well to heed the warning.

Thought: 'It is better to be oppressed than an oppressor' (G. Scroggie).

James 5.7-12

There are two Greek words which are sometimes translated 'patience', and we have both of them in this passage. The one means very much what we mean by patience. It contains the idea of longsuffering. It is formed on exactly the model of a word which means 'short-tempered' and is its opposite, i.e. 'long-tempered'. It is a refusal to give way to provocation. It is a readiness to put up with contradiction and baseless opposition. It is a steady refusal to lose one's temper in the face of frustration. There is nothing that one can do about this kind of opposition except be provoked by it or endure it. It is this that James has in mind when he speaks of the farmer. There is nothing he can do about the weather, or the seasons. When he has planted his crop he must wait patiently. But in his patient waiting he knows that the time of harvest is surely coming. And the Christian knows that the time of this world's harvest is coming. He must endure innumerable provocations and frustrations. But he can bear them all with patience, for he knows that his Lord will one day come. The last word is not with those who provoke and frustrate. The last word is with the Lord. Since His coming is sure we may settle our hearts (8).

The other word means steadfastness rather than patience. It is the attitude of the soldier who in the midst of the hardest battle is not dismayed by the hard knocks he receives but lays about him with a right good will. There is an air of activity, even aggressiveness, about it. James uses this word of Job (11). That patriarch came through triumphant. While perhaps James does not want us to differentiate too sharply between his two words they do have different emphases and we can profit by reflecting on both. James' final statement in v. 11 should be borne in mind in all troubles. The Lord who permits them is compassionate and merciful.

Verse 12 reminds us that our word should be reliable always. James is not concerned with the problem of oaths in law courts and the like. He is saying that in ordinary life our word should not need to be bolstered by an oath before it can be accepted.

James 5.13-20

Throughout this Epistle we have seen that James is strongly practical. He is greatly concerned with the way Christians live out their faith. Now in his concluding section he gives attention to prayer, possibly the most powerful weapon in the Christian's armoury, and certainly a potent factor in the everyday life of the believer. He relates prayer to suffering and to sickness. In the latter case he suggests that the elders of the church should pray over the sick man and anoint him with oil in the Lord's name (14). Many have pointed out that in heathen religions there was widespread use of incantations and the like in times of sickness, and the thought is that James is advocating a Christian practice that would replace this kind of thing. Be that as it may, his emphasis is not on the oil but on prayer. It is 'the prayer of faith' that 'will save the sick man' (15). James also sees this as connected with the man's spiritual condition. Forgiveness of sins is to be sought and will be granted. This is the point also of the mutual confession advocated in v. 16. It is not a sacramental confession but a mutual sharing of grief, with prayer for healing. Christians should be concerned about one author's spiritual condition and be constant in prayer for each other. James goes on to cite Elijah as a well-known example of the power of prayer. That power, which caused first drought and then rain, he feels, is very applicable to believers.

This brings him on to his final topic, that of soul-winning. To bring men back from sin to Christ is to bring them into salvation. It will cover all their sins. Nothing could be more worthwhile.

In all our concern for sickness and sinners we should not overlook the fact that James has something for those whose souls are in health (13). The cheerful should sing praise. It is God who is the source of all their blessings and it is well that they recognize it.

Questions for further study and discussion on James 3–5

1. What are your own sins of the tongue? How can you guard against them?
2. What is the relevance for our generation of James' words about war?
3. Apply James' teaching on doing the will of God to your own situation.
4. In what circumstances in modern life may we apply the teachings of James about patience and endurance?
5. Discuss the relation between prayer and the cure of sickness.

1 and 2 Peter, Jude

INTRODUCTION

1 Peter was written to the scattered Christians of northern and western Asia Minor, an area which was mainly outside the sphere of Paul's missionary work. Various references make it clear that the majority of the intended readers were Gentiles. Silvanus (5.12), i.e. Silas, Paul's companion on his second missionary journey, may have interested Peter in the area. The excellent Greek is probably due to Silvanus having acted as scribe. The letter was probably written from Rome (5.13), possibly after the beginning of Nero's persecution.

The language of *2 Peter* is very different, but this can be explained by Peter's using a different scribe, for there is no marked difference in thought. The recipients of the letter are not named, but since this letter was perhaps the last book to be accepted into the Canon, it was probably not written to an influential church. The chief reason why many reject the Petrine authorship is the way he speaks of Paul's letters (3.15 f.), but the argument is hardly valid. The same may be said of the use of *Jude*, the message of which Peter may have wished to make better known.

Jude was almost certainly written by our Lord's brother of that name. The fact that most of the letter was taken up by Peter into his second letter suggests that it was originally addressed to a limited circle. It is concerned with those who were both false teachers and false livers, as were so many who were influenced by early Gnosticism, cf. Rev. 2,3.

1 Peter 1.1-9   The Preciousness of Faith

With the doubtful exception of Gal. 6.16, the name Israel is not applied to the Church in the N.T., but the various descriptions of it are. Peter uses here and in 2.11 three such terms. 'Dispersion' (1) was the regular term for the Jew living outside Palestine; the Christian's homeland is heaven. 'Exiles' (also in 2.11, cf. 1.17), better, sojourners, is rendered excellently 'who lodge for a while' by the NEB. The stress is on the short while we are here. Then there is 'aliens' in 2.11. The stress is that the Christian, not being a citizen of this world, cf. Phil. 3.20, has no rights here. They are Christians by a threefold act of the Trinity (though the word is not used):

chosen by the Father, made holy by the Spirit, consecrated by the blood of the Son (see NEB).

'Grace and peace' (2): the former includes the experience of God's covenant love, the latter the opening of God's treasure chamber. This fact leads to a benediction. 'Blessed' (3) virtually means that we accept this in gratitude on bended knees. Central is Jesus' resurrection. His new life has started a new life in us which expects to reach Him in heaven. He is our inheritance which we shall obtain at His coming. Because it is a person, not a thing, it is 'imperishable' (4), etc. While it is there secure for us in heaven, we are kept for Him down here, because 'the power from without corresponds to the faith within' (Hort).

We can never be sure of anything until it has been tested—'temptations' (6, AV[KJV]) had this meaning earlier—and so we must pass through testings or 'trials' (6), which can be very painful. Paul assures us we shall never be overtested (1 Cor. 10.13), and the outcome is that we know our faith is not merely something we have produced, but it has been given us by God. Victory in trial shows that the faith came from God, so it is 'precious' (7), and can be the cause of praise and glory. Peter was doubtless thinking of Christ's words to Thomas (John 20.29), when he wrote 'without having seen Him' (8). The rendering of 'the salvation of your souls' (9) can be misleading. For the Bible the soul is the whole of a man including his body.

Thought: Salvation is complete!

1 Peter 1.10-12   The Faith of the Prophets

Peter's readers might legitimately have asked why *their* faith should be so specially important. Where Paul referred to Abraham and *Hebrews* to a long line of the faithful, Peter turned to the prophets. In contrast to the predominant modern view, which sees them as little more than clear-sighted interpreters of their own time, he followed the Rabbinic maxim, 'No prophet ever prophesied except for the days of the Messiah.' This did not mean that they did not prophesy for their own time—stupidity was not one of the Rabbinic faults—but that they saw their own time in the light of the day of the Lord. Peter said that they were so convinced that they were giving God's message, that they committed themselves to it before they knew to whom it applied or when it would come to fulfilment.

To be noted is that they showed deeper interest in the salvation (10) than in the time (11). The term 'the Spirit of Christ' is found again in Rom. **8.9**. Here it means that they were so possessed by the Spirit of the Messiah that they were able to see coming suffering and glory with His eyes.

In addition, however, they saw that they were foretelling the salvation of those to whom Peter was writing, i.e. the Church. It has often been suggested that the prophets could not discern the interval between the first and second comings of Christ, just as when a man viewing two parallel ranges of mountains from a distance cannot know the deep valley that separates them. With all the truth in this view it is inadequate. Throughout the O.T. God is praised as Saviour. But there is always an element of inadequacy in it and hence a looking to the future. This is succinctly summed up in Heb. **11.39** f. Not only has Christ entered into His glory (Luke **24.26**), but we share in it, e.g. Gal. **2.20**; Col. **3.1–4**. It is not merely that we shall experience 'the powers of the world to come', but we have tasted them already (Heb. **6.5**). Eternity is projected into time, the glory of Christ may be seen in the Church before His return. and therefore the salvation which the prophets hoped for has become a reality through our faith.

1 Peter 1.13-21   The Life of Faith

So wonderful is our salvation that 'angels stoop down to look' (12), so Peter turns to our responsibility. His readers were to 'pull themselves together'. The growing hostility to the Christians which came to a climax in the Neronian persecution in Rome, doubtless copied in the provinces, evidently made them feel a little sorry for themselves. It is not clear whether we are to take 'be sober' literally or as 'perfectly self-controlled' (NEB); Eph. **5.18** is sufficient evidence that undue drinking did take place. They were to set their hope 'fully': there is always the temptation to hope that there may be some private relaxation. Selwyn is probably correct with 'the blessing that is being conferred on you in the Lord's appearing.'

Since their hope was set on the future, they had to be 'obedient' (14). The combination of 'passions' and 'ignorance' strongly suggests Gentile readers. Since they were children, they should show the character of the Father (15–17). Note that v. 16, just like Lev. **19.2**, can just as well be rendered 'You will be holy . . .' Sanctification, the making holy, is the work of the Holy Spirit, who separates those for God—the meaning of holy—who are willing to be separated. 'Stand in awe' (NEB), or conduct yourselves 'reverently' (Selwyn), is better than 'fear' (17). 'Your exile': cf. note on **1.1**.

'You were ransomed' (18): to ransom or redeem belongs to the standard language of salvation in the O.T. The question to whom the price is paid is never raised; what is of importance is that God frees the slave. It is Mark **10**.45 that makes clear that a price has to be paid, though even here no recipient is suggested. The 'futile ways' (18) are probably idolatry. Many are tempted to think of God like an earthly ruler, adapting his policy to circumstances. Even if the AV(KJV) of 2 Sam. **14**.14 were correct (see RSV), it would not be a revelation of God's way of working, but the crafty argument of Joab and the woman. The cross is an essential part of God's purpose antedating the creation (20). Neither the fall of Satan nor of man took God by surprise. 'At the end of the times' (20), or ages; we are in the final age already, though only those who know Christ can enjoy the powers of the coming age.

Thought: We must not tarnish God's triumph.

1 Peter 1.22—2.3   The Soil for Love

Great though faith is, it takes second place to love. Peter remembered that his passionate devotion to his Master brought him a stinging rebuke (Matt. **16**.23) and did not keep him from denying Him. Christian love is a fruit of the Spirit, borne by the 'purified soul (22). The NEB gets the sense '. . . you have purified your souls until you feel sincere affection.' The evil things mentioned in 2.1 are weeds which effectively smother the growth of love. Some of those who complain of lack of love may find the clue to their trouble here. It may seem strange, but love is not one of those quiet virtues that grows best when least observed; the more we actually love, the more we shall be able to. Furthermore it is a long-term virtue. Many think that life is so short that they dare not give themselves unrestrainedly in love. We have been reborn for eternity, and love is one of the few things we can carry with us.

'Pure spiritual milk' (2): it is very doubtful whether Peter is making the distinction found in Heb. **5**.12–14; 1 Cor. **3**.1 f., where milk represents the simpler and more fundamental facts of the gospel. For the babe to remain in good health and grow, he needs food regularly. The adult may be able to fast or go on iron rations for days at a time, but not the baby. That is why regular habits of Bible study and prayer are so important for the new convert. 'Pure' (2): unadulterated. For us adulteration means the addition of some noxious substance, but here any addition is implied. The uninterested, blinded outsider may need some bait to get him to listen. For the baby, born by the work of the Holy Spirit, such things are unnecessary. We must not water down our teaching, or add the sugar of sentimentality. On the other hand we must not offer that dehydration of the Word, which we call theology.

Thought: Be sure to speak a good word for your Lord.

1 Peter 2.4-10   The Honour of Christ's People

There is a complete change of subject. In a theological treatise this would be strange, but not in a letter. There are many examples of this in Paul's writings. Up to this point Peter has been thinking of his readers as individuals, but now of them as linked together in the Church. A comparison of vs. 6–8 with Rom. 9.33; Acts 4.11; Mark 12.10 f., will show that the N.T. wove together Isa. 8.14 f.; 28.15f.; Psa. 118.19–23, and applied them to Christ. We know from Qumran that such linking of Scripture was already common there.

'That living stone' (4): the Greek word implies not a rock, as in Matt. 16.18, but one that has been shaped, cf. Heb. 2.10,18; 5.9, etc. It is not merely to the eternal Son of God that we come, but to Jesus, the God-man. If He was shaped, so are we, so that all together we may form a spiritual temple, cf. 1 Cor. 3.16 f.; 2 Cor. 6.16–18; Eph. 2.19–22. In the notes on Rev. 21.22. there are comments on a temple as that which separates God from man; here the temple enables God to live among men, even though they reject Him. Not the church building, but the company of faithful Christians is the house of God.

Because the temple is built with living stones, they are simultaneously the priests that minister in it. The 'spiritual sacrifices' (5) are not that of Rom. 12.1, which is individual. These refer to the work of the local church as an organism. They include the worship of the church, but surely also all those activities that reveal the character of God to men. The very vagueness of Peter's language indicates that he was not thinking of something limited and definite.

The quotations that follow do not link logically with v.5, but with Peter's thought as a whole. 'He is precious' (7); it is doubtful whether this is the meaning. We should probably take it as 'To you who believe He is honour', i.e. belief ensures honour to those who believe. The NEB rendering, 'The great worth of which it speaks is for you', expresses this thought. The honour is the spiritual reality of the promise made to Israel (Exod. 19.5 f.). 'A royal priesthood' in the light of the O.T. and Rev. 1.6 (see notes) probably means a priesthood in the service of the King, i.e. God. 'A holy nation': both in Hebrew and Greek, the word for nation is that used for the nations in general, the Gentiles; it is holiness that makes Israel and the Church different.

1 Peter 2.11-17   Caesar and God

Once again the subject changes. Peter urges his readers to behave as 'aliens' and sojourners (see note on 1.1) should, cf. Phil. 3.17–21. As aliens in this world there is no compulsion for them to live as worldlings. The world will malign them (12)—the foreigner is always suspect—but on the day of judgement ('visitation') it will acknowledge the truth before God; in Josh. 7.19 the phrase is used in the sense of 'tell the truth'.

For vs. 13, 14, cf. Rom. 13.1–7. The Christian is a free man (16), a citizen of heaven (Phil. 3.20), and yet he is to accept the world-order around him. That is because it is based on law, and the apostles knew that bad law is better than lawlessness and chaos. They would not have regarded the totalitarian tendency to 'legalize' the wrongs it has committed as the rule of law. The difference is that under law one knows what is prohibited, under chaos one is at the mercy of those in power at the moment. The quiet bearing of injustice under the guise of law is always harder than plotting the overthrow of the unjust, but it is also always more effective in the long run.

Later portions of the letter make it clear that Peter knew that his readers might and would suffer for their loyalty to God, e.g. 3.13–17; 4.1, 12–16, but that did not alter the principle. If Christ suffered unjustly, so can we. When Jesus said, 'Give to Caesar the things that are Caesar's, and to God the things that are God's' (Mark 12.17), we often overlook that what is Caesar's has been given him by God. To most believers comes the moment when they have to say to those in authority in the home, the church, the State, 'Here I take my stand; I can do nothing else, so help me God.' When this happens there is suffering and blessing. Unfortunately most of us take our stand on ground of our choosing, not Christ's; then there is strife and division, not blessing. So often difficulties arise because we do not honour *all* men (17); we regard them as potential salvation fodder, but no more.

Thought: God rules in the affairs of men.

Slavery was legal, and God had given His qualified recognition of it by legislating about it. So slaves—not 'servants' (18)—provided perhaps the extremest and most painful example of being subject to human institutions (13). Though little slavery remains in the world today there is much subordination: economic, social, traditional. Sometimes it is good and right, sometimes abhorrent. Whenever the attempt to throw it off is made we discover that where there is no inner freedom, outward freedom leads only to new slavery. In addition, men are discovering that where they are not willing to serve, they will not be served in the hour of need.

It was Christ who came not to be served but to serve (Mark 10.45), so He is the pattern for those who serve. If the slave is willing to serve for Christ's sake, as his God-given vocation, then the sting of slavery has gone. He is also the example for those who suffer injustice and abuse from those who abuse their positions (21–23). Few Christians grasp what a privilege it is (painful, of course) to be allowed to share the injustice Christ suffered.

The RSV margin is correct in v. 24, cf. NEB. Peter here assumes, but does not stress, the death of Christ; it is that which went before and prepared for that death that occupies him. Jesus was not suddenly identified with our sins when the nails were driven into His hands and feet. All that had gone before was part of His self-identification with our sins. He carried them 'to the tree', the burden becoming heavier as He went. While to render John the Baptist's words, 'Behold, the Lamb of God, who takes away the sin of the world' (John 1.29), is to draw out their full meaning, literally he said, 'Who carries the sin of the world'.

Concepts like these throw light on Paul's remarkable statement in Col. 1.24. We cannot share in Christ's atoning work, except to profit from it, but we can share in His sufferings. When we think of His life, we are apt to think of Him living under Jewish law, the law of God, even if distorted by Pharisaic reasoning. We forget that Palestine was under Roman colonial law as well, with all its brutality and frequent arbitrariness.

Thought: Christ is the special Patron of those who serve.

Questions for further study and discussion on 1 Peter chs. 1,2

1. What does the phrase 'exiles (sojourners) of the Dispersion' (1.1) suggest concerning the Christian's proper attitude to the

world and the State? (See **1.17**; **2.11–17**, and collect other N.T. references, e.g. Phil. **3.20**; Rom. **12,13.**)

2. Starting from **2.4,5**, discuss the Christian's responsibility in and to the Church.
3. How can **2.18–20** be applied to modern conditions of employment, with (*a*) a Christian, and (*b*) a non-Christian, employer?
4. In what ways do both this passage and 1 John 3 link together the themes of sinful behaviour and brotherly love?

1 Peter 3.1-7 Marriage

From slavery, and by implication, all similar forms of subjection, Peter passes to marriage. He uses the same word, 'submissive', for the wife as for the slave (**2.**18) and the younger church member (**5.5**). The NEB is correct in the first two cases in rendering 'accept the authority', and this would have been best in the third as well. God has ordered His creation on the basis of authority and subordination, and Peter is calling on us to respect God's order. Relative subordination in this world disappears in a common subordination to Christ, before whom we all stand on the same footing. The difficulty felt in Peter's teaching by many today would in great measure vanish, if we took 'honour all men' (**2.**17) seriously. Not 'obey', but 'honour' is the difficult word for many in the marriage promise.

Some of his readers were women married to unbelievers, Jewish or pagan (1). Peter says it is their lives rather than their words that may win their husbands. Both Paul, in 1 Tim. **2.**9f., and Peter concentrate on the same point. The 'hair-do', the ornaments and the striking dresses, where they are not intended to put the neighbours' noses out of joint, are to boost the woman's ego. In contrast to modern concepts the Church's wedding robe in Rev. **19.**8 (see note) is for the glory of the Bridegroom. The women Peter describes are dressing for themselves, not their husbands. Phillips may be correct in paraphrasing, 'do not give way to hysterical fears' (6). Many marriages are wrecked by deep-rooted fears. If a woman simply trusts her marriage, children and husband to God and does not think she must fight to preserve it, she will find fear vanishing.

When he turns to the husbands, Peter does not rise to the heights of Eph. **5.**25, but he should be understood in the same way. 'With understanding' (NEB) is far superior to 'considerately' (7). It is true of us all that 'we are fearfully and wonderfully made', but this is truer of the woman than of the man. By the time a young husband has really come to understand his wife—and great consideration is needed for this—he will find that she will probably want to accept his authority. If he does not remember that she is his equal spiritually, he will diminish his own spiritual standing and not be able to pray properly (7).

1 Peter 3.8-12   Mutual Submission

Just as in Eph. 5.21,22, Peter sees marriage as only a special case of general relationships. While 'unity of spirit' (8) is created by the Holy Spirit, it is far more than the one Spirit living in us all. If I do not try to find out what my fellow Christian is thinking, I cannot be one with him. If I do not discover what he is feeling, I cannot suffer with him, the meaning of 'sympathy'. 'A tender heart', literally, 'with healthy intestines'; it means a well-balanced reaction to the situation of those I meet. I must neither be carried away by my feelings, nor deal with him purely intellectually. 'The humble mind' enables me to show him the honour that is his by right (2.17) and by the fact that, like me, he is God's child. Should anyone object that too high a standard is being demanded, Peter quotes Christ's own words (Matt. 5.39,44). The 'blessing' we obtain is found in Matt. 5.45. Sometimes we feel that someone deserves an 'ear-ful' of what he is really like ('reviling') or a dose of his own medicine ('return evil'); we should remember Christ's words then (Matt. 5.45,48).

Peter develops the thought of the blessing by quoting Psa. 34.12–16. The two features stressed are a check on one's words, i.e. not reviling, and turning from evil. The blessing is life, good days, and prayers that are heard. When we hear complaints about discord in the local church, lack of love, and unkind actions and judgements, we should do well to look at the one who complains. Very often his own life is an epitome of the things he complains about. We may give him the benefit of the doubt and say he did not begin the trouble, but he has seen to it that the troubles continue.

Thought: If we want others to be different let us set them an example.

1 Peter 3.13-22   Christ's Triumph

It might be argued that self-assertion is necessary in this evil world. 'God cares for those who care for themselves' is a frequently met maxim. Peter makes no secret of the probability that they will have to suffer for righteousness' sake. Apparent defeat will be merely the way to victory. It should be noted, however, that we are far more likely to suffer, if we are zealous for other people to do right, than if the zeal is applied to our own lives (13).

Christ's death combined with His resurrection represents God's greatest triumph (18). In the natural realm ('in the flesh') He was put to death; in the spiritual realm He was made alive—His bodily resurrection is the sequel to, and the consequence of, this, cf. Acts 2.24. In the course of which ('in which') He made proclamation of His triumph ('preached') to the angels ('spirits'; the word is not used of dead men) imprisoned in the days of Noah, cf. Jude 6. They had done their very best to destroy the world (Gen. 6.1-8), and had apparently succeeded, for all but eight persons were over-whelmed by the Flood. To them, and presumably to any other fallen angels awaiting their final judgement, came the knowledge that their utmost efforts had been defeated. The idea that Christ was pro-claiming His salvation to those overwhelmed by the Flood does not seem to play any part here, the more so as they were merely a special case of a common problem (see notes on Rev. 20.11-15).

The transference of thought to Christian baptism (21) is an easy one, but there is much to be said for the theory that this letter represents an expansion of a baptismal sermon. Baptism springs from Christ's triumph, cf. Rom 6.3 f. The Ark was the symbol of God's triumph and saving power in the midst of corruption, and so is baptism. 'Not as a removal of dirt from the body' (21): the 'baptisms' of Qumran were largely an extension of the ceremonial washings of the Temple and of the Pharisees (Mark 7.3 f.) intended to remove physical defilement. Baptism so cleanses the inner man, or represents his cleansing, that 'with a good conscience we can appeal to God' or 'make a pledge to Him for a new life'. The RSV 'an appeal to God for a clear conscience' is improbable, and the other rendering should have appeared at least in the margin.

Thought: The eye of faith sees the Ark, not the flood-waters.

1 Peter 4.1-11
Life in the Last Days

Not the fear of death, but of dying, dogs the feet of very many Christians. Christ's sufferings (1) are His death; so the Christian's death will mean triumph, i.e. 'ceasing from sin'. But in the measure in which he shares Christ's sufferings he will cease sinning, for he places himself by so doing under 'the will of God' (2).

The Jew was notorious among the Gentiles for his refusal to share their meals and junketings, so vs. 3,4 are very strong evidence that the bulk of Peter's readers were Gentiles. It is likely that the AV (KJV) 'abominable idolatries' (3) is preferable to 'lawless idolatry'. We are not called on to sit in judgement on the immorality around us; we have simply to proclaim that there will be a Divine judgement. We do not escape this judgement by death. Though the Christian dead (6) received the common judgement of the flesh, i.e. death, they will live. So for the others there will be the second death (Rev. 20.14).

'Keep sane' (7): 'Keep your heads' (Selwyn). The final failure of man's devices, of which there is so much in *Revelation*, should find the believer untroubled and prayerful. It is particularly in a time of chaos that the basic virtues find their place. Love can be very difficult when all around men are losing their heads. 'Love covers a multitude of sins' (8): this may well be a saying of Christ's. Its meaning is not clear, for it means more than that love veils the sin of others, cf. 1 Cor. 13.7. Certainly where a person is outstandingly known for love, most people are likely to overlook shortcomings that might otherwise be glaring. Even more, true love can turn others to the source of love, so that they may see Him 'covering' their sins by His blood. 'Hospitality' (9); where church meetings were in private houses, and where there was a tendency to move round so as not to draw undue attention to any one meeting place, hospitality in the widest sense could be a heavy burden. 'A gift' (10) can have a wide range of meaning. The one-sidedness of modern church thought is shown by the exaltation of speaking (11), whereas every form of 'service', because given by Christ, ranks equal with it in the right place.

Thought: God gives the strength to use the gifts He has given.

1 Peter 4.12-19   God's Judgement

Judgement begins 'with the household of God' (17). One of the less considered tensions in Christian theology is that between justification and judgement. This judgement may be experienced in three ways. The tension of Rom. 7.24 f. may be intensified by earlier evil living, especially if it was in defiance of the known will of God. Then there is suffering for the failure of the present, e.g. 1 Cor. 11.29–32 and the warnings to the Seven Churches (Rev. 2,3). Thirdly, there are certain things against which we are specially warned, e.g. Mark 9.42 (does a Christian never do this?); Heb. 4.1; 10.26–31. The clue is probably given by 1 Cor. 11.31.

Here Peter is considering the suffering of Christians as members of the Church, rather than as individuals. Because the Church has fallen short and falls short, its innocent members must suffer together with the guilty. Innocent? All too often wrongdoing in the local church has been possible because of the laxity of standards. Neither now nor before the judgement seat of Christ can the Lord be indifferent to ungodly living and low standards (2 Cor. 5.10).

If we suffer through no fault of ours, we should rejoice that the judgements of God are doing their work and that we are permitted to share in the sufferings of Christ (13, Col. 1.24). We must, however, be careful. Experience suggests that when we are most wronged, we have by omissions or commissions often helped to create the situation in which we were wronged. God is not interested in legal technicalities.

'The spirit of glory and of God' (14): here glory, literally, the glory, is the equivalent of the Shekinah, or abiding presence of God, i.e. Jesus Christ, cf. John 1.14. So the phrase means the Spirit of Christ in all His glory and of God. 'Mischief-maker' (15): the Greek word in this form occurs only twice, and its meaning is far from certain. Phillips takes it as 'spy', the NEB as 'infringing the rights of others'; the more usual interpretation is 'busybody'. In any case it means putting your nose in where it does not belong. We are slow to learn that where God wants us to intervene in another's life He will give us the knowledge to let us do it with proper effect.

Thought: God never calls black white!

1 Peter 5.1-5 The Elders

Acts shows us clearly enough Peter as the leader of the Twelve, and equally clearly he never forgot the especial charge laid on him to be a shepherd of God's people (John 21.15–17). This will have been his motive in writing the letter, for there is no evidence that he had ever worked in the area to which it is addressed. So he has a special word of exhortation for the elders in the churches to which his letter was sent. He avoids the word shepherd with reference to himself, except by implication, when he calls Christ 'the chief Shepherd' (4), because in the figurative language of the O.T. the shepherd is the king. It is, however, unfortunate that it has been forgotten that true elders are vice-regents. So important are they that Peter claims no authority over them but simply calls himself a 'fellow elder' (1). Yet he had a claim to be heard. He had witnessed the sufferings of

Christ and had seen the Transfiguration—'the glory that is to be revealed' (2 Pet. 1.16–18).

There are three sets of contrasts: 'constraint', 'shameful gain', 'domineering'—'willingly', 'eagerly', 'examples'; in each case there is a logical and spiritual link. The 'constraint' today comes very often from the failure of the church to realize that the very real spiritual gifts a young man may have do not necessarily qualify him as an elder and pastor. It comes, too, from those who should be pastors, but do not wish to accept the responsibility. The 'crown' is more specifically the victor's crown in the games, cf. 1 Cor. 9.25 and NEB 'garland'.

The principle of authority applies in the church as everywhere else (5), see notes on 3.1. Many of our difficulties today come from the elders assuming that because they have authority they have knowledge, and from a younger generation believing that their far more extensive education implies spiritual maturity. Both sides need 'humility' (5). We tend not to take John 7.15,16 sufficiently seriously. Arguing from what we think Jesus should have known, we attribute His authority as a teacher to His knowledge, while He claims it comes from His Father.

Question: What will become of my work if God opposes me?

1 Peter 5.6-14   God's Certain Care

'Humble yourselves' (6); Selwyn points out that it is really 'Allow yourselves to be humbled; accept your humiliations.' 'The mighty hand of God', whether it acts directly, or through persons and things around us, brings us down. There are few things so disgusting or, perhaps, ludicrous, as a person looking for opportunities to be humble. Where God does it, it should be a cause of praise, for we know we shall be exalted, when we can stand the testing involved. The AV(KJV) of v. 7 is misleading, and so to some extent the RSV, for there is no inner link of meaning between 'anxieties . . . cares'. NEB expresses it better, 'Cast all your cares on Him, for you are His charge.'

That God has a concern for us comes not merely from our being His children, but from our being involved in the rear-guard action that Satan still wages against Him (8,9). The lion is at its least dangerous, when it roars. The hunting lion can be amazingly quiet; the roaring (Amos 3.4) comes when the prey has been secured. So the picture is of a lion trying to do by bluff and intimidation, what it cannot do by stealth and strength. For the idea behind 'the God of all grace' (10) see Phil. **4.19**. Peter does not minimize the power of persecution—after all he had collapsed at the jeers of a servant-girl—but he promises that even if we are shaken by it, God will 'restore' (make good what has gone wrong), 'establish' (set us more firmly on our true foundation), and 'strengthen' (where weakness has been revealed, provide the strength).

Papias, as early as the second century, understood 'Babylon' to mean Rome. It is not likely that Babylon in Mesopotamia or the one in Egypt would have been suggested, had not some wished to weaken the tradition linking Peter with Rome. The mention of 'Mark', who is linked both with Peter and Rome, supports the traditional view. 'She who is at Babylon' is, of course, the church there, cf. 2 John 1,13.

Questions for further study and discussion on 1 Peter chs. 3–5

1. How would you rephrase 3.1–7 to meet modern conditions?
2. List the mutual responsibilities and attitudes which are essential to the proper functioning of the marriage relationship.
3. What reasons for joy in suffering persecution does Peter list (**4.12–14**)? Look up references concerning our Lord's and Peter's attitudes to persecution.
4. What duties and dangers are inherent in shepherding the flock of God, and what are the essential qualifications (**5.1–4**; Ezek. **34**; John **21.15–17**)?

2 Peter 1.1-11 Christian Growth

There is little doubt that Simeon Peter (1, NEB) is correct, cf. Acts **15.14**. If his first letter, cf. **3.1**, was 1 Peter, then this will have been written when the Neronian persecution was reaching its height. This is sufficient reason for the lack of details about the recipients. 'Obtained' (1): inadequate; the word means to obtain by lot or Divine decree, i.e. all personal merit is excluded. There is only one true 'faith'; the gifts that follow it are diverse. The only linguistically valid interpretation of 'our God and Saviour Jesus Christ' is that Jesus is being called God, cf. **1.11**; **2.20**; **3.18**; Tit. **2.13**. For 'grace and peace' (2) see note on 1 Pet. **1.2**; the covenant love and riches of God are constant, but our knowledge of God teaches us to draw on them.

In John **17.3** knowledge and salvation are linked (3). While God may reveal to us individually the implications of salvation (1

427

John 2.26 f.), yet it is a surer method to give us the promises of Scripture (4), which are always greater than our interpretation of them at any given time. The promises do not deliver us from corruption, but stir us up to claim deliverance. With vs. 5–7, cf. Rom. 5.3–5; Gal. 5.22 f. 'Virtue' (5): it is a pity that the link with v. 3 has not been indicated, where the word is rendered 'excellence'; the quality is something coming from God. 'Knowledge' is not that human quality condemned by Paul in *1 Corinthians*, but a gift from the Holy Spirit giving us true balance in judgement. 'Self-control' (6) without knowledge and balance is likely to become asceticism or fanaticism; similarly 'steadfastness' without self-control is liable to lead to an explosion. 'Godliness', cf. v. 3: piety (NEB) or devotion to God (Phillips) are preferable; it refers to a visible quality in life, our attitude to God expressed in actions. The difference between 'brotherly affection' (7, cf. 1 Pet. 1.22; 3.8) and 'love' is not made clear. The former probably has more of the emotional about it.

The child that stops growing becomes a monstrosity. When a man stops developing mentally he has taken the first step to senility. This is even truer with spiritual growth, the more so as the purpose of our salvation is that we should become like Christ, cf. 2 Cor. 3.18; 1 John 3.2. 'To confirm your call' (10): the necessity to respond to God's call does not end with conversion.

Question: Have you stopped growing?

2 Peter 1.12-18 The Assurance of Christ's Return

At the time he wrote this letter Peter was already an old man as things were then reckoned. It is not likely that he had had a special revelation of his coming·death (14); it is more likely that he foresaw that the prediction of John 21.18 would soon come to pass. This latter is referred to in v. 15. They would be able to refer to it at any time.

Clearly the difficulty in the minds of those to whom he was writing was not the resurrection of Christ, but that the One who had lived here in humility could ever conquer the world—the dream of the Church in the days of its dominance, that it would conquer the world for Jesus, had not crossed their mind. Indications of this doubt may be traced here and there in *1 Peter*. If Christ could not keep His own from suffering, how could He triumph? So Peter reminds us that he had seen His Divine 'majesty' (16)—the word is not used of men—break through on the Mount of Transfiguration.

428

This had been confirmed by the glory which came from the majesty on high and the voice which acknowledged Him (17). In other words, His earthly poverty and humility had been assumed and were not the expression of His real nature, cf. Phil. 2.5–8. Equally then, the humility and poverty of the Church were a cloak hiding its true nature.

Today, also, every effort is being made to show that the N.T. teaching about the Return of Christ is mere myth (16); it is doubtful whether the term 'cleverly devised' would even be granted to such attempts! We may differ about the how and when, but the N.T. teaches clearly that the Creator of the world came into His creation (John 1.10 f.) and won or redeemed it for Himself. Whatever the future of the world (see notes on Rev. 21,22), He does not abandon His creation to futility (Rom. 8.18–23), but will achieve His original purpose with it. The world, too, is capable of transformation.

Thought: We are to witness the vindication of Christ as Creator as well as Saviour.

2 Peter 1.19—2.3   The Interpretation of Prophecy

We have today a strong and growing stress on religious experience. In so far as this is Spirit produced, it is valid and not to be despised. But even Peter let his experience on the Mount of Transfiguration step into second place behind the prophetic Scriptures, which for him included the *Pentateuch* and the historical books from *Joshua* to *2 Kings*, apart from *Ruth*. 'We have the prophetic word made more sure' (19): the Greek is ambiguous. It may mean as in the NEB margin, 'In the message of the prophets we have something still more certain'. It is not so important, for Peter does not ask his readers to look away from the prophets but rather 'to pay attention' (19). For 'the morning star' see note on Rev. 22.16.

There are certain points to be remembered about prophecy. The oriental 'lamp' illuminated only the immediate surroundings. Prophecy is not that we should know the details of the future, but that we may understand the future, when it becomes the present. Then no prophecy 'is of any private interpretation'; since prophecy came from the Holy Spirit, it must be interpreted by the Holy Spirit. The Church is far from infallible, but an interpretation rejected by spiritual men after due thought and prayer is not likely to be correct. It also means, however, that since prophecy is a unity because it all comes from the same Spirit, we have no right to take a passage and interpret it in isolation from the rest. Our greatest weakness in Biblical exegesis, and not merely in our interpretation of prophecy, comes from our frequent ignoring of this principle. The prophets 'were impelled by the Holy Spirit' (21, NEB). Peter is not denying the very real personal contribution of the prophet to his message, but that it was in any way something thought out and shaped by him.

Yet 'false prophets' (1) there have been, just as there are false teachers. Much in the later prophetic writing is devoted to false prophets; see especially Jer. 23.9–40. The characteristics of the false teachers are that in one way or another they disown their Master (NEB), they are licentious, and they exploit their hearers. The proportions of these vary from false teacher to false teacher, but they are always present. Peter is not thinking of those who do not claim to be Christians.

2 Peter 2.4-16   False Prophets and Teachers

Peter in this chapter largely reproduces Jude 4–16. The humility which is apparent in both his letters probably made him consider that Jude had expressed himself far better than he could.

The remarkable thing about the false prophets and teachers (1) is that they ignore the long list of warning judgements. 'The angels when they sinned' (4): cf. note on 1 Pet. 3.19 f. Clearly this does not refer to Satan. 'Cast them into hell', literally into Tartarus; it is a pity that RSV has translated as it has, for hell has taken on the meaning of Gehenna, or the lake of fire (Rev. 19.20; 20.14). Tartarus was the lowest abyss of Hades. The Flood and the destruction of Sodom and Gomorrah left an indelible impression on Israel. 'Lot' (7) is mentioned, as is 'Noah' (5), to make quite clear that these catastrophes were not merely natural events. The deliverance of the only righteous people among those destroyed showed God's guiding hand over all. 'Defiling passion' (10): the presence of false teaching shows itself almost invariably in an ascetic depreciation of marriage or in a denial of its bonds. 'Despise authority': those whom Peter condemns either thought they could prophesy by their own impulse or denied the apostolic authority in the Church.

'They are not afraid to revile' (10); for the comment on this verse and the next see that on Jude 8,9; Peter abbreviates here. By their despising God's order they have sunk to the level of animals (12) and will go to their destruction blindly. 'To revel in the daytime' (13): contrast Peter's indignant comment in Acts 2.15. Work is also part of God's order, not merely a result of the fall (Gen. 2.15).

430

The NEB gets the sense better, 'While they sit with you at table they are an ugly blot on your company, because they revel in their own deceptions' (13b). 'Eyes full of adultery' (14): they are not merely driven by an insatiable sexual urge; it obtains a special relish in its defiance of the seventh commandment. It is interesting that of the three names given in Jude 11 Peter restricts himself to Balaam. He was a true prophet and feared God. But when the price was big enough he listened to money rather than God. Though he would not prophesy falsely against Israel, he was willing to lead him astray (Num. 31.16).

Thought: The false teacher is worse than the atheist. The latter says there is no God and acts accordingly; the former speaks in His name and defies Him.

2 Peter 2.17-22   False Prophets and Teachers

The tragic description continues. The worst about these men is the way they fail those who put their trust in them. Two pictures are used. 'Waterless springs' (17): for the implications, cf. Job 6.15-20. In the drier Mediterranean lands the traveller plans his route by the known springs and wells. If one of these fails, it means, possibly, death. From these men there comes a sound as of abundance of water springing up, but when one comes to them one finds only wind. Then they are 'mists driven by a storm'. On the wings of the storm-wind, a mist covers the parched land which longs for rain. When the sun comes out again, it is clear that all that has come is a humidity that has merely raised false hopes. The sun is hotter than ever and the mist has vanished into nothingness. The proverb quoted in v. 22 indicates that these men had never been changed. They had genuinely been drawn to Christ and had found much in the teaching of His messengers that fascinated them. But instead of submitting themselves to Him as Lord they tried to force Him into their systems and philosophies.

This description will be of value to us only as we first look to see how far we are tainted with the danger. It is so easy to demand that Christ conform to our emotional experiences—and others' also—or to our preconceived ideas of what they should be. If we are truly regenerated persons, this will lead merely to our making true Christianity revolve around an experience instead of Christ. All those who come to us with infallible recipes for blessing or signs of spirituality fall into this category. Alternately, we shall so stress one aspect of truth that the whole picture of Christ becomes distorted, or much truth is excluded from the framework we have so strictly drawn. Most of our sects and divisions are due to this. The great danger is that if we persist in this course, we shall find our sense of our own importance so growing that the Person of Christ grows dimmer and marginal. Finally, we worship not Him but our idea of Him. Once that has happened only the grace of God can set limits to the evil into which we may fall.

When we have judged ourselves, we shall be better fitted to estimate Christian teachers around us. Beware of the man who makes himself the measuring-rod of truth and condemns all who do not conform. Beware of the man who exalts his experience above the Scriptures and who lets the moral law of God sit lightly on him. Beware of the man who seems to have one eye on his hearers' purses. Such men may be all right, but they stand in slippery places.

2 Peter 3.1-7   Scoffers

Peter now returns to the subject of the Second Coming. The very formality of v. 1 shows that ch. 2 was a digression, caused probably by his recent reading of *Jude*. Far more important than false teachers is our attitude to the Return. After all, if our attention is fixed on Christ and His Coming, we are not likely to be led astray by the false prophets and teachers. 'The commandment of the Lord' (2) refers to His statements in passages like Matt. 24,25; Mark 13; Luke 12.32–48; 17.22–37; 21.5–36, with their repetition of the command to watch. 'Through your apostles': the epistles are full of admonitions reinforcing Christ's command. *1 and 2 Thessalonians* make it clear that the Second Advent must have played a large part in Paul's preaching and teaching in Thessalonica, cf. especially 1 Thess. 5.1,2; 2 Thess. 2.5.

There is no reason for identifying the 'scoffers' (3) with the false teachers of ch. 2, though from the nature of their doctrines the Second Advent will have played little or no part in their thinking. 'Following their own passions' (3): cf. NEB 'and live self-indulgent lives'. The future implies that the scoffers are there and will continue, for, in company with the other apostles, Peter regarded the period of the Church as 'the last days', cf. 1 John 2.18; Rom. 13.12. These scoffers were men who wanted to live 'natural' lives bounded by the here and now. The concept of a God who can break into history and transform it is abhorrent to them. They may appeal to science as a justification but their god is man-made security.

432

Peter reminds them that in the Flood there was already a drastic recreating of the earth. His words are a warning against a minimizing of the Flood, but equally to read into them a meaning in conflict with all the evidence of science is foolish. Peter is not giving a new revelation of how *Genesis* is to be understood. Since the Flood, though a destruction, was a recreating, so the fire (7) will be a recreating, cf. Rev. 21.1 (see notes).

Thought: If God broke into human history in Jesus, is there any reason why He should not do it again?

2 Peter 3.8-13   New Heavens and a New Earth

One of the oldest and most enduring delusions in the Church is the assumption that v. 8 gives us a yard-stick by which to measure God's time. Although archaeology has moved the indubitable evidence for the existence of *homo sapiens*, i.e. rational man as the Bible knows him, to before 8,000 B.C.—this is distinct from the claim that man-like creatures existed long before this—there are still many who are working on the basis of a Divine week, the last day of which is the Millennium (Rev. 20.6). Had Peter meant anything like this he would have told his readers to stop thinking about the Second Coming. He means that since God's thoughts are not ours, we cannot interpret the 'soon' and 'quickly' of the Advent (see notes on Rev. 22.6f.). If we grow tired waiting, let us remember that it is for the good of others.

We shall always be plagued by those who insist on finding in Scripture what is not there; it appeals to their vanity. So we are told that v. 10 together with vs. 7,12 refer to the blowing up of the earth by a nuclear explosion. Such an idea has its place in science fiction but not in sober Biblical exposition. The earth is God's, and neither Satan nor men can destroy it. What man's puny A and H bombs have shown is that God can burn up the world by using natural law as easily as He destroyed life on it by water.

The rendering 'hastening' (12) is linguistically possible but theologically an abomination! It is made quite clear in Scripture, cf. Mark 13.32, that the day of the Coming lies in God's sovereignty, as is indeed implied by vs. 8 f. We must therefore follow the margin and NEB in rendering 'earnestly desiring' or 'look eagerly'.

Peter held the universal N.T. hope that this earth had its future in God's plans (13). The 'new heavens' are our atmosphere, not the home of God, see note on Rev. **21.1**. 'Righteousness' is conformity to God's will and standards.

Thought: Time is part of man's nature, not God's. We must learn to live in the present of God's activity.

2 Peter 3.14-18   Life in the Light of the Coming

Peter sets two ideals before his readers. When Christ comes they should be 'without spot or blemish' (14), cf. Eph. **5.27**. We are not called to approximate to some abstract ideal. We are to let the Holy Spirit work out the perfection of what we are. God made us all different, and those differences are preserved in time and doubtless in eternity. It is the flaws and stains for which God is not answerable that are to vanish. Then we are to be 'at peace' (14). Does the thought of His Coming stir any fears in us? If so we are not at peace with Him. Do our circumstances create anxiety in us? Then we do not enjoy His peace, i.e. God's riches in Christ Jesus.

We sometimes complain that there are things hard to understand in the Bible, as though God were small enough to be comprehended by our formulas. Even Peter, the fisherman, found Paul, the scholar, hard to understand at times (16). Where we find such difficulties we should humbly tell God and our fellow men that we do not understand. Not so the proud man. He must find a meaning, even if he twists the Scriptures and deduces doctrines dishonouring to God and harmful to man (16 f.).

Peter's last word is 'grow' (18). That is one of the wonders of being a Christian. We have all eternity to grow in, and eternity will be insufficient to exhaust the wonders of God.

Thought: Beware of controversy, for in controversy we are most likely to twist Scripture to suit our views.

Questions for further study and discussion on 2 Peter

1. What does 'faith' mean to Peter (**1.1,5**)? Compare his treatment with that of Paul and James.
2. What positive lessons concerning the understanding of the Bible can be gained from **1.20** f.? What other Scriptures are relevant to this subject?
3. Remembering the abundance of Christian cults, whose members visit from door to door, what should be (*a*) our attitude towards, and (*b*) method of dealing with, such false teachers?
4. In the light of ch. 3, how should the doctrine of the Second Coming affect our living?

There is such a striking similarity between the introduction to this
letter and the introduction to the Fourth Gospel (John 1.1-18) that
it seems fairly certain that the letter was a covering document for
the Gospel or that it was written shortly afterwards to develop certain concepts in it. The Gospel was written 'that you may believe
. . . and that believing you may have life' (John 20.31), and this
letter 'that you may know you have eternal life' (5.13). So the Gospel begins with the Word (John 1.1), and this letter with the Word
of life (1), because by experiencing Him, Christians have come to
know the One who has brought life (John 1.4).

Verse 1 amalgamates John 1.1 and 14. The one controversy in
the fourth and fifth centuries that never received a satisfying answer
was how God could become man; there should never have been
controversy, because Matt. 11.27 gave due warning that an answer
would not be found. No one stresses the deity of Christ more clearly
than John, but equally His manhood is as clearly demonstrated.
We have to lean back and try to let the wonder penetrate us. On
the one hand He was 'the Word of life which was from the beginning'
and on the other He was 'looked upon' and 'touched' (1).

When we think of 'eternal', or everlasting, 'life' (2) our tendency
is to stress its endlessness, but for John it is, above all, that which
was 'with the Father.' The presence of the tree of life in Eden,
cf. Rev. 22.2, reminds us that man was not created immortal, but
capable of not dying. Immortality belongs only to God (1 Tim.
6.16), and by giving Himself to us in Jesus Christ, He gives also
immortality.

'Fellowship' (3) means having something in common. Christian
fellowship is not based on common doctrine—that is the weakness
of the denomination based on a detailed doctrinal basis, though this
may be justified in a society which has been formed for a special
purpose—but on sharing a common God and Saviour (3). 'We
are writing' (4): the 'we' is emphatic. It is a letter from one who has
had contact with the Incarnate Word during the days of His flesh
('we' is merely the normal style for letters, now mainly reserved for
newspaper editors, though it is the more appropriate here, for John
knew that all of his aposotolic brothers would have agreed with
him). True unity in Christ produces true joy (4).

*Question: How far do we know true fellowship with our fellow
Christians?*

We saw that fellowship with our fellow Christians depended on our fellowship with God. If there is that in us which God cannot share, there can be no true fellowship with Him. For the antithesis between light and darkness, see notes on Rev. 21.25; 22.5. To understand v. 5 we should think of the effects of a car's headlights, or even more, of a searchlight beam; with them we have either light or darkness; there is no intermediate zone. Man may hesitate to judge another, but for God the issue is clear-cut; a man is either in the dark or in the light. Because God is light, we can know Him and His will, but it involves our laying ourselves bare to the revealing light as well.

We have here a darkness-light parallelism, each on an ascending scale; on the dark side are vs. 6, 8, 10, on the light side vs. 7,9; 2.1. First, we have the man who does not recognize the darkness, i.e. the lack of fellowship with God in which he lives (6). This is followed by the person claiming perfection at any given moment (8), and finally, in v. 10 there is the one who denies that he has ever sinned or shows any of its imperfections (the perfect tense in Greek). It is probable, however, that John is not thinking merely of the man who has persuaded himself that darkness is light and that he is mysteriously right and all others wrong, but also, of the man who in any given position claims complete rightness. With the ascending darkness of sin there is also the increasing power of Christ. In v. 9 we have the need of definite confession of the sin. Finally, in 2.1 we have the awakened sinner calling on Christ to deal with the serious situation in which he finds himself.

The way to fellowship with our brothers is through fellowship with God, but lack of fellowship with our brothers will reveal that we are out of fellowship with God (7). This verse also encourages us to avoid an undue preoccupation with our sins. Unless it is something serious we have persisted in, it is sufficient to walk in the light.

Thought: Concentrate on Christ, not on yourself.

1 John 2.1-6

Jesus Christ Our Advocate

John was an old man when he wrote his letter, so 'My little children' (1) comes appropriately from him. We shall see what he means by 'that you may not sin' when we deal with 3.9; here we content ourselves with the remedy for sin. 'Advocate' is a linguistically accurate rendering of 'Paraclete', a term used in some of our hymns for the Holy Spirit. It is used of the Holy Spirit in John 14.16,26; 15.26;

16.7, and of the Lord Himself here. Obviously the same rendering should be used throughout if possible, for the Holy Spirit is 'another' Paraclete. The NEB does this with Advocate, although here it is placed in the margin. The Paraclete is the One whom one calls to one's side—Latin, *ad-vocatus*. This may be for help, for advice, for comfort, for representation. Behind all these lies the assumption that one hands over one's affairs completely to one's Advocate. He cannot act adequately unless one does. 'Jesus Christ the righteous': the implication of 'righteous' is that He completely meets the Father's standards.

'Expiation' (2): AV(KJV) 'propitiation'. The latter means to appease (God's) anger, the former to make good harm done. Neither is really an ideal translation, for in the N.T. the word and its cognates are used to express the Hebrew word *kipper* and its related forms in the O.T. This, translated atone, atonement, mercy-seat, has fundamentally the idea of covering (of sin). Hence the NEB rendering 'He is Himself the remedy for the defilement of our sins', and Phillips 'the One who made personal atonement for our sins', though not ideal, bring out the inner meaning.

Knowing Him (3,4), cf. John 17.3, is virtually equivalent to walking in the light. Fellowship with God implies keeping His commandments. In addition, if we do hand our affairs over to Christ, it implies that we shall not be concerned with this or that commandment, but that His Word becomes an indwelling power (5). Then John passes over to a more personal expression. Walking in the light can be taken impersonally, but abiding in Him (6), cf. John 15.4–10, indicates the believer's personal link with his Saviour. It is possible to stress Jesus as the pattern for our lives in a way that overshadows His atoning work, but for all that it is an essential part of the gospel.

Thought: There is nothing to fear, if we have handed everything over to Christ.

1 John 2.7-17   The Commandment of Love

Words divorced from events can be very empty things. So it is with our Lord's 'new commandment' (John 13.34; 15.12,17)—the fact that John does not specify it explicitly till 3.11,23, shows the close link of *1 John* with the Gospel. It is not a new commandment, because we find it already in Lev. 19.18. The very question in Luke 10.29 shows how relatively shallow was the way in which it was understood. The moment Jesus linked it with Himself He transformed it, so that it became a new commandment. As the implications of

437

Christ's work became ever clearer in the Church (8), the darkness which hid the implications of Lev. **19**.18 was vanishing. 'He who . . . hates his brother' (9): the linguistic use of the O.T., e.g. Mal. **1**.2 f., and our Lord's teaching, e.g. Matt. **5**.43–48, make clear that no shadow-land is being left between love and hatred. Hatred is quite simply absence of love, and love must be understood in the light of Christ's life. Sin can be so evil, that it is sometimes very hard to hate the sin and love the sinner, especially when he loves his sin. So John makes his words turn on love to one's 'brother' (9–11) in faith instead of to the outsider.

John then gives what should be the characteristics of the developing Christian. To begin with there must be the knowledge of forgiveness (12) and of God's desire that men should be saved (13). The strength and courage of the Christian who has grown to man's stature are seen in his victory over the 'evil one' (13 f.) and his knowledge of God's will. Full maturity is shown by a true understanding of 'Him who is from the beginning' (13 f.), i.e. Jesus Christ. It would be well to compare these standards with much that is stressed today.

Wherever man is organized for business or pleasure without thought of God there we have the world (15). 'The things in the world' are man's works for his glory and pride, and not God's creation. No thing is in itself worldly; it is man's attitude, 'the lust of the flesh and the lust of the eyes and the pride of life', that makes it so. So while experience may show that certain things are dangerous or disadvantageous to the Christian, the vital question to ask is why he wants something, or why he wishes to do it. For Christ's teaching on the subject, see Matt. **6**.19–21, 24–34; Luke **16**.9–13.

Thought: Seek the things that are above, where Christ is.

1 John 2.18-27   The Anointing of the Holy Spirit

The Christian who has learnt how to look on society with the eyes of God is not likely to be misled by those false teachers whom John calls 'antichrists' (18). 'Anti' means 'in place of'; hence, antichrist may mean one who displaces Christ by claiming to be more important, or one who is the outspoken enemy of Christ. The latter is the sense in which we generally use the term and make it equivalent to 'the man of lawlessness' (2 Thess. **2**.3) or the 'beast' (Rev. **13**.1). Here John uses it for teachers who claimed to be Christians (19) but denied that Jesus was God's King (the Christ, 22). Since God is the Father primarily in virtue of Jesus Christ as His Son, and not in virtue of His creation of man, to deny the sonship of Jesus is to deny the fatherhood of God (22).

Scripture must be interpreted in its context. The AV(KJV) 'ye know all things' (20) is based on inferior manuscripts. To every true Christian the Holy Spirit gives an anointing and so he has an intuitive, inner knowledge of certain basic facts—'you all know'. This knowledge is not something that makes teaching and the study of the Scriptures unnecessary, nor does it introduce us to secrets of which the Bible says nothing. It is rather an intuitive knowledge that certain teaching is false (27), cf. John 10.5,27. One of the greatest difficulties for young Christians is when they find this inner light decried and they are virtually forced to assent to propositions which they know to be false. This inner light can easily be distinguished from the intellectualism that challenges established Christian doctrine. It will never deny the Scriptures; if it does, it is not of God.

It should be specially noted that John shows no distress at the fact that these antichrists were once church members (19). He was evidently confident that in the local church where Christ was Lord the false teacher would soon be too uncomfortable to stay for long. The mention of 'the last hour' (18, cf.notes on 2 Pet. 3.3) is intended to bring out that just as Jesus Christ brought the revelation of God to its earthly climax, so also it brings out the revelation of the climax of sin's rebellion.

Thought: Do not be afraid of being led by the Holy Spirit.

1 John 2.28—3.3 Our Hope

It is of little importance whether a man has much or little knowledge of Christ, whether his spiritual growth has been fast or slow. If he is abiding in Christ, the Spirit of Christ (cf. 1 Pet 1.11) is doing His transforming work in him, and he will welcome the returning Christ with all the simplicity of the child. It is the Christian who has chosen his own way that will 'shrink from Him in shame' (28), for the emptiness of his character will at once have become apparent. In v. 29; 3.7, we have one of the most important principles of the Christian life. We can teach correct doctrine to a parrot, but correct life comes only from the Holy Spirit.

Through our misunderstanding of the use of Father for God— see note on 2.22—we have largely lost the thrill of being able to say 'Father' to God, as indeed is revealed by so many of our public prayers. 'Children of God' (1) reflects Hebraic thought and implies that we reveal His character. We have become so hypnotized by correctness of doctrine that we fail to remember that it is correctness of life that matters. Since the world did not understand the Son of God, we cannot expect it to understand His sons and daughters, cf. John 15.18 f.; Matt. 10.24 f. There are very few who can predict the development of the child by looking at him; so it is with the Christian. There is little point in speculating about the transformed resurrection body; what is important is that we shall be like Him, 'like God in Christ' (Westcott), of the same nature. No wonder the one who has not allowed the Holy Spirit to do His work 'will shrink from Him in shame'.

No one can purify himself in the first place. That must be done by Christ as we trust in Him. But once we have been purified we can keep away from that which we know will defile us. The little child hauled out of the coal bunker cannot clean itself up, but it can keep away from the coal in future. No wonder John can extol the love of the Father. He who has really been gripped by this hope is not likely to be worried by worldliness. The glory of Christ causes the best of man's dreams to grow pale.

Thought: If you do not want to be like Christ, be assured that His likeness will never be forced on you.

Questions for further study and discussion on 1 John 1.1–3.3

1. What is the real basis of Christian fellowship? See 1.7; 1 Cor. 1.9; Phil. 1.7; 2.1; Tit. 1.4.
2. Consider the place given to keeping commandments in the Christian life.
3. With the help of a concordance study the occurrence of the word 'world' in the N.T., and determine its various usages. How will our understanding of this word affect our daily living?
4. What is the relationship between the abiding of God's Word in us and our abiding in Him (ch.2)? Does the former make the latter automatic?
5. In view of 3.2 f. what place should the Second Coming have in Christian proclamation?

1 John 3.4-10   The Reborn Man Cannot Sin

'Sin is lawlessness' (4): this does not mean that it is a breach of the law of Moses or of any specific command, cf. Rom. 5.13 f. Sin is the setting up of oneself as one's own law and authority. 'It is the assertion of the selfish will against a paramount authority.'

The distinction between 'sins' and 'sin' (5) is vital to our understanding of the passage. Sins are the result of an inner principle of sin. The knowledge that Christ has borne our sins reconciles us to God, but our coming to Him and being reborn implies a treatment of the root rebellion of sin. One cannot abide in Him, or even know or see Him and remain rebellious against the law of God (6). The one 'born of God' (9)—the verb is perfect, i.e. the life continues and develops—will not continue in rebellion against God. Furthermore this birth means that something of 'God's nature' has been implanted in a person, so it is impossible that he should be in rebellion. But John fully shares Paul's attitude expressed in Rom. 7.7–25. The vanishing of the old nature awaits Christ's coming (3.2), and so falling short is bound to continue (1.8). See also 5.14–18. That this is the correct interpretation is seen by the fact that John sees sin particularly in two things: the consistent failure to try to achieve God's standards ('whoever does not do right'), and to 'love his brother' (10), in other words, it is a question of attitude rather than acts.

Human thought naturally expresses itself in alternatives, in either . . . or. Either a man is a sinner or sinless. Divine truths normally express themselves in both . . . and, or neither . . . nor. It is the latter we are dealing with here. Regenerate man is neither sinless nor a rebel against God. If a man is in rebellion against God, he should not expect his claim to be a Christian to be taken seriously. If we find him falling short of God's will, provided he does not deny the fact, it is rather a testimony to what God has already done.

Thought: God transforms; He does not force His children into a mould.

1 John 3.11-24   Love in Action

While 'that we should love one another' (11) represents the goal of the message rather than its terms, we may well ask how far this could be affirmed of the normal presentation of the gospel today. Though none of those who reads this is likely ever to murder another, Christ has warned us that anger and insult rank along with it in God's sight (Matt. 5.22). So many of us criticize, impute motives, quietly stand in another's way because his life is an implicit criticism of ours, and his acts are more clearly blessed than ours (12). We should not wonder if the world hates us (13); indeed the wonder should be, if it does not. But what are we to say of the petty hatred and spite of our fellow Christians? We have to hold in spiritual balance the truths

441

that hatred, i.e. lack of love, is murder (15), and that love is not a natural thing but the result of rebirth (14). The love John is writing about is Christ's love (16; **4.**19). 'He laid down His life' (16): the translation is unsatisfactory. He gave up His self and this culminated in death (Phil. **2.**5–8). Similarly, we have to give up our selves; whether this ends in premature death—unlike Jesus we have to die!— or not depends entirely on God's will. 'The world's goods' (17): the NEB is more likely to be correct with 'enough to live on' than Phillips with 'the well-to-do man'. The giving out of our superfluity is taken for granted; it is the lowering of our own standard of living that is being considered. Note, too, that John is not writing about turning away the beggar, but of responding to what our eyes have seen. Love sharpens vision.

The fruit of love is confidence (19; **4.**18). The Greek of vs. 19,20 is far from easy. The sense seems to be that if our heart, i.e. our conscience, condemns us, (there is no suggestion that the condemnation is mistaken), then the knowledge that we love the brethren enables us confidently to trust in the grace of God, who has given us new life, for He is greater than any shortcoming of ours. On the other hand we do not have confidence for unfettered asking (22) until the voice of conscience is satisfied (21), for we could be asking amiss. The summary of the O.T. law (Mark **12.**29–31) is here rephrased as trust in Jesus Christ ('believe in the name') and love of the brethren (23). There is a double abiding. Our abiding in Him depends on our doing His will. His abiding in us is by His Spirit (24).

Thought: Tragic is the plight of the man who resists the urge of the Spirit to unite him to Christ.

1 John 4.1-12 Love is Supreme

At the end of ch. 3 John mentioned the Holy Spirit for the first time, even though He is implicit in a passage like **2.**20. The reason immediately becomes obvious. Then as now there were those who preferred the 'gifts of the Spirit' to the more costly 'fruit of the Spirit'. They might not show much love, but they did display spiritual gifts, in this case prophetic (1). John did not deny the fact of spirit activity, for there are spirits other than the Holy Spirit (1). The acknowledgement of the Incarnation was a sure test (2), for apparently it had brought the spirits in a special way under the control of the name of Jesus Christ (Mark **16.**17; Acts **19.**13). 'The spirit of antichrist' (3): see note on **2.**18. Stress on these phenomena, even if they are superficially harmless and orthodox, deflects attention from Christ. Their attractiveness is that 'they are of the world' (5), i.e. they appeal to the natural man. Ultimately, we may know the validity of a teacher's message by those whom he attracts (6).

John then dismisses these people by returning to the subject of love, the primacy of which remains absolute, cf. 1 Cor. **13**.1–3, and it is the one certain test of a man's standing before God. Snaith in writing of the love of God in the O.T. has called it election love, because it is always seen in action. So here, too, the love of God is characterized by God's sending (9), cf. John 3.16. God's love is always prior and basic (10). One of the basic stresses in *Hosea* lies just here. Since God had included all Israel in His covenant love, for one Israelite to wrong another was to deny the relation of covenant love that God had set up. 'Love me, love my dog' is a down-to-earth version of what is being stressed here.

It goes further. 'No man has ever seen God' (12): we know Him by what He has done for us, above all in Jesus Christ, in whom He became visible, and by what He has worked in our fellow men. So long as our love to God is a matter of feelings towards Him, or even expressed in the living of a moral life, it is a static love. Once it shows itself in action towards those whom God has loved, it 'is perfected in us'.

1 John 4.13-21 God is Love

At this point John pauses and picks up some of the strands of his message. Verse 13 looks back to 3.24; v. 14 to **1**.2; **2**.2; v. 15 to 3.23 f. The basis of everything is that the Father sent and the Son saved. We accept this in our confession of Jesus as the Son of God, and to us the proof of this is the possession of the Holy Spirit.

'Thus we have come to know and believe the love which God has for us' (16a, NEB): the climax of our union with God is a fusion of experience and faith, not concerned with abstract theology but with the expression of God's love, not merely to me, but also to others.

A new section begins with 'God is love', cf. NEB. We may not qualify this in any way, but equally we may not preach it to those who have not experienced it. Since it is an abstract statement, we must make it concrete in Christ and in our own lives, otherwise men will interpret it by their own concepts of love. Where man and God are linked in love, the love of God flows to man, and through him out to his fellow man and back to God, thus causing 'the day of judgement' (17) to take on another aspect. Even in this world we show by our love that we are like Him. To those who are strangers to God, or who have just come into living contact with Him, we have to bring 'theologies of the atonement' to demonstrate that Christ's death was more than just the tragic death of a very good and noble man. Caught up in the sphere of love both doubts and fears vanish.

'There is no fear in love' (18) does not exclude the possibility of God's discipline or even of the tendency of the old nature to shrink back. 'Punishment' here is almost fear of the consequences, for it is retributory punishment and not discipline, cf. Heb. 12.5–11, that is being considered. In God's love this is excluded for those who are linked to Him by the bonds of love. There is not even the fear of our love breaking down, for it is His love (19). Man's love can discriminate, God's does not, so to hate my brother is to make a mockery of the love to God I claim (20). In any case my attitude towards the one I see daily is a sure token of my attitude towards the One I have never seen.

1 John 5.1-12 The Three Witnesses

'Christ' in Greek is not a proper name but a title, and a most unusual one for John's contemporaries. The challenge is to believe that Jesus is God's Messiah, i.e. His King and Representative. Once again we have the stress that love is a relationship within the family (1). As such it is not primarily emotional but derives its nature from God. If we have the right relation to God and 'obey His commandments' (2), our love to God's fellow children will look after itself, because obedience is a sign of our love to God. Obedience is 'not burdensome' (3), because we share a common character with God, cf. Matt. 11.30. Yet we may never think that the Christian life is something merely automatic. There is the continuous conflict with the world, which demands the continued use of 'our faith' (4), which must give Jesus His full position (5).

The verse numbering of RSV hides the fact that v. 7 of AV(KJV) has been omitted, certainly correctly. The statement about the three witnesses in heaven is found in Latin sources in the 5th century, but no Greek manuscript before the 13th century contains it. With its omission we find the justification for our confession of Jesus as the Son of God. John's thought is hard to follow in detail, and there is point in Law's view (*The Tests of Life*) that we have 'a summary . . . intended to recall fuller oral exposition'.

While 'water and blood' (6) have some relation to John 19.34, the different order shows that primarily it refers to His baptism and

444

death. In contrast, the reference to the Spirit is in the present and must refer to His witness in the Church. So the 'three witnesses' (8) are the Spirit (mentioned first!), Baptism and the Lord's Supper. The blessing on the sacraments, when rightly used, from generation to generation, shows that God has approved of them, and so the three are God's testimony (9). Where men accept God's objective testimony, they receive a subjective inner testimony as well. Men may disbelieve us with impunity, but to disbelieve God is to charge Him with being a liar. To believe is life, to disbelieve is death (12).

Thought: In your witness do not place yourself between God and man.

1 John 5.13-21   Sin unto Death

In the concluding section of the letter, John brings together a number of his main points. Certainty of salvation ('eternal life') is not a necessity, but it certainly makes the Christian walk easier and more triumphant (13). When we love (3.21-23) we shall know the will of the Beloved, and so we shall ask according to His will and obtain it (14). Neither need we wait for the visible answer (15).

It is a pity that the RSV and NEB do not keep 'a sin unto death' (16 f.), for as Westcott points out, the Greek means 'tending to death' —only God can ultimately classify sin. John is writing about believers (16), and the Roman Catholic concept of mortal sin, i.e. one that will bring a man to hell, if not repented of, has no Scriptural justification. Especially in the light of 1 Cor. 11.30 there is no reason why we should not take death and life literally. All sin within the Church is unspeakably serious for it mars the witness of the body of Christ. In the story of Ananias and Sapphira we have God visiting such persons with death (Acts 5.1-11). Paul envisages the notorious sinner as handed over to Satan for the destruction of the flesh (1 Cor. 5.5). Because of the serious lack of discipline in the Church, we seldom see John's teaching being applied, but this does not alter God's attitude towards the sin of Christians.

The mention of this possibility of sin causes John to stress once again that it is really a contradiction in terms (18). The combination, however, makes clear that we must regard the state of not sinning as the normal, not as the impossible. The child can deny his parentage, but cannot undo it.

Because there was a time when it appeared that the Church had Christianized Europe and many of its colonies, the distinction between the true Church and the world became blurred. It remains

445

true, however, that the world (see note on **2.15**) is always in opposition to God, and whether it knows it or not, under the control of Satan.

'To know Him who is true' (20): cf. Rev. **19.11**. There 'reliable' is the better rendering, but here 'real' (NEB) is perhaps best, for it is contrasted with 'idols' (21). The Greek word implies an image without inner reality, or a shadow. God is real; man's desires are vain shadows.

Thought: 'On Christ, the solid Rock, I stand.'

Questions for further study and discussion on 1 John 3.4–5.21

1. Starting from **3.4** collect and analyse the Biblical descriptions of sin. What do these teach us about man?
2. In the light of **3.16b** (cf. Acts **20.24**; Phil. **2.30**; Rev. **12.11**) how can we express the radical character of Christian love in our present environment?
3. In **4.2** John goes beyond the simple test of 1 Cor. **12.3**; do we need a more elaborate test than John's in the present-day Church?
4. What does it mean to have victory over the world (**5.4**)? Look up 'overcome' in a concordance.
5. Does the Bible make any excuses for unbelief? How should our answer to this affect our evangelism?

2 John 1-6   The Primacy of Love

Neither contents nor tradition give any idea of the date of this short letter, or of its recipient. The style suggests a date near that of *1 John*. If that is so, the worsening position of the Church in the Roman empire would explain its essential anonymity.

'The elder' (1): cf. 1 Pet. **5.1**. John is not claiming apostolic authority. 'The elect lady': the position might explain the omission of the name, but contrast 3 John 1. The use of the same term in v. 13, however, suggests strongly that a personified local church is intended. This is strengthened by his statement that all who know the truth share his outlook. 'The truth' (2) is, of course, Christ, cf. John **14.6**. 'Grace' (3) is God's free covenant love; 'mercy', or better, 'compassion', is His understanding of the Church's position and weakness as it faces the increasing hostility of the Roman power; 'peace' is the inner quiet from having all the resources of God at one's disposal.

'Some of your children' (4): this otherwise strange remark becomes clear, if we understand it to mean that John had met some of the recipient church's members when they were on their travels. In this case it does not imply that the others had lapsed. John was living at a time when false teachers were rife, and so the churches were making their first steps towards tighter organization and formulation of doctrine, to exclude them. John approves, but he sees the danger. So he urges that first things be placed first, i.e. love. Where there is true love the false teacher will find himself ignored. 'That you follow love' (6): if this were the correct translation it would mean seeing Jesus as the personification of love. The AV(KJV) 'that ye should walk in it', is, however, correct, or as expressed by the NEB 'to be your rule of life'. Since it is Divine love John is writing about, it is neither weak nor sentimental. It will not compromise nor call evil good, nor false true.

Thought: Love is a soil in which falsehood cannot grow.

2 John 7-13   Plague Carriers

For v. 7, cf. notes on 1 John 2.18; 4.3. In one way or another the false teacher tries to diminish the importance of Christ in order to stress his doctrine. Whenever anyone suggests that his views should take priority in a Christian's life and thinking, he has become an antichrist. Unbalanced doctrine, even if not positively false, leads to unbalanced thought and action, and this will lead to an unbalanced reward, i.e. something will be missing (8). 'Anyone who goes ahead' (9): Phillips gets the meaning excellently with, 'The man who is so "advanced" that he is not content with what Christ taught.' Where true love exists, there will be the willingness to believe that God's love has revealed all that is necessary, and that, in any case, ideas that only puzzle my fellow Christians have no real place in Christian teaching. We generally assume they are too uneducated, too conservative, too unintelligent (how loving!) to understand; love would suggest that it is their spirituality that makes them turn from my ideas. The refusal of greeting (10) shows that John is not writing about the casual stranger, whose views would be unknown, but about the known teacher claiming the right to propagate his views. To receive him would be as senseless as welcoming the carrier of plague or other major infectious disease. Probably John was thinking of certain teachers going round the area, but he did not wish to put too much on paper, lest the letter fall into the hands of the authorities. The man who has given himself to the perversion of truth will also twist the fact that I have given him hospitality, and will claim that my action has given him a testimonial of respectability.

It is not always wise to write too much. Very much harm has been done to Christian work in the mission field and in lands hostile to Christianity by enthusiastic reports that have fallen into the wrong hands. So John was prepared to leave what else was to be said until he could visit the church to which he had sent his warning.

Question: Do my pet views enhance the glory of Christ?

3 John 1-8   A Hospitable Home

There are no grounds for separating this short letter widely in time from *1* and *2 John*. In other words it was probably written towards the end of the first century. 'Elder' (1): see notes on 2 John 1; 1 Pet. 5.1. The apostles were authorities on doctrine, but they could not impose their will on an already established church. John writes with the authority due to the senior elder of the church in Ephesus— at least so tradition says—but that does not give him power over another church. 'Gaius' was a common name at the time. Three or possibly four other men of that name are mentioned in the N.T., and we can hardly identify him with any of them. The salutation suggests that he may have been ill, and even that he may have been involved in some difficulties. John had no doubt of his spiritual state. Gaius may well have been a convert of John's (4). 'The truth of your life' (3) does not refer to doctrinal purity, but to a harmony between words, actions and character.

Here we have the opposite of 2 John 10 f. For reasons connected with Diotrephes (9) the church in which Gaius was a member had not welcomed wandering preachers as they should. Gaius had evidently taken them in and been taken to task by the church for so doing. John expresses the hope that he will so do again (6), for they refused to accept any form of payment from the 'heathen' to whom they had preached. The obvious distinction between them and the false teachers was that they were not seeking to influence the church at all; they were missionaries to the heathen around. The regulations of Matt. 10.5–13 could apply only partially because they were preaching, not to God-fearing Jews, but to idolatrous pagans. If it is asked

448

why the church that sent them out did not provide for their needs, it may be suggested that it was often inadvisable for such travellers to carry much money. Until the local synagogue rejected Paul's teaching, he could rely on Jewish hospitality, but those days were long past.

Thought: We do not have to preach to share the preacher's work.

3 John 9-15 The Church Dictator

The trouble in the church was due to Diotrephes (9), 'who wants to be head of everything' (Phillips). No false doctrine is attributed to him; it was simply that he felt he had to have a finger in every pie. It is not clear whether the 'something' John had written to the church was a protest to the church for the way it had behaved or a few lines commending the travelling preachers. Since he is not likely to have written so lightly about a formal protest, it was probably the latter. Diotrephes probably objected to the fact that the letter had not been addressed to him personally and that he had not been consulted in advance. He will have had no objection to the preachers as such.

Diotrephes was not yet a bishop; they developed later. His authority was limited, and the only way he could counteract John's lines of commendation was to slander him. This has remained to this day one of the most effective ways of undermining true spiritual authority. There can be little doubt that the NEB is correct in v. 10 with 'and tries to expel them from the congregation'. There is no evidence that Gaius had been excommunicated, though Diotrephes would doubtless have been pleased to get rid of him. While John could not order the church about, he had the right to expose what had happened, when he visited the church. The 'authority' (9) which Diotrephes had not recognized, was to commission the preachers. 'Demetrius' (12) had probably resisted him and been bitterly attacked.

Diotrephes has always been in the church, and has probably done more harm than false teachers. There is always the willingness to let the 'willing horse' carry more than his share of the church burdens. This, of course, robs the less gifted of their opportunities of service. Sometimes the 'willing horse' is motivated purely by the spirit of service; then he normally has a break-down. Sometimes it is the drive to get his nose in everywhere. If this is allowed, the day comes when he is felt to be

449

indispensable and he becomes a dictator. Then he grumbles because no one seems willing to pull his weight!

Thought: 'Through love be servants of one another' (*Gal.* **5**.13).

Jude 1-7   There is Judgement on Godlessness

The bulk of this short letter is reproduced in 2 Pet. **2**, and the notes on that chapter should be referred to. In our study of it we must remember that we are dealing with two phenomena which need not be linked. It is a pungent attack on men who, while genuinely attracted to certain features of Christianity, had no real claim to the name. Today they are represented by some of the modern cults and certain theosophical groups. Then they represented a widespread antinomian, anti-moral movement, which was not confined to Christian circles, though they found the rapidly growing, enthusiastic groups a useful base. Such an outlook is sweeping over us again today, but for the most part it has no interest in Christianity, or the churches.

Jude, cf. Mark **6**.3, is Judas or Judah, the third of Jesus' brothers; apart from this letter nothing is known of him. Hegesippus tells us that his grandsons were brought before the Emperor Domitian (A.D. 81–98) as members of the House of David, and hence possible rallying points for Jewish disaffection. When he found they were mere peasants, he sent them home. The NEB gives the sense better in v. 1, 'to those whom God has called, who live in the love of God the Father and in the safe keeping of Jesus Christ.'

Jude had been wanting to write to his unnamed readers when a sudden danger made it necessary (3). 'To contend': there is no necessary connection with physical fighting in the word. 'Once for all': hence new ideas and revelations just cannot be true. These men (4) found acceptance in Christian circles by hiding their views at first. The foretelling of their coming is found in passages like Matt. **24**.5,24. 'Our only Master and Lord': Master is a strong word, used in 1 Pet. **2**.18 for a slave-owner. Only here and in 2 Pet. **2**.1 is it applied to Jesus Christ, to show how wicked their action was. Their denial was by a life and teaching completely contrary to His.

He said their doom had been foretold (4), and this he demonstrates by listing some of the judgements on similar men in the past. As Paul makes clear in 1 Cor. **10**.6–8, one of the chief sins of the Israelites in the wilderness was immorality. We

450

know from Jewish writings that 'the angels' (6) were above all those mentioned in Gen. **6.**2,4, cf. note on 1 Pet. **3.**19 f. On the basis of Gen. **19.**4–11, it is assumed in Jewish tradition that the sin of Sodom and Gomorrah was above all unnatural vice, though this is hardly borne out by Ezek. **16.**49 f. 'Eternal fire' means fire that blotted out the cities for ever.

Thought: The best way of contending for the truth is living it.

Jude 8-16   The Ungodliness of the Ungodly

Jude calls the doctrines of these teachers dreams (8); they had no solid basis. They degraded the human body, ignored authority ordained by God and insulted those to whom God had given glory by the position He had granted them. One feature of Jude is his familiarity with Jewish apocalyptic and pseudepigraphic writings. In v. 9 he quotes from *The Assumption of Moses*. It is immaterial whether it is factual; this is how one should behave in the presence of God's great officials. Satan acted as a sort of public prosecutor, cf. Job **1.**6–12; **2.**1–6; Zech. **3.**1–5; Luke **22.**31. These men had destroyed their higher nature by their dreams, and so they had become like animals to be destroyed by their passions. Cain committed murder because his brother's life rebuked his (see note on 1 John **3.**12). For Balaam, see note on 2 Pet. **2.**15; he was willing to flout God's will for money. Korah rebelled against God-given authority (Num. **16.**1–35).

'These are blemishes on your love feasts' (12): this is the way it is taken in 2 Pet. **2.**13, where an almost identical Greek word is used. There is, however, much to be said for taking the word here as meaning 'hidden reefs', hence Phillips 'these men are a menace'. The picture is of them sitting in the love feasts of the local church threatening the spiritual life of those around them by their conversation and selfish conduct. Like 'waterless clouds' they have a promise of good things but give nothing; 'fruitless trees in late autumn' will bear no fruit, cf. Mark **11.**12–14,20, and none in the future because they have no roots. The 'sea' (13) is the O.T. symbol for chaos and lawlessness, cf. Isa. **57.**20. The 'wandering stars' are probably comets.

In vs. 14,15 we have a quotation from *The Book of Enoch*, a Jewish pseudepigraph. There is no importance in the fact that this is an extra-canonical book, for Jude could have easily found similar statements in the canon. The tense is the prophetic

451

perfect, i.e. that foretold is so certain, that it can be described as though it had already happened. It was the constant use of 'ungodly' that commended the passage to Jude. They were 'loud-mouthed boasters' with small people, but flatterers of the great (16).
Thought: Jesus Christ died for these people also.

Jude 17-25   Our Defence against the Godless

Such predictions had been given by the apostles—Jude does not claim the rank—quite frequently; this is the force of the tense in v. 18. Examples are Acts **20**.29; 1 Tim. **4**.1; 2 Tim. **3**.1 f.; **4**.3. We have the general sense of them in v. 18. One of the characteristics of such people is the divisions they cause (19). Since they care only for themselves, they care nothing for the unity of the Church. Though they are completely unspiritual, they claim to be spiritual teachers.

The defence against such teachers is fourfold. Our faith (20) is only the beginning. We have to build up a rounded Christian character on it. Then we must 'pray in the Holy Spirit', cf. Rom. **8**.26 f. This means that we must allow God's Spirit to mould our thoughts, cf. 1 John **5**.14 f. 'Keep yourselves in the love of God' (21): the love of God is always there, but we can cut ourselves from it by sin. A thin blind can shut out the sunlight. Above all, there is the waiting for the return of Christ. It has a strange power to bring matters into true perspective, and inspire us to try to save others.

The final doxology faces facts squarely. On the one hand is man in his imperfection, who can be helped to stand when he is in danger of falling, and kept unblemished though not perfect; on the other hand is God with all glory, majesty, dominion and authority. The two are linked by Jesus Christ, the God-man.
Prayer: Lord, teach us to see Thee in Thy greatness and man in his smallness.

Questions for further study and discussion on 2 and 3 John and Jude

1. At least one modern commentator has criticized the stern attitude of 2 John 9-11: do you think this attitude ought to be practised today? If so, how?
2. What was there about Gaius that especially called forth John's love for him (3 John 1)?

3. Study the N.T. teaching on Christian hospitality and support (3 John 5-8).
4. How should the local church deal with a modern Diotrephes? What does the N.T. teach on church discipline?
5. Note the strong denunciations of Jude: what is the right balance between denunciation of sinners and attempts to save them, and how do we preserve it?

Revelation

INTRODUCTION

When it is rightly understood, the *Revelation* is one of the most important books in the Bible. Though it was not the last to be written, it fittingly stands at the end of the N.T., for in many ways it picks up themes, which have their start in *Genesis*, and brings them and others to a focus.

There are three main recognized methods of interpreting the book, though each is capable of almost infinite subdivision. The Praeterist sees the whole book, except the final couple of chapters, as referring to and fulfilled in the time in which it was written. The Historicist sees the history of the Church depicted in broad outline from ch. 4 onwards. The Futurist considers chs. 2,3 to be an outline of Church history, while everything from ch. 4 onwards is still future. The first two are obviously inadequate, the third must wait for the future before it can be judged, but its treatment of chs. 2,3 does not give us much confidence in its attempts to peer into the future. Best is to accept the opening words as a guide and to look on it as 'a revelation of Jesus Christ'. These notes adopt this method, though the obviously future elements are treated as such. Only rarely are the three schools of interpretation mentioned.

The language of the book is very largely symbolic. This symbolism is sometimes taken from contemporary apocalyptic writings, more often from the O.T., especially *Ezekiel* and *Daniel*. Both the nature of symbolism and its use are made clear in the notes.

There are no real grounds for doubting that the John who

wrote the book was the apostle of the same name. It is more likely to have been written in the reign of the Emperor Domitian (A.D. 81–96) than in that of Nero (54–68).

Revelation 1.1-8   Greetings from the Triune God

Fundamentally 'the Preacher' was correct in maintaining that 'there is nothing new under the sun' (Eccles. 1.9), for neither the nature of God, of Satan, nor of man changes. Hence the same patterns keep on recurring, though doubtless they may reach a climax before the Second Advent. This justifies the stress on 'the time is near' (3). Jesus is the Coming One, and Christians are intended to be kept awake by seeing signs of that coming in the things that happen. Hence it would be unfair to say that the Praeterist or Historicist was spiritually wrong in his interpretation.

We may look on Jesus in two ways. He is the eternal Word of God (John 1.1–18), but He is also that Word once in time made flesh for us, keeping His humanity for ever. It is these two aspects that are united in this portion; in v. 2 'word' should probably have a capital letter. Before Greek philosophical skill led to our formulation of the doctrine of the Trinity, there was really no other way of expressing this mystery. God as the one 'who is to come' (8) is Jesus Christ (7). If God is the A and the Z, the modern English for 'Alpha and Omega' (8), Jesus calls Himself 'the first and the last' (17), cf. also 22.12 f. For 'the seven spirits' (4), cf. Isa. 11.2; the Holy Spirit is meant, but Hebrew thought allowed each of His attributes to be considered separately; seven is the number of perfection and completeness. There is nothing outside His power and influence.

The Greek of *Revelation* is most unusual and it is likely that we should take v. 6 as in Exod. 19.6, to which it obviously refers. We are not merely under God's sovereignty, the force of 'kingdom', cf. v. 9, but we have also the right of unhindered access to Him, the force of priests, Zech. 12.10 refers only to the Jew, but v. 7 extends the truth to all, for in the sight of God all are responsible for the crucifixion. The expression 'the clouds' (7), means that He comes from God as God's representative (cf. Dan. 7.13).

Thought: The main thoughts of Revelation are so understandable that there is a blessing on its public reading.

454

If, as seems almost certain, *Revelation* was written c. A.D. 90 during Domitian's persecution, John will have been getting on for eighty, when he was condemned to hard labour in the quarries of Patmos. This must have been physically crushing for a man of his age, but though he had no day off and little leisure, he could still be 'in the Spirit' (10). It is unlikely that the Lord's day means Sunday; it corresponds rather to the Day of the Lord in the O.T., meaning the period in which the judgements of God are abroad in the world as He sets up His universal rule. While the visions may perhaps span a long period in the history of the Church, they are looking to and preparing for the Second Coming. 'The seven churches' (11) are literal, and a Bible map will show that they come in the natural order for a messenger carrying the letters; seven, however, indicates that we may expect to find all forms of church experience paralleled here. The force of 'angels' (20) is not clear; it may mean their guardian angels, cf. Matt. 18.10. Neither bishops nor the churches' messengers to John carries conviction.

The description of the glorified Christ is almost completely symbolic. 'One like a son of man' (13), cf. Dan. 7.13—human, yet with heavenly glory. 'A long robe', cf. Isa. 6.1; the length of His garment showed His dignity as king and priest. The 'girdle' by its material showed the wearer's rank; that it was 'round His breast' means that it was not holding up His robe, i.e. He was at rest, His work done. 'His hair' (14), cf. Dan. 7.9; He is simultaneously one like a son of man and the Ancient of Days, depicted with white hair because He has existed from all eternity. The description of His eyes reflects Dan. 10.6; for Him to see means purification or destruction. 'His feet' (15) showed that there had been no defilement from the paths of earth He had trodden. 'Like the sound of many waters' (15), cf. Ezek. 1:24; to stand by a rockbound coast in a storm or a mighty waterfall and let the noise possess you will give the sense. The 'two-edged sword' (16) reminds us of Heb. 4.12 f. The 'right hand' (17) is a symbol of strength and protection, so it also imparts strength. 'I died' (18): better, 'I became dead' (RV), for it refers to a deliberate and voluntary action. 'Hades' (Heb. *Sheol*) is not hell, but where the souls of the dead await the resurrection and judgement.

Question: How great is Jesus to you?

The Seven Churches

of

Revelation

MYSIA

O   2O   4OMiles

– – – Route for delivery of letters

● Adramyttium

Pergamum

Ancyra ●

Thyatira

L Y D I A

Magnesia ●

Sardis

Smyrna

Philadelphia

Ephesus ●

Tralles ●

Hierapolis ●

Antioch ●

Laodicea ● Colossae

Samos

● Miletus

C A R I A

The operative word in all the seven letters is 'I know'. Our knowledge of ourselves is at the best distorted by self-interest, ignorance and prejudice. We see in part and we know in part. Christ's knowledge is complete, objective and constructive. He rebukes so as to restore.

The church in Ephesus, founded by Paul, and later, John's home, had all the makings of an ideal church. It not only did what it should, but continued when the ground was stony and the going hard. It was not influenced by outward appearances, but tested the claims of those who claimed special gifts and position (2, 'apostles'). But though it had not grown weary in well doing (3), the original motives and driving force had gone (4). The rendering 'abandoned' (4) should make us sit up. The AV(KJV) 'lost' may make us think of a very human cooling of ardour, something that is inevitable when love is thought of as mainly or entirely a matter of feelings. But here was the deliberate adoption of a lower standard. The works had ceased to be the outpouring of love and had become essentially legalistic, for the demands of love were proving too costly. Where this happens in a church, it is near spiritual death.

The root of the matter was still there, however, as was seen in their treatment of the Nicolaitans (6), i.e. the followers of one Nicolaus, of whom absolutely nothing is known. Certain popular guesses are best disregarded. That love was there was shown by their hating, neither the heretics nor their teaching, but their works. A teaching, however plausible, which produces the wrong results, must be false; if the results are right, its errors must be marginal. Love will always detect the loveless life, even if it is bewildered by the loveless teaching.

'To him who conquers' (7): to be accounted righteous by faith is only the beginning of a life terminating with the victor's crown of righteousness (2 Tim. 4.8). Eternal life comes through the act of faith, but the rewards through a life of faith. The conqueror knows he will be a member of the Church glorified, the new Jerusalem, where the tree of life is (22.2).

Thought: What excuse will I give Christ for failure?

Photo: Street of Curates at Ephesus

Photo: Amphitheatre at Pergamum

Smyrna was a much smaller town than Ephesus, and so the church there, even though it was probably much smaller, was much more obvious to its neighbours and correspondingly persecuted. As a result they were poor (9), probably in numbers, spiritual gift and possessions, things that so often go together. So Jesus reminded them of His victory (8), and that they were rich (9), for to the poor in spirit comes the guarantee of living under the kingly rule of God (Matt. **5.**3).

Evidently their chief difficulties came from the local Jews. Satan is the accuser and slanderer—the meaning of *diabolos* (Devil). So apparently they had both accused the church and slandered it, cf. Acts 13.45,50; 14.2,19; 17.5–8,13; 18.12 f. For the denial that they were really Jews (9), cf. Rom. 2.28 f. This kind of attitude is far too common among Christians, when they speak of movements they dislike or reject. We picture them as we feel they should be, and we allow report to feature as fact.

Even though it is usual for Church histories to describe the nearly three hundred years of persecution by the Roman authorities under ten major heads, this does not justify us in equating the church in Smyrna with that of the period of persecution. Probably the significance of the 'ten days' (10) is that the Lord of the Church both gives it over to persecution and so controls the persecutors, that He can foretell the time of its ending before it begins.

Because Christ was raised from the dead, physical death should have no terrors for us, even if it can be very painful. The death to be feared is the second, spiritual death (11, cf. Matt. **10.**28). There are Christians who, though they will not be burnt, will as it were be singed. Probably no one knows the full implication of being saved 'but only as through fire' (1 Cor. 3.15). Though there is no suggestion of purgatory in it, it certainly implies more than the loss of one's life-work.

Thought: The poor church enjoys the riches of no condemnation.

Revelation 2.12-17   Hard By Satan's Throne

Pergamum had once been the important capital of an independent little kingdom, but now its political importance was merely a memory and it had been outshone commercially by Ephesus. It remained famous for the temple of Zeus which topped its

458

hill—'Satan's throne' (13). Life was dominated by it, and its priests had early claimed the life of Antipas, who is otherwise unknown. In such surroundings there had to be a clear-cut response to the official paganism of the city, which presented no difficulty to the true believer. More subtle by far was the suggestion that he should recognize the hidden truth in it, an attitude that is all too prevalent in theoretical missionary thinking today. The mention of 'Balaam' (14, see Num. **25.**1–9,16–18; **31.**8,16) shows that the syncretism they were threatened by was a grosser form of Gnosticism, in which the initiates were encouraged to indulge in sins of the flesh to show that they had risen above the restraints of the Law. If you meet such a one, for they still exist, shun him; he is a carrier of spiritual plague. The mention in the same context of the 'Nicolaitans' (15, cf. v. 6) suggests that Nicolaus' teaching was also a Gnostic one, though probably not so gross. When a church permits such things, God's judgement on the sinner will affect it as well (16).

'The hidden manna' (17) in its literal meaning looks back to the jar of manna placed in the Ark (Exod. **16.**33; Heb. **9.**4), the contents of which were controlled solely by God. In the context we have true spiritual secrets, 'the name' and the nourishment, in contrast to the spurious wisdom and secrets of the Gnostics. For some there is always a very strong pull towards the idea that there are special teachings and meanings in the Bible which can be appreciated only by the *élite*. When such teaching is met, we should not stop to ask whether it is true—though it is well to remember that the unprovable has little to commend it—but whether it brings us to closer personal intimacy with God.

Thought: Beware of those who wish to reduce the Bible to a book of doctrine; it is the record of God's mighty acts explained by God's prophets.

Revelation 2.18-29 A Mixed Church

The church in Thyatira was a strange mixture. On the one hand it excelled that in Ephesus in its Christian life and labour (19, cf. vs. 2,3), because their mounting scale showed that their love had not grown cold (cf. v. 4). Had Lydia (Acts **16.**14) perhaps returned home? On the other hand it had gone further than any of the other churches in yielding to the immoral Gnostic teaching around (20).

'Jezebel' was evidently one of those women with pronounced

psychic powers who have a strange influence on otherwise level-headed Christians. The name given her—it is hardly likely to have been her real one—links her with Ahab's wife, a lady who showed sufficient respect for the God of Israel to let her children's names include His and who doubtless attended her husband's worship of Jehovah, but whose real religion was the gross nature worship of Tyre with its deification of sex. In Ephesus and Pergamum it is a syncretistic corruption of Christianity that is condemned, but here the adoption of another religion —'adultery' (22)—which would involve suffering and death for its propagators and followers.

It is impossible to be sure whether 'the deep things of Satan' (24) refers to 'Jezebel's' teaching or to some other form of Gnostic aberration. There are those who delight in penetrating beyond the veiled hints in the Bible about the powers of evil that surround us. At the best their teaching deflects our attention from Jesus Christ, at the worst it defiles heart and mind. There is normally spiritual pride behind it. Have you noticed that the O.T. never describes the heathen religions that surrounded and influenced Israel? Not evil but its remedy should be our interest.

He who conquers in the Thyatiran situation is the man whose heart and mind are satisfied and filled with his Lord. So his reward is that he lives in the hope of the coming dawn (cf. v. 28 with 22.16), and that he shares in his Lord's rule (26,27). This point will be of special importance in our study of ch. 12.

The picture of the rod of iron is taken from Psa. 2.9. We must choose whether we are to be shepherded and defended by the Lord's rod (Psa. 23.4) or broken in pieces by it.

Revelation 3.1-6 A Dead Church

Doctors are given to post-mortems to discover the cause of death, and they are doubtless very often justified. Though we very often indulge in them, post-mortems on spiritual deaths seldom serve a good purpose, and so we have none on Sardis. Today there is much controversy on when a person should be reckoned as medically dead. Though the church in Sardis was dead to all appearance—only the name for a short and honourable past remained—yet the Giver of life could see that a flicker of life still remained (2), and for Him that is a ground of hope.

Many of us would doubtless have told the few who were true (4) that they should come out of a dead church and be separate. However much this may have been historically necessary from time to time—in many cases the loyal ones were thrown out— there is no Scriptural justification for the proliferation of denominations in Protestantism.

Their white garments speak not merely of purity but also of life in the midst of death. For many the thought of names being blotted out of 'the book of life' (5) raises major theological difficulties. This is due to a widespread popular watering down and distortion of what may for convenience be called Calvinist teaching, though Calvin would have disowned it. It is the belief that because a person has prayed certain words, passed through certain routines, etc., he is thereby saved and saved eternally. The only proof of life is life, and the only proof of salvation is a changed life. The blotting out is presumably of that which man had assumed as certain, cf. John 20.23. The man who is content to die spiritually will not be forced by Christ to live, whatever protestations to the contrary he may have made at some time.

It should be specially noted what is said about the works of Sardis (2). Evidently in the sight of man they were admirable. It is possible for a church to get into a routine which can go on very happily even while it is dying on its feet. A great need in the Church today is for those with spiritual discernment. All too often the life of a local church is judged by pure externals, even by its numbers.

Thought: 'Every one should remain in the state in which he was called' (1 Cor. 7.20).

Revelation 3.7-13   Weak but Triumphant

The picture of 'the key of David' (7) is taken from Isa. 22.22; it speaks of Christ's kingly rule within the people of God, here the local church. The deduction from the 'open door' (8) is that there are locked ones as well. Many spend the best years of their lives battering at these and wondering why there is no clear call and blessing. Just as others cannot shut the door Christ has opened for us, so we cannot open the doors He has locked. The door, i.e. the opportunities of service, will always be propor-

Photo: Restored synagogue at Sardis

Photo: Ruins of Laodicea

tionate to our 'power' (8)—whatever we may not be able to do, we can always keep Christ's command ('My word') and not deny His character ('My name') by our lives. For v. 9 see notes on 2.9.

There is no point in interpreting 'the hour of trial' (10) as the great tribulation, the more so as 'the hour of testing' is the true rendering. There are recurrent judgements of God, nation-wide, even world-wide, which reveal the true nature of those who pass through them. The church in Philadelphia had already shown this, and therefore there was no need of further testing: for a similar thought, cf. 1 Pet. 4.1.

We hear too much today of crusades, campaigns and advances, and not enough of 'keep' (10), 'hold fast' (11), 'stand' (Eph. 6.13,14). All too often more ground is lost by erosion in the church than is gained by these advances. The promise to such people, the conquerors, who have 'little power' is that they will become 'pillars' in God's temple (12). Though the promise is for the future, its reality is very often worked out in the present. The strength of the pillar is that it is rock and that it is based on rock. They are rock because the name, i.e. character, of Christ is written upon them. The features of Jerusalem's name that must be intended are 'holy' (21.10) and 'new'. One is holy when one belongs to and is set apart for God. Hence there is no going out. The feature implied by 'new' in Jerusalem and in Jesus' 'own new name' is a disclosure of riches and wonder only half guessed by men.

Thought: My very little becomes very much in Jesus' hands.

Revelation 3.14-22   Too Rotten to be Wicked

The last of the seven churches, Laodicea, stands lower than any of the others, even than that of Sardis. Notice that neither false doctrine nor evil living is affirmed of it. Its sin is that of Ephesus, but on a very much worse level. Ephesus had loved, and its abandoning of its first love was visible to the human eye only by comparision with what it had once been. It is doubtful whether Laodicea had fallen, for it is doubtful whether it had had anything to fall from. To the purely superficial observer it probably seemed to be what it thought itself to be (17). That is why in the introduction the unshakeable validity of Christ's judgement is stressed. As 'the prime source of all God's creation' (14, NEB) 'all things were created through Him and

462

for Him' (Col. 1.16, cf. Col. 1.17 f.), and so He can judge both action and motive accurately.

Both love and hatred make us very sensitive to the views of others; self-satisfaction and lukewarmness lead us to ignore their judgements. The easiest way with such people is to leave them 'to stew in their own juice', but love will reprove, and where possible deflate (19). There are few things more painful than to be entertained out of a sense of duty, so we have the picture of the Lord waiting outside the life of the lukewarm believer (20). Though we are entirely justified in using this verse in appealing to those who have no living knowledge of Christ, we should never forget that it was first said to those who claimed to be Christians. If we shut our eyes and ears to the fact that there are many Christians who have no personal experience of Christ, we only deceive ourselves. God never accepts divided loyalty, and this lukewarmness is the result of it. True fellowship in this life must involve conquering, because we cannot involve Christ in our defeats; they are evidence of the lack of His presence. Conquest means quite simply that the fellowship begun in this life is continued in eternity (21). The one difference is that at this time He transforms the humble life and home I can offer Him into His palace; then He will welcome me to His palace as one who will rule with Him, cf. 20.4,6.

Thought: The cure for lukewarmness is to ask Christ to share every department of our life.

Questions for further study and discussion on Revelation chs. 1–3

1. Note down what is said in 1.5–8 concerning (*i*) the Person of Christ and (*ii*) the Work of Christ. To what extent does this serve as a guide for Christian preaching and teaching concerning our Lord today?
2. Since John was writing to a local congregation, try to relate his message in 2.1–7 to your own local church.
3. 'I know your tribulation' (2.9). Note down facts concerning the persecution of Christians around the world of which you are aware and collect additional information from Christian papers and societies. What positive results can come from this exercise?
4. The loyal Christians in Sardis (3.1–6) were told to 'strengthen what remains'. How would you go about this if you were in such a church? Why were they not commanded to separate from it?

5. If reading 3.14–22 has pointed to the need for revival in your own church, what are the priorities which should occupy its members, beginning at yourself?

Revelation 4.1-8 The Throne of God

It is reasonably certain that the vision of God on His throne introduces us to a new chapter of His activity upon earth, but our identification of that moment in time will not help us to understand the vision better. The once widely held view that 'Come up hither' (1) refers to the Rapture of the Church (1 Thess. 4.16 f.) is based on an inferior text in 5.10, where the AV(KJV) has the first person, but RSV, correctly, the third.

'A throne' (2) is the symbol of rule, cf. Isa. 6.1. No more than in Isa. 6 or Ezek. 1.26 f. is there any attempt to describe God. The transparency (3) symbolizes inner purity. Perfection is indicated by the complete rainbow of one colour, contrasted with the part rainbow with broken colours we see on earth. 'The twenty-four elders' (4) are high angelic rulers; we meet this number elsewhere, e.g. 21.12–14, so they may be the guardians of the true Israel and the Church. For the 'lightning, voices, thunder' (5), cf. Exod. 20.18; Heb. 12.18 ff. Grace does not abolish law but puts it in its perfect context. 'The seven spirits of God'; see note on 1.4. For 'the sea of glass' (6), cf. Ezek. 1.22, 26; Exod. 24.10; it separates the purity of heaven from the sinfulness of earth. It is completely transparent for those who look down from there to us, but us it dazzles, hiding the glory from the eyes of sinful man.

The 'four living creatures' are the four cherubim of Ezek. 1.5–10; 10.15. It is immaterial that they are somewhat differently described, for the description is symbolic, cf. Ezek. 41.18 f., where they have only two faces. They are almost certainly also the seraphim (= the burning ones) of Isa. 6.2, as is suggested by their song. They are the representatives of God's earthly creation. The importance God attaches to it—not merely to man—is shown by their being the guardians of God's throne, or, in the symbolism of the mercy seat, His throne itself. All Biblical revelation is given to man for man, so we have God's estimate of the home He made for man. If God became man on earth, how wonderful must man and man's home be; if He died for man, how fallen must man be! Therefore, lest man who

464

receives the revelation should be proud, the song of the cherubim begins with the declaration of God's holiness, His separation from sinful man.

Revelation 4.9—5.5 The Book of the Future

From v. 9 it is clear that v. 8 is only a summary of the song of the living creatures. Since what follows primarily concerns the earth and the perfect working out of God's purposes for it, the distinctive feature of their song is thanks, in contrast to the worship of the elders; they worship in admiration, the living creatures in gratitude.

As the sequel shows, the 'scroll' (1) is the book of the future. It is in God's 'right hand' to show His control over it; it is written on both sides to show that none can add to it, and it is sealed so that none can bring it to pass before the time. We do not always sufficiently realize that Jesus Christ as the righteous and victorious Man has a special place in God's purposes. It is as Man that He is man's Saviour and man's Judge (John 5.27). Equally man's future history is entrusted into His hands. So, mysteriously, God allows the working out of His purposes to be linked with men. 'God's fellow-workers' (1 Cor. 3.9, NEB) is far more than a pious phrase.

As early as Gen. 49.9 the lion is associated with the tribe of Judah, and traditionally the tribe used the lion on its standard. So when the Conqueror is called 'the Lion of the tribe of Judah' (5), more than a contrast with the following 'Lamb' (6) is intended. He is the fulfilment of the prophecy of Gen. 49.9 in a higher sense than Jacob can have foreseen. 'The Root of David': cf. 22.16, where its meaning is made clear; it is probably based on Isa. 11.10, quoted in Rom. 15,12. David was considered to be the great glory of Judah, with the Messiah no more than a second David. John affirms that not only is Jesus greater than His ancestor David, but that David's greatness was entirely due to the will, planning, and strength of his 'Son', whom he yet called 'Lord' (Mark 12.35–37).

Thought: If Jesus' victory is so great that He is the Controller of the future, cannot we trust Him to control our lives in the present?

The RSV, following the AV(KJV), has sadly missed the force of v. 6. The Lamb was 'in the very middle of the throne' (NEB, Phillips). He was not 'among the elders' but in the middle of the circle formed by them and the living creatures (NEB). In other words, He occupied the central position even before He took the scroll. 'With the marks of slaughter upon him' (NEB) is preferable to 'as though it had been slain', for it makes it clearer that sacrificial death is meant. The lexicons give no support to the sentimental tradition, that we should translate 'little lamb'. The horn is a symbol of strength. In 12.3 and 13.1 the number of horns is linked with Dan. 7.7 and must be interpreted in the light of it. Here the number is clearly symbolic, the perfect number representing perfect strength, just as the 'seven eyes' show perfect knowledge.

'The prayers of God's people' (8, NEB) have such an inherent value, since they are a testimony to God's salvation and power, that they can make the worship of heaven even sweeter. Men admire ability and force; the operative word in heaven is 'worthy' (9,12).

In the dominant Greek philosophical thought of John's day matter was not merely inferior to spirit but was positively a limitation on it, and therefore evil. O.T. thought is radically opposed to this throughout. As soon as the Hebrew Christian was squeezed out of the Church, and the O.T. was increasingly neglected, Christian theology was poisoned by this Greek concept. This earth was regarded as evil and destined to be destroyed once its purpose as a testing ground for man was accomplished. The true Biblical concept was retained mainly by those regarded as sectarians or ignorant. We are told in Gen. 1.31 that God saw that all that He had made was very good. This creation has been in measure marred by human sin, but to assume that this means its destruction is to affirm God's defeat, at least in one sphere. Hence in the worship of the Lamb we find the creation anticipating its deliverance (13, cf. Rom. 8.19–22). So, too, the elders see the goal of redemption in 'they shall reign on earth' (10). This is equivalent to affirming that man will reach the original purpose of his creation, viz. having dominion (Gen. 1.26,28). We shall see this thought taken up again at the end of the book, which ends on earth and not in heaven, or which brings heaven down to earth rather than earth up to heaven.

There are three basic principles in this section which must be grasped. (*i*) All four riders are essentially evil. Yet all four had been written beforehand in the scroll by God. The suffering of the world is not evidence of an imperfect control by God, or even of an imperfect witness by the Church. (*ii*) Nothing happens until the Lamb breaks the seals one by one. The development of human history is in the hand of Christ, and it is all working towards a predetermined end. (*iii*) It is the living creatures, the cherubim, who call on the riders to appear. Though the outcome is suffering for the creation they represent, they welcome it because it means the approach of final deliverance for the world.

Whether or not a closer historical interpretation can be given to the four riders, it is clear that they primarily represent the four main aspects of war. War is the supreme evidence for the fallen state and inner depravity of man, and so writers constantly try to justify and glamorize it more than most other evils. Its roots lie in covetousness, in the desire to possess that which belongs to others, and often in the instinct of self-preservation rooted in lack of trust in God. It always issues in theft on a grand scale with murder as its climax.

Traditionally the first rider is very often interpreted as being Jesus Christ issuing forth on His conquest of the world by the preaching of the gospel. The mention of the bow, which is never used elsewhere as a Christian symbol, should have been a sufficient warning. In addition, symbolism has an inner cohesion, which is denied when we suggest that the rider is Christ at the moment when as Lamb He is opening the seals.

Part of the attraction of war is the repeated belief that an opportunity exists for an almost bloodless victory march. Very often those who yield to this temptation find that they succeed, and the world justifies them, for they seem to guarantee peace over a wide area. In fact, sooner or later, they cause only the bitterer hostilities, which are represented by the second rider. After bloodshed and pillage there follow shortage, rationing and hunger. Then it is only a short step to famine, plague and death, and the inrush of wild animals, over which man should rule.

It is often very difficult to establish causal connections, to be sure which is cause and which effect, or whether both alike are evidence of the depravity of the human heart. It is a fact of experience, however, that the breakdown of society, linked with war and the persecution of God's people, go hand in hand. So after we have seen the horrors of war we are introduced to the sufferings of the saints.

Many interpretations of 'the altar' (9) have been offered. It could be the golden altar of incense, which is not specifically mentioned until **8.3**, but this does not explain why the souls of the martyrs are under it—note that the same word, 'slain', is used for the Lamb in **5.6**, cf. also John **16.2**. It is probably better to understand it as the earth, which has been sanctified to God by the blood of the martyrs from Abel onwards. The abode of the dead is always pictured as under the earth. It is often said that the Second Coming is delayed so that the total number of the elect may be gathered into the Church. Here (11) the delay is so that the total of the martyrs may be complete! The 'white robe' is a guarantee of the verdict, when they stand before Christ's judgement seat, cf. 2 Tim. **4.8**. It would be dangerous to draw conclusions from this passage about the amount the righteous dead know, but it certainly affirms their consciousness, as against those who teach 'soul sleep', and that they are not yet in heaven, even if the altar mentioned is there.

The language of vs. 12–14 was a commonplace in apocalyptic and eschatological literature. If we realize this, it will keep us from attributing scientifically impossible meanings to it. In general the pictures speak of the collapse and vanishing of all that seems fixed and stable in life. Nothing human can endure, if the 'earthquake' is sufficiently strong; the 'sun' and 'moon' not merely give light but also fix the seasons (Gen. **1.14–18**). The 'stars' speak of God's sustaining role (Isa. **40.26**, Psa. **147.4**), and their vanishing is linked with the rolling up of the sky in Isa. **34.4**. Just as the 'island' (14) seems to provide fixity in the midst of the stormy seas, so the 'mountain' seems to be the most stable element in a changing landscape, cf. Pss. **46.2**; **121.1**; Isa. **54.10**; Jer. **4.24**. The 'great men' (15–17) recognize the disasters for what they are, for by that time the gospel has been preached to all nations (Matt. **24.14**).

Though most expositors who take this book seriously will regard this chapter as indubitably future, there are spiritual principles in it which are applicable to all times.

Dan. 7.2 explains v. 1. Long before Abraham the term 'the four corners of the earth' was used to imply universality. The 'sea' is the lawless chaos of the nations, the 'earth' is according to context either Palestine or the lands where God's law is respected, cf. 12.16, and the 'trees' the rulers and leaders. The 'winds' represent unrest and war. Repeatedly in Scripture we find a gap between the pronouncement of judgement and its fulfilment, between disaster as a warning and disaster as final. So it is here, but it is made clear (3) that the delay is less to give those who have had their warning time to repent and more to prepare those of the saints who are to pass through the intensified judgements to come. This preparation is not one of learning how to adopt a protective colouring, but the making obvious of their faith. The seal on their foreheads is where it cannot be hidden. Both seal and the sealed are apparently explained in 14.1.

In *Revelation* the distinction between true Israel and the victorious Church is reduced to a minimum (see note on 4.4). So there is little point in arguing how the Israelite tribes are to be understood. We should probably interpret in the light of 14.1. Of importance is that all God's chosen are represented, in full number, twelve, and in ample number, 12,000. The symbolic number does not suggest that each group must of necessity be equal.

Great play has sometimes been made with the fact that Dan is apparently not included. This is one of the pieces of 'evidence' adduced for the baseless theory that the Antichrist is to come from the tribe of Dan. In fact, it is strange that along with 'Joseph' (8) 'Manasseh' also (6) is mentioned and that apparently in an unnatural position. Dan and Naphtali are generally coupled together, so it is probable that in an early manuscript Dan was read as Man, which was then interpreted as an abbreviation for Manasseh.

Thought: God's choice is perfect and its fulfilment is perfect.

In the earlier part of this chapter we saw the people of God at a given moment, and its number seemed terribly small. But when it is seen as a whole, it is 'a great multitude which no man could number' (9). There is no suggestion here that God's sealing is a guarantee of physical protection. Because the Church is the body of Christ here on earth, it has the privilege of sharing in His sufferings, cf. Col. 1.24; 2 Tim. 3.12. Whatever the details of Christ's Second Coming and the relation of the Rapture to it (1 Thess. 4.17), it is a sad fact that for very many the main stress has been laid on the 'fact' that the believer is not to pass through the great tribulation. For some, at any rate, this stress has led to a shrinking from suffering and the regarding of persecution, when it has come, as a strange thing. The sad fruits of this attitude can easily be met both at home and in many part of the mission field.

The redeemed are apparently pictured as standing even nearer the throne than the elders and the living creatures. The 'white robes' (9) are the victor's dress, but it is due to Christ's death that they are white. The 'palm branch' takes the place of the olive or laurel crown of the winner in the Greek games, the change being almost certainly to link them with John 12.13, to show that their victory was through Jesus and by the same path as His. Their position is as it should be, for where Christ is, there His people should be, too. The worship of v. 12 throws light on Eph. 3.10, for 'principalities and powers' need be understood in a bad sense only where the context demands it. The wisdom, power and love of God are specially displayed by the triumph of the Church by His grace in the midst of tribulation.

The 'elder' (13) can teach us a lesson in communication; he knew that John did not know, but he did not force the information on him. By his question he gave John the possibility of asking—'Sir, you know' (14) is a polite question—and ensured his participation. With v. 15, cf. 22.3 f. and the notes on the passage. We have the redeemed here as God's kingdom, under His protection, and His priests (cf. 1.6). There is an obvious reference to Psa. 23 in vs. 16,17. All that man experiences of God's grace on earth is only a foretaste of heaven.

Thought: Our triumph on earth can call out the highest praise of God in heaven.

Questions for further study and discussion on Revelation chs. 4–7
1. What are common concepts about God? Compare these with **4.8,11**. What needs to be emphasized concerning Him in the Church and in contemporary society?
2. Compare the qualities of the 'Lion' and the 'Lamb' as they find expression in the life of Christ.
3. Consider the statement 'The martyrs cry for vengeance (**6.9–11**)—not from personal spite, but as with the psalmist, that the honour of God may be vindicated'. Should this attitude be reflected in our lives? Does this conflict with Christlike compassion?
4. What place should the wrath of God occupy in our proclamation of the Christian faith? With the aid of a concordance note the frequency with which this concept recurs in Scripture.

Revelation 8.1-6   The Lamb's Work is Finished

Today there is a growing agreement .that chs. 4–20 should be divided into a number of approximately parallel sections (**4.1–8.1; 8.2–11.19; 12.1–14.20; 15.1–16.21; 17.1–19.21**). They start at varying points but all terminate at the point of Christ's return. If that is so, **8.1** is the end of the section that began with **4.1**. When the seventh seal is broken, the silence shows that there is nothing more in the scroll. The glorified and victorious Church has echoed the 'It is finished' of its Lord. Nothing remains but for the Lamb to take up His power upon earth. Even so He can wait; the Lord knows no haste in the fulfilment of His purposes.

With v. 2 we go back in time, probably to the fifth seal. (**6.9**) and see the judgements of God in more detail. As was mentioned on **6.9**, the golden 'altar' (3) is a new feature. Heb. **9.3** f. tell us that it belonged to the Holy of Holies, i.e. this is a mere shadow of the heavenly reality. Incense has a double meaning. It is that which goes up, and so it can represent prayer (**5.8**), but it also hides (Lev. **16.12** f.). So here it is that which hides God from man (Isa. **6.4**, 'smoke'), symbolized by the veil of the Tabernacle. This is a warning against taking symbolism as a sort of mathematical game in which, for the solver, two terms are interchangeable. If it were so, it would be no more than a poetic device. The seven trumpets speak primarily of God's wrath on men from whom He is hidden.

In favour of a link with **6.9** f. is the fact that the censer used for the offering of the prayers and incense is now used for the

471

hurling of fire on the earth, prophetic of the woes to come. The fulfilment of the prayers of the martyred saints might seem a long time coming, but it was sure.

Thought: Among the virtues we must learn is patience. More harm is done through haste than slowness.

Revelation 8.7-13

God Turns the Wisdom of the Wise to Folly

The essentially symbolic nature of the woes announced is seen most clearly in v. 12. A disaster to sun and moon would decrease the total quantity of light given or reflected by them. What it could not do would be to cause darkness for a third of the night and day. Phillips' rendering shows his awareness of this, but its legitimacy may be questioned. In fact one third, and similar proportions, are a regular feature of such prophecies, cf. Zech. 13.8 f.; Ezek. 5.2,12. Major, but not irreparable disaster is indicated. At the first God's judgements are intended to be educative. It is only when they are ignored that they finally overwhelm mankind in disaster.

The reading 'eagle' (13) is justified not merely by very strong manuscript support, but also by the impossibility of explaining its presence, if 'angel', as in the AV(KJV), had been original. It must symbolize war, and the sequel in ch. 9 supports this. That being so, we may infer that the sufferings under the first three trumpets were from natural catastrophes. The fourth probably represents the trouble caused by the failure of the leaders when faced with these things. Such persons repeatedly seek to justify themselves by turning to war, in the hope that the people will forget their failures, when faced with greater perils.

There is an undue willingness in certain circles to see in any disastrous natural phenomenon a sign of the near coming of Christ. It would be far better, if we were to stress that they show most effectively the hollowness of man's claim to dominate nature. In many cases, as in China a few years ago, they are in addition clearly a Divine answer to the claim that man has everything under control, and so he does not need God, even if He exists. Politicians, who believe that they are masters in their own house and have no need of Divine guidance and help, find these visitations of nature especially galling. They cannot

472

humble themselves to confess that there are forces completely outside their control.

Thought: 'If God wills' is not a pious formula, but a serious statement of fact. He has all the forces of nature at His command to stop us, if He wishes to.

Revelation 9.1-12 An Invasion of Demons

Efforts to identify the scourge here described with some known nation past or present have carried little conviction, but an application of symbolism may help us. The 'star fallen from heaven' (1) will be as symbolic as in 8.12; in the light of 12.9, Luke 10.18, it may well be Satan that is meant. He does not possess the key of 'the shaft of the abyss' (NEB)—the rendering 'bottomless pit' is justified neither by the Greek nor by common sense—it is given him, obviously by the Lamb. However much Satan may wish to wreck God's work, he is the agent of His will, cf. Job 1,2.

Those that rise from the abyss are obviously demons, but the demon has seldom, if ever, power over nature as such—they are not to harm the grass or trees (4)—but over evil men whom they enter and control. Hence they cannot hurt those with God's seal. The predominant impression they create is of the beast—'horses' (7)—for the demon-possessed is always essentially sub-human, even where this is not immediately clear. He claims to rise above human limitations, hence the 'crown' (7). The reference to 'women's hair' (8) may be to remind us that the inrush of evil is almost always linked with an apparent glorification of sex, which always leads to its debasement. They are pictured as an army. There are many periods when evil puts on the mask of goodness, even as Satan may appear as an angel of light, but there are others, and we are passing through one now, when evil is in embattled opposition to God. We find ourselves in the position of Eph. 6.10–18, when we may be thankful, if we have been able to do no more than stand our ground. 'Abaddon', cf. Job 26.6; 28.22; 31.12; Psa. 88.11; Prov. 15.11; 27.20, means, like 'Apollyon', destruction, and is another name for death or Sheol. Demon influence tortures man first of all, and in the end destroys him.

Of special importance is the mention of 'five months' (5,10). This is the first of numerous passages where a fixed number is

473

mentioned. It is not the interpretation of the period that is important, but that we realize that the apparent triumph of evil is God-permitted and controlled, its very beginning and ending being fixed in advance.

Revelation 9.13-21 Evil Let Loose

The forces in this section are as clearly demonic as in the previous one, though probably physical as well as spiritual warfare is intended. Here again there is an exact indication of time given, in this case of when the disaster is to break out (15). Its duration is governed by the time taken to accomplish their task. It should be noted that, because the evil done seems to be physical rather than spiritual, there is no mention of God's people being spared, cf. v. 4.

No explanation is given as to who 'the four angels' (14) may be; that they are bound suggests that they are fallen ones; that they are four—see note on 7.1—may imply that they represent the fallen angels as a whole, and they may be the otherwise unexplained 'cavalry' (16). The Euphrates (14) seems to play a symbolic part in Biblical thinking. It served as a kind of symbolic frontier between civilization and barbarism. Civilization, in Johannine language, the world, is on the one hand a gift of God (Rom. 13.1), on the other it has been twisted by Satan and evil men into an obstacle to the advance of God's will and rule. So God has repeatedly allowed the stable world to be rocked to its foundations by the inrush of barbarism. Sometimes it has been like a tidal wave of barbarian destruction, which in due course has ebbed again. Sometimes their way has been prepared by propaganda, as with the inrush of Communism, which has often effectively destroyed all desire to resist. It should not be forgotten that the totalitarian systems of our day are essentially a perverted Communism, a seeking to use Satan to drive out sin. We should be staggered, could we reckon how many lives have been lost through Communism, Nazism and Fascism of various kinds.

Whenever such judgements have come, the result has always been the same. Men have never turned as a body from the worship of their false gods, and from their crimes, whether they are crude ones like those mentioned in vs. 20 f. or the rather more subtle ones of today. If anything, disaster is explained away by saying that the worship of these gods had not been thorough

474

enough. 'Sorceries' (21) is probably not a satisfactory rendering; it probably refers to drug traffic, either to murder or to create willingness to sin.

Revelation 10.1-11 The Mystery of God Draws to an End

It is generally agreed that there are two visions (10.1–11; 11.1–13) which form a parenthesis before the blowing of the seventh trumpet in 11.15. So far as the former is concerned, there is no evidence that it should be fitted into the developing revelation, however this is understood. It is rather a message to the seer, returned for a moment to earth—the angel came down (1)—for if we respond to revelation we may expect more to be given us.

The identity of the 'angel' (1) is immaterial. The various attributes, like cloud, rainbow, sun, are not to identify him with Christ, but are to make it clear that he is speaking with the authority of God. The 'little scroll' (2) is not that of 5.1, but looks back to Ezek. 2.9–3.3, and is John's continuing message. It is smaller, because no man in his personal ministry can hope to do justice to every aspect of God's revelation. The message concerned the people of God ('the land') and the nations at large ('the sea'). 'The seven thunders' (3) did not merely sound, they spoke (NEB). No indication of their nature or of what they said is given. They may have given revelation beyond what John had to reveal; we must confine ourselves to what God teaches us. On the other hand it may have been the opposition of apparently authoritative circles. We are not to record and so give longer life to voices that oppose God's revelation.

The rendering of the AV(KJV) and RV text in v. 6 ('there shall be time no longer') is unfortunate; it has given rise to unprofitable theories about the timelessness of eternity and its consequent stagnation. God's 'mystery' (7), or 'hidden purpose' (NEB), has been revealed, but our full understanding of it awaits the end of present history. The subtle difference between v. 10 and Ezek. 3.3 should be noted. There is a bitter element in the gospel which cannot be eliminated without distorting it. It is a fragrance from death to death among those who are perishing (2 Cor. 2.15 f.). At the age he had reached, relaxation from his labours would have seemed natural for John. There is no doubt, however, that his Gospel and letters were written after this. Though John is called the apostle of love, he has some of the sternest and straightest language in the Bible about lovelessness and sin.

Thought: When God teaches us, it is that we may teach others.

There is no part of *Revelation* which has lent itself more to fanciful interpretations than this, but we shall ignore them. No description of the measuring is given. It was doubtless performed in vision, for it seems to be a temple on earth, and that in Jerusalem had already been destroyed by Titus. The measuring is doubtless of the same nature as the sealing in 7.3, i.e. the guaranteeing of God's care, and the temple is God's people, cf. Eph. 2.19–22; 2 Cor. 6.16; once again there is no need to distinguish between the Church and the true Israel. There are no grounds for identifying it with the temple of 11.19. 'The court outside' (2), the court of the Gentiles, represents all that mixed multitude which at most times is associated with the people of God, cf. Isa. 1.12. For the 'forty-two months' in v. 2, cf. 11.3; 12.6,14; 13.5; it is the same period as that in Dan. 7.25; 12.7. We need not doubt that there will be a fulfilment in a later day, when the time will be literally fulfilled, but it is also symbolic, for it represents half the great week of God's purposes, nor may we forget that in Dan. 9.24 we are dealing with a day equalling a year. So long God can allow His adversaries to have their way.

The 'two witnesses' (3) are linked through v. 4 with Zech. 4, where they are Zerubbabel and Joshua. Without our ruling out the possibility of literal fulfilment, we should recognize that they speak to us of due leadership within the people of God, who maintain its witness. The triumph of the beast (7) links with 13.7, where it is imperative that a wide meaning be found. We should note the short period of the beast's triumph compared to the length of the witness.

The same movement within a narrower and wider meaning is seen in the description of the city (8). While in its narrower sense it refers to Jerusalem, the description 'great city' asks us to look outwards. Jerusalem is compared with Sodom in Isa. 1.9f.; Ezek. 16.46–56, but never with Egypt. What is true of apostate Jerusalem is true of apostate civilization generally. The disciples understood this, cf. Acts 4.25–27.

Question: Are you willing to be defeated for Jesus' sake?

Revelation 11.15-19 Christ is King!

We now reach the same point as 8.1. The apparent difference and even contradiction is due to the nature of symbolism. A symbol never claims to represent more than one aspect of the truth. Therefore two symbols may be used for the same event, which at first sight are incompatible. Silence (8.1) brought out the completion of Christ's work in the Church. Here we have the response of the heavenly powers to it.

'The kingdom of the world' (15): very much better is 'the sovereignty of the world' (NEB) or 'the kingship of the world' (Phillips); see note on 1.6. God has always ruled the world, but the majority of men have been in revolt against Him. Since God willed to control the animal creation through man (Gen. 1.26–28; Psa. 8.5–8; Heb. 2.5–9), man's revolt and fall mean that God's rule in the animal world is only partially discernible. At this point we see Phil. 2.10 f. about to go into effect.

If we are to understand the frequent prosperity and well-being of the wicked—there are many exceptions; while Stalin died in his bed as an old man, Mussolini died by violence and Hitler by his own hand—we must grasp that the sufferings of this present time are seldom God's punishment, which awaits the final judgement. They are partly the sequel of broken law, but even more God's effort to bring man to his senses. The sufferings that precede the coming of Christ, 'the birth pangs of the Messiah' (Mark 13.8), which have been repeatedly foreshadowed in history, are intended to break man's will to resist, even though they do not necessarily bring him to faith.

'Thy wrath' (18): God's wrath is essentially 'the wrath to come' (1 Thess. 1.10, cf. 1 Thess. 5.9; Matt. 3.7); that is why the NEB renders very well, 'Thy day of retribution'. It is revealed in man's sufferings and above all in his being 'given up' (Rom. 1.24,26,28), but all this is only a foretaste of that to come, which finds its climax in the seven plagues (15.1). We should avoid replacing wrath by anger. There is normally an element of reaction to the wrong done to oneself in anger; in God's wrath there is merely the reaction to the wrong done to others. The climax of God's judgement is on 'the destroyers of the earth' (18).

For the temple in heaven (19), cf. 15.5. Presumably we are to infer that the earthly Tabernacle and Temple are merely symbols of the heavenly reality seen in ch.4.

Questions for further study and discussion on Revelation chs. 8–11

1. Does God use disasters to punish men? Have they any other function? Note the disasters of the O.T.: earthquake (*Amos*), famine (*Amos*), foreign powers (Isa.10), locusts and drought (*Joel*).

477

2. The new age in which we now live has changed the status of Satan. How far? Examine his activities, not only in the light of *Revelation*, but in the rest of the N.T.
3. What were the bitter-sweet results of the Word of God in the experience of John and, more particularly, in the life of Paul? Is it possible to have one without the other?
4. Have we any way of knowing today whether the end is near?
5. Why must imagery and metaphor be used to describe spiritual realities?

Revelation 12.1-6   Satan and the People of God

Again a new section begins; 'And' (1) is only the introduction common in Hebrew narrative. The measure of time (6) puts it before **11.3**, but more we cannot say. Few passages of Scripture have given rise to more diverse interpretations, so the following must be regarded merely as an effort to take the symbolism seriously.

The section **12.1-14.5** is played out on three levels: the throne of God (Mount Zion), heaven, and earth; they are to be understood of spiritual status, not of physical position, cf. Eph. **2.6**. The sun, moon and stars link the woman with Israel (Gen. 37.9), to be understood, as elsewhere in *Revelation*, as the people of God. The 'red dragon' (3) is identified with the devil (9). It is red because Satan is a murderer from the beginning (John **8.44**). The heads and horns are identical with those of the second beast (**13.1**); it is easier to explain them in the latter (see notes), so we may assume that Satan is thus pictured in order to show that the second beast is a real reproduction on earth of Satan and his system. If in the first the diadems are on the heads, in the second on the horns, it shows that the sovereignty is only delegated in the second. In v. 4 we have an intensification of Dan. **8.10**; here it probably refers to the seducing of many of the angelic host.

What of the 'male child' (5)? The apparently obvious meaning is Jesus, but why should there be a reference back to His birth? In addition, v. 5 would be a strange summary of His earthly work. Chapters **2.26** f.; **20.4** suggest that he personifies the conquerors, the true Church within the Church that claims the name, cf. **14.1-5**; Eph. **5.27**.

The woman is seen in heaven and on earth, i.e. the 'wilderness' (6). This is the contrast between the people of God as seen by God, and in their humiliation as seen by man, as they are judged by God and man to be. When they are most despised by man, they are most in

478

the place prepared by God for them, and where they will find God's provision.

Revelation 12.7-12 The Defeat of Satan

Popular Christian fantasy, basing itself on this passage, Isa. **14.12**, etc., has pictured a war in which God's angels led by Michael threw Satan and his angels out of heaven long before the creation of man. There is no Scriptural warrant for this, least of all in this passage.

What is depicted is something within the range of events described by *Revelation* and affecting its readers (12). What is more, the defeat of Satan is merely symbolic, for the victory has been won by the conquerors within the Church (11), thus almost certainly confirming the interpretation given to the male child (5). Whether or not this scene has a yet future application and climax, it has worked itself out throughout the history of the Church. They had conquered Godwards by their trust in Christ's death, and manwards by their witness. Because in both directions they had renounced trust in what they did themselves, 'they loved not their lives even unto death' (11). This must not be understood merely as a willingness to embrace a martyr's death, but also as a renunciation of success as the world inside and outside the Church esteems it.

By their victory they first of all shut the mouth of Satan (= the Accuser). As the image of Christ was formed in them, cf. 2 Cor. 3.18, they demonstrated to the world that Satan is not its ruler and that there is a greater power than his, thus depriving him of his place in man's esteem. Doubtless there will be a great, final demonstration of this, but it is something that has had to be worked out anew in each new generation. The Church is never in greater danger than when it is acclaimed by the world, for it may allow itself to be persuaded that there is some merit in it, and that there is something it can achieve. When the Church allows its task and methods to be dictated by the world, it is the subtle recognition of the wisdom of Satan, prince of this world.

Perhaps the most important lesson of this section is that we must not look on the Church merely as the sphere of salvation, but as that of God's continuing victory in Christ. The body of Christ is no mere empty metaphor but a living reality, cf. Eph. **1**.22 f. (NEB); 3.10; Col. **1**.24.

Revelation 12.13-17

We have to distinguish between the willingness to suffer martyrdom (11) and the foolhardy challenging of death. Jesus Himself commanded His disciples to flee to another city when they were persecuted (Matt. 10.23), implying that the message would be better spread that way. Here (14) we see the people of God going underground for the time being, something that has been more frequent and more fruitful than is often realized. The wings symbolize the speed at which it happens. There is always a danger, when the Church becomes too anchored and hampered by physical things which restrict its mobility.

The symbolism in vs. 15,16 is probably clear in general outline but difficult to apply in detail. The earth always stands symbolically for that which is firm and steadfast, and hence law-abiding. Sometimes, but hardly here, it represents Israel as the people under God's law. The water-floods, whether the sea, or as here a river in spate, represent the nations in their lawlessness and rebellion against God. So the picture is of Satan loosing mob violence against the Church, as he has so often done. Indeed, in every age State action against the Church has often been based on popular demand. Here, however, the forces of law and order react against the mob violence and foil it. But as ch. 13 shows us, this merely means that subtlety is substituted for force by the enemy.

Satan changes his attack from the Church as such to its members. The description of them (17) precludes any interpretation that they are those left behind at the Rapture. They are surely the male child unrecognized in their humble state.

Thought: Keeping the commandments of God and witnessing go together.

Revelation 13.1-10

In Dan. 7.3 four beasts come out of the sea. Here there is only one (1), but it combines the traits of the first three (2, cf. Dan. 7.4–6), and as it develops, it shows another trait, its mouth, which links it with the fourth (5, Dan. 7.8,20); this is in any case shown by its horns (1, Dan. 7.7). As Dan. 7.17 makes clear, the beast is both a man and a system. It is in fact the summing up of an age-old system, which John calls the world, and of a line of men who have sought to rule in defiance of God's will. Its last stage is merely the climax of what has been all along. It comes out of the sea (1), i.e. it is the product of mankind in rebellion against God; it is a beast, because man in revolt against God is sub-human. Even the mortally wounded head (3) is only a special case of a common phenomenon. Repeatedly in human history a system or ruler is saved when at the apparent point of death. This is regarded as proof of divine favour, and honour and validity are attributed which are in fact a worship of Satan.

Far more effective than mob violence against the believer is to embrace him in the omnicompetent, authoritarian State, which may give lip-service to God, but by its claims blasphemes Him. The dragon may give the beast his power (2), but only God can allow it to make war on the saints and conquer them (7), and doubtless it is also God who gives it its authority (cf. Rom. 13.1), though its length is strictly limited (5). From v. 7 we see that these principles are world-wide.

In the Holy Communion we take the bread as symbol of Christ's body of humiliation, not of His glorified body. Similarly the Church follows in the steps of His humiliation, even though it may enjoy hours of popular favour, as He did. Periodically, not only in the end time, the Church knows the bitterness of apparent defeat and death. Only so can God separate the true from the false. Natural man's sights are set on the present or immediate future, the spiritual man's on the end of the age, when Christ returns and true judgement is meted out (10), cf. 14.16–20.

Question: Do you expect more from life than Jesus did, cf. Matt. 10.24,25?

Revelation 13.11-18   The Mark of the Beast

The very fact that the second beast rises out of 'the earth' (11) suggests its nature. It represents every organization that claims to accept God's law, but is opposed to its spirit. Very much ingenuity has been used in interpreting the number of the beast (18), and some of the interpretations may have a limited validity. But 'wisdom', and not a knowledge of Greek, or even Hebrew, is called for (18). The RSV is among the few translations that realizes that 'the number of a man' is a false translation; 'it is a human number', or the number of mankind. Seven is symbolically the perfect number, God's number; six is the number of man at his best. 666 is man at the climax of his achievement, but still falling short of the perfection of 777. The details of the vision are not so important as the

481

realization that we have essentially the worship of man depicted, which is indirectly the worship of Satan, as lord of the world.

There are times when the killing of those who refuse to worship (15) is to be taken literally; sometimes no more than the squeezing out of the non-conformist is involved. The reference is not to ration cards, though these show how easily the vision can be carried out, but to the raising of human organizations, particularly those of the State, to complete power. There was a time, when either by the inefficiency of the State machine, or by moving to virgin lands, men could opt out. Today this has become impossible, and it is merely a question of how much authority the State chooses to exert. The fact that in almost every land liberal, not necessarily Christian, men are alarmed by the growth of State power shows how far we have gone.

Perhaps our greatest danger is the belief that we extend our influence by increasing and strengthening our Christian organizations. However pure their doctrine, they are in danger of being caught up in the orbit of the second beast. One of the saddest lessons from the Communist and Nazi dictatorships is the way in which they have been able to capture and, in great measure, use completely admirable church organizations.

Thought: One of the Christian's greatest problems is to hold in balance subjection to the authorities with a rejection of the Satanic powers that use them.

Revelation 14.1-5   The Conquerors

Though Mt. Zion is repeatedly used as a symbol for God's throne among men, it is never so used for something future, separated from this earth; see especially Heb. 12.22, which speaks of a present reality. It seems to be the symbolic expression here of Eph. 2.6. We return to the 'male child' and see what his being caught up to the throne of God really meant.

The conquering Christian lives on two planes simultaneously. One we saw in 13.7, but all the time the beast seemed to be triumphing he was in fact being conquered. The mention of the Father's name (1) is a reminder that it is possible to develop a worship of the purely earthly Jesus of Nazareth, which is as one-sided as the ignoring of His earthly life.

The literal rendering of v. 4, 'These are they who did not defile themselves with women, for they are virgins' has led to a false exaltation of celibacy. Such an understanding assumes that the whole company is male, which is never otherwise suggested, and it commits the cardinal fault in exegesis of taking a symbolic passage literally. It also assumes that marriage causes some form of defilement. Over half the instances of the word-groups of adultery and fornication (whoredom) in the O.T. are applied to the worship of other gods, or to a conception of Jehovah which He refused to recognize, and that is surely the meaning here. In this day of the overvaluing of sex, every young Christian should consider passages like Matt. **19.**10–12; 1 Cor. **7.**7,8,25,26,32–35 prayerfully, but let him not forget that under other circumstances Paul commanded marriage (1 Tim. **5.**14). Above all there is never any suggestion that celibacy increases a person's standing as a Christian; most of the apostles were married (1 Cor. **9.**5).

It should be specially noted that the evidence that they 'follow the Lamb wherever He goes' (4) is that they do not lie (5). Lies are caused by two things, fear and pride, which cause personal desires to take the chief place. Both disappear in the presence of Christ; cf. also **21.**8,27; **22.**15.

This close contact with their Lord also enables them to understand Him and the purposes of God better and more clearly. It is this that is implied by the 'new song' (3) that others could not learn. Salvation does not depend on understanding God and what He has done in this way; scholarship will not teach it and spiritual exaltation will not give it. It comes from fellowship and obedience, and the two cannot really be separated.

Revelation 14.6-13   God Has the Last Word

It is probably best to see in **14.**6–20 the climax of the vision of **12.**1–**14.**5, and its inevitable outcome. The Victorian period with its frills and furbelows, its knick-knacks and aspidistras, loved complication, and so many saw in the 'eternal gospel' (6) a special and different one for the world after the rapture of the Church. Today we are learning that God's greatness is seen above all in a simplicity too great for man to grasp. The expression of the gospel at any time takes on a special form, for it should always be adapted to the circumstances of the hearers (note the indefinite article in RSV), but essentially it is eternal and unchangeable. A preaching of the cross that neglects the eternal sovereignty of God is always less than the gospel.

Here in the face of the apparent triumph of the beast the abiding sovereignty of God is proclaimed. This is reinforced by the fall of

483

'Babylon' (8), both ecclesiastical and commercial (see notes on chs. 17,18), which means the humbling of human pride. So then the third call is for mental and spiritual revolt against the enthralment of the beast (9), which for so long had bedazzled men. The true Christian does not and will not worship the beast. The one who has been misled and has worshipped him in ignorance is given the opportunity of repentance.

We tend to smile indulgently at the practice of keeping up with the Joneses, but we repeatedly fail to see what it hides. It puts what I have before what I am, and makes possessions the standard of judgement; it exalts the temporary above the eternal. It is the implicit rejection of all that Jesus' life meant. When such people are faced with the realities of eternity, it means torment.

The last mile of the road, the last lap of the race, the last round of the fight, is always the hardest. The clear evidence that the systems of this world are breaking down and chaos is coming in will be the most taxing for the Church. Even today so many feel that there should be rest rather than light at eventide. It will be extra hard for those who die just as they fancy they can see the light of Christ's return on the horizon. So there is a special word of encouragement for them (13).

Revelation 14.14-20 The Harvest

The great difference between Biblical religion and probably all others is its sense of final purpose. Islam and Mahayana Buddhism believe in a judgement after death, but neither sees any real purpose behind the world process. Equally, modern philosophies including Marxism and Humanism may offer motives for what is considered good behaviour, but they have no real goal for human history. For the Bible human history is surely, if very slowly, moving towards that moment when God's triumph will be obvious, not so much because He crushes opposition—if that were His purpose, He could and would have done so long ago—but because the harvest is ripe, and the difference between wheat and tares is finally obvious. His goal is that man should accept His will, and that this acceptance be seen as man's greatest good. 'One like a son of man' (14): from the context it seems improbable that Jesus Christ is meant, cf. also Matt. 13.39,41,49.

If here the contrast is between grain and grapes, it is not a disparagement of the latter, or of the wine made from them—they can be used of the fruit borne by the Christian (John 15.2,5)—but be-

484

cause of the picture offered by the treading of the grapes in the wine press (19.15; Isa. 63.3). 'Outside the city' (20): normally a wine press would be outside the city walls. Here, however, 'the city' is probably Jerusalem. This would link it with what is normally called the battle of Armageddon (16.16), though this is in fact merely mentioned as the mustering place for the army. The implications of the last battle will be dealt with when commenting on 19.11–21. Here it is sufficient to underline that the vision deals with the results of active and deliberate opposition to God.

'The angel who has power over fire' (18): the Greek is 'the fire'. Probably lightning is meant. This was regarded in the ancient world as peculiarly the expression of God's power, and in its suddenness and devastating destruction still reminds man of his weakness and insignificance.

Question: If man chooses to fight God, why should he be saved from the consequences?

Questions for further study and discussion on Revelation chs. 12–14

1. What factors account for the persecution of Christian churches? What may be deduced from the fact that the western churches are relatively free from persecution?
2. What is involved in the statement 'They loved not their lives even unto death' (12.11)? Examine this in the light of the teaching of our Lord, John and Paul.
3. Chapters 12,13 say much about Satan's attack on the Church. Which methods does he employ most successfully today?
4. Examine the N.T. references to antichrist and antichrists. What are the characteristics and functions involved?
5. What rule of life is set out for Christians in 13.10? Using a concordance see how this is stressed in the N.T.

Revelation 15.1-8   The Seven Last Plagues

In this chapter we find ourselves at the same point in the development in God's purposes as 7.9–17 and 19.1–10. The rapture of the Church is past (14.14 f.), and the grape harvest (14.17–20) is about to be reaped. We here see that the plagues are an interpretation of the treading out of the grapes. There are 'seven plagues' (1); for reasons mentioned earlier they are the full, perfect and final pouring out of God's wrath. We shall be safe in assuming that they occupy very little time.

485

The 'sea of glass' (2) is that of 4.6, but where it formerly merely dazzled the earth-dweller, now, once the Church has gone, the signs of the imminent judgement ('fire') befleck it. The 'harps of God' (2): better 'the harps which God had given them' (NEB). 'The song of Moses and . . . of the Lamb' (3): as has been repeatedly said, John does not draw any clear distinction between the true Israel and the conquering Church; here both are represented, hence the double song. Yet Israel can sing the song of the Lamb, for all the time it had looked forward to His coming, even if it had not recognized Him, and the Church can sing the song of Moses, for Christ is the completion of the O.T. and of its hope (John 8.56). 'The song of Moses' refers back to Exod. 15.1–18. It matters very little whether we read 'King of the ages' (3) or 'of the nations'. The song of triumph recognizes that God has not merely guided and ruled His people, but has guided (Amos 9.7) and overruled the nations which did not accept Him, as well as the ages to which human thinkers could give no meaning.

'The temple of the tent of witness' (5): far better 'the sanctuary of the heavenly Tent of Testimony' (NEB); for the concept, cf. Heb. 8.5. The angels have, like the Lord (1.13), their breasts girded with golden girdles to show that they act as His representatives. The Tent was filled with smoke so that none could enter (8), for those on whom the plagues were to fall had made their choice, and it was too late to repent.

Thought: If you say No often enough, God will take you at your word.

Revelation 16.1-7 The First Three Plagues

Since all the plagues are future, every attempt to give a definitive explanation to the symbolism is likely to fall short. Yet here, as elsewhere in the book, we shall probably do better taking the details symbolically rather than literally.

We live in a time when most still try to keep a façade of respectability for their lives, and it is still possible for many in the public eye to hush up scandals until after their death. The minority who do not trouble about appearances nevertheless try to justify their actions by terms like freedom and self-expression, a brushing away of hypocrisy, etc. Now, however, the reality of an evil life is to be made clear to all; the inner is to become visible.

One of the results of the gospel was very gradually to teach Christendom that violence was evil, and murder a unique sin. This recognition was always superficial; with the increasing rejection of the gospel violence has become a commonplace, and we find even Christian ministers advocating the use of violence to right wrongs. Hence murder has become only one crime among many. With the removal of the Church, murder and violence become the characteristic of the nations—'the sea' (3); in O.T. thought 'the blood of a dead man' means life violently taken.

Since 'the angel of water' (5) approves of the third plague, it is clear that 'the rivers and fountains of water' (4) are something good. In Eastern Mediterranean lands water is the most important of the gifts of heaven, and, except in Egypt, it comes through rain at the right time. So we should probably think of a breakdown of the great uniformities of nature (Gen. 8.22) and of God's beneficent providence (Matt. 5.45). It is a sign of human pride that so few today are any longer prepared to see the hand of God in drought and flood, storm and unseasonable weather. The picture of blood is taken from Exod. 7.17-21. Just as we can only infer the causes of the first plague in Egypt, so we must reserve judgement here; in both cases blood refers to the colour, not composition of the water. The first two plagues strike at man's pride in himself and the society he has created, the third at his vaunted domination of nature.

When we hear 'the altar cry' (7), we are fairly safe in interpreting it as of the earth as in 6.9. The O.T. concept of the involvement of the soil in the life of those that live on it has been almost completely lost today.

Thought: Man can achieve the worth-while only by God's permission.

Revelation 16.8-16 Keep Awake!

Since none of the other heavenly bodies is here mentioned with 'the sun' (8), there is no reason why we should not take it literally. A very small rise in the sun's inner temperature could raise that of the earth to an almost unbearable level beside causing major natural disasters by the melting of glaciers and the polar ice-caps. The darkness over the beast's capital (Babylon?) and the heart of his kingdom is doubtless to be explained as in Exod. 10.21. Drought and great heat—nor may we exclude the possibility of volcanic action (18,19)—create the conditions for a major sand storm. The result of these two plagues justify the grape harvest of judgement (14.17-20). The man who does not respond to God's love will not humble himself before His judgements.

For the symbolic meaning of the Euphrates see note on **9.14**. We are probably intended to see the breakdown of civilization under the inrush of the underprivileged peoples from all sides—not only the east is intended. Faced with the breakdown of all that Satanic wiles, human pride and religious self-confidence had created, the three beasts plan a supreme come-back. Since the war on the saints (**13.**7) is not to be understood literally, neither should that on God. Armageddon is named as the mustering place, not the battle ground. Since it is the largest plain in Palestine, it points to the size of the forces involved. There is no suggestion of an attack on Jerusalem; we must beware how we try to piece different prophecies into a tidy unity, as though they were bits of a jig-saw. The mustering is done by 'demonic spirits' (14), so it seems that a supreme effort is being made to get men to abjure God.

In spite of their horror, the plagues are merely intensifications of what has already happened, just as the plagues on Egypt were of natural troubles that have often stricken the land. So Christian readers are warned that the judgements of God are abroad in the land and so they must keep awake (15), cf. 1 Thess. **5.**2–8. The temple area was a fortress and Levitical troops used to be on duty at night. At an unpredictable hour the 'captain of the temple' used to make his rounds. Should he find a sentry asleep, he took a torch from one of the escort and set his clothes on fire; with morning light his burnt appearance proclaimed to all his companions his failure in his duty, cf. 1 John **2.**28.

Revelation 16.17-21   It is Done!

We have again reached the same point as **8.**1; **11.**15–19; **14.**17–20. Though there is no connection, the fear shown by so many of atomic fallout will show what the pouring of the last bowl 'into the air' (17) means. Everywhere, with no nook or cranny left for safety, the wrath of God floats down on men, leaving nothing more to be awaited. With v. 18, cf. **8.**5; if the divisions of the book suggested are correct, it is an intensification we are now dealing with, but it is one of the signs which justify us in thinking that God constantly causes man to experience foreshadowings of what is to be.

The meaning of the great city (19) was discussed in the notes on **11.**8; cf. also **17.**9,18. Though there is no reason why Jerusalem should not be included, it is most doubtful whether any exclusive reference to it is intended. The first two cities recorded in the Bible are Enoch (Gen. **4.**17) and Babel (Gen. **11.**4), and both were expressions of lack of trust in God, cf. Heb. **11**.10. What is here being proclaimed is the complete destruction of man's last line of defence against both God and chaos.

'Great Babylon' (19): though Babylon is not mentioned in Scripture between Gen. **11**.9—Babel is the Hebrew name for Bab-ili, which we render Babylon—and the days of Hezekiah, it had a position all its own in Hebrew thought. Though it had little political importance between its capture by the Kassites in 1530 B.C. and its being made the capital of a Chaldean empire in 626 B.C., it was the virtually undisputed commercial and religious capital of the Fertile Crescent. So it is the personification, so to speak, for the Bible, of man organized for financial profit, and of man-made religion in all its attractive sophistry. These are the two aspects which are dealt with in chs. **17** (religion) and **18** (commerce). If we compare *Nahum* and *Habakkuk*, we shall learn something of the different impression created by the pride and cruelty of Assyria and the corruption of human nature which the prophet saw in Babylon.

'Hailstones' (21): cf. Job 38.22 f. For the inhabitants of the Eastern Mediterranean lands it was a supreme sign that something was wrong with the world, when the rain which was the supreme blessing could become a threat to life and property as it was turned to ice. So hail was looked on supremely as a sign of Divine intervention and anger; here it can be anything that carries that message.

Revelation 17.1-6 Babylon the Harlot

It is the religious aspect of Babylon we are here considering. She is called 'the great harlot' (1) because false religion, like false sex, cheats; it gives only a counterfeit, never the reality. She is riding 'a scarlet beast' (3), which is later clearly identified with that of **13**.1, or sitting on 'many waters' (1), rightly rendered 'the ocean' (NEB), cf. v. 15; Dan. 7.2, i.e. the nations. Here we have religion not as a political organization, but as exercising power through the State. This involves 'the harlot' in supporting the State; that is the price she must pay for power. Since God and the world are in irreconcilable conflict, religion must adopt the world's values to retain its position. So she is seen in 'a wilderness' (3); she kills true spiritual life.

Marx, when he said, 'Religion is the opium of the people', probably did not know that he was repeating the maxim of one of the Cromwellian Levellers or Fifth Monarchy men. In its original sense it is true. Every religious system, to preserve its own existence,

489

is tempted to preach obedience to something in addition to Christ. In the measure it does this it belongs to the harlot. We may think that one system more than others is the harlot, but John makes no effort to identify her. We may also think that for someone to belong to such a system automatically taints him. Experience has shown that Christ leaves some of His choicest saints in such churches, that they may resist, often at great loss, the lust for power and the demand for obedience where it must not be given.

While it is the beast that persecutes, the impulse comes from the harlot (cf. 13.16, where the second beast is referred to that represents the religious side of persecution). The official world has normally very little fear of the saint, for it knows that he has no itch to rule, no desire to seize power. It has been only when rulers have deified themselves, like the Roman emperors, or have claimed religious power they had no right to, like some Reformation monarchs, or virtually deified the State, like modern totalitarian systems, that the secular power has persecuted in its own interests. We are told the harlot was 'drunk' (6). That is one of the worst aspects of persecution. Once it starts, it seems to know no bounds; this is as true when it is done in the name of orthodoxy as in that of false teaching.

Revelation 17.7-18   The Fate of the Harlot

John tells us that when he saw the harlot, 'I was greatly astonished' (6, NEB). If it were not that we are so familiar with the existence and history of the official Church, we should probably be so, too. At the time the Roman Empire was turning itself into a god; it was uninterested in religious systems unless they claimed first place, and then it persecuted them. So in that sense the beast 'is not' (8). From the time of Constantine the new alliance began. Wherever European civilization has become dominant, in one way or another the story has repeated itself. Even in the United States, where established religion is barred by the constitution, the Christian churches enjoy much privilege.

Though Rome is not the only city to have been built on seven hills—the same is asserted of Jerusalem—there can be no doubt that it looms large in the picture, and we need not be surprised that for the Reformers the identification of the harlot with the Roman Catholic Church was almost an article of faith. This is the more natural, if we remember that Constantinople (as later Moscow) had claimed to be the heir of Rome. In so symbolic a book we may, however, question an interpretation that may deflect attention from

490

one's own denomination. We have met seven before, and the hills are the symbol of stability. At all times the established church has been the chief supporter of the establishment. The identification of the harlot with organized society is seen in her being called 'the great city' (18).

There is a tendency in some circles to link certain modern church groupings with the harlot. All church groupings that aim at or exercise power fall into her orbit. So do the organizations set up to fight them. Every church organization seeking power and setting its own claims for loyalty has been so drawn.

In the end the beast tires of the harlot and destroys her. This is a process that began with the French Revolution, if not earlier. It has been greatly advanced by the rise of Marxism and totalitarianism. Already politicians have little time for the pronouncements of Church circles. The final overthrow of the harlot, when the world will appear unmasked as unashamedly anti-God, will show that the end is very near.

Questions for further study and discussion on Revelation chs. 15-17

1. Compare the Song of Moses (Exod. 15) with 15.3 f. What connection is there between these two songs? What concepts concerning God are emphasized? Do they figure prominently in our worship?
2. Note the recurring phrase 'they did not repent' (ch. 16). Why do people react to disaster in this way?
3. Have the judgements of God been neglected in contemporary preaching? If so, how can this be rectified without negating the fact of His love?
4. What concept of God has the modern man? How would you seek to present a balanced N.T. picture of God to the non-Christian? Where would you start and how would you proceed?
5. What is blasphemy?

Revelation 18.1-8   Babylon the Great

How inextricably the harlot church and human society are intertwined is shown by the difficulty in realizing that we have moved to another Babylon. The passage is shot through with memories of the prophets, e.g. Isa. 13.21; 14.23; 34.11,13; Jer. 50.39; 51.37 for v. 2, and Jer. 50.15; 51.9; Isa. 47.7,8; Zeph. 2.13 for vs. 6,7.

The call to come out of her, which shows that in v. 2 we have the

491

'prophetic perfect', i.e. that which is about to happen is spoken of as though it has already occurred, is parallel to 2 Cor. 6.14–18, which is quoted from Isa. 52.11. It is to be noted that in none of the three cases is there any question of leaving some form of corrupt Christianity, whether doctrine or life is involved. Here it refers to the money-based commercial power-system that dominates our society. In certain Christian circles a faith mission or 'to live by faith' implies a claim to be looking to God alone for daily needs. Though such an expression has no real Biblical justification and can be very uncharitable towards some other Christian workers, it is a tacit recognition of the difficulty of refusing to conform to the present world system. It is almost always easier to separate oneself from what one deems to be incorrect churchmanship than to abandon the mutual benefit system of the world. The call reflects the position in 13.16, and is addressed to those who by continued conformity risk their souls; coming out would preserve their souls even though it risked their bodies.

We are reminded of Psa. 137.7–9 by v. 6. One of the achievements of Babylon is to hide from us the worst evils it commits. Even the Press watch-dog is apt to deal with evil facts as the cinema does with the heroine lost in the African jungle. She may emerge in rags, but she looks as though she had just left the beauty parlour. Somehow the real evil in evil is normally eliminated before it reaches us in print and picture. On the other hand we have 'selective condemnation', where we see only those evils that are committed by those outside our political views and ideologies. The call of vs. 4–8 reminds us that evil when seen by heaven is blacker. 'To know all is to forgive all' is not one of God's maxims!

Thought: Lot was not the only righteous man that has lived in Sodom.

Revelation 18.9-19   The Lament over Babylon

There is no more honourable call open to man than to be king, as the term was and should be understood, for the king should make God's rule real to his subjects. But few have been the kings who realized their high calling and so have gone down in history as 'the Good'. By most it was understood not as a call to serve but to be served, cf. Mark 10.42–44. For them Babylon was the means by which they received the baubles their office brought them; hence their lamentation (10).

The real losers are the merchants. We should read through their list carefully, weighing each item and asking ourselves how necessary it is (12,13). Few of the goods will pass the scrutiny of eternity, though some may make life easier and more pleasant. The list ends with 'slaves'. It does not matter whether we take 'human souls' as a qualification (so RSV), or render 'and the lives of men' (NEB). Commerce is bitterly condemned here and in the O.T., because normally it pays so little attention to the good of those involved in it. Today it is often merely a question whether human labour or machines are cheaper. This is not a condemnation of commerce, but of commerce as it has been twisted by the world. It is clear that God so made the world that no individual or country can be completely autonomous. For modern life even giants like the USA and Russia are not completely self-supporting. Perhaps the most telling condemnation of it is 1 Kings 10.22, with which compare 1 Kings 10.16–21,27.

The selfishness of the whole business is seen in the fact that kings, merchants and sailors alike think merely of what they have lost. There is no sign of sympathy with those who have perished, not even with those with whom they had personal business links. We need to put the person of our Lord against this background and then reread Matt. 6.25–34. Teaching, which seems idealistic and even impossible, becomes possible in the light of Christ and practical in the light of Babylon's end.

Thought: Seek the things that are above where Christ is.

Revelation 18.20-24   The Doom of Babylon

It is very strange that the RSV should have taken v. 20 as the close of the mariners' lament. If it were so, their sudden recognition of the role of heaven, and the justification of those who had lost their lives in or through Babylon would run counter to the whole trend of the chapter. Rather, v. 20 would seem to be John's own comment, showing his deep satisfaction. The NEB seems to be correct in rendering, 'for in the judgement against her He has vindicated your cause!' Whether we think of Babylon as a place or a system, as religious or commercial, there seems no reason why its judgement should anticipate the general judgement. It could have been swept away in the dust caused by the Return, cf. Dan. 2.34 f. But even under the conditions of this age it had to be shown that in the end Lowell's lines do not apply:

'Truth for ever on the scaffold,
Wrong for ever on the throne.'

493

There follows the symbolic sign of the doom of Babylon (21), cf. Jer. 51.63 f. It should be noted that we are not told exactly how Babylon the harlot and the city perish. The foretelling of Scripture is to enable us to recognize God's hand, when He brings His purpose to pass, not to enable us to flaunt our knowledge by being able to tell people exactly how things are to come about.

Just as the destruction of the harlot is not something sudden like a bolt out of the blue, but is being foreshadowed by much that has happened during the past two centuries, so too, just at the time when international commerce seems to have reached its height, there are growing signs of its breaking down.

The harlot offers man second-rate religion, the outward appearance without the inner reality. International commerce draws the world closer together, not to create true brotherhood, but to make exploitation easier. The true believer, by true fellowship with his Lord and true brotherhood with his fellow, shows up the hollowness of Babylon. That is why he is hated and persecuted.

Thought: The love of money is a root of all manner of evil.

Revelation 19.1-5   Joy in Heaven

We are accustomed to think of joy in heaven over a sinner that repents. Here it is ultimately over those who will never be able to repent. This may seem frightful, until we remember that it is over those who made it so hard for others to believe, those who fought to the last against the truth, those who were the incarnation of Satan's hatred even as the Church is of Christ's love. In addition, Christ in His judgement of the great white throne can discriminate between those who had sold themselves to the Satanic powers for gain and power, and those deluded ones who were swept along by the current of the age.

The NEB does well to render 'the roar of a vast throng' (1); it reverberates like peals of thunder, cf. v. 6. 'The smoke from her' (3); for mortal minds it is as difficult to conceive of perfect sinless bliss as of utter, inexorably just condemnation. Therefore both are described in purely symbolic language, which should always be treated as such. The best chapter to study the symbolic language of judgement is probably Isa. 34. In vs. 1–4 we have universal judgement involving even the heavenly bodies (but are they rulers?); the earth is strewn with corpses and the mountains flow with blood. In v. 5 the general judgement is particularized by Edom, and in vs. 6,7 we have the soil manured with fat and blood. In vs. 8–10 we have it as active volcanic waste—note v, 10b—but in vs. 11–17 it is inhabited by animals, real and mythological, that do not live among pitch and brimstone. From this we should grasp that we do not have any unitary picture of judgement; we are allowed to judge of its reality by the juxtaposition of mutually incompatible pictures which give some idea of the awefulness of God's judgement. The picture of smoke continually rising (19.3, cf. 18.18; Isa. 34.10) is taken from Gen. 19.28, thus linking the destruction of Babylon with that of Sodom and Gomorrah.

Thought: It is a fearful thing to fall into the hands of the living God.

Revelation 19.6-10   The Marriage of the Lamb

The concept of Israel as the wife of Jehovah is at least as old as *Hosea*, and figures prominently in *Jeremiah* and *Ezekiel* as well as the second half of *Isaiah*. The thought behind it is partly that of God's love, partly of His covenant loyalty, partly that Israel by representing Jehovah 'completes' Him upon earth. The concept was then taken over by the Church, especially as Christ = Messiah = King, and a king must have a people. When that people was thought of as expressing His character, the picture of the vine and branches was used (John 15.1–8), the fruit being the fruit of the Spirit (Gal. 5.22 f.). When the Church is looked on as serving and representing Christ, it is called His body. When the fellowship between the Church and its Saviour is stressed, then it is His wife (Eph. 5.21–33; this passage shows that there is no contradiction between the pictures of body and wife). Since engagement in Israel was equivalent to marraige, the Church can be called the wife of Christ now, but the fullness awaits the victory of Christ through the Church.

One of the loveliest pictures in the N.T. has been obscured in the AV(KJV); 'the fine linen is the righteous deeds of the saints' (8). The picture evoked is of a great loom in heaven; every righteous deed, i.e. every act produced by our being accounted righteous in Christ, is carried up to the angel weaver, who incorporates it in the material of the wedding dress, designed to bring glory to the Bridegroom, not the bride.

Needless discussion has raged around 'Blessed are those who are invited' (9), cf. the Ten Virgins (Matt. 25.1–13). By its nature, symbolism is never the complete expression of truth. Terms like body and wife refer to the Church corporate, local or universal, and not to the individual. Hence in symbolic language we can have the wedding feast and yet those who compose the wife, the conquerors, invited to it.

'For testimony to Jesus is the spirit that inspires prophets' (10, NEB, margin) seems to give the meaning best. The angel refused to let his testimony bring him worship, i.e. honour. Wherever the prophet brings honour to himself instead of Jesus, his message is not from God. The interpreter of prophecy who draws attention to others than Jesus, or to himself by his cleverness, has lost his way.

Thought: At the name of Jesus every knee shall bow.

Revelation 19.11-21   The Victorious Word of God

The Word of God, a title hinted at in 1.2,16 and given in John 1.1, comes victoriously (13). Jesus Christ has been the perfect expression and performer of God's will from beginning to end. The only weapon mentioned is His sword (21), which is His words; a similar concept is found in 2 Thess. 2.8. If there is war at all in this passage, it is spiritual and not physical. In fact it is questionable whether there is war at all. How can any stand against the unveiled glory of Christ?

'A white horse' (11): the sign of the conqueror, cf. 6.2. 'Faithful and True', i.e. Trustworthy and Dependable. 'Like a flame of fire' (12), cf. 1.14. 'Many diadems', in contrast to the seven (12.3) and ten (13.1); all authority is Christ's. The name known only to Himself (12) probably refers to the very widely spread superstition in antiquity that knowledge of a man's or god's name can give power over him; none can control the Lord, and there is no formula of words that can force Him to do our bidding. 'Dipped in blood' (13): not 'sprinkled with' as in the margin. Sprinkling was for cleansing from sin; here it is His own blood and replaces 'as though He had been slain' in the description of the Lamb (5.6). 'The armies of heaven' (14): this is a victory parade. 'Wine press' (15): see notes on 14.19. 'His thigh' (16): this probably means His girdle.

The call of the angel (17) does not invalidate the earlier remark about the absence of fighting. The symbolism of war is carried on throughout. The enemies of Christ are destroyed that they may await the general resurrection. If the beast and the false prophet are treated differently, it is because they are systems and not merely persons, cf. also 20.14, where death and Hades are also so treated. This should warn us against dogmatism in our understanding of 'the lake of fire' (20). The picture is symbolic, but that does not entitle us to strip it of meaning. Symbolism always expresses less than the

whole truth. The modern reaction against the crudities of the mediaeval concept of hell should merely be a challenge to us to envisage
something worse and more tragic for those who find their eternal
destiny there.

Revelation 20.1-6   The Millennium

There is always a strong temptation for the theologian to try to
avoid the obvious teaching of symbolism, if it does not fit in with
his theories. Now that so much more is known of Talmudic and
Inter-Testamental Jewish writings, it is beyond dispute that John
is referring to the 'days of the Messiah', the period which links this
age with the world to come. Any other interpretation would force
on the prophecy a meaning its first hearers could not have understood.

Two interpretations seem compatible with this. One claims that
the triumph of Christ in 19.11–21 is purely spiritual and that it is
followed by a long period of the triumphant Church bringing
blessing to the world before the final revolt and the return of Christ
in judgement. The fact that Augustine, and after him most in the
mediaeval Church, thought that they had already entered the Millennium does not invalidate this interpretation. The other is that
19.11–21 shows the return of Christ, and that the Millennium
follows it, the world being in some way under the personal rule of
Christ. This view has more difficulties in it than its supporters often
realize, but it certainly fits the evidence of the N.T. better. Rightly
understood the two views are not so far apart as is often thought.
Both should see Christ's triumph through the Church, and both
should look to the future for the open revelation of it.

The purpose of the long history of God's dealings with men is to
make them realize that only through complete trust in and obedience
to God can there be true blessing. The final lesson that men have to
learn is that the root of the trouble is *in* them and not outside;
so Satan, having been defeated, is for the time being rendered in-
capable of doing his work.

While there is not much about 'the first resurrection' (5) in the
N.T., it is indubitably there. It is implied in Luke 14.14 and probably in 1 Cor. 15.23; it is stated in 1 Thess. 4.16 and probably in
the Greek of Phil. 3.11. Since all resurrection is the outcome of
Christ's, the N.T. avoids giving the impression that the earlier resurrection of the conquerors is in any way a result of their own
merits. The nature of the 'judgement' (4) is not specified, but there is

no indication that it has anything to do with the dead. There is, however, no suggestion of sinlessness during the Millennium.

Revelation 20.7-15 The Final Judgement

Organized evil and opposition to God need a leader, and so Satan is released to show that essentially man has not changed. Gog and Magog, cf. Ezek. 38.2,3, seem to represent all those peoples who have been on the fringe of civilization and therefore only marginally involved with the beast. The use of 'camp' (9) may be an indication that even the Millennium is not the final goal of the Church, cf. Heb. 11.10; Rev. 21.2, though Phillip's translation 'the army of the saints defending the beloved city' is worthy of consideration. It is striking how little is told us of the Millennium.

The One who sits on the 'great white throne' (11) is presumably Jesus Christ, cf. John 5.22,27. The throne represents rule, and white purity. Faced by it even material creation cannot abide it; 21.1 makes clear, however, that there is no thought of the abolition of the world. The 'books' (12), cf. Dan. 7.10, are doubtless the record of human history, though we should hesitate to take them literally. We should remember that this is genuine judgement, not merely a parade for condemnation, though there are those who appear only to hear the sentence, cf. John 3.18. The books give evidence of the man's life and character, but the verdict is based on 'the book of life'; in other words, acquittal is by grace. The idea that the book of life is opened merely to show that a man's name is not there is almost blasphemous. We may be certain that the hardened Jew (Rom. 11.25), the Gentile who has never heard, and all those who have seen and heard only perversions of the gospel, will be treated accordingly. We can accept without hesitation that the Judge, who was the sin offering for all men, will say to some, 'Your life shows that if you had heard, or heard properly, you would have believed.' We may imagine some of those who had never heard falling at His feet in adoration, as they recognize the One they had always longed for. We are not entitled to think that Satan will have the satisfaction of drawing the bulk of mankind with him to hell. That some will be lost we know; our estimate of how many will be saved is likely to depend on our estimate of the power and love of God.

'The second death' (14): it might be better, if we were to use this term rather than hell. Death is that which makes it impossible for man to accomplish his dreams and God's will. As he stands before

Photo: A scroll of the Word of Truth

'And he who sat upon the throne said,
  "Behold, I make all things new."
Also he said,
  "Write this, for these words are trustworthy and true."
And he said to me,
  "It is done! I am the Alpha and the Omega, the beginning and the end. To the thirsty I will give water without price from the fountain of the water of life. He who conquers shall have this heritage, and I will be his God and he shall be my son."'
(Revelation **21**.5–7)

the great white throne he knows what he is and what he has missed, but there remains no hope of ever changing or achieving.

Questions for further study and discussion on Revelation chs. 18–20

1. What is meant by Babylon?
2. Note the emphasis on wealth and luxury in ch. **18**. What does the N.T. have to say concerning riches and those who have them?
3. Note those portions in *Revelation* which give praise to God and Christ. For what specific reasons is praise given?
4. Bearing in mind **19.**8 show from 1 John and Matt. **25** that the thought of the coming of Christ is meant to spur us on to greater holiness of life.
5. 'Persecution' and 'expansion' are two key words in Church history. Illustrate this from *Acts* and later Church history.
6. What does the Bible teach about Satan?
7. Who will be judged, and on what basis?

Revelation 21.1-8   God with Man

'A new heaven' (1): this is the same word as in **20.**11; it is the sky and not God's home that is meant. The word for new in Greek implies that there is some link with the old, just as there is between our resurrection bodies and those that now are. The 'new Jerusalem' is the wife of the Lamb (9), i.e. the glorified Church. Contrary to popular opinion the age to come does not see the abolition of this creation in favour of heaven—that is a legacy of Greek thought with its despising of the material—but its transformation through its being linked with heaven by the glorified Church. 'With men' (3): not the Church but the new nations (24). It is likely that we should translate v. 3 as 'God-with-them shall Himself be their God' (NEB, margin), i.e. we have finally the complete fulfilment of the promise of Isa. 7.14.

In this section of *Revelation* we do not merely have a picture of the future, for the Bible is never interested in the future merely as future, but in its bearing on our lives in the present. So repeatedly there is a message addressed to the reader, e.g. vs. 5–8. 'Trustworthy and true' (5): the same as the name in **19.**11—as the speaker so His words. 'It is done' (6); what John had seen was not to find its fulfilment until many centuries had rolled by, but since God is the Creator and Sustainer from beginning to end, His decree would bring the vision to certain fruition.

Those who are finally to enjoy these things must be like Christ (1 John 3.2) and be God's sons because they have been transformed into the image of the Son of God. Exclusion is due to lack of Christlikeness. The sins mentioned fall into three categories. Liars (cf. 14.5), cowards, faithless persons (i.e. those who having no faith in God cannot be trusted) are those who fear their fellow men rather than God, and who place the judgement of man above that of God. The murderers and fornicators destroy the lives of men that are and of the children that have not yet been conceived. Then there are the idolaters, those who would make God in their own image, and the sorcerers, those who seek to twist God round their own will by magic of all kinds; such men are polluted, for they have no interest in the cleansing that only God can offer.

Thought: You can be made new!

Revelation 21.9-21   The New Jerusalem

It has already been pointed out that we are dealing with the glorified Church (9). If the gates have the names of 'the twelve tribes' (12), and the foundations those of 'the twelve apostles' (14), it means that the true Israel and the victorious Church, whose essential unity of being has been assumed throughout the book, have now coalesced, though we are not told how. Those who speak of a heavenly calling for the Church and an earthly one for the Jew are correct only on a short-term view.

'Twelve thousand stadia' are about 1500 miles. A perfect cube (16) of such dimensions makes no practical sense, especially if it has a wall only '144 cubits' (17), i.e. 216 feet, high. We can, however, interpret it in terms of Ezek. 40.2 and see a pyramid-shaped mountain. But instead of there being a relatively small temple on the summit, the city, which received only passing notice in Ezek. 48.30–35 (note the twelve gates), has now filled the mountain, cf. also Dan. 2.35; Isa. 11.9. The measurements are, of course, as symbolic as the city itself. Spurgeon in one of his lectures made fun of the literalist by calculating the size of the oyster needed to produce 'a pearl' (21) large enough to form a city gate, and speculated on the kind of sea needed to grow such an oyster. Those used to abstract or poetic thought can be satisfied with 'having the glory of God' (11), but for the more primitive or childlike mind this has to be expressed in material terms.

Eight of the precious stones in vs. 19 f. are found in the standard Greek translation of Exod. 28.17–20, though not in this order. It is a safe guess then that they are meant to be the twelve stones of the breastplate of judgement, the Greek version available to John using other names in the missing positions. If this is so, any symbolic meaning in the stones must be sought in their O.T. significance. The walls are founded on judgement, but also, on the love and thought of God, for the breastplate was worn over Aaron's heart. Yet the values of the city are not those of this world, for gold, for which many men will sell their souls, is of no more value than to be used as a paving material to be trodden underfoot.

Revelation 21.22—22.5   I Saw No Temple There

We think of a temple normally as a place where men worship God. In fact, both with the Tabernacle and the Temple the real purpose was to separate the worshippers from God. Into the Holy of Holies with its cherub throne for God, only the High Priest could come one day in the year; only priests were allowed in the Holy Place, and that when they were carrying out their duties. Into the court of the Tabernacle and the inner court of the Temple the ceremonially clean Israelite man could enter only as he brought his sacrifices. In the Tabernacle court there was no room for the woman or the man without a sacrifice. In the Temple John had known, the Court of the Israelite, the Courts of the Women and of the Gentiles had decreasing stages of sanctity, but in the strictest sense they were not part of the sanctuary. The reason for the separation was to keep apart Divine holiness and human sin. Already Jeremiah foresaw the day when Jerusalem, not the Ark, would 'be called the throne of the Lord' (Jer. 3.17). Now the vision is fulfilled. Sin has gone, so the dividing walls have, too (22).

'Night shall be no more' (5,25); physical conditions under the conditions of eternity are unknowable. Once again we have symbolism, where night and darkness represent evil, sin and absence of God, cf. John 1.5; 1 John 1.5, even as the sea in 21.1 is once again lawlessness.

One of the great weaknesses of traditional theology is that it tends to overlook in practice the universality of atonement and makes the Church the only sphere of salvation. Yet we have 'the nations . . . and the kings of the earth' (24) in addition to the city, i.e. the Church. Among them there is not perfection, for unlike the Church they need 'healing' (2) even in eternity.

We are given three aspects of the eternal state. 'His servants', literally slaves, 'shall worship Him' (3); neither the Christian's

501

title nor occupation, cf. Rom. **12.**1, has changed, only the degree of perfection. 'They shall see His face' (4): though we now see in a mirror dimly (1 Cor. **13.**12), the fellowship implied has already begun. 'His name shall be on their foreheads': this awaits Christ's coming (1 John 3.2), but the process of transformation is already going on (2 Cor. 3.18), cf. **14.**1.

Thought: The life of eternity begins down here.

Revelation 22.6-15 I Come Quickly!

For v. 6, cf. **19.**11; **21.**5. We meet a crux in interpretation in vs. 6,7; '. . . what must soon take place . . . I am coming soon', cf. **3.**11; **22.**20. It is increasingly being claimed that the apostles were mistaken about our Lord's teaching on His return, or even that they projected their own ideas into His teaching. Hence, it is suggested, we need not take the Second Advent teaching of the N.T. seriously. The one answer we may not give is that the time-measure used is God's, cf. note on 2 Pet. 3.8. The answer lies in another direction. If the exposition has achieved its purpose, it will have made clear the timelessness of so much in *Revelation*, so that men were justified in thinking that its prophecies were going into effect in their day. It is not important when Christ comes but that He comes, and that there has never been a time since the destruction of Jerusalem when He could not have come. It is our attitude to the Coming that matters, cf. 2 Tim. **4.**8, and we are meant to be on the watch.

'I fell down to worship' (8), cf. **19.**10: the Greek word is used of any act of profound respect, especially prostration, to high-ranking persons as well as gods. Hence it is used frequently in the N.T. in settings where 'worship' is misleading. John, the Jew, could never have thought of worshipping an angel. It is his extreme respect that is being rejected. Those entrusted with the Word are apt to expect undue honour from men, cf. John 5.43 f.

In v. 11 we have neither indifference to men's salvation, nor a suggestion that there is no hope for those mentioned. The man who has taken in the warnings of 'this book' (10) and has gone his way unchanged has little hope of changing. While we may not exclude hope so long as there is life, we should have little for the man who has repeatedly heard and repeatedly rejected. Theoretically 'the gates' should come before 'the tree of life' (14), but since both are pictures of Christ, it represents the normal order. He who practises falsehood will come to love it (15). 'The dogs': cf. Matt **7.**6;

Phil. 3.2, an epithet often applied by the Jews to the heathen. It is doubtful whether 'depraved' (Phillips) is an adequate rendering; rather the person without a sense of values or morals is intended— the dog was the scavenger of the ancient city.

Revelation 22.16-21   Come, Lord Jesus!

For 'the root and the offspring of David' (16), cf. 5.5. While we are accustomed to think of the O.T. as being summed up in Jesus Christ, we must never forget that it is also the unfolding of His will. 'The bright morning star': two lines of thought converge here. He is the star of Num. 24.17, proclaimed by the star of Matt. 2.2. He is also the abiding hope as the night grows long, proclaiming that dawn cannot be far off.

It is normal to take 'Come' (17) as a call to Christ, as in v. 20. In the context, however, it is more likely to be the appeal to those outside. Day has not yet come, so while the day star is yet to be seen, the continued appeal goes out.

For anyone to add to or subtract from the Scriptures is a spiritual hardihood for which a man will have to give his answer in the judgement. But that is not the point of vs. 18,19, which refer only to *Revelation*. In looking at the world around us it is easy for one with a reputation as a prophetic expert to convince himself that he is witnessing the fulfilment of the prophecy and so quietly to twist it slightly to prove his thesis. On the other hand, passages that do not suit it can be quietly ignored. It is this way of treating prophecy that has brought it into such disrepute.

For those who live where man has not befouled the world, it can be very beautiful. Man has created much which must arouse our admiration and regard in art, music, architecture and literature, though part of his handiwork suggests hell rather than heaven for its place of origin. Married love and the family are such that God is willing to use their language to express His relationship to His people. But over the best there lies the shadow of death, reminding us that sin has left its mark on all. Once the light of the Coming falls on the scene around us, it is like the traditional transformation scene in the pantomime, where all relationships are changed. *Revelation* has showed us that beauty and ease for the Christian are merely the calm at the centre of the cyclone, while the attractiveness of the world hides the corruption beneath. So the heart cries yearningly, 'Come, Lord Jesus!' Till He does, it remains true:

Yea, thro' life, death, thro' sorrow and thro' sinning
He shall suffice me, for He hath sufficed:
Christ is the end, for Christ was the beginning,
Christ the beginning, for the end is Christ.

Thought: The grace of the Lord Jesus is sufficient even for me.

Questions for further study and discussion on Revelation chs. 21,22

1. What does the N.T. teach about heaven?
2. What do we learn from 22.11a and Rom. 1.18–32 about (*i*) God and (*ii*) man?
3. What can be said with certainty about the Second Coming?
4. How is the sovereignty of God in the world depicted in *Revelation*?
5. For what reasons was the *Revelation* written? Are these relevant today?
6. In what sense can more that one interpretation of *Revelation* be valid?